T0364986

Toyota Corolla
Service and Repair Manual

Jay Storer and John H Haynes

Models covered

(3259 - 304 - 10AH2)

All Toyota Corolla Hatchback, Liftback, Saloon and Estate petrol engine models,
including special/limited editions
1332 cc, 1587 cc & 1762 cc petrol engines

Does not cover Diesel engine models

© Haynes Group Limited 2005

A book in the **Haynes Service and Repair Manual Series**

ISBN **978 0 85733 590 6**

British Library Cataloguing in Publication Data
A catalogue record for this book is available from the British Library.

Haynes Group Limited
Haynes North America, Inc

www.haynes.com

Disclaimer

There are risks associated with automotive repairs. The ability to make repairs depends on the individual's skill, experience and proper tools. Individuals should act with due care and acknowledge and assume the risk of performing automotive repairs.

The purpose of this manual is to provide comprehensive, useful and accessible automotive repair information, to help you get the best value from your vehicle. However, this manual is not a substitute for a professional certified technician or mechanic.

This repair manual is produced by a third party and is not associated with an individual vehicle manufacturer. If there is any doubt or discrepancy between this manual and the owner's manual or the factory service manual, please refer to the factory service manual or seek assistance from a professional certified technician or mechanic.

Even though we have prepared this manual with extreme care and every attempt is made to ensure that the information in this manual is correct, neither the publisher nor the author can accept responsibility for loss, damage or injury caused by any errors in, or omissions from, the information given.

Contents

LIVING WITH YOUR TOYOTA COROLLA

Roadside Repairs

MAINTENANCE

Contents

Toyota Corolla models are available in three-, four-, and five-door Saloon, Liftback, Hatchback and Estate body styles.

The transversely mounted in-line four-cylinder engines used in these vehicles are available in 1.3L, 1.6L and 1.8L versions.

The engine drives the front wheels through either a five-speed manual or a three- or four-speed automatic transmission via independent driveshafts.

Independent suspension, featuring coil spring/strut damper units, is used on all four wheels. The rack-and-pinion steering unit is mounted behind the engine with power-assistance available either as standard or optional equipment.

The brakes are disc at the front and drumsor discs at the rear, depending on model, with servo-assistance standard. An Anti-lock Braking System (ABS) is available on some models.

Provided that regular servicing is carried out in accordance with the manufacturer's recommendations, the Toyota Corolla should prove extremely reliable and economical. The engine compartment is well-designed, and most of the items needing frequent attention are easily accessible.

Your Toyota Corolla Manual

The aim of this manual is to help you get the best value from your vehicle. It can do so in several ways. It can help you decide what work must be done (even should you choose to get it done by a garage), provide information on routine maintenance and servicing, and give a logical course of action and diagnosis when random faults occur. However, it is hoped that you will use the manual by tackling the work yourself. On simpler jobs, it may even be quicker than booking the car into a garage and going there twice, to leave and collect it. Perhaps most important, a lot of money can be saved by avoiding the costs a garage must charge to cover its labour and overheads.

The manual has drawings and descriptions to show the function of the various components, so that their layout can be understood. Then the tasks are described and photographed in a clear step-by-step sequence.

Acknowledgements

Thanks are due to Somerset County Cars, Taunton. Thanks are also also due to Draper Tools Limited, who provided some of the workshop tools, and to all those people at Sparkford who helped in the production of this manual.

We take great pride in the accuracy of information given in this manual, but vehicle manufacturers make alterations and design changes during the production run of a particular vehicle of which they do not inform us. No liability can be accepted by the authors or publishers for loss, damage or injury caused by any errors in, or omissions from, the information given.

Toyota Corolla 1.6 GLi 4-door

Toyota Corolla 1.3 GLi 2-door

Notes for UK readers

Because this manual was originally written in the US, its layout differs slightly from our current UK-originated manuals and the technical terminology used throughout the manual is in the US style. The UK equivalent of US components and various other US words is given in the Section headed *Use of English*. It should be remembered that the project vehicle used in the main Chapters of the manual was a left-hand drive model; therefore, the position of the steering wheel, steering column, clutch and brake pedals, etc. will be on the opposite side of the vehicle on UK models. It should also be noted that some of the components shown in the photographs and illustrations will not be fitted to UK specification vehicles. Where this affects a specific procedure, it will be noted in the accompanying text or caption.

All Specifications appear in Imperial form; the equivalent metric values can be calculated using the Conversion factors page.

Toyota Corolla 1.3 GLi Estate

Working on your car can be dangerous. This page shows just some of the potential risks and hazards, with the aim of creating a safety-conscious attitude.

General hazards

Scalding

• Don't remove the radiator or expansion tank cap while the engine is hot.
• Engine oil, automatic transmission fluid or power steering fluid may also be dangerously hot if the engine has recently been running.

Burning

• Beware of burns from the exhaust system and from any part of the engine. Brake discs and drums can also be extremely hot immediately after use.

Crushing

• When working under or near a raised vehicle, always supplement the jack with axle stands, or use drive-on ramps. *Never venture under a car which is only supported by a jack.*

• Take care if loosening or tightening high-torque nuts when the vehicle is on stands. Initial loosening and final tightening should be done with the wheels on the ground.

Fire

• Fuel is highly flammable; fuel vapour is explosive.
• Don't let fuel spill onto a hot engine.
• Do not smoke or allow naked lights (including pilot lights) anywhere near a vehicle being worked on. Also beware of creating sparks (electrically or by use of tools).
• Fuel vapour is heavier than air, so don't work on the fuel system with the vehicle over an inspection pit.
• Another cause of fire is an electrical overload or short-circuit. Take care when repairing or modifying the vehicle wiring.
• Keep a fire extinguisher handy, of a type suitable for use on fuel and electrical fires.

Electric shock

• Ignition HT voltage can be dangerous, especially to people with heart problems or a pacemaker. Don't work on or near the ignition system with the engine running or the ignition switched on.

• Mains voltage is also dangerous. Make sure that any mains-operated equipment is correctly earthed. Mains power points should be protected by a residual current device (RCD) circuit breaker.

Fume or gas intoxication

• Exhaust fumes are poisonous; they often contain carbon monoxide, which is rapidly fatal if inhaled. Never run the engine in a confined space such as a garage with the doors shut.
• Fuel vapour is also poisonous, as are the vapours from some cleaning solvents and paint thinners.

Poisonous or irritant substances

• Avoid skin contact with battery acid and with any fuel, fluid or lubricant, especially antifreeze, brake hydraulic fluid and Diesel fuel. Don't syphon them by mouth. If such a substance is swallowed or gets into the eyes, seek medical advice.
• Prolonged contact with used engine oil can cause skin cancer. Wear gloves or use a barrier cream if necessary. Change out of oil-soaked clothes and do not keep oily rags in your pocket.
• Air conditioning refrigerant forms a poisonous gas if exposed to a naked flame (including a cigarette). It can also cause skin burns on contact.

Asbestos

• Asbestos dust can cause cancer if inhaled or swallowed. Asbestos may be found in gaskets and in brake and clutch linings. When dealing with such components it is safest to assume that they contain asbestos.

Special hazards

Hydrofluoric acid

• This extremely corrosive acid is formed when certain types of synthetic rubber, found in some O-rings, oil seals, fuel hoses etc, are exposed to temperatures above 400°C. The rubber changes into a charred or sticky substance containing the acid. *Once formed, the acid remains dangerous for years. If it gets onto the skin, it may be necessary to amputate the limb concerned.*
• When dealing with a vehicle which has suffered a fire, or with components salvaged from such a vehicle, wear protective gloves and discard them after use.

The battery

• Batteries contain sulphuric acid, which attacks clothing, eyes and skin. Take care when topping-up or carrying the battery.
• The hydrogen gas given off by the battery is highly explosive. Never cause a spark or allow a naked light nearby. Be careful when connecting and disconnecting battery chargers or jump leads.

Air bags

• Air bags can cause injury if they go off accidentally. Take care when removing the steering wheel and/or facia. Special storage instructions may apply.

Diesel injection equipment

• Diesel injection pumps supply fuel at very high pressure. Take care when working on the fuel injectors and fuel pipes.

⚠ *Warning: Never expose the hands, face or any other part of the body to injector spray; the fuel can penetrate the skin with potentially fatal results.*

Remember...

DO

• Do use eye protection when using power tools, and when working under the vehicle.

• Do wear gloves or use barrier cream to protect your hands when necessary.

• Do get someone to check periodically that all is well when working alone on the vehicle.

• Do keep loose clothing and long hair well out of the way of moving mechanical parts.

• Do remove rings, wristwatch etc, before working on the vehicle – especially the electrical system.

• Do ensure that any lifting or jacking equipment has a safe working load rating adequate for the job.

DON'T

• Don't attempt to lift a heavy component which may be beyond your capability – get assistance.

• Don't rush to finish a job, or take unverified short cuts.

• Don't use ill-fitting tools which may slip and cause injury.

• Don't leave tools or parts lying around where someone can trip over them. Mop up oil and fuel spills at once.

• Don't allow children or pets to play in or near a vehicle being worked on.

As the main part of this book has been written in the US, it uses the appropriate US component names, phrases, and spelling. Some of these differ from those used in the UK. Normally, these cause no difficulty, but to make sure, a glossary is printed below. When ordering spare parts, remember the parts list may use some of these words:

AMERICAN	ENGLISH	AMERICAN	ENGLISH
Aluminum	Aluminium	Muffler	Silencer
Antenna	Aerial	Odor	Odour
Authorized	Authorised	Oil pan	Sump
Auto parts stores	Motor factors	Open flame	Naked flame
Axleshaft	Halfshaft	Panel wagon/van	Van
Back-up	Reverse	Parking brake	Handbrake
Barrel	Choke/venturi	Parking light	Sidelight
Block	Chock	Pinging	Pinking
Box-end wrench	Ring spanner	Piston pin or wrist pin	Gudgeon pin
Bushing	Bush	Piston pin or wrist pin	Small end, little end
Carburetor	Carburettor	Pitman arm	Drop arm
Center	Centre	Power brake booster	Servo unit
Coast	Freewheel	Primary shoe (of brake)	Leading shoe (of brake)
Color	Colour	Prussian blue	Engineer's blue
Convertible	Drop head coupe	Pry	Prise (force apart)
Cotter pin	Split pin	Prybar	Lever
Counterclockwise	Anti-clockwise	Prying	Levering
Countershaft (of gearbox)	Layshaft	Quarter window	Quarterlight
Dashboard	Facia	Recap	Retread
Denatured alcohol	Methylated spirit	Release cylinder	Slave cylinder
Dome lamp	Interior light	Repair shop	Garage
Driveaxle	Driveshaft	Replacement	Renewal
Driveshaft	Propeller shaft	Ring gear (of differential)	Crownwheel
Fender	Wing/mudguard	Rocker panel (beneath doors)	Sill panel (beneath doors)
Firewall	Bulkhead	Rod bearing	Big-end bearing
Flashlight	Torch	Rotor/disk	Disc (brake)
Float bowl	Float chamber	Secondary shoe (of brake)	Trailing shoe (of brake)
Floor jack	Trolley jack	Sedan	Saloon
Freeway, turnpike etc	Motorway	Setscrew, Allen screw	Grub screw
Freeze plug	Core plug	Shock absorber, shock	Damper
Frozen	Seized	Snap-ring	Circlip
Gas tank	Petrol tank	Soft top	Hood
Gasoline (gas)	Petrol	Spacer	Distance piece
Gearshift	Gearchange	Spare tire	Spare wheel
Generator (DC)	Dynamo	Spark plug wires	HT leads
Ground (electrical)	Earth	Spindle arm	Steering arm
Header	Exhaust manifold	Stabilizer or sway bar	Anti-roll bar
Heat riser	Hot spot	Station wagon	Estate car
High	Top gear	Stumbles	Hesitates
Hood (engine cover)	Bonnet	Tang or lock	Tab washer
Installation	Refitting	Throw-out bearing	Thrust bearing
Intake	Inlet	Tie-rod or connecting rod (of steering)	Trackrod
Jackstands	Axle stands	Tire	Tyre
Jumper cable	Jump lead	Transmission	Gearbox
Keeper	Collet	Troubleshooting	Fault finding/diagnosis
Kerosene	Paraffin	Trunk	Boot (luggage compartment)
Knock pin	Roll pin	Turn signal	Indicator
Lash	Clearance	TV (throttle valve) cable	Kickdown cable
Lash	Free-play	Unpublicized	Unpublicised
Latch	Catch	Valve cover	Rocker cover
Latches	Locks	Valve lifter	Tappet
License plate	Number plate	Valve lifter or tappet	Cam follower or tappet
Light	Lamp	Vapor	Vapour
Lock (for valve spring retainer)	Split cotter (for valve spring cap)	Vise	Vice
Lopes	Hunts	Wheel cover	Roadwheel trim
Lug nut/bolt	Wheel nut/bolt	Whole drive line	Transmission
Metal chips or debris	Swarf	Windshield	Windscreen
Misses	Misfires	Wrench	Spanner

The following pages are intended to help in dealing with common roadside emergencies and breakdowns. You will find more detailed fault finding information at the back of the manual, and repair information in the main chapters.

If your car won't start and the starter motor doesn't turn

☐ If it's a model with automatic transmission, make sure the selector is in 'P' or 'N'.
☐ Open the bonnet and make sure that the battery terminals are clean and tight.
☐ Switch on the headlights and try to start the engine. If the headlights go very dim when you're trying to start, the battery is probably flat. Get out of trouble by jump starting (see next page) using a friend's car.

If your car won't start even though the starter motor turns as normal

☐ Is there fuel in the tank?
☐ Is there moisture on electrical components under the bonnet? Switch off the ignition, then wipe off any obvious dampness with a dry cloth. Spray a water-repellent aerosol product (WD-40 or equivalent) on ignition and fuel system electrical connectors like those shown in the photos. Pay special attention to the ignition coil wiring connector and HT leads.

A Check that the spark plug wires are securely connected at the spark plugs . . .

B . . . and at the connections on the distributor

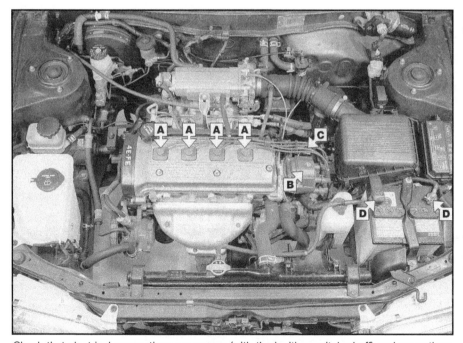

Check that electrical connections are secure (with the ignition switched off) and spray them with a water dispersant spray like WD40 if you suspect a problem due to damp

C Check that all ignition wiring connectors such as this at the distributor are secure and spray with water dispersant if necessary

D Check the security and condition of the battery terminals

Jump starting

When jump-starting a car using a booster battery, observe the following precautions:

✔ Before connecting the booster battery, make sure that the ignition is switched off.

✔ Ensure that all electrical equipment (lights, heater, wipers, etc) is switched off.

✔ Take note of any special precautions printed on the battery case.

✔ Make sure that the booster battery is the same voltage as the discharged one in the vehicle.

✔ If the battery is being jump-started from the battery in another vehicle, the two vehicles MUST NOT TOUCH each other.

✔ Make sure that the transmission is in neutral (or PARK, in the case of automatic transmission).

HAYNES HiNT *Jump starting will get you out of trouble, but you must correct whatever made the battery go flat in the first place. There are three possibilities:*

1 *The battery has been drained by repeated attempts to start, or by leaving the lights on.*

2 *The charging system is not working properly (alternator drivebelt slack or broken, alternator wiring fault or alternator itself faulty).*

3 *The battery itself is at fault (electrolyte low, or battery worn out).*

1 Connect one end of the red jump lead to the positive (+) terminal of the flat battery

2 Connect the other end of the red lead to the positive (+) terminal of the booster battery.

3 Connect one end of the black jump lead to the negative (-) terminal of the booster battery

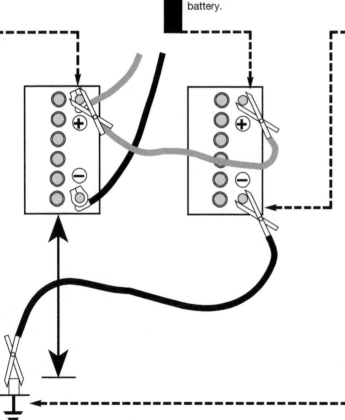

4 Connect the other end of the black jump lead to a bolt or bracket on the engine block, well away from the battery, on the vehicle to be started.

5 Make sure that the jump leads will not come into contact with the fan, drive-belts or other moving parts of the engine.

6 Start the engine using the booster battery and run it at idle speed. Switch on the lights, rear window demister and heater blower motor, then disconnect the jump leads in the reverse order of connection. Turn off the lights etc.

Wheel changing

Some of the details shown here will vary according to model. For instance, the location of the spare wheel and jack is not the same on all cars. However, the basic principles apply to all vehicles.

Warning: Do not change a wheel in a situation where you risk being hit by another vehicle. On busy roads, try to stop in a lay-by or a gateway. Be wary of passing traffic while changing the wheel - it is easy to become distracted by the job in hand.

Preparation

☐ When a puncture occurs, stop as soon as it is safe to do so.
☐ Park on firm level ground, if possible, and well out of the way of other traffic.
☐ Use hazard warning lights if necessary.

☐ If you have one, use a warning triangle to alert other drivers of your presence.
☐ Apply the handbrake and engage first or reverse gear (or Park on models with automatic transmission.

☐ Chock the wheel diagonally opposite the one being removed – a couple of large stones will do for this.
☐ If the ground is soft, use a flat piece of wood to spread the load under the jack.

Changing the wheel

1 From inside the luggage compartment, remove the trim panel and remove the jack.

2 Lift up the floor covering and unscrew the spare wheel retainer. Lift out the wheel, tool kit and wheelbrace. Place the chock, supplied in the tool kit, in front of the wheel diagonally opposite the one to be changed.

3 Use the removal tool supplied in the tool kit to remove the wheel trim. Then, using the wheelbrace, slacken the wheel nuts. by half a turn.

4 Locate the jack below the reinforced jacking point on the sill and on firm ground (don't jack the car at any other points on the sill).

5 Turn the jack handle clockwise until the wheel is raised clear of the ground, remove the wheel nuts and lift the wheel clear.

6 Position the spare wheel then install and tighten the nuts. Lower the car and tighten the wheel nuts in the sequence shown.

Finally...

☐ Install the wheel trim.

☐ Remove the wheel chocks.

☐ Stow the jack and tools in the correct locations in the car.

☐ Check the tyre pressure on the wheel just fitted. If it is low, or if you don't have a pressure gauge with you, drive slowly to the nearest garage and inflate the tyre to the right pressure.

☐ Have the damaged tyre or wheel repaired as soon as possible.

Identifying leaks

Puddles on the garage floor or drive, or obvious wetness under the bonnet or underneath the car, suggest a leak that needs investigating. It can sometimes be difficult to decide where the leak is coming from, especially if the engine bay is very dirty already. Leaking oil or fluid can also be blown rearwards by the passage of air under the car, giving a false impression of where the problem lies.

 Warning: Most automotive oils and fluids are poisonous. Wash them off skin, and change out of contaminated clothing, without delay.

 The smell of a fluid leaking from the car may provide a clue to what's leaking. Some fluids are distinctively coloured. It may help to clean the car carefully and to park it over some clean paper overnight as an aid to locating the source of the leak.
Remember that some leaks may only occur while the engine is running.

Sump oil

Engine oil may leak from the drain plug...

Oil from filter

...or from the base of the oil filter.

Gearbox oil

Gearbox oil can leak from the seals at the inboard ends of the driveshafts.

Antifreeze

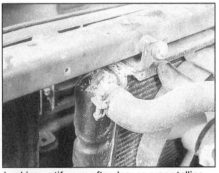

Leaking antifreeze often leaves a crystalline deposit like this.

Brake fluid

A leak occurring at a wheel is almost certainly brake fluid.

Power steering fluid

Power steering fluid may leak from the pipe connectors on the steering rack.

Towing

When all else fails, you may find yourself having to get a tow home – or of course you may be helping somebody else. Long-distance recovery should only be done by a garage or breakdown service. For shorter distances, DIY towing using another car is easy enough, but observe the following points:
☐ Use a proper tow-rope – they are not expensive. The vehicle being towed must display an 'ON TOW' sign in its rear window.
☐ Always turn the ignition key to the 'on' position when the vehicle is being towed, so

that the steering lock is released, and that the direction indicator and brake lights will work.
☐ Only attach the tow-rope to the towing eyes provided.
☐ Before being towed, release the handbrake and select neutral on the transmission.
☐ Note that greater-than-usual pedal pressure will be required to operate the brakes, since the vacuum servo unit is only operational with the engine running.
☐ On models with power steering, greater-than-usual steering effort will also be required.

☐ The driver of the car being towed must keep the tow-rope taut at all times to avoid snatching.
☐ Make sure that both drivers know the route before setting off.
☐ Only drive at moderate speeds and keep the distance towed to a minimum. Drive smoothly and allow plenty of time for slowing down at junctions.
☐ On models with automatic transmission, special precautions apply. If in doubt, do not tow, or transmission damage may result.

Every 250 miles or weekly, whichever comes first

- [ ] Check the engine oil level
- [ ] Check the engine coolant level
- [ ] Check the windscreen washer fluid level
- [ ] Check the brake fluid level
- [ ] Check the tyres and tyre pressures

Every 4500 miles (7500 km) or 6 months - whichever comes first

- [ ] Replace the engine oil and filter

Note: *Frequent oil and filter changes are good for the engine. We recommend changing the oil at the mileage specified here, or at least twice a year if the mileage covered is less.*

Every 9000 miles (15 000 km) or 6 months - whichever comes first

In addition to the items listed above, carry out the following:

- [ ] Check manual transmission oil level
- [ ] Check automatic transmission fluid level
- [ ] Check engine coolant strength
- [ ] Check the condition of the drivebelt(s), and replace if necessary
- [ ] Check the spark plugs and ignition system
- [ ] Check the evaporative loss emission control equipment
- [ ] Hose and fluid leak check
- [ ] Check and adjust the brake pedal
- [ ] Check the brake vacuum servo unit, hose and non-return check-valve
- [ ] Check and adjust the handbrake
- [ ] Check the front and (where applicable) rear brake pads and discs and replace if necessary*
- [ ] Check (where applicable) the rear brake shoes and drums and replace if necessary*
- [ ] Check the exhaust system
- [ ] Check the steering and suspension components for condition and security*
- [ ] Check the condition of the driveshafts, CV joints and boots*
- [ ] Check the battery electrolyte level and terminals
- [ ] Check the tightness of the roadwheel nuts
- [ ] Wheel alignment check
- [ ] Check the headlight beam alignment
- [ ] Lubricate door and bonnet hinges
- [ ] Adjust the washer jets
- [ ] Check, and if necessary replace the wiper blades
- [ ] Check the condition, operation and security of all seat belts
- [ ] Check the body for corrosion

*This should be performed more frequently if the vehicle is used in Severe Conditions (ie towing a trailer, repeated short distances, dusty conditions etc).

Every 18 000 miles (30 000 km) or 12 months - whichever comes first

In addition to the items listed above, carry out the following:

- [ ] Replace the spark plugs
- [ ] Replace the fuel filter*
- [ ] Replace the air filter element*

*This should be performed more frequently if the vehicle is used in Severe Conditions (ie towing a trailer, repeated short distances, dusty conditions etc).

Every 24 months

- [ ] Change the brake fluid

Every 36 000 miles (60 000 km)

- [ ] Change the manual transmission oil*
- [ ] Change the automatic transmission fluid*
- [ ] Change the engine coolant

*This should be performed more frequently if the vehicle is used in Severe Conditions (ie towing a trailer, repeated short distances, dusty conditions etc).

Every 54 000 miles (90 000 km)

- [ ] Check and adjust the valve clearances

Every 63 000 miles (105 000 km)

- [ ] Replace the timing belt

Advanced driving

Many people see the words 'advanced driving' and believe that it won't interest them or that it is a style of driving beyond their own abilities. Nothing could be further from the truth. Advanced driving is straightforward safe, sensible driving - the sort of driving we should all do every time we get behind the wheel.

An average of 10 people are killed every day on UK roads and 870 more are injured, some seriously. Lives are ruined daily, usually because somebody did something stupid. Something like 95% of all accidents are due to human error, mostly driver failure. Sometimes we make genuine mistakes - everyone does. Sometimes we have lapses of concentration. Sometimes we deliberately take risks.

For many people, the process of 'learning to drive' doesn't go much further than learning how to pass the driving test because of a common belief that good drivers are made by 'experience'.

Learning to drive by 'experience' teaches three driving skills:

☐ Quick reactions. (Whoops, that was close!)
☐ Good handling skills. (Horn, swerve, brake, horn).
☐ Reliance on vehicle technology. (Great stuff this ABS, stop in no distance even in the wet...)

Drivers whose skills are 'experience based' generally have a lot of near misses and the odd accident. The results can be seen every day in our courts and our hospital casualty departments.

Advanced drivers have learnt to control the risks by controlling the position and speed of their vehicle. They avoid accidents and near misses, even if the drivers around them make mistakes.

The key skills of advanced driving are **concentration,** effective all-round **observation, anticipation** and **planning.** When **good vehicle handling** is added to these skills, all driving situations can be approached and negotiated in a safe, methodical way, leaving nothing to chance.

Concentration means applying your mind to safe driving, completely excluding anything that's not relevant. Driving is usually the most dangerous activity that most of us undertake in our daily routines. It deserves our full attention.

Observation means not just looking, but seeing and seeking out the information found in the driving environment.

Anticipation means asking yourself what is happening, what you can reasonably expect to happen and what could happen unexpectedly. (One of the commonest words used in compiling accident reports is 'suddenly'.)

Planning is the link between seeing something and taking the appropriate action. For many drivers, planning is the missing link.

If you want to become a safer and more skilful driver and you want to enjoy your driving more, contact the Institute of Advanced Motorists at www.iam.org.uk, phone 0208 996 9600, or write to IAM House, 510 Chiswick High Road, London W4 5RG for an information pack.

Chapter 1
Routine maintenance and servicing

Contents

Degrees of difficulty

| Easy, suitable for novice with little experience | | Fairly easy, suitable for beginner with some experience | | Fairly difficult, suitable for competent DIY mechanic | | Difficult, suitable for experienced DIY mechanic | | Very difficult, suitable for expert DIY or professional | |

Recommended lubricants and fluids

Engine oil	Multigrade engine oil, viscosity SAE 15W/40, 10W/30 or 20W/50 to API SG or better
Coolant	Ethylene glycol-based antifreeze and soft water
Automatic transmission	
Fluid	Dexron type II automatic transmission fluid (ATF)
Differential lubricant	Dexron type II automatic transmission fluid (ATF)
Manual transmission oil	Hypoid gear oil, viscosity SAE 75W/90 to API GL5
Brake fluid	Hydraulic fluid to SAE J1703F or DOT 3
Clutch fluid	Hydraulic fluid to SAE J1703F or DOT 3
Power steering system	Dexron type II automatic transmission fluid (ATF)

Choosing your engine oil

Engines need oil, not only to lubricate moving parts and minimise wear, but also to maximise power output and to improve fuel economy.

HOW ENGINE OIL WORKS

• Beating friction

Without oil, the moving surfaces inside your engine will rub together, heat up and melt, quickly causing the engine to seize. Engine oil creates a film which separates these moving parts, preventing wear and heat build-up.

• Cooling hot-spots

Temperatures inside the engine can exceed 1000° C. The engine oil circulates and acts as a coolant, transferring heat from the hot-spots to the sump.

• Cleaning the engine internally

Good quality engine oils clean the inside of your engine, collecting and dispersing combustion deposits and controlling them until they are trapped by the oil filter or flushed out at oil change.

OIL CARE - FOLLOW THE CODE

To handle and dispose of used engine oil safely, always:

• *Avoid skin contact with used engine oil. Repeated or prolonged contact can be harmful.*
• *Dispose of used oil and empty packs in a responsible manner in an authorised disposal site. Call 0800 663366 to find the one nearest to you. Never tip oil down drains or onto the ground.*

Capacities*

Engine oil (including filter)
1.3L engine	5.0 Imp pints
1.6L engine	5.2 Imp pints
1.8L engine	6.6 Imp pints

Coolant
  1.3L engine
Manual transmission with air conditioning	8.6 Imp pints
Manual transmission without air conditioning	8.0 Imp pints
Automatic transmission	8.2 Imp pints

  1.6L engine
Manual transmission with air conditioning	9.6 Imp pints
Manual transmission without air conditioning	8.8 Imp pints
Automatic transmission	9.2 Imp pints
1.8L engine	9.8 Imp pints
Fuel tank	11.0 Imp gallons
Manual transmission	4.6 Imp pints

Automatic transmission (drain and refill)
Three-speed	4.4 Imp pints
Differential	2.4 Imp pints
Four-speed	5.4 Imp pints

* All capacities approximate. Add as necessary to bring up to appropriate level.

Engine

Valve clearances (engine cold)

Intake valve	0.006 to 0.010 inch

Exhaust valve

1.3L engine	0.012 to 0.016 inch
1.6L and 1.8L engines	0.010 to 0.014 inch

Cooling system

Thermostat rating

Starts to open	190-degrees F
Fully open	212-degrees F

Fuel system

Fuel grade	95 RON unleaded. Leaded fuel (eg UK "4-star") must not be used

Ignition system

	Type	Electrode gap
Spark plugs:		
All engines	Bosch FR 78	Not adjustable
Spark plug wire resistance	10,000 to 25,000 ohms	
Engine firing order	1-3-4-2 (No 1 cylinder at timing belt end of engine)	

Clutch

Pedal freeplay	3/16 to 5/8 inch

Pedal height

Right-hand drive models	5-3/4 inches
Left-hand drive models	6 inches

Braking system

Disc brake pad lining thickness (minimum)	1/16 inch
Drum brake shoe lining thickness (minimum)	1/16 inch
Parking brake adjustment	4 to 7 clicks

Suspension and steering

Steering wheel freeplay limit	1-3/16 inch
Balljoint allowable movement	0 inch

Tyre pressures (cold)

	Front	Rear
1.3L engine models	36 psi	36 psi
1.6L engine models	37 psi	37 psi
1.8L engine models	35 psi	33 psi

Note: Pressures apply only to original equipment tyres at speeds of up to 100 mph and may vary if any other make or type is fitted; check with the tyre manufacturer or supplier for correct pressures, if necessary. For pressures at higher speeds, or when carrying heavy loads, consult the vehicle's handbook or your Toyota dealer.

Torque wrench settings

	Ft-lbs
Automatic transmission	
Three-speed	
Pan bolts	4
Filter bolts	4
Drain plug	13
Four-speed	
Pan bolts	4
Filter bolts	7
Drain plug	36
Manual transmission drain and filler plugs	29
Spark plugs	13
Seat bolts/nuts	27
Wheel nuts	76

Note: *The following schedule is based on that given for North American models. For a schedule more applicable to the United Kingdom market, refer to the "Notes for UK readers" section in the beginning of this Manual.*

The maintenance intervals in this manual are provided with the assumption that you, not the dealer, will be doing the work. These are the minimum maintenance intervals recommended by the factory for vehicles that are driven daily. If you wish to keep your vehicle in peak condition at all times, you may wish to perform some of these procedures even more often. Because frequent maintenance enhances the efficiency, performance and resale value of your car, we encourage you to do so. If you drive in dusty areas, tow a trailer, idle or drive at low speeds for extended periods or drive for short distances (less than four miles) in below freezing temperatures, shorter intervals are also recommended.

When your vehicle is new, it should be serviced by a factory authorized dealer service department to protect the factory warranty. In many cases, the initial maintenance check is done at no cost to the owner.

Every 250 miles or weekly, whichever comes first

- ☐ Check the engine oil level (Section 3)
- ☐ Check the engine coolant level (Section 3)
- ☐ Check the windscreen washer fluid level (Section 3)
- ☐ Check the brake fluid level (Section 3)
- ☐ Check the tyres and tyre pressures (Section 4)

Every 3000 miles or 3 months, whichever comes first

All items listed above plus:
- ☐ Check the power steering fluid level (Section 5)
- ☐ Check the automatic transmission fluid level (Section 6)
- ☐ Change the engine oil and oil filter (Section 7)

Every 7500 miles or 6 months, whichever comes first

- ☐ Inspect and replace if necessary the windscreen wiper blades (Section 8)
- ☐ Check the clutch pedal for proper freeplay (Section 9)
- ☐ Check and service the battery (Section 10)
- ☐ Check and adjust if necessary the engine drivebelts (Section 11)
- ☐ Inspect and replace if necessary all underbonnet hoses (Section 12)
- ☐ Check the cooling system (Section 13)
- ☐ Rotate the tyres (Section 14)

Every 15 000 miles or 12 months, whichever comes first

All items listed above plus:
- ☐ Inspect the brake system (Section 15)*
- ☐ Replace the air filter (Section 16)
- ☐ Inspect the fuel system (Section 17)
- ☐ Check the three-speed automatic transmission lubricant level (Section 18)
- ☐ Check the manual transmission lubricant level (Section 19)
- ☐ Inspect the suspension and steering components (Section 20)*
- ☐ Check the driveshaft boots (Section 21)

Every 30 000 miles or 2 years, whichever comes first

All items listed above plus:
- ☐ Replace the fuel filter (Section 22)
- ☐ Check and replace if necessary the spark plugs (Section 23)
- ☐ Inspect and replace if necessary the spark plug leads, distributor cap and rotor (Section 24)
- ☐ Service the cooling system (drain, flush and refill) (Section 25)
- ☐ Inspect the evaporative emissions control system(Section 26)
- ☐ Inspect the exhaust system (Section 27)
- ☐ Change the automatic transmission fluid and filter and differential lubricant (Section 28)**
- ☐ Change the manual transmission lubricant (Section 29)**
- ☐ Check and replace if necessary the PCV valve (Section 30)

Every 60 000 miles or 4 years, whichever comes first

- ☐ Check and adjust the valve clearances (Section 31)
- ☐ Replace the timing belt (Chapter 2A)

* This item is affected by "severe" operating conditions as described below. If your vehicle is operated under "severe" conditions, perform all maintenance indicated with an asterisk (*) at 3000 mile/3 month intervals. Severe conditions are indicated if you mainly operate your vehicle under one or more of the following conditions:
   Operating in dusty areas
   Towing a trailer
   Idling for extended periods and/or low speed operation
   Operating when outside temperatures remain below freezing and when most trips are less than 4 miles

** If operated under one or more of the following conditions, change the manual or automatic transmission fluid and differential lubricant every 15,000 miles:
   In heavy city traffic where the outside temperature regularly reaches 90-degrees F (32-degrees C) or higher
   In hilly or mountainous terrain
   Frequent trailer pulling

1 Introduction

This chapter is designed to help the home mechanic maintain the Toyota Corolla for peak performance, economy, safety and long life.

On the following pages is a master maintenance schedule, followed by sections dealing specifically with each item on the schedule. Visual checks, adjustments, component replacement and other helpful items are included. Refer to the **accompanying illustrations** of the engine compartment and the underside of the vehicle for the location of various components.

Servicing your Corolla in accordance with the mileage/time maintenance schedule and the following Sections will provide it with a planned maintenance program that should result in a long and reliable service life. This is a comprehensive plan, so maintaining some items but not others at the specified service intervals will not produce the same results.

As you service your Corolla, you will discover that many of the procedures can - and should - be grouped together because of the nature of the particular procedure you're performing or because of the close proximity of two otherwise unrelated components to one another.

For example, if the vehicle is raised for any reason, you should inspect the exhaust, suspension, steering and fuel systems while you're under the vehicle. When you're rotating the tyres, it makes good sense to check the brakes and wheel bearings since the wheels are already removed.

Finally, let's suppose you have to borrow or rent a torque wrench. Even if you only need to tighten the spark plugs, you might as well check the torque of as many critical fasteners as time allows.

The first step of this maintenance program is to prepare yourself before the actual work begins. Read through all sections pertinent to the procedures you're planning to do, then make a list of and gather together all the parts and tools you will need to do the job. If it looks as if you might run into problems during a particular segment of some procedure, seek advice from your local parts man or dealer service department.

Engine compartment component locations
- Right-hand drive 1.3L (4E-FE engine) model

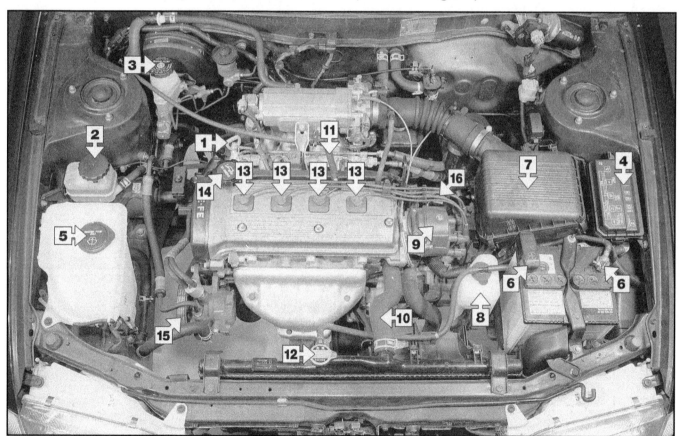

1	Engine oil dipstick	5	Windscreen washer fluid reservoir	9	Distributor	13	Spark plug
2	Power steering fluid reservoir	6	Battery terminals	10	Radiator hose	14	Oil filler cap
3	Brake fluid reservoir	7	Air cleaner assembly	11	PCV valve	15	Drivebelt
4	Fuse block	8	Coolant reservoir	12	Radiator cap	16	HT leads

Engine compartment component locations - left-hand drive 1.8L (7A-FE engine) model (1.6L engine models similar)

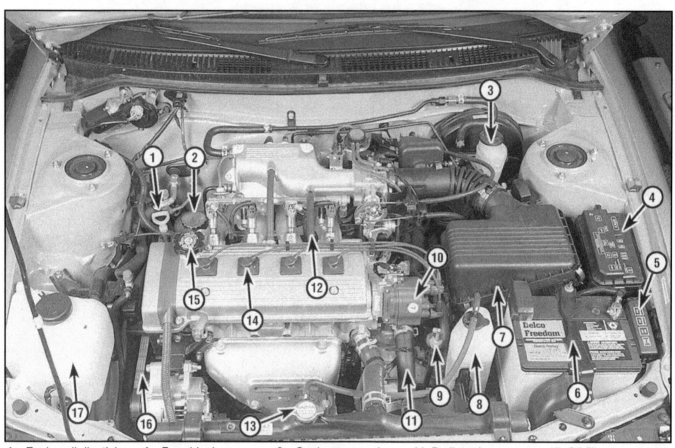

1	Engine oil dipstick	**4**	Fuse block	**8**	Coolant reservoir	**11**	Radiator hose
2	Power steering fluid reservoir	**5**	Relay block	**9**	Automatic transmission dipstick	**12**	PCV valve
3	Brake fluid reservoir	**6**	Battery	**10**	Distributor	**13**	Radiator cap
		7	Air cleaner assembly			**14**	Spark plug

15	Oil filler cap
16	Drivebelt
17	Windscreen washer fluid reservoir

Typical engine compartment underside components

1 Driveshaft boot	**4** Steering gear boot	**7** Radiator drain fitting
2 Automatic transmission drain plug	**5** Engine oil drain plug	**8** Engine oil filter
3 Exhaust system catalytic converter	**6** Front suspension strut unit	**9** Front disc brake caliper

Typical rear underside components

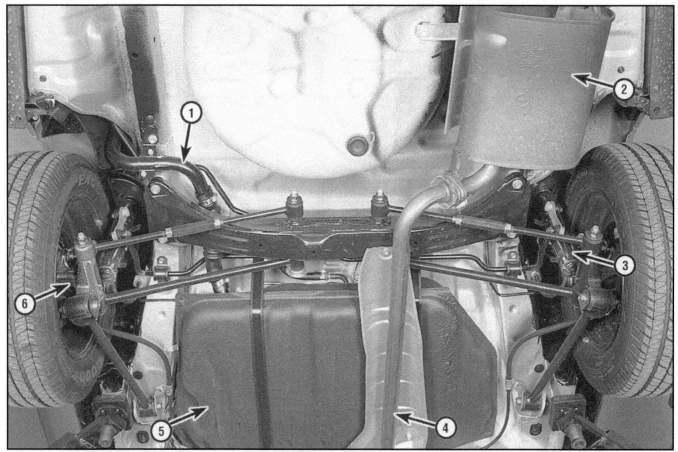

1 Petrol tank filler pipe	**3** Suspension strut	**5** Petrol tank
2 Muffler (silencer)	**4** Exhaust system	**6** Rear brake assembly

2 Tune-up general information

The term tune-up is used in this manual to represent a combination of individual operations rather than one specific procedure.

If, from the time the vehicle is new, the routine maintenance schedule is followed closely and frequent checks are made of fluid levels and high wear items, as suggested throughout this manual, the engine will be kept in relatively good running condition and the need for additional work will be minimized.

More likely than not, however, there will be times when the engine is running poorly due to lack of regular maintenance. This is even more likely if a used vehicle, which has not received regular and frequent maintenance checks, is purchased. In such cases, an engine tune-up will be needed outside of the regular routine maintenance intervals.

The first step in any tune-up or engine diagnosis to help correct a poor running engine would be a cylinder compression check. A check of the engine compression (Chapter 2 Part B) will give valuable information regarding the overall performance of many internal components and should be used as a basis for tune-up and repair procedures. If, for instance, a compression check indicates serious internal engine wear, a conventional tune-up will not help the running condition of the engine and would be a waste of time and money.

The following series of operations are those most often needed to bring a generally poor running engine back into a proper state of tune.

Minor tune-up

Clean, inspect and test the battery (Section 10)
Check all engine related fluids (Section 3)
Check and adjust the drivebelts (Section 11)
Replace the spark plugs (Section 23)
Inspect the distributor cap and rotor (Section 24)
Inspect the spark plug and coil leads (Section 24)
Check all underbonnet hoses (Section 12)
Check the cooling system (Section 13)
Check the air filter (Section 16)

Major tune-up

All items listed under Minor tune-up, plus . . .
Check the ignition system (Section 24)
Check the charging system (Chapter 5)
Check the fuel system (Section 17)
Replace the air filter (Section 16)
Replace the distributor cap and rotor (Section 24)
Replace the spark plug leads (Section 24)

3.2 The engine oil dipstick is located on the right rear side of the engine

3 Fluid level checks

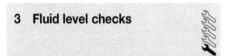

1 Fluids are an essential part of the lubrication, cooling, brake, clutch and other systems. Because these fluids gradually become depleted and/or contaminated during normal operation of the vehicle, they must be periodically replenished. See *Recommended lubricants and fluids* at the beginning of this Chapter before adding fluid to any of the following components. **Note:** *The vehicle must be on level ground before fluid levels can be checked.*

Engine oil

2 The engine oil level is checked with a dipstick located at the back side of the engine **(see illustration)**. The dipstick extends through a metal tube from which it protrudes down into the engine oil pan.
3 The oil level should be checked before the vehicle has been driven, or about 15 minutes after the engine has been shut off. If the oil is checked immediately after driving the vehicle, some of the oil will remain in the upper engine components, producing an inaccurate reading on the dipstick.
4 Pull the dipstick from the tube and wipe all the oil from the end with a clean rag or paper towel. Insert the clean dipstick all the way back into its metal tube and pull it out again. Observe the oil at the end of the dipstick. At its highest point, the level should be between the L and F marks **(see illustration)**.
5 It takes one US quart of oil to raise the level from the L mark to the F mark on the dipstick. Do not allow the level to drop below the L mark or oil starvation may cause engine damage. Conversely, overfilling the engine (adding oil above the F mark) may cause oil fouled spark plugs, oil leaks or oil seal failures.
6 Remove the threaded cap from the valve cover to add oil **(see illustration)**. Use a funnel to prevent spills. After adding the oil, install the filler cap hand tight. Start the engine and look carefully for any small leaks around the oil filter or drain plug. Stop the engine and check the oil level again after it has had sufficient time to drain from the upper block and cylinder head galleys.

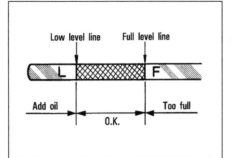

3.4 The oil level should be at or near the F mark - if it isn't, add enough oil to bring the level to near the F mark (it takes approximately two pints to raise the level from the L to the F mark)

7 Checking the oil level is an important preventive maintenance step. A continually dropping oil level indicates oil leakage through damaged seals, from loose connections, or past worn rings or valve guides. If the oil looks milky in colour or has water droplets in it, a cylinder head gasket may be blown. The engine should be checked immediately. The condition of the oil should also be checked. Each time you check the oil level, slide your thumb and index finger up the dipstick before wiping off the oil. If you see small dirt or metal particles clinging to the dipstick, the oil should be changed (Section 7).

Engine coolant

 Warning: Do not allow antifreeze to come in contact with your skin or painted surfaces of the vehicle. Flush contaminated areas immediately with plenty of water. Don't store new coolant or leave old coolant lying around where it's accessible to children or pets - they're attracted by its sweet smell and may drink it. Ingestion of even a small amount of coolant can be fatal! Wipe up garage floor and drip pan spills immediately. Keep antifreeze containers covered and repair cooling system leaks as soon as they're noticed.
8 All vehicles covered by this manual are equipped with a pressurized coolant recovery system. A white coolant reservoir located in the left front corner of the engine compartment is connected by a hose to the base of the coolant filler cap **(see illustration)**. As the coolant heats up during engine operation, coolant can escape through a pressurized filler cap, then through a connecting hose into the reservoir. As the engine cools, the coolant is automatically drawn back into the cooling system to maintain the correct level.
9 The coolant level should be checked regularly. It must be between the Full and Low lines on the tank. The level will vary with the temperature of the engine. When the engine is cold, the coolant level should be at or slightly above the Low mark on the tank. Once the engine has warmed up, the level should be at

3.6 The threaded oil filler cap is located on the valve cover - always make sure the area around the opening is clean before unscrewing the cap to prevent dirt from contaminating the engine

or near the Full mark. If it isn't, allow the fluid in the tank to cool, then remove the cap from the reservoir and add coolant to bring the level up to the Full line. Use only ethylene/glycol type coolant and water; do not use supplemental inhibitor additives. If only a small amount of coolant is required to bring the system up to the proper level, water can be used. However, repeated additions of water will dilute the recommended antifreeze and water solution. In order to maintain the proper ratio of antifreeze and water, it is advisable to top up the coolant level with the correct mixture. Refer to your owner's handbook for the recommended ratio.
10 If the coolant level drops within a short time after replenishment, there may be a leak in the system. Inspect the radiator, hoses, engine coolant filler cap, drain plugs, air bleeder plugs and water pump. If no leak is evident, have the radiator cap pressure tested by your dealer.

 Warning: Never remove the radiator cap or the coolant recovery reservoir cap when the engine is running or has just been shut down, because the cooling system is hot. Escaping steam and scalding liquid could cause serious injury.

3.8 The coolant reservoir is located next to the battery - make sure the level is between Low and Full marks on the reservoir

3.14 The windscreen washer fluid reservoir tank is located on the right front corner of the engine compartment

3.17 The brake fluid level should be kept between the MIN and MAX marks on the translucent plastic reservoir - lift up the cap to add fluid

11 If it is necessary to open the radiator cap, wait until the system has cooled completely, then wrap a thick cloth around the cap and turn it to the first stop. If any steam escapes, wait until the system has cooled further, then remove the cap.

12 When checking the coolant level, always note its condition. It should be relatively clear. If it is brown or rust-coloured, the system should be drained, flushed and refilled. Even if the coolant appears to be normal, the corrosion inhibitors wear out with use, so it must be replaced at the specified intervals.

13 Do not allow antifreeze to come in contact with your skin or painted surfaces of the vehicle. Flush contacted areas immediately with plenty of water.

Windscreen washer fluid

14 Fluid for the windscreen washer system is stored in a plastic reservoir which is located on the right side of the engine compartment (see illustration). In milder climates, plain water can be used to top up the reservoir, but the reservoir should be kept no more than two-thirds full to allow for expansion should the water freeze. In colder climates, the use of a specially designed windscreen washer fluid, available at your dealer and any auto parts store, will help lower the freezing point of the fluid. Mix the solution with water in accordance with the manufacturer's directions on the container. Do not use regular antifreeze. It will damage the vehicle's paint.

Battery electrolyte

15 On models not equipped with a sealed battery, unscrew the filler/vent cap and check the electrolyte level. It must be between the upper and lower levels. It the level is low, and add distilled water. Install and securely retighten the cap.

Caution: Overfilling the cells may cause electrolyte to spill over during periods of heavy charging, causing corrosion or damage.

Brake and clutch fluid

16 The brake master cylinder is mounted on the front of the servo unit in the engine compartment. The clutch cylinder used on vehicles with manual transmissions is located next to the master cylinder.

17 To check either the fluid level of the brake master cylinder or clutch reservoir, simply look at the MAX and MIN marks on the reservoirs (see illustration). The level should be at or near the maximum fill line for both reservoirs.

18 If the level is low for either reservoir, wipe the top of the reservoir cover with a clean rag to prevent contamination of the brake or clutch system before lifting the cover.

19 Add only the specified brake fluid to the brake or clutch reservoir (refer to *Recommended lubricants and fluids* at the front of this chapter or to your owner's handbook). Mixing different types of brake fluid can damage the system. Fill the brake master cylinder reservoir only to the dotted line - this brings the fluid to the correct level when you put the cover back on.

⚠ *Warning: Use caution when filling either reservoir - brake fluid can harm your eyes and damage painted surfaces. Do not use brake fluid that has been opened for more than one year (even if the cap has been on) or has been left open. Brake fluid absorbs moisture from the air. Excess moisture can cause a dangerous loss of braking.*

20 While the reservoir cap is removed, inspect the master cylinder reservoir for contamination. If deposits, dirt particles or water droplets are present, the system should be drained and refilled (see Chapter 8 for clutch reservoir or Chapter 9 for brake reservoir).

21 After filling the reservoir to the proper level, make sure the lid is properly seated to prevent fluid leakage and/or system pressure loss.

22 The brake fluid in the master cylinder will drop slightly as the brake pads at each wheel wear down during normal operation. If the

master cylinder requires repeated replenishing to keep it at the proper level, this is an indication of leakage in the brake system, which should be corrected immediately. Check all brake lines and connections, along with the wheel cylinders and servo (see Section 15 for more information).

23 If, upon checking the master cylinder fluid level, you discover one or both reservoirs empty or nearly empty, the brake system must be diagnosed immediately (see Chapter 9).

4 Tyre and tyre pressure checks

1 Periodic inspection of the tyres may spare you from the inconvenience of being stranded with a flat tyre. It can also provide you with vital information regarding possible problems in the steering and suspension systems before major damage occurs.

2 Normal tread wear can be monitored with a simple, inexpensive device known as a tread depth indicator (see illustration). When the tread depth reaches the specified minimum, replace the tyre(s).

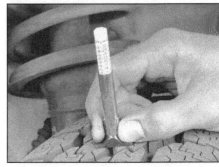

4.2 A tyre tread depth indicator should be used to monitor tyre wear - they are available at auto parts stores and service stations and cost very little

Tyre Tread Wear Patterns

Shoulder Wear

**Underinflation
(wear on both sides)**
Check and adjust pressures

**Incorrect wheel camber
(wear on one side)**
Repair or renew suspension parts

Hard cornering
Reduce speed!

Centre Wear

Overinflation
Check and adjust pressures

If you sometimes have to inflate your car's tyres to the higher pressures specified for maximum load or sustained high speed, don't forget to reduce the pressures to normal afterwards.

Toe Wear

Incorrect toe setting
Adjust front wheel alignment

Note: The feathered edge of the tread which characterises toe wear is best checked by feel.

Uneven Wear

Incorrect camber or castor
Repair or renew suspension parts

Malfunctioning suspension
Repair or renew suspension parts

Unbalanced wheel
Balance tyres

Out-of-round brake disc/drum
Machine or renew

3 Note any abnormal tread wear. Tread pattern irregularities such as shown above **(see illustration)** are indications of front end alignment and/or balance problems. If any of these conditions are noted, take the vehicle to a tyre shop or service station to correct the problem.

4 Look closely for cuts, punctures and embedded nails or tacks. Sometimes a tyre will hold its air pressure for a short time or leak down very slowly even after a nail has embedded itself into the tread. If a slow leak persists, check the valve stem core to make sure it is tight **(see illustration)**. Examine the tread for an object that may have embedded itself into the tyre. If a puncture is suspected, it can be easily verified by spraying a solution

of soapy water onto the puncture area **(see illustration)**. The soapy solution will bubble if there is a leak. Unless the puncture is inordinately large, a tyre shop or garage can usually repair the punctured tyre.

5 Carefully inspect the inner sidewall of each tyre for evidence of brake fluid leakage. If you see any, inspect the brakes immediately.

6 Correct tyre air pressure adds miles to the lifespan of the tyres, improves mileage and enhances overall ride quality. Tyre pressure cannot be accurately estimated by looking at a tyre, particularly if it is a radial. A tyre pressure gauge is therefore essential. Keep an accurate gauge in the glovebox. The pressure gauges fitted to the nozzles of air hoses at petrol stations are often inaccurate.

7 Always check tyre pressure when the tyres are cold. "Cold," in this case, means the vehicle has not been driven over a mile in the three hours preceding a tyre pressure check. A pressure rise of four to eight pounds is not uncommon once the tyres are warm.

8 Unscrew the valve cap protruding from the wheel or hubcap and push the gauge firmly onto the valve **(see illustration)**. Note the reading on the gauge and compare this figure to the recommended tyre pressure shown in this Chapter's Specifications. Be sure to reinstall the valve cap to keep dirt and moisture out of the valve stem mechanism. Check all five tyres and, if necessary, add enough air to bring them up to the recommended pressure levels.

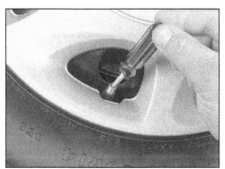

4.4a If a tyre loses air on a steady basis, check the valve core first to make sure it's snug (special inexpensive wrenches are commonly available at parts stores)

4.4b If the valve core is tight, raise the corner of the vehicle with the low tyre and spray a soapy water solution onto the tread as the tyre is turned slowly - slow leaks will cause small bubbles to appear

4.8 To extend the life of your tyres, check the air pressure at least once a week with an accurate gauge (don't forget the spare!)

5.2 The power steering fluid reservoir is located either at the right side of the engine compartment, or at the right rear corner of the engine as shown here (arrowed)

5.6 On this type of reservoir, the power steering fluid is checked with a dipstick which is part of the cap - the fluid level varies with temperature, so the fluid can be checked hot or cold

Every 3000 miles or 3 months

5 Power steering fluid level check

1 Unlike manual steering, the power steering system relies on fluid which may, over a period of time, require replenishing.
2 The fluid reservoir for the power steering pump is located either at the right side of the engine compartment behind the washer fluid reservoir, or at the right rear corner of the engine next to the engine oil level dipstick (see illustration).
3 For the check, the front wheels should be pointed straight-ahead and the engine should be off.
4 Use a clean rag to wipe off the reservoir cap and the area around the cap. This will help prevent any foreign matter from entering the reservoir during the check.
5 Twist off the cap and check the temperature of the fluid by dipping the fluid with your finger.
6 According to reservoir type, the fluid level is checked in one of two ways. Where the reservoir is remotely sited at the right side of the engine compartment, level marks are stamped on the side of the reservoir, and the reservoir is transparent, so you can see the fluid level inside. Where the reservoir is mounted on the engine, a dipstick incorporated in the reservoir cap is used to check the level. With the cap removed, wipe off the fluid with a clean rag, reinsert it, then withdraw it and read the fluid level. On both reservoir types, the level should be at the top of the HOT mark if the fluid was hot to the touch. It should be at the top of the COLD mark if the fluid was cool to the touch. Note that the marks (HOT and COLD) are on opposite sides of the reservoir or dipstick (see

illustration). At no time should the fluid level drop below the lower mark for each heat range.
7 If additional fluid is required, pour the specified type directly into the reservoir, using a funnel to prevent spills.
8 If the reservoir requires frequent fluid additions, all power steering hoses, hose connections, the power steering pump and the rack and pinion assembly should be carefully checked for leaks.

6 Automatic transmission fluid level check

1 The level of the automatic transmission fluid should be carefully maintained. Low fluid level can lead to slipping or loss of drive, while overfilling can cause foaming, loss of fluid and transmission damage.
2 The transmission fluid level should only be

checked when the transmission is hot (at its normal operating temperature). If the vehicle has just been driven over 10 miles (15 miles in a cold climate), and the fluid temperature is 160 to 175-degrees F, the transmission is hot. *Caution: If the vehicle has just been driven for a long time at high speed or in city traffic in hot weather, or if it has been pulling a trailer, an accurate fluid level reading cannot be obtained. Allow the fluid to cool down for about 30 minutes.*
3 Park the vehicle on level ground, set the parking brake and start the engine. While the engine is idling, depress the brake pedal and move the selector lever through all the gear ranges, beginning and ending in Park.
4 With the engine still idling, remove the dipstick from its tube (see illustration). Check the level of the fluid on the dipstick (see illustration) and note its condition.
5 Wipe the fluid from the dipstick with a clean rag and reinsert it back into the filler tube until the cap seats.

6.4a The automatic transmission dipstick (arrowed) is located in a tube which extends forward from the transmission toward the radiator

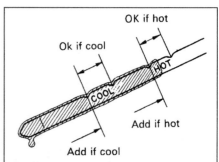

6.4b If the automatic transmission fluid is cold, the level should be between the two lower notches; if it's at operating temperature, the level should be between the two upper notches

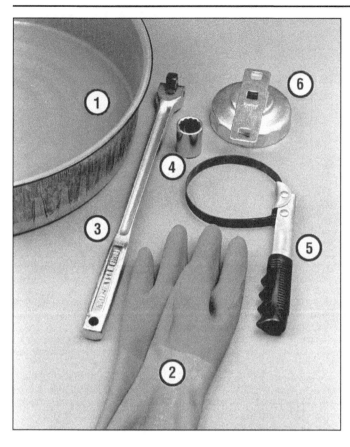

◀ **7.2 These tools are required when changing the engine oil and filter**

1 **Drain pan** - *It should be fairly shallow in depth, but wide in order to prevent spills*
2 **Rubber gloves** - *When removing the drain plug and filter, it is inevitable that you will get oil on your hands (the gloves will prevent burns)*
3 **Breaker bar** - *Sometimes the oil drain plug is pretty tight and a long breaker bar is needed to loosen it*
4 **Socket** – *To be used with the breaker bar or a ratchet (must be the correct size to fit the drain plug)*
5 **Filter wrench** - *This is a metal band-type wrench, which requires clearance around the filter to be effective*
6 **Filter wrench** - *This type fits on the bottom of the filter and can be turned with a ratchet or beaker bar (different size wrenches are available for different types of filters)*

7.7 Use a proper size box-end wrench or socket to remove the oil drain plug and avoid rounding it off

6 Pull the dipstick out again and note the fluid level. If the transmission is cold, the level should be in the COLD or COOL range on the dipstick. If it is hot, the fluid level should be in the HOT range. If the level is at the low side of either range, add the specified automatic transmission fluid through the dipstick tube with a funnel.

7 Add just enough of the recommended fluid to fill the transmission to the proper level. It takes about one pint to raise the level from the low mark to the high mark when the fluid is hot, so add the fluid a little at a time and keep checking the level until it is correct.

8 The condition of the fluid should also be checked along with the level. If the fluid at the end of the dipstick is black or a dark reddish brown colour, or if it emits a burned smell, the fluid should be changed (see Section 28). If you are in doubt about the condition of the fluid, purchase some new fluid and compare the two for colour and smell.

7 Engine oil and oil filter change

1 Frequent oil changes are the best preventive maintenance the home mechanic can give the engine, because ageing oil becomes diluted and contaminated, which leads to premature engine wear.

2 Make sure that you have all the necessary tools before you begin this procedure **(see illustration)**. You should also have plenty of rags or newspapers handy for mopping up any spills.

3 Access to the underside of the vehicle is greatly improved if the vehicle can be lifted on a hoist, driven onto ramps or supported by jack stands.

⚠ *Warning: Do not work under a vehicle which is supported only by a bumper, hydraulic or scissors-type jack.*

4 If this is your first oil change, get under the vehicle and familiarize yourself with the location of the oil drain plug. The engine and exhaust components will be warm during the actual work, so try to anticipate any potential problems before the engine and accessories are hot.

5 Park the vehicle on a level spot. Start the engine and allow it to reach its normal operating temperature (the needle on the temperature gauge should be at least above the bottom mark). Warm oil and sludge will flow out more easily. Turn off the engine when it's warmed up. Remove the filler cap from the valve cover.

6 Raise the vehicle and support it on jack stands.

⚠ *Warning: To avoid personal injury, never get beneath the vehicle when it is supported by*

only by a jack. The jack provided with your vehicle is designed solely for raising the vehicle to remove and replace the wheels. Always use jack stands to support the vehicle when it becomes necessary to place your body underneath the vehicle.

7 Being careful not to touch the hot exhaust components, place the drain pan under the drain plug in the bottom of the pan and remove the plug **(see illustration)**. You may want to wear gloves while unscrewing the plug the final few turns if the engine is really hot.

8 Allow the old oil to drain into the pan. It may be necessary to move the pan farther under the engine as the oil flow slows to a trickle. Inspect the old oil for the presence of metal shavings and chips.

9 After all the oil has drained, wipe off the drain plug with a clean rag. Even minute metal particles clinging to the plug would immediately contaminate the new oil.

10 Clean the area around the drain plug opening, reinstall the plug and tighten it securely, but do not strip the threads.

11 Move the drain pan into position under the oil filter.

12 Remove all tools, rags, etc. from under the vehicle, being careful not to spill the oil in the drain pan, then lower the vehicle.

13 Loosen the oil filter **(see illustration)** by turning it anti-clockwise with the filter wrench.

7.13 The oil filter is usually on very tight, so you'll need a filter wrench for removal - DO NOT use the wrench to tighten the new filter

7.15 Lubricate the oil filter gasket with clean engine oil before installing the filter on the engine

Any standard filter wrench should work. Once the filter is loose, use your hands to unscrew it from the block. Just as the filter is detached from the block, immediately tilt the open end up to prevent the oil inside the filter from spilling out.

 Warning: The engine exhaust manifold may still be hot, so be careful.

14 With a clean rag, wipe off the filter mounting surface on the block. If a residue of old oil is allowed to remain, it will smoke when the block is heated up. It will also prevent the new filter from seating properly. Also make sure that the none of the old gasket remains stuck to the mounting surface. It can be removed with a scraper if necessary.

15 Compare the old filter with the new one to make sure they are the same type. Smear some engine oil on the rubber gasket of the new filter and screw it into place **(see illustration)**. Because overtightening the filter will damage the gasket, do not use a filter wrench to tighten the filter. Tighten it by hand until the gasket contacts the seating surface. Then seat the filter by giving it an additional 3/4-turn.

16 Add new oil to the engine through the oil filler cap in the valve cover. Use a spout or funnel to prevent oil from spilling onto the top of the engine. Pour three US quarts of fresh oil into the engine. Wait a few minutes to allow the oil to drain into the pan, then check the level on the oil dipstick (see Section 3 if necessary). If the oil level is at or near the F mark, install the filler cap hand tight, start the engine and allow the new oil to circulate.

17 Allow the engine to run for about a minute. While the engine is running, look under the vehicle and check for leaks at the oil pan drain plug and around the oil filter. If either is leaking, stop the engine and tighten the plug or filter slightly.

18 Wait a few minutes to allow the oil to trickle down into the pan, then recheck the level on the dipstick and, if necessary, add enough oil to bring the level to the F mark.

19 During the first few trips after an oil change, make it a point to check frequently for leaks and proper oil level.

20 The old oil drained from the engine cannot be re-used in its present state and should be discarded. Check with your local refuse disposal company, disposal facility or environmental agency to see if they will accept the oil for recycling. Don't pour used oil into drains or onto the ground. After the oil has cooled, it can be drained into a suitable container (capped plastic jugs, topped bottles, etc.) for transport to one of these disposal sites.

Every 7500 miles or 6 months

8 Windscreen wiper blade inspection and replacement

1 The windscreen wiper and blade assembly should be inspected periodically for damage, loose components and cracked or worn blade elements.

2 Road film can build up on the wiper blades and affect their efficiency, so they should be washed regularly with a mild detergent solution.

3 The action of the wiping mechanism can loosen bolts, nuts and fasteners, so they should be checked and tightened, as necessary, at the same time the wiper blades are checked.

4 If the wiper blade elements are cracked, worn or warped, or no longer clean adequately, they should be replaced with new ones.

5 Remove the wiper blade assembly from the arm by pushing on the release lever, then sliding the assembly down and out of the hook in the end of the arm **(see illustration)**.

6 Detach the blade insert element and pull it out of the right end of the wiper frame **(see illustration)**.

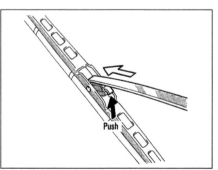

8.5 Push on the release lever and slide the wiper assembly down out of the hook in the end of the wiper arm

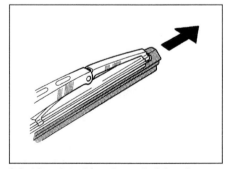

8.6 After detaching the end of the element, slide it out of the end of the frame

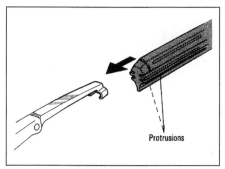

8.7 Insert the end of the element with the protrusions in first

7 Insert the new element end with the small protrusions into the right side of the wiper frame **(see illustration)**. Slide the element fully into place, then seat the protrusions in the end of the frames to secure it.

9 Clutch pedal freeplay check and adjustment

1 Press down lightly on the clutch pedal and, with a small steel ruler, measure the distance that it moves freely before the clutch resistance is felt **(see illustration)**. The freeplay should be within the specified limits. If it isn't, it must be adjusted.
2 Loosen the locknut on the pedal end of the clutch pushrod **(see illustration)**.
3 Turn the pushrod until pedal freeplay and pushrod freeplay are correct.
4 Tighten the locknut.
5 After adjusting the pedal freeplay, check the pedal height from the pedal pad to the asphalt sheet on the floor.
6 If pedal height is incorrect, loosen the locknut and turn the stopper bolt until the height is correct. Tighten the locknut.

10 Battery check, maintenance and charging

Warning: Certain precautions must be followed when checking and servicing the battery. Hydrogen gas, which is highly flammable, is always present in the battery cells, so keep lighted tobacco and all other open flames and sparks away from the battery. The electrolyte inside the battery is actually dilute sulphuric acid, which will cause injury if splashed on your skin or in your eyes. It will also ruin clothes and painted surfaces. When removing the battery cables, always detach the negative cable first and hook it up last!

General checks

1 A routine preventive maintenance program for the battery in your vehicle is the only way

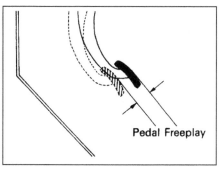

9.1 To check clutch pedal freeplay, measure the distance between the natural resting place of the pedal and the point at which you encounter resistance

to ensure quick and reliable starts. But before performing any battery maintenance, make sure that you have the proper equipment necessary to work safely around the battery **(see illustration)**.
2 There are also several precautions that should be taken whenever battery maintenance is performed. Before servicing the battery, always turn the engine and all accessories off and disconnect the cable from the negative terminal of the battery.
Caution: If the stereo in your vehicle is equipped with an anti-theft system, make sure you have the correct activation code before disconnecting the battery.
3 The battery produces hydrogen gas, which is both flammable and explosive. Never create a spark, smoke or light a match around the battery. Always charge the battery in a ventilated area.

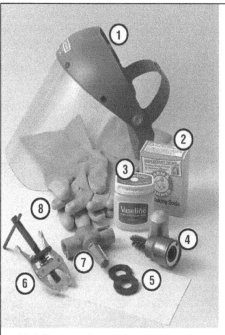

10.1 Tools and materials required for battery maintenance

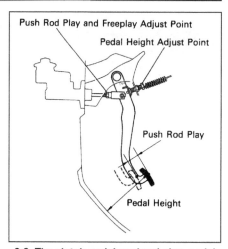

9.2 The clutch pedal pushrod play, pedal height and freeplay adjustments are made by loosening the locknut and turning the threaded adjuster

4 Electrolyte contains poisonous and corrosive sulphuric acid. Do not allow it to get in your eyes, on your skin on your clothes. Never ingest it. Wear protective safety glasses when working near the battery. Keep children away from the battery.
5 Note the external condition of the battery. If the positive terminal and cable clamp on your vehicle's battery is equipped with a rubber protector, make sure that it's not torn or damaged. It should completely cover the terminal. Look for any corroded or loose connections, cracks in the case or cover or loose hold-down clamps. Also check the entire length of each cable for cracks and frayed conductors.

1 *Face shield/safety goggles - When removing corrosion with a brush, the acidic particles can easily fly up into your eyes*
2 *Baking soda - A solution of baking soda and water can be used to neutralize corrosion*
3 *Petroleum jelly - A layer of this on the battery posts will help prevent corrosion*
4 *Battery post/cable cleaner - This wire brush cleaning tool will remove all traces of corrosion from the battery posts and cable clamps*
5 *Treated felt washers - Placing one of these on each post, directly under the cable clamps, will help prevent corrosion*
6 *Puller - Sometimes the cable clamps are very difficult to pull off the posts, even after the nut/bolt has been completely loosened. This tool pulls the clamp straight up and off the post without damage*
7 *Battery post/cable cleaner - Here is another cleaning tool which is a slightly different version of number 4 above, but it does the same thing*
8 *Rubber gloves - Another safety item to consider when servicing the battery; remember that's acid inside the battery*

10.6a Battery terminal corrosion usually appears as light, fluffy powder

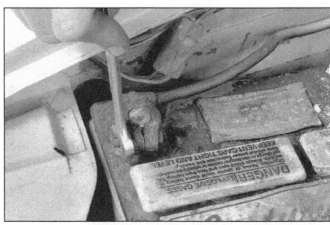

10.6b Removing a cable from the battery post with a wrench - sometimes a pair of special battery pliers are required for this procedure if corrosion has caused deterioration of the nut hex (always remove the ground (-) cable first and hook it up last!)

6 If corrosion, which looks like white, fluffy deposits **(see illustration)** is evident, particularly around the terminals, the battery should be removed for cleaning. Loosen the cable clamp bolts with a wrench, being careful to remove the ground cable first, and slide them off the terminals **(see illustration)**. Then disconnect the hold-down clamp bolt and nut, remove the clamp and lift the battery from the engine compartment.

7 Clean the cable clamps thoroughly with a battery brush or a terminal cleaner and a solution of warm water and baking soda **(see illustration)**. Wash the terminals and the top of the battery case with the same solution but make sure that the solution doesn't get into the battery. When cleaning the cables, terminals and battery top, wear safety goggles and rubber gloves to prevent any solution from coming in contact with your eyes or hands. Wear old clothes too - even diluted sulphuric acid splashed onto clothes will burn holes in them. If the terminals have been extensively corroded, clean them up with a terminal cleaner **(see illustration)**. Thoroughly wash all cleaned areas with plain water.

8 Make sure that the battery tray is in good condition and the hold-down nut and bolt are tight **(see illustration)**. If the battery is removed from the tray, make sure no parts remain in the bottom of the tray when the battery is reinstalled. When reinstalling the hold-down clamp bolt or nut, do not overtighten it.

Electrolyte level check

9 On batteries with removable cell covers, the electrolyte level in the battery should be checked (and if necessary topped up) at regular intervals; the check should be made more often if the car is operated in high ambient temperature conditions. "Maintenance-free" batteries (usually identifiable by a label on the battery top) do not require topping-up and the cell covers are not removable.

10 On some batteries, the case is translucent and incorporates minimum (or lower) and maximum (or upper) level marks; with the vehicle parked on level ground, the electrolyte level in each cell must be maintained between these marks. On batteries without a translucent case and suitable level marks, the general rule is that the electrolyte level must be maintained just above the top of the cell plates.

11 If topping up is necessary, remove the cell covers from the top of the battery then carefully add distilled or de-ionized water to raise the electrolyte level in each cell, but do not overfill. With the electrolyte level replenished, refit the cell covers.

Cleaning

12 Corrosion on the hold-down components, battery case and surrounding areas can be removed with a solution of water and baking soda. Thoroughly rinse all cleaned areas with plain water.

13 Any metal parts of the vehicle damaged by corrosion should be covered with a zinc-based primer, then painted.

Charging

 Warning: When batteries are being charged, hydrogen gas, which is very explosive and flammable, is produced. Do not smoke or allow open flames near a charging or a recently charged battery. Wear eye protection when near the battery during charging. Also, make sure the charger is unplugged before connecting or disconnecting the battery from the charger.

10.7a When cleaning the cable clamps, all corrosion must be removed (the inside of the clamp is tapered to match the taper on the post, so don't remove too much material)

10.7b Regardless of the type of tool used to clean the battery posts, a clean, shiny surface should be the result

10.8 Make sure the battery clamp nut and bolt (arrowed) are tight

14 Slow-rate charging is the best way to restore a battery that's discharged to the point where it will not start the engine. It's also a good way to maintain the battery charge in a vehicle that's only driven a few miles between starts. Maintaining the battery charge is particularly important in the winter when the battery must work harder to start the engine and electrical accessories that drain the battery are in greater use.

15 It's best to use a one or two-amp battery charger (sometimes called a "trickle" charger). They are the safest and put the least strain on the battery. They are also the least expensive. For a faster charge, you can use a higher amperage charger, but don't use one rated more than 1/10th the amp/hour rating of the battery. Rapid boost charges that claim to restore the power of the battery in one to two hours are hardest on the battery and can damage batteries not in good condition. This type of charging should only be used in emergency situations.

16 The average time necessary to charge a battery should be listed in the instructions that come with the charger. As a general rule, a trickle charger will charge a battery in 12 to 16 hours.

11 Drivebelt check, adjustment and replacement

Check

1 The alternator, power steering pump and air conditioning compressor drivebelts, also referred to as simply "fan" belts, are located at the right end of the engine. The good condition and proper adjustment of the alternator belt is critical to the operation of the engine. Because of their composition and the high stresses to which they are subjected, drivebelts stretch and deteriorate as they get older. They must therefore be periodically inspected.

2 The number of belts used on a particular vehicle depends on the engine type and accessories installed. One belt transmits power from the crankshaft to the water pump and alternator. If the vehicle is equipped with power steering and/or air conditioning, a separate belt (or two separate belts) are used to drive these components.

3 With the engine off, open the bonnet and locate the drivebelts. With a flashlight, check each belt for separation of the adhesive rubber on both sides of the core, core separation from the belt side, a severed core, separation of the ribs from the adhesive rubber, cracking or separation of the ribs, and torn or worn ribs or cracks in the inner ridges of the ribs **(see illustration)**. Also check for fraying and glazing, which gives the belt a shiny appearance. Both sides of the belt should be inspected, which means you will have to twist the belt to check the underside. Use your fingers to feel the belt where you can't see it. If any of the above conditions are evident, replace the belt (go to Step 8).

4 To check the tension of each belt, the following rule of thumb method is recommended: Push firmly on the belt with your thumb at a distance halfway between the pulleys and note how far the belt can be pushed (deflected). Measure this deflection with a ruler **(see illustration)**. The belt should deflect 1/4-inch if the distance from pulley center to pulley center is between 7 and 11 inches; the belt should deflect 1/2-inch if the distance from pulley center to pulley center is between 12 and 16 inches.

Adjustment

5 Two adjustment methods are used for the drivebelts according to their arrangement. On all models, the alternator drivebelt is adjusted by loosening the mounting and adjustment/lock bolts then moving the alternator either by hand, or by turning the adjuster bolt, as necessary while checking the tension in accordance with one of the above methods. Tighten the mounting and adjustment/lock bolts when the tension is correct. To adjust the tension of the other belts, first check to see if an idler pulley is used in the belt arrangement. If an idler pulley is fitted, loosen the idler pulley lock nut and turn the adjusting bolt **(see**

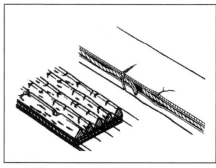

11.3 Check the multi-ribbed belt for signs of wear like these – if the belt looks worn, replace it

illustration). Measure the belt tension in accordance with one of the above methods. Repeat this step until the drivebelt is adjusted correctly then tighten the idler pulley locknut. If an idler pulley is not fitted, adjustment is carried out at the power steering pump. Loosen the adjustment bolt that secures the pump to the slotted bracket and pivot the pump (away from the engine to tighten the belt, toward it to loosen it). Repeat the procedure until the drivebelt tension is correct and tighten the bolt.

Replacement

6 To replace a belt, follow the above procedures for drivebelt adjustment but slip the belt off the relevant pulleys and remove it. Depending on which belt you are replacing, it will probably be necessary to remove an outer belt first because of the way they are arranged on the pulleys. Because of this, and because belts tend to wear out more or less together, it is a good idea to replace all the belts at the same time. Mark each belt and its appropriate pulley groove so the replacement belts can be installed in their proper positions.

7 Take the old belts to the parts store in order to make a direct comparison for length, width and design.

8 After replacing the drivebelt, make sure that it fits properly in the ribbed grooves in the pulleys **(see illustration)**. It is essential that the belt be properly centered.

9 Adjust the belt(s) in accordance with the procedure outlined above.

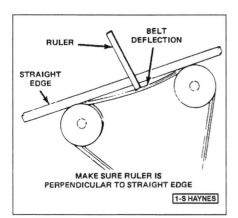

11.4 Measuring drivebelt deflection with a straightedge and ruler

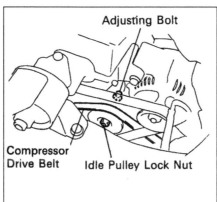

11.5 After loosening the idler pulley lock nut, turn the adjusting bolt

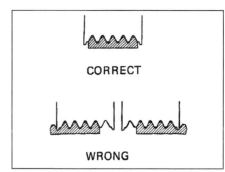

11.8 When installing a multi-ribbed belt, make sure that it is centered - it must not overlap either edge of the pulley

12 Underbonnet hose check and replacement

Caution: Replacement of air conditioning hoses must be left to a dealer service department or air conditioning shop that has the equipment to depressurize the system safely. Never remove air conditioning components or hoses until the system has been depressurized.

General

1 High temperatures in the engine compartment can cause the deterioration of the rubber and plastic hoses used for engine, accessory and emission systems operation. Periodic inspection should be made for cracks, loose clamps, material hardening and leaks.
2 Information specific to the cooling system hoses can be found in Section 13.
3 Some, but not all, hoses are secured to the fittings with clamps. Where clamps are used, check to be sure they haven't lost their tension, allowing the hose to leak. If clamps aren't used, make sure the hose has not expanded and/or hardened where it slips over the fitting, allowing it to leak.

Vacuum hoses

4 It's quite common for vacuum hoses, especially those in the emissions system, to be colour-coded or identified by coloured stripes moulded into them. Various systems require hoses with different wall thickness, collapse resistance and temperature resistance. When replacing hoses, be sure the new ones are made of the same material.
5 Often the only effective way to check a hose is to remove it completely from the vehicle. If more than one hose is removed, be sure to label the hoses and fittings to ensure correct installation.
6 When checking vacuum hoses, be sure to include any plastic T-fittings in the check. Inspect the fittings for cracks and the hose where it fits over the fitting for distortion, which could cause leakage.
7 A small piece of vacuum hose (1/4-inch inside diameter) can be used as a steth-oscope to detect vacuum leaks. Hold one end of the hose to your ear and probe around vacuum hoses and fittings, listening for the "hissing" sound characteristic of a vacuum leak.

 Warning: When probing with the vacuum hose stethoscope, be very careful not to come into contact with moving engine components such as the drivebelts, cooling fan, etc.

Fuel hoses

 Warning: There are certain precautions which must be taken when inspecting or servicing fuel system comp-onents. Work in a well ventilated area and do not allow open flames (cigarettes, appliance pilot lights, etc.) or bare light bulbs near the work area. Mop up any spills immediately and do not store fuel soaked rags where they could ignite.

8 Check all rubber fuel lines for deterioration and chafing. Check especially for cracks in areas where the hose bends and just before fittings, such as where a hose attaches to the fuel filter.
9 High quality fuel line, specifically designed for fuel injection systems, must be used for fuel line replacement.

 Warning: Never use anything other than the proper fuel line for fuel line replacement.

10 Spring-type clamps are commonly used on fuel lines. These clamps often lose their tension over a period of time, and can be "sprung" during removal. Replace all spring-type clamps with screw clamps whenever a hose is replaced.

Metal lines

11 Sections of metal line are often used for fuel line between the fuel pump and fuel

ALWAYS CHECK FOR CHAFED OR BURNED AREAS THAT MAY CAUSE AN UNTIMELY AND COSTLY FAILURE.

SOFT HOSE INDICATES INSIDE DETERIORATION. THIS DETERIORATION CAN CONTAMINATE THE COOLING SYSTEM AND CAUSE PARTICLES TO CLOG THE RADIATOR.

HARDENED HOSE CAN FAIL AT ANY TIME. TIGHTENING HOSE CLAMPS WILL NOT SEAL THE CONNECTION OR STOP LEAKS.

SWOLLEN HOSE OR OIL SOAKED ENDS INDICATE DANGER AND POSSIBLE FAILURE FROM OIL OR GREASE CONTAMINATION. SQUEEZE THE HOSE TO LOCATE CRACKS AND BREAKS THAT CAUSE LEAKS.

13.4 Hoses, like drivebelts, have a habit of failing at the worst possible time - to prevent the inconvenience of a blown radiator or heater hose, inspect them carefully as shown here

injection unit. Check carefully to be sure the line has not been bent or crimped and that cracks have not started in the line.
12 If a section of metal fuel line must be replaced, only seamless steel tubing should be used, since copper and aluminum tubing don't have the strength necessary to withstand normal engine vibration.
13 Check the metal brake lines where they enter the master cylinder and brake proportioning unit (if used) for cracks in the lines or loose fittings. Any sign of brake fluid leakage calls for an immediate thorough inspection of the brake system.

13 Cooling system check

1 Many major engine failures can be attributed to a faulty cooling system. If the vehicle is equipped with an automatic transmission, the cooling system also cools the transmission fluid and thus plays an important role in prolonging transmission life.
2 The cooling system should be checked with the engine cold. Do this before the vehicle is driven for the day or after the engine has been shut off for at least three hours.
3 Remove the radiator cap by turning it to the left until it reaches a stop. If you hear a hissing sound (indicating there is still pressure in the system), wait until it stops. Now press down on the cap with the palm of your hand and continue turning to the left until the cap can be removed. Thoroughly clean the cap, inside and out, with clean water. Also clean the filler neck on the radiator. All traces of corrosion should be removed. The coolant inside the radiator should be relatively transparent. If it's rust-coloured, the system should be drained and refilled (see Section 25). If the coolant level isn't up to the top, add additional antifreeze/coolant mixture (see Section 3).
4 Carefully check the large upper and lower radiator hoses along with the smaller diameter heater hoses which run from the engine to the firewall. Inspect each hose along its entire length, replacing any hose which is cracked, swollen or shows signs of deterioration. Cracks may become more apparent if the hose is squeezed (see illustration). Regardless of condition, it's a good idea to replace hoses with new ones every two years.
5 Make sure that all hose connections are tight. A leak in the cooling system will usually show up as white or rust-coloured deposits on the areas adjoining the leak. If wire-type clamps are used at the ends of the hoses, it may be a good idea to replace them with more secure screw-type clamps.
6 Use compressed air or a soft brush to remove bugs, leaves, etc. from the front of the radiator or air conditioning condenser. Be careful not to damage the delicate cooling fins or cut yourself on them.

7 Every other inspection, or at the first indication of cooling system problems, have the cap and system pressure tested. If you don't have a pressure tester, most repair shops will do this for a minimal charge.

14 Tyre rotation

1 The tyres should be rotated at the specified intervals and whenever uneven wear is noticed. Since the vehicle will be raised and the tyres removed anyway, check the brakes (see Section 15) at this time.
2 Radial tyres must be rotated in a specific pattern **(see illustration)**.
3 Refer to the information in *"Jacking and*

vehicle support" at the rear of this manual for the proper procedures to follow when raising the vehicle and changing a tyre. If the brakes are to be checked, do not apply the parking brake. Make sure the tyres are blocked to prevent the vehicle from rolling.
4 Preferably, the entire vehicle should be raised at the same time. This can be done on a hoist or by jacking up each corner and then lowering the vehicle onto jack stands placed under the frame rails. Always use four jack stands and make sure the vehicle is firmly supported.
5 After rotation, check and adjust the tyre pressures as necessary and be sure to check the nut tightness.
6 For further information on the wheels and tyres, refer to Chapter 10.

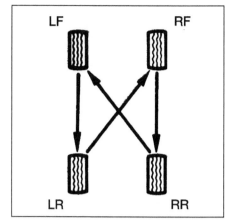

14.2 The recommended tyre rotation pattern for these vehicles

Every 15 000 miles or 12 months

15 Brake check

Note: *For detailed photographs of the brake system, refer to Chapter 9.*
1 In addition to the specified intervals, the brakes should be inspected every time the wheels are removed or whenever a defect is suspected. Any of the following symptoms could indicate a potential brake system defect: The vehicle pulls to one side when the brake pedal is depressed; the brakes make squealing or dragging noises when applied; brake travel is excessive; the pedal pulsates; brake fluid leaks, usually onto the inside of the tyre or wheel.
2 The disc brake pads have built-in wear indicators which should make a high-pitched squealing or scraping noise when they are worn to the replacement point. When you hear this noise, replace the pads immediately or expensive damage to the discs can result.
3 Loosen the wheel nuts.

4 Raise the vehicle and place it securely on jack stands.
5 Remove the wheels (see *"Jacking and vehicle support"* at the rear of this book, or your owner's handbook, if necessary).

Disc brakes

6 There are two pads - an outer and an inner - in each caliper. The pads are visible through small inspection holes in each caliper **(see illustration)** .
7 Check the pad thickness by looking at each end of the caliper and through the inspection hole in the caliper body. If the lining material is less than the thickness listed in this Chapter's Specifications, replace the pads. **Note:** *Keep in mind that the lining material is riveted or bonded to a metal backing plate and the metal portion is not included in this measurement.*
8 If it is difficult to determine the exact thickness of the remaining pad material by the above method, or if you are concerned about the condition of the pads, remove the caliper(s), then remove the pads from the calipers for further inspection (refer to Chapter 9).

9 Once the pads are removed from the calipers, clean them with brake cleaner and re-measure them with a small steel pocket ruler or a vernier caliper.
10 Measure the disc thickness with a micrometer to make sure that it still has service life remaining. If any disc is thinner than the specified minimum thickness, replace it (refer to Chapter 9). Even if the disc has service life remaining, check its condition. Look for scoring, gouging and burned spots. If these conditions exist, remove the disc and have it resurfaced (see Chapter 9).
11 Before installing the wheels, check all brake lines and hoses for damage, wear, deformation, cracks, corrosion, leakage, bends and twists, particularly in the vicinity of the rubber hoses at the calipers. Check the clamps for tightness and the connections for leakage. Make sure that all hoses and lines are clear of sharp edges, moving parts and the exhaust system. If any of the above conditions are noted, repair, reroute or replace the lines and/or fittings as necessary (see Chapter 9).

Rear drum brakes

12 To check the brake shoe lining thickness without removing the brake drums, remove the rubber plug from the backing plate and use a flashlight to inspect the linings **(see illustration)**. For a more thorough brake inspection, follow the procedure below.
13 Refer to Chapter 9 and remove the rear brake drums.

⚠️ *Warning: Brake dust produced by lining wear and deposited on brake components contains asbestos, which is hazardous to your health. DO NOT blow it out with compressed air and DO NOT inhale it! DO NOT use petrol or solvents to remove the dust. Brake system cleaner should be used to flush the dust into a drain pan. After the*

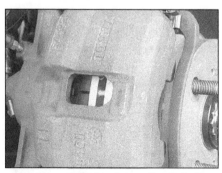

15.6 You will find an inspection hole like this in each caliper - placing a steel ruler across the hole should enable you to determine the thickness of remaining pad material for both inner and outer pads

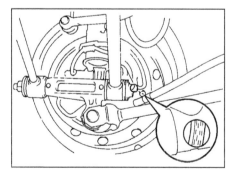

15.12 A quick check of the remaining drum brake shoe lining material can be made by removing the rubber plug in the backing plate and looking through the inspection hole

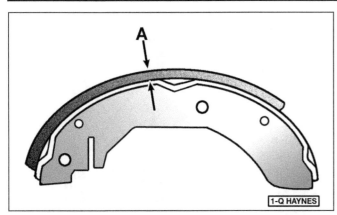

15.15 If the lining is bonded to the brake shoe, measure the lining thickness from the outer surface to the metal shoe, as shown here; if the lining is riveted to the shoe, measure from the lining outer surface to the rivet head

15.17 Carefully peel back the wheel cylinder boot and check for leaking fluid indicating that the cylinder must be replaced or rebuilt

brake components are wiped clean with a damp rag, dispose of the contaminated rag(s) and solvent in a covered and labelled container. Try to use non-asbestos replacement parts whenever possible.

14 Note the thickness of the lining material on the rear brake shoes **(see illustration)** and look for signs of contamination by brake fluid and grease.

15 If the lining material is within 1/16-inch of the recessed rivets or metal shoes, replace the brake shoes with new ones. The shoes should also be replaced if they are cracked, glazed (shiny lining surfaces) or contaminated with brake fluid or grease. See Chapter 9 for the replacement procedure.

16 Check the shoe return and hold-down springs and the adjusting mechanism to make sure they're installed correctly and in good condition. Deteriorated or distorted springs, if not replaced, could allow the linings to drag and wear prematurely.

17 Check the wheel cylinders for leakage by carefully peeling back the rubber boots **(see illustration)**. If brake fluid is noted behind the boots, the wheel cylinders must be replaced (see Chapter 9).

18 Check the drums for cracks, score marks, deep scratches and hard spots, which will appear as small discoloured areas. If imperfections cannot be removed with emery cloth, the drums must be resurfaced by an automotive machine shop (see Chapter 9 for more detailed information).

19 Install the brake drums (see Chapter 9).

20 Install the wheels and nuts.

21 Remove the jack stands and lower the vehicle.

22 Tighten the wheel nuts to the torque listed in this Chapter's Specifications.

Vacuum servo check

23 Sit in the driver's seat and perform the following sequence of tests.

24 With the engine stopped, depress the brake pedal several times - the travel distance should not change.

25 With the brake fully depressed, start the engine - the pedal should move down a little when the engine starts.

26 Depress the brake, stop the engine and hold the pedal in for about 30 seconds - the pedal should neither sink nor rise.

27 Restart the engine, run it for about a minute and turn it off. Then firmly depress the brake several times - the pedal travel should decrease with each application.

28 If your brakes do not operate as described above when the preceding tests are performed, the servo unit is either in need of repair or has failed. Refer to Chapter 9 for the removal procedure.

Parking brake

29 Slowly pull up on the parking brake and count the number of clicks you hear until the handle is up as far as it will go. The adjustment is correct if you hear the specified number of clicks. If you hear more or fewer clicks, it's time to adjust the parking brake (refer to Chapter 9).

30 An alternative method of checking the parking brake is to park the vehicle on a steep hill with the parking brake set and the transmission in Neutral. If the parking brake cannot prevent the vehicle from rolling, it is in need of adjustment (see Chapter 9).

16 Air filter replacement

1 The air filter is located inside a housing at the left side of the engine compartment.

2 To remove the air filter, release the four spring clips that keep the two halves of the air cleaner housing together, then lift the cover up and remove the air filter element **(see illustrations)**.

3 Inspect the outer surface of the filter element. If it is dirty, replace it. If it is only moderately dusty, it can be re-used by blowing it clean from the back to the front surface with compressed air. Because it is a pleated paper type filter, it cannot be washed or oiled. If it cannot be cleaned satisfactorily with compressed air, discard and replace it. While the cover is off, be careful not to drop anything down into the housing.

Caution: Never drive the vehicle with the air cleaner removed. Excessive engine wear could result and backfiring could even cause a fire under the bonnet.

4 Wipe out the inside of the air cleaner housing.

5 Place the new filter into the air cleaner housing, making sure it seats properly.

6 Installation of the cover is the reverse of removal.

16.2a Detach the clips and separate the cover from the air cleaner housing

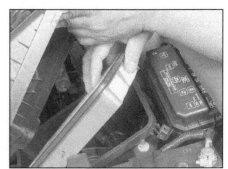

16.2b Hold the cover up out of the way and lift the element out

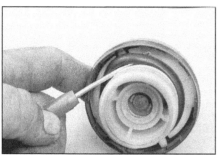

17.2 Use a small screwdriver to carefully pry out the old gasket - take care not to damage the cap

17 Fuel system check

 Warning: Certain precautions should be observed when inspecting or servicing the fuel system components. Work in a well ventilated area and do not allow open flames (cigarettes, appliance pilot lights, etc.) near the work area. Mop up spills immediately and do not store fuel soaked rags where they could ignite. It is a good idea to keep a dry chemical (Class B) fire extinguisher near the work area any time the fuel system is being serviced.

1 If you smell petrol while driving or after the vehicle has been sitting in the sun, inspect the fuel system immediately.

2 Remove the fuel filler cap and inspect if for damage and corrosion. The gasket should have an unbroken sealing imprint. If the gasket is damaged or corroded, remove it and install a new one **(see illustration)**.

3 Inspect the fuel feed and return lines for cracks. Make sure that the threaded flare-nut type connectors which secure the metal fuel lines to the fuel injection system and the banjo bolts which secure the banjo fittings to the in-line fuel filter are tight.

4 Since some components of the fuel system - the fuel tank and part of the fuel feed and return lines, for example - are underneath the vehicle, they can be inspected more easily with the vehicle raised on a hoist. If that's not possible, raise the vehicle and support it securely on jack stands.

5 With the vehicle raised and safely supported, inspect the fuel tank and filler neck for punctures, cracks and other damage. The connection between the filler neck and the tank is particularly critical. Sometimes a rubber filler neck will leak because of loose clamps or deteriorated rubber **(see illustration)**. These are problems a home mechanic can usually rectify.

 Warning: Do not, under any circumstances, try to repair a fuel tank (except rubber components). A welding torch or any open flame can easily cause fuel vapours inside the tank to explode.

17.5 Inspect the filler hose for cracks and make sure the clamps are tight

6 Carefully check all rubber hoses and metal lines leading away from the fuel tank. Check for loose connections, deteriorated hoses, crimped lines and other damage. Carefully inspect the lines from the tank to the fuel injection system. Repair or replace damaged sections as necessary (see Chapter 4).

18 Automatic transmission differential lubricant level check (three-speed only)

1 The three-speed automatic transmission differential has a separate lubricant supply with a check/fill plug which must be removed to check the level. If the vehicle is raised to gain access to the plug, be sure to support it safely on jack stands - DO NOT crawl under the vehicle when it's supported only by the jack.

2 Remove the filler plug from the front of the differential **(see illustration)**.

3 Use your little finger as a dipstick to make sure the lubricant level is even with the bottom of the plug hole. If not, use a syringe or a gear oil pump to add the recommended lubricant (see this Chapter's Specifications) until it just starts to run out of the opening.

4 Install the plug and tighten it securely.

19 Manual transmission lubricant level check

1 The manual transmission does not have a dipstick. To check the fluid level, raise the

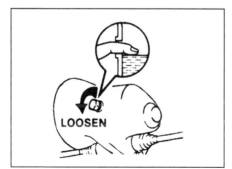

19.1 Use your finger as a dipstick to check the manual transmission lubricant level

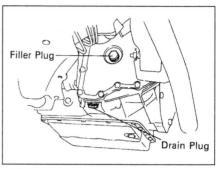

18.2 Differential filler and drain plug details (three-speed automatic transmission)

vehicle and support it securely on jack stands. On the lower front side of the transmission housing, you will see a plug **(see illustration)**. Remove it. If the lubricant level is correct, it should be up to the lower edge of the hole.

2 If the transmission needs more lubricant (if the level is not up to the hole), use a syringe or a gear oil pump to add more. Stop filling the transmission when the lubricant begins to run out the hole.

3 Install the plug and tighten it securely. Drive the vehicle a short distance, then check for leaks.

20 Steering and suspension check

Note: *For detailed illustrations of the steering and suspension components, refer to Chapter 10.*

With the wheels on the ground

1 With the vehicle stopped and the front wheels pointed straight-ahead, rock the steering wheel gently back and forth. If freeplay **(see illustration)** is excessive, a front wheel bearing, steering column shaft, intermediate shaft, lower arm balljoint or steering system joint is worn or the steering gear is out of adjustment or broken. Refer to Chapter 10 for the appropriate repair procedure.

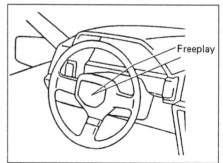

20.1 Steering wheel freeplay is the amount of travel between an initial steering input and the point at which the front wheels begin to turn (indicated by a slight resistance)

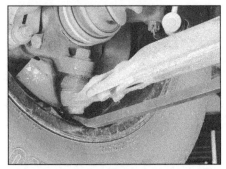

20.7 To check a balljoint for wear, raise the vehicle and support it on jack stands, place a 7-inch thick block of wood under the tyre, block the wheel with chocks and lower the jack until there is about half a load on the coil spring - then move the lower arm up and down with a prybar to make sure there is no play in the balljoint (if there is, replace it)

20.8 Push on the balljoint boot to check for damage

21.2 Flex the driveshaft boots by hand to check for cracks and/or leaking grease

2 Other symptoms, such as excessive vehicle body movement over rough roads, swaying (leaning) around corners and binding as the steering wheel is turned, may indicate faulty steering and/or suspension components.

3 Check the shock absorbers by pushing down and releasing the vehicle several times at each corner. If the vehicle does not come back to a level position within one or two bounces, the shocks/struts are worn and must be replaced. When bouncing the vehicle up and down, listen for squeaks and noises from the suspension components. Additional information on suspension components can be found in Chapter 10.

Under the vehicle

4 Raise the vehicle with a floor jack and support it securely on jack stands. See *"Jacking and vehicle support"* at the rear of this book for the proper jacking points.

5 Check the tyres for irregular wear patterns

and proper inflation. See Section 4 in this Chapter for information regarding tyre wear and Chapter 10 for the wheel bearing replacement procedures.

6 Inspect the universal joint between the steering shaft and the steering gear housing. Check the steering gear housing for grease leakage or oozing. Make sure that the dust seals and boots are not damaged and that the boot clamps are not loose. Check the steering linkage for looseness or damage. Check the tie-rod ends for excessive play. Look for loose bolts, broken or disconnected parts and deteriorated rubber bushings on all suspension and steering components. While an assistant turns the steering wheel from side to side, check the steering components for free movement, chafing and binding. If the steering components do not seem to be reacting with the movement of the steering wheel, try to determine where the slack is located.

7 Check the balljoints for wear by placing a 7-inch thick wooden block under each tyre. Lower the jack until there is about half a load on the coil spring. Make sure that the front wheels are in a straight-forward position and block the wheel with chocks. Move each lower arm up and down with a pry bar (see

illustration) to ensure that its balljoint has no play. If any balljoint does have play, replace it. See Chapter 10 for the front balljoint replacement procedure.

8 Inspect the balljoint boots for damage and leaking grease (see illustration). Replace the balljoints with new ones if they are damaged (see Chapter 10).

21 Driveshaft boot check

1 The driveshaft boots are very important because they prevent dirt and water from entering and damaging the constant velocity (CV) joints. Oil and grease can cause the boot material to deteriorate prematurely, so it's a good idea to wash the boots with soap and water. Because it constantly pivots back and forth following the steering action of the front hub, the outer CV boot wears out sooner and should be inspected regularly.

2 Inspect the boots for tears and cracks as well as loose clamps (see illustration). If there is any evidence of cracks or leaking lubricant, they must be replaced (see Chapter 8).

Every 30 000 miles or 2 years

22 Fuel filter replacement

1 Disconnect the negative battery cable.
Caution: If the stereo in your vehicle is equipped with an anti-theft system, make sure you have the correct activation code before disconnecting the battery.

2 The canister filter is mounted in a bracket on the firewall near the left side of the car.

3 Remove any components that would interfere with access to the top of the filter.

4 Using a backup wrench to steady the filter, remove the threaded banjo bolt at the top and loosen the fitting at the bottom of the fuel filter

(use a flare-nut wrench if possible) (see illustrations).

5 Remove both bracket bolts from the firewall and remove the old filter and the filter support bracket assembly.

6 Note that the inlet and outlet pipes are clearly labelled on their respective ends of the filter and that the flanged end of the filter faces down. Make sure the new filter is installed so that it's facing the proper direction as noted above. When correctly installed, the filter should be installed so that the outlet pipe faces up and the inlet pipe faces down.

7 Using the new crush washers provided by the filter manufacturer, install the inlet and outlet fittings and tighten them securely.

8 The remainder of installation is the reverse of the removal procedure.

22.4a Using a backup wrench, remove the banjo bolt at the top and . . .

22.4b . . . loosen the fitting at the bottom of the filter

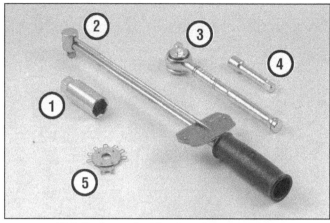

23.1 Tools required for changing spark plugs

1 **Spark plug socket** - This will have special padding inside to protect the spark plug porcelain insulator
2 **Torque wrench** - Although not mandatory, use of this tool is the best way to ensure that the plugs are tightened properly
3 **Ratchet** - Standard hand tool to fit the plug socket
4 **Extension** - Depending on model and accessories, you may need special extensions and universal joints to reach one or more of the plugs
5 **Spark plug gap gauge** - This gauge for checking the gap comes in a variety of styles. Make sure the gap for your engine is included

23 Spark plug check and replacement

1 Spark plug replacement requires a spark plug socket which fits onto a ratchet wrench. This socket is lined with a rubber grommet to protect the porcelain insulator of the spark plug and to hold the plug while you insert it into the spark plug hole. You will also need a wire-type feeler gauge to check and adjust the spark plug gap and a torque wrench to tighten the new plugs to the specified torque **(see illustration)**.
2 If you are replacing the plugs, purchase the new plugs, adjust them to the proper gap and then replace each plug one at a time. **Note:** *When buying new spark plugs, it's essential that you obtain the correct plugs for your specific vehicle. This information can be found in the Specifications Section at the beginning of this Chapter, on the Vehicle Emissions Control Information (VECI) label (where fitted) located on the underside of the bonnet or in the owner's handbook. If these sources specify different plugs, purchase the spark plug type specified on the VECI label because that information is provided specifically for your engine.*
3 Inspect each of the new plugs for defects. If there are any signs of cracks in the porcelain insulator of a plug, don't use it.

4 Check the electrode gaps of the new plugs. Check the gap by inserting the wire gauge of the proper thickness between the electrodes at the tip of the plug **(see illustration)**. The gap between the electrodes should be identical to that listed in this Chapter's Specifications or on the VECI label. If the gap is incorrect, use the notched adjuster on the feeler gauge body to bend the curved side electrode slightly **(see illustration)**.
Caution: Some plugs are supplied with the gap pre-set. There is no need to adjust them.
5 If the side electrode is not exactly over the center electrode, use the notched adjuster to align them.

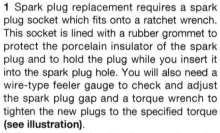

23.4a Spark plug manufacturers recommend using a wire-type gauge when checking the gap - if the wire does not slide between the electrodes with a slight drag, adjustment is required

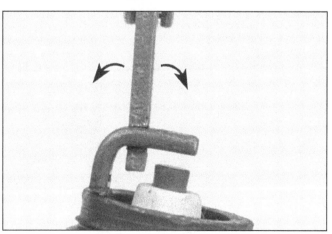

23.4b To change the gap, bend the side electrode only, as indicated by the arrows, and be very careful not to crack or chip the porcelain insulator surrounding the center electrode

23.6 When removing the spark plug wires, pull only on the boot and use a twisting/pulling motion

23.8 Use a spark plug socket with a long extension to unscrew the spark plug

Removal

6 To prevent the possibility of mixing up spark plug leads, work on one spark plug at a time. Remove the wire and boot from one spark plug. Grasp the boot - not the cable - as shown, give it a half twisting motion and pull straight up **(see illustration)**.

7 If compressed air is available, blow any dirt or foreign material away from the spark plug area before proceeding (a common bicycle pump will also work).

8 Remove the spark plug **(see illustration)**. Examination of the spark plugs will give a good indication of the condition of the engine. If the insulator nose of the spark plug is clean and white, with no deposits, this is indicative of a weak mixture or too hot a plug (a hot plug transfers heat away from the electrode slowly, a cold plug transfers heat away quickly).

9 If the tip and insulator nose are covered with hard black-looking deposits, then this is indicative that the mixture is too rich. Should the plug be black and oily, then it is likely that the engine is fairly worn, as well as the mixture being too rich. If the insulator nose is covered with light tan to greyish-brown deposits, then the mixture is correct and it is likely that the engine is in good condition.

Installation

10 Prior to installation, it's a good idea to coat the spark plug threads with anti-seize compound **(see illustration)**. Also, it's often difficult to insert spark plugs into their holes without cross-threading them. To avoid this possibility, fit a short piece of 3/8-inch ID rubber hose over the end of the spark plug **(see illustration)**. The flexible hose acts as a universal joint to help align the plug with the plug hole. Should the plug begin to cross-thread, the hose will slip on the spark plug, preventing thread damage. Tighten the plug to the torque listed in this Chapter's Specifications.

11 Attach the plug lead to the new spark plug, again using a twisting motion on the boot until it is firmly seated on the end of the spark plug.

12 Follow the above procedure for the remaining spark plugs, replacing them one at a time to prevent mixing up the spark plug leads.

24 Spark plug lead, distributor cap and rotor check and replacement

1 The spark plug leads should be checked whenever new spark plugs are installed.

2 Begin this procedure by making a visual check of the spark plug leads while the engine is running. In a darkened garage (make sure there is ventilation) start the engine and observe each plug lead. Be careful not to come into contact with any moving engine parts. If there is a break in the lead, you will see arcing or a small spark at the damaged area. If arcing is noticed, make a note to obtain new leads, then allow the engine to cool and check the distributor cap and rotor.

3 The spark plug leads should be inspected one at a time to prevent mixing up the order, which is essential for proper engine operation. Each original plug lead should be numbered to help identify its location. If the number is illegible, a piece of tape can be marked with the correct number and wrapped around the plug lead.

4 Disconnect the plug lead from the spark plug. A removal tool can be used for this purpose or you can grasp the rubber boot, twist the boot half a turn and pull the boot free. Do not pull on the lead itself.

5 Check inside the boot for corrosion, which will look like a white crusty powder.

6 Push the lead and boot back onto the end of the spark plug. It should fit tightly onto the end of the plug. If it doesn't, remove the lead and use pliers to carefully crimp the metal connector inside the lead boot until the fit is snug.

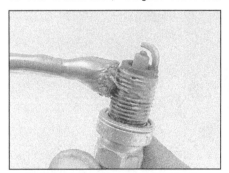

23.10a Apply a thin coat of anti-seize compound to the spark plug threads

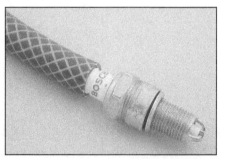

23.10b A length of 3/8-inch ID rubber hose will save time and prevent damaged threads when installing the spark plugs

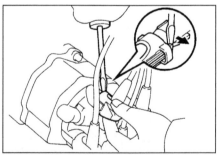

24.8 Use a small screwdriver to lift the lock claw up when detaching the spark plug boot from the distributor

24.11a Remove the two screws (arrowed) and detach the distributor cap

24.11b Inspect the distributor cap for carbon tracks, charred or eroded terminals and other damage (if in doubt about its condition, install a new one)

7 Using a clean rag, wipe the entire length of the lead to remove built-up dirt and grease. Once the lead is clean, check for burns, cracks and other damage. Do not bend the lead sharply, because the conductor might break.

8 Disconnect the lead from the distributor cap, using a small screwdriver to lift up on the lock claw (see illustration). Check for corrosion and a tight fit. Replace the lead in the distributor cap.

9 Inspect the remaining spark plug leads, making sure that each one is securely fastened at the distributor and spark plug when the check is complete.

10 If new spark plug leads are required, purchase a set for your specific engine model. Pre-cut lead sets with the boots already installed are available. Remove and replace the leads one at a time to avoid mix-ups in the firing order.

11 Detach the distributor cap by removing the two retaining screws (see illustration). Look inside it for cracks, carbon tracks and worn, burned or loose contacts (see illustration).

12 Pull the rotor off the distributor shaft and examine it for cracks and carbon tracks (see illustration). Replace the cap and rotor if any damage or defects are noted.

13 It is common practice to install a new cap and rotor whenever new spark plug leads are installed, but if you wish to continue using the old cap, check the resistance between the spark plug leads and the cap first (see illustration). If the indicated resistance is more than the maximum value listed in this Chapter's Specifications, replace the cap and/or leads.

14 When installing a new cap, remove the leads from the old cap one at a time and attach them to the new cap in the exact same location – do not simultaneously remove all the leads from the old cap or firing order mix-ups may occur.

25 Cooling system servicing (draining, flushing and refilling)

⚠️ Warning: Do not allow engine coolant (antifreeze) to come in contact with your skin or painted surfaces of the vehicle. Rinse off spills immediately with plenty of water. Antifreeze is highly toxic if ingested. Never leave antifreeze laying around in an open container or in puddles on the floor; children and pets are attracted by its sweet smell and may drink it. Check with local authorities about disposing of used antifreeze. Many communities have collection centers which will see that antifreeze is disposed of safely.

1 Periodically, the cooling system should be drained, flushed and refilled to replenish the antifreeze mixture and prevent formation of rust and corrosion, which can impair the performance of the cooling system and cause engine damage. When the cooling system is serviced, all hoses and the radiator cap should be checked and replaced if necessary.

Draining

2 Apply the parking brake and block the wheels. If the vehicle has just been driven, wait several hours to allow the engine to cool down before beginning this procedure.

3 Once the engine is completely cool, remove the radiator cap.

4 Move a large container under the radiator drain to catch the coolant. Attach a 3/8-inch inner diameter hose to the drain fitting to direct the coolant into the container (some models are already equipped with a hose), then open the drain fitting (a pair of pliers may be required to turn it) (see illustration).

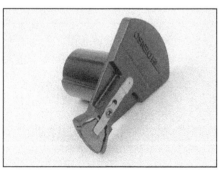

24.12 Check the rotor for damage, wear and corrosion (if in doubt about its condition, buy a new one)

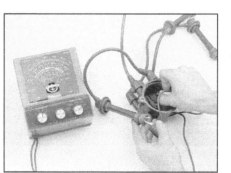

24.13 Measure the resistance value of the distributor cap and the spark plug wires - if it exceeds the specified maximum value, replace either the cap, the wires, or both

25.4 On most models you will have to remove a cover for access to the radiator drain fitting located at the bottom of the radiator - before opening the valve, push a short section of 3/8-inch ID hose onto the plastic fitting to prevent the coolant from splashing

25.5 After draining the radiator, be sure to fully drain the cooling system by removing the block drain plug (arrowed) located on the side of the engine block

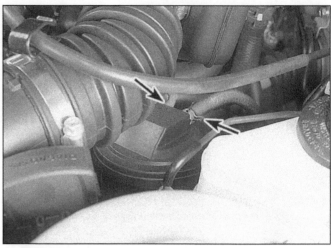

26.2 Check the evaporative emissions control canister for damage and the hose connections for cracks and damage (arrowed)

5 After the coolant stops flowing out of the radiator, move the container under the engine block drain plug **(see illustration)**. Loosen the plug and allow the coolant in the block to drain.

6 While the coolant is draining, check the condition of the radiator hoses, heater hoses and clamps (refer to Section 12 if necessary).

7 Replace any damaged clamps or hoses (see Chapter 3).

Flushing

8 Once the system is completely drained, flush the radiator with fresh water from a garden hose until water runs clear at the drain. The flushing action of the water will remove sediments from the radiator but will not remove rust and scale from the engine and cooling tube surfaces.

9 These deposits can be removed by the chemical action of a cleaner. Follow the procedure outlined in the manufacturer's instructions. If the radiator is severely corroded, damaged or leaking, it should be removed (see Chapter 3) and taken to a radiator repair shop.

10 Remove the overflow hose from the coolant recovery reservoir. Drain the reservoir and flush it with clean water, then reconnect the hose.

Refilling

11 Close and tighten the radiator drain. Install and tighten the block drain plug.

12 Place the heater temperature control in the maximum heat position.

13 Slowly add new coolant (a 50/50 mixture of water and antifreeze) to the radiator until it's full. Add coolant to the reservoir up to the lower mark.

14 Leave the radiator cap off and run the engine in a well-ventilated area until the thermostat opens (coolant will begin flowing through the radiator and the upper radiator hose will become hot).

15 Turn the engine off and let it cool. Add more coolant mixture to bring the level back up to the lip on the radiator filler neck.

16 Squeeze the upper radiator hose to expel air, then add more coolant mixture if necessary. Replace the radiator cap.

17 Start the engine, allow it to reach normal operating temperature and check for leaks.

26 Evaporative emissions control system check

1 The function of the evaporative emissions control system is to draw fuel vapours from the fuel tank and fuel system, store them in a charcoal canister and then burn them during normal engine operation.

2 The most common symptom of a fault in the evaporative emissions system is a strong fuel odour in the engine compartment. If a fuel odour is detected, inspect the charcoal canister, located at the front of the engine compartment. Check the canister and all hoses for damage and deterioration **(see illustration)**.

3 The evaporative emissions control system is explained in more detail in Chapter 6.

27 Exhaust system check

1 With the engine cold (at least three hours after the vehicle has been driven), check the complete exhaust system from its starting point at the engine to the end of the tailpipe. This should be done on a hoist where unrestricted access is available.

2 Check the pipes and connections for evidence of leaks, severe corrosion or damage. Make sure that all brackets and hangers are in good condition and tight.

3 At the same time, inspect the underside of the body for holes, corrosion, open seams, etc. which may allow exhaust gases to enter the passenger compartment. Seal all body openings with silicone or body putty.

4 Rattles and other noises can often be traced to the exhaust system, especially the mounts and hangers. Try to move the pipes, muffler and catalytic converter. If the components can come in contact with the body or suspension parts, secure the exhaust system with new mounts **(see illustration)**.

5 Check the running condition of the engine by inspecting inside the end of the tailpipe. The exhaust deposits here are an indication of engine state-of-tune. If the pipe is black and sooty or coated with white deposits, the engine is in need of a tune-up, including a thorough fuel system inspection.

28 Automatic transmission/differential fluid and filter change

1 At the specified time intervals, the automatic transmission and differential fluid should be drained and replaced.

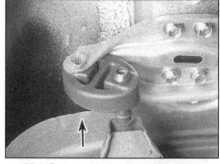

27.4 Be sure to check each exhaust system rubber hanger (arrowed) for damage

28.7 On three-speed models, you'll need an Allen wrench to remove the transmission drain plug

28.8a After loosening the front bolts, remove the rear transmission pan bolts and . . .

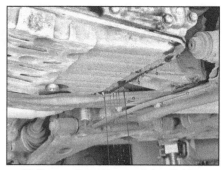

28.8b . . . allow the remaining fluid to drain out

2 Before beginning work, purchase the specified transmission fluid (see *Recommended fluids and lubricants* at the front of this Chapter).

3 Other tools necessary for this job include jack stands to support the vehicle in a raised position, wrenches, drain pan capable of holding at least four US quarts, newspapers and clean rags.

4 The fluid should be drained immediately after the vehicle has been driven. Hot fluid is more effective than cold fluid at removing built up sediment.

 Warning: Fluid temperature can exceed 350-degrees F in a hot transmission. Wear protective gloves.

5 After the vehicle has been driven to warm up the fluid, raise it and place it on jack stands for access to the transmission and differential drain plugs.

6 Move the necessary equipment under the vehicle, being careful not to touch any of the hot exhaust components.

7 Place the drain pan under the drain plug in the transmission pan and remove the drain plug with the Allen wrench **(see illustration)**. Be sure the drain pan is in position, as fluid will come out with some force. Once the fluid is drained, reinstall the drain plug securely.

8 Remove the front transmission pan bolts, then loosen the rear bolts and carefully pry the pan loose with a screwdriver and allow the remaining fluid to drain **(see illustrations)**.

Once the fluid had drained, remove the bolts and lower the pan.

9 Remove the filter retaining bolts, disconnect the clip (some models) and lower the filter from the transmission **(see illustration)**. Be careful when lowering the filter as it contains residual fluid.

10 Place the new filter in position, connect the clip (if equipped) and install the bolts. Tighten the bolts to the torque listed in the Specifications Section at the beginning of this Chapter.

11 Carefully clean the gasket surfaces of the fluid pan, removing all traces of old gasket material. Noting their location, remove the magnets, wash the pan in clean solvent and dry it with compressed air. Be sure to clean and reinstall any magnets **(see illustration)**.

12 Install a new gasket, place the fluid pan in position and install the bolts in their original positions. Tighten the bolts to the torque listed in this Chapter's Specifications.

13 Locate the differential drain plug. Place the drain pan underneath the plug, remove it with the Allen wrench and drain the fluid **(see illustrations)**. When the differential fluid has drained, reinstall the plug securely.

14 Referring to Section 18, add new fluid of the specified type (see *Specifications*) to the differential until it begins to run out of the filler hole.

Caution: Do not overfill. The automatic transmission and the differential are separate units.

28.9 Remove the filter bolts and lower the filter (be careful, there will be some residual fluid) - note that here one of the pan magnets is stuck to the filter (arrowed); be sure to clean any magnets and return them to the pan

15 Lower the vehicle.

16 With the engine off, add new fluid to the transmission through the dipstick tube (see *Recommended fluids and lubricants* for the fluid type and capacity). Use a funnel to prevent spills. It is best to add a little fluid at a time, continually checking the level with the dipstick (see Section 6). Allow the fluid time to drain into the pan.

17 Start the engine and shift the selector into all positions from P through L, then shift into P and apply the parking brake.

18 With the engine idling, check the fluid level. Add fluid up to the Cool level on the dipstick.

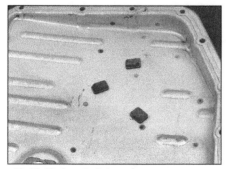

28.11 Noting their locations, remove any magnets and wash them and the pan in solvent before reinstalling them

28.13a Use an Allen wrench to remove the differential drain plug (three-speed models)

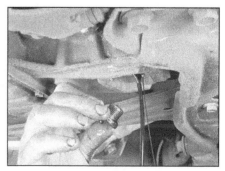

28.13b Be careful when removing the plug because the fluid usually comes out with some force

30.2 Grasp the hose securely and pull the PCV valve out of the cover

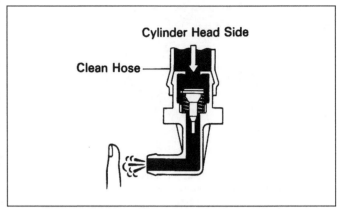

30.4 To check the PVC valve, first attach a clean section of hose to the cylinder head side of the valve and blow through it - air should pass through easily - then blow through the intake manifold side of the valve and verify that air passes through with difficulty

29 Manual transmission lubricant change

1 Remove the drain plug(s) and drain the fluid.
2 Reinstall the drain plug(s) securely.
3 Add new fluid until it is even with the lower edge of the filler hole (Section 19). See *Recommended lubricants and fluids* for the specified lubricant type.

30 Positive Crankcase Ventilation (PCV) valve and hose check and replacement

1 The PCV valve and hose is located in the valve cover.
2 Pull the PCV valve from the cover (see illustration).
3 With the engine idling at normal operating temperature, place your finger over the end of the valve. If there's no vacuum at the valve,

check for a plugged hose or valve. Replace any plugged or deteriorated hoses.
4 Turn off the engine. Remove the PCV valve from the hose. Connect a clean piece of hose and blow through the valve from the valve cover (cylinder head) end. If air will not pass through the valve in this direction, replace it with a new one (see illustration).
5 When purchasing a replacement PCV valve, make sure it's for your particular vehicle and engine size. Compare the old valve with the new one to make sure they're the same.

Every 60 000 miles or 4 years

31 Valve clearance check and adjustment

Note: *The following procedure requires the use of a special valve lifter tool. It is impossible to perform this task without it.*
1 Disconnect the negative cable from the battery.

⚠ *Warning: These models are equipped with airbags. The airbag is armed and can deploy (inflate) anytime the battery is connected. To prevent accidental deployment (and possible injury), turn the ignition key to LOCK and disconnect the negative battery cable whenever working near airbag components. After the battery is disconnected, wait at least two minutes*

before beginning work (the system has a back-up capacitor that must fully discharge). For more information on the airbag system see Chapter 12.
Caution: If the stereo in your vehicle is equipped with an anti-theft system, make sure you have the correct activation code before disconnecting the battery.
2 Disconnect the spark plug leads (Section 24) and remove any other components that will interfere with valve cover removal.
3 Blow out the recessed area around the spark plug openings with compressed air, if available, to remove any debris that might fall into the cylinders, then remove the spark plugs (see Section 23).
4 Remove the valve cover (refer to Chapter 2A).
5 Refer to Chapter 2A and position the number 1 piston at TDC on the compression stroke.
6 Measure the clearances of the indicated valves with feeler gauges (see illustrations). Record the measurements which are out of specification. They will be used later to determine the required replacement shims.
7 Turn the crankshaft one complete revolution and realign the timing marks. Measure the remaining valves (see illustration).

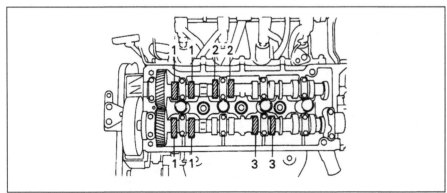

31.6a When the no. 1 piston is at TDC on the compression stroke, the valve clearance for the No. 1 and No. 3 cylinder exhaust valves and the No. 1 and No. 2 cylinder intake valves can be measured

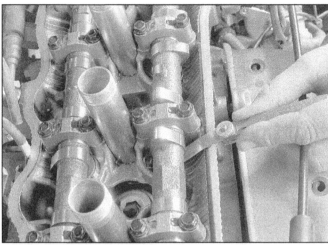

31.6b Check the clearance for each valve with a feeler gauge of the specified thickness - if the clearance is correct, you should feel a slight drag on the gauge as you pull it out

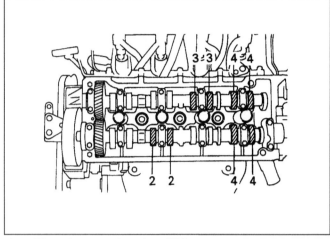

31.7 When the no. 4 piston is at TDC on the compression stroke, the valve clearance for the No. 2 and No. 4 exhaust valves and the No. 3 and No. 4 intake valves can be measured

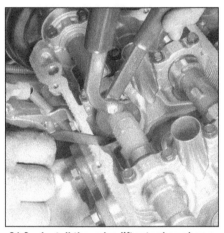

31.9a Install the valve lifter tool as shown and squeeze the handles together to depress the valve lifter, then hold the lifter down with the smaller tool so the shim can be removed

8 After all the valves have been measured, turn the crankshaft pulley until the camshaft lobe above the first valve which you intend to adjust is pointing upward, away from the shim.

9 Position the notch in the valve lifter toward the spark plug. Then depress the valve lifter with the special valve lifter tools (see illustration). Place the special valve lifter tool in position as shown, with the longer jaw of the tool gripping the lower edge of the cast lifter boss and the upper, shorter jaw gripping the upper edge of the lifter itself. Depress the valve lifter by squeezing the handles of the valve lifter tool together, then hold the lifter down with the smaller tool and remove the larger one. Remove the adjusting shim with a small

screwdriver or a pair of tweezers (see illustrations). Note that the wire hook on the end of some valve lifter tool handles can be used to clamp both handles together to keep the lifter depressed while the shim is removed.

10 Measure the thickness of the shim with a micrometer (see illustration). To calculate the correct thickness of a replacement shim that will place the valve clearance within the specified value, use the following formula:

$N = T + (A - V)$

T = thickness of the old shim
A = valve clearance measured
N = thickness of the new shim
V = desired valve clearance (see this Chapter's Specifications)

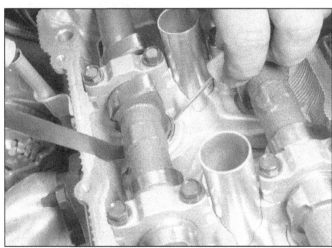

31.9b Keep pressure on the lifter with the smaller tool and remove the shim with a small screwdriver . . .

31.9c . . . a pair of tweezers or a magnet as shown here

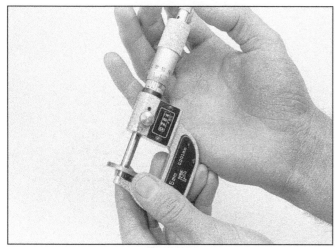

31.10 Measure the shim thickness with a micrometer

Shim No.	Thickness	Shim No.	Thickness
1	2.55 (0.1004)	9	2.95 (0.1161)
2	2.60 (0.1024)	10	3.00 (0.1181)
3	2.65 (0.1043)	11	3.05 (0.1201)
4	2.70 (0.1063)	12	3.10 (0.1220)
5	2.75 (0.1083)	13	3.15 (0.1240)
6	2.80 (0.1102)	14	3.20 (0.1260)
7	2.85 (0.1122)	15	3.25 (0.1280)
8	2.90 (0.1142)	16	3.30 (0.1299)

New shim thickness mm (in.)

31.11 Valve adjusting shim thickness chart

11 Select a shim with a thickness as close as possible to the valve clearance calculated. Shims, which are available in 17 sizes in increments of 0.0020-inch (0.050 mm), range in size from 0.0984-inch (2.500 mm) to 0.1299-inch (3.300 mm) **(see illustration)**. **Note:** *Through careful analysis of the shim sizes needed to bring the out-of-specification valve clearance within specification, it is often possible to simply move a shim that has to come out anyway to another valve lifter requiring a shim of that particular size, thereby reducing the number of new shims that must be purchased.*

12 Place the special valve lifter tool in position as shown in illustration 31.9a, with the longer jaw of the tool gripping the lower edge of the cast lifter boss and the upper, shorter jaw gripping the upper edge of the lifter itself, press down the valve lifter by squeezing the handles of the valve lifter tool together and install the new adjusting shim (note that the wire hook on the end of one valve lifter tool handle can be used to clamp the handles together to keep the lifter depressed while the shim is inserted. Measure the clearance with a feeler gauge to make sure that your calculations are correct.

13 Repeat this procedure until all the valves which are out of clearance have been corrected.

14 Installation of the spark plugs, valve cover, spark plug leads and boots, etc. is the reverse of removal.

Chapter 2 Part A
Engine in-car repair procedures

Contents

Degrees of difficulty

| **Easy,** suitable for novice with little experience | **Fairly easy,** suitable for beginner with some experience | **Fairly difficult,** suitable for competent DIY mechanic 🔧 | **Difficult,** suitable for experienced DIY mechanic 🔧 | **Very difficult,** suitable for expert DIY or professional 🔧 |

Specifications

General

Engine type	DOHC, in-line four-cylinder, four valves per cylinder
Cylinder numbers (timing belt end-to-transmission end)	1-2-3-4
Firing order	1-3-4-2
Displacement	
4E-FE engine	1.3L (1332 cc)
4A-FE engine	1.6L (1587 cc)
7A-FE engine	1.8L (1762 cc)

Timing belt

Tensioner spring free length	
1.3L engine	1.512 inches
1.6L engine	1.390 inches
1.8L engine	1.252 inches
Timing belt deflection	0.20 to 0.24 inch

Oil pump

	Standard	Service limit
Rotor-to-body clearance		
1.3L engine	0.0039 to 0.0083 inch	0.0098 inch
1.6L and 1.8L engines	0.0031 to 0.0071 inch	0.0079 inch
Rotor tip clearance		
1.3L engine	0.0024 to 0.0059 inch	0.0079 inch
1.6L and 1.8L engines	0.0010 to 0.0033 inch	0.0079 inch
Rotor-to-cover clearance		
1.3L engine	0.1142 to 0.1146 inch	0.1169 inch
1.6L and 1.8L engines	0.0010 to 0.0033 inch	0.0039 inch

Camshaft

Journal diameters
   1.3L engines .... 0.9035 to 0.9041 inch
   1.6L and 1.8L engines
      Exhaust camshaft, No. 1 journal .... 0.9822 to 0.9829 inch
      All others .... 0.9035 to 0.9041 inch
Bearing oil clearance
   Standard .... 0.0014 to 0.0028 inch
   Service limit .... 0.0039 inch
Runout limit .... 0.0016 inch
Lobe height, intake camshaft
   1.3L engine
      Standard .... 1.6343 to 1.6378 inches
      Service limit, minimum .... 1.6283 inches
   1.6L engine
      Standard .... 1.6776 to 1.6815 inches
      Service limit, minimum .... 1.6614 inches
   1.8L engine
      Standard .... 1.6450 to 1.6539 inches
      Service limit, minimum .... 1.6339 inches
Lobe height, exhaust camshaft
   1.3L engine
      Standard .... 1.6264 to 1.6303 inches
      Service limit, minimum .... 1.6205 inches
   1.6L and 1.8L engines
      Standard .... 1.6520 to 1.6560 inches
      Service limit, minimum .... 1.6358 inches
Camshaft thrust clearance (endplay)
   Intake camshaft
      1.3L engine
         Standard .... 0.0018 to 0.0039 inch
         Service limit, minimum .... 0.0047 inch
      1.6L and 1.8L engines
         Standard .... 0.0012 to 0.0033 inch
         Service limit, maximum .... 0.0043 inch
   Exhaust camshaft
      1.3L engine
         Standard .... 0.0018 to 0.0039 inch
         Service limit, minimum .... 0.0047 inch
      1.6L and 1.8L engines
         Standard .... 0.0014 to 0.0035 inch
         Service limit, maximum .... 0.0043 inch
Camshaft gear spring free length
   1.3L engine .... 0.886 to 0.902 inch
   1.6L and 1.8L engines .... 0.669 to 0.693 inch
Camshaft gear backlash
   Standard .... 0.0008 to 0.0079 inch
   Service limit .... 0.0188 inch
Valve lifter
   Diameter
      1.3L engine .... 1.1014 to 1.1018 inches
      1.6L and 1.8L engines .... 1.2191 to 1.2195 inches
   Bore diameter
      1.3L engine .... 1.1024 to 1.1032 inches
      1.6L and 1.8L engines .... 1.2205 to 1.2215 inches
Lifter oil clearance
   1.3L engine
      Standard .... 0.0006 to 0.0018 inch
      Service limit .... 0.0039 inch
   1.6L and 1.8L engines
      Standard .... 0.0009 to 0.0023 inch
      Service limit .... 0.0028 inch

Torque wrench settings

	Ft-lbs
Intake manifold bolts	14
Intake manifold brace bolts	
1.3L engine	
At manifold	14
At block	14
1.6L and 1.8L engines	
At manifold	14
At block	29
Intake air chamber (plenum) cover (1.6L and 1.8L engines)	14
Exhaust manifold nuts/bolts	
1.3L engine	35
1.6L and 1.8L engines	25
Exhaust manifold brace bolts (1.6L and 1.8L engines)	43
Crankshaft pulley-to-crankshaft bolt	
1.3L engine	112
1.6L and 1.8L engines	87
Flywheel/driveplate bolts	
1.3L engine	65
1.6L and 1.8L engines	
Flywheel (manual transmission)	58
Driveplate (automatic transmission)	47
Idler pulley bolts	
1.3L engine	
Upper pulley to cylinder head	14
Lower pulley to cylinder block	20
1.6L and 1.8L engines	27
Cylinder head bolts	
1.3L engine	
Step 1	33
Step 2	Tighten an additional 90-degrees
1.6L and 1.8L engines	
Step 1	22
Step 2	Tighten an additional 90-degrees
Step 3	Tighten an additional 90-degrees
Camshaft bearing cap bolts	9
Camshaft sprocket bolt	
1.3L engine	37
1.6L and 1.8L engines	43
Oil pump bolts	
1.3L engine	9
1.6L and 1.8L engines	16
Oil pick-up/strainer nuts/bolts	
1.3L engine	8
1.6L and 1.8L engines	7
Oil pan bolts	
1.3L engine	7
1.6L engine	4
1.8L engine	
Reinforcement section-to-block	12
Pan-to-reinforcement section	4
Centre chassis brace bolts	45
Engine/transmission stiffener bolts (1.6L engine)	17
Rear crankshaft oil seal retainer bolts	
1.3L engine	5
1.6L and 1.8L engines	7

1 General information

This Part of Chapter 2 is devoted to in-vehicle engine repair procedures. All information concerning engine removal and installation and engine block and cylinder head overhaul can be found in Part B of this Chapter.

The following repair procedures are based on the assumption that the engine is installed in the vehicle. If the engine has been removed from the vehicle and mounted on a stand, many of the steps outlined in this Part of Chapter 2 will not apply.

The Specifications included in this Part of Chapter 2 apply only to the procedures contained in this Part. Part B of Chapter 2 contains the Specifications necessary for cylinder head and engine block rebuilding.

During the years covered by this manual, the four-cylinder engines in the Corolla are designated the 4E-FE (1.3L), 4A-FE (1.6L) and the 7A-FE (1.8L). The three engines are almost identical, and incorporate dual overhead camshafts (DOHC) and four valves per cylinder.

2 Repair operations possible with the engine in the vehicle

Many major repair operations can be accomplished without removing the engine from the vehicle.

Clean the engine compartment and the exterior of the engine with some type of degreaser before any work is done. It will make the job easier and help keep dirt out of the internal areas of the engine.

Depending on the components involved, it may be helpful to remove the bonnet to improve access to the engine as repairs are performed (refer to Chapter 11 if necessary). Cover the bumpers to prevent damage to the paint. Special pads are available, but an old bedspread or blanket will also work.

If vacuum, exhaust, oil or coolant leaks develop, indicating a need for gasket or seal replacement, the repairs can generally be made with the engine in the vehicle. The intake and exhaust manifold gaskets, oil pan gasket, crankshaft oil seals and cylinder head gasket are all accessible with the engine in place.

Exterior engine components, such as the intake and exhaust manifolds, the oil pan, the oil pump, the water pump, the starter motor, the alternator, the distributor and the fuel system components can be removed for repair with the engine in place, although when replacing the oil pump an engine hoist is required to support the engine from above, while the right engine mount is removed.

Since the cylinder head can be removed without removing the engine, camshaft and valve component servicing can also be accomplished with the engine in the vehicle. Replacement of the timing belt and pulleys is also possible with the engine in the vehicle.

In extreme cases caused by a lack of necessary equipment, repair or replacement of piston rings, pistons, connecting rods and rod bearings is possible with the engine in the vehicle. However, this practice is not recommended because of the cleaning and preparation work that must be done to the components involved.

3 Top Dead Centre (TDC) for number one piston - locating

Note: *The following procedure is based on the assumption that the distributor is correctly installed. If you are trying to locate TDC to install the distributor correctly, piston position must be determined by feeling for compression at the number one spark plug hole, then aligning the ignition timing marks as described in Step 8.*

1 Top Dead Centre (TDC) is the highest point in the cylinder that each piston reaches as it travels up the cylinder bore. Each piston reaches TDC on the compression stroke and again on the exhaust stroke, but TDC generally refers to piston position on the compression stroke.

2 Positioning the piston(s) at TDC is an essential part of many procedures such as camshaft and timing belt/pulley removal and distributor removal.

3 Before beginning this procedure, be sure to place the transmission in Neutral and apply the parking brake or block the rear wheels. Also, disable the ignition system by detaching the coil wire from the centre terminal of the distributor cap and grounding it on the block with a jumper wire. Remove the spark plugs (see Chapter 1).

4 In order to bring any piston to TDC, the crankshaft must be turned using one of the methods outlined below. When looking at the timing belt end of the engine, normal crankshaft rotation is clockwise.

  a) *The preferred method is to turn the crankshaft with a socket and ratchet attached to the bolt threaded into the front of the crankshaft. Apply pressure on the bolt in a clockwise direction only. Never turn the bolt anti-clockwise.*

  b) *If an assistant is available to turn the ignition switch to the Start position in short bursts, you can get the piston close to TDC without a remote starter switch. Make sure your assistant is out of the vehicle, away from the ignition switch, then use a socket and ratchet as described in paragraph a) to complete the procedure.*

5 Note the position of the terminal for the number one spark plug wire on the distributor cap. If the terminal isn't marked, follow the plug wire from the number one cylinder spark plug to the cap.

6 Use a felt-tip pen or chalk to make a mark on the distributor body directly under the number one terminal.

7 Detach the cap from the distributor and set it aside (see Chapter 1 if necessary).

8 Turn the crankshaft until the notch in the crankshaft pulley is aligned with the 0 on the timing plate located at the front of the engine **(see illustration)**.

9 Look at the distributor rotor - it should be pointing directly at the mark you made on the distributor body. If so, you are at TDC for number 1.

10 If the rotor is 180-degrees off, the number one piston is at TDC on the exhaust stroke.

11 To get the piston to TDC on the compression stroke, turn the crankshaft one complete turn (360-degrees) clockwise. The rotor should now be pointing at the mark on the distributor. When the rotor is pointing at the number one spark plug wire terminal in the distributor cap and the ignition timing marks are aligned, the number one piston is at TDC on the compression stroke. **Note:** *If it's impossible to align the ignition timing marks when the rotor is pointing at the mark on the distributor body, the timing belt may have jumped teeth on the pulleys or may have been installed incorrectly.*

12 After the number one piston has been positioned at TDC on the compression stroke, TDC for any of the remaining pistons can be located by turning the crankshaft and following the firing order. Mark the remaining spark plug wire terminal locations on the distributor body just like you did for the number one terminal, then number the marks to correspond with the cylinder numbers. As you turn the crankshaft, the rotor will also turn. When it's pointing directly at one of the marks on the distributor, the piston for that particular cylinder is at TDC on the compression stroke.

4 Valve cover - removal and installation

Removal

1 Disconnect the negative cable from the battery.
Caution: If the stereo in your vehicle is equipped with an anti-theft system, make sure you have the correct activation code before disconnecting the battery.

2 Detach the PCV hoses from the valve cover.

3 Remove the spark plug wires from the spark plugs, handling them by the boots, not pulling on the wires.

4 On 1.6L and 1.8L engines, remove two bolts at the timing-belt end of the valve cover, then pull up the wiring harness cover and wiring **(see illustration)**.

5 Remove the valve cover mounting nuts, then detach the valve cover and gasket from the cylinder head **(see illustration)**. If the valve cover is stuck to the cylinder head, bump the end with a wood block and a hammer to jar it loose. If that doesn't work, try to slip a flexible putty knife between the cylinder head and valve cover to break the seal.
Caution: Don't pry at the valve cover-to-cylinder head joint or damage to the sealing surfaces may occur, leading to oil leaks after the valve cover is reinstalled.

3.8 Align the crankshaft drivebelt pulley notch (arrowed) with the 0 (zero) on the timing plate

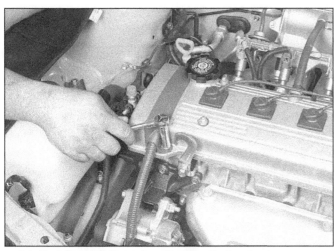

4.4 On 1.6L and 1.8L engines, remove the two harness-cover mounting bolts at the right end of the valve cover, allowing the wiring harness to be pulled up and clear of the valve cover

4.5 On 1.6L and 1.8L engines the valve cover is held in place by four nuts (arrowed). There is an additional nut at the front on 1.3L engines

Installation

6 The mating surfaces of the housing or cylinder head and valve cover must be clean when the valve cover is installed. The rubber sealing gasket can be re-used unless it has high mileage and the rubber has hardened or cracked, then pull out the rubber seal and clean the mating surfaces with lacquer thinner or acetone. Install a new rubber gasket, pressing it evenly into the groove around the underside of the valve cover. If there's residue or oil on the mating surfaces when the valve cover is installed, oil leaks may develop. **Note:** *Make sure that the spark plug tube gaskets are in place on the underside of the valve cover before reinstalling it* **(see illustration)**.

7 Apply RTV sealant near the rubber plug, cam seal cap and distributor.

8 Position a new gasket on the cylinder head, then install the valve cover and nuts.

9 Tighten the nuts in three or four equal steps.

10 Reinstall the remaining parts, run the engine and check for oil leaks.

---

5 Intake manifold - removal and installation

Removal

Note: *If the intake manifold is to be unbolted only for removal of the cylinder head, then the intake manifold can simply be unbolted from the cylinder head and pushed toward the firewall, without disconnecting any hoses, wires or linkage. The following procedure is for complete removal of the manifold from the vehicle.*

1 Disconnect the negative cable from the battery.

Caution: If the stereo in your vehicle is equipped with an anti-theft system, make

sure you have the correct activation code before disconnecting the battery.

2 Refer to Chapter 4 to remove the throttle body and linkages, and safely relieve the fuel system pressure.

3 Label and detach the PCV and vacuum hoses connected to the intake manifold, including those from the MAP sensor, vacuum servo unit and the air conditioning idle-up actuator **(see illustration)**.

4 The intake manifold can be removed with the injectors and fuel rail in place. If the injectors are to be removed from the intake manifold, refer to Chapter 4.

5 Disconnect the electrical connector from the EGR valve (where fitted), label and disconnect the vacuum hose, and unbolt the EGR pipe from the intake manifold (see Chapter 4). Set the EGR assembly aside. On 1.3L engines, disconnect the air control valve electrical connector and the hoses from the air pipe at the rear of the manifold.

4.6 The valve cover gasket (left arrow) is a rubber O-ring seal - it can be re-used if it hasn't hardened - make sure the spark plug tube seals (arrowed) are in place before replacing the valve cover

5.3 The various hoses should be marked to insure correct reinstallation

5.6a From underneath the vehicle, remove the bolt retaining this brace (arrowed) to the intake manifold (intake manifold removed for clarity)

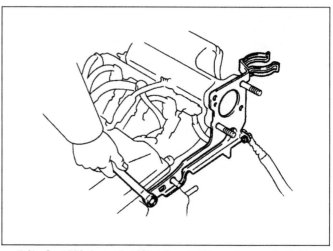

5.6b On 1993 through 1995 1.6 and 1.8L engines, unbolt this intake manifold brace from the cylinder head

6 Unbolt the upper end of the intake manifold-to-block brace (accessible from under the vehicle), and on 1993 through 1995 1.6L and 1.8L engines, remove the intake manifold-to-cylinder head brace from the cylinder head (see illustrations).

7 Remove the ground strap and mounting nuts/bolts, then detach the manifold from the engine (see illustrations). Note: From under the vehicle, it will be necessary to unbolt the wiring harness, the lower intake manifold bolts, and the two nuts securing the pair of steel lines to the underside of the intake manifold.

Installation

8 Clean the mating surfaces of the intake manifold and the cylinder head mounting surface with lacquer thinner or acetone. If the gasket shows signs of leaking, have the manifold checked for warpage at an automotive machine shop and resurfaced if necessary.

9 On 1.6L and 1.8L engines, the manifold is a two-piece design, and a new gasket set may include the gasket for the air chamber cover. Unless the engine has high mileage or you suspect a vacuum leak at the mating surfaces, don't unbolt the air chamber cover. If it's necessary to replace the gasket, unbolt the cover, clean the surfaces, position the new gasket and reinstall the cover. Tighten the cover bolts to the torque listed in this Chapter's Specifications.

10 Install a new gasket, then position the manifold on the cylinder head and install the nuts/bolts.

11 Tighten the nuts/bolts in three or four equal steps to the torque listed in this Chapter's Specifications. Work from the centre out towards the ends to avoid warping the manifold.

12 Install the remaining parts in the reverse order of removal.

13 Before starting the engine, check the throttle linkage for smooth operation.

14 Run the engine and check for coolant and vacuum leaks.

15 Road test the vehicle and check for proper operation of all accessories, including the cruise control system, if equipped.

6 Exhaust manifold - removal and installation

Warning: The engine must be completely cool before beginning this procedure.

Removal

1 Disconnect the negative cable from the battery.
Caution: If the stereo in your vehicle is equipped with an anti-theft system, make sure you have the correct activation code before disconnecting the battery.

5.7a From underneath the vehicle, unbolt the wiring harness (right arrow) from the water neck and cylinder head, then remove the lower manifold bolts (left arrow indicates one, of the four bolts)

5.7b Remove the intake manifold bolts/nuts and remove the intake manifold

6.2 Remove the five upper heat insulator bolts (arrowed) - 1.8L engine shown

2 Remove the upper heat insulator from the manifold (see illustration). Note: There may also be a lower heat insulator, but this is attached to the manifold from underneath and does not need to be removed.
3 Apply penetrating oil to the exhaust manifold mounting nuts/bolts, and the nuts retaining the exhaust pipe to the manifold. After the nuts have soaked, remove the nuts retaining the exhaust pipe to the manifold (see Chapter 4).
4 Where fitted, unbolt the exhaust manifold brace (see illustration).
5 Remove the nuts/bolts and detach the manifold and gasket (see illustration).

Installation

6 Use a scraper to remove all traces of old gasket material and carbon deposits from the manifold and cylinder head mating surfaces. If the gasket was leaking, have the manifold checked for warpage at an automotive machine shop and resurfaced if necessary.
7 Position a new gasket over the cylinder head studs. Note: The marks on the gasket should face out (away from the cylinder head) and the arrow should point toward the rear (transmission end) of the engine.
8 Install the manifold and thread the mounting nuts/bolts into place.
9 Working from the centre out, tighten the nuts/bolts to the torque listed in this Chapter's Specifications in three or four equal steps.
10 Reinstall the remaining parts in the reverse order of removal.

7.7 With the belts removed, unbolt and remove the air conditioning idler pulley (arrow, shown from below through the right fenderwell on a 1.8L engine)

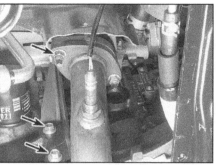

6.4 Remove the upper bolt retaining the exhaust brace to the manifold (top arrow), and loosen the two bolts retaining the brace to the block (lower arrows)

11 Run the engine and check for exhaust leaks.

7 Timing belt and sprockets - removal, inspection and installation

Removal

1 Disconnect the negative cable from the battery.
Caution: If the stereo in your vehicle is equipped with an anti-theft system, make sure you have the correct activation code before disconnecting the battery.
2 Block the rear wheels and set the parking brake.
3 Loosen the nuts on the right front wheel and raise the vehicle. Support the front of the vehicle securely on jackstands.
4 Remove the right front wheel and bumper apron seal.
5 Remove the spark plugs (see Chapter 1).
6 Remove the drivebelts (see Chapter 1).
7 Remove the air conditioning compressor belt idler pulley (see illustration).
8 Unbolt the cruise control actuator (if equipped) and set it aside.
9 Refer to Section 4 and remove the valve cover.
10 Support the engine from underneath with a jack (use a wood block on the jack, but

7.12 Use a pry bar wedged into the flywheel (arrowed) to keep the engine from rotating while loosening the crankshaft pulley bolt

6.5 Remove the bolts and nuts and remove the exhaust manifold

don't place the block under the oil pan drain plug. Note: If you're planning on removing the oil pan in addition to the timing belt, support the engine with a hoist from above (see Chapter 2B).
11 Position the number one piston at TDC on the compression stroke (see Section 3).
12 Pry the flywheel inspection cover out (see Chapter 7A) and wedge a large screwdriver into the flywheel teeth to hold the engine while an assistant loosens the crankshaft pulley bolt (see illustration).
13 The crankshaft pulley should slide off the crankshaft without a puller (see illustration).
14 Remove the two (1.3L engine) or three (1.6L and 1.8L engines) timing belt covers (see illustration).
15 Remove the timing belt guide from the crankshaft, noting that the cupped side faces out and the smooth side is next to the belt.
16 If you plan to re-use the timing belt, apply match marks on the sprocket and belt and an arrow indicating direction of rotation on the belt.
17 Loosen the belt tensioner adjustment bolt, pry the tensioner to the left and retighten the bolt in this position (see illustration). Slip the timing belt off the sprocket. If you're removing the belt for camshaft seal replacement or cylinder head removal, it isn't necessary to detach the belt from the crankshaft sprocket, or unbolt the right engine mount. If you are removing the belt completely, remove the two nuts from the right engine mount (from underneath) and the bolt from above (see illustrations).

7.13 After removing the center bolt, remove the crankshaft pulley

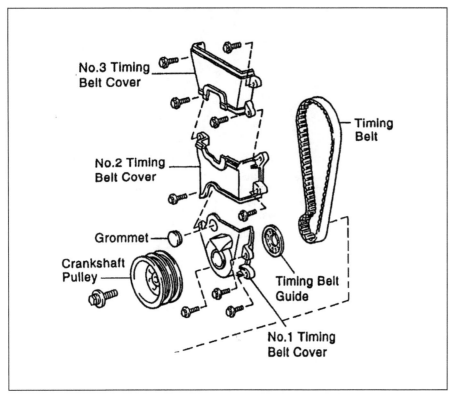

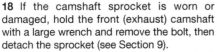

7.14 1.6L and 1.8L engine timing belt cover details. There are only two covers on the 1.3L engine

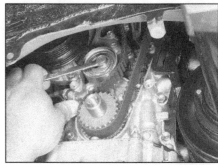

7.17a Loosen the center bolt on the belt tensioner, pry it to the rear of the car, then retighten to keep tension off the belt for removal/installation

7.17b With the engine supported by a jack, remove these two nuts (arrowed) from the right engine mount

18 If the camshaft sprocket is worn or damaged, hold the front (exhaust) camshaft with a large wrench and remove the bolt, then detach the sprocket (see Section 9).

19 Slip the timing belt off the crankshaft sprocket and remove it. If the sprocket is worn or damaged, or if you need to replace the crankshaft front oil seal, remove the sprocket from the crankshaft. Before removing it, paint matching marks on the crankshaft sprocket and the oil pump case, so that you can find the TDC position without the crankshaft pulley in place **(see illustration)**.

Inspection

Caution: Do not bend, twist or turn the timing belt inside out. Do not allow it to come in contact with oil, coolant or fuel. Do not utilize timing belt tension to keep the camshaft or crankshaft from turning when installing the sprocket bolts. Do not turn the crankshaft or camshaft more than a few degrees (if necessary for tooth alignment) while the timing belt is removed.

20 If the timing belt broke during engine operation, the belt may have been contaminated or over-tightened.

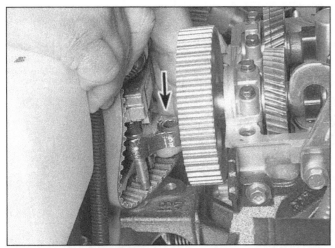

7.17c Remove the upper engine mount bolt (arrowed) and lower the engine, then pull the upper part of the mount up (the rubber will allow movement) until the belt can be slipped out between the upper and lower sections of the mount - this saves removing the mount completely

7.19 The crankshaft sprocket should slide off the crankshaft easily - If its stuck, protect the oil pump case with rags and pry the sprocket off with two screwdrivers. While the engine is at TDC, paint marks (arrowed) on the crankshaft sprocket and oil pump case, so you can find TDC without the crankshaft pulley in place

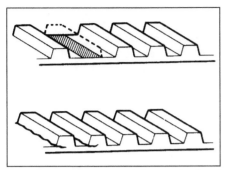

7.21 Check the timing belt for cracked and missing teeth

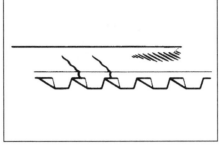

7.22 If the face of the belt is cracked or worn, check the idler pulleys for nicks or burrs

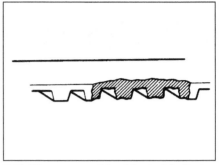

7.23 Wear on one side of the belt indicates sprocket misalignment problems

Caution: If the timing belt broke during engine operation, the valves may have come in contact with the pistons, causing damage. Check the valve clearance (see Chapter 1) - bent valves usually will have excessive clearance, indicating damage that will require cylinder head removal to repair.

21 If the belt teeth are cracked or missing **(see illustration)**, the distributor, oil pump or camshafts may have seized.

22 If there is noticeable wear or cracks on the face of the belt, check to see if there are nicks or burrs on the idler pulleys **(see illustration)**.

23 If there is wear or damage on only one side of the belt, check the belt guide and the alignment of the sprockets **(see illustration)**.

24 Replace the timing belt with a new one if obvious wear or damage is noted or if it is the least bit questionable. Correct any problems which contributed to belt failure prior to belt installation. **Note:** *Professionals recommend replacing the belt whenever it is removed, since belt failure can lead to expensive engine damage. The manufacturer recommends replacing the belt at approximately 60,000-mile intervals.*

25 Release the bolt on the belt tensioner, then remove the tensioner and its spring.

Check the idler for free rotation and measure the spring's free length **(see illustration)**. Replace the spring if it doesn't meet Specifications. reinstall the tensioner and spring. On 1.3L engines, also check the condition of the upper idler pulley and replace it, by removing the center securing bolt, if obvious wear or damage is noted. Fit the new idler and tighten the securing bolt to the torque listed in this Chapter's Specifications.

Installation

26 Remove all dirt, oil and grease from the timing belt area at the front of the engine.

27 Recheck the camshaft and crankshaft timing marks to be sure they are properly aligned **(see illustration)**. If the camshaft sprocket had been removed, reinstall it with the timing mark hole in the sprocket aligned with the notch in the front bearing cap of the exhaust camshaft. Make sure the crankshaft sprocket is still aligned at the TDC marks you made in Step 19.

28 Install the timing belt on the crankshaft and camshaft sprockets. If the original belt is being reinstalled, align the marks made during removal.

29 Slip the belt guide onto the crankshaft with the cupped side facing out.

30 Reinstall the lower timing belt cover and crankshaft pulley and recheck the TDC marks.

31 Keeping tension on the side of the belt nearest the front of the vehicle, loosen the idler pulley bolt 1/2-turn, allowing the spring to apply pressure to the idler pulley.

32 Slowly turn the crankshaft clockwise two complete revolutions (720-degrees), then tighten the idler pulley mounting bolt to the torque listed in this Chapter's Specifications. Measure the deflection of the belt on the radiator side, halfway between the camshaft and crankshaft sprockets, and compare it to this Chapter's Specifications.

33 Recheck the timing marks. With the crankshaft at TDC for number one cylinder, the hole in the camshaft sprocket must align with the timing mark **(see illustration 7.27)**. If the marks are not aligned exactly, repeat the belt installation procedure.

Caution: DO NOT start the engine until you're absolutely certain that the timing belt is installed correctly. Serious and costly engine damage could occur if the belt is installed out-of-time.

34 Reinstall the remaining parts in the reverse order of removal.

35 Run the engine and check for proper operation.

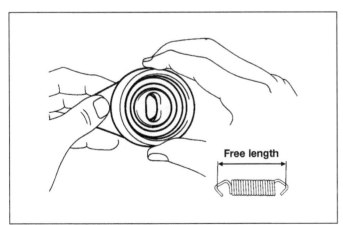

7.25 Check the idler pulley bearing for smooth operation and measure the free length of the tension spring for comparison to this Chapter's Specifications

Free length

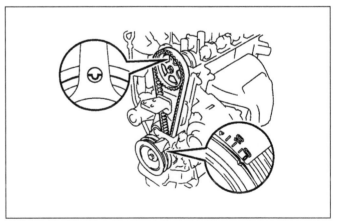

7.27 The camshaft sprocket is at TDC when the hole in the sprocket lines up with the notch in the front bearing cap

8.2a Wrap tape around the screwdriver tip and carefully work the crankshaft front oil seal out of the bore - DO NOT nick or scratch the crankshaft in the process!

8 Crankshaft front oil seal - replacement

1 Remove the timing belt and crankshaft sprocket (see Section 7).
2 Note how far the seal is recessed in the bore, then carefully pry it out of the oil pump housing with a screwdriver or seal removal tool (see illustration). Don't scratch the housing bore or damage the crankshaft in the process (if the crankshaft is damaged, the new seal will end up leaking). Note: *The seal may be easier to remove if the old seal lip is cut with a sharp utility knife first* (see illustration).
3 Clean the bore in the housing and coat the outer edge of the new seal with engine oil or multi-purpose grease. Apply moly-base grease to the seal lip.
4 Using a socket with an outside diameter slightly smaller than the outside diameter of the seal, carefully drive the new seal into place with a seal driver or large socket (see

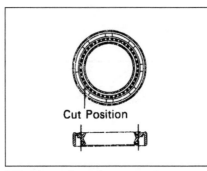

8.2b The seal may be removed more easily by carefully cutting the lip as indicated

illustration). Make sure it's installed squarely and driven in to the same depth as the original. If a socket isn't available, a short section of large diameter pipe will also work. Check the seal after installation to make sure the spring didn't pop out of place.
5 Reinstall the crankshaft sprocket and timing belt (see Section 7).
6 Run the engine and check for oil leaks at the front seal.

9 Camshaft oil seal - replacement

1 Refer to Section 4 and remove the valve cover, then remove the timing belt.
2 Use a large wrench to hold the exhaust camshaft at its hex portion, while removing the bolt from the camshaft sprocket (see illustration), then pull off the sprocket.
3 Note how far the seal is seated in the bore, then carefully pry it out with a small screwdriver (see illustration). Don't scratch the bore or damage the camshaft in the process (if the camshaft is damaged, the new seal will end up leaking).
4 Clean the bore and coat the outer edge of the new seal with engine oil or multi-purpose grease. Apply multi-purpose grease to the seal lip.

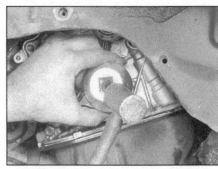

8.4 Gently drive the new seal into place with the spring side installed toward the engine

5 Using a socket with an outside diameter slightly smaller than the outside diameter of the seal, carefully drive the new seal into place with a seal installer or large socket. Make sure it's installed squarely and driven in to the same depth as the original. If a socket isn't available, a short section of pipe will also work. Note: *There isn't much room for a hammer, so you can also pry between the engine mount and the socket to press the seal in* (see illustration).
6 Reinstall the camshaft sprocket and timing belt (see Section 7). Refer to Section 4 and reinstall the valve cover.
7 Run the engine and check for oil leaks at the camshaft seal.

10 Camshafts and valve lifters - removal, inspection and installation

Note: *Before beginning this procedure, obtain two 6 x 1.0 mm, bolts 16 to 20 mm long. They will be referred to as service bolts in the text.*

1.3L engine
Removal
1 Remove the valve cover as described in Section 4.
2 Refer to Section 3 and place the engine on TDC for number 1 cylinder.

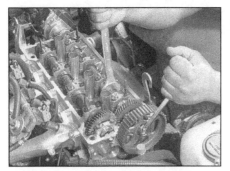

9.2 Use an end wrench to hold the camshaft while removing the camshaft sprocket bolt

9.3 Carefully pry the camshaft seal out of the bore - DO NOT nick or scratch the camshaft journal

9.5 The new camshaft seal can be pressed into place squarely with an appropriate-size socket and a pry bar working against the engine mount

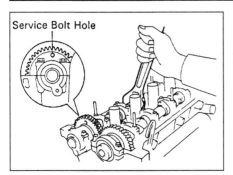

10.5 On 1.3L engines, position the intake camshaft so that the service bolt hole in the camshaft gear is uppermost

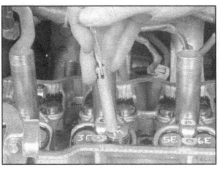

10.12a Mark the lifters/shims (I for intake, E for exhaust, and number their location) and remove them with a magnetic tool

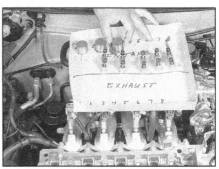

10.12b Mark up a cardboard box to store the lifters/shims and bearing caps

3 Remove the distributor (see Chapter 5). Remove the timing belt and camshaft sprocket (see Sections 7 and 9).

4 Measure the camshaft thrust clearance (endplay) with a dial indicator **(see illustration 10.50)**. If the clearance is greater than the service limit, replace the camshaft and/or the cylinder head.

5 Position the intake camshaft so that the service bolt hole in the camshaft gear is uppermost **(see illustration)**. This will position the intake camshaft lobes so the camshaft will be pushed up evenly by valve spring pressure. *Caution: This positioning is important to avoid damaging the cylinder head or camshaft as the camshaft is removed.*

6 Remove the four bolts and the front bearing caps from the intake and exhaust camshafts. Remove the housing plug from its location in front of the intake camshaft, and remove the oil seal from the exhaust camshaft.

7 Secure the intake camshaft sub-gear to the main gear by installing one of the service bolts into the threaded hole **(see illustration 10.53)**.

8 Following the reverse of the tightening sequence **(see illustration 10.42)**, loosen the remaining exhaust camshaft bearing cap bolts in 1/4-turn increments until the bolts can be removed by hand. Lift the bearing caps straight up and off.

Caution: As the centre bearing cap bolts are being loosened, make sure the camshaft is moving up evenly. If one end or the other stops moving and the cam gets cocked, start over by reinstalling the bearing caps. DO NOT try to pry or force the camshaft out.

9 Lift the exhaust camshaft straight up and out of the cylinder head.

10 Following the reverse of the tightening sequence **(see illustration 10.39)**, loosen the remaining intake camshaft bearing cap bolts in 1/4-turn increments until the bolts can be removed by hand. Lift the bearing caps straight up and off.

Caution: As the centre bearing cap bolts are being loosened, make sure the camshaft is moving up evenly. If one end or the other stops moving and the cam gets cocked, start over by reinstalling the bearing caps. DO NOT try to pry or force the camshaft out.

11 Lift the intake camshaft straight up and out of the cylinder head.

12 Clean the oil off the valve lifter shims, mark them with a felt-tip marker and remove the lifters, keeping the shims with their lifters **(see illustration)**. Store the camshaft bearing caps, lifters and shims so they can be reinstalled without mixing them up **(see illustration)**.

10.13 With the hex portion of the intake camshaft clamped in a vise, use a spanner to relieve the tension on the service bolt, remove the bolt, then release the tension on the subgear

13 Position the intake camshaft in a vise, clamping it on the hex portion. Using a two-pin spanner, rotate the sub-gear clockwise and remove the service bolt from the threaded hole, then allow the sub-gear to rotate back until all tension is relieved **(see illustration)**.

14 Remove the sub-gear snap-ring **(see illustration)**. The wave washer, sub-gear and camshaft gear spring can now be removed from the camshaft **(see illustration)**.

10.14a Remove the snap-ring with a pair of snap-ring pliers

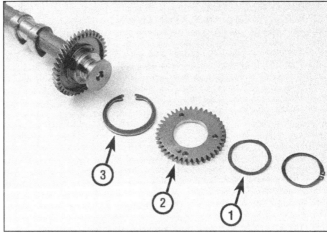

10.14b Remove the wave washer (1), the camshaft sub-gear (2) and the gear spring (3)

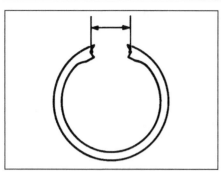

10.15 Measure the distance between the ends of the camshaft gear spring

10.16 Wipe off the oil and inspect each lifter for wear and scuffing

Inspection

15 Measure the free length (distance between the ends) of the camshaft gear spring **(see illustration)** and compare it to this Chapter's Specifications. If not as specified, replace the spring.

16 Inspect each lifter for scuffing and score marks **(see illustration)**.

17 Measure the outside diameter of each lifter and the corresponding lifter bore inside diameter. Subtract the lifter diameter from the lifter bore diameter to determine the oil clearance. Compare it to this Chapter's

Specifications. If the oil clearance is excessive, a new cylinder head and/or new lifters will be required.

18 Visually examine the cam lobes and bearing journals for score marks, pitting, galling and evidence of overheating (blue, discoloured areas). Look for flaking away of the hardened surface layer of each lobe.

19 Using a micrometer, measure the height of each camshaft lobe **(see illustration)**. Compare your measurements with this Chapter's Specifications. If the height for any one lobe is less than the specified minimum, replace the camshaft.

20 Using a micrometer, measure the diameter of each journal at several points **(see illustration)**. Compare your measurements with this Chapter's Specifications. If the diameter of any one journal is less than specified, replace the camshaft.

21 Check the oil clearance for each camshaft journal as follows:

a) Clean the bearing caps and the camshaft journals with lacquer thinner or acetone.

b) Carefully lay the camshaft(s) in place in the cylinder head. Don't install the lifters or intake camshaft sub-gear and don't use any lubrication.

c) Lay a strip of Plastigauge on each journal.

d) Install the bearing caps with the arrows pointing toward the front (timing belt end) of the engine **(see illustration)**.

e) Tighten the bolts to the torque listed in this Chapter's Specifications in 1/4-turn increments. **Note:** Don't turn the camshaft while the Plastigauge is in place.

f) Remove the bolts and detach the caps.

g) Compare the width of the crushed Plastigauge (at its widest point) to the scale on the Plastigauge envelope **(see illustration)**.

h) If the clearance is greater than specified, replace the camshaft and/or cylinder head.

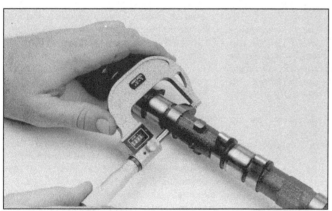

10.19 Measure the lobe heights on each camshaft - if any lobe height is less than the specified allowable minimum, replace that camshaft

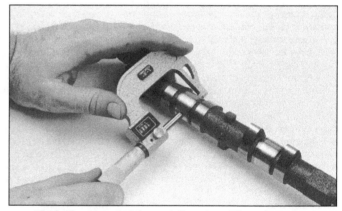

10.20 Measure each journal diameter with a micrometer (if any journal measures less than the specified limit, replace the camshaft)

10.21a The camshaft bearing caps are numbered and have an arrow that should face the timing belt end of the engine

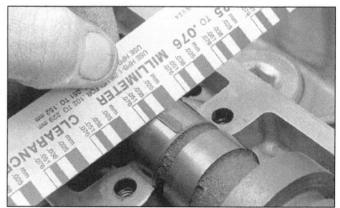

10.21b Compare the width of the crushed Plastigauge to the scale on the envelope to determine the oil clearance

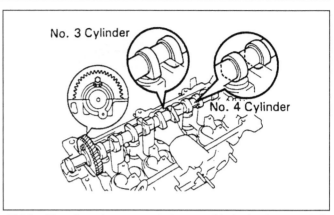

10.22 Position a dial indicator as shown here to measure gear backlash - hold one camshaft steady with a wrench while moving the other camshaft with another wrench

10.32a Align the exhaust camshaft gear with the intake camshaft gear by matching up the timing marks on the gears

i)   *Scrape off the Plastigauge with your fingernail or the edge of a credit card - don't scratch or nick the journals or bearing caps.*

22 With the caps reinstalled temporarily, use a dial indicator to measure the backlash between the two camshaft gears. Hold one camshaft from turning (using a wrench on the hex portion) while measuring the movement in the other camshaft gear, and compare the results to Specifications **(see illustration)**. If the backlash is beyond Specifications, replace both camshafts.

Installation

23 Reassemble the intake camshaft sub-gear. Install the camshaft gear spring, sub-gear and wave washer. Secure them with the snap-ring **(see illustrations 10.14a and 10.14b)**.
24 Refer to Step 7 and install a service bolt.
25 Apply moly-base grease or engine assembly lube to the intake valve lifters, then install them in their original locations. Make sure the valve adjustment shims are in place on the lifters.
26 Apply moly-base grease or engine assembly lube to the intake camshaft lobes and bearing journals.

27 Position the intake camshaft so that the service bolt hole in the camshaft gear is uppermost then place the camshaft in position **(see illustration 10.5)**.
28 Install the intake camshaft bearing caps, (except the front cap) in numerical order with the arrows pointing toward the timing belt end of the engine.
29 Tighten the bearing cap bolts uniformly and alternately, in several stages, until the caps are snug with the cylinder head. Do not tighten the bolts to the full torque setting at this stage.
30 Apply moly-base grease or engine assembly lube to the exhaust valve lifters, then install them in their original locations. Make sure the valve adjustment shims are in place on the lifters.
31 Apply moly-base grease or engine assembly lube to the exhaust camshaft lobes and bearing journals.
32 Align the exhaust camshaft gear with the intake camshaft gear by matching up the timing marks on the gears **(see illustration)**.
Caution: On some engines there are two sets of timing marks - ensure that the correct ones are aligned (see illustration).
33 Roll the exhaust camshaft down into position. Turn the intake camshaft back and

forth a little until the exhaust camshaft sits in the bearings evenly.
34 Install the exhaust camshaft bearing caps (except the front cap) in numerical order with the arrows pointing toward the timing belt end of the engine.
35 Tighten the bearing cap bolts uniformly and alternately, in several stages, until the caps are snug with the cylinder head. Do not tighten the bolts to the full torque setting at this stage.
36 Remove the service bolt from the intake camshaft gear.
37 Apply a thin coat of RTV sealant to the intake camshaft front bearing-cap-to-cylinder-head mating surface. **Note:** *The cap must be installed immediately or the sealer will dry prematurely.* Install the cap and tighten the two bearing cap bolts uniformly and alternately, in several stages, until the cap is snug with the cylinder head. Do not tighten the bolts to the full torque setting at this stage.
38 Install the housing plug to its location in front of the intake camshaft.
39 Following the recommended sequence **(see illustration)**, tighten all the intake camshaft bearing cap bolts uniformly to the torque listed in this Chapter's Specifications.

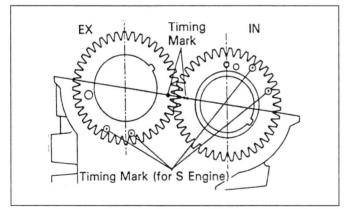

10.32b On some 1.3L engines there are two sets of timing marks - DO NOT use the timing marks for the engine when installing the camshafts and gears

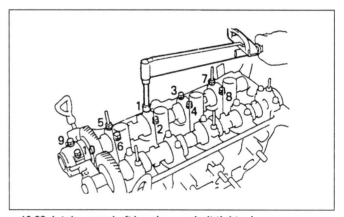

10.39 Intake camshaft bearing cap bolt tightening sequence - 1.3L engine

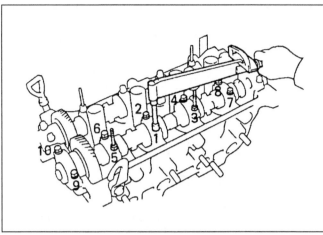

10.42 Exhaust camshaft bearing cap bolt tightening sequence - 1.3L engine

10.50 Mount a dial indicator as shown to measure camshaft endplay - with the dial zeroed, pry the camshaft forward and back and read the endplay on the dial

40 Lubricate the lips of a new exhaust camshaft oil seal with engine oil or multi-purpose grease and install the seal in the cylinder head. Push the seal fully into the recess in the head.

41 Apply a thin coat of RTV sealant to the exhaust camshaft front bearing-cap-to-cylinder-head mating surface. **Note:** *The cap must be installed immediately or the sealer will dry prematurely.* Install the cap and tighten the two bearing cap bolts uniformly and alternately, in several stages, until the cap is snug with the cylinder head. Do not tighten the bolts to the full torque setting at this stage.

42 Following the recommended sequence **(see illustration)**, tighten all the exhaust camshaft bearing cap bolts uniformly to the torque listed in this Chapter's Specifications.

43 Turn the camshafts through one or two revolutions and check that the timing marks are still aligned.

44 Install the timing belt sprocket on the exhaust camshaft and tighten the bolt to the torque listed in this Chapter's Specifications. Prevent the camshaft from turning by holding it with a wrench on the large hex.

45 Install the timing belt (see Section 7).

46 The remainder of installation is the reverse of the removal procedure.

1.6L and 1.8L engines

Removal

47 Remove the valve cover as described in Section 4.

48 Refer to Section 3 and place the engine on TDC for number 1 cylinder. Apply a dab of paint to the camshaft gear TDC alignment marks (the marks where the gears mesh just at the valve cover/head interface line). **Note:** *There are two sets of marks on the camshaft gears. The marks that align at TDC are for TDC reference only, the other two marks are used to align the camshafts during installation.*

49 Remove the distributor (see Chapter 5). Remove the timing belt and camshaft sprocket (see Sections 7 and 9).

50 Measure the camshaft thrust clearance (endplay) with a dial indicator **(see illustration)**. If the clearance is greater than the service limit, replace the camshaft and/or the cylinder head.

51 Position the knock pin in the EXHAUST camshaft just above the top of the cylinder head **(see illustration)**. This will position the intake camshaft lobes so the camshaft will be pushed up evenly by valve spring pressure. *Caution: This positioning is important to avoid damaging the cylinder head or camshaft as the camshaft is removed.*

52 Remove the two bolts and the front bearing cap from the intake camshaft **(see illustration)**.

53 Secure the intake camshaft sub-gear to the main gear by installing one of the service bolts into the threaded hole **(see illustration)**.

54 Following the reverse of the tightening sequence **(see illustration 10.76)**, loosen the remaining intake camshaft bearing cap bolts in 1/4-turn increments until the bolts can be removed by hand. Lift the bearing caps straight up and off. *Caution: As the centre bearing cap bolts are being loosened, make sure the camshaft is moving up evenly. If one end or the other stops moving and the cam gets cocked, start over by reinstalling the bearing caps. DO NOT try to pry or force the camshaft out.*

55 Lift the camshaft straight up and out of the cylinder head.

56 Position the knock pin in the exhaust camshaft at approximately the 5 o'clock position **(see illustration)**.

57 Remove the front (timing belt end) exhaust camshaft bearing cap bolts and detach the bearing cap and oil seal. *Caution: Do not pry the cap off. If it doesn't come loose easily, leave it in place without bolts.*

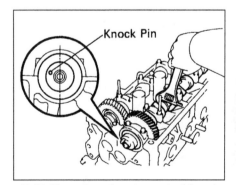

10.51 Place the exhaust camshaft knock pin between the 9 o'clock and 10 o'clock position

10.52 Remove the two bolts and the front camshaft bearing cap from the intake camshaft

10.53 Install a service bolt through the sub-gear and thread it into the main gear (arrowed)

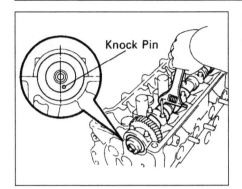

10.56 Turn the exhaust camshaft until the knock pin is pointed at about the 5 o'clock position

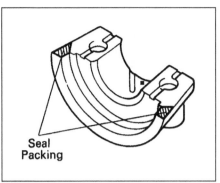

10.67 Apply sealer to the shaded areas of the front exhaust camshaft bearing cap

58 Following the reverse of the tightening sequence **(see illustration 10.69)**, loosen the remaining exhaust camshaft bearing cap bolts in 1/4-turn increments until the bolts can be removed by hand. Lift off the bearing caps. *Caution: As the centre bearing cap bolts are being loosened, make sure the camshaft is moving up evenly. If one end or the other stops moving and the cam gets cocked, start over by reinstalling the bearing caps and resetting the knock pin. DO NOT try to pry or force the camshaft out.*

59 Lift the camshaft straight up and out of the cylinder head.

60 Clean the oil off the valve lifter shims, mark them with a felt-tip marker and remove the lifters, keeping the shims with their lifters **(see illustration 10.12a)**. Store the camshaft bearing caps, lifters and shims so they can be reinstalled without mixing them up **(see illustration 10.12b)**.

61 Position the intake camshaft in a vise, clamping it on the hex portion. Using a two-pin spanner, rotate the sub-gear clockwise and remove the service bolt from the threaded hole, then allow the sub-gear to rotate back until all tension is relieved **(see illustration 10.13)**.

62 Remove the sub-gear snap-ring **(see illustration 10.14a)**. The wave washer, sub-gear and camshaft gear spring can now be removed from the camshaft **(see illustration 10.14b)**.

Inspection

63 Follow the instructions given in steps 15 to 22.

Installation

64 Apply moly-base grease or engine assembly lube to the exhaust valve lifters, then install them in their original locations. Make sure the valve adjustment shims are on place on the lifters.

65 Apply moly-base grease or engine assembly lube to the exhaust camshaft lobes and bearing journals.

66 Position the exhaust camshaft in the cylinder head with the knock pin at approximately the 5 o'clock position **(see illustration 10.56)**.

67 Apply a thin coat of RTV sealant to the outer edge of the front bearing-cap-to-cylinder-head mating surface **(see illustration)**. Note: *The cap must be installed immediately or the sealer will dry prematurely.*

68 Install the exhaust camshaft bearing caps in numerical order with the arrows pointing toward the timing belt end of the engine.

69 Following the recommended tightening sequence **(see illustration)**, tighten the bearing cap bolts in 1/4-turn increments to the torque listed in this Chapter's Specifications.

70 Refer to Section 9 and install a new camshaft oil seal.

71 Reassemble the intake camshaft sub-gear. Install the camshaft gear spring, sub-gear and wave washer. Secure them with the snap-ring **(see illustrations 10.14a and 10.14b)**.

72 Refer to Step 53 and install a service bolt.

73 Apply moly-base grease or engine assembly lube to the intake valve lifters, then install them in their original locations. Make sure the valve adjustment shims are in place on the lifters.

74 Apply moly-base grease or engine assembly lube to the intake camshaft lobes and bearing journals.

75 Rotate the EXHAUST camshaft until the knock pin is positioned between the 9 o'clock and 10 o'clock position **(see illustration 10.51)**.

76 Align the intake camshaft gear with the exhaust camshaft gear by matching up the *installation* marks on the gears **(see illustration)**.

Caution: There are two sets of marks. Do not use the TDC marks you applied paint to in Step 48. The camshaft installation marks are the only marks that are duplicated on both front and rear sides of the two camshaft gears.

77 Roll the intake camshaft down into position. Turn the exhaust camshaft back and forth a little until the intake camshaft sits in the bearings evenly.

78 Install the intake camshaft bearing caps in numerical order with the arrows pointing toward the timing belt end of the engine.

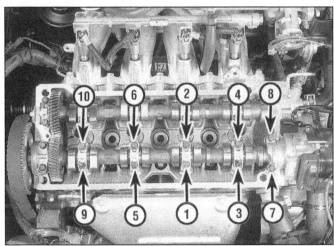

10.69 Exhaust camshaft bearing cap bolt tightening sequence - 1.6L and 1.8L engines

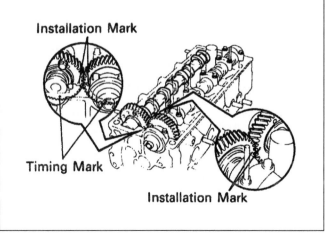

10.76 Align the camshaft gears as shown here - use the installation marks, NOT the TDC marks

10.79 Intake camshaft bearing cap bolt tightening sequence -
1.6L and 1.8L engines

11.14 If the cylinder head is stuck, pry only at the overhang,
not between the mating surfaces

79 Following the recommended sequence **(see illustration)**, tighten the bearing cap bolts in 1/4-turn increments to the torque listed in this Chapter's Specifications.

80 Remove the service bolt from the intake camshaft gear.

81 Install the timing belt sprocket on the exhaust camshaft and tighten the bolt to the torque listed in this Chapter's Specifications. Prevent the camshaft from turning by holding it with a wrench on the large hex.

82 Install the timing belt (see Section 7).

83 The remainder of installation is the reverse of the removal procedure.

11 Cylinder head - removal and installation

Note: *The engine must be completely cool before beginning this procedure.*

Removal

1 Disconnect the negative cable from the battery.

Caution: If the stereo in your vehicle is equipped with an anti-theft system, make sure you have the correct activation code before disconnecting the battery.

2 Drain the coolant from the engine block and radiator (see Chapter 1).

3 Drain the engine oil and remove the oil filter (see Chapter 1).

4 Remove the throttle body, fuel injectors and fuel rail (see Chapter 4).

5 Remove the intake manifold (see Section 5).

6 Remove the exhaust manifold (see Section 6).

Note: *It is possible to leave the intake and exhaust manifolds attached to the cylinder head, to be removed along with the cylinder head for disassembly on the bench.*

7 Remove the timing belt and camshaft sprocket (see Sections 7 and 9).

8 Remove the camshafts and lifters (see Section 10).

9 Remove the alternator and distributor (see Chapter 5).

10 Unbolt the power steering pump and set the pump aside without disconnecting the hoses.

11 Label and remove any remaining items, such as coolant fittings, tubes, cables, hoses or wires.

12 Refer to Chapter 3 and detach the water necks from each end of the cylinder head. At this point the cylinder head should be ready for removal.

13 Using an 8 mm hex-head socket bit and a breaker bar, loosen the cylinder head bolts in 1/4-turn increments until they can be removed by hand. Loosen the cylinder head bolts in the reverse of the recommended tightening sequence **(see illustrations 11.25a and 11.25b)** to avoid warping or cracking the cylinder head.

14 Lift the cylinder head off the engine block. If it's stuck, very carefully pry up at the transmission end, beyond the gasket surface **(see illustration)**.

15 Remove all external components from the cylinder head to allow for thorough cleaning and inspection. See Chapter 2B, for cylinder head servicing procedures.

Installation

16 The mating surfaces of the cylinder head and block must be perfectly clean when the cylinder head is installed.

17 Use a gasket scraper to remove all traces of carbon and old gasket material **(see illustration)**, then clean the mating surfaces with lacquer thinner or acetone. If there's oil on the mating surfaces when the cylinder head is installed, the gasket may not seal correctly and leaks could develop. When working on the block, stuff the cylinders with clean shop rags to keep out debris. Use a vacuum cleaner to remove material that falls into the cylinders.

18 Check the block and cylinder head mating surfaces for nicks, deep scratches and other damage. If damage is slight, it can be removed with a file; if it's excessive, machining may be the only alternative.

19 Use a tap of the correct size to chase the threads in the cylinder head bolt holes, then clean the holes with compressed air - make sure that nothing remains in the holes.

⚠ *Warning: Wear eye protection when using compressed air!*

11.17 Remove all traces of old gasket material - the cylinder head and block mating surfaces must be perfectly clean to ensure a good gasket seal

11.22 Place the new cylinder head gasket over the dowels in the block, noting the markings for UP on the gasket

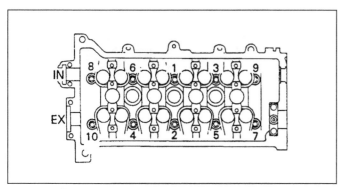

11.25a Cylinder head bolt tightening sequence - 1.3L engine

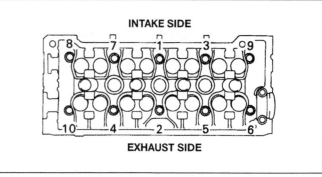

11.25b Cylinder head bolt tightening sequence - 1.6L and 1.8L engines

20 Mount each bolt in a vise and run a die down the threads to remove corrosion and restore the threads. Dirt, corrosion, sealant and damaged threads will affect torque readings.

21 Install the components that were removed from the cylinder head.

22 Position the new gasket over the dowel pins in the block **(see illustration)**.

23 Carefully set the cylinder head on the block without disturbing the gasket.

24 Before installing the cylinder head bolts, apply a small amount of clean engine oil to the threads and under the bolt heads.

25 Install the bolts in their original locations and tighten them finger tight. Install the shorter bolts along the intake side of the cylinder head and the longer bolts along the exhaust side. Following the recommended sequence, tighten the bolts in two steps for 1.3L engines and in three steps for 1.6L and 1.8L engines to the torque listed in this Chapter's Specifications **(see illustrations)**. Steps 2 and 3 of the tightening sequence require the bolts to be angle-tightened. If you don't have an angle-torque attachment for your torque wrench, simply apply a paint mark at one edge of each cylinder head bolt and tighten the bolt until that mark is 90 degrees from where you started (Step 2). On 1.6L and 1.8L engines, tighten the bolts an additional

90 degrees so after Step 3, the marks will be 180 degrees from where they started.

26 The remaining installation steps are the reverse of removal. **Note:** *If the semi-circular rubber plug had been removed from the cylinder head (ahead of the intake camshaft), reinstall it with some RTV sealant.*

27 Check and adjust the valve clearances as necessary (see Chapter 1).

28 Refill the cooling system, install a new oil filter and add oil to the engine (see Chapter 1).

29 Run the engine and check for leaks. Set the ignition timing (see Chapter 5) and road test the vehicle.

12 Oil pan - removal and installation

Removal

1 Disconnect the negative cable from the battery. **Caution: If the stereo in your vehicle is equipped with an anti-theft system, make sure you have the correct activation code before disconnecting the battery.**

2 Set the parking brake and block the rear wheels.

3 Raise the front of the vehicle and support it securely on jackstands.

4 Remove the two plastic splash shields under the engine.

5 Drain the engine oil and remove the oil filter (see Chapter 1). Remove the oil dipstick.

6 Disconnect the electrical connector to the oxygen sensor (see Chapter 6).

7 Remove the two nuts retaining the front exhaust pipe to the exhaust manifold, then the two bolts/nuts connecting the pipe to the rear of the exhaust system (see Chapter 4).

8 Remove the two front bolts of the longitudinal chassis brace and the two nuts securing the radiator-side engine mount **(see illustration)**.

1.3L and 1.6L engines

9 On 1.6L engines, unbolt and remove the block-to-transmission brace **(see illustration)**.

10 Remove the bolts and detach the oil pan. If it's stuck, pry it loose very carefully with a small screwdriver or putty knife **(see illustration)**. Don't damage the mating surfaces of the pan and block or oil leaks could develop.

1.8L engine

11 The 1.8L engine uses a steel oil pan mounted to a large cast aluminum reinforcement section that stiffens the block/transmission mounting. There is no separate engine/transmission brace as on the 1.6L engine. **Note:** *The manufacturer uses a very tough sealant on the oil pan flange which make the steel and aluminum components*

12.8 Remove the front bolts of the chassis brace (arrowed) - for better access for oil pan removal, you'll have to insert a large pry bar between the brace and the chassis to pry the brace down

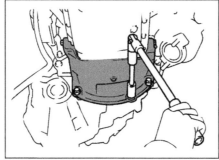

12.9 Unbolt the block-to-transaxle brace on 1.6L engines

12.10 Carefully pry the oil pan away from the block - if the mating surfaces are damaged, oil leaks could develop

12.12 Remove the bolts and nuts securing the oil pan to the reinforcement section, then break its seal with a putty knife

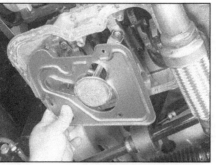

12.13 Remove the oil baffle plate and the pick-up tube/strainer

12.15a Unbolt the six fasteners inside the area concealed by the oil pan - one is an Allen-head bolt (arrowed)

12.15b To access the bolts between the reinforcement section and the transaxle (arrowed), you'll need to bend the exhaust pipe down at its flex joint and pry the longitudinal chassis brace down

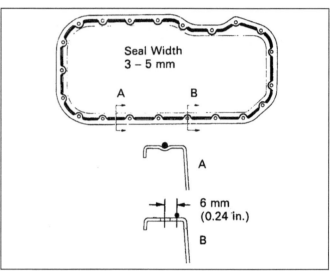

12.20a RTV sealant application details - 1.6L engine oil pan (1.3L engine similar)

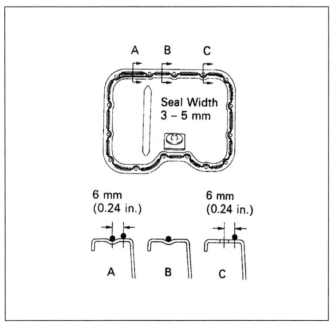

12.20b RTV sealant application details - 1.8L engine oil pan

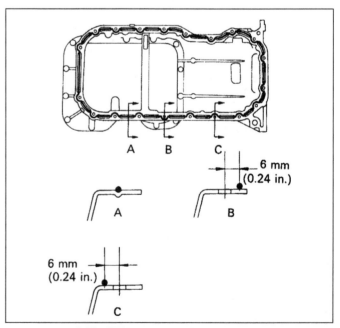

12.20c RTV sealant application details - 1.8L engine aluminum reinforcement section

13.3 Remove the bolt (arrowed) and withdraw the crankshaft position sensor from the oil pump body

13.4 Remove the oil pump body-to-block bolts (arrowed)

13 Oil pump - removal, inspection and installation

Removal

1 Remove the oil dipstick, oil pan, baffle plate (1.8L engine only) and the oil pick-up/strainer assembly (see Section 12).

2 Support the engine securely from above and remove the timing belt, idler pulley and spring, crankshaft pulley, crankshaft sprocket and, on 1.3L engines, the oil pump sprocket (see Section 7).

3 Where fitted, remove the crankshaft position sensor **(see illustration)**. Unbolt and remove the oil dipstick pipe. On 1.3L engines, remove the oil pressure relief valve from the crankcase.

4 Remove the bolts and detach the oil pump body from the engine **(see illustration)**. You may have to pry carefully between the front main bearing cap and the pump body with a screwdriver, or tap behind the oil pump with a soft-faced hammer. On 1.3L engines, remove the O-ring.

5 Use a scraper to remove all traces of sealant and old gasket material from the pump body and engine block, then clean the mating surfaces with lacquer thinner or acetone.

6 Remove the five Torx screws (1.6L and 1.8L engines) and separate the pump cover from the body. Lift out the drive and driven rotors **(see illustrations)**.

7 Remove the oil pressure relief valve snap-ring retainer, spring and piston.

> **Warning: The spring is tightly compressed - be careful and wear eye protection.**

difficult to separate. *Take your time and use a putty knife rather than a screwdriver to break the seal.*

12 Remove the bolts and stud nuts around the perimeter of the oil pan, then carefully pry between the steel and aluminum sections to loosen the oil pan **(see illustration)**. Be careful not to gouge the softer aluminum or distort the flange of the steel pan.

13 Remove the two bolts and two nuts retaining the oil baffle and remove the baffle **(see illustration)**.

14 Unbolt the pick-up tube/oil strainer assembly and remove it for cleaning.

15 If necessary, remove the bolts and nuts retaining the aluminum reinforcement section to the block and transmission **(see illustrations)**. Carefully pry the aluminum section down without gouging the sealing surface. Six of the fasteners are inside the area originally covered by the oil pan. *Caution: Do not pry on the reinforcement section until you are certain all fasteners are removed. There are two Allen bolts near the right front which will require using a ball-hex wrench to remove. If you don't have this type wrench (which allows you to turn an Allen bolt from a slight angle), you will have to move the air conditioning compressor and bracket (see Chapter 3) to allow using a L-shaped Allen wrench.*

Installation

16 Use a scraper to remove all traces of old gasket material and sealant from the block and oil pan. Clean the mating surfaces with lacquer thinner or acetone.

17 Make sure the threaded bolt holes in the block are clean.

18 Check the oil pan flange for distortion, particularly around the bolt holes. If necessary, place the oil pan on a wood block and use a hammer to flatten and restore the gasket surface.

19 Inspect the oil pump pick-up tube assembly for cracks and a blocked strainer. On 1.3L and 1.6L engines, if the pick-up was removed, clean it thoroughly and install it now, using a new O-ring or gasket. Tighten the nuts/bolts to the torque listed in this Chapter's Specifications.

20 Apply a 5 mm (approximately) wide bead of RTV sealant to the oil pan flange (1.3L and 1.6L engines) or reinforcement section (1.8L engine) **(see illustrations)**. **Note:** *Installation must be completed within 5 minutes once the sealer has been applied.*

21 Carefully position the oil pan or reinforcement section on the engine block and install the bolts. Working from the centre out. Tighten the bolts to the torque listed in this Chapter's Specifications in three or four steps. On 1.8L engines, reinstall the oil baffle plate and the pick-up tube/strainer. Be sure to use a new gasket on the pick-up tube. On 1.8L engines, apply RTV to the oil pan flange and install it after the aluminum reinforcement section has been sealed and tightened to specifications.

22 The remainder of installation is the reverse of removal. Be sure to add oil and install a new oil filter. Use new gasket/seals on the front exhaust pipe.

23 Run the engine and check for oil pressure and leaks.

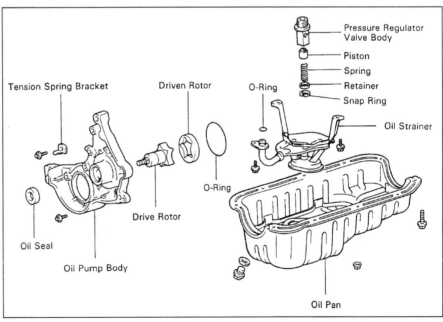

13.6a Oil pump components - 1.3L engine

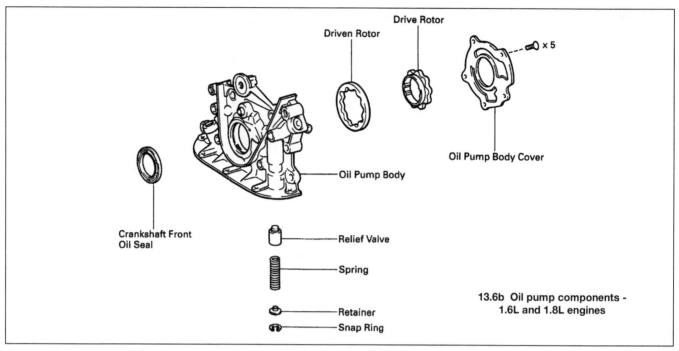

Driven Rotor

Drive Rotor

× 5

Oil Pump Body

Oil Pump Body Cover

Crankshaft Front
Oil Seal

Relief Valve

Spring

Retainer

Snap Ring

13.6b Oil pump components -
1.6L and 1.8L engines

Inspection

8 Clean all components with solvent, inspect them for wear and damage.
9 Check the oil pressure relief valve piston sliding surface and valve spring. If either the spring or the valve is damaged, they must be replaced as a set.
10 Check the driven rotor-to-body clearance, rotor-to-cover clearance and drive rotor tip clearance with a feeler gauge (see illustrations) and compare the results to this Chapter's Specifications. If any clearance is excessive, replace the rotors as a set. If necessary, replace the oil pump body.

Installation

11 Lubricate all rotors with clean engine oil and place them in the pump body with the marks facing in (1.3L engine) or out (1.6L and 1.8L engines) (see illustration 13.10c).
12 Pack the pump cavity with petroleum jelly, attach the pump cover and tighten the screws.
13 Lubricate the oil pressure relief valve piston with clean engine oil and reinstall the valve components in the pump body or crankcase.
14 On 1.3L engines, apply a 5 mm wide bead of RTV sealant to the pump body as shown (see illustration) and locate a new O-ring in the body groove. On 1.6L and 1.8L engines, place a new gasket on the engine block (the dowel pins should hold it in place).
15 Position the pump assembly against the block and install the mounting bolts. On 1.6L and 1.8L engines, make sure that the flats on the oil pump drive rotor aligns with the flats on the crankshaft (see illustration).
16 Tighten the bolts to the torque listed in this Chapter's Specifications in three or four steps. Follow a criss-cross pattern to avoid warping the body.
17 Reinstall the remaining parts in the reverse order of removal.
18 Using a new gasket, install the oil pick-up tube/strainer assembly and baffle plate (see Section 12). Tighten the fasteners to the torque listed in this Chapter's Specifications. When reinstalling the dipstick tube, use a new O-ring on the oil-pump end.
19 Add oil, start the engine and check for oil pressure and leaks.
20 Recheck the engine oil level.

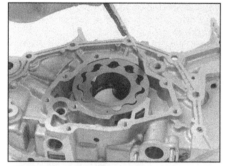

13.10a Measure the driven rotor-to-body clearance with a feeler gauge. The pump used on 1.3L engines is a different type but the inspection procedures are the same

13.10b Using a straight-edge and feeler gauge, measure the rotor-to-cover clearance

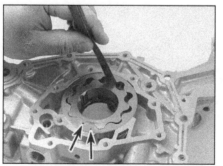

13.10c Measure the rotor tip clearance with a feeler gauge - on 1.6L and 1.8L engines, install the rotors with the marks facing out (arrowed)

13.15 When installing the oil pump on 1.6L and 1.8L engines, align the flats in the pump rotor with the flats on the crankshaft (arrowed)

14 Flywheel/driveplate - removal and installation

Removal

1 Raise the vehicle and support it securely on jackstands, then refer to Chapter 7 and remove the transmission.
2 Remove the pressure plate and clutch disc (Chapter 8) (manual transmission equipped vehicles).
3 Use a centre punch or paint to make alignment marks on the flywheel/driveplate and crankshaft to ensure correct alignment during reinstallation **(see illustration)**.
4 Remove the bolts that secure the flywheel/driveplate to the crankshaft. If the crankshaft turns, wedge a screwdriver in the ring gear teeth to jam the flywheel **(see illustration 7.12)**.
5 Remove the flywheel/driveplate from the crankshaft. Since the flywheel is fairly heavy, be sure to support it while removing the last bolt. Some automatic transmission equipped vehicles have spacers on both sides of the driveplate **(see illustration)**. Keep them with the driveplate.

⚠ **Warning: The ring-gear teeth may be sharp, wear gloves to protect your hands.**

Installation

6 Clean the flywheel to remove grease and oil. Inspect the surface for cracks, rivet grooves, burned areas and score marks. Light scoring can be removed with emery cloth. Check for cracked and broken ring gear teeth. Lay the flywheel on a flat surface and use a straight-edge to check for warpage.
7 Clean and inspect the mating surfaces of the flywheel/driveplate and the crankshaft. If the crankshaft rear seal is leaking, replace it before reinstalling the flywheel/driveplate (see Section 15).

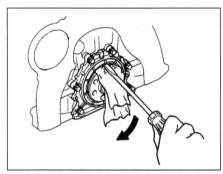

15.2 The quick way to replace the rear crankshaft oil seal is to simply pry the old one out with a screwdriver, lubricate the crankshaft journal and the lip of the new seal with moly-base grease and push the new seal into place - the seal lip is very stiff and can be easily damaged during installation if you're not careful

14.3 Mark the flywheel/driveplate and the crankshaft so they can be reassembled in the same relative positions

8 Position the flywheel/driveplate against the crankshaft. Be sure to align the marks made during removal. Note that some engines have an alignment dowel or staggered bolt holes to ensure correct installation. Before installing the bolts, apply thread-locking compound to the threads.
9 Wedge a screwdriver in the ring gear teeth to keep the flywheel/driveplate from turning and tighten the bolts to the torque listed in this Chapter's Specifications. Follow a criss-cross pattern and work up to the final torque in three or four steps.
10 The remainder of installation is the reverse of the removal procedure.

15 Rear main oil seal - replacement

1 Remove the transmission (see Chapter 7). Remove the rear end plate.
2 The seal can be replaced without removing the oil pan or seal retainer. However, this method is not recommended because the lip of the seal is quite stiff and it's possible to cock the seal in the retainer bore or damage it during installation. If you want to take the chance, pry out the old seal with a screwdriver

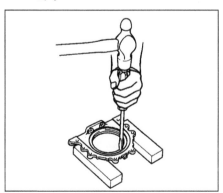

15.5 After removing the retainer assembly from the block, support it between two wooden blocks and drive out the old seal with a screwdriver and hammer

14.5 On vehicles equipped with a spacer plate, note the position of the locating pin (arrowed)

(see illustration). Apply multi-purpose grease to the crankshaft seal journal and the lip of the new seal and carefully push the new seal into place. The lip is stiff so carefully work it onto the seal journal of the crankshaft with a smooth object like the end of an extension as you tap the seal into place. Don't rush it or you may damage the seal.
3 The following method is recommended but requires resealing the rear of the oil pan (see Section 12) and removing the seal retainer.
4 After removing the two rearmost oil pan bolts that go into the seal retainer, break the seal between the rear of the oil pan and the bottom of the seal retainer with a putty knife. Remove the bolts, detach the seal retainer and remove all the old gasket material. remove the sealant from the top of the oil pan flange. **Note:** *Cover the open area of the oil pan with clean rags to keep debris out while bracing the pan flange.*
5 Position the seal and retainer assembly between two wood blocks on a workbench and drive the old seal out from the back side with a screwdriver **(see illustration)**.
6 Drive the new seal into the retainer with a wood block **(see illustration)** or a section of pipe slightly smaller in diameter than the outside diameter of the seal.

15.6 Drive the new seal into the retainer with a wood block or a section of pipe - make sure that you don't cock the seal in the retainer bore

7 Lubricate the crankshaft seal journal and the lip of the new seal with multi-purpose grease. Position a new gasket on the engine block. Apply a bead of RTV sealant to the exposed portion of oil pan flange and particularly at the pan-to-block mating surface.

8 Slowly and carefully push the seal and retainer onto the crankshaft. The seal lip is stiff, so work it onto the crankshaft with a smooth object such as the end of an extension as you push the retainer against the block.

9 Install and tighten the retainer bolts to the torque listed in this Chapter's Specifications.

10 The remainder of installation is the reverse of removal.

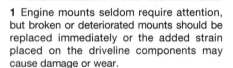

16 Engine mounts - check and replacement

1 Engine mounts seldom require attention, but broken or deteriorated mounts should be replaced immediately or the added strain placed on the driveline components may cause damage or wear.

Check

2 During the check, the engine must be raised slightly to remove the weight from the mounts.

3 Raise the vehicle and support it securely on jackstands, then position a jack under the engine oil pan. Place a large wood block between the jack head and the oil pan, then carefully raise the engine just enough to take the weight off the mounts. Do not position the wood block under the drain plug.

 Warning: DO NOT place any part of your body under the engine when it's supported only by a jack!

4 Check the mounts **(see illustration)** to see if the rubber is cracked, hardened or separated from the metal plates. Sometimes the rubber will split right down the centre.

5 Check for relative movement between the mount plates and the engine or frame (use a large screwdriver or pry bar to attempt to move the mounts). If movement is noted, lower the engine and tighten the mount fasteners.

6 Rubber preservative should be applied to the mounts to slow deterioration.

Replacement

7 Disconnect the negative battery cable from the battery, then raise the vehicle and support it securely on jackstands (if not already done). Support the engine as described in Step 3.

Caution: If the stereo in your vehicle is equipped with an anti-theft system, make sure you have the correct activation code before disconnecting the battery.

8 To remove the right engine mount, remove the two nuts from underneath, one bolt from above, and the upper section will separate from the engine bracket **(see illustrations 7.17b and 7.17c)**.

9 Remove the mount-to-chassis nuts and detach the mount.

10 To remove the rear engine mount, pull the rubber plugs from the longitudinal chassis brace to access the two nuts.

11 To remove the front engine mount, remove the two nuts retaining the insulator to the longitudinal chassis brace **(see illustration 12.8)**, then the three nuts retaining the insulator to the chassis.

12 Installation is the reverse of removal. Use thread locking compound on the mount bolts/nuts and be sure to tighten them securely.

13 See Chapter 7 for transmission mount replacement.

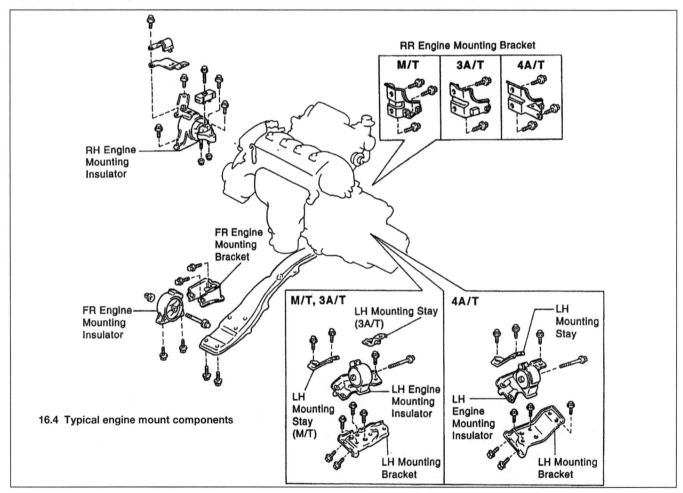

16.4 Typical engine mount components

Chapter 2 Part B
Engine removal and overhaul procedures

Contents

Degrees of difficulty

Easy, suitable for novice with little experience	**Fairly easy,** suitable for beginner with some experience	**Fairly difficult,** suitable for competent DIY mechanic	**Difficult,** suitable for experienced DIY mechanic	**Very difficult,** suitable for expert DIY or professional

Specifications

General

Displacement	
4E-FE engine	1.3L (1332 cc)
4A-FE engine	1.6L (1587 cc)
7A-FE engine	1.8L (1762 cc)
Cylinder compression pressure @ 250 rpm	
Standard	
1.3L engine	185 psi
1.6L and 1.8L engines	191 psi
Minimum	142 psi
Oil pressure (engine warm)	
At idle	4.3 psi minimum
At 3000 rpm	36 to 71 psi

Cylinder head

Warpage limits	
Block surface	0.0020 inch
Manifold surfaces	0.0039 inch

Engine block

Deck warpage limit	0.0020 inch
Cylinder bore diameter	
1.3L engine	
Standard	
Mark 1	2.9134 to 2.9138 inches
Mark 2	2.9138 to 2.9142 inches
Mark 3	2.9142 to 2.9146 inches
Service limit	2.9224 inches
1.6L and 1.8L engines	
Standard	
Mark 1	3.1890 to 3.1894 inches
Mark 2	3.1894 to 3.1898 inches
Mark 3	3.1898 to 3.1902 inches
Service limit	3.1982 inches
Taper and out-of-round limits	0.0008 inch

Valves and related components

Valve margin width
Standard . . . .   0.031 to 0.047 inch
Minimum . . . .   0.020 inch
Valve stem diameter
Intake . . . .   0.2350 to 0.2356 inch
Exhaust . . . .   0.2348 to 0.2354 inch
Valve stem-to-guide clearance
Intake
Standard . . . .   0.0010 to 0.0024 inch
Service limit . . . .   0.0031 inch
Exhaust
Standard . . . .   0.0012 to 0.0026 inch
Service limit . . . .   0.0039 inch
Valve spring
Out-of-square limit . . . .   0.079 inch
Free length
1.3L engine . . . .   1.569 inches
1.6L and 1.8L engines . . . .   1.669 inches

Crankshaft and connecting rods

Connecting rod journal
Diameter
1.3L and 1.6L engine . . . .   1.5742 to 1.5748 inches
1.8L engine . . . .   1.8893 to 1.8898 inches
Taper and out-of-round limits . . . .   0.0002 inch
Bearing oil clearance
Standard
1.3 L . . . .   0.0006 to 0.0019 inch
1.6L . . . .   0.0008 to 0.0020 inch
1.8L . . . .   0.0008 to 0.0017 inches
Service limit . . . .   0.0031 inch
Connecting rod side clearance (endplay)
Standard
1.3L engine . . . .   0.0059 to 0.0138 inch
1.6L and 1.8L engines . . . .   0.0059 to 0.0098 inch
Service limit
1.3L engine . . . .   0.0177 inch
1.6L and 1.8L engines . . . .   0.0118 inch
Main bearing journal
Diameter
1.3L engine . . . .   1.8498 to 1.8504 inches
1.6L and 1.8L engines . . . .   1.8891 to 1.8898 inches
Taper and out-of-round limits . . . .   0.0008 inch
Runout limit
1.3L engine . . . .   0.0024 inch
1.6L and 1.8L engines . . . .   0.0012 inch
Bearing oil clearance
Standard . . . .   0.0006 to 0.0013 inch
Service limit . . . .   0.0031 inch
Crankshaft endplay
Standard
1.3L engine . . . .   0.0008 to 0.0079 inch
1.6L and 1.8L engines . . . .   0.0008 to 0.0087 inch
Service limit . . . .   0.0118 inch
Thrust washer thickness . . . .   0.0961 to 0.0980 inch

Pistons and rings

Piston diameter
1.3L engine
Mark 1 . . . .   2.9094 to 2.9098 inches
Mark 2 . . . .   2.9098 to 2.9102 inches
Mark 3 . . . .   2.9102 to 2.9106 inches
1.6L and 1.8L engines
Mark 1 . . . .   3.1852 to 3.1856 inches
Mark 2 . . . .   3.1856 to 3.1860 inches
Mark 3 . . . .   3.1860 to 3.1864 inches

Piston-to-bore clearance
  Standard . . . . 0.0033 to 0.0041 inch
  Service limit . . . . 0.0051 inch
Piston ring end gap
  1.3L engine
    No. 1 (top) compression ring
      Standard . . . . 0.0102 to 0.0142 inch
      Service limit . . . . 0.0374 inch
    No. 2 (middle) compression ring
      Standard . . . . 0.0059 to 0.0118 inch
      Service limit . . . . 0.0354 inch
    Oil ring
      Standard . . . . 0.0051 to 0.0150 inch
      Service limit . . . . 0.0386 inch
  1.6L and 1.8L engines
    No. 1 (top) compression ring
      Standard . . . . 0.0098 to 0.0138 inch
      Service limit . . . . 0.0413 inch
    No. 2 (middle) compression ring
      Standard . . . . 0.0138 to 0.0197 inch
      Service limit . . . . 0.0472 inch
    Oil ring
      Standard . . . . 0.0039 to 0.0157 inch
      Service limit . . . . 0.0413 inch
Piston ring groove clearance
  No. 1 (top) compression ring . . . . 0.0018 to 0.0033 inch
  No. 2 (middle) compression ring . . . . 0.0012 to 0.0028 inch

Torque wrench settings*   **Ft-lbs**
Main bearing cap bolts 44
Connecting rod cap nuts/bolts
  1.3L engine 29
  1.6L engine
    Step 1 22
    Step 2 . . . . Tighten an additional 90-degrees
  1.8L engine
    Step 1 18
    Step 2 . . . . Tighten an additional 90-degrees
* **Note:** *Refer to Part A for additional torque specifications.*

---

1 General information

Included in this portion of Chapter 2 are the general overhaul procedures for the cylinder head(s) and internal engine components.

The information ranges from advice concerning preparation for an overhaul and the purchase of replacement parts to detailed, step-by-step procedures covering removal and installation of internal engine components and the inspection of parts.

The following Sections have been written based on the assumption that the engine has been removed from the vehicle. For information concerning in-vehicle engine repair, as well as removal and installation of the external components necessary for the overhaul, see Chapter 2A and Section 8 of this Chapter.

The Specifications included in this Part are only those necessary for the inspection and overhaul procedures which follow. Refer to Part A for additional Specifications.

2 Engine overhaul - general information

It's not always easy to determine when, or if, an engine should be completely overhauled, as a number of factors must be considered.

High mileage is not necessarily an indication that an overhaul is needed, while low mileage doesn't preclude the need for an overhaul. Frequency of servicing is probably the most important consideration. An engine that's had regular and frequent oil and filter changes, as well as other required maintenance, will most likely give many thousands of miles of reliable service. Conversely, a neglected engine may require an overhaul very early in its life.

Excessive oil consumption is an indication that piston rings, valve seals and/or valve guides are in need of attention. Make sure that oil leaks aren't responsible before deciding that the rings and/or guides are bad. Perform a cylinder compression check to determine the extent of the work required (see Section 4). Also check the vacuum readings under various conditions (see Section 3).

Check the oil pressure with a gauge installed in place of the oil pressure sending unit **(see illustrations)** and compare it to this Chapter's Specifications. If it's extremely low, the bearings and/or oil pump are probably worn out.

2.4a The oil pressure can be checked by removing the sending unit and installing a pressure gauge in its place

2.4b The oil pressure sending unit (arrowed) is located in the right front corner of the engine block, near the oil filter

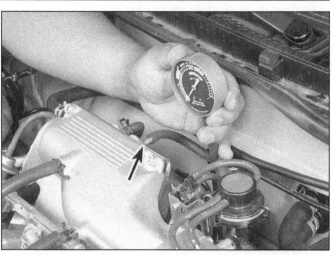

3.4 The vacuum gauge is easily attached to this unused port (arrowed) on the intake manifold

Loss of power, rough running, knocking or metallic engine noises, excessive valve train noise and high fuel consumption rates may also point to the need for an overhaul, especially if they're all present at the same time. If a complete tune-up doesn't remedy the situation, major mechanical work is the only solution.

An engine overhaul involves restoring the internal parts to the specifications of a new engine. During an overhaul, the piston rings are replaced and the cylinder walls are reconditioned (rebored and/or honed). If a rebore is done by an automotive machine shop, new oversize pistons will also be installed. The main bearings, connecting rod bearings and camshaft bearings are generally replaced with new ones and, if necessary, the crankshaft may be reground to restore the journals. Generally, the valves are serviced as well, since they're usually in less-than-perfect condition at this point. While the engine is being overhauled, other components, such as the distributor, starter and alternator, can be rebuilt as well. The end result should be a like new engine that will give many trouble free miles. **Note:** *Critical cooling system components such as the hoses, drivebelts, thermostat and water pump should be replaced with new parts when an engine is overhauled. The radiator should be checked carefully to ensure that it isn't clogged or leaking (see Chapter 3). If you purchase a rebuilt engine or short block, some rebuilders will not warranty their engines unless the radiator has been professionally flushed. Also, we don't recommend overhauling the oil pump - always install a new one when an engine is rebuilt.*

Before beginning the engine overhaul, read through the entire procedure to familiarize yourself with the scope and requirements of the job. Overhauling an engine isn't difficult, but it is time-consuming. Plan on the vehicle being tied up for a minimum of two weeks, especially if parts must be taken to an automotive machine shop for repair or reconditioning. Check on availability of parts and make sure that any necessary special tools and equipment are obtained in advance. Most work can be done with typical hand tools, although a number of precision measuring tools are required for inspecting parts to determine if they must be replaced. Often an automotive machine shop will handle the inspection of parts and offer advice concerning reconditioning and replacement. **Note:** *Always wait until the engine has been completely disassembled and all components, especially the engine block, have been inspected before deciding what service and repair operations must be performed by an automotive machine shop.* Since the block's condition will be the major factor to consider when determining whether to overhaul the original engine or buy a rebuilt one, never purchase parts or have machine work done on other components until the block has been thoroughly inspected. As a general rule, time is the primary cost of an overhaul, so it doesn't pay to install worn or substandard parts.

As a final note, to ensure maximum life and minimum trouble from a rebuilt engine, everything must be assembled with care in a spotlessly-clean environment.

3 Vacuum gauge diagnostic checks

A vacuum gauge provides valuable information about what is going on in the engine at a low cost. You can check for worn rings or cylinder walls, leaking head or intake manifold gaskets, incorrect fuel and emission control adjustments, restricted exhaust, stuck or burned valves, weak valve springs, improper ignition or valve timing and ignition problems.

Unfortunately, vacuum gauge readings are easy to misinterpret, so they should be used in conjunction with other tests to confirm the diagnosis.

Both the absolute readings and the rate of needle movement are important for accurate interpretation. Most gauges measure vacuum in inches of mercury (in-Hg). As vacuum increases (or atmospheric pressure decreases), the reading will increase. Also, for every 1,000 foot increase in elevation above sea level, the gauge readings will decrease about one inch of mercury.

Connect the vacuum gauge directly to intake manifold vacuum, not to ported (above the throttle plate) vacuum **(see illustration)**. Be sure no hoses are left disconnected during the test or false readings will result.

Before you begin the test, allow the engine to warm up completely. Block the wheels and set the parking brake. With the transmission in neutral (or Park, on automatics), start the engine and allow it to run at normal idle speed.

⚠ **Warning: Carefully inspect the fan blades for cracks or damage before starting the engine. Keep your hands and the vacuum tester clear of the fan and do not stand in front of the vehicle or in line with the fan when the engine is running.**

Read the vacuum gauge; an average, healthy engine should normally produce between 17 and 22 inches of vacuum with a fairly steady needle.

Refer to the following vacuum gauge readings and what they indicate about the engines condition:

1 A low steady reading usually indicates a leaking gasket between the intake manifold and throttle body, a leaky vacuum hose, late ignition timing or incorrect camshaft timing. Check ignition timing with a timing light and eliminate all other possible causes, utilizing the tests provided in this Chapter before you remove the timing belt cover to check the timing marks.

2 If the reading is three to eight inches below normal and it fluctuates at that low reading, suspect an intake manifold gasket leak at an intake port or a faulty injector.

3 If the needle has regular drops of about two to four inches at a steady rate the valves are probably leaking. Perform a compression or leak-down test to confirm this.

4 An irregular drop or down-flick of the needle can be caused by a sticking valve or an ignition misfire. Perform a compression or leak-down test and check the spark plugs.

5 A rapid vibration of about four in-Hg vibration at idle combined with exhaust smoke indicates worn valve guides. Perform a leak-down test to confirm this. If the rapid vibration occurs with an increase in engine speed, check for a leaking intake manifold gasket or head gasket, weak valve springs, burned valves or ignition misfire.

6 A slight fluctuation, say one inch up and down, may mean ignition problems. Check all the usual tune-up items and, if necessary, run the engine on an ignition analyzer.

7 If there is a large fluctuation, perform a compression or leak-down test to look for a weak or dead cylinder or a blown head gasket.

8 If the needle moves slowly through a wide range, check for a clogged PCV system, incorrect idle fuel mixture, throttle body or intake manifold gasket leaks.

9 Check for a slow return after revving the engine by quickly snapping the throttle open until the engine reaches about 2,500 rpm and let it shut. Normally the reading should drop to near zero, rise above normal idle reading (about 5 in-Hg over) and then return to the previous idle reading. If the vacuum returns slowly and doesn't peak when the throttle is snapped shut, the rings may be worn. If there is a long delay, look for a restricted exhaust system (often the muffler or catalytic converter). An easy way to check this is to temporarily disconnect the exhaust ahead of the suspected part and redo the test.

4 Cylinder compression check

1 A compression check will tell you what mechanical condition the upper end (pistons, rings, valves, head gaskets) of your engine is in. Specifically, it can tell you if the compression is down due to leakage caused by worn piston rings, defective valves and seats or a blown head gasket. **Note:** *The engine must be at normal operating temperature and the battery must be fully charged for this check.*

2 Begin by cleaning the area around the spark plugs before you remove them (compressed air should be used, if available, otherwise a small brush or even a bicycle tyre pump will work). The idea is to prevent dirt from getting into the cylinders as the compression check is being done.

3 Remove all of the spark plugs from the engine (see Chapter 1).

4 Block the throttle wide open.

5 Detach the coil wire from the centre of the distributor cap and ground it on the engine block. Use a jumper wire with alligator clips on each end to ensure a good ground. It is also a good idea to pull the EFI fuse from the fuse panel to disable the fuel pump during the compression test.

6 Install the compression gauge in the spark plug hole **(see illustration)**.

7 Crank the engine over at least seven compression strokes and watch the gauge. The compression should build up quickly in a healthy engine. Low compression on the first stroke, followed by gradually increasing pressure on successive strokes, indicates worn piston rings. A low compression reading on the first stroke, which doesn't build up during successive strokes, indicates leaking valves or a blown head gasket (a cracked head could also be the cause). Deposits on the undersides of the valve heads can also cause low compression. Record the highest gauge reading obtained.

8 Repeat the procedure for the remaining cylinders and compare the results to this Chapter's Specifications.

9 Add some engine oil (about three squirts from a plunger-type oil can) to each cylinder, through the spark plug hole, and repeat the test.

10 If the compression increases after the oil is added, the piston rings are definitely worn. If the compression doesn't increase significantly, the leakage is occurring at the valves or head gasket. Leakage past the valves may be caused by burned valve seats and/or faces or warped, cracked or bent valves.

11 If two adjacent cylinders have equally low compression, there's a strong possibility that the head gasket between them is blown. The appearance of coolant in the combustion chambers or the crankcase would verify this condition.

4.6 A compression gauge with a threaded fitting for the spark plug hole is preferred over the type that requires hand pressure to maintain the seal - be sure to block open the throttle valve as far as possible during the compression check!

12 If one cylinder is 20-percent lower than the others, and the engine has a slightly rough idle, a worn exhaust lobe on the camshaft could be the cause.

13 If the compression is unusually high, the combustion chambers are probably coated with carbon deposits. If that's the case, the cylinder head(s) should be removed and decarbonized.

14 If compression is way down or varies greatly between cylinders, it would be a good idea to have a leak-down test performed by an automotive repair shop. This test will pinpoint exactly where the leakage is occurring and how severe it is.

5 Engine removal - methods and precautions

If you've decided that an engine must be removed for overhaul or major repair work, several preliminary steps should be taken.

Locating a suitable place to work is extremely important. Adequate work space, along with storage space for the vehicle, will be needed. If a shop or garage isn't available, at the very least a flat, level, clean work surface made of concrete or asphalt is required.

Cleaning the engine compartment and engine before beginning the removal procedure will help keep tools clean and organized.

An engine hoist or A-frame will also be necessary. Make sure the equipment is rated in excess of the combined weight of the engine and transmission. Safety is of primary importance, considering the potential hazards involved in lifting the engine out of the vehicle.

If the engine is being removed by a novice, a helper should be available. Advice and aid from someone more experienced would also be helpful. There are many instances when one person cannot simultaneously perform all of the operations required when lifting the engine out of the vehicle.

Plan the operation ahead of time. Arrange for or obtain all of the tools and equipment you'll need prior to beginning the job. Some of the equipment necessary to perform engine removal and installation safely and with relative ease are (in addition to an engine hoist): a heavy duty floor jack, complete sets of wrenches and sockets as described in the rear of this manual, wooden blocks and plenty of rags and cleaning solvent for mopping up spilled oil, coolant and gasoline. If the hoist must be rented, make sure that you arrange for it in advance and perform all of the operations possible without it beforehand. This will save you money and time.

Plan for the vehicle to be out of use for quite a while. A machine shop will be required to perform some of the work which the do-it-yourselfer can't accomplish without special equipment. These shops often have a busy schedule, so it would be a good idea to consult them before removing the engine in order to accurately estimate the amount of time required to rebuild or repair components that may need work.

Always be extremely careful when removing and installing the engine. Serious injury can result from careless actions. Plan ahead, take your time and a job of this nature, although major, can be accomplished successfully.

6 Engine - removal and installation

Note: *Read through the entire Section before beginning this procedure. The factory recommends removing the engine and transmission from the top as a unit, then separating the engine from the transmission on the shop floor. If the transmission is not being serviced, it is possible to leave the transmission in the vehicle and remove the engine from the top by itself, by removing the crankshaft pulley and tilting up the timing belt end of the engine for clearance.*

Removal

Warning: These models are equipped with airbags. The airbag is armed and can deploy (inflate) anytime the battery is connected. To prevent accidental deployment (and possible injury), turn the ignition key to LOCK and disconnect the negative battery cable whenever working near airbag components. After the battery is disconnected, wait at least two minutes before beginning work (the system has a back-up capacitor that must fully discharge). For more information see Chapter 12.

1 Relieve the fuel system pressure (see Chapter 4).

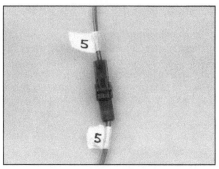

6.7 Label both ends of each wire and hose before disconnecting it

2 Disconnect the negative cable from the battery.
Caution: If the stereo in your vehicle is equipped with an anti-theft system, make sure you have the correct activation code before disconnecting the battery.
3 Remove the battery and battery tray.
4 Place protective covers on the bumpers and cowl and remove the bonnet (see Chapter 11).
5 Remove the air cleaner assembly (see Chapter 4).
6 Raise the vehicle and support it securely on jackstands. Drain the cooling system and engine oil and remove the drivebelts (see Chapter 1).
7 Clearly label, then disconnect, all vacuum lines, coolant and emissions hoses, wiring harness connectors, ground straps and fuel lines. Masking tape and/or a touch up paint applicator work well for marking items **(see illustration)**. Take instant photos or sketch the locations of components and brackets.
8 Remove the windscreen washer tank and coolant reservoir tank.
9 Remove the cooling fan(s) and radiator (see Chapter 3).
10 Disconnect the heater hoses.
11 Release the residual fuel pressure in the tank by removing the fuel tank cap, then

detach the fuel lines connecting the engine to the chassis (see Chapter 4). Plug or cap all open fittings.
12 Disconnect the throttle linkage, transmission Throttle Valve (TV) linkage and speed control cable, if equipped, from the engine (see Chapter 4).
13 Remove the battery and battery tray (see Chapter 5).
14 Refer to Part A of this Chapter and remove the intake and exhaust manifolds.
15 On power steering-equipped vehicles, unbolt the power steering pump. If clearance allows, tie the pump aside without disconnecting the hoses. If necessary, remove the pump (see Chapter 10).
16 On air-conditioned models, unbolt the compressor and set it aside. Do not disconnect the refrigerant hoses. **Note:** *Wire the compressor out of the way with a coat hanger, don't let the compressor hang on the hoses.*
17 Attach a lifting sling to the engine. Position a hoist and connect the sling to it. Take up the slack until there is slight tension on the hoist.
18 Refer to Chapter 8 and remove the driveshafts.
19 Remove the through-bolt holding the rear (firewall side) engine mount to its engine bracket, then pull the rubber access plugs from the longitudinal engine brace and remove the four nuts and five bolts **(see Chapter 7A).**
20 Refer to Part A of this Chapter and remove the drivebelts, water pump pulley and crankshaft pulley.
21 Remove the bolt securing the radiator-side engine mount to the chassis.
22 On automatic transmission-equipped models, pry out the plastic torque converter dust shield from the lower bellhousing. Remove the torque converter-to-driveplate fasteners (see Chapter 7B) and push the converter back slightly into the bellhousing.

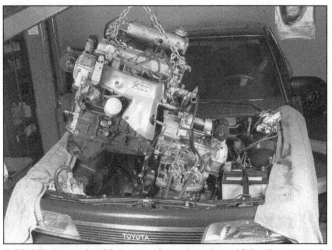

6.26 Lift the engine high enough to clear the vehicle, then move it away and lower the hoist - this engine is being removed with the transaxle still attached

6.27 Lower the engine outside of the vehicle, remove the driveplate, and attach the engine to a suitable workstand

23 Remove the engine-to-transmission bolts and separate the engine from the transmission (see Chapter 7A). The torque converter should remain in the transmission. **Note:** *If the transmission is to be removed at the same time, the left-side engine mount should be disconnected, along with any wires, cables or hoses connected to the transmission. The engine-to-transmission bolts should remain in place at this time.*

24 Recheck to be sure nothing except the mounts are still connecting the engine to the vehicle or to the transmission. Disconnect and label anything still remaining.

25 Support the transmission with a floor jack. Place a block of wood on the jack head to prevent damage to the transmission. Remove the bolts from the engine mounts, leaving those attached to the transmission in place.

 Warning: Do not place any part of your body under the engine/transmission when it's supported only by a hoist or other lifting device.

26 Slowly lift the engine (or engine/transmission) out of the vehicle **(see illustration)**. It may be necessary to pry the mounts away from the frame brackets. **Note:** *When removing the engine from a manual transmission equipped vehicle and the transmission is to remain in the vehicle, you may have to use the jack supporting the transmission to tilt the transmission enough to allow the engine to be angled forward and up out of the vehicle.*

27 Move the engine away from the vehicle and carefully lower the hoist until the engine can be set on the floor; or remove the flywheel/driveplate and mount the engine on an engine stand **(see illustration)**. **Note:** *On automatic transmission-equipped models, mark the front and rear spacer plates (where fitted) and keep them with the driveplate.*

Installation

28 Check the engine/transmission mounts. If they're worn or damaged, replace them.

29 On manual transmission-equipped models, inspect the clutch components (see Chapter 8) and on automatic models inspect the converter seal and bushing.

30 On automatic transmission-equipped models, apply a dab of grease to the nose of the converter.

31 Carefully guide the transmission into place, following the procedure outlined in Chapter 7A or 7B. **Caution:** *Do not use the bolts to force the engine and transmission into alignment. They may crack or damage major components.*

32 Install the engine-to-transmission bolts and tighten them to the torque listed in the Chapter 7 Specifications.

33 Attach the hoist to the engine and carefully lower the engine/transmission assembly into the engine compartment. **Note:** *If the engine was removed with the*

transmission remaining in the car, lower the engine into the car until an assistant can help you line up the dowel pins on the block with the transmission. Some twisting and angling of the engine and/or the transmission will be necessary to secure proper alignment of the two.

34 Install the mount bolts and tighten them securely.

35 Reinstall the remaining components and fasteners in the reverse order of removal.

36 Add coolant, oil, power steering and transmission fluids as needed (see Chapter 1).

37 Run the engine and check for proper operation and leaks. Shut off the engine and recheck the fluid levels.

7 Engine rebuilding alternatives

The do-it-yourselfer is faced with a number of options when performing an engine overhaul. The decision to replace the engine block, piston/connecting rod assemblies and crankshaft depends on a number of factors, with the number one consideration being the condition of the block. Other considerations are cost, access to machine shop facilities, parts availability, time required to complete the project and the extent of prior mechanical experience on the part of the do-it-yourselfer.

Some of the rebuilding alternatives include:

Individual parts - If the inspection procedures reveal that the engine block and most engine components are in re-usable condition, purchasing individual parts may be the most economical alternative. The block, crankshaft and piston/connecting rod assemblies should all be inspected carefully. Even if the block shows little wear, the cylinder bores should be surface honed.

Short engine - A short engine consists of an engine block with a crankshaft and piston/connecting rod assemblies already installed. All new bearings are incorporated and all clearances will be correct. The existing camshafts, valve train components, cylinder head and external parts can be bolted to the short engine with little or no machine shop work necessary.

Reconditioned engine - A reconditioned engine usually consists of a short engine plus an oil pump, oil pan, cylinder head, valve cover, camshaft and valve train components, timing sprockets and timing belt covers. All components are installed with new bearings, seals and gaskets incorporated throughout. The installation of manifolds and external parts is all that's necessary.

Give careful thought to which alternative is best for you and discuss the situation with local automotive machine shops, auto parts dealers and experienced rebuilders before ordering or purchasing replacement parts.

8 Engine overhaul - disassembly sequence

1 It's much easier to disassemble and work on the engine if it's mounted on a portable engine stand. A stand can often be rented quite cheaply from an equipment rental yard. Before the engine is mounted on a stand, the flywheel/driveplate and rear oil seal retainer should be removed from the engine.

2 If a stand isn't available, it's possible to disassemble the engine with it blocked up on the floor. Be extra careful not to tip or drop the engine when working without a stand.

3 If you're going to obtain a reconditioned engine, all external components must come off first, to be transferred to the replacement engine, just as they will if you're doing a complete engine overhaul yourself. These include:

Alternator and brackets
Emissions control components
Distributor, spark plug wires and spark plugs
Thermostat and housing cover
Water pump and remaining cooling system components
EFI components
Intake/exhaust manifolds
Oil filter
Engine mounts
Clutch and flywheel/driveplate
Engine rear plate

Note: *When removing the external components from the engine, pay close attention to details that may be helpful or important during installation. Note the installed position of gaskets, seals, spacers, pins, brackets, washers, bolts and other small items.*

4 If you're obtaining a short engine, which consists of the engine block, crankshaft, pistons and connecting rods all assembled, then the cylinder head, oil pan and oil pump will have to be removed as well from your engine so that your short engine can be turned in to the rebuilder as a core. See *Engine rebuilding alternatives* for additional information regarding the different possibilities to be considered.

5 If you're planning a complete overhaul, the engine must be disassembled and the internal components removed in the following order **(see illustration)**.

Intake and exhaust manifolds
Valve cover
Timing belt covers
Timing belt and sprockets
Cylinder head
Oil pan
Oil pump
Piston/connecting rod assemblies
Crankshaft rear oil seal retainer
Crankshaft and main bearings

6 Before beginning the disassembly and overhaul procedures, make sure the following

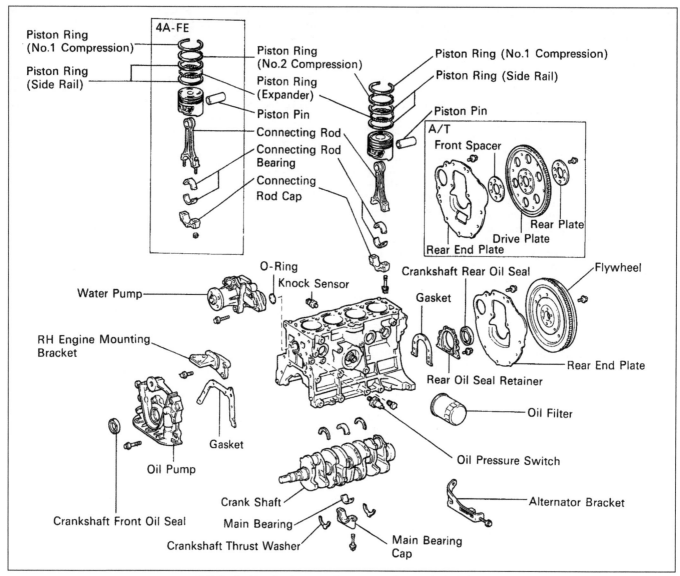

8.5 Typical engine lower end components - exploded view

items are available. Also, refer to Section 21 for a list of tools and materials needed for engine reassembly.

Common hand tools
Small cardboard boxes or plastic bags for storing parts
Gasket scraper
Ridge reamer
Micrometers
Telescoping gauges
Dial indicator set
Valve spring compressor
Cylinder surfacing hone
Piston ring groove-cleaning tool
Electric drill motor
Tap and die set
Wire brushes
Oil gallery brushes
Cleaning solvent

9 Cylinder head - disassembly

Note: *New and rebuilt cylinder heads are commonly available for most engines at dealerships and auto parts stores. Due to the fact that some specialized tools are necessary for the disassembly and inspection procedures, and replacement parts may not be readily available, it may be more practical and economical for the home mechanic to purchase a replacement head rather than taking the time to disassemble, inspect and recondition the original.*

1 Cylinder head disassembly involves removal of the intake and exhaust valves and related components. It's assumed that the lifters and camshafts have already been removed (see Part A as needed).

2 Before the valves are removed, arrange to label and store them, along with their related components, so they can be kept separate and reinstalled in the same valve guides they are removed from **(see illustration)**.

3 Compress the springs on the first valve with a spring compressor and remove the keepers **(see illustration)**. Carefully release the valve spring compressor and remove the retainer, the spring and the spring seat (if used).

Caution: Be very careful not to nick or otherwise damage the lifter bores when compressing the valve springs. Note: If your spring compressor does not have an end with cut-outs on the side (such as the one shown), an adapter is available to use with a standard spring compressor.

9.2 A small plastic bag, with an appropriate label, can be used to store the valve components so they can be kept together and reinstalled in the correct guide

4 Pull the valve out of the head, then remove the oil seal from the guide. If the valve binds in the guide (won't pull through), push it back into the head and deburr the area around the keeper groove with a fine file or whetstone.
5 Repeat the procedure for the remaining valves. Remember to keep all the parts for each valve together so they can be reinstalled in the same locations.
6 Once the valves and related components have been removed and stored in an organized manner, the head should be thoroughly cleaned and inspected. If a complete engine overhaul is being done, finish the engine disassembly procedures before beginning the cylinder head cleaning and inspection process.

10 Cylinder head - cleaning and inspection

1 Thorough cleaning of the cylinder head(s) and related valve train components, followed by a detailed inspection, will enable you to decide how much valve service work must be done during the engine overhaul. **Note:** *If the*

engine was severely overheated, the cylinder head is probably warped (see Step 12).

Cleaning

2 Scrape all traces of old gasket material and sealing compound off the head gasket, intake manifold and exhaust manifold sealing surfaces. Be very careful not to gouge the cylinder head. Special gasket-removal solvents that soften gaskets and make removal much easier are available at auto parts stores.
3 Remove all built up scale from the coolant passages.
4 Run a stiff wire brush through the various holes to remove deposits that may have formed in them. If there are heavy rust deposits in the water passages, the bare head should be professionally cleaned at a machine shop.
5 Run an appropriate-size tap into each of the threaded holes to remove corrosion and thread sealant that may be present. If compressed air is available, use it to clear the holes of debris produced by this operation.

 Warning: Wear eye protection when using compressed air!

6 Clean the exhaust and intake manifold stud threads with a wire brush.
7 Clean the cylinder head with solvent and dry it thoroughly. Compressed air will speed the drying process and ensure that all holes and recessed areas are clean. **Note:** *Decarbonizing chemicals are available and may prove very useful when cleaning cylinder heads and valve train components. They are very caustic and should be used with caution. Be sure to follow the instructions on the container.*
8 Clean the lifters with solvent and dry them thoroughly. Compressed air will speed the drying process and can be used to clean out the oil passages. Don't mix them up during the cleaning process; keep them in a box with numbered compartments.

9 Clean all the valve springs, spring seats, keepers and retainers with solvent and dry them thoroughly. Work on the components from one valve at a time to avoid mixing up the parts.
10 Scrape off any heavy deposits that may have formed on the valves, then use a motorized wire brush to remove deposits from the valve heads and stems. Again, make sure the valves don't get mixed up.

Inspection

Note: *Be sure to perform all of the following inspection procedures before concluding that machine shop work is required. Make a list of the items that need attention. The inspection procedures for the lifters and camshafts, can be found in Part A.*

Cylinder head

11 Inspect the head very carefully for cracks, evidence of coolant leakage and other damage. If cracks are found, check with an automotive machine shop concerning repair. If repair isn't possible, a new cylinder head should be obtained.
12 Using a straight-edge and feeler gauge, check the head gasket mating surface for warpage **(see illustration)**. If the warpage exceeds the limit found in this Chapter's Specifications, it can be resurfaced at an automotive machine shop.
13 Examine the valve seats in each of the combustion chambers. If they're pitted, cracked or burned, the head will require valve service that's beyond the scope of the home mechanic.
14 Check the valve stem-to-guide clearance with a small hole gauge and micrometer, or a small dial bore gauge **(see illustration)**. Also, check the valve stem deflection with a dial indicator attached securely to the head. The valve must be in the guide and approximately 1/16-inch off the seat. The total valve stem movement indicated by the gauge needle must be noted, then divided by two to obtain

9.3 Compress the spring until the keepers can be removed with a small magnetic screwdriver or needle-nose pliers

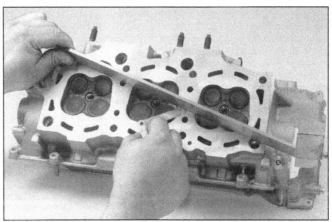

10.12 Check the cylinder head gasket surfaces for warpage by trying to slip a feeler gauge under the precision straight-edge (see the Specifications for the maximum warpage allowed and use a feeler gauge of that thickness)

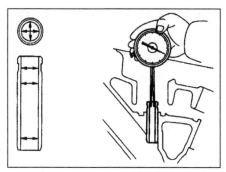

10.14 Use a small dial bore gauge to determine the inside diameter of the guides

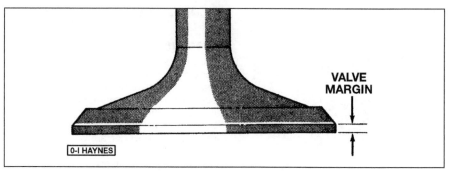

10.16 The margin width on each valve must be as specified (if no margin exists, the valve cannot be re-used)

the actual clearance value. If it exceeds the stem-to-guide clearance limit found in this Chapter's Specifications, the valve guides should be replaced. After this is done, if there's still some doubt regarding the condition of the valve guides they should be checked by an automotive machine shop (the cost should be minimal). **Note:** *Most home mechanics will not have a precision small bore gauge, but your local machine shop can measure the guides for you.*

Valves

15 Carefully inspect each valve face for uneven wear, deformation, cracks, pits and burned areas. Check the valve stem for scuffing and galling and the neck for cracks. Rotate the valve and check for any obvious indication that it's bent. Look for pits and excessive wear on the end of the stem. The presence of any of these conditions indicates the need for valve service by an automotive machine shop.

16 Measure the margin width on each valve **(see illustration)**. Any valve with a margin narrower than that listed in this Chapter's Specifications will have to be replaced with a new one.

Valve components

17 Check each valve spring for wear (on the ends) and pits. Measure the free length and compare it to this Chapter's Specifications **(see illustration)**. Any springs that are shorter than specified have sagged and should not be re-used. The tension of all springs should be pressure checked with a special fixture before

deciding that they're suitable for use in a rebuilt engine (take the springs to an automotive machine shop for this check).
18 Stand each spring on a flat surface and check it for squareness **(see illustration)**. If any of the springs are distorted or sagged, replace all of them with new parts.
19 Check the spring retainers and keepers for obvious wear and cracks. Any questionable parts should be replaced with new ones, as extensive damage will occur if they fail during engine operation.
20 Any damaged or excessively worn parts must be replaced with new ones.
21 If the inspection process indicates that the valve components are in generally poor condition and worn beyond the limits specified, which is usually the case in an engine that's being overhauled, reassemble the valves in the cylinder head and refer to Section 11 for valve servicing recommendations.

11 Valves - servicing

1 Because of the complex nature of the job and the special tools and equipment needed, servicing of the valves, the valve seats and the valve guides, commonly known as a valve job, should be done by a professional.
2 The home mechanic can remove and disassemble the head(s), do the initial cleaning and inspection, then reassemble and deliver them to a dealer service department or

an automotive machine shop for the actual service work. Doing the inspection will enable you to see what condition the head(s) and valve train components are in and will ensure that you know what work and new parts are required when dealing with an automotive machine shop.
3 The dealer service department, or automotive machine shop, will remove the valves and springs, recondition or replace the valves and valve seats, recondition the valve guides, check and replace the valve springs, spring retainers and keepers (as necessary), replace the valve seals with new ones, reassemble the valve components and make sure the installed spring height is correct. The cylinder head gasket surface will also be resurfaced if it's warped.
4 After the valve job has been performed by a professional, the head(s) will be in like new condition. When the heads are returned, be sure to clean them again before installation on the engine to remove any metal particles and abrasive grit that may still be present from the valve service or head resurfacing operations. Use compressed air, if available, to blow out all the oil holes and passages.

12 Cylinder head - reassembly

1 Regardless of whether or not the head was sent to an automotive machine shop for valve servicing, make sure it's clean before beginning reassembly. Note that there are several small core plugs (also called freeze plugs or expansion plugs) in the head. These should be replaced whenever the engine is overhauled or the cylinder head is reconditioned (see Section 15 for replacement procedure).
2 If the head was sent out for valve servicing, the valves and related components will already be in place. Begin the reassembly procedure with Step 8.
3 Install new seals on each of the valve guides. **Note:** *Intake and exhaust valves require different seals - DO NOT mix them up!* Gently tap each intake valve seal into place until it's seated on the guide **(see illustration)**.

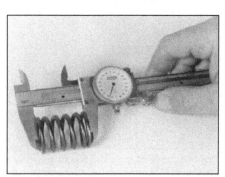

10.17 Measure the free length of each valve spring with a dial or vernier caliper

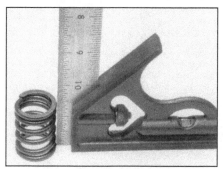

10.18 Check each valve spring for squareness

Caution: Don't hammer on the valve seals once they're seated or you may damage them. Don't twist or cock the seals during installation or they won't seat properly on the valve stems.

4 Beginning at one end of the head, lubricate and install the first valve. Apply moly-base grease or clean engine oil to the valve stem.

5 Drop the spring seat or shim(s) over the valve guide and set the valve spring and retainer in place.

6 Compress the springs with a valve spring compressor and carefully install the keepers in the upper groove, then slowly release the compressor and make sure the keepers seat properly. Apply a small dab of grease to each keeper to hold it in place if necessary **(see illustration)**.

7 Repeat the procedure for the remaining valves. Be sure to return the components to their original locations - don't mix them up!

8 Check the valve spring installed height with a dial or vernier caliper.

13 Pistons/connecting rods - removal

Note: *Prior to removing the piston/connecting rod assemblies, remove the cylinder head, the oil pan and the oil pump pick-up tube by*

13.1 A ridge reamer is required to remove the ridge from the top of each cylinder - do this before removing the pistons!

12.3 Gently tap the valve seals (arrowed) into place with a deep socket and hammer - the intake seals are painted brown or grey, while the exhaust seals are painted black (don't mix them up)

referring to the appropriate Sections in Chapter 2A.

1 Use your fingernail to feel if a ridge has formed at the upper limit of ring travel (about 1/4-inch down from the top of each cylinder). If carbon deposits or cylinder wear have produced ridges, they must be completely removed with a special tool **(see illustration)**. Follow the manufacturer's instructions provided with the tool. Failure to remove the ridges before attempting to remove the piston/connecting rod assemblies may result in piston damage.

2 After the cylinder ridges have been removed, turn the engine upside-down so the crankshaft is facing up.

3 Before the connecting rods are removed, check the endplay with feeler gauges. Slide them between the first connecting rod and the crankshaft throw until the play is removed **(see illustration)**. The endplay is equal to the thickness of the feeler gauge(s). If the endplay exceeds the specified service limit, new connecting rods will be required. If new rods (or a new crankshaft) are installed, the endplay may fall under the service limit (if it does, the rods will have to be machined to restore it - consult an automotive machine shop for advice if necessary). Repeat the procedure for the remaining connecting rods.

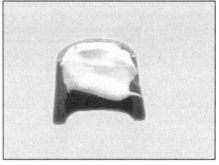

12.6 The small valve stem keepers are easier to position when coated with grease

4 Check the connecting rods and caps for identification marks. If they aren't plainly marked, use a small centre punch to make the appropriate number of indentations on each rod and cap (1, 2, 3, etc., depending on the engine type and cylinder they're associated with) **(see illustration)**.

5 Loosen each of the connecting rod cap nuts 1/2-turn at a time until they can be removed by hand. Remove the number one connecting rod cap and bearing insert. Don't drop the bearing insert out of the cap. **Note:** *The 1.3L and 1.6L engines use conventional rod bolts (pressed into the rod) and nuts, while the 1.8L engine uses cap bolts that go through the rod cap and screw into the rod.*

6 Slip a short length of plastic or rubber hose over each connecting rod cap bolt to protect the crankshaft journal and cylinder wall as the piston is removed **(see illustration)**.

7 Remove the bearing insert and push the connecting rod/piston assembly out through the top of the engine. Use a wooden hammer handle to push on the upper bearing surface in the connecting rod. If resistance is felt, double-check to make sure that all of the ridge was removed from the cylinder.

8 Repeat the procedure for the remaining cylinders. **Note:** *Turn the crankshaft as needed to put the rod to be removed close to parallel with the cylinder bore, i.e. don't try to drive it out while at a large angle to the bore.*

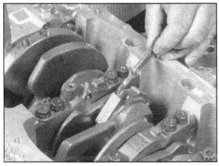

13.3 Check the connecting rod side clearance with a feeler gauge as shown here

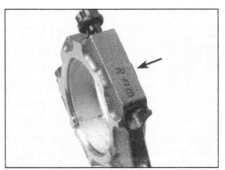

13.4 The rods and caps should be marked to indicate which cylinder they're installed in - do not confuse the markings shown here as rod numbers; these are bearing size identifications

13.6 To prevent damage to the crankshaft journals and cylinder walls, slip sections of hose over the rod bolts before removing the pistons

9 After removal, reassemble the connecting rod caps and bearing inserts in their respective connecting rods and install the cap nuts/bolts finger tight. Leaving the old bearing inserts in place until reassembly will help prevent the connecting rod bearing surfaces from being accidentally nicked or gouged.

10 Don't separate the pistons from the connecting rods (see Section 18 for additional information).

14 Crankshaft - removal

Note: *The crankshaft can be removed only after the engine has been removed from the vehicle. It's assumed that the flywheel or driveplate, crankshaft sprocket, timing belt, oil pan, oil pick-up tube, oil pump and piston/connecting rod assemblies have already been removed. The rear main oil seal and retainer must be removed from the block before proceeding with crankshaft removal.*

1 Before the crankshaft is removed, check the endplay. Mount a dial indicator with the stem in line with the crankshaft and touching one of the crank throws **(see illustration)**.

2 Push the crankshaft all the way to the rear and zero the dial indicator. Next, pry the crankshaft to the front as far as possible and check the reading on the dial indicator. The distance that it moves is the endplay. If it's greater than specified, check the crankshaft thrust surfaces for wear. If no wear is evident, new thrust washers should correct the endplay.

3 If a dial indicator isn't available, feeler gauges can be used. Gently pry or push the crankshaft all the way to the front of the engine. Slip feeler gauges between the crankshaft and the front face of the number 3 (thrust) main bearing to determine the clearance **(see illustration)**.

4 Check the main bearing caps to see if they're marked to indicate their locations. They should be numbered consecutively from the front of the engine to the rear. If they aren't, mark them with number stamping dies or a centre punch. Main bearing caps

14.1 Checking crankshaft endplay with a dial indicator

generally have a cast-in arrow, which points to the front of the engine. Loosen the main bearing cap bolts 1/4-turn at a time each, in the reverse order of the recommended tightening sequence **(see illustration 23.12)**, until they can be removed by hand.

5 Gently tap the caps with a soft-face hammer, then separate them from the engine block. If necessary, use the bolts as levers to remove the caps. Try not to drop the bearing inserts if they come out with the caps.

6 Carefully lift the crankshaft out of the engine. It may be a good idea to have an assistant available, since the crankshaft is quite heavy. With the bearing inserts in place in the engine block and main bearing caps or cap assembly, return the caps to their respective locations on the engine block and tighten the bolts finger tight.

15 Engine block - cleaning

Caution: The core plugs (also known as freeze or soft plugs) may be difficult or impossible to retrieve if they're driven completely into the block coolant passages.

1 Using the blunt end of a punch, tap in on the outer edge of the core plug to turn the plug sideways in the bore. Then using pliers, pull the core plug from the engine block **(see illustrations)**.

14.3 Checking crankshaft endplay with a feeler gauge

2 Using a gasket scraper, remove all traces of gasket material from the engine block. Be very careful not to nick or gouge the gasket sealing surfaces.

3 Remove the main bearing caps or cap assembly and separate the bearing inserts from the caps and the engine block. Tag the bearings, indicating which cylinder they were removed from and whether they were in the cap or the block, then set them aside.

4 Remove all of the threaded oil gallery plugs from the block. The plugs are usually very tight - they may have to be drilled out and the holes re-tapped. Use new plugs when the engine is reassembled.

5 If the engine is extremely dirty, it should be taken to an automotive machine shop to be steam cleaned or hot tanked.

6 After the block is returned, clean all oil holes and oil galleries one more time. Brushes specifically designed for this purpose are available at most auto parts stores. Flush the passages with warm water until the water runs clear, dry the block thoroughly and wipe all machined surfaces with a light, rust preventive oil. If you have access to compressed air, use it to speed the drying process and to blow out all the oil holes and galleries.

⚠ *Warning: Wear eye protection when using compressed air!*

7 If the block isn't extremely dirty or sludged up, you can do an adequate cleaning job with hot soapy water and a stiff brush. Take plenty

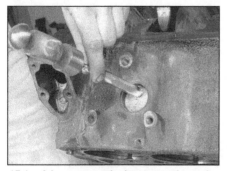

15.1a A hammer and a large punch can be used to knock the core plugs sideways in their bores

15.1b Pull the core plugs from the block with pliers

15.8 All bolt holes in the block - particularly the main bearing cap and head bolt holes - should be cleaned and restored with a tap (be sure to remove debris from the holes after this is done)

15.10 A large socket on an extension can be used to drive the new core plugs into the bores

of time and do a thorough job. Regardless of the cleaning method used, be sure to clean all oil holes and galleries very thoroughly, dry the block completely and coat all machined surfaces with light oil.
8 The threaded holes in the block must be clean to ensure accurate torque readings during reassembly. Run the proper size tap into each of the holes to remove rust, corrosion, thread sealant or sludge and restore damaged threads **(see illustration)**. If possible, use compressed air to clear the holes of debris produced by this operation. Now is a good time to clean the threads on the head bolts and the main bearing cap bolts as well.
9 Reinstall the main bearing caps and tighten the bolts finger tight.
10 After coating the sealing surfaces of the new core plugs with sealant, install them in the engine block **(see illustration)**. Make sure they're driven in straight and seated properly or leakage could result. Special tools are available for this purpose, but a large socket, with an outside diameter that will just slip into the core plug, a 1/2-inch drive extension and a hammer will work just as well.
11 Apply non-hardening sealant to the new oil gallery plugs and thread them into the holes in the block. Make sure they're tightened securely.
12 If the engine isn't going to be reassembled right away, cover it with a large plastic bag to keep it clean.

16 Engine block - inspection

1 Before the block is inspected, it should be cleaned as described in Section 15.
2 Visually check the block for cracks, rust and corrosion. Look for stripped threads in the threaded holes. It's also a good idea to have the block checked for hidden cracks by an automotive machine shop that has the special equipment to do this type of work, especially if the vehicle had a history of overheating or using coolant. If defects are found, have the block repaired, if possible, or replaced.

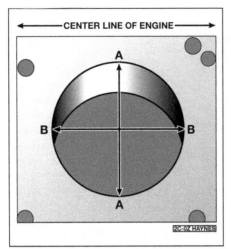

16.4a Measure the diameter of each cylinder at a right angle to engine centerline (A), and parallel to engine centerline (B) - out-of-round is the difference between A and B; taper is the difference between A and B at the top of the cylinder and A and B at the bottom of the cylinder

3 Check the cylinder bores for scuffing and scoring.
4 Check the cylinders for taper and out-of-round conditions as follows **(see illustrations)**:
5 Measure the diameter of each cylinder at the top (just under the ridge area), centre and bottom of the cylinder bore, parallel to the crankshaft axis.
6 Next, measure each cylinder's diameter at the same three locations perpendicular to the crankshaft axis.
7 The taper of each cylinder is the difference between the bore diameter at the top of the cylinder and the diameter at the bottom. The out-of-round specification of the cylinder bore is the difference between the parallel and perpendicular readings. Compare your results to this Chapter's Specifications.
8 If the cylinder walls are badly scuffed or scored, or if they're out-of-round or tapered beyond the limits given in this Chapter's Specifications, have the engine block rebored and honed at an automotive machine shop. If a rebore is done, oversize pistons and rings will be required.

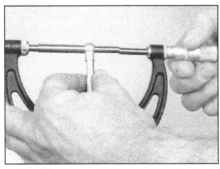

16.4c The gauge is then measured with a micrometer to determine the bore size

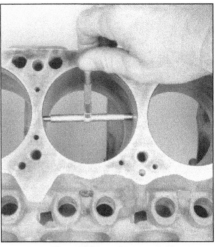

16.4b The ability to "feel" when the telescoping gauge is at the correct point will be developed over time, so work slowly and repeat the check until you're satisfied that the bore measurement is accurate

9 Using a precision straight-edge and feeler gauge, check the block deck (the surface that mates with the cylinder head) for distortion **(see illustration)**. If it's distorted beyond the specified limit, it can be resurfaced by an automotive machine shop.
10 If the cylinders are in reasonably good condition and not worn to the outside of the limits, and if the piston-to-cylinder clearances can be maintained properly, then they don't have to be rebored. Honing is all that's necessary (refer to Section 17).

17 Cylinder honing

1 Prior to engine reassembly, the cylinder bores must be honed so the new piston rings will seat correctly and provide the best possible combustion chamber seal. **Note:** *If you don't have the tools or don't want to tackle the honing operation, most automotive machine shops will do it for a reasonable fee.*

16.9 Check the block deck for distortion with a precision straightedge and feeler gauges

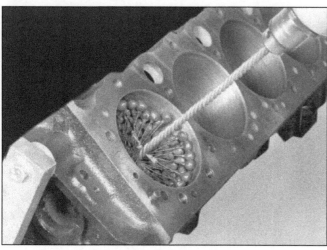

17.3a A "bottle brush" hone will produce better results if you have never done cylinder honing before

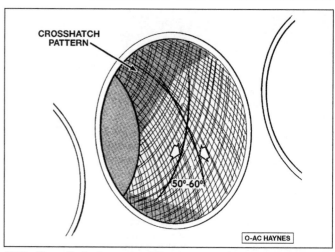

CROSSHATCH PATTERN

50°-60°

O-AC HAYNES

17.3b The cylinder hone should leave a smooth, crosshatch pattern with the lines intersecting at approximately a 60-degree angle

2 Before honing the cylinders, install the main bearing caps or cap assembly (without bearing inserts) and tighten the bolts to the specified torque.

3 Two types of cylinder hones are commonly available - the flex hone or "bottle brush" type and the more traditional surfacing hone with spring-loaded stones. Both will do the job, but for the less-experienced mechanic the "bottle brush" hone will probably be easier to use. You'll also need some kerosene or honing oil, rags and an electric drill motor. The drill motor should be operated at a steady, slow speed. Use a large 1/2-inch drill or a 3/8-inch variable-speed drill. Proceed as follows:

 Warning: Be sure to wear safety goggles or a face shield!

a) *Mount the hone in the drill motor, compress the stones and slip it into the first cylinder (see illustration).*
b) *Lubricate the cylinder with plenty of honing oil, turn on the drill and move the hone up-and-down in the cylinder at a pace that will produce a fine crosshatch pattern on the cylinder walls. Ideally, the crosshatch lines should intersect at approximately a 60-degree angle (see illustration). Be sure to use plenty of lubricant and don't take off any more material than is absolutely necessary to produce the desired finish. Note: Piston ring manufacturers may specify a smaller crosshatch angle than the traditional 60-degrees - read and follow any instructions included with the new rings.*
c) *Don't withdraw the hone from the cylinder while it's running. Instead, shut off the drill and continue moving the hone up-and-down in the cylinder until it comes to a complete stop, then compress the stones and withdraw the hone. If you're using a "bottle brush" type hone, stop the drill motor, then turn the chuck in the normal direction of rotation while withdrawing the hone from the cylinder.*

d) *Wipe the oil out of the cylinder and repeat the procedure for the remaining cylinders.*
4 After the honing job is complete, chamfer the top edges of the cylinder bores with a small file so the rings won't catch when the pistons are installed. Be very careful not to nick the cylinder walls with the end of the file.
5 The entire engine block must be washed again very thoroughly with warm, soapy water to remove all traces of the abrasive grit produced during the honing operation. **Note:** *The bores can be considered clean when a lint-free white cloth - dampened with clean engine oil - used to wipe them out doesn't pick up any more honing residue, which will show up as grey areas on the cloth. Be sure to run a brush through all oil holes and galleries and flush them with running water.*
6 After rinsing, dry the block and apply a coat of light rust preventive oil to all machined surfaces. Wrap the block in a plastic trash bag to keep it clean and set it aside until reassembly.

18 Pistons/connecting rods - inspection

1 Before the inspection process can be carried out, the piston/connecting rod assemblies

must be cleaned and the original piston rings removed from the pistons. **Note:** *Always use new piston rings when the engine is reassembled.*
2 Using a piston ring installation tool, carefully remove the rings from the pistons. Be careful not to nick or gouge the pistons in the process.
3 Scrape all traces of carbon from the top of the piston. A hand-held wire brush or a piece of fine emery cloth can be used once the majority of the deposits have been scraped away. Do not, under any circumstances, use a wire brush mounted in a drill motor to remove deposits from the pistons. The piston material is soft and may be eroded away by the wire brush.
4 Use a piston ring groove-cleaning tool to remove carbon deposits from the ring grooves. If a tool isn't available, a piece broken off the old ring will do the job. Be very careful to remove only the carbon deposits - don't remove any metal and do not nick or scratch the sides of the ring grooves (see illustrations).
5 Once the deposits have been removed, clean the piston/rod assemblies with solvent and dry them with compressed air (if available). Make sure the oil return holes in the back sides of the ring grooves and the oil hole in the lower end of each rod are clear.

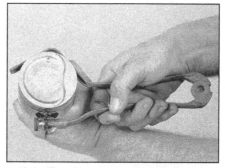

18.4a The ring grooves can be cleaned with a special tool, as shown here . . .

18.4b . . . or a section of a broken ring

6 If the pistons and cylinder walls aren't damaged or worn excessively, and if the engine block is not rebored, new pistons won't be necessary. Normal piston wear appears as even vertical wear on the piston thrust surfaces and slight looseness of the top ring in its groove. New piston rings, however, should always be used when an engine is rebuilt.

7 Carefully inspect each piston for cracks around the skirt, at the pin bosses and at the ring lands.

8 Look for scoring and scuffing on the thrust faces of the skirt, holes in the piston crown and burned areas at the edge of the crown. If the skirt is scored or scuffed, the engine may have been suffering from overheating and/or abnormal combustion, which caused excessively high operating temperatures. The cooling and lubrication systems should be checked thoroughly. A hole in the piston crown is an indication that abnormal combustion (pre-ignition) was occurring. Burned areas at the edge of the piston crown are usually evidence of spark knock (detonation). If any of the above problems exist, the causes must be corrected or the damage will occur again. The causes may include intake air leaks, incorrect air/fuel mixture, incorrect ignition timing and EGR system malfunctions.

9 Corrosion of the piston, in the form of small pits, indicates that coolant is leaking into the combustion chamber and/or the crankcase. Again, the cause must be corrected or the problem may persist in the rebuilt engine.

10 Measure the piston ring groove clearance by laying a new piston ring in each ring groove and slipping a feeler gauge in beside it **(see illustration)**. Check the clearance at three or four locations around each groove. Be sure to use the correct ring for each groove - they are different. If the clearance is greater than that listed in this Chapter's Specifications, new pistons will have to be used.

11 Check the piston-to-bore clearance by measuring the bore (see Section 16) and the piston diameter. Make sure the pistons and bores are correctly matched. Measure the piston across the skirt, at a 90-degree angle to the piston pin **(see illustration)**. Subtract the piston diameter from the bore diameter to obtain the clearance. If it's greater than specified, the block will have to be rebored and new pistons and rings installed.

12 Check the piston-to-rod clearance by twisting the piston and rod in opposite directions. Any noticeable play indicates excessive wear, which must be corrected.

13 If the pistons must be removed from the connecting rods for any reason, the piston/connecting rod assemblies should be taken to an automotive machine shop, for the interference fit gudgeon pins to be pressed out. The rods can also be checked for bend and twist at this time, and then the new pistons can be installed.

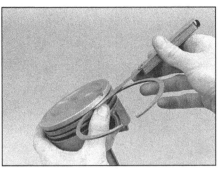

18.10 Check the ring groove clearance with a feeler gauge at several points around the groove

14 Check the connecting rods for cracks and other damage. Temporarily remove the rod caps, lift out the old bearing inserts, wipe the rod and cap bearing surfaces clean and inspect them for nicks, gouges and scratches. After checking the rods, replace the old bearings, slip the caps into place and tighten the nuts finger tight. **Note:** *If the engine is being rebuilt because of a connecting rod knock, be sure to install new rods.*

19 Crankshaft - inspection

1 Clean the crankshaft with solvent and dry it with compressed air (if available).

2 Check the main and connecting rod bearing journals for uneven wear, scoring, pits and cracks.

3 Remove all burrs from the crankshaft oil holes with a stone, file or scraper.

4 Clean the oil holes with a stiff brush and flush them with solvent.

5 Check the rest of the crankshaft for cracks and other damage. It should be magnafluxed to reveal hidden cracks - an automotive machine shop will handle the procedure.

6 Using a micrometer, measure the diameter of the main and connecting rod journals and compare the results to this Chapter's Specifications **(see illustration)**. By

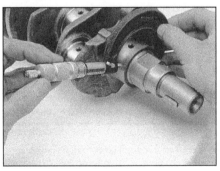

19.6 Measure the diameter of each crankshaft journal at several points to detect taper and out-of-round conditions

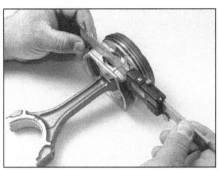

18.11 Measure the piston diameter at a 90-degree angle to the piston pin, at the bottom of the piston pin area - a precision caliper may be used if a micrometer isn't available

measuring the diameter at a number of points around each journal's circumference, you'll be able to determine whether or not the journal is out-of-round. Take the measurement at each end of the journal, near the crank throws, to determine if the journal is tapered. Crankshaft runout should be checked also, but large V-blocks and a dial indicator are needed to do it correctly. If you don't have the equipment, have a machine shop check the runout.

7 If the crankshaft journals are damaged, tapered, out-of-round or worn beyond the limits given in the Specifications, have the crankshaft reground by an automotive machine shop. Be sure to use the correct size bearing inserts if the crankshaft is reconditioned.

8 Check the oil seal journals at each end of the crankshaft for wear and damage. If the seal has worn a groove in the journal, or if it's nicked or scratched, the new seal may leak when the engine is reassembled. In some cases, an automotive machine shop may be able to repair the journal by pressing on a thin sleeve. If repair isn't feasible, a new or different crankshaft should be installed.

9 Refer to Section 20 and examine the main and rod bearing inserts.

20 Main and connecting rod bearings - inspection and selection

Inspection

1 Even though the main and connecting rod bearings should be replaced with new ones during the engine overhaul, the old bearings should be retained for close examination, as they may reveal valuable information about the condition of the engine **(see illustration)**.

2 Bearing failure occurs because of lack of lubrication, the presence of dirt or other foreign particles, overloading the engine and corrosion. Regardless of the cause of bearing failure, it must be corrected before the engine is reassembled to prevent it from happening again.

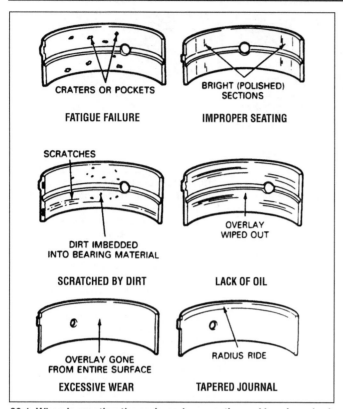

20.1 When inspecting the main and connecting rod bearings, look for these problems

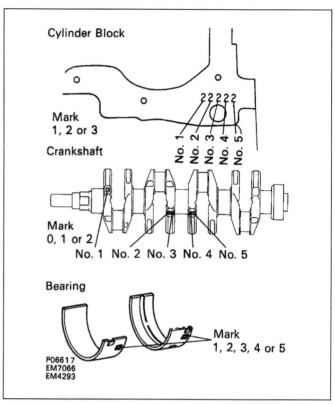

20.10 Main bearing selection details for 1.6L and 1.8L engines. On 1.3L engines, the numbers shown here on the crankshaft are not used

3 When examining the bearings, remove them from the engine block, the main bearing caps, the connecting rods and the rod caps and lay them out on a clean surface in the same general position as their location in the engine. This will enable you to match any bearing problems with the corresponding crankshaft journal.

4 Dirt and other foreign particles get into the engine in a variety of ways. It may be left in the engine during assembly, or it may pass through filters or the PCV system. It may get into the oil, and from there into the bearings. Metal chips from machining operations and normal engine wear are often present. Abrasives are sometimes left in engine components after reconditioning, especially when parts are not thoroughly cleaned using the proper cleaning methods. Whatever the source, these foreign objects often end up embedded in the soft bearing material and are easily recognized. Large particles will not embed in the bearing and will score or gouge the bearing and journal. The best prevention for this cause of bearing failure is to clean all parts thoroughly and keep everything spotlessly clean during engine assembly. Frequent and regular engine oil and filter changes are also recommended.

5 Lack of lubrication (or lubrication breakdown) has a number of interrelated causes. Excessive heat (which thins the oil), overloading (which squeezes the oil from the bearing face) and oil leakage or throw off (from excessive bearing clearances, worn oil pump or high engine speeds) all contribute to lubrication breakdown. Blocked oil passages, which usually are the result of misaligned oil holes in a bearing shell, will also oil starve a bearing and destroy it. When lack of lubrication is the cause of bearing failure, the bearing material is wiped or extruded from the steel backing of the bearing. Temperatures may increase to the point where the steel backing turns blue from overheating.

6 Driving habits can have a definite effect on bearing life. Low speed operation in too high a gear (lugging the engine) puts very high loads on bearings, which tends to squeeze out the oil film. These loads cause the bearings to flex, which produces fine cracks in the bearing face (fatigue failure). Eventually the bearing material will loosen in pieces and tear away from the steel backing. Short trip driving leads to corrosion of bearings because insufficient engine heat is produced to drive off the condensed water and corrosive gases. These products collect in the engine oil, forming acid and sludge. As the oil is carried to the engine bearings, the acid attacks and corrodes the bearing material.

7 Incorrect bearing installation during engine assembly will lead to bearing failure as well. Tight-fitting bearings leave insufficient bearing oil clearance and will result in oil starvation. Dirt or foreign particles trapped behind a bearing insert result in high spots on the bearing which lead to failure.

Selection

8 If the original bearings are worn or damaged, or if the oil clearances are incorrect (see Section 23 or 25), the following procedures should be used to select the correct new bearings for engine reassembly. However, if the crankshaft has been reground, new undersize bearings must be installed - the following procedure should not be used if undersize bearings are required! The automotive machine shop that reconditions the crankshaft will provide or help you select the correct size bearings. Regardless of how the bearing sizes are determined, use the oil clearance, measured with Plastigauge, as a guide to ensure the bearings are the right size.

Main bearings

9 If you need to use a STANDARD size main bearing, install one that has the same number as the original bearing (see illustration 20.10 for the bearing number locations). There are three (1.3L engine) or five (1.6L and 1.8L engines) sizes of main bearings.

10 If the number on the original main bearing has been obscured, locate the main journal grade numbers stamped into the oil pan mating surface on the engine block and, on 1.6L and 1.8L engines, on the crankshaft counterweights (see illustration).

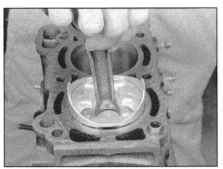

22.3 When checking piston ring end gap, the ring must be square in the cylinder bore (this is done by pushing the ring down with the top of a piston as shown)

11 On 1.3L engines, check the number stamped on the block mating surface for the cylinder in question. Obtain new main bearings of the same number as the relevant numbers on the block. On 1.6L and 1.8L engines, adding the block number to the crank number for a particular journal will give the recommended bearing size.

Connecting rod bearings

12 If you need to use a STANDARD size rod bearing, install one that has the same number as the number stamped into the connecting rod cap **(see illustration 13.4)**.

All bearings

13 Remember, the oil clearance is the final judge when selecting new bearing sizes. If you have any questions or are unsure which bearings to use, get help from a dealer parts or service department.

21 Engine overhaul - reassembly sequence

1 Before beginning engine reassembly, make sure you have all the necessary new parts, gaskets and seals as well as the following items on hand:

Common hand tools
A 1/2-inch drive torque wrench
Piston ring installation tool
Piston ring compressor
Short lengths of rubber or plastic hose to fit over connecting rod bolts
Plastigauge
Feeler gauges
A fine-tooth file
New engine oil
Engine assembly lube or moly-base grease
Gasket sealer
Thread locking compound

2 In order to save time and avoid problems, engine reassembly must be done in the following general order:

Piston rings (Part B)
Crankshaft and main bearings (Part B)
Piston/connecting rod assemblies (Part B)

22.4 With the ring square in the cylinder, measure the end gap with a feeler gauge

Rear main (crankshaft) oil seal (Part B)
Cylinder head and lifters (Part A)
Camshafts (Part A)
Oil pump (Part A)
Timing belt and sprockets (Part A)
Timing belt covers (Part A)
Oil pick-up (Part A)
Oil pan (Part A)
Intake and exhaust manifolds (Part A)
Valve cover (Part A)
Flywheel/driveplate (Part A)

22 Piston rings - installation

1 Before installing the new piston rings, the ring end gaps must be checked. It's assumed that the piston ring groove clearance has been checked and verified correct (see Section 18).

2 Lay out the piston/connecting rod assemblies and the new ring sets so the ring sets will be matched with the same piston and cylinder during the end gap measurement and engine assembly.

3 Insert the top (number one) ring into the first cylinder and square it up with the cylinder walls by pushing it in with the top of the piston **(see illustration)**. The ring should be near the bottom of the cylinder, at the lower limit of ring travel.

4 To measure the end gap, slip feeler gauges between the ends of the ring until a gauge

22.9a Install the spacer/expander in the oil control ring groove

equal to the gap width is found **(see illustration)**. The feeler gauge should slide between the ring ends with a slight amount of drag. Compare the measurement to that found in this Chapter's Specifications. If the gap is larger or smaller than specified, double-check to make sure you have the correct rings before proceeding.

5 If the gap is too small, replace the rings - DO NOT file the ends to increase the clearance.

6 Excess end gap isn't critical unless it's greater than the service limit listed in this Chapter's Specifications. Again, double-check to make sure you have the correct rings for your engine.

7 Repeat the procedure for each ring that will be installed in the first cylinder and for each ring in the remaining cylinders. Remember to keep rings, pistons and cylinders matched up.

8 Once the ring end gaps have been checked/corrected, the rings can be installed on the pistons.

9 The oil control ring (lowest one on the piston) is usually installed first. It's composed of three separate components. Slip the spacer/expander into the groove **(see illustration)**. If an anti-rotation tang is used, make sure it's inserted into the drilled hole in the ring groove. Next, install the lower side rail. Don't use a piston ring installation tool on the oil ring side rails, as they may be damaged. Instead, place one end of the side rail into the groove between the spacer/expander and the ring land, hold it firmly in place and slide a finger around the piston while pushing the rail into the groove **(see illustration)**. Next, install the upper side rail in the same manner.

10 After the three oil ring components have been installed, check to make sure that both the upper and lower side rails can be turned smoothly in the ring groove.

11 The number two (middle) ring is installed next. It's usually stamped with a mark which must face up, toward the top of the piston. **Note:** *Always follow the instructions printed on the ring package or box - different manufacturers may require different approaches. Do not mix up the top and middle rings, as they have different cross-sections.*

22.9b DO NOT use a piston ring installation tool when installing the oil ring side rails

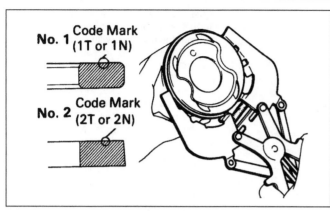

22.12 Install the compression rings with a ring expander - the mark must face up

23.10 Lay the Plastigauge strips (arrowed) on the main bearing journals, parallel to the crankshaft centerline

12 Use a piston ring installation tool and make sure the ring's identification mark is facing the top of the piston, then slip the ring into the middle groove on the piston (see illustration). Don't expand the ring any more than necessary to slide it over the piston.

13 Install the number one (top) ring in the same manner. Make sure the mark is facing up. Be careful not to confuse the number one and number two rings.

14 Repeat the procedure for the remaining pistons and rings.

23 Crankshaft - installation and main bearing oil clearance check

1 Crankshaft installation is the first major step in engine reassembly. It's assumed at this point that the engine block and crankshaft have been cleaned, inspected and repaired or reconditioned.

2 Position the engine with the bottom facing up.

3 Remove the main bearing cap bolts and lift out the caps. Lay the caps out in the proper order.

4 If they're still in place, remove the old bearing inserts from the block and the main

bearing caps. Wipe the main bearing surfaces of the block and caps with a clean, lint free cloth. They must be kept spotlessly clean!

Main bearing oil clearance check

5 Clean the back sides of the new main bearing inserts and lay the bearing half with the oil groove in each main bearing saddle in the block. Lay the other bearing half from each bearing set in the corresponding main bearing cap. Make sure the tab on each bearing insert fits into the recess in the block or cap. Also, the oil holes in the block must line up with the oil holes in the bearing insert.

Caution: Do not hammer the bearings into place and don't nick or gouge the bearing faces. No lubrication should be used at this time.

6 The thrust bearings (washers) must be installed in the number three cap and saddle.

7 Clean the faces of the bearings in the block and the crankshaft main bearing journals with a clean, lint free cloth. Check or clean the oil holes in the crankshaft, as any dirt here can go only one way - straight through the new bearings.

8 Once you're certain the crankshaft is clean, carefully lay it in position in the main bearings.

9 Before the crankshaft can be permanently installed, the main bearing oil clearance must be checked.

10 Trim several pieces of the appropriate size Plastigauge (they must be slightly shorter than the width of the main bearings) and place one piece on each crankshaft main bearing journal, parallel with the journal axis (see illustration).

11 Clean the faces of the bearings in the caps and install the caps in their respective positions (don't mix them up) with the arrows pointing toward the front of the engine. Don't disturb the Plastigauge. Apply a light coat of oil to the bolt threads and the under-sides of the bolt heads, then install them.

12 Following the recommended sequence (see illustration), tighten the main bearing cap bolts, in three steps, to the torque listed in this Chapter's Specifications. Don't rotate the crankshaft at any time during this operation!

13 Remove the bolts and carefully lift off the main bearing caps. Keep them in order. Don't disturb the Plastigauge or rotate the crankshaft. If any of the main bearing caps are difficult to remove, tap them gently from side-to-side with a soft-face hammer to loosen them.

14 Compare the width of the crushed Plastigauge on each journal to the scale printed

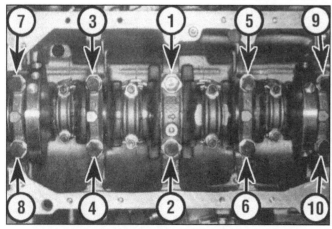

23.12 Main bearing cap bolt tightening sequence

23.14 Compare the width of the crushed Plastigauge to the scale on the envelope to determine the main bearing oil clearance (always take the measurement at the widest point of the Plastigauge) - be sure to use the correct scale; standard and metric scales are included

23.19a Rotate the thrust washer into position with the oil grooves facing OUT

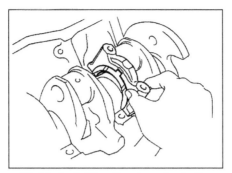

23.19b Install the thrust washer in the number three cap with the oil grooves facing OUT

on the Plastigauge envelope to obtain the main bearing oil clearance **(see illustration)**. Check the Specifications to make sure it's correct.

15 If the clearance is not as specified, the bearing inserts may be the wrong size (which means different ones will be required - see Section 20). Before deciding that different inserts are needed, make sure that no dirt or oil was between the bearing inserts and the caps or block when the clearance was measured. If the Plastigauge is noticeably wider at one end than the other, the journal may be tapered (see Section 19).

16 Carefully scrape all traces of the Plastigauge material off the main bearing journals and/or the bearing faces. Don't nick or scratch the bearing faces.

Final crankshaft installation

17 Carefully lift the crankshaft out of the engine. Clean the bearing faces in the block, then apply a thin, uniform layer of clean moly-base grease or engine assembly lube to each of the bearing surfaces. Coat the thrust washers as well.

18 Lubricate the crankshaft surfaces that contact the oil seals with moly-base grease, engine assembly lube or clean engine oil.

19 Make sure the crankshaft journals are clean, then lay the crankshaft back in place in

the block. Clean the faces of the bearings in the caps, then apply lubricant to them. Install the caps in their respective positions with the arrows pointing toward the front of the engine. **Note:** *Be sure to install the thrust washers with the number 3 main journal.* The upper (block side) thrust washers can be rotated into position around the crank with the crank in the block, with the thrust washer grooves facing OUT. The tanged lower thrust washers should be placed on the caps with their grooves OUT and the tangs fitting into the cap slots **(see illustrations)**.

20 Apply a light coat of oil to the bolt threads and the undersides of the bolt heads, then install them. Tighten all main bearing cap bolts to the torque listed in this Chapter's Specifications, following the recommended sequence.

21 Rotate the crankshaft a number of times by hand to check for any obvious binding.

22 Check the crankshaft endplay with a feeler gauge or a dial indicator as described in Section 14. The endplay should be correct if the crankshaft thrust faces aren't worn or damaged and new thrust washers have been installed.

23 Install a new rear main oil seal, then bolt the retainer to the block (see Section 24).

24 Rear main oil seal installation

1 The crankshaft must be installed first and the main bearing caps bolted in place, then the new seal should be installed in the retainer and the retainer bolted to the block.

2 Check the seal contact surface on the crankshaft very carefully for scratches and nicks that could damage the new seal lip and cause oil leaks. If the crankshaft is damaged, the only alternative is a new or different crankshaft.

3 The old seal can be removed from the retainer by driving it out from the back side with a hammer and punch **(see illustration)**. Be sure to note how far it's recessed into the bore before removing it; the new seal will have to be recessed an equal amount. Be very careful not to scratch or otherwise damage the bore in the retainer or oil leaks could develop.

4 Make sure the retainer is clean, then apply a thin coat of engine oil to the outer edge of the new seal. The seal must be pressed squarely into the bore, so hammering it into place isn't recommended. If you don't have access to a press, sandwich the housing and seal between two smooth pieces of wood and press the seal into place with the jaws of a large vise. The pieces of wood must be thick enough to distribute the force evenly around the entire circumference of the seal. Work slowly and make sure the seal enters the bore squarely.

5 As a last resort, the seal can be tapped into the retainer with a hammer. Use a block of wood to distribute the force evenly and make sure the seal is driven in squarely **(see illustration)**.

6 The seal lips must be lubricated with clean engine oil or moly-based grease before the seal/retainer is slipped over the crankshaft and bolted to the block, using a new gasket.

7 Tighten the bolts a little at a time to the torque listed in Chapter 2A Specifications.

24.3 After removing the retainer from the block, support it on a couple of wood blocks and drive out the old seal with a punch or screwdriver and hammer

24.5 Drive the new seal into the retainer with a wood block or a section of pipe, if you have one large enough - make sure you don't cock the seal in the retainer bore

25 Pistons/connecting rods - installation and rod bearing oil clearance check

1 Before installing the piston/connecting rod assemblies, the cylinder walls must be perfectly clean, the top edge of each cylinder must be chamfered, and the crankshaft must be in place.

2 Remove the cap from the end of the number one connecting rod (refer to the marks made during removal). Remove the original bearing inserts and wipe the bearing surfaces of the connecting rod and cap with a clean, lint-free cloth. They must be kept spotlessly clean.

3 Clean the back side of the new upper bearing insert, then lay it in place in the connecting rod. Make sure the tab on the bearing fits into the recess in the rod so the oil holes line up **(see illustration)**. Don't hammer the bearing insert into place and be very careful not to nick or gouge the bearing face. Don't lubricate the bearing at this time.

4 Clean the back side of the other bearing insert and install it in the rod cap. Again, make sure the tab on the bearing fits into the recess in the cap, and don't apply any lubricant. It's critically important that the mating surfaces of the bearing and connecting rod are perfectly clean and oil free when they're assembled.

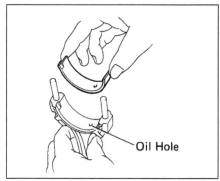

25.3 Align the oil hole in the bearing with the oil hole in the rod

5 Position the piston ring gaps at staggered intervals around the piston **(see illustrations)**.

6 Slip a section of plastic or rubber hose over each connecting rod cap bolt to protect the cylinder bore.

7 Lubricate the piston and rings with clean engine oil and attach a piston ring compressor to the piston. Leave the skirt protruding about 1/4-inch to guide the piston into the cylinder. The rings must be compressed until they're flush with the piston.

8 Rotate the crankshaft until the number one connecting rod journal is at BDC (bottom dead centre) and apply a coat of engine oil to the cylinder wall.

9 With the dimple or arrow on top of the piston **(see illustration)** facing the front of the engine, gently insert the piston/connecting rod assembly into the number one cylinder bore and rest the bottom edge of the ring compressor on the engine block.

10 Tap the top edge of the ring compressor to make sure it's contacting the block around its entire circumference.

11 Gently tap on the top of the piston with the end of a wooden hammer handle **(see illustration)** while guiding the end of the connecting rod into place on the crankshaft journal. The piston rings may try to pop out of the ring compressor just before entering the cylinder bore, so keep some downward pressure on the ring compressor. Work slowly, and if any resistance is felt as the piston enters the cylinder, stop immediately. Find out what's hanging up and fix it before proceeding.

Caution: Do not, for any reason, force the piston into the cylinder - you might break a ring and/or the piston.

12 Once the piston/connecting rod assembly is installed, the connecting rod bearing oil clearance must be checked before the rod cap is permanently bolted in place.

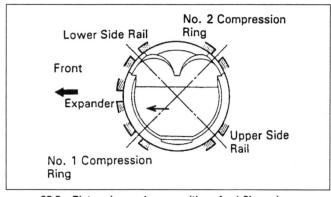

25.5a Piston ring end gap positions for 1.3L engines

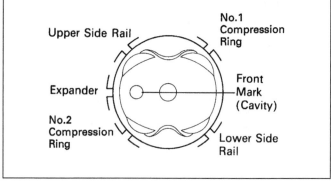

25.5b Piston ring end gap positions for 1.6L and 1.8L engines

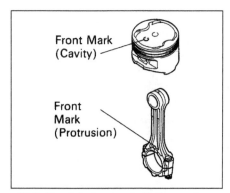

25.9 Check to be sure both the mark on the piston and the mark on the connecting rod are aligned as shown

25.11 The piston can be driven (gently) into the cylinder bore with the end of a wooden or plastic hammer handle

25.13 Lay the Plastigauge strips on each rod bearing journal, parallel to the crankshaft centerline

25.15 Install the connecting rod caps with the front mark (arrowed) facing the timing belt end of the engine, and torque to Specifications - for the 90-degree second step (1.6L and 1.8L engines only), use an angle gauge as shown, or paint reference marks on the rod and the socket

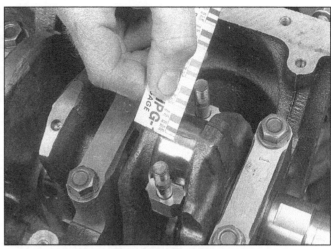

25.17 Measure the width of the crushed Plastigauge to determine the rod bearing oil clearance (be sure to use the correct scale - standard and metric scales are included)

Connecting rod bearing oil clearance check

13 Cut a piece of the appropriate size Plastigauge slightly shorter than the width of the connecting rod bearing and lay it in place on the number one connecting rod journal, parallel with the journal axis **(see illustration)**.

14 Clean the connecting rod cap bearing face, remove the protective hoses from the connecting rod bolts and install the rod cap. Make sure the mating mark on the cap is on the same side as the mark on the connecting rod. Check the cap to make sure the front mark is facing the timing belt end of the engine.

15 Apply a light coat of oil to the undersides of the nuts, then install and tighten them to the torque listed in this Chapter's Specifications. Use a thin-wall socket to avoid erroneous torque readings that can result if the socket is wedged between the rod cap and nut. If the socket tends to wedge itself between the nut and the cap, lift up on it slightly until it no longer contacts the cap. Do not rotate the crankshaft at any time during this operation. **Note:** *On 1.6L and 1.8L engines, after reaching the specified step one torque, tighten each nut an additional 90-degrees (1/4-turn)* **(see illustration)**.

16 Remove the nuts and detach the rod cap, being very careful not to disturb the Plastigauge.

17 Compare the width of the crushed Plastigauge to the scale printed on the Plastigauge envelope to obtain the oil clearance **(see illustration)**. Compare it to this Chapter's Specifications to make sure the clearance is correct.

18 If the clearance is not as specified, the bearing inserts may be the wrong size (which means different ones will be required). Before deciding that different inserts are needed,

make sure that no dirt or oil was between the bearing inserts and the connecting rod or cap when the clearance was measured. Also, recheck the journal diameter. If the Plastigauge was wider at one end than the other, the journal may be tapered (refer to Section 19).

Final connecting rod installation

19 Carefully scrape all traces of the Plastigauge material off the rod journal and/or bearing face. Be very careful not to scratch the bearing, use your fingernail or the edge of a credit card to remove the Plastigauge.

20 Make sure the bearing faces are perfectly clean, then apply a uniform layer of clean moly-base grease or engine assembly lube to both of them. You'll have to push the piston higher into the cylinder to expose the face of the bearing insert in the connecting rod, be sure to slip the protective hoses over the rod bolts first.

21 Slide the connecting rod back into place on the journal, remove the protective hoses from the rod cap bolts, install the rod cap and tighten the nuts to the torque listed in this Chapter's Specifications.

22 Repeat the entire procedure for the remaining pistons/connecting rods.

23 The important points to remember are:
a) *Keep the back sides of the bearing inserts and the insides of the connecting rods and caps perfectly clean when assembling them.*
b) *Make sure you have the correct piston/rod assembly for each cylinder.*
c) *The dimple or arrow on the piston must face the front of the engine.*
d) *Lubricate the cylinder walls with clean oil.*
e) *Lubricate the bearing faces when installing the rod caps after the oil clearance has been checked.*

24 After all the piston/connecting rod assemblies have been properly installed, rotate the crankshaft a number of times by hand to check for any obvious binding.

25 As a final step, the connecting rod endplay must be checked. Refer to Section 13 for this procedure.

26 Compare the measured endplay to this Chapter's Specifications to make sure it's correct. If it was correct before disassembly and the original crankshaft and rods were reinstalled, it should still be right. If new rods or a new crankshaft were installed, the endplay may be inadequate. If so, the rods will have to be removed and taken to an automotive machine shop for re-sizing.

26 Initial start-up after overhaul

 Warning: Have a fire extinguisher handy when starting the engine for the first time.

1 Once the engine has been installed in the vehicle, double-check the engine oil and coolant levels.

2 With the spark plugs out of the engine and the ignition system and fuel pump disabled (see Section 4), crank the engine until oil pressure registers on the gauge or the light goes out.

3 Install the spark plugs, hook up the plug wires and restore the ignition system and fuel pump functions (see Section 4).

4 Start the engine. It may take a few moments for the fuel system to build up pressure, but the engine should start without a great deal of effort.

5 After the engine starts, it should be allowed to warm up to normal operating temperature. While the engine is warming up, make a thorough check for fuel, oil and coolant leaks.

6 Shut the engine off and recheck the engine oil and coolant levels.

7 Drive the vehicle to an area with minimum traffic, accelerate from 30 to 50 mph, then allow the vehicle to slow to 30 mph with the throttle closed. Repeat the procedure 10 or 12 times. This will load the piston rings and cause them to seat properly against the cylinder walls. Check again for oil and coolant leaks.

8 Drive the vehicle gently for the first 500 miles (no sustained high speeds) and keep a constant check on the oil level. It is not unusual for an engine to use oil during the run-in period.

9 At approximately 500 to 600 miles, change the oil and filter.

10 For the next few hundred miles, drive the vehicle normally. Do not pamper it or abuse it.

11 After 2000 miles, change the oil and filter again and consider the engine run-in.

Chapter 3
Cooling, heating and air conditioning systems

Contents

Degrees of difficulty

Easy, suitable for novice with little experience	Fairly easy, suitable for beginner with some experience	Fairly difficult, suitable for competent DIY mechanic	Difficult, suitable for experienced DIY mechanic	Very difficult, suitable for expert DIY or professional

Specifications

General
Radiator cap pressure rating	10.7 to 14.9 psi
Thermostat rating	183 to 203 degrees F
Air conditioning system refrigerant type	
1993	R-12
1994 and later	R-134a

Torque wrench settings
	Ft-lbs
Thermostat cover bolts	
4E-FE engines	4
4A-FE and 7A-FE engines	7
Water pump-to-block bolts	
4E-FE engines	14
4A-FE and 7A-FE engines	11

1 General information

Engine cooling system

All vehicles covered by this manual employ a pressurized engine cooling system with thermostatically-controlled coolant circulation (**see illustration**). An impeller type water pump mounted on the front of the block pumps coolant through the engine. The coolant flows around each cylinder and toward the rear of the engine. Cast-in coolant passages direct coolant around the intake and exhaust ports, near the spark plug areas and in proximity to the exhaust valve guides.

A wax-pellet type thermostat is located in the thermostat housing at the transmission end of the engine. During warm up, the closed thermostat prevents coolant from circulating through the radiator. When the engine reaches normal operating temperature, the thermostat opens and allows hot coolant to travel through the radiator, where it is cooled before returning to the engine.

The cooling system is sealed by a pressure-type radiator cap. This raises the boiling point of the coolant, and the higher boiling point of the coolant increases the cooling efficiency of the radiator. If the system pressure exceeds the cap pressure-relief value, the excess pressure in the system forces the spring-loaded valve inside the cap off its seat and allows the coolant to escape through the overflow tube into a coolant reservoir. When the system cools, the excess coolant is automatically drawn from the reservoir back into the radiator.

The coolant reservoir does double duty as both the point at which fresh coolant is added to the cooling system to maintain the proper fluid level and as a holding tank for overheated coolant.

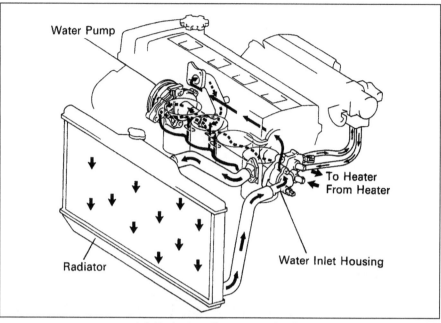

1.1 Typical cooling system details

This type of cooling system is known as a closed design because coolant that escapes past the pressure cap is saved and reused.

Heating system

The heating system consists of a blower fan and heater core located within the heater box under the right end of the dashboard, the inlet and outlet hoses connecting the heater core to the engine cooling system and the heater/air conditioning control head on the dashboard (**see illustration**). Hot engine coolant is circulated through the heater core. When the heater mode is activated, a flap door opens to expose the heater box to the passenger compartment. A fan switch on the control head activates the blower motor, which forces air through the core, heating the air.

Air conditioning system

The air conditioning system consists of a condenser mounted in front of the radiator, an evaporator mounted adjacent to the heater core, a compressor mounted on the engine, a filter-drier which contains a high pressure relief valve and the plumbing connecting all of the above.

A blower fan forces the warmer air of the passenger compartment through the evaporator core (sort of a radiator-in-reverse), transferring the heat from the air to the refrigerant. The liquid refrigerant boils off into low pressure vapor, taking the heat with it when it leaves the evaporator. The compressor keeps refrigerant circulating through the system, pumping the warmed coolant through the condenser where it is cooled and then circulated back to the evaporator.

2 Antifreeze - general information

⚠️ *Warning: Do not allow antifreeze to come in contact with your skin or painted surfaces of the vehicle. Rinse off spills immediately with plenty of water. Antifreeze is highly toxic if ingested. Never leave antifreeze lying around in an open container or in puddles on the floor; children and pets are attracted by its sweet smell and may drink it. Check with local authorities about disposing of used antifreeze. Many communities have collection centres which will see that antifreeze is disposed of safely. Never dump used antifreeze on the ground or into drains.*

1.6 Underdash arrangement of the blower unit, evaporator unit and heater core

2.4 An inexpensive hydrometer can be used to test the condition of your coolant

The cooling system should be filled with a water/ethylene-glycol based antifreeze solution, which will prevent freezing down to at least -20 degrees F, or lower if local climate requires it. It also provides protection against corrosion and increases the coolant boiling point.

The cooling system should be drained, flushed and refilled every 30,000 miles or every two years (see Chapter 1). The use of antifreeze solutions for periods of longer than two years is likely to cause damage and encourage the formation of rust and scale in the system. If your tap water is "hard", i.e. contains a lot of dissolved minerals, use distilled water with the antifreeze.

Before adding antifreeze to the system, check all hose connections, because antifreeze tends to search out and leak through very minute openings. Engines do not normally consume coolant. Therefore, if the level goes down, find the cause and correct it.

The exact mixture of antifreeze-to-water you should use depends on the relative weather conditions. The mixture should contain at least 50 percent antifreeze, but should never contain more than 70 percent antifreeze. Consult the mixture ratio chart on the antifreeze container before adding coolant. Hydrometers are available at most auto parts stores to test the ratio of antifreeze to water **(see illustration)**. Use antifreeze which meets the vehicle manufacturer's specifications.

3 Thermostat - check and replacement

 Warning: Do not attempt to remove the radiator cap, coolant or thermostat until the engine has cooled completely.

Check

1 Before assuming the thermostat is responsible for a cooling system problem, check the coolant level (Chapter 1), drivebelt tension (Chapter 1) and temperature gauge (or light) operation.
2 If the engine takes a long time to warm up (as indicated by the temperature gauge or

heater operation), the thermostat is probably stuck open. Replace the thermostat with a new one.
3 If the engine runs hot, use your hand to check the temperature of the radiator top hose. If the hose is not hot, but the engine is, the thermostat is probably stuck in the closed position, preventing the coolant inside the engine from traveling through the radiator. Replace the thermostat.
Caution: Do not drive the vehicle without a thermostat. The computer may stay in open loop and emissions and fuel economy will suffer.
4 If the radiator top hose is hot, it means that the coolant is flowing and the thermostat is open. Consult the Fault Finding Section at the rear of this manual for further diagnosis.

Replacement

5 Disconnect the negative cable from the battery.
Caution: If the stereo in your vehicle is equipped with an anti-theft system, make sure you have the correct activation code before disconnecting the battery.
6 Drain the coolant from the radiator (see Chapter 1).
7 Disconnect the cooling fan temperature switch connector from the thermostat cover located just under the distributor at the left end of the cylinder head **(see illustration)**.
8 Detach the thermostat cover from the housing. Be prepared for some coolant to spill as the gasket seal is broken. The radiator hose can be left attached to the cover, unless the cover itself is to be replaced.
9 Remove the thermostat, noting the direction in which it was installed in the cover or housing, and thoroughly clean the sealing surfaces **(see illustration)**.
10 Fit a new gasket onto the thermostat **(see illustration)**. Make sure it is evenly fitted all the way around.
11 On 4A-FE and 7A-FE engines, install the thermostat and the cover, positioning the jiggle pin at the highest point. On 4E-FE engines, position the thermostat in the cover with the jiggle pin aligned with the raised projection on the cover, then install the cover and thermostat.

3.9 The thermostat is installed with the spring end towards the cylinder head

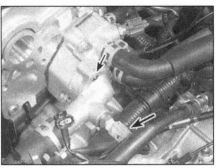

3.7 Disconnect the cooling fan temperature switch connector (arrowed) and remove the two nuts (arrow indicates the upper nut) retaining the thermostat cover to the housing

12 Tighten the cover fasteners to the torque listed in this Chapter's Specifications and reinstall the remaining components in the reverse order of removal.
13 Refill the cooling system (see Chapter 1), run the engine and check for leaks and proper operation.

4 Engine cooling fan and relay - check and replacement

 Warning: To avoid possible injury, keep clear of the fan blades, as they may start turning at any time!

Check

1 If the radiator fan won't shut off when the engine is cool, disconnect the wiring connector from the cooling fan temperature switch **(see illustration 3.7)**. With the key ON, the fan should now operate. If not, check the fan relay, wiring between the temperature switch and the relay, and the fan motor itself.
2 The cooling fan temperature switch can be tested for continuity with an ohmmeter. Disconnect the wiring connector and attach one lead of the ohmmeter to the prong on the switch, and the other lead to the body of the switch **(see illustration)**. When the engine is

3.10 The thermostat gasket, which is actually a grooved sealing ring, fits around the edge of the thermostat

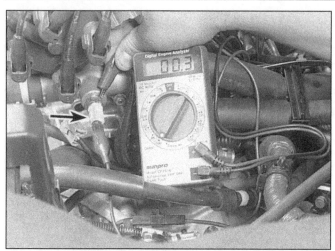

4.2 The temperature switch (arrowed) for the electric cooling fan control is mounted in the thermostat cover - test for continuity with one lead on the terminal and one on the switch body

4.3 Disconnect the fan wiring connector (arrowed) and connect jumper wires directly to the positive and negative terminals of the battery - this view is from below on the driver's side

cold (below 180-degrees F) there should be continuity. When the engine is warm (above 199-degrees F), there should be NO continuity.

3 To test an inoperative fan motor (one that doesn't come on when the engine gets hot or when the air conditioner is on), first check the fuses and/or fusible links (see Chapter 12). Then disconnect the electrical connector at the motor and use fused jumper wires to connect the fan directly to the battery **(see illustration)**. If the fan still does not work, replace the fan motor.

 Warning: Do not allow the test clips to contact each other or any metallic part of the vehicle.

4 If the motor tested OK in the previous test but is still inoperative, then the fault lies in the relays, fuse, or wiring. The fan relay and main engine relay can be tested as described below.

Relay check

5 Locate the main relay box, located in the engine compartment, on the left-side. Air-conditioned models have extra relays in a separate box next to the battery **(see illustration)**.

6 Remove the No 1 cooling fan relay and, using an ohmmeter, test for continuity as shown **(see illustration)**. Both Nippondenso and Bosch-made relays are used, and the terminals are numbered differently. Be sure to test either relay as shown in the illustration.

7 If the fan relays check OK, remove the main engine relay and test it as shown **(see illustration)**. There should be continuity between terminals 3 and 5, and between 2 and 4. There should be NO continuity between terminals 1 and 2. With battery voltage applied across terminals 3 and 5, there should be continuity between 1 and 2, and NO continuity between 2 and 4. If both relays test OK, we recommend you take the vehicle to a dealer or other qualified repair facility for further diagnosis, due to the complexity and variety of the circuits involved.

Replacement

8 Disconnect the negative battery cable. *Caution: If the stereo in your vehicle is equipped with an anti-theft system, make sure you have the correct activation code before disconnecting the battery.*

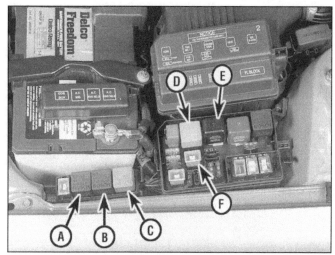

4.5 Main relay box - main engine relay, AC relay and fan relay locations:

A Air conditioning relay
B No. 3 cooling fan relay
C No. 2 cooling fan relay
D No. 1 cooling fan relay
E Main engine relay
F Fan circuit breaker

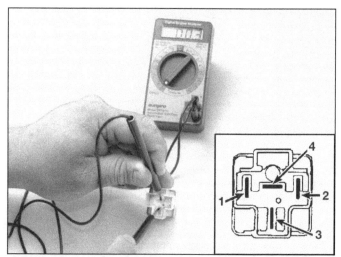

4.6 Test the No 1 cooling fan relay (Nippondenso) for continuity - with no voltage applied, there should be continuity between 1 and 2, and 3 and 4 - with voltage applied across 1 and 2, there should be NO continuity between 3 and 4. On Bosch relays, disregard the numbers on the terminals, test it just like this Nippondenso relay

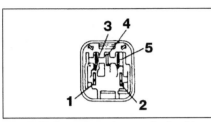

4.7 Main engine relay terminal guide

9 Disconnect the wiring connector at the fan motor. **Note:** *Models equipped with air-conditioning have two cooling fans. The one on the front side of the radiator is cooling fan No 2, which provides additional cooling when the air conditioning is on. This fan and its relay can be tested and removed/replaced with the same procedures as the engine cooling fan No 1* **(see illustrations).**

10 Drain enough coolant to disconnect the upper radiator hose at the radiator (see Chapter 1), then disconnect the coolant overflow hose from the top of the radiator.

11 Unbolt the fan shroud from the radiator and lift the fan/shroud assembly from the vehicle **(see illustration).**

4.11 Remove the two lower fan shroud bolts from below, then the two top fasteners (arrowed) and lift out the cooling fan and shroud assembly

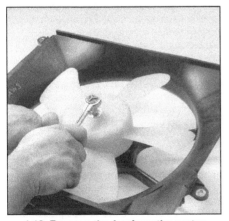

4.12 Remove the fan from the motor

4.9a The air conditioning fan in front of the radiator is mounted on the right-side with a plastic pin (arrowed) - the right arrow indicates the wiring connector

12 Hold the fan blades and remove the fan retaining nut (and spacer, if equipped) **(see illustration)**. **Note:** *On air-conditioned models, the No 2 (condenser) cooling fan blade is retained by a clip, not a nut.*

13 Unbolt the fan motor from the shroud **(see illustration)**.

14 Installation is the reverse of removal.

5   Radiator and coolant reservoir - removal and installation

⚠ **Warning: Do not start this procedure until the engine is completely cool.**

Radiator

1 Disconnect the negative battery cable. *Caution: If the stereo in your vehicle is equipped with an anti-theft system, make sure you have the correct activation code before disconnecting the battery.*

4.13 Remove the motor from the shroud

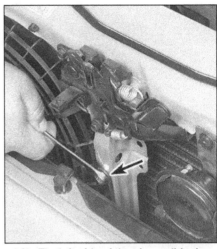

4.9b The left-side of the air conditioning fan is mounted with a bolt at the bonnet latch support (arrowed) and one lower bolt accessible through the hole in the bumper cover

2 Drain the coolant into a container (see Chapter 1).

3 Remove both the upper and lower radiator hoses.

4 Disconnect the reservoir hose from the radiator filler neck.

5 Remove the cooling fan (see Section 4).

6 If equipped with an automatic transmission, disconnect the fluid cooler lines from the radiator **(see illustration)**. Place a drip pan to catch the fluid and cap the fittings.

7 Remove the two upper radiator mounting brackets **(see illustration)**. **Note:** *The bottom of the radiator is retained by grommeted projections that fit into holes in the body.*

8 Lift out the radiator **(see illustration)**. Be aware of dripping fluids and the sharp fins.

9 With the radiator removed, it can be inspected for leaks, damage and internal blockage. If in need of repairs, have a professional radiator workshop or dealer service department perform the work as special techniques are required.

5.6 Remove the automatic transmission fluid cooler lines and the lower radiator hose (arrowed)

5.7 Remove the upper hold-down clamps from each end of the radiator

5.8 Remove the radiator carefully, and do not lose the rubber mounts - they must be in place on the bottom projections when the radiator is reinstalled

5.15 Pull the coolant reservoir hose assembly (left arrow), then pull the reservoir bottle out of its bracket (right arrow)

10 Bugs and dirt can be cleaned from the radiator with compressed air and a soft brush. Don't bend the cooling fins as this is done.

 Warning: Wear eye protection when using compressed air.

11 Installation is the reverse of the removal procedure. Be sure the rubber mounts are in place on the bottom of the radiator.
12 After installation, fill the cooling system with the proper mixture of antifreeze and water. Refer to Chapter 1 if necessary.
13 Start the engine and check for leaks. Allow the engine to reach normal operating temperature, indicated by both radiator hoses becoming hot. Recheck the coolant level and add more if required.
14 On automatic transmission equipped models, check and add fluid as needed.

Coolant reservoir

15 On most models, the coolant reservoir simply pulls up and out of the bracket next to the battery **(see illustration)**.
16 Pour the coolant into a container. Wash out and inspect the reservoir for cracks and chafing. Replace it if damaged.
17 Installation is the reverse of removal.

---

6 Water pump - check

1 A failure in the water pump can cause serious engine damage due to overheating.
2 With the engine running and warmed to normal operating temperature, squeeze the upper radiator hose. If the water pump is working properly, a pressure surge should be felt as the hose is released.

 Warning: Keep hands away from fan blades!

3 Water pumps are equipped with weep or vent holes **(see illustration 7.14)**. If a failure occurs in the pump seal, coolant will leak from this hole. In most cases it will be necessary to use a flashlight to find the hole on the water

pump by looking through the space behind the pulley just below the water pump shaft.
4 If the water pump shaft bearings fail there may be a howling sound at the front of the engine while it is running. Bearing wear can be felt if the water pump pulley is rocked up and down. Do not mistake drivebelt slippage, which causes a squealing sound, for water pump failure. Spray automotive drivebelt dressing on the belts to eliminate the belt as a possible cause of the noise.

---

7 Water pump - removal and installation

 Warning: Do not start this procedure until the engine is completely cool.

Removal

4E-FE engines

1 Disconnect the negative battery cable and drain the cooling system (see Chapter 1).
Caution: If the stereo in your vehicle is equipped with an anti-theft system, make sure you have the correct activation code before disconnecting the battery.
2 Refer to Chapter 12 and remove the alternator.

7.11 Use a screwdriver to pry the wiring clip out of the dipstick tube bracket, then remove the one bolt retaining the dipstick tube to the engine and pull the tube out

3 Remove the nut and two bolts retaining the intake manifold stay at the rear of the engine and remove the stay.
4 Remove the water inlet hose and bypass hose from the water inlet at the rear of the water pump. Remove the retaining bolt and pull the water inlet pipe from the water pump. Collect the sealing O-ring from the end of the pipe.
5 Remove the oil dipstick. Remove the bolt retaining the dipstick tube and alternator adjustment arm to the engine and pull the dipstick tube from the oil pump housing.
6 Remove the bolt and two nuts retaining the water pump to the engine block and remove the water pump assembly. The pulley can remain on the water pump during removal.
7 Disassemble the water pump and replace the gaskets. Thoroughly clean all sealing surfaces, removing all traces of old sealant from the housing-to-engine mating faces. Re-assemble the water pump using new gaskets.

4A-FE and 7A-FE engines

8 Disconnect the negative battery cable and drain the cooling system (see Chapter 1).
Caution: If the stereo in your vehicle is equipped with an anti-theft system, make sure you have the correct activation code before disconnecting the battery.
9 Refer to Chapter 1 and remove the power steering belt, alternator/water pump belt and air conditioning belt. Then remove the upper power steering mounting bracket.
10 Refer to Chapter 2A and remove the valve cover and the upper timing belt covers.
11 Remove the oil dipstick. Remove the bolt retaining the dipstick tube to the engine and pull the dipstick tube from the oil pump housing **(see illustration)**.
12 Behind the water pump, remove the two nuts retaining the right-side water neck to the cylinder head, and unplug the water temperature gauge sender connector from the sender **(see illustration)**.
13 Remove the three bolts retaining the water pump to the engine block and remove the water pump and water neck assembly. The pulley can remain on the water pump during removal **(see illustrations)**.

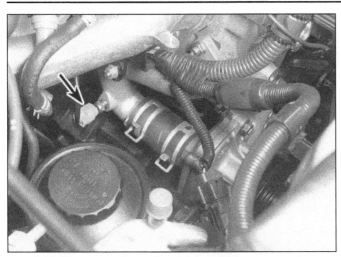

7.12 Disconnect the coolant temperature gauge sender (arrowed) from the water neck

7.13a From above, remove the two nuts (smaller arrows) retaining the water neck to the cylinder head, then remove the top bolt (larger arrow) from the water pump

14 Disassemble the water pump and replace the gaskets. Thoroughly clean all sealing surfaces, removing the O-ring and cleaning the groove **(see illustration)**. Re-assemble the water pump using new gaskets.

Installation

4E-FE engines

15 Obtain a tube of sealant (available from Toyota dealers) and apply a 1/8-inch band of the sealant to the sealing groove on the housing, following the instructions supplied with the sealant.
16 Install the pump assembly to the block and secure with the bolt and two nuts.
17 Install the remaining parts in the reverse order of removal. When reinstalling the dipstick tube, use a new O-ring where it pushes into the oil pump. Also use a new O-ring on the water inlet pipe.

18 With installation complete, wait at least two hours for the sealant to set then refill the cooling system (see Chapter 1), run the engine and check for leaks and proper operation.

4A-FE and 7A-FE engines

19 Using a new O-ring, install the pump assembly to the block. Use a new gasket on the water neck. **Note:** *If the pump has been replaced after many miles of usage, it's a good idea to also replace the hose connecting the water pump to the water neck.*
20 Install the remaining parts in the reverse order of removal. When reinstalling the dipstick tube, use a new O-ring where it pushes into the oil pump.
21 Refill the cooling system (see Chapter 1), run the engine and check for leaks and proper operation.

8 Coolant temperature gauge sender unit - check and replacement

 Warning: Do not start this procedure until the engine is completely cool.

Check

1 If the coolant temperature gauge is inoperative, check the fuses first (see Chapter 12).
2 If the temperature gauge indicates excessive temperature after running awhile, see the Fault Finding Section in the rear of the manual.
3 If the temperature gauge indicates Hot as soon as the engine is started from cold, disconnect the wire at the coolant temperature sender. The sender is located on

7.13b From below, remove the two remaining water pump assembly-to-block bolts - do not remove the bolts retaining the pump halves together until the assembly is removed from the block

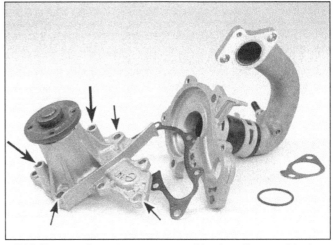

7.14 Remove the water pump assembly, then disassemble the pump and replace the gaskets - The three small arrows indicate the water pump-to-block bolts, while the two larger arrows indicate the weep holes

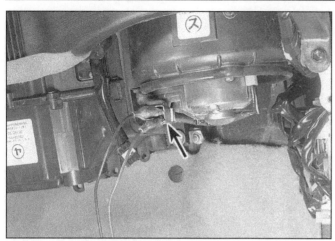 

9.4 With the connector disconnected from the blower motor, apply fused power and ground to the motor terminals (arrowed) - replace the blower if it doesn't operate

9.6 Blower motor resistor location (arrowed) - the resistor is retained by two screws

the side of the thermostat housing on 4E-FE engines, and on the water pump water neck on 4A-FE and 7A-FE engines. If the gauge reading drops, replace the sending unit. If the reading remains high, the wire to the gauge may be shorted to ground or the gauge is faulty.

4 If the coolant temperature gauge fails to show any indication after the engine has been warmed up, (approximately 10 minutes) and the fuses checked out OK, shut off the engine. Disconnect the wire at the sender unit and, using a jumper wire, connect the wire to a clean ground on the engine. Briefly turn on the ignition without starting the engine. If the gauge now indicates Hot, replace the sender unit.

5 If the gauge fails to respond, the circuit may be open or the gauge may be faulty - see Chapter 12 for additional information.

Replacement

6 Drain the coolant (see Chapter 1).
7 Disconnect the wiring connector from the sender unit.
8 Using a deep socket or a wrench, remove the sender unit.
9 Install the new unit and tighten it securely. Do not use thread sealer as it may electrically insulate the sender unit.

9.9 Remove the three screws and lower the blower motor from the housing

10 Reconnect the wiring connector, refill the cooling system and check for coolant leakage and proper gauge function.

9 Blower unit - check, removal and installation

Check

1 The blower unit is located in the passenger compartment above the right front footwell. If the blower doesn't work, check the fuse and all connections in the circuit for looseness and corrosion. Make sure the battery is fully charged.

2 Remove the glove compartment liner, the glove compartment door and the right lower dash panel (see Chapter 11).

3 If the blower motor does not operate, disconnect the electrical connector at the blower motor, turn the ignition key On (engine not running) and check for battery voltage on the black wire terminal with the blower speed switch ON. If battery voltage is not present, there is a problem in the ignition feed circuit.

4 If battery voltage is present, reconnect the terminal to the blower motor and backprobe the black/white wire with a jumper wire connected to ground. If the motor still does not operate, the motor is probably faulty. Apply fused power and ground connections to the blower motor terminals, if the motor does not operate, replace the motor **(see illustration)**.

5 If the motor is good, but doesn't operate at any speed, the heater/air conditioning control switch is probably faulty. Remove the control assembly (see Section 11) and check for continuity through the switch in each position.

6 If the blower motor operates at High speed, but not at one or more of the lower speeds, check the blower motor resistor, located under the instrument panel on the passenger side **(see illustration)**.

Removal

7 Disconnect the electrical connector from the blower motor resistor. Remove the screws and withdraw the resistor from the housing.
8 Using a continuity tester on the blower motor resistor, there should be continuity between all terminals. If not, replace the resistor.
9 If the blower motor must be replaced, remove the bracket retaining the wiring connector to the blower, then remove the three mounting screws and lower the blower assembly from the housing **(see illustration)**. The fan can be removed and reused on the new blower motor.

Installation

10 Installation is the reverse of removal. Check for proper operation.

10 Heater core - removal and installation

⚠ *Warning: These models are equipped with airbags. The airbag is armed and can deploy (inflate) anytime the battery is connected. To prevent accidental deployment (and possible injury), turn the ignition key to LOCK and disconnect the negative battery cable whenever working near airbag components. After the battery is disconnected, wait at least two minutes before beginning work (the system has a back-up capacitor that must fully discharge). For more information see Chapter 12.*

Note 1: *The following procedure details removing the heater core assembly by itself, but it is much easier to remove the heater core housing if the evaporator (cooling) assembly is removed first, although this necessitates having the refrigerant discharged and recovered before work begins. See Section 16*

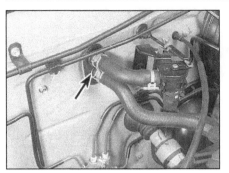

10.3 Disconnect the heater hoses at the firewall (arrowed)

10.7 Remove the right dashboard-to-floor brace - besides the mounting bolts (arrowed), you must also unbolt several ground wires from the brace before removing it

10.8 Remove the center ventilation duct

for evaporator removal, and do not discharge the refrigerant without reading the Warning in Section 12.

Note 2: *The factory recommends removal of the entire instrument panel and dropping the steering column to remove the heater core. This involves disconnecting numerous electrical connectors and there is the potential for breakage of delicate plastic tabs on various components. This is a difficult job for the average home mechanic. It is possible to remove the heater core assembly without removing the dash, and is the procedure outlined below.*

Removal

1 Disconnect the negative cable from the battery.

Caution: If the stereo in your vehicle is equipped with an anti-theft system, make sure you have the correct activation code before disconnecting the battery.

2 Drain the cooling system (see Chapter 1).

3 Working in the engine compartment, disconnect the heater hoses at the firewall **(see illustration)**. Push the rubber seal around the hoses toward the inside of the vehicle, releasing it from the sheet metal.

4 Refer to Chapters 11 and 12 and remove the centre console, glove compartment, glove compartment liner, ashtray, radio and centre dash bezels.

5 Refer to Section 11 of this Chapter to remove the heater/air conditioning controls.

6 Refer to Chapter 6 and remove the ECM without disconnecting the connectors. Set the ECM aside to allow room under the heater core housing.

7 There are two gold-coloured metal braces from the dashboard to the floor. The left one should be unbolted from the floor, but it need not be entirely removed from the vehicle. The right brace should be unbolted and removed **(see illustration)**.

Caution: There are Phillips screws retaining the brace to the backside of the dash plastic. Use the right size Phillips bit and be careful. Seat your screwdriver squarely into

the slots while removing them. They are in tight and the heads could strip.

8 Unbolt and remove the centre ventilation duct **(see illustration)**.

9 Remove the heater duct/control door that is directly above and in front of the heater unit **(see illustration)**.

10 Loosen the nuts on the studs that retain the left side of the evaporator housing (see Section 16). There are three studs retaining the heater unit to the firewall. Remove the nuts from these studs **(see illustrations)**.

11 Pull the heater unit out from behind the dash **(see illustration)**. Keep plenty of towels or rags on the carpeting to catch any coolant that may drip.

10.9 Pull up and out on this duct/door assembly (arrowed) then pull it down and out to allow more working room around the heater unit

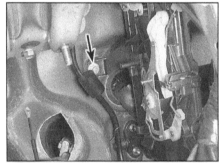

10.10a Remove the nut from the stud near the upper arm of the accelerator pedal (arrowed)

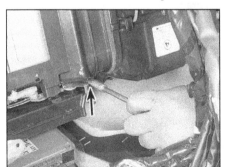

10.10b Remove the stud/nut located at the lower right corner of the heater core housing (arrowed)

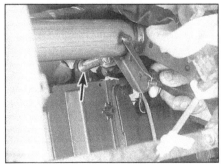

10.10c Remove the last nut from the stud at the upper right corner (arrowed) of the heater core housing

10.11 After the housing tabs clear the firewall studs and the housing is clear of the lip on the evaporator housing, pull the heater unit down and out to the right

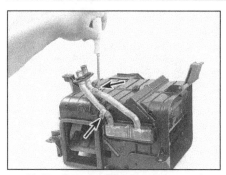

10.12a Remove the two screws and clamps (arrowed) . . .

10.12b . . . then slide the heater core out of the housing

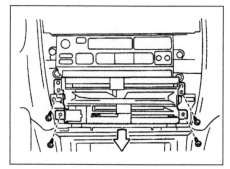

11.4 Remove these screws to release the control panel

Caution: *Work slowly and carefully to avoid breaking any plastic components during removal. The assembly must be pulled out (toward the rear of the vehicle) far enough for the plastic tabs to clear the firewall studs and then moved to the left to clear the lip of the evaporator housing before pulling the unit down and out.*

12 Once the heater unit is removed from the vehicle, remove the clamps retaining the heater core tubes to the housing. Slide the core out of the housing **(see illustrations)**.

Installation

13 Installation is the reverse order of removal. **Note:** *The nuts used on the firewall studs for both the heater core housing and the evaporator housing are designed for one-time use on the assembly line. After removing them, purchase new metric nuts and lockwashers to reinstall the housing to the studs.*

14 Refill the cooling system, reconnect the battery and run the engine. Check for leaks and proper system operation.

11 Heater and air conditioning control assembly - check, removal and installation

⚠️ **Warning:** *These models are equipped with airbags. The airbag is armed and can deploy (inflate) anytime the battery is connected. To prevent accidental deployment (and possible injury), turn the ignition key to LOCK and disconnect the negative battery cable whenever working near airbag components. After the battery is disconnected, wait at least two minutes before beginning work (the system has a back-up capacitor that must fully discharge). For more information see Chapter 12.*

Removal and installation

1 Disconnect the negative cable from the battery.

Caution: *If the stereo in your vehicle is equipped with an anti-theft system, make sure you have the correct activation code before disconnecting the battery.*

2 Remove the centre cluster trim panels (see Chapter 11).

3 Pull off the control knobs.

4 Remove the mounting screws located on the front of the control assembly **(see illustration)**.

5 Pull the control out slightly. Twist the flags on the control cable mounts and remove the cables from the control **(see illustration)**. Disconnect the electrical connectors.

6 Installation is the reverse of the removal procedure.

7 Run the engine and check for proper functioning of the heater (and air conditioning, if equipped).

Cable adjustment

8 With the cables attached at the control end and the control assembly installed in the dash, adjust the cables at their ends. The controls should be set to: RECIRC, COOL, and DEF.

9 To adjust the air inlet damper control cable set the damper lever to RECIRC, install the cable and clamp it in place **(see illustration)**.

10 To adjust the air mix control cable, set the air mix damper to COOL, install the cable and lock the clamp while applying slight pressure on the outer cable **(see illustration)**.

11 To adjust the mode damper control cable, set the mode damper to the DEF mode, hook the cable end on and tighten the clamp **(see illustration)**.

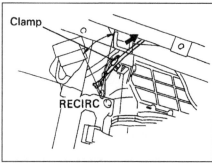

11.5 Twist the plastic flag (arrowed) on each cable to release it from the control unit, then lift the cable end eye off the control lever pin

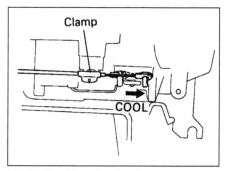

11.9 To adjust the air inlet damper cable, move the arm away from the firewall, attach the cable end and tighten the clamp

11.10 To adjust the air mix control cable, push the lever away from the cable clamp and tighten the clamp

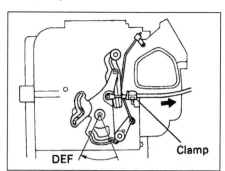

11.11 Adjust the mode damper control cable with the lever is pulled toward the cable clamp, then tighten the clamp

11.12 With the air conditioning switch On, there should be continuity between terminals 5 and 6; and 1 and 3

Electrical checks

12 Check the air conditioning switch continuity. When the switch is pushed in (ON), there should be continuity between 5 and 6, and 1 and 3 **(see illustration)**.

13 Test the blower speed control switch for continuity **(see illustration)**. If the switch fails any of the tests, replace the control assembly.

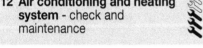

12 Air conditioning and heating system - check and maintenance

Air conditioning system

Warning: The air conditioning system is under high pressure. Do not loosen any hose fittings or remove any components until the system has been discharged. Air conditioning refrigerant may only be discharged by a dealer service department

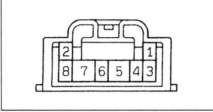

11.13 The blower speed selector switch should exhibit continuity as follows:

Low - between 3 and 7
M1 - between 3, 7 and 8
M2 - between 3, 6 and 7
HI - between 3, 5 and 7

or an automotive air conditioning repair facility. Always wear eye protection when disconnecting air conditioning system fittings even after the system has been discharged.

1 The following maintenance checks should be performed on a regular basis to ensure that the air conditioner continues to operate at peak efficiency **(see illustration)**:
a) *Inspect the condition of the compressor drivebelt. If it is worn or deteriorated, replace it (see Chapter 1).*
b) *Check the drivebelt tension and, if necessary, adjust it (see Chapter 1).*
c) *Inspect the system hoses. Look for cracks, bubbles, hardening and deterioration. Inspect the hoses and all fittings for oil bubbles or seepage. If there*

is any evidence of wear, damage or leakage, replace the hose(s).
d) *Inspect the condenser fins for leaves, bugs and any other foreign material that may have embedded itself in the fins. Use a "fin comb" or compressed air to remove debris from the condenser.*

2 It's a good idea to operate the system for about ten minutes at least once a month. This is particularly important during the winter months because long term non-use can cause hardening, and subsequent failure, of the seals.

3 Leaks in the air conditioning system are best spotted when the system is brought up to operating temperature and pressure, by running the engine with the air conditioning ON for five minutes. Shut the engine off and inspect the air conditioning hoses and connections. Traces of oil usually indicate refrigerant leaks.

4 Because of the complexity of the air conditioning system and the special equipment required to effectively work on it, any work on the system should be left to a professional technician.

5 If the air conditioning system doesn't operate at all, check the fuse panel and the air conditioning relay, located in the fuse/relay box in the engine compartment. Refer to Sections 4, 9 and 11 for electrical checks of heating/air conditioning system components.

6 The most common cause of poor cooling is simply a low system refrigerant charge. If a noticeable drop in cool air output occurs, the following quick check will help you determine if the refrigerant level is low.

Checking the refrigerant charge

7 Warm the engine up to normal operating temperature.

8 Place the air conditioning temperature selector at the coldest setting and put the blower at the highest setting. Open the doors (to make sure the air conditioning system doesn't cycle off as soon as it cools the passenger compartment).

9 With the compressor engaged - the clutch will make an audible click and the centre of the clutch will rotate. After the system reaches operating temperature, feel the two pipes connected to the evaporator at the firewall **(see illustration)**.

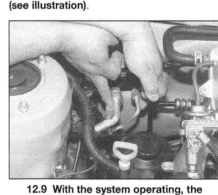

12.9 With the system operating, the evaporator outlet line (large tubing) should feel slightly warmer than the inlet line (small tubing)

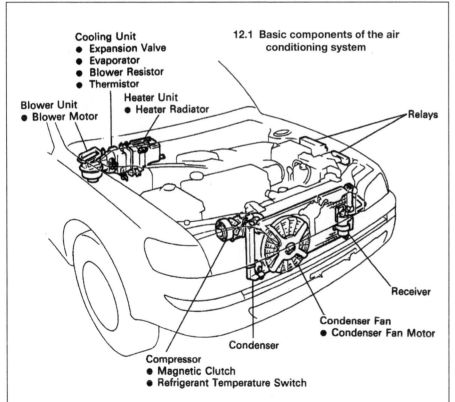

Cooling Unit
● Expansion Valve
● Evaporator
● Blower Resistor
● Thermistor

Heater Unit
● Heater Radiator

Blower Unit
● Blower Motor

12.1 Basic components of the air conditioning system

Relays

Receiver

Condenser Fan
● Condenser Fan Motor

Condenser

Compressor
● Magnetic Clutch
● Refrigerant Temperature Switch

12.10 Check the temperature of the output air in the center register with a thermometer - it should be 35-40 degrees F below the ambient air temperature

12.11 The sight glass is located on top of the receiver/drier (arrowed)

10 The pipe leading from the condenser outlet to the evaporator (small tubing) should be cold, and the evaporator outlet line (the larger tubing that leads back to the compressor) should be slightly colder (3 to 10 degrees F). If the evaporator outlet is considerably warmer than the inlet, the system needs a charge. Insert a thermometer in the centre air distribution duct while operating the air conditioning system **(see illustration)** - the temperature of the output air should be 35 to 40 degrees F below the ambient air temperature (down to approximately 40 degrees F). If the ambient (outside) air temperature is very high, say 110 degrees F, the duct air temperature may be as high as 60 degrees F, but generally the air conditioning is 35 to 40 degrees F cooler than the ambient air. If the air isn't as cold as it used to be, the system probably needs a charge. Further inspection or testing of the system is beyond the scope of the home mechanic and should be left to a professional.
11 Inspect the sight glass If the refrigerant looks foamy when running, it's low **(see illustration)**. When ambient temperatures are very hot, bubbles may show in the sight glass even with the proper amount of refrigerant. With the proper amount of refrigerant, when the air conditioning is turned off, the sight glass should show refrigerant that foams, then clears.
12 If the previous checks indicate that the refrigerant charge is low, take the vehicle to a Toyota dealer or automotive air conditioning repair facility to have the system recharged.

Heating systems

13 If the air coming out of the heater vents isn't hot, the problem could stem from any of the following causes:
  a) *The thermostat is stuck open, preventing the engine coolant from warming up enough to carry heat to the heater core. Replace the thermostat (see Section 3).*

  b) *A heater hose is blocked, preventing the flow of coolant through the heater core. Feel both heater hoses at the firewall. They should be hot. If one of them is cold, there is an obstruction in one of the hoses or in the heater core, or the heater control valve is shut. Detach the hoses and back flush the heater core with a water hose. If the heater core is clear but circulation is impeded, remove the two hoses and flush them out with a water hose.*
  c) *If flushing fails to remove the blockage from the heater core, the core must be replaced. (see Section 10).*
14 If the blower motor speed does not correspond to the setting selected on the blower switch, the problem could be a bad fuse, circuit, switch, blower motor resistor or motor (see Sections 9 and 11).
15 If there isn't any air coming out of the vents:
  a) *Turn the ignition ON and activate the fan control. Place your ear at the heating/air conditioning register (vent) and listen. Most motors are audible. Can you hear the motor running?*

13.3 After the system has been discharged, unbolt the two refrigerant lines from the top of the receiver/drier and cap them - there is one bolt and one screw to remove (arrowed)

  b) *If you can't (and have already verified that the blower switch and the blower motor resistor are good), the blower motor itself is probably bad (see Section 9).*
16 If the carpet under the heater core is damp, or if antifreeze vapor or steam is coming through the vents, the heater core is leaking. Remove it (see Section 10) and install a new unit (most radiator workshops will not repair a leaking heater core).
17 Inspect the drain hose from the heater/air conditioning assembly at the right side of the firewall, make sure it is not clogged.

13 Air conditioning receiver/drier - removal and installation

Warning: The air conditioning system is under high pressure. Do not loosen any hose fittings or remove any components until the system has been discharged. Air conditioning refrigerant may only be discharged by a dealer service department or an automotive air conditioning repair facility. Always wear eye protection when disconnecting air conditioning system fittings even after the system has been discharged.

Removal

1 Have the refrigerant discharged and recovered by a Toyota dealer or automotive air conditioning repair facility.
2 Refer to Chapter 11 and remove the grille.
3 Disconnect the refrigerant lines **(see illustration)** from the receiver/drier and cap the open fittings to prevent entry of moisture.
4 Loosen the pinch bolt and slip the receiver/drier out of the bracket.

Installation

5 Installation is the reverse of removal.
6 Have the system evacuated, charged and leak tested by the workshop that discharged it.

14.4 Disconnect the wiring harness connector (large arrow) at the compressor, then unbolt the flanges (two smaller arrows) and detach the refrigerant lines from the compressor

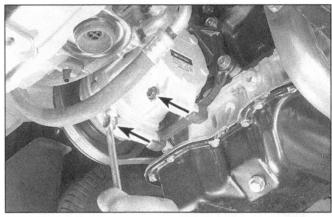

14.5 Remove the compressor mounting bolts (arrows indicate the two bottom bolts, two more are near the top of the compressor) and remove the compressor

14 Air conditioning compressor - removal and installation

Warning: The air conditioning system is under high pressure. Do not loosen any hose fittings or remove any components until the system has been discharged. Air conditioning refrigerant may only be discharged by a dealer service department or an automotive air conditioning repair facility. Always wear eye protection when disconnecting air conditioning system fittings even after the system has been discharged.

Removal

1 Have the refrigerant discharged and recovered by a Toyota dealer or automotive air conditioning repair facility.
2 Disconnect the negative cable from the battery.
Caution: If the stereo in your vehicle is equipped with an anti-theft system, make sure you have the correct activation code before disconnecting the battery.

3 Remove the drivebelt from the compressor (see Chapter 1).
4 Detach the wiring connector and disconnect the refrigerant lines **(see illustration)**.
5 Unbolt the compressor and lift it from the vehicle **(see illustration)**.
6 If a new or rebuilt compressor is being installed, follow the directions supplied with the compressor regarding the proper level of oil prior to installation.

Installation

7 Installation is the reverse of removal. Replace any O-rings with new ones specifically made for the type of refrigerant in your system and lubricate them with refrigerant oil, also designed specifically for your system.
8 Have the system evacuated, recharged and leak tested by the workshop that discharged it.

15 Air conditioning condenser - removal and installation

Warning: The air conditioning system is under high pressure. Do not loosen any hose fittings

or remove any components until the system has been discharged. Air conditioning refrigerant may only be discharged by a dealer service department or an automotive air conditioning repair facility. Always wear eye protection when disconnecting air conditioning system fittings even after the system has been discharged.

Removal

1 Have the refrigerant discharged and recovered by a Toyota dealer or automotive air conditioning repair facility.
2 Remove the radiator as described in Section 5.
3 Remove the grille and right headlight assembly for access (see Chapter 11). Disconnect the condenser inlet and outlet fittings **(see illustration)**. Cap the open fittings immediately to keep moisture and contamination out of the system. **Note:** *The left-side fitting is connected to the receiver/drier (see Section 13).*
4 Remove the two condenser mounting bolts, pull the condenser back and lift it out **(see illustration)**.

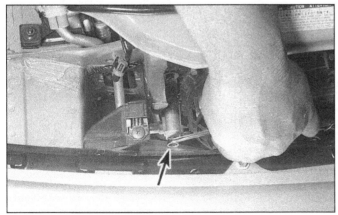

15.3 Disconnect the refrigerant line on the right side by unbolting this flange (arrowed)

15.4 Remove the condenser mounting bolts - there is one bolt at each end (right side shown)

Installation

5 Install the condenser, brackets and bolts, making sure the rubber cushions fit on the mounting points properly.

6 Reconnect the refrigerant lines, using new O-rings where needed. If a new condenser has been installed, add approximately 1.4 to 1.7 ounces of new refrigerant oil of the correct type.

7 Reinstall the remaining parts in the reverse order of removal.

8 Have the system evacuated, charged and leak tested by the workshop that discharged it.

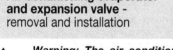

16 Air conditioning evaporator and expansion valve - removal and installation

⚠ *Warning: The air conditioning system is under high pressure. Do not loosen any hose fittings or remove any components until the system has been discharged. Air conditioning refrigerant may only be discharged by a dealer service department or an automotive air conditioning repair*

16.2b Use a back-up wrench when disconnecting the air conditioning lines at the firewall

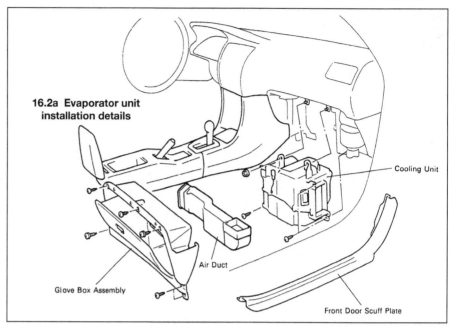

16.2a Evaporator unit installation details

Cooling Unit

Air Duct

Glove Box Assembly

Front Door Scuff Plate

facility. Always wear eye protection when disconnecting air conditioning system fittings even after the system has been discharged.

Removal

1 Have the refrigerant discharged and recovered by a Toyota dealer or automotive air conditioning repair facility.

2 Remove the glove compartment assembly **(see illustration)**. Disconnect the air conditioning lines at the firewall, use a back-up wrench so as not to damage the fittings **(see illustration)**. Cap the open fittings after disassembly to prevent the entry of air or dirt.

3 Remove two nuts and three screws retaining the evaporator unit to the firewall and pull the unit out of the vehicle **(see illustration 16.2a)**.

4 With the evaporator unit on the bench, remove the screws and clips and separate the top and bottom halves of the case and pull out the evaporator **(see illustration)**.

5 Pull the thermistor sensor probe from the evaporator core and unbolt the expansion valve and the two short refrigerant lines **(see illustration 16.4)**.

6 The evaporator core can be cleaned with a "fin comb" and blown off with compressed air **(see illustration)**.

⚠ *Warning: Be sure to wear eye protection when using compressed air.*

Installation

7 If the evaporator core is replaced with a new unit, add 1.4 ounces of new refrigerant oil of the correct type to the system.

8 The remainder of the installation is the reverse of the removal process. Be sure to use new O-rings, and new gaskets on the expansion valve.

9 Have the system evacuated, charged and leak tested by the workshop that discharged it.

16.6 The fins of the core can be cleaned with a fin comb -use the side of the tool with the correct fins-per-inch spacing for your core

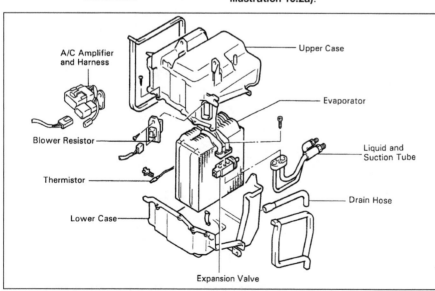

A/C Amplifier and Harness

Upper Case

Evaporator

Blower Resistor

Liquid and Suction Tube

Thermistor

Drain Hose

Lower Case

Expansion Valve

16.4 Separate the two halves of the evaporator housing and remove the core

Chapter 4
Fuel and exhaust systems

Contents

Degrees of difficulty

Easy, suitable for novice with little experience	**Fairly easy,** suitable for beginner with some experience	**Fairly difficult,** suitable for competent DIY mechanic	**Difficult,** suitable for experienced DIY mechanic	**Very difficult,** suitable for expert DIY or professional

Specifications

Fuel system

Fuel pressure
  Ignition ON, engine not running

1.3L engine	40.8 to 41.7 psi
1.6L and 1.8L engines	38 to 44 psi

  Engine idling
    Vacuum sensing hose detached

1.3L engine	40.8 to 41.7 psi
1.6L and 1.8L engines	38 to 44 psi

    Vacuum sensing hose attached

1.3L engine	33 to 37 psi
1.6L and 1.8L engines	31 to 37 psi
Fuel system hold pressure	21 psi
Fuel injector resistance	13.4 to 14.2 ohms
Idle Air Control (IAC) valve resistance (1.6L and 1.8L engines)	19 to 23 ohms
Air control valve resistance (1.3L engines)	30 to 33 ohms
Air conditioning idle-up valve solenoid resistance	30 to 34 ohms

Idle speed

Automatic transmission	750 rpm
Manual transmission	700 rpm

Torque wrench settings

Ft-lbs

Throttle body mounting bolts/nuts

1.3L engine	9
1.6L and 1.8L engines	16
Fuel rail mounting bolts	14
Fuel line fittings	22

Fuel pressure regulator bolts

1.3L engine	6
1.6L and 1.8L engines	7

1 General information

The fuel system consists of a fuel tank, an electric fuel pump (located in the fuel tank), an EFI/fuel pump relay, fuel injectors, a fuel pressure regulator, an air cleaner assembly and a throttle body unit. All models covered by this manual are equipped with the Multi Point Fuel Injection (MPFI) system.

Multi Point Fuel Injection (MPFI) system

Multi point fuel injection uses timed impulses to sequentially inject the fuel directly into the intake port of each cylinder. The injectors are controlled by the Electronic Control Module (ECM). The ECM monitors various engine parameters and delivers the exact amount of fuel, in the correct sequence, into the intake ports. The throttle body serves only to control the amount of air passing into the system. Because each cylinder is equipped with an injector mounted immediately adjacent to the intake valve, much better control of the fuel/air mixture ratio is possible.

Fuel pump and lines

Fuel is circulated from the fuel tank to the fuel injection system, and back to the fuel tank, through a pair of metal lines running along the underside of the vehicle. An electric fuel pump is attached to the fuel sending unit inside the fuel tank. A vapor return system routes all vapors and hot fuel back to the fuel tank through a separate return line.

The fuel pump will operate as long as the engine is cranking or running and the ECM is receiving ignition reference pulses from the electronic ignition system (see Chapter 5). If there are no reference pulses, the fuel pump will shut off after 2 or 3 seconds.

Exhaust system

The exhaust system includes a manifold fitted with an exhaust oxygen sensor, a catalytic converter, an exhaust pipe, and a muffler.

The catalytic converter is an emission control device added to the exhaust system to reduce pollutants. A single-bed converter is used in combination with a three-way (reduction) catalyst. Refer to Chapter 6 for more information regarding the catalytic converter.

2 Fuel pressure relief

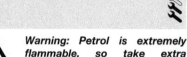

⚠️ *Warning: Petrol is extremely flammable, so take extra precautions when you work on any part of the fuel system. Don't smoke or allow open flames or bare light bulbs near the work area, and don't work in a garage where a natural gas-type appliance (such as a water heater or a clothes dryer) with a pilot light is present. Since petrol is carcinogenic, wear latex gloves when there's a possibility of being exposed to fuel, and, if you spill any fuel on your skin, rinse it off immediately with soap and water. Mop up any spills immediately and do not store fuel-soaked rags where they could ignite. The fuel system is under constant pressure, so, if any fuel lines are to be disconnected, the fuel pressure in the system must be relieved first. When you perform any kind of work on the fuel system, wear safety glasses and have a Class B type fire extinguisher on hand.*

1 Before servicing any fuel system component, you must relieve the fuel pressure to minimize the risk of fire or personal injury.

2 Remove the fuel filler cap - this will relieve any pressure built up in the tank.

3 Remove the radio (see Chapter 12) and cup holder for access to the circuit opening relay. Unplug the electrical connector from the relay **(see illustration)**.

4 Start the engine and wait for the engine to stall, then turn the ignition key to Off.

5 The fuel system is now depressurized. **Note:** *Place a rag around the fuel line before removing any hose clamp or fitting to prevent any residual fuel from spilling onto the engine.*

6 Before working on the fuel system, disconnect the cable from the negative terminal of the battery.
Caution: If the stereo in your vehicle is equipped with an anti-theft system, make sure you have the correct activation code before disconnecting the battery.

7 Reconnect the relay then install the radio when the job is completed.

3 Fuel pump/fuel pressure - check

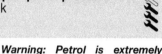

⚠️ *Warning: Petrol is extremely flammable, so take extra precautions when you work on any part of the fuel system. Don't smoke or allow open flames or bare light bulbs near the work area, and don't work in a garage where a natural gas-type appliance (such as a water heater or a clothes dryer) with a pilot light is present. Since petrol is carcinogenic, wear latex gloves when there's a possibility of being exposed to fuel, and, if you spill any fuel on your skin, rinse it off immediately with soap and water. Mop up any spills immediately and do not store fuel-soaked rags where they could ignite. The fuel system is under constant pressure, so, if any fuel lines are to be disconnected, the fuel pressure in the system must be relieved first. When you perform any kind of work on the fuel system, wear safety glasses and have a Class B type fire extinguisher on hand.*

Fuel pump operation check

1 Turn ON the ignition switch (but do not start the engine).

2 On all 1993, and 1994 models and 1995 models with the 1.3L or 1.6L engine, bridge terminals +B and FP of the test connector with a jumper wire **(see illustration)**. **Note:** *On 1995 1.8L engines and all 1996 models (with the OBD II on-board diagnostic system), it is not possible to power the fuel pump using the test connector. On these models, start the engine to obtain fuel pressure readings.*

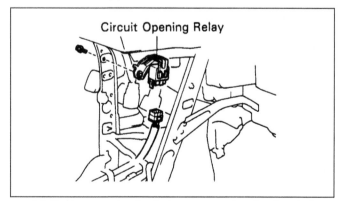

2.3 To depressurize the fuel system, unplug the electrical connector from the circuit opening relay, start the engine and allow it to stall

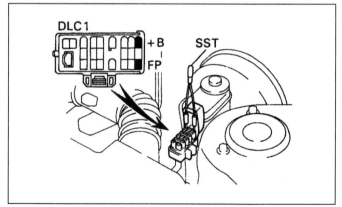

3.2 Bridge terminals FP and +B on the test connector using a jumper wire or paper clip

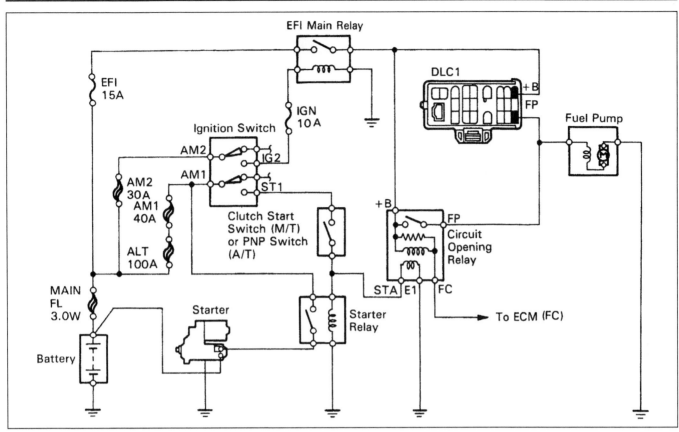

3.6a Typical electrical schematic of the fuel pump circuit

3 The fuel pump is now activated. Listen for fuel pump noises from the fuel tank (under the rear seat) and verify that there is pressure in the hose from the fuel filter.

4 Remove the jumper wire. Close the cap on the test connector.

5 Turn the ignition switch OFF.

6 If the fuel pump did not operate, inspect the following electrical components: the EFI 15-amp fuse and the ignition switch 30-amp fuse (AM2) **(see illustration)** and/or the EFI main relay and the circuit opening relay (see Steps 33 through 38), the fuel pump **(see illustration)**; and the wiring and electrical connectors (see the wiring diagrams at the end of the book).

Fuel pressure check

7 A fuel pressure gauge, capable of measuring a minimum of 50-psi, equipped with a banjo fitting on the end of the hose (Toyota special service tool no. SST 09268-45012) is required for the following procedure. There are a couple of alternatives if you are unable to obtain the special Toyota fuel

pressure gauge set:
a) *Obtain a 12 mm banjo fitting that will adapt to your fuel pressure gauge hose with a hose clamp.*
b) *If you can't find the correct size banjo fitting, obtain a 12 mm bolt with 1.25 mm thread pitch, cut the head off and drill a hole through the centre and one through the side, perpendicular to the lengthwise hole. Add a locknut with the same thread pitch and seal the threads with teflon tape* **(see illustration).**

3.6b Check for battery voltage directly at the fuel pump electrical connector on the top of the fuel tank

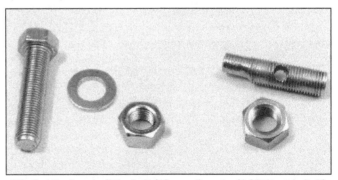

3.7 Cut the head off the bolt (12 mm diameter/1.25 thread pitch) and drill a hole directly through the bolt, lengthwise. Grind the end to accept the pressure gauge hose and drill another hole to allow system pressure to flow. It is important that this hole is drilled in the correct location. The easiest method is to use the banjo bolt that was removed from the fuel filter and place it directly next to the tool for the correct alignment of this passage for fuel flow

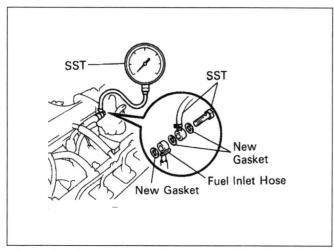

3.11a If the factory tools are available, install the fuel pressure gauge onto the end of the fuel rail

3.11b If you are using the homemade tool, install the fuel pressure gauge to the top of the fuel filter (located in the engine compartment)

8 Remove the fuel tank cap to relieve any pressure that has built up in the tank.

9 Verify that the battery voltage is 12 volts or more (see Chapter 5).

10 Relieve the fuel pressure (see Section 2).

11 There are two methods possible for testing the fuel pressure:

a) If you have the special banjo fitting (Toyota tool number SST 09268-45012) required to attach the fuel pressure gauge, remove the fuel rail bolt at the end of the fuel rail and install the special tool into the fuel rail (see illustration).

b) If you have constructed the drilled-out bolt and locknut tool, detach one side of the fuel filter (see illustration) and install the fuel pressure gauge at this point.

12 To attach the fuel pressure gauge:

a) If you are using the factory setup, use the special banjo fitting on the fuel rail to attach the fuel pressure gauge to the fuel rail. Be sure to use crush washers on both sides of the banjo fitting.

b) If you are using a drilled-out 12 mm bolt, working in the engine compartment, attach the bolt to the fuel filter, tighten the locknut and attach the fuel pressure gauge hose with a hose clamp.

3.20 First check the fuel pressure without vacuum applied to the fuel pressure regulator and then with vacuum applied - fuel pressure should DECREASE as vacuum INCREASES

13 Wipe off any petrol that has leaked out of the fuel rail (or filter).

14 Place the transmission in Neutral (manual) or Park (automatic) and apply the parking brake.

15 On all 1993, and 1994 models and 1995 models with the 1.3L or 1.6L engine, bridge terminals +B and FP of the test connector (see illustration 3.2). Note: On 1995 1.8L engines and 1996 models (with OBD II), it is not possible to power the fuel pump using the test connector. On these models, start the engine to obtain fuel pressure readings.

16 Turn the ignition to ON (engine not running). Measure the fuel pressure and compare it to the fuel pressure listed in this Chapter's Specifications.

a) If the pressure is high, check for a restricted fuel return line. If the line is clear, replace the pressure regulator.

b) If the pressure is low, pinch the fuel return line. If the pressure goes up, replace the fuel pressure regulator. If the pressure does not increase, check the fuel feed line, the fuel pump and the fuel filter.

17 Remove the jumper wire from the service electrical connector or fuel pump connector.

18 Start the engine.

a) Measure the fuel pressure at idle and compare your reading to the fuel pressure listed in this Chapter's Specifications.

b) If the pressure is not as specified, check the vacuum sensing hose and fuel pressure regulator (see Steps 20 through 24).

19 Stop the engine and verify that the fuel pressure remains at 21 psi or more for five minutes after the engine is turned off. If the pressure bleeds down, the fuel pressure regulator, the fuel pump or a fuel injector may be leaking.

Fuel pressure regulator check

20 Disconnect and plug the vacuum hose from the fuel pressure regulator and connect a hand-held vacuum pump to the regulator. Start the engine and read the fuel pressure

gauge without vacuum applied to the fuel pressure regulator. Apply vacuum to the regulator and check the fuel pressure again (see illustration). The fuel pressure should decrease as vacuum increases. Compare your readings with the values listed in this Chapter's Specifications.

21 Reconnect the vacuum hose to the regulator and check the fuel pressure at idle, comparing your reading with the value listed in this Chapter's Specifications. Disconnect the hose and watch the gauge - the pressure should jump up to the maximum specified pressure as soon as the hose is disconnected. If the pressure at idle was too high (with the hose disconnected), connect a vacuum gauge to the hose and check for vacuum (see illustration). If there is no reading on the gauge, check the air intake plenum and intake manifold for a vacuum leak.

22 If the fuel pressure is LOW, pinch the fuel return line shut and watch the gauge. If the pressure doesn't rise, the fuel pump is defective or there is a restriction in the fuel feed line. If the pressure rises sharply, replace the fuel pressure regulator (see Section 13).

23 If the indicated fuel pressure is too high, relieve the fuel pressure (see Section 2), disconnect the fuel return line and blow

3.21 Connect a vacuum gauge to the vacuum line leading to the fuel pressure regulator and check the vacuum source

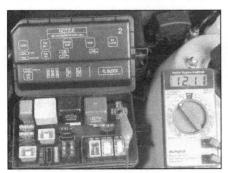

3.30 Locate and remove the EFI relay and check for battery voltage to the relay with the ignition key ON

3.31 Remove the circuit opening relay and check for battery voltage

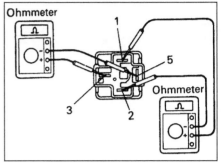

3.33 EFI main relay checks on Nippondenso style relay

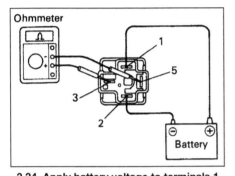

3.34 Apply battery voltage to terminals 1 and 2 and check for continuity between terminals 3 and 5

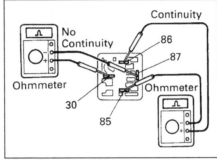

3.35 EFI main relay checks on Bosch style relay

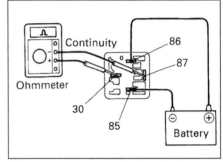

3.36 Apply battery voltage to terminals 85 and 86 and confirm that continuity exists across terminals 87 and 30

through it to check for blockage. If there is no blockage, replace the fuel pressure regulator (see Section 13).

24 If the fuel pressure does not fluctuate as described in Step 21, replace the fuel pressure regulator (see Section 13).

25 Carefully remove the fuel pressure gauge. Be sure to cover the fitting with a rag before loosening it.

26 Using new sealing washers, reattach the pipe banjo fitting to the fuel rail.

27 Wipe up any spilled petrol.

28 Start the engine and check for leaks.

EFI main relay and circuit opening relay checks

Voltage checks

29 There are two relays involved in the fuel pump circuit. First, test for battery voltage to the EFI main relay and then the circuit opening relay.

30 Remove the EFI main relay from the electrical connector and with the ignition key ON (engine not running), check for battery voltage (see illustration).

31 If battery voltage is present, insert the relay back into the connector and check for battery voltage at the circuit opening relay (see accompanying illustration and illustration 2.3). This will require removal of the radio (see Chapter 12).

32 If battery voltage is present at the relay connectors, check the relays.

EFI main relay (Nippondenso type)

33 Using an ohmmeter, check for continuity across terminals 1 and 2 (see illustration). Check that there is no continuity across terminals 3 and 5.

34 Apply battery voltage across terminals 1 and 2 (see illustration). Using an ohmmeter, check for continuity across terminals 3 and 5. Continuity should exist. If the test results are incorrect, replace the relay.

EFI main relay (Bosch type)

35 Using an ohmmeter, check for continuity across terminals 86 and 85 (see illustration). Check that there is no continuity across terminals 87 and 30.

36 Apply battery voltage across terminals 86 and 85 (see illustration). Using an ohmmeter, check for continuity across terminals 87 and 30. Continuity should exist. If the test results are incorrect, replace the relay.

Circuit opening relay

37 Using an ohmmeter, check for continuity across terminals ST and E1 (see illustration). Also, check for continuity across +B and FC. Check that there is no continuity across terminals +B and FP.

38 Apply battery voltage across terminals ST and E1 (see illustration). Using an ohmmeter, check for continuity across terminals +B and FP. Continuity should exist. If the test results are incorrect, replace the relay.

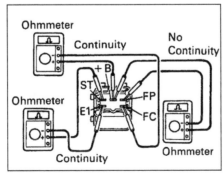

3.37 Circuit opening relay checks

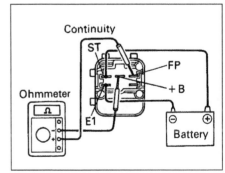

3.38 Apply battery voltage to ST and E1 and check for continuity across terminals FP and +B

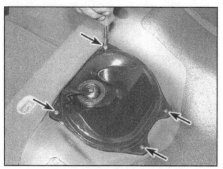

4.4 Remove the fuel pump/fuel level sending unit access cover screws (arrowed) and lift the cover off

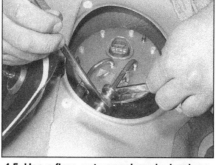

4.5 Use a flare-nut wrench and a back-up wrench to remove the fuel feed line; remove the clamp and hose from the fuel return line fitting

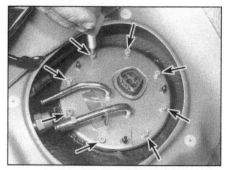

4.6 Remove the fuel pump/sending unit assembly mounting bolts (arrowed)

4 Fuel pump - removal and installation

Warning: Petrol is extremely flammable, so take extra precautions when you work on any part of the fuel system. Don't smoke or allow open flames or bare light bulbs near the work area, and don't work in a garage where a natural gas-type appliance (such as a water heater or a clothes dryer) with a pilot light is present. Since petrol is carcinogenic, wear latex gloves when there's a possibility of being exposed to fuel, and, if you spill any fuel on your skin, rinse it off immediately with soap and water. Mop up any spills immediately and do not store fuel-soaked rags where they could ignite. The fuel system is under constant pressure, so, if any fuel lines are to be disconnected, the fuel pressure in the system must be relieved first. When you perform any kind of work on the fuel system, wear safety glasses and have a Class B type fire extinguisher on hand.*

Removal

1 Remove the fuel tank cap.
2 Disconnect the cable from the negative terminal of the battery.
Caution: If the stereo in your vehicle is equipped with an anti-theft system, make sure you have the correct activation code before disconnecting the battery.
3 Remove the rear seat from inside the passenger compartment (see Chapter 11).
4 Remove the fuel pump/sending unit access cover **(see illustration)**.
5 Disconnect the electrical connector. Disconnect the fuel lines **(see illustration)**.
6 Remove the fuel pump/sending unit retaining bolts **(see illustration)**.
7 Carefully withdraw the fuel pump/fuel level sending unit assembly from the fuel tank **(see illustration)**.
8 Pry the lower end of the fuel pump loose from the bracket **(see illustration)**.
9 Remove the rubber cushion from the lower end of the fuel pump.

10 Remove the clip securing the inlet screen to the pump.
11 Remove the screen and inspect it for contamination. If it is dirty, replace it.
12 If you are only replacing the fuel pump inlet screen, install the new screen, the clip and the rubber cushion, push the lower end of the pump back into the bracket and install the pump/sending unit assembly in the fuel tank.
13 If you are replacing the fuel pump, remove the hose clamp at the upper end of the pump and disconnect the pump from the hose **(see illustration)**.
14 Disconnect the wires from the pump terminals and remove the pump **(see illustration)**.

Installation

15 Installation is the reverse of removal.

5 Fuel level sending unit - check and replacement

Warning: Petrol is extremely flammable, so take extra precautions when you work on any part of the fuel system. Don't smoke or allow open flames or bare light bulbs near the work area, and don't work in a garage where a natural gas-type appliance (such as a water heater or a clothes dryer) with a pilot light is present. Since petrol is carcinogenic, wear latex

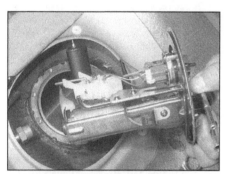

4.7 Lift the fuel pump/sending unit assembly from the fuel tank at an angle so as not to damage the inlet screen or float arm

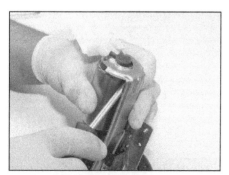

4.8 Separate the fuel pump from the frame by gently prying outward

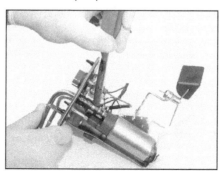

4.13 Remove the clamp from the fuel pump outlet hose

4.14 Remove the electrical connector from the fuel pump

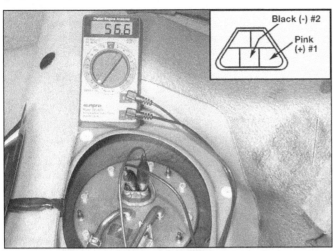
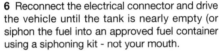

5.4 Position the probes of the ohmmeter onto terminals 1 and 2 and observe the fuel level sending unit resistance

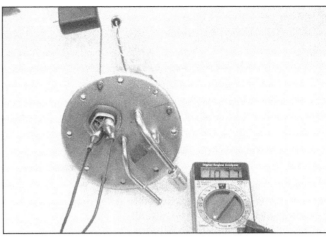

5.8 An accurate check of the sending unit can be made by removing it from the fuel tank and observing the resistance with the float down (empty) and then up (full)

gloves when there's a possibility of being exposed to fuel, and, if you spill any fuel on your skin, rinse it off immediately with soap and water. Mop up any spills immediately and do not store fuel-soaked rags where they could ignite. The fuel system is under constant pressure, so, if any fuel lines are to be disconnected, the fuel pressure in the system must be relieved first. When you perform any kind of work on the fuel system, wear safety glasses and have a Class B type fire extinguisher on hand.

Check

1 Before performing any tests on the fuel level sending unit, completely fill the tank with fuel.

2 Remove the rear seat and the fuel pump/sending unit access cover **(see illustration 4.4)**.

3 Disconnect the fuel level sending unit electrical connector located on top of the fuel tank.

4 Position the ohmmeter probes on the electrical connector terminals (terminals pink (+) and black (-) check for resistance **(see illustration)**. Use the 200-ohm scale on the ohmmeter.

5 With the fuel tank completely full, the resistance should be about 4.0 ohms.

6 Reconnect the electrical connector and drive the vehicle until the tank is nearly empty (or siphon the fuel into an approved fuel container using a siphoning kit - not your mouth.

7 Check the resistance. The resistance of the sending unit should now be about 110 ohms.

8 If the readings are incorrect, replace the sending unit. **Note:** *The test can also be performed with the fuel level sending unit removed from the fuel tank. Using an ohmmeter, check the resistance of the sending unit with the float arm completely down (tank empty) and with the arm up (tank full)* **(see illustration)**. *The resistance should change steadily from 110 ohms to approximately 2.0 to 4.0 ohms.*

Replacement

9 Remove the fuel pump/fuel level sending unit assembly from the fuel tank (see Section 4).

10 Carefully angle the sending unit out of the opening without damaging the fuel level float located at the bottom of the assembly **(see illustration 4.7)**.

11 Disconnect the electrical connectors from the sending unit **(see illustration)**.

12 Remove the screw from the side of the sending unit bracket and separate the sending unit from the assembly **(see illustration)**.

13 Installation is the reverse of removal.

6 Fuel lines and fittings - inspection and replacement

 Warning: Petrol is extremely flammable, so take extra precautions when you work on any part of the fuel system. Don't smoke or allow open flames or bare light bulbs near the work area, and don't work in a garage where a natural gas-type appliance (such as a water heater or a clothes dryer) with a pilot light is present. Since petrol is carcinogenic, wear latex gloves when there's a possibility of being exposed to fuel, and, if you spill any fuel on your skin, rinse it off immediately with soap and water. Mop up any spills immediately and do not store fuel-soaked rags where they could ignite. The fuel system is under constant pressure, so, if any fuel lines are to be disconnected, the fuel pressure in the system must be relieved first. When you perform any kind of work on the fuel system, wear safety glasses and have a Class B type fire extinguisher on hand.

Inspection

1 Once in a while, you will have to raise the vehicle to service or replace some component (an exhaust pipe hanger, for example). Whenever you work under the vehicle, always inspect fuel lines and all fittings and connections for damage or deterioration.

2 Check all hoses and pipes for cracks, kinks, deformation or obstructions.

3 Make sure all hoses and pipe clips attach their associated hoses or pipes securely to the underside of the vehicle.

4 Verify all hose clamps attaching rubber hoses to metal fuel lines or pipes are snug enough to assure a tight fit between the hoses and pipes.

5.11 Remove the electrical connector from the fuel level sending unit

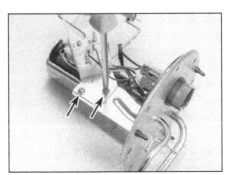

5.12 Remove the screws that retain the fuel level sending unit

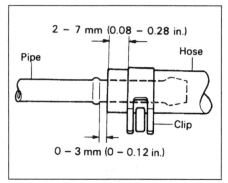

6.6 When attaching a section of rubber hose to a metal fuel line, be sure to overlap the hose as shown, secure it to the line with a new hose clamp of the proper type

Replacement

5 If you must replace any damaged sections, use original equipment replacement hoses or pipes constructed from exactly the same material as the section you are replacing. Do not install substitutes constructed from inferior or inappropriate material or you could cause a fuel leak or a fire.

6 Always, before detaching or disassembling any part of the fuel line system, note the routing of all hoses and pipes and the orientation of all clamps and clips to assure that replacement sections are installed in exactly the same manner. When attaching hoses to metal lines, overlap them as shown **(see illustration)**.

7 Before detaching any part of the fuel system, be sure to relieve the fuel line and tank pressure by removing the fuel tank cap and disconnecting the battery. Cover the fitting being disconnected with a rag to absorb any fuel that may spray out.

7 Fuel tank - removal and installation

 Warning: Petrol is extremely flammable, so take extra precautions when you work on any part of the fuel system. Don't smoke or allow open flames or bare light bulbs near the work area, and don't work in a garage where a natural gas-type appliance (such as a water heater or a clothes dryer) with a pilot light is present. Since petrol is carcinogenic, wear latex gloves when there's a possibility of being exposed to fuel, and, if you spill any fuel on your skin, rinse it off immediately with soap and water. Mop up any spills immediately and do not store fuel-soaked rags where they could ignite. The fuel system is under constant pressure, so, if any fuel lines are to be disconnected, the fuel pressure in the system must be relieved first. When you perform any kind of work on the fuel system, wear safety glasses and have a Class B type fire extinguisher on hand.

Removal

1 This procedure is much easier to perform if the fuel tank is empty. Some models may have a drain plug for this purpose. If for some reason the drain plug can't be removed, postpone the job until the tank is empty or siphon the fuel into an approved container using a siphoning kit (available at most auto parts stores).

 Warning: Do not start the siphoning action by mouth!

2 Remove the fuel filler cap to relieve fuel tank pressure. Relieve the fuel system pressure (see Section 2)

3 Detach the cable from the negative terminal of the battery.
Caution: If the stereo in your vehicle is equipped with an anti-theft system, make sure you have the correct activation code before disconnecting the battery.

4 If the tank is full or nearly full, drain the fuel into an approved container.

5 Raise the vehicle and place it securely on jackstands.

6 Familiarize yourself with the layout of the fuel tank assembly before proceeding **(see illustration)**.

7 Remove the centre exhaust pipe and the heat insulator from the vehicle (see Section 14).

8 Support the fuel tank with a floor jack. Place a sturdy plank between the jack head and the fuel tank to protect the tank.

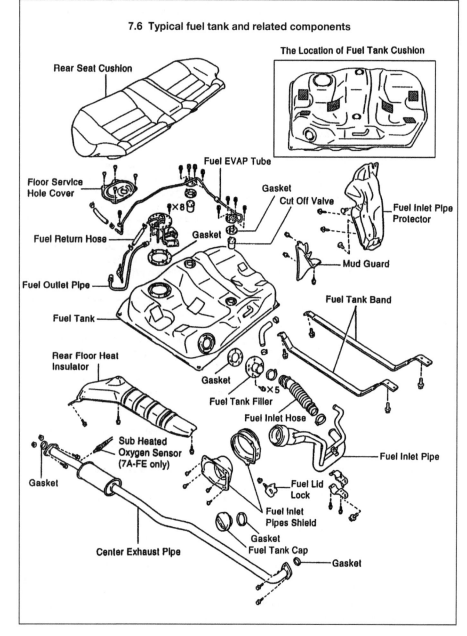

7.6 Typical fuel tank and related components

The Location of Fuel Tank Cushion

Rear Seat Cushion

Floor Service Hole Cover

Fuel EVAP Tube

Gasket

Cut Off Valve

Fuel Inlet Pipe Protector

Fuel Return Hose

Gasket

Mud Guard

Fuel Outlet Pipe

Fuel Tank

Fuel Tank Band

Rear Floor Heat Insulator

Gasket

Sub Heated Oxygen Sensor (7A-FE only)

Fuel Tank Filler

Fuel Inlet Hose

Gasket

Fuel Inlet Pipe

Fuel Lid Lock

Fuel Inlet Pipes Shield

Gasket
Fuel Tank Cap

Center Exhaust Pipe

Gasket

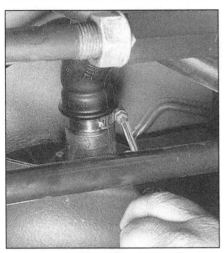

7.9a Remove the clamp that retains the fuel filler hose

7.9b Loosen the clamp and detach the fuel vapor line from the fuel tank

7.10 Remove the tank strap bolts (arrowed) from the body

9 Disconnect the fuel lines, the vapor return line and the fuel filler hose **(see illustrations)**. **Note:** *Be sure to plug the hoses to prevent leakage and contamination of the fuel system.*
10 Remove the bolts from the fuel tank retaining straps **(see illustration)**.
11 Lower the tank enough to disconnect the electrical connector and ground strap from the fuel pump/fuel gauge sending unit, if you have not already done so.
12 Remove the tank from the vehicle.

Installation

13 Installation is the reverse of removal.

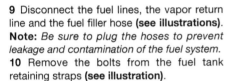

8 Fuel tank cleaning and repair - general information

1 Any repairs to the fuel tank or filler neck should be carried out by a professional who has experience in this critical and potentially dangerous work. Even after cleaning and flushing of the fuel system, explosive fumes can remain and ignite during repair of the tank.
2 If the fuel tank is removed from the vehicle, it should not be placed in an area where sparks or open flames could ignite the fumes coming out of the tank. Be especially careful inside garages where a natural gas-type appliance is located, because the pilot light could cause an explosion.

9 Air cleaner assembly - removal and installation

Removal

1 Detach the clips and remove the air filter and the filter element (see Chapter 1).
2 Disconnect the air intake hose from the assembly.

3 Remove the three bolts and remove the air cleaner assembly from the engine compartment **(see illustration)**.

Installation

4 Installation is the reverse of removal.

10 Accelerator cable - removal, installation and adjustment

Removal

1 Detach the cable from the negative terminal of the battery.
Caution: If the stereo in your vehicle is equipped with an anti-theft system, make sure you have the correct activation code before disconnecting the battery.
2 Loosen the locknut on the threaded portion of the throttle cable at the throttle body **(see illustration)**.

9.3 Remove the bolts (arrowed) that retain the air cleaner housing to the engine compartment

10.2 Loosen the locknuts on the accelerator cable

10.3 Rotate the throttle lever and remove the cable end from the slot

3 Rotate the throttle lever and slip the cable end out of the slot in the lever **(see illustration).**
4 Detach the throttle cable from the accelerator pedal **(see illustration).** Remove the two bolts securing the cable retainer to the firewall.
5 From inside the vehicle, pull the cable through the firewall.

Installation and adjustment

6 Installation is the reverse of removal. Make sure the cable casing grommet seats properly in the firewall.

10.4 Separate the cable from the accelerator pedal assembly and slide the cable end out of the slot (arrowed) in the housing

7 To adjust the cable, fully depress the accelerator pedal and check that the throttle is fully opened.
8 If not fully opened, loosen the locknuts, depress accelerator pedal and adjust the cable until the throttle is fully open.
9 Tighten the locknuts and recheck the adjustment. Make sure the throttle closes fully when the pedal is released.

11 Electronic Fuel Injection (EFI) system - general information

1 These models are equipped with an Electronic Fuel Injection (EFI) system. The EFI system is composed of three basic subsystems: fuel system, air induction system and electronic control system **(see illustration).**

Fuel system

2 An electric fuel pump located inside the fuel tank supplies fuel under constant pressure to the fuel rail, which distributes fuel evenly to all injectors. From the fuel rail, fuel is injected into the intake ports, just above the intake valves, by fuel injectors. The amount of fuel supplied by the injectors is precisely controlled by an Electronic Control Module (ECM). A pressure regulator controls system pressure in relation to intake manifold vacuum. A fuel filter between the fuel pump and the fuel rail filters fuel to protect the components of the system.

Air induction system

3 The air induction system consists of an air filter housing, the throttle body and the duct connecting the two. An Intake Air Temperature (IAT) sensor monitors the temperature of the incoming air. This information helps the ECM determine the amount of fuel to be injected by the injectors.

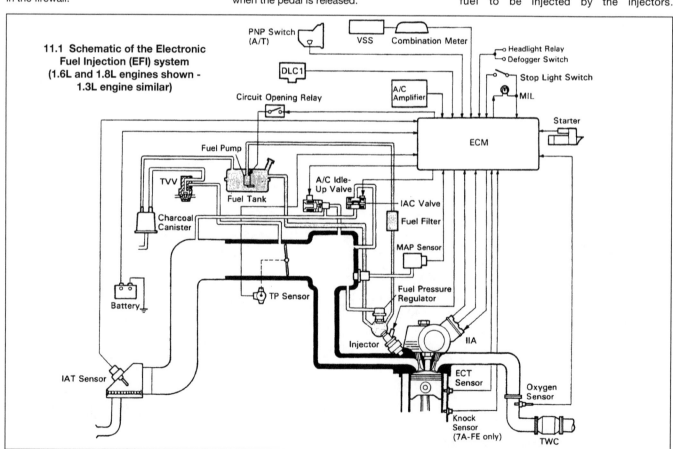

11.1 Schematic of the Electronic Fuel Injection (EFI) system (1.6L and 1.8L engines shown - 1.3L engine similar)

12.6 With the engine off, use aerosol carburetor cleaner (make sure it is safe for use with catalytic converters and oxygen sensors), a toothbrush and a rag to clean the throttle body - open the throttle plate so you can clean behind it

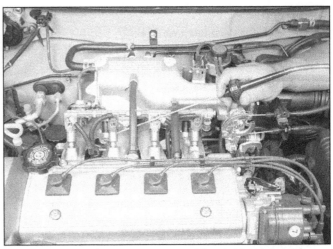

12.7 Use a stethoscope or a screwdriver to determine if the injectors are working properly - they should make a steady clicking sound that rises and falls with engine speed changes

The throttle plate inside the throttle body is controlled by the driver. As the throttle plate opens, the speed of the incoming air increases, which lowers the temperature of the air. The IAT sensor sends this information to the ECM and the ECM signals the injectors to increase the amount of fuel delivered to the intake ports.

Electronic control system

4 The Computer Control System controls the EFI and other systems by means of an Electronic Control Module (ECM), which employs a microcomputer. The ECM receives signals from a number of information sensors which monitor such variables as intake air temperature, throttle angle, coolant temperature, engine rpm, vehicle speed and exhaust oxygen content. These signals help the ECM determine the injection duration necessary for the optimum air/fuel ratio. Some of these sensors and their corresponding ECM-controlled relays are not contained within EFI components, but are located throughout the engine compartment. For further information regarding the ECM and its relationship to the engine electrical and ignition system, see Chapter 6.

12 Electronic Fuel Injection (EFI) system - check

1 Check the ground wire connections for tightness. Check all wiring and electrical connectors that are related to the system. Loose electrical connectors and poor grounds can cause many problems that resemble more serious malfunctions.
2 Check to see that the battery is fully charged, as the control unit and sensors depend on an accurate supply voltage in order to properly meter the fuel.

3 Check the air filter element - a dirty or partially blocked filter will severely impede performance and economy (see Chapter 1).
4 If a blown fuse is found, replace it and see if it blows again. If it does, search for a grounded wire in the harness related to the system.
5 Check the air intake duct from the air cleaner housing to the intake manifold for leaks, which will result in an excessively lean mixture. Also check the condition of the vacuum hoses connected to the intake manifold.
6 Remove the air intake duct from the throttle body and check for carbon and residue build-up. If it's dirty, clean it with aerosol carburetor cleaner (make sure the can says it's safe for use with oxygen sensors and catalytic converters) and a toothbrush (see illustration).
7 With the engine running, place a stethoscope against each injector, one at a time, and listen for a clicking sound, indicating

operation (see illustration). If you don't have an automotive stethoscope you can use a long screwdriver; just place the tip of the screwdriver against the injector body and press your ear against the handle.
8 If there is a problem with an injector, purchase a special injector test light ("noid" light) and install it into the injector electrical connector (see illustration). Start the engine and make sure that each injector connector flashes the noid light. This will test for the proper voltage signal to the injector.
9 With the engine OFF and the fuel injector electrical connectors disconnected, measure the resistance of each injector (see illustration). Each injector should measure about 13.4 to 14.2 ohms. If not, the injector is probably faulty.
10 The remainder of the system checks should be left to a dealer service department or other qualified repair workshop, as there is a chance that the control unit may be damaged if not performed properly.

12.8 Install the "noid" light into the fuel injector electrical connector and check to see that it blinks with the engine running

12.9 Using an ohmmeter, measure the resistance across the terminals of the injector

13 Electronic Fuel Injection (EFI) system - component check and replacement

⚠ *Warning: Petrol is extremely flammable, so take extra precautions when you work on any part of the fuel system. Don't smoke or allow open flames or bare light bulbs near the work area, and don't work in a garage where a natural gas-type appliance (such as a water heater or a clothes dryer) with a pilot light is present. Since petrol is carcinogenic, wear latex gloves when there's a possibility of being exposed to fuel, and, if you spill any fuel on your skin, rinse it off immediately with soap and water. Mop up any spills immediately and do not store fuel-soaked rags where they could ignite. The fuel system is under constant pressure, so, if any fuel lines are to be disconnected, the fuel pressure in the system must be relieved first. When you perform any kind of work on the fuel system, wear safety glasses and have a Class B type fire extinguisher on hand.*

Caution: If the stereo in your vehicle is equipped with an anti-theft system, make sure you have the correct activation code before disconnecting the battery.

Throttle body

Check

1 Verify that the throttle linkage operates smoothly.
2 Start the engine, detach each vacuum hose and, using a vacuum gauge, check there is no vacuum at idle, but that there is vacuum at all other times.

Replacement

 Warning: Wait until the engine is completely cool before beginning this procedure.

3 Drain the cooling system (see Chapter 1) then detach the cable from the negative terminal of the battery (see the **Caution** at the beginning of this Section).
4 Loosen the hose clamps and remove the air intake duct.
5 Detach the accelerator cable from the throttle lever (see Section 10).
6 Where applicable, detach the throttle cable bracket and set it aside (it's not necessary to detach the throttle cable from the bracket).
7 If your vehicle is equipped with an automatic transmission, detach the throttle valve (TV) cable from the throttle linkage (see Chapter 7B), detach the TV cable brackets from the engine and set the cable and brackets aside.

13.10 A typical throttle body is retained by four bolts/nuts (arrowed)

8 Clearly label, then detach, all vacuum and coolant hoses from the throttle body.
9 Disconnect the electrical connector from the throttle position sensor (TPS).
10 Remove the four throttle body mounting bolts **(see illustration)**. On some engines there are two bolts and two nuts.
11 Detach the throttle body and gasket **(see illustration)** from the intake manifold.
12 Using a soft brush and carburetor cleaner, thoroughly clean the throttle body casting, then blow out all passages with compressed air.

Caution: Do not clean the throttle position sensor with anything. Just wipe it off carefully with a clean, soft cloth.

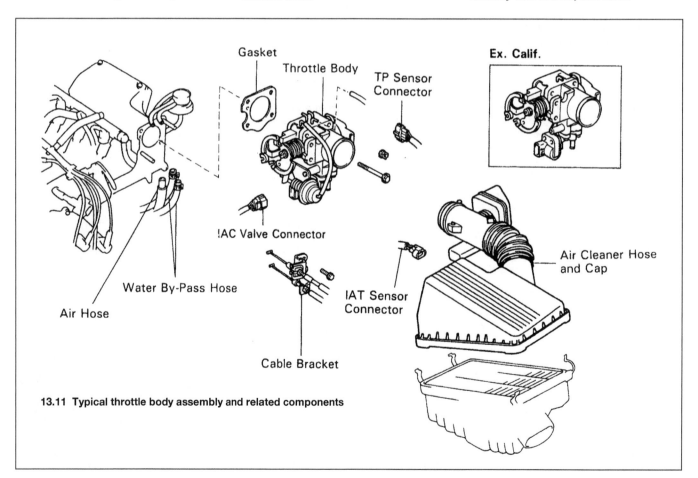

13.11 Typical throttle body assembly and related components

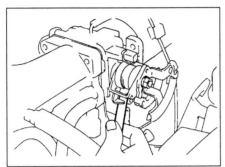

13.16 To check the throttle position sensor (TPS), insert a feeler gauge of the specified thickness (0.50 or 0.70 mm - 1.3L engine; 0.40 or 0.90 mm - 1.6L and 1.8L engines) between the throttle stop screw and the stop lever

13 Installation of the throttle body is the reverse of removal.
14 Be sure to tighten the throttle body mounting bolts to the torque listed in this Chapter's Specifications. Refill the cooling system (see Chapter 1) when you're done.

Throttle position sensor (TPS)

Check

15 Disconnect the electrical connector from the throttle position sensor (TPS). On California models, apply vacuum to the throttle positioner.
16 Insert feeler gauges of the specified thicknesses between the throttle stop screw and the stop lever (see illustration).

17 Using an ohmmeter, measure the resistance between the indicated terminal pairs, with the different thickness feeler gauges inserted (see illustrations).
18 If the resistance is not as specified, insert a 0.70 mm (0.028 in.) feeler gauge (1.6L and 1.8L engines) or 0.60 mm (0.024 in.) feeler gauge (1.3L engine) between the throttle stop

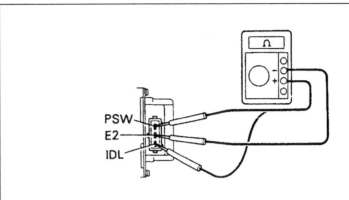

Clearance between lever and stop screw	Between terminals	Continuity
0.50 mm (0.020 in.)	IDL — E2	Continuity
0.70 mm (0.028 in.)	IDL — E2	No continuity
Throttle valve fully open	PSW — E2	Continuity

13.17a Use this terminal guide and the continuity table to check the TPS on 1.3L engines

screw and lever, and connect the ohmmeter to terminals IDL and E2. Loosen the TPS mounting screws and slowly rotate the sensor clockwise until the ohmmeter reads infinity.
19 Tighten the mounting screws, and using the proper feeler gauges, recheck the continuity between the specified terminals.

Replacement

20 If adjustment doesn't bring the sensor within specifications, disconnect it, remove the screws and replace it with a new one (see illustration), then adjust it as described in Step 18.

Fuel pressure regulator

Check

21 Refer to the fuel pump/fuel pressure check procedure (see Section 3).

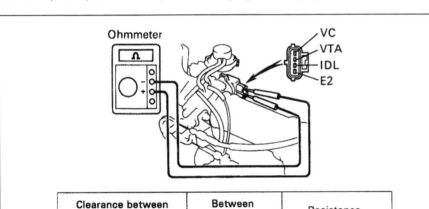

Clearance between lever and stop screw	Between terminals	Resistance
0 mm (0 in.)	VTA — E2	0.2 — 6.0 kΩ
0.40 mm (0.016 in.)	IDL — E2	2.3 kΩ or less
0.90 mm (0.035 in.)	IDL — E2	Infinity
Throttle valve fully open	VTA — E2	3.3 — 10.0 kΩ
—	VC — E2	4.0 — 8.5 kΩ

13.17b Use this terminal guide and the continuity table to check the TPS on 1.6L and 1.8L engines

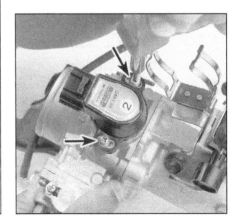

13.20 Remove the two set screws (arrowed) to change the TPS

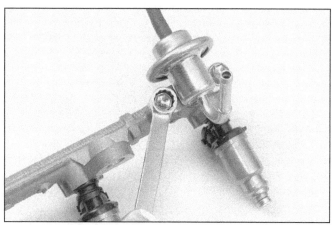

13.26 To remove the fuel pressure regulator from the fuel rail, detach the fuel return hose, remove the two regulator bolts (arrowed) and separate the regulator from the fuel rail (fuel rail removed for clarity)

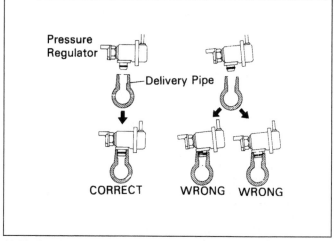

13.27 If the fuel pressure regulator is cocked during installation, it will not seal properly

Replacement

22 Relieve the fuel pressure (see Section 2) and detach the cable from the negative terminal of the battery (see the **Caution** at the beginning of this Section).

23 Detach the vacuum sensing hose from the regulator.

24 Place a metal container or workworkshop towel under the fuel return hose.

25 On 1.3L engines, remove the fuel return hose banjo bolt and washers, then disconnect the return hose from the regulator. On 1.6L and 1.8L engines, slide the clamp down the hose and remove the fuel return hose from the regulator.

26 Remove the pressure regulator mounting bolts **(see illustration)** and detach the pressure regulator from the fuel rail.

27 Use a new O-ring and make sure that the pressure regulator is installed properly on the fuel rail **(see illustration)**.

28 The remainder of installation is the reverse of removal. On 1.3L engines, use new copper washers each side of the banjo fitting.

Idle air control (IAC) valve (1.6L and 1.8L engines)

Note: *The minimum idle speed is pre-set at the factory and should not require adjustment under normal operating conditions; however if the throttle body has been replaced or you suspect the minimum idle speed has been tampered with (for example, if the idle speed screw was removed from the throttle body) have the vehicle checked by a dealer service department or a qualified automotive repair workworkshop.*

Check

29 Apply the parking brake, shift the transmission to Neutral (manual) or Park (automatic) and block the drive wheels. Install the lead of a tachometer to the IG (–) terminal on the test connector **(see illustration)**. Start the engine and allow it to reach normal operating temperature. Check the idle speed and compare it to the idle speed listed in this Chapter's Specifications.

30 Using a jumper wire, bridge terminals TE1 and E1 of the test connector **(see illustration)**.

31 The engine speed should increase to approximately 1000 to 1200 rpm for five seconds then return to normal idle speed.

a) *If the engine speed changes as described, the IAC valve is okay.*

b) *If the engine speed does not change as described, measure the IAC valve resistance.*

32 Remove the jumper wire.

33 Disconnect the IAC valve electrical connector.

34 Measure the resistance between the middle terminal and each of the other two outer terminals **(see illustration)**. Compare your results to the IAC valve resistance in this Chapter's Specifications.

a) *If the resistance is as specified, the IAC valve is okay (but there may be a problem with the wiring or the ECM).*

b) *If the resistance is not as specified, replace the IAC valve.*

35 Connect the IAC valve electrical connector.

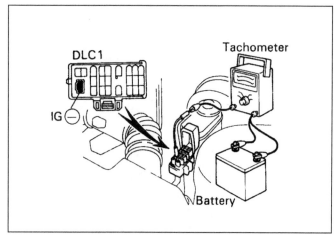

13.29 Install the lead from the tachometer into the IG (-) terminal of the test connector located in the corner of the engine compartment

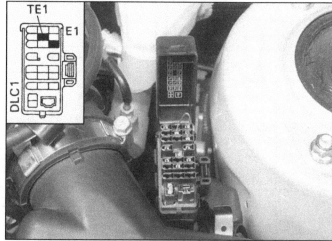

13.30 To test the IAC motor, locate the test connector and using a jumper wire or paper clip, bridge terminals TE1 and E1

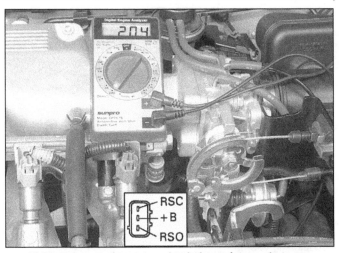

13.34 Using an ohmmeter, check the resistance between +B and RSC or RSO

13.37 Remove the mounting screws that retain the IAC valve to the throttle body

Replacement

36 Remove the throttle body (see Steps 3 through 11). **Note:** *The IAC valve and assembly are difficult to reach, therefore it is recommended to remove the throttle body so that the new IAC valve assembly can be installed properly.*

37 Remove the mounting screws and detach the IAC valve and gasket **(see illustration)**.

38 If the IAC assembly was replaced, be sure to install the Temperature Vacuum Valve (TVV) from the original assembly into the new unit (if equipped).

39 Installation of the IAC valve is the reverse of removal. Be sure to use a new gasket when installing the IAC valve.

Fuel rail and fuel injectors

Check

40 Refer to the fuel injection system checking procedure (see Section 12).

Replacement

41 Relieve the fuel pressure (see Section 2).

42 Detach the cable from the negative terminal of the battery (see the **Caution** at the beginning of this Section).

43 Remove the PCV hose from the cylinder head and intake manifold.

44 On 1.6L and 1.8L engines, remove the air intake plenum (see Steps 65 through 74).

45 Carefully mark each injector connector with a felt pen or paint **(see illustration)**. Disconnect the fuel injector electrical connectors and set the injector wire harness aside. On 1.3L engines remove the bolt and detach the harness from the air intake plenum stay bar. Remove the nut and bolt, then remove the stay bar.

46 Detach the vacuum sensing hose from the fuel pressure regulator.

47 Disconnect the fuel lines from the fuel pressure regulator and the fuel rail.

48 Remove the fuel rail mounting bolts **(see illustration)**.

49 Remove the fuel rail with the fuel injectors attached **(see illustration)**.

50 Remove the fuel injector(s) from the fuel rail and set them aside in a clearly labeled storage container.

51 If you intend to re-use the same injectors, replace the grommets and O-rings **(see illustrations)**.

52 Installation of the fuel injectors is the reverse of removal.

53 Tighten the fuel rail mounting bolts to the torque listed in this Chapter's Specifications.

Air conditioning idle-up valve

Check

54 Apply the parking brake, shift the transmission to Neutral (manual) or Park (automatic) and block the drive wheels. Install the lead of a tachometer to the IG (–) terminal

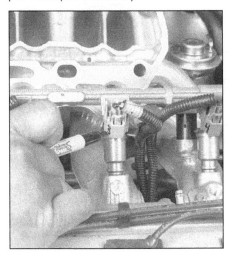

13.45 Number each injector electrical connector before disconnecting them from the fuel rail

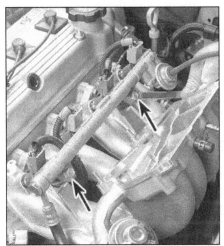

13.48 Remove the bolts (arrowed) that retain the fuel rail to the intake manifold

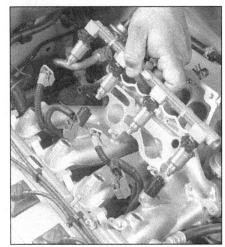

13.49 Lift the fuel rail assembly from the engine. Beware of any fuel that may spill out of the fuel pressure regulator or fuel rail while you are lifting it out

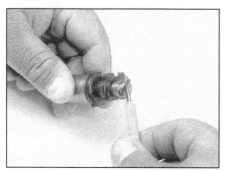

13.51a Remove the O-ring from the injector

13.51b Remove the grommet from the top of the injector

13.51c Remove the O-rings from the bores in the intake manifold

on the test connector (see illustration 13.29). Start the engine and allow it to reach normal operating temperature and idle speed, then turn the air conditioning system ON.

55 Using a jumper wire, bridge terminals TE1 and E1 of the check electrical connector.

56 Verify that the engine speed increases to approximately 1,000 to 1,200 rpm for approximately three seconds after engaging the test terminals, then returns to normal. After 15 seconds check the idle speed again, it should be approximately 100 rpm greater than normal.

a) If the engine speed changes as described, the air conditioning idle-up valve is okay.

b) If the rpm increases more than 100 rpm, adjust the rpm range by turning the adjustment screw accordingly.

c) If the engine speed does not change or if it decreases, measure the air conditioning idle-up valve resistance.

57 Remove the jumper wire.

58 Disconnect the air conditioning idle-up valve electrical connector (see illustration).

59 Measure the resistance between the terminals (see illustration). It should be between 30 and 34 ohms.

a) If the resistance is as specified, the air conditioning idle-up valve is okay (but there may be a problem with the wiring or the ECM).

b) If the resistance is not as specified, replace the valve (see below).

60 Apply battery voltage across the terminals and check that air flows from port E to port F (see illustration) . Note: Port E is the top port and port F is the bottom port. Remove battery voltage and observe that air does not flow from port E through port F.

61 If the test results are incorrect, replace the air conditioning idle-up valve.

Replacement

62 Remove the mounting screws and detach the idle-up valve and gasket.

63 Installation of the idle-up valve is the reverse of removal.

64 Be sure to use a new gasket when installing the idle-up valve.

Air intake plenum (1.6L and 1.8L engines)

Removal

 Warning: Wait until the engine is completely cool before beginning this procedure.

65 Detach the cable from the negative terminal of the battery (see the **Caution** at the beginning of this Section).

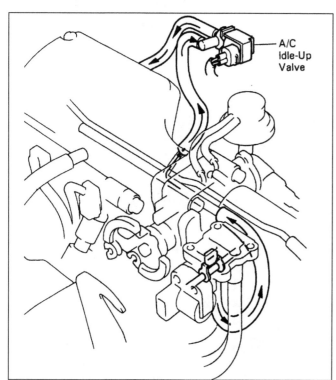

13.58 Schematic of the air conditioning idle-up system

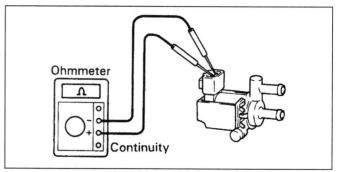

13.59 Check for continuity on the air conditioning idle-up solenoid

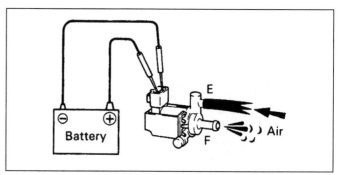

13.60 With battery voltage applied to the solenoid, air should flow through port E and out port F

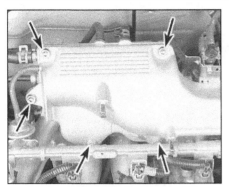

13.73 Remove the bolts (arrowed) that retain the air intake plenum to the intake manifold

66 Disconnect the electrical connectors at the IAC valve, throttle position sensor (TPS) and EGR/EVAP canister control solenoid.

67 Detach the accelerator cable (see Section 10) and transmission linkage (see Chapter 7) from the throttle body assembly.

68 Remove the accelerator cable from the intake manifold (see Section 10).

69 Clearly label, then detach, the vacuum lines from air intake plenum, the EGR valve (where fitted) and the fuel pressure regulator.

70 Detach the PCV system by disconnecting the hose from the fitting on the air intake plenum.

71 Remove the plenum bracket and bolt (if equipped).

72 Detach the coolant hoses from the throttle body and plug them.

73 Remove the air intake plenum retaining bolts **(see illustration)** and the lower (side) retaining bolts.

74 Remove the air intake plenum and throttle body as an assembly from the lower intake manifold.

Installation

75 Be sure to clean and inspect the mounting surface of the lower intake manifold (see Chapter 2A) and the air intake plenum before positioning the new gasket onto the lower intake mounting face. Install the air intake plenum and throttle body assembly onto the intake manifold. Ensure the gasket remains in place. Install the upper intake manifold

retaining bolts and tighten the bolts to the torque listed in Chapter 2A Specifications. Installation is otherwise the reverse of removal.

Air control valve (1.3L engine)

Check

76 Disconnect the air control valve electrical connector - the valve is located on the right-side of the intake manifold.

77 Measure the resistance between the valve terminals. It should be between 30 and 33 ohms.
  a) *If the resistance is as specified, the air control valve is okay.*
  b) *If the resistance is not as specified, replace the valve (see below).*

78 Blow through the port at the diaphragm end and check that no air flows from the lower outlet port.

79 Apply battery voltage across the terminals and check that air flows from the diaphragm port to the outlet port F.

80 If the test results are incorrect, replace the air control valve.

Replacement

81 Remove the mounting screws and detach the valve and gasket.

82 Installation of the valve is the reverse of removal.

14 Exhaust system servicing - general information

> *Warning: Inspection and repair of exhaust system components should be done only after the system components have cooled completely.*

1 The exhaust system consists of the exhaust manifold, catalytic converter, the muffler, the tailpipe and all connecting pipes, brackets, hangers and clamps. The exhaust system is attached to the body with mounting brackets and rubber hangers **(see illustration over-leaf)**. If any of these parts are damaged or deteriorated, excessive noise and vibration will be transmitted to the body.

2 Conducting regular inspections of the exhaust system will keep it safe and quiet. Look for any damaged or bent parts, open seams, holes, loose connections, excessive corrosion or other defects which could allow exhaust fumes to enter the vehicle. Deteriorated exhaust system components should not be repaired - they should be replaced with new parts.

3 If the exhaust system components are extremely corroded or rusted together, they will probably have to be cut from the exhaust system. The convenient way to accomplish this is to have a muffler repair workworkshop remove the corroded sections with a cutting torch. If, however, you want to save money by doing it yourself and you don't have an oxy/acetylene welding outfit with a cutting torch, simply cut off the old components with a hack-saw. If you have compressed air, special pneumatic cutting chisels can also be used. If you do decide to tackle the job at home, be sure to wear eye protection to protect your eyes from metal chips and work gloves to protect your hands.

4 Here are some simple guidelines to apply when repairing the exhaust system:
  a) *Work from the back to the front when removing exhaust system components.*
  b) *Apply penetrating oil to the exhaust system component fasteners to make them easier to remove.*
  c) *Use new gaskets, hangers and clamps when installing exhaust system components.*
  d) *Apply anti-seize compound to the threads of all exhaust system fasteners during reassembly.*
  e) *Be sure to allow sufficient clearance between newly installed parts and all points on the underbody to avoid overheating the floor pan and possibly damaging the interior carpet and insulation. Pay particularly close attention to the catalytic converter and its heat shield.*

> *Warning: The catalytic converter operates at very high temperatures and takes a long time to cool. Wait until it's completely cool before attempting to remove the converter. Failure to do so could result in serious burns.*

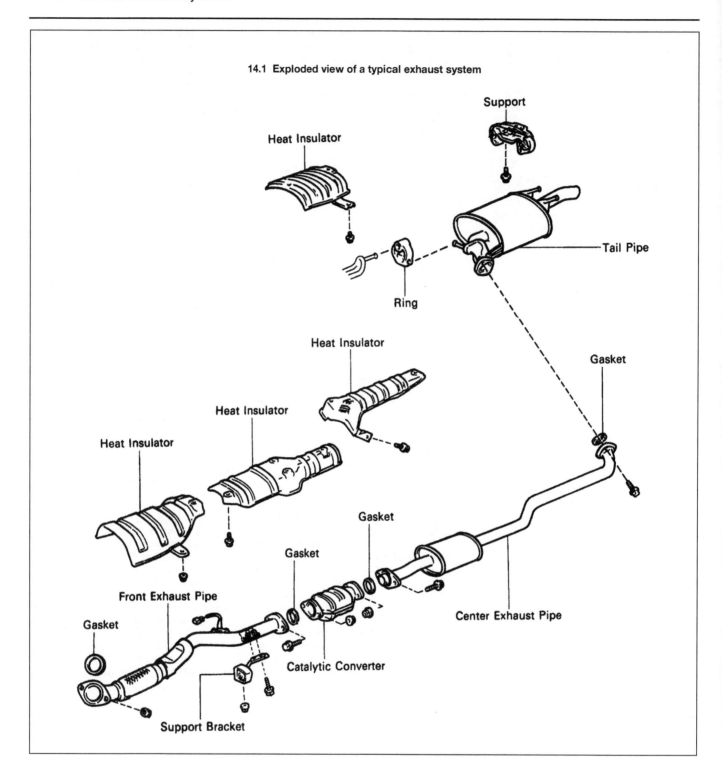

14.1 Exploded view of a typical exhaust system

Chapter 5
Engine electrical systems

Contents

Degrees of difficulty

| Easy, suitable for novice with little experience | | Fairly easy, suitable for beginner with some experience | | Fairly difficult, suitable for competent DIY mechanic | | Difficult, suitable for experienced DIY mechanic | | Very difficult, suitable for expert DIY or professional | |

Specifications

Ignition timing (all models)
With test terminals TE1 and E1 earthed .... 10-degrees BTDC
Without test terminals TE1 and E1 earthed
   4E-FE engines .... 6 to 18-degrees BTDC
   4A-FE and 7A-FE engines .... 5 to 15-degrees BTDC

Ignition coil resistance (cold)
Distributors with internal igniters
   Primary resistance .... 1.11 to 1.75 ohms
   Secondary resistance .... 9.0 to 15.7k ohms
Distributors with external igniters
   Primary resistance .... 0.36 to 0.55 ohms
   Secondary resistance .... 9.0 to 15.4k ohms

Distributor
Air gap .... 0.008 to 0.016 inch
Pick-up coil resistance
  Distributors with internal igniters
    Cold (below 103-degrees F)
      G+ to G- terminals .... 185 to 275 ohms
      NE+ to NE- terminals .... 370 to 550 ohms
    Hot (above 104-degrees F)
      G+ to G- terminals .... 240 to 325 ohms
      NE+ to NE- terminals .... 475 to 650 ohms
  Distributors with external igniters
    Cold (below 103-degrees F)
      G+ to G- terminals .... 185 to 275 ohms
      NE+ to NE- terminals .... 1,630 to 2,740 ohms
    Hot (above 104-degrees F)
      G+ to G- terminals .... 240 to 325 ohms
      NE+ to NE- terminals .... 2,065 to 3,225 ohms

Charging system

Charging voltage	13.9 to 15.1 volts
Standard amperage	
All lights and accessories turned off	Less than 10 amps
Headlights (hi-beam) and heater blower motor turned on	30 amps or more
Alternator brush length	
Standard	13/32-inch
Minimum	1/16-inch

1 General information

The engine electrical systems include all ignition, charging and starting components. Because of their engine related functions, these components are discussed separately from chassis electrical devices such as the lights, the instruments, etc. (which are included in Chapter 12).

Always observe the following precautions when working on the electrical systems:

a) *Be extremely careful when servicing engine electrical components. They are easily damaged if checked, connected or handled improperly.*

b) *Never leave the ignition switch on for long periods of time (10 minutes maximum) with the engine off.*

c) *Don't disconnect the battery cables while the engine is running.*

d) *Maintain correct polarity when connecting a battery cable from another vehicle during jump starting.*

e) *Always disconnect the negative cable first and hook it up last or the battery may be shorted by the tool being used to loosen the cable clamps.*

It's also a good idea to review the safety-related information regarding the engine electrical systems located in the Safety first section near the front of this manual before beginning any operation included in this Chapter.

2 Battery - emergency jump starting

Refer to the *Jump starting* procedure at the front of this manual.

3 Battery - removal and installation

Removal

1 Starting with the negative battery cable **(see illustration)**, disconnect both cables from the battery terminals.

Caution: If the stereo in your vehicle is equipped with an anti-theft system, make sure you have the correct activation code before disconnecting the battery.

2 Remove the battery hold-down clamp.

3 Lift out the battery. Be careful, it's heavy.

4 While the battery is out, inspect the carrier (tray) for corrosion.

5 If you are replacing the battery, make sure that you get one that's identical, with the same dimensions, amperage rating, cold cranking rating, etc. as the original.

Installation

6 Installation is the reverse of removal.

4 Battery cables - check and replacement

Caution: If the stereo in your vehicle is equipped with an anti-theft system, make sure you have the correct activation code before disconnecting the battery.

Check

1 Periodically inspect the entyre length of each battery cable for damage, cracked or burned insulation and corrosion. Poor battery cable connections can cause starting problems and decreased engine performance.

2 Check the cable-to-terminal connections at the ends of the cables for cracks, loose wire strands and corrosion. The presence of white, fluffy deposits under the insulation at the cable terminal connection is a sign that the cable is corroded and should be replaced. Check the terminals for distortion, missing mounting bolts and corrosion.

3 When removing the cables, always disconnect the negative cable first and hook it up last or the battery may be shorted by the tool used to loosen the cable clamps. Even if only the positive cable is being replaced, be

3.1 To remove the battery, detach the negative battery cable first, then the positive cable, remove the hold-down strap nut and bolt (arrows) and remove the hold-down strap

sure to disconnect the negative cable from the battery first (see Chapter 1 for further information regarding battery cable removal).

Replacement

4 Disconnect the old cables from the battery, then trace each of them to their opposite ends and detach them from the starter solenoid and earth terminals. Note the routing of each cable to ensure correct installation.

5 If you are replacing either or both of the old cables, take them with you when buying new cables. It is vitally important that you replace the cables with identical parts. Cables have characteristics that make them easy to identify: positive cables are usually red, larger in cross-section and have a larger diameter battery post clamp; earth cables are usually black, smaller in cross-section and have a slightly smaller diameter clamp for the negative post.

6 Clean the threads of the solenoid or earth connection with a wire brush to remove rust and corrosion.

> **HAYNES HINT** *Apply a light coat of battery terminal corrosion inhibitor, or petroleum jelly, to the threads to prevent future corrosion.*

7 Attach the cable to the solenoid or earth connection and tighten the mounting nut/bolt securely.

8 Before connecting a new cable to the battery, make sure that it reaches the battery post without having to be stretched.

9 Connect the positive cable first, followed by the negative cable.

5 Ignition system - general information and precautions

General information

1 There are two types of ignition systems equipped on the models covered by this manual - the external igniter system or the internal igniter system. On the latter ignition system, the igniter is located within the distributor housing. On both systems the ignition coil is mounted inside the distributor.

2 The electronic ignition system includes the ignition switch, the battery, the igniter, the pick-up coil, the ignition coil, the primary (low voltage) and secondary (high voltage) wiring circuits, the distributor and the spark plugs. The ignition system is controlled by the

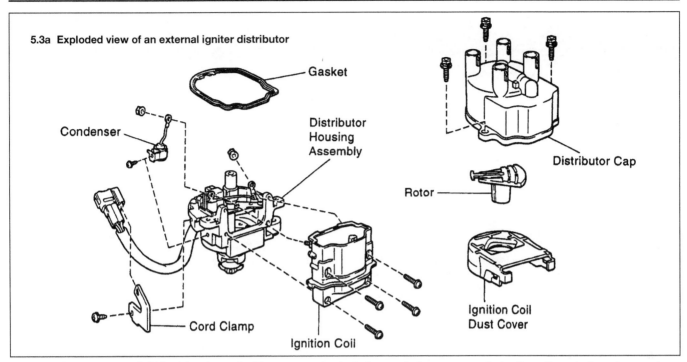

5.3a Exploded view of an external igniter distributor

Electronic Control Module (ECM). Using data provided by information sensors which monitor various engine functions (such as rpm, intake air volume, engine temperature, etc.), the ECM ensures a perfectly timed spark under all conditions. This system is known as Electronic Spark Advance (ESA).

3 The breakerless ignition systems are divided into two groups; external igniter distributors and internal igniter distributors **(see illustrations)**. When diagnosing these units, be sure to make all the necessary ignition system checks before replacing any components, as they are expensive and usually non-returnable.

Precautions

4 When working on the ignition system, take the following precautions:

a) *Do not keep the ignition switch on for more than 10 seconds if the engine will not start.*

b) *Always connect a tachometer in accordance with the manufacturer's instructions. Some tachometers may be incompatible with this ignition system. Consult a dealer service department before buying a tachometer for use with this vehicle.*

c) *Never allow the ignition coil terminals to touch earth. Earthing the coil could result in damage to the igniter and/or the ignition coil.*

d) *Do not disconnect the battery when the engine is running.*

e) *Make sure the igniter is properly earthed.*

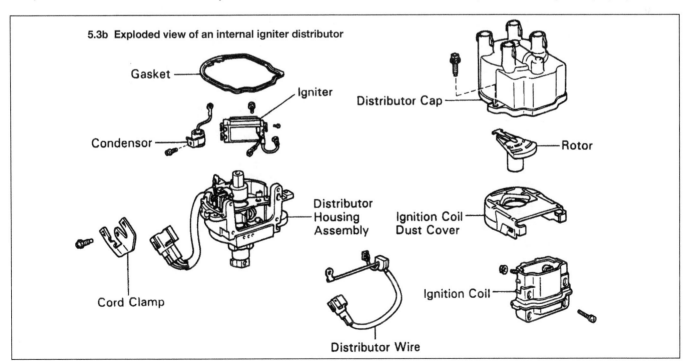

5.3b Exploded view of an internal igniter distributor

6.1 To use a calibrated ignition tester (available at most auto parts stores), remove an ignition wire from a cylinder, connect the spark plug boot to the tester and clip the tester to a good ground - if there is enough voltage to fire the plug, sparks will be clearly visible between the electrode tip and the tester body as the engine is turned over

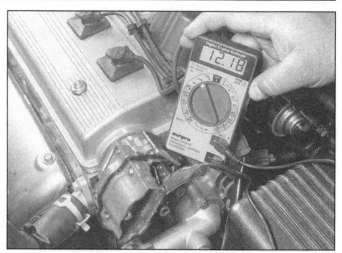

6.7 Check for battery voltage to the positive side (+) of the ignition coil

6 Ignition system - check

⚠️ **Warning: Because of the high voltage generated by the ignition system, extreme care should be taken whenever an operation is performed involving ignition components. This not only includes the igniter, coil, distributor and spark plug wires, but related components such as plug connectors, tachometer and other test equipment also.**

1 If the engine turns over but won't start, disconnect the spark plug wire from any spark plug and attach it to a calibrated tester (available at most auto parts stores) **(see illustration)**. Connect the clip on the tester to a bolt or metal bracket on the engine. If you're unable to obtain a calibrated ignition tester,

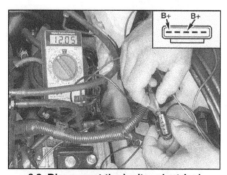

6.9 Disconnect the igniter electrical connector and with the ignition key ON (engine not running), check for battery voltage to the igniter (external igniter shown - on models with an internal igniter, check for voltage on the brown wire to the igniter)

remove the wire from one of the spark plugs and using an insulated tool, pull back the boot and hold the end of the wire about 1/4-inch from a good earth.

2 Crank the engine and watch the end of the tester or spark plug wire to see if a bright blue, well-defined sparks occur.

3 If sparks occur, sufficient voltage is reaching the plug to fire it (repeat the check at the remaining plug wires to verify that the distributor cap and rotor are OK). However, the plugs themselves may be fouled, so remove and check them as described in Chapter 1.

4 If no sparks or intermittent sparks occur, remove the distributor cap and check the cap and rotor as described in Chapter 1. If moisture is present, dry out the cap and rotor, then reinstall the cap and repeat the spark test.

5 If there's still no spark, detach the coil secondary wire from the distributor cap and hook it up to the tester (reattach the plug wire to the spark plug), then repeat the spark check. Again, if you don't have a tester, hold the end of the wire about 1/4-inch from a good earth.

6 If sparks now occur, the distributor cap, rotor or plug wire(s) may be defective.

7 If no sparks occur, check the primary wire connections at the coil to make sure they're clean and tight. Check for voltage to the coil on the primary circuit from the ignition switch **(see illustration)**. Check the ignition coil (see Section 7) and the distributor pick-up coil (see Section 11). Make any necessary repairs, then repeat the check again.

8 If there's still no spark, the coil-to-cap wire may be bad (check the resistance with an ohmmeter and compare it to the spark plug wire resistance Specifications found in Chapter 1). If a known good wire doesn't

make any difference in the test results, the igniter may be defective.

9 Check for battery voltage to the igniter **(see illustration)** with the ignition key ON, engine not running. If voltage is available and there is still no spark, replace the igniter (see Section 10).

7 Ignition coil - check and replacement

Caution: If the stereo in your vehicle is equipped with an anti-theft system, make sure you have the correct activation code before disconnecting the battery.

Check

1 Detach the cable from the negative terminal of the battery (see the **Caution** above).

2 Remove the plastic shield from the coil **(see illustration)**.

3 Remove the mounting bolts from the coil electrical connectors and install the ohmmeter probes.

7.2 Carefully pry the plastic shield at the locking tab to release it from the ignition coil

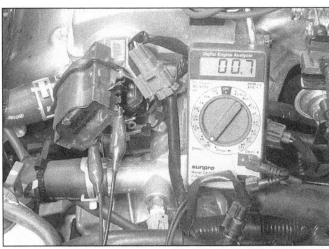

7.4a To check the primary resistance of the coil, measure the resistance between the positive and the negative terminals

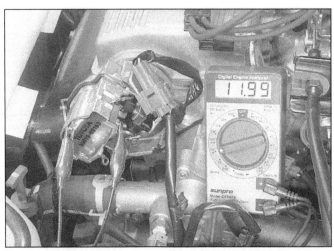

7.4b To check the secondary resistance of the coil, measure the resistance between the positive terminal and the high tension terminal

4 Using an ohmmeter:

a) *Measure the resistance between the positive and negative terminals of the coil* **(see illustration)**. *Compare your reading with the specified coil primary resistance listed in this Chapter's Specifications.*

b) *Measure the resistance between the positive terminal and the high tension terminal* **(see illustration)**. *Compare your reading with the specified coil secondary resistance listed in this Chapter's Specifications.*

5 If either of the above tests yield resistance values outside the specified amount, replace the coil.

Replacement

6 Detach the cable from the negative terminal of the battery (see the **Caution** above).

7 Remove the heat shield from the coil.

8 Label and disconnect the wires from the coil terminals.

9 Remove the coil mounting screws **(see illustration)**.

10 Installation is the reverse of removal.

---

8 Distributor - removal and installation

Removal

1 Detach the cable from the negative battery terminal.

Caution: If the stereo in your vehicle is equipped with an anti-theft system, make sure you have the correct activation code before disconnecting the battery.

2 Disconnect the electrical connectors from the distributor.

3 Look for a raised "1" on the distributor cap. This marks the location for the number one cylinder spark plug wire terminal. If the cap does not have a mark for the number one terminal, locate the number one spark plug and trace the wire back to the terminal on the cap.

4 Remove the distributor cap (see Chapter 1) and turn the engine over until the rotor is pointing toward the number one spark plug terminal (see locating TDC procedure in Chapter 2A).

5 Make a mark on the edge of the distributor base directly below the rotor tip and in line with it. Also, mark the distributor base and the engine block to ensure that the distributor is installed correctly **(see illustration)**.

7.9 Remove the retaining screws (arrows) and lift the coil from the distributor housing

8.5 Paint or scribe a mark (arrow) on the edge of the distributor housing immediately below the rotor tip to ensure that the rotor is pointing in the same direction when the distributor is reinstalled. Also, paint or scribe another mark across the cylinder head and the distributor body (arrow) to ensure that the distributor is aligned correctly when it is reinstalled

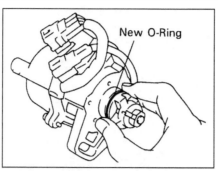

8.7 Remove the hold-down bolt from the distributor body and pull the distributor straight out

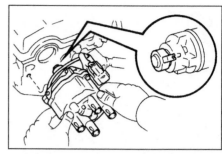

8.8 Install a new O-ring in to the groove in the distributor housing

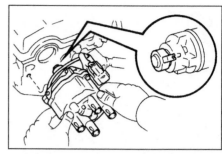

8.9 If you have set the engine at TDC compression for number one cylinder, align the cut-out portion of the coupling with the groove in the distributor housing

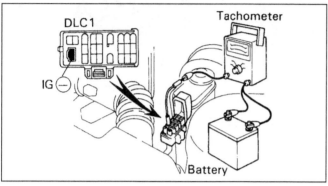

9.1 Connect the tachometer lead to the IG terminal of the test connector

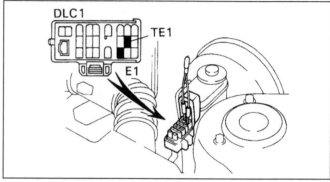

9.2 Attach a jumper wire between terminals E1 and TE1 of the test connector

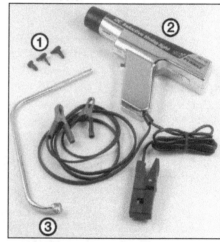

9.3 Tools needed to check and adjust the ignition timing

6 If equipped with collar bolts, loosen but do not remove the two bolts in the distributor collar. This will give the distributor shaft clearance.

7 Remove the distributor hold-down bolt **(see illustration)**, then pull the distributor straight out to remove it.

Caution: DO NOT turn the crankshaft while the distributor is out of the engine, or the alignment marks will be useless.

Installation

Note: *If the crankshaft has been moved while the distributor is out, locate Top Dead Centre (TDC) for the number one piston (see Chapter 2A) and position the distributor and the rotor accordingly.*

8 Install a new O-ring onto the distributor housing **(see illustration)**.

9 Align the cut-out portion of the coupling with the groove in the housing **(see illustration)**.

10 Insert the distributor into the engine in exactly the same relationship to the block that it was in when removed.

11 If the distributor does not seat completely, recheck the alignment marks between the distributor base and the block to verify that the distributor is in the same position it was in before removal. Also check the rotor to see if it's aligned with the mark you made on the edge of the distributor base.

12 Loosely install the distributor hold-down bolt(s).

13 Installation is the reverse of removal.

14 Check the ignition timing (see Section 9) and tighten the distributor hold-down bolt securely.

9 Ignition timing - check and adjustment

Note: *The following ignition timing procedure applies to most models covered by this manual. However, if the procedure specified on the VECI label of your vehicle differs from this one, use the procedure found on the VECI label.*

1 Connect a tachometer according to the manufacturer's specifications **(see illustration)**.

2 Locate the diagnostic connector and insert a jumper wire between terminals E1 and TE1 **(see illustration)**.

3 With the ignition switch off, connect a timing light according to the manufacturer's specifications **(see illustration)**. Most timing lights are powered by the battery. Also, an inductive style pick-up is installed onto the number one cylinder spark plug wire.

4 Locate the timing marks on the front cover and the crankshaft pulley.

1 *Vacuum plugs - Vacuum hoses will, in most cases, have to be disconnected and plugged. Molded plugs in various shapes and sizes are available for this*

2 *Inductive pick-up timing light - Flashes a bright, concentrated beam of light when the number one spark plug fires. Connect the leads according to the instructions supplied with the light*

3 *Distributor wrench - On some models, the hold-down bolt for the distributor is difficult to reach and turn with conventional wrenches or sockets. A special wrench like this must be used*

5 Start the engine and allow it to warm up to normal operating temperature (upper radiator hose hot). Verify that the engine idle is correct (see Chapter 4 Specifications). Aim the timing light at the timing scale on the front cover **(see illustration)**. The mark on the crankshaft pulley should line up with the 10-degree mark on the scale. If necessary, loosen the distributor hold-down bolt and slowly rotate the distributor until the timing marks align. Tighten the hold-down bolt and recheck the timing.

6 Remove the jumper wire from the diagnostic connector and confirm that the ignition timing advances in accordance with the figures listed in this Chapter's Specifications.

7 Turn the engine off and remove the tachometer and the timing light.

10 Igniter - replacement

1 Detach the cable from the negative terminal of the battery.

Caution: If the stereo in your vehicle is equipped with an anti-theft system, make sure you have the correct activation code before disconnecting the battery.

Externally mounted igniter

2 Disconnect the electrical connector from the igniter.

3 Remove the screws from the bracket assembly and pull the igniter/bracket assembly out of the engine compartment **(see illustration)**.

4 Installation is the reverse of removal.

Internally mounted igniter

5 Remove the ignition coil from the distributor (see Section 7).

9.5 Point the timing light at the timing marks with the engine at idle

6 Disconnect the electrical connector from the igniter.

7 Remove the screws from the igniter assembly and pull the igniter/bracket assembly out of the engine compartment **(see illustration 5.3b)**.

8 Installation is the reverse of removal.

11 Pick-up coil - check and replacement

Pick-up coil check

1 Disconnect the electrical connector at the distributor and using an ohmmeter, measure the resistance between the pick-up coil terminals **(see illustration)**.

2 Compare the measurements to those listed in this Chapter's Specifications. If the resistance is not as specified, replace the pick-up coil.

Air gap check

3 Detach the cable from the negative terminal of the battery.

10.3 Remove the igniter screws (arrows) and lift the igniter from the engine compartment

Caution: If the stereo in your vehicle is equipped with an anti-theft system, make sure you have the correct activation code before disconnecting the battery.

4 Remove the distributor from the engine (see Section 8).

5 Using a brass feeler gauge, measure the gap between the signal rotor and the pick-up coil projection **(see illustration)**. Compare your measurement to the air gap listed in this Chapter's Specifications. If the air gap is not as specified, replace the distributor, as the air gap is not adjustable. Excessive air gap is usually a sign of wear in the distributor shaft bushing.

Replacement

6 Detach the cable from the negative terminal of the battery.

Caution: If the stereo in your vehicle is equipped with an anti-theft system, make sure you have the correct activation code before disconnecting the battery.

7 Remove the distributor from the engine (see Section 8).

8 Remove the coil from the distributor (see Section 7).

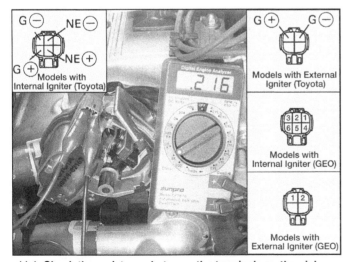
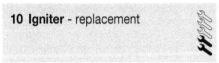

11.1 Check the resistance between the terminals on the pick-up coil indicated in this Chapter's Specifications.

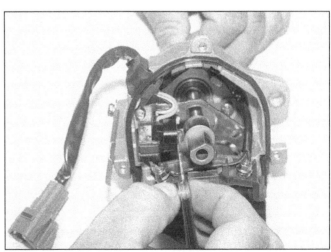

11.5 Measure the air gap between the signal rotor and the pick-up coil projection - if the gap is not within specification, replace the distributor

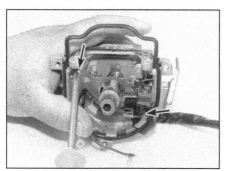

11.9 Remove the pick-up coil setscrews (arrows)

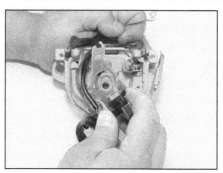

11.10 Lift the pick-up coil from the distributor

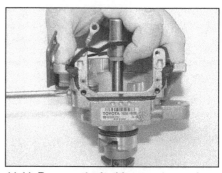

11.11 Remove the ignition condenser from the distributor

9 Remove the set screws that retain the pick-up coil to the distributor **(see illustration)**.
10 Remove the pick-up coil from the distributor **(see illustration)**.
11 Remove the condenser from the distributor **(see illustration)** and replace it.
12 Installation is the reverse of removal.

12 Charging system - general information and precautions

General information

The charging system includes the alternator, an internal voltage regulator, a charge indicator, the battery, a fusible link and the wiring between all the components **(see illustration)**. The charging system supplies electrical power for the ignition system, the lights, the radio, etc. The alternator is driven by a drivebelt at the front of the engine.

These models are equipped with either a Nippondenso or a Delco alternator.

The purpose of the voltage regulator is to limit the alternator's voltage to a preset value. This prevents power surges, circuit overloads, etc., during peak voltage output.

The fusible link is a short length of insulated wire integral with the engine compartment wiring harness **(see illustration)**. The link is several wire gauges smaller in diameter than the circuit it protects. See Chapter 12 for additional information regarding fusible links.

The charging system doesn't ordinarily require periodic maintenance. However, the drivebelt, battery and wires and connections should be inspected at the intervals outlined in Chapter 1.

The dashboard warning light should come on when the ignition key is turned to Start, then should go off immediately. If it remains on, there is a malfunction in the charging system. Some vehicles are also equipped with a voltage gauge. If the voltage gauge indicates abnormally high or low voltage, check the charging system (see Section 13).

Precautions

Be very careful when making electrical circuit connections to a vehicle equipped with an alternator and note the following:

a) *When reconnecting wires to the alternator from the battery, be sure to note the polarity.*

b) *Before using arc welding equipment to repair any part of the vehicle, disconnect the wires from the alternator and the battery terminals.*

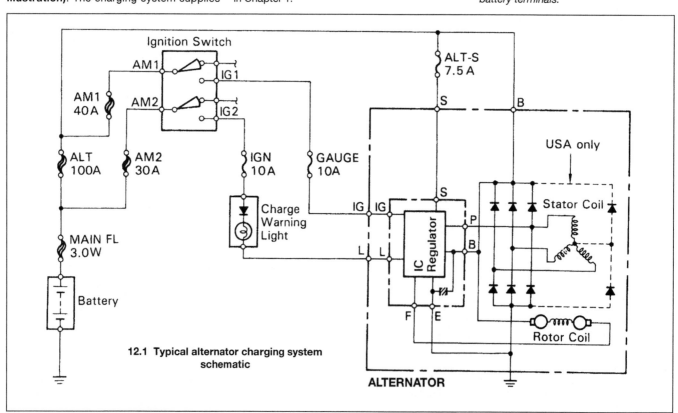

12.1 Typical alternator charging system schematic

IGN Fuse (10A)

GAUGE Fuse (10A)

Generator

ALT-S Fuse (7.5A)

MAIN FUSIBLE LINK (3.0W)

ALT H-Fuse (100A)

AM2 H-Fuse (30A)

AM1 H-Fuse (40A)

12.4 Typical charging system fuses and fusible link

c) *Never start the engine with a battery charger connected.*

d) *Always disconnect both battery leads before using a battery charger.*

e) *The alternator is driven by an engine drivebelt which could cause serious injury if your hand, hair or clothes become entangled in it with the engine running.*

f) *Because the alternator is connected directly to the battery, it could arc or cause a fire if overloaded or shorted out.*

g) *Wrap a plastic bag over the alternator and secure it with rubber bands before steam cleaning the engine.*

13 Charging system - check

1 If a malfunction occurs in the charging circuit, don't automatically assume that the alternator is causing the problem. First check the following items:

a) *Check the drivebelt tension and its condition. Replace it if worn or deteriorated.*

b) *Make sure the alternator mounting and adjustment bolts are tight.*

c) *Inspect the alternator wiring harness and the electrical connectors at the alternator and voltage regulator. They must be in good condition and tight.*

d) *Check the fusible link located at the positive battery cable or the large main fuses in the engine compartment. If it's burned, determine the cause, repair the circuit and replace the link or fuse (the vehicle won't start and/or the accessories won't work if the fusible link or fuse blows).*

e) *Check all the fuses that are in series with the charging system circuit* **(see illustration 12.4)**. *The location of these fuses and fusible links may vary from year and model but the designations are the same; main fusible link 3.0W, Alt H fuse (80 or 100 amp), AM1 (40 amp), AM2 (30 amp), IG (10 amp), Gauge 10A, and ALT-S (7.5 amp).*

f) *Start the engine and check the alternator for abnormal noises (a shrieking or squealing sound indicates a bad bushing).*

g) *Check the specific gravity of the battery electrolyte. If it's low, charge the battery (doesn't apply to maintenance free batteries).*

h) *Make sure that the battery is fully charged (one bad cell in a battery can cause overcharging by the alternator).*

i) *Disconnect the battery cables (negative first, then positive).*

Caution: If the stereo in your vehicle is equipped with an anti-theft system, make sure you have the correct activation code before disconnecting the battery. Inspect the battery posts and the cable clamps for corrosion. Clean them thoroughly if necessary (see Section 4 and Chapter 1). Reconnect the positive cable, then the negative cable.

2 Using a voltmeter, check the battery voltage with the engine off. It should be approximately 12 volts.

3 Start the engine and check the battery voltage again. It should now be approximately 13.5 to 15.1 volts.

4 Turn on the headlights. The voltage should drop and then come back up, if the charging system is working properly.

5 If the voltage reading is greater than the specified charging voltage, replace the voltage regulator (see Section 15).

6 If the voltmeter reading is less than standard voltage, check the regulator and alternator as follows.

7 Remove the rear cover from the alternator. Earth terminal F **(see illustration)**, start the engine, check the voltage at the battery and compare your reading to the standard voltage.

a) *If the voltmeter reading is greater than standard voltage, replace the regulator.*

b) *If the voltmeter reading is less than standard voltage, check the alternator (or have it checked by a dealer service department if you do not have an ammeter).*

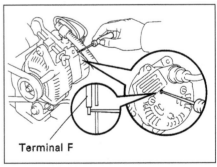

Terminal F

13.7 If the alternator is putting out less than standard voltage, ground terminal F, start the engine and check the voltage at the battery - if the reading is greater than standard voltage, replace the regulator; if the reading is less than standard, check the alternator or have it checked by a dealer service departmentor other qualified repair shop

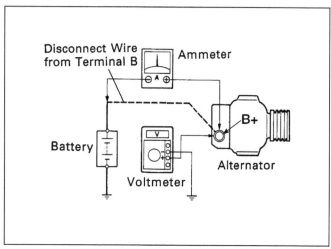

13.8 Hook up an ammeter as shown to check alternator output

14.2 Disconnect the electrical connections from the alternator

8 If you have an ammeter, hook it up to the charging system as shown (**see illustration**). If you don't have an ammeter, you can also use an inductive-type current indicator. This device is inexpensive, readily available at auto parts stores and accurate enough to perform simple amperage checks like the following test.

9 With the engine running at 2000 rpm, check the reading on the ammeter with all accessories and lights off, then again with the high-beam headlights on and the heater blower switch turned to the HI position. Compare your readings to the standard amperage listed in this Chapter's Specifications.

10 If the ammeter reading is less than standard amperage, repair or replace the alternator.

14 Alternator - removal and installation

Removal

1 Detach the cable from the negative terminal of the battery.

Caution: If the stereo in your vehicle is equipped with an anti-theft system, make sure you have the correct activation code before disconnecting the battery.

2 Detach the electrical connectors from the alternator (**see illustration**).

3 Loosen the alternator adjustment, pivot and lock bolts (**see illustration**) and detach the drivebelt.

4 Remove the adjustment and lock bolts from the alternator adjustment bracket.

5 Separate the alternator and bracket from the engine.

6 If you are replacing the alternator, take the old alternator with you when purchasing a replacement unit. Make sure that the new/rebuilt unit is identical to the old alternator. Look at the terminals - they should be the same in number, size and locations as the terminals on the old alternator. Finally, look at the identification markings - they will be stamped in the housing or printed on a tag or plaque affixed to the housing. Make sure that these numbers are the same on both alternators.

7 Many new/rebuilt alternators do not have a pulley installed, so you may have to switch the pulley from the old unit to the new/rebuilt one. When buying an alternator, find out the workshop's policy regarding installation of pulleys - some workshops will perform this service free of charge.

Installation

8 Installation is the reverse of removal.

9 After the alternator is installed, adjust the drivebelt tension (see Chapter 1).

10 Check the charging voltage to verify proper operation of the alternator (see Section 13).

15 Alternator components - check and replacement

Disassembly

1 Remove the alternator (see Section 14) and place it on a clean workbench.

2 Remove the rear cover nuts, the nut and terminal insulator and the rear cover (**see illustrations**).

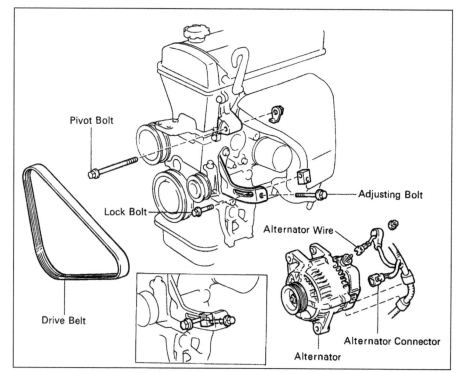

14.3 Alternator installation details

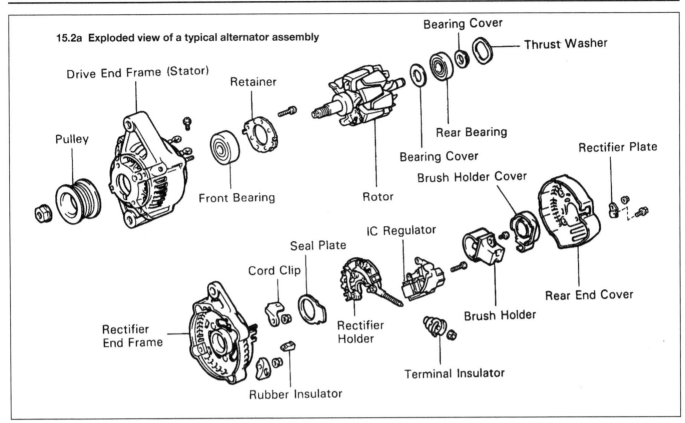

15.2a Exploded view of a typical alternator assembly

3 Remove the five voltage regulator and brush holder mounting screws **(see illustration)**.

15.2b Remove the three nuts from the rear cover

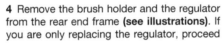

4 Remove the brush holder and the regulator from the rear end frame **(see illustrations)**. If you are only replacing the regulator, proceed

15.2c Take the nut, washer and insulator off terminal B and remove the alternator end cover

15.3 Once the rear cover is removed, remove the five screws (arrows) that retain the voltage regulator and the brush holder

15.4a Remove the brush holder

to Step 8, install the new unit, reassemble the alternator and install it on the engine (see Section 14). If you are going to replace the brushes, proceed with the next Step.
5 Measure the exposed length of each brush **(see illustration)** and compare it to the minimum length listed in this Chapter's Specifications. If the length of either brush is less than the specified minimum, replace the brushes and brush holder assembly. **Note:** *On some models, it may be necessary to solder the new brushes in place.*
6 Make sure that each brush moves smoothly in the brush holder.
7 Remove the rectifier assembly **(see illustration)**. Remove the four rubber insulators and the seal plate.
8 Scribe or paint marks on the front and rear end frame housings of the alternator to facilitate reassembly.

15.4b Remove the regulator

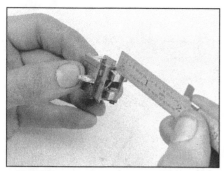

15.5 Measure the exposed length of the brushes and compare your measurements to the specified minimum length to determine if they should be replaced

15.7 Remove the mounting screws (arrows) that retain the rectifier assembly

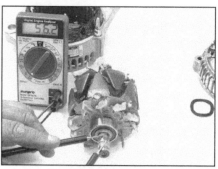

15.12a Continuity should exist between the rotor slip rings

9 Remove the nut retaining the pulley to the rotor shaft and remove the pulley.

10 Remove the four nuts retaining the front and rear end frames together, then separate the rear end frame assembly from the front end frame **(see illustration 15.2)**.

11 Remove the thrust washer and remove the rotor from the front end frame.

Component checks

12 Check for an open between the two slip rings **(see illustration)**. There should be 2 to 4 ohms resistance between the slip rings. Check for earths between each slip ring and the rotor **(see illustration)**. There should be no continuity (infinite resistance) between the rotor and either slip ring. If the rotor fails either test, or if the slip rings are excessively worn, the rotor is defective.

13 Check for opens between each end terminal of the stator windings **(see illustration)**. If either reading is high (infinite resistance), the stator is defective. Check for a earthed stator winding between each stator terminal and the frame. If there's continuity between any stator winding and the frame the stator is defective.

14 Check the positive and negative rectifiers.
a) *First start the checks on the positive diode assembly by touching the positive probe of the ohmmeter onto the diode terminal and the negative probe onto one of the other designated diode terminals* **(see illustration)**. *Then reverse the probes and check again* **(see illustration)**. *The diode should have continuity with the ohmmeter one way and no continuity when the probes are reversed* **(see illustration)**. *Check each of the terminals in this manner. If any of the diodes fail the test, the diode assembly is defective.*
b) *Now, check the negative diode assembly by touching the negative probe of the ohmmeter onto the NEGATIVE TERMINALS* **(see illustration)** *and the other probe onto each rectifier terminal. Reverse the polarity (reverse probes) and check to make sure there is no continuity in one position and continuity in the other position. Check each of the terminals in this manner. If any of the diodes fail the test, the diode assembly is defective.*

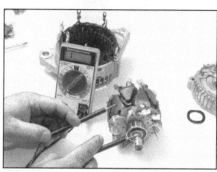

15.12b Check the continuity between the rotor and the slip rings. There should be NO continuity

Reassembly

15 Install the components in the reverse order of removal, noting the following:

16 Install the brush holder by depressing each brush with a small screwdriver to clear the shaft **(see illustration)**.

17 Install the voltage regulator and brush holder screws into the rear frame.

18 Install the rear cover and tighten the three nuts securely.

19 Install the terminal insulator and tighten it with the nut.

20 Install the alternator (see Section 14).

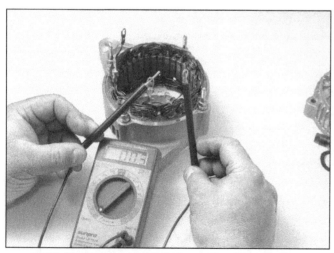

15.13 Check for continuity between the stator windings

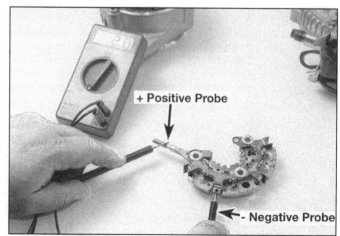

15.14a Position the positive probe of the ohmmeter onto the diode assembly positive post and the negative probe to ground. Continuity should exist

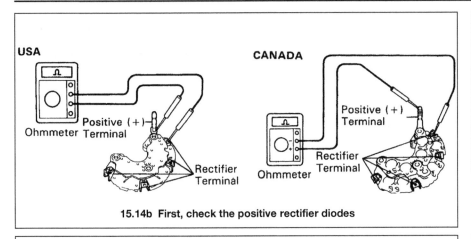

15.14b First, check the positive rectifier diodes

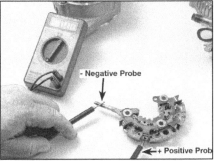

15.14c Switch the polarity of the ohmmeter probes and confirm that now there is NO continuity within the diodes. Check each diode (four total) individually

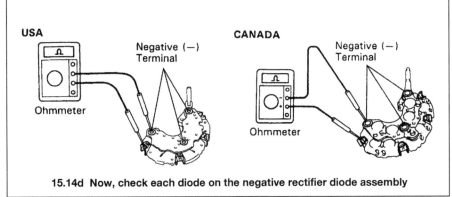

15.14d Now, check each diode on the negative rectifier diode assembly

15.16 To facilitate installation of the brush holder, depress each brush with a small screwdriver to clear the shaft

16 Starting system - general information and precautions

General information

The function of the starting system is to turn over the engine quickly enough to allow it to start.

The system consists of the battery, the starter motor, the starter solenoid and the electrical circuit connecting the components. The solenoid is mounted directly on the starter motor **(see illustration)**.

The solenoid/starter motor assembly is installed on the upper part of the engine, next to the transmission bellhousing.

When the ignition key is turned to the START position, the starter solenoid is actuated through the starter control circuit. The starter solenoid then connects the battery to the starter. The battery supplies the electrical energy to the starter motor, which does the actual work of cranking the engine.

The starter motor on a vehicle equipped with a manual transmission can be operated only when the clutch pedal is depressed; the starter on a vehicle equipped with an automatic transmission can be operated only when the transmission selector lever is in Park or Neutral.

Precautions

Always observe the following precautions when working on the starting system:

a) Excessive cranking of the starter motor can overheat it and cause serious damage. Never operate the starter motor for more than 15 seconds at a time without pausing to allow it to cool for at least two minutes.
b) The starter is connected directly to the battery and could arc or cause a fire if mishandled, overloaded or short circuited.

c) Always detach the cable from the negative terminal of the battery before working on the starting system.

Caution: If the stereo in your vehicle is equipped with an anti-theft system, make sure you have the correct activation code before disconnecting the battery.

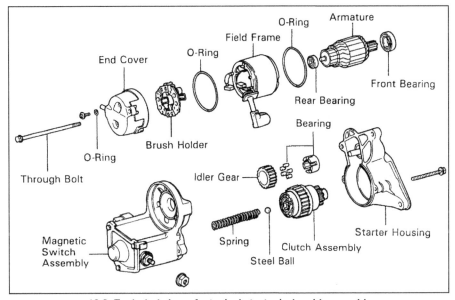

16.2 Exploded view of a typical starter/solenoid assembly

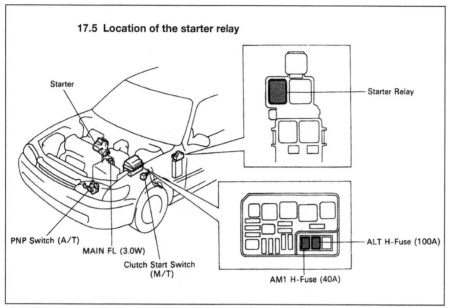

17.5 Location of the starter relay

Starter

Starter Relay

PNP Switch (A/T)

MAIN FL (3.0W)

Clutch Start Switch (M/T)

ALT H-Fuse (100A)

AM1 H-Fuse (40A)

17 Starter motor - testing in vehicle

Note: Before diagnosing starter problems, make sure the battery is fully charged.

1 If the starter motor does not turn at all when the switch is operated, make sure that the shift lever is in Neutral or Park (automatic transmission) or that the clutch pedal is depressed (manual transmission).

2 Make sure that the battery is charged and that all cables, both at the battery and starter solenoid terminals, are clean and secure.

3 If the starter motor spins but the engine is not cranking, the overrunning clutch in the starter motor is slipping and the starter motor must be replaced.

4 If, when the switch is actuated, the starter motor does not operate at all but the solenoid clicks, then the problem lies with either the battery, the main solenoid contacts or the starter motor itself (or the engine is seized).

5 If the solenoid plunger cannot be heard when the switch is actuated, the battery is bad, the fusible link is burned (the circuit is open), the starter relay **(see illustration)** is defective or the starter solenoid itself is defective. **Note:** *Follow the relay testing procedure in Chapter 4, Section 3 to diagnose a defective relay.*

6 To check the solenoid, connect a jumper lead between the battery (+) and the ignition switch terminal (the small terminal) on the solenoid. If the starter motor now operates, the solenoid is OK and the problem is in the ignition switch, Neutral start switch or in the wiring.

7 If the starter motor still does not operate, remove the starter/solenoid assembly for disassembly, testing and repair.

8 If the starter motor cranks the engine at an abnormally slow speed, first make sure that the battery is charged and that all terminal connections are tight. If the engine is partially seized, or has the wrong viscosity oil in it, it will crank slowly.

9 Run the engine until normal operating temperature is reached, then disconnect the coil wire from the distributor cap and earth it on the engine.

10 Connect a voltmeter positive lead to the battery positive post and connect the negative lead to the negative post.

11 Crank the engine and take the voltmeter readings as soon as a steady figure is indicated. Do not allow the starter motor to turn for more than 15 seconds at a time. A reading of nine volts or more, with the starter motor turning at normal cranking speed, is normal. If the reading is nine volts or more but the cranking speed is slow, the motor is faulty. If the reading is less than nine volts and the cranking speed is slow, the solenoid contacts are probably burned, the starter motor is bad, the battery is discharged or there is a bad connection.

18 Starter motor - removal and installation

Note: *The starter/solenoid assembly cannot be repaired using separate components. In the event of failure, exchange the starter/solenoid assembly for a new or rebuilt complete unit.*

Removal

1 Detach the cable from the negative terminal of the battery.

Caution: If the stereo in your vehicle is equipped with an anti-theft system, make sure you have the correct activation code before disconnecting the battery.

2 Remove the battery from the engine compartment.

3 Disconnect and remove the cruise control assembly from the engine compartment (see Chapter 12).

4 Detach the electrical connectors from the starter/solenoid assembly.

5 Remove the starter motor mounting bolts **(see illustration)**.

6 Remove the bracket from the upper section of the starter/solenoid assembly. **Note:** *It is necessary to loosen one or two of the bracket bolts to allow the starter/solenoid assembly to partially drop down to gain access to the remaining bracket assembly bolts and hardware.*

Installation

7 Installation is the reverse of removal.

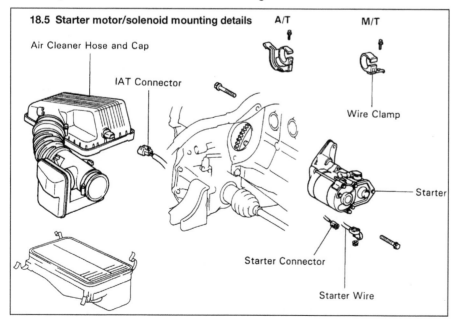

18.5 Starter motor/solenoid mounting details

A/T   M/T

Air Cleaner Hose and Cap

IAT Connector

Wire Clamp

Starter

Starter Connector

Starter Wire

Chapter 6
Emissions and engine control systems

Contents

Degrees of difficulty

Easy, suitable for novice with little experience		**Fairly easy,** suitable for beginner with some experience		**Fairly difficult,** suitable for competent DIY mechanic		**Difficult,** suitable for experienced DIY mechanic		**Very difficult,** suitable for expert DIY or professional	

Specifications

EGR temperature sensor resistance

112-degrees F	69 to 89 k-ohms
212-degrees F	11 to 15 k-ohms
302-degrees F	2 to 4 k-ohms

1 General information

To minimize pollution of the atmosphere from incompletely burned and evaporating gases and to maintain good driveability and fuel economy, a number of emission control systems are used on these vehicles, according to market territory **(see illustrations)**. They include the:

  Positive Crankcase Ventilation (PCV) system
  Evaporative Emission Control (EVAP) system
  Exhaust Gas Recirculation (EGR) system (not UK models)
  Three-way catalytic converter (TWC) system
  Electronic Fuel Injection (EFI) system

The Sections in this Chapter include general descriptions, checking procedures within the scope of the home mechanic and component replacement procedures (when possible) for each of the systems listed above.

Before assuming an emissions control system is malfunctioning, check the fuel and ignition systems carefully (see Chapters 4 and 5). The diagnosis of some emission control devices requires specialized tools, equipment and training. If checking and servicing become too difficult or if a procedure is beyond the scope of your skills, consult your dealer service department or other repair workshop.

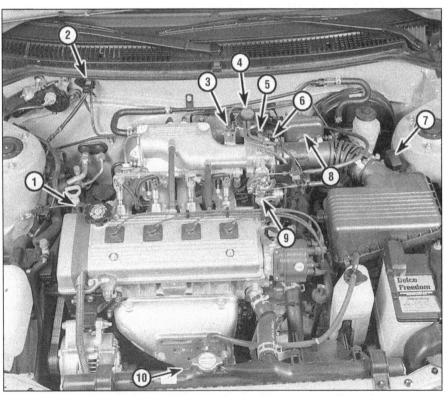

1.1a Emission and engine control components on the 1.8L engine

1 *Crankshaft Position sensor*	4 *EGR vacuum modulator**	8 *Air intake resonator*
2 *MAP sensor*	5 *EGR valve**	9 *IAC valve*
3 *EGR vacuum switching*	6 *Throttle Position Sensor*	10 *Oxygen sensor*
valve*	7 *Test terminal*	* *Not fitted to UK models*

1.1b Locations of the emission and engine control components

Combination Meter

A/C Idle-up VSV

A/C Amplifier

Fuel Pump

Manifold Absolute Pressure Sensor

Throttle Position Sensor

Injector

IIA

Engine Coolant Temp. Sensor

Main Oxygen Sensor*¹

Ignition Switch

Circuit Opening Relay

Engine Control Module

Data Link Connector 1

Idle Air Control Valve

Oxygen Sensor

Park/Neutral Position Switch*²

Intake Air Temp. Sensor

Vehicle Speed Sensor

Sub-Oxygen Sensor*¹

*¹: Applicable only to California specification vehicles.
*²: Applicable only to automatic transaxle vehicles.

This doesn't mean, however, that emission control systems are particularly difficult to maintain and repair. You can quickly and easily perform many checks and do most of the regular maintenance at home with common tune-up and hand tools. **Note:** *The most frequent cause of emissions problems is simply a loose or broken electrical connector or vacuum hose, so always check the electrical connectors and vacuum hoses first.*

Pay close attention to any special precautions outlined in this Chapter. It should be noted that the illustrations of the various systems may not exactly match the system installed on your vehicle because of changes made by the manufacturer during production or from year-to-year.

Models for some markets have a Vehicle Emissions Control Information (VECI) label and a vacuum hose diagram located on the

bonnet **(see illustrations)**. These contain important emissions specifications and setting procedures, and a vacuum hose schematic with emissions components identified. When servicing the engine or emissions systems, on models so equipped, the VECI label in your particular vehicle should always be checked for up-to-date information.

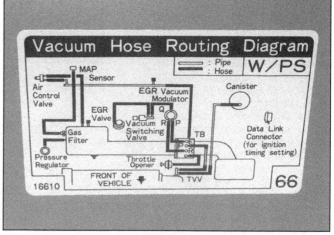

1.6a The Vehicle Emissions Control Information (VECI) label contains such essential information as the types of emission control systems installed on the engine, the idle speed and ignition timing specifications

1.6b The VECI label also contains the vacuum hose routing diagram

2 Electronic control system - general information and ECM removal and installation

General information

1 The fuel injection system is controlled by means of a microcomputer known as the Electronic Control Module (ECM).

2 The ECM receives signals from various sensors which monitor changing engine operating conditions such as intake air volume, intake air temperature, coolant temperature, engine rpm, acceleration/deceleration, exhaust oxygen content, etc. These signals are utilized by the ECM to determine the correct fuel injection duration.

3 The system is analogous to the central nervous system in the human body: The sensors (nerve endings) constantly relay signals to the ECM (brain), which processes the data and, if necessary, sends out a command to change the operating parameters of the engine (body).

4 Here's a specific example of how one portion of this system operates: An oxygen sensor, located in the exhaust manifold, constantly monitors the oxygen content of the exhaust gas. If the percentage of oxygen in the exhaust gas is incorrect, an electrical signal is sent to the ECM. The ECM takes this information, processes it and then sends a command to the fuel injection system telling it to change the air/fuel mixture. This happens in a fraction of a second and it goes on continuously when the engine is running. The end result is an air/fuel mixture ratio which is constantly maintained at a predetermined ratio, regardless of driving conditions.

5 In the event of a sensor malfunction, a backup circuit will take over to provide driveability until the problem is fixed.

Precautions

Warning: These models are equipped with airbags. The airbag is armed and can deploy (inflate) anytime the battery is connected. To prevent accidental deployment (and possible injury), turn the ignition key to LOCK and disconnect the negative battery cable whenever working near airbag components. After the battery is disconnected, wait at least two minutes before beginning work. This system has a back-up capacitor that must fully discharge. For more information, see Chapter 12.

Caution: If the stereo in your vehicle is equipped with an anti-theft system, make sure you have the correct activation code before disconnecting the battery.

6 Follow these steps:
a) *Always disconnect the power by either turning off the ignition switch or disconnecting the battery terminals before unplugging any electrical connectors.*

b) *When installing a battery, be particularly careful to avoid reversing the positive and negative battery cables.*
c) *Do not subject EFI components, emissions-related components or the ECM to severe impact during removal or installation.*
d) *Do not be careless during troubleshooting. Even slight terminal contact can invalidate a testing procedure and damage one of the numerous transistor circuits.*
e) *Never attempt to work on the ECM or open the ECM cover.*
f) *If you are inspecting electronic control system components during rainy weather, make sure that water does not enter any part. When washing the engine compartment, do not spray these parts or their electrical connectors with water.*

ECM removal and installation

7 Disconnect the negative cable from the battery (see Chapter 5).
Caution: If the stereo in your vehicle is equipped with an anti-theft system, make sure you have the correct activation code before disconnecting the battery.
8 Remove the lower finish panel on the passenger side under the glove compartment (see Chapter 11).
9 Remove the centre console from the passenger compartment (see Chapter 11).
10 Disconnect the electrical connectors from the ECM **(see illustration)**. Each connector has a locking tab which must be disengaged before the connector is unplugged.
11 Remove the bolts from the ECM brackets.
12 Lift the ECM from the vehicle.
13 Installation is the reverse of removal.

3 On Board Diagnosis (OBD) system - description and trouble code access

Note: *This procedure does not include the diagnostic codes or the code extracting procedure for 1996 models equipped with the OBD II system. These models require a special SCAN tool to read out the various levels of*

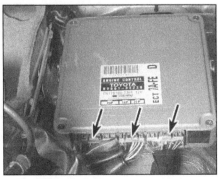

2.10 The ECM is located behind the center console - CAREFULLY disconnect the electrical connectors (arrowed)

coded information. Have the 1996 models diagnosed by a dealer service department or other qualified repair workshop in the event of computer failure.

General information

The ECM contains a built-in self-diagnosis system which detects and identifies malfunctions occurring in the network. When the ECM detects a problem, three things happen: the CHECK ENGINE light comes on, the trouble is identified and a diagnostic code is recorded and stored. The ECM stores the failure code assigned to the specific problem area until the diagnosis system is canceled by removing the EFI fuse with the ignition switch off.

The CHECK ENGINE warning light, which is located on the instrument panel, comes on when the ignition switch is turned to ON and the engine is not running. When the engine is started, the warning light should go out. If the light remains on, the self-diagnosis system has detected a malfunction.

Obtaining diagnostic code output

1 To obtain an output of diagnostic codes, verify first that the battery voltage is above 11 volts, the throttle is fully closed, the transmission is in Neutral, the accessory switches are off and the engine is at normal operating temperature.
2 Turn the ignition switch to ON (engine not running). Do not start the engine.
3 Use a jumper wire to bridge terminals TE1 and E1 of the test connector **(see illustration)**.
Note: *The self-diagnosis system can be accessed by using either test terminal number 1 (engine compartment) or test terminal number 2 (under driver's dash).*
4 Read the diagnosis code as indicated by the number of flashes of the "CHECK ENGINE" light on the dash. Normal system operation is indicated by Code No. 1 (no malfunctions) for all models. The "CHECK

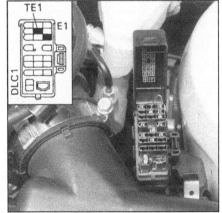

3.3 To access the self diagnosis system, locate the test connector in the engine compartment and using a jumper wire or paper clip, bridge terminals TE1 and E1

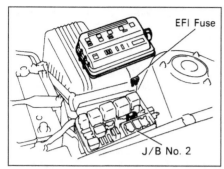

3.7 Typical location of the 15A EFI fuse

ENGINE" light displays a Code No. 1 by blinking once every 0.25 seconds. Each code will be displayed by first blinking the first digit of the code, then pause, and blink the second digit of the code. For example; Code 24 (IAT sensor) will flash two times, pause, and then flash four times. Each flash will be the exact same length but the distinction will be the pause that separates the digits of the code. Only code 1 (normal operation) will flash continuously without a pause.

5 If there are any malfunctions in the system, their corresponding trouble codes are stored in computer memory and the light will blink the requisite number of times for the indicated trouble codes. If there's more than one trouble code in the memory, they'll be displayed in numerical order (from lowest to highest) with a pause between each one. After the code with the largest number of flashes has been displayed, there will be another pause and then the sequence will begin all over again.
Note: *The diagnostic trouble codes 25, 26, 27 and 71 use a special diagnostic capability called "two-trip detection logic". With this system, when a malfunction is first detected, it is temporarily stored into the ECM on the first*

trip. The engine must be turned off and the vehicle taken on another trip to allow the malfunction to be stored permanently in the ECM. This will distinguish a true problem from a false alarm on vehicles with these particular codes entered into the ECM. Normally the self-diagnosis system will detect the malfunctions, but in the event the home mechanic wants to double-check the diagnosis by canceling the codes and rechecking, then it will be necessary to go on two test drives to confirm any malfunctions with these particular codes.

6 To ensure correct interpretation of the flashing "CHECK ENGINE" light, watch carefully for the interval between the end of one code and the beginning of the next; otherwise, you will become confused by the apparent number of flashes and misinterpret the display (the length of this interval varies with the model year).

Cancelling a diagnostic code

7 After the malfunctioning component has been repaired/replaced, the trouble codes stored in computer memory must be canceled. To accomplish this, simply remove the 15A EFI fuse **(see illustration)** for at least 10 seconds with the ignition switch off.

8 A stored code can also be canceled by removing the cable from the negative battery terminal, but other memory systems (such as the clock and radio presets) will also be canceled.
Caution: If the stereo in your vehicle is equipped with an anti-theft system, make sure you have the correct activation code before disconnecting the battery.

9 If the diagnosis code is not canceled, it will be stored by the ECM and appear with any new codes in the event of future trouble.

10 Should it become necessary to work on engine components requiring removal of the battery terminal, always check to see if a diagnostic code has been recorded before disconnecting the battery.

Diagnostic trouble codes

11 Refer to the table on the opposite page.

---

4   Information sensors

Note: *Refer to Chapters 4 and 5 for additional information on the location and the diagnostic procedures for the sensors that are not directly covered in this Section.*

Coolant temperature sensor

General description

1 The coolant temperature sensor is a thermistor (a resistor which varies the value of its voltage output in accordance with temperature changes). As the sensor temperature DECREASES, the resistance values will INCREASE. As the sensor temperature INCREASES, the resistance values will DECREASE **(see illustration)**. A failure in this sensor circuit should set a Code 22. This code indicates a failure in the coolant temperature sensor circuit, so in most cases the appropriate solution to the problem will be either repair of a connector or wire, or replacement of the sensor.

Check

2 To check the sensor, disconnect the electrical connector and measure the resistance across the sensor terminals **(see illustration)**. With the engine completely cold (68-degrees F) the resistance should be 2,000 to 3,000 ohms.

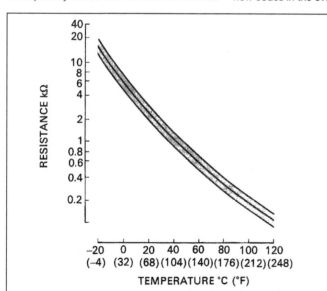

4.1 Compare the indicated resistance values specified on this graph - note that as the temperature increases (as the engine warms up) the resistance decreases

4.2 To check the coolant temperature sensor, use an ohmmeter to measure the resistance between the two sensor terminals

On Board Diagnosyic system - Diagnostic trouble codes

Code	Circuit or system	Diagnosis	Trouble area
1	Normal	The CHECK ENGINE light flashes on and off rapidly when no codes are identified	
12	RPM signal	No rpm signal to the ECM within several seconds after the engine is cranked	Distributor or circuit Crankshaft position sensor or circuit ECM or circuit
13	RPM signal	No rpm signal to the ECM with engine speed above 1,500 rpm	Distributor or circuit Crankshaft position sensor or circuit ECM or circuit
14	Ignition signal	No ignition signal to the ECM	Igniter or circuit Ignition coil Ignition switch or circuit ECM
16	ECM control signal	Problem between the engine controls and transmission controls inside the ECM	ECM
21	Main oxygen sensor	Problem in the main oxygen sensor circuit	Main oxygen sensor or circuit ECM
22	Coolant temperature	Open or short in the coolant temperature sensor circuit	Coolant Temperature sensor or circuit ECM
24	Intake air temperature sensor	Open or short in the intake air temperature sensor circuit	Intake air temperature sensor or circuit ECM
25	Oxygen sensor or circuit	An excessively lean air/fuel ratio has been indicated by the oxygen sensor circuit	Injector or circuit Oxygen sensor or circuit ECM Fuel pressure regulator Coolant temperature sensor or circuit Intake air temperature sensor or circuit Vacuum or exhaust leak Contaminated fuel Ignition system
26	Oxygen sensor or circuit	An overly rich air/fuel ratio has been indicated by the oxygen sensor circuit	Injector or injector circuit Coolant temperature sensor or circuit Oxygen sensor or circuit Intake air temperature sensor or circuit Fuel pressure regulator EVAP system EGR system MAP sensor or circuit ECM Air intake system
27	Sub-oxygen sensor	Open or shorted circuit in the sub-oxygen sensor circuit	Sub-oxygen sensor or circuit ECM
31	MAP sensor	Open or short in MAP sensor circuit	MAP sensor or circuit ECM
41	Throttle position sensor	Open or short in the throttle position sensor circuit	Throttle position sensor or circuit ECM
42	Vehicle speed sensor	No speed signal for 8 seconds when the engine speed is between 3,000 and 5,000 rpm and the transmission is in gear	Vehicle speed sensor or circuit ECM Speedometer Instrument panel printed circuit
43	Starter signal	No starter signal to the ECM until engine speed reaches 800 rpm with the vehicle not moving	Starter signal circuit Ignition switch ECM
51	Switch condition signal	No throttle position signal, gear selector signal or air conditioning signal to the ECM	Air conditioning switch or circuit Air conditioning amplifier Neutral Start switch Throttle Position sensor ECM
52	Knock sensor signal	Open or short circuit in knock sensor circuit	Knock sensor or circuit ECM
71	EGR system	EGR temperature signal is too low	EGR system (EGR valve, hoses, etc.) EGR temperature sensor or circuit EGR vacuum switching valve ECM

4.3 Use a voltmeter and probe the coolant temperature sensor connector for reference voltage with the ignition key ON (engine not running). It should be approximately 5.0 volts

4.13 Insert a pin into the backside of the oxygen sensor connector on the correct terminal and check for a millivolt output signal generated by the sensor

Next, start the engine and warm it up until it reaches operating temperature (180-degrees F) - the resistance should be 200 to 400 ohms. **Note:** *If necessary, remove the sensor and perform the tests in a pan of heated water to simulate the conditions. Compare the resistance values with the accompanying graph.*
3 If the resistance values of the coolant temperature sensor are correct, check the circuit for the proper signal voltage. Turn the ignition key ON (engine not running) and check for reference voltage **(see illustration)**. It should be approximately 5 volts.

Replacement

4 To remove the sensor, depress the locking tabs, unplug the electrical connector, then carefully unscrew the sensor.
Caution: Handle the coolant sensor with care. Damage to this sensor will affect the operation of the entyre fuel injection system.
5 Before installing the new sensor, wrap the threads with Teflon sealing tape to prevent leakage and thread corrosion.
6 Installation is the reverse of removal.

Oxygen sensor

General description

7 These models are equipped with either a single oxygen sensor system or a dual-stage oxygen sensor system. On dual-stage systems, the main oxygen sensor is mounted ahead of the front catalytic converter and monitors the exhaust gases exiting the engine. The sub oxygen sensor monitors the exhaust gases after they have passed through the front catalytic converter. Each oxygen sensor monitors the oxygen content of the exhaust gas stream. The oxygen content in the exhaust reacts with the oxygen sensor to produce a voltage output which varies from 0.1-volt (high oxygen, lean mixture) to 0.9-volts (low oxygen, rich mixture). The ECM constantly monitors this variable voltage

output to determine the ratio of oxygen to fuel in the mixture. The ECM alters the air/fuel mixture ratio by controlling the pulse width (open time) of the fuel injectors. A mixture ratio of 14.7 parts air to 1 part fuel is the ideal mixture ratio for minimizing exhaust emissions, thus allowing the catalytic converter to operate at maximum efficiency. It is this ratio of 14.7 to 1 which the ECM and the oxygen sensor attempt to maintain at all times.
8 The oxygen sensor produces no voltage when it is below its normal operating temperature of about 600-degrees F. During this initial period before warm-up, the ECM operates in open loop mode.
9 If the engine reaches normal operating temperature and/or has been running for two or more minutes, and if the main oxygen sensor is producing a steady signal voltage below 0.70-volts at 1,500 or more rpm, the ECM will set a Code 21. Code 27 will indicate a problem with the sub oxygen sensor.
10 When there is a problem with the oxygen sensor or its circuit, the ECM operates in the open loop mode - that is, it controls fuel delivery in accordance with a programmed default value instead of feedback information from the oxygen sensor.
11 The proper operation of the oxygen sensor depends on four conditions:
a) *Electrical - The low voltages generated by the sensor depend upon good, clean connections which should be checked whenever a malfunction of the sensor is suspected or indicated.*
b) *Outside air supply - The sensor is designed to allow air circulation to the internal portion of the sensor. Whenever the sensor is removed and installed or replaced, make sure the air passages are not restricted.*
c) *Proper operating temperature - The ECM will not react to the sensor signal until the sensor reaches approximately*

600-degrees F. This factor must be taken into consideration when evaluating the performance of the sensor.
d) *Unleaded fuel - The use of unleaded fuel is essential for proper operation of the sensor. Make sure the fuel you are using is of this type.*
12 In addition to observing the above conditions, special care must be taken whenever the sensor is serviced.
a) *The oxygen sensor has a permanently attached pigtail and electrical connector which should not be removed from the sensor. Damage to or removal of the pigtail or electrical connector can adversely affect operation of the sensor.*
b) *Grease, dirt and other contaminants should be kept away from the electrical connector and the louvered end of the sensor.*
c) *Do not use cleaning solvents of any kind on the oxygen sensor.*
d) *Do not drop or roughly handle the sensor.*
e) *The silicone boot must be installed in the correct position to prevent the boot from being melted and to allow the sensor to operate properly.*

Check

13 To check the oxygen sensor use a digital voltmeter to monitor the millivolt signal from the oxygen sensor during actual operating conditions. Locate the oxygen sensor electrical connector and backprobe the black wire on the harness side of the oxygen sensor connector **(see illustration)**. To properly backprobe the connector insert a long straight pin (a T-pin is preferred) alongside the wire until the pin contacts the metal wire terminal inside the connector. Connect the positive probe of a voltmeter onto the pin and the negative probe to ground.
14 Start the engine and monitor the voltage signal (millivolts) of the main oxygen sensor as the engine warms-up. The oxygen sensor will

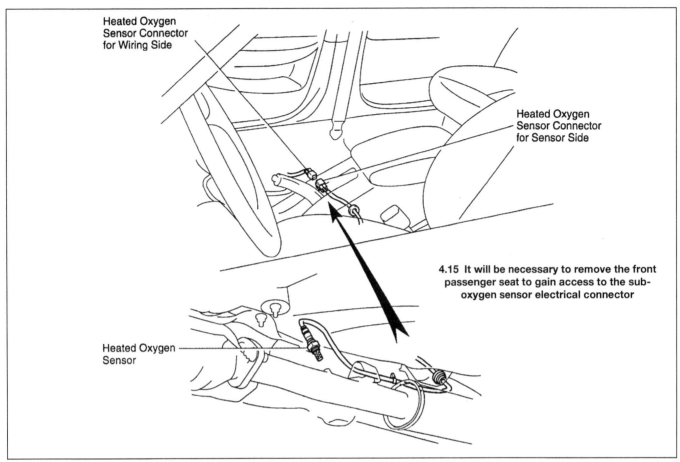

Heated Oxygen
Sensor Connector
for Wiring Side

Heated Oxygen
Sensor Connector
for Sensor Side

4.15 It will be necessary to remove the front passenger seat to gain access to the sub-oxygen sensor electrical connector

Heated Oxygen
Sensor

produce a steady voltage signal at first (open loop) of approximately 0.1 to 0.2 volts with the engine cold. After a period of approximately two minutes, the engine will reach operating temperature and the oxygen sensor voltage will fluctuate between 0.1 to 0.9 volts (closed loop). If the oxygen sensor fails to operate as described, replace it.

15 To check the sub-oxygen sensor, locate the electrical connector **(see illustration)** and

check it in the same manner as the main oxygen sensor.

16 Also check the sub-oxygen sensor heater (if equipped) as follows: Disconnect the oxygen sensor electrical connector and connect an ohmmeter between the +B and HT terminals on the oxygen sensor side of the connector **(see illustration)**. It should measure approximately 11.0 to 17.0 ohms. **Note:** *Not all models are equipped with a*

heated oxygen sensor. Models with heated oxygen sensors will be equipped with a four-wire electrical connector.

17 Check for proper supply voltage to the oxygen sensor heater. With the ignition key ON (engine not running), check for battery voltage at the black/red wire (positive +) and the blue/black wire (negative -) on the harness side of the connector **(see illustration)**.

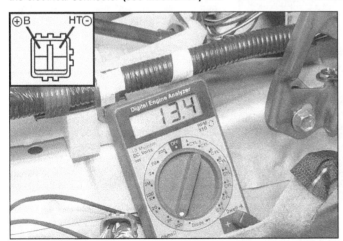

4.16 To test the oxygen sensor heater, disconnect the harness connector and check the resistance across terminals HT and +B of the oxygen sensor connector. It should be between 11 to 17 ohms

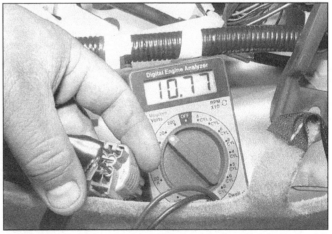

4.17 Check for the voltage to the heater on the black/red wire (+) and the blue/black wire (-). It should be approximately 12 volts (battery voltage)

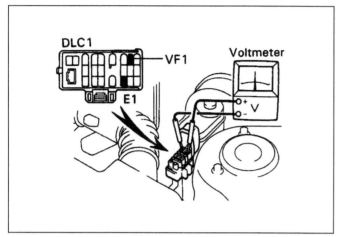

4.18 Connect the probes of the voltmeter to terminals VF1 (+) and E1 (-), raise the engine speed to 2,500 rpm and jump terminals TE1 and E1 with a jumper wire or paper clip

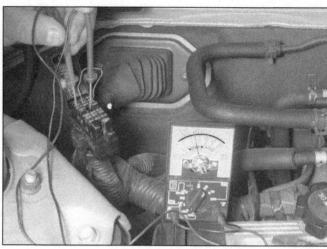

4.19 With terminals TE1 and E1 of the test connector jumpered observe the number of needle sweeps in a 10-second time period

18 On 1993 and 1994 models, it's also possible to check the oxygen sensor in another manner. With the engine completely warmed up and the oxygen sensor connected, connect a voltmeter to the test connector VF1 (positive probe +) and E1 (negative probe -) **(see illustration)**. **Note:** *Use only an analog type voltmeter because it will be necessary to watch the needle fluctuations.*

19 Run the engine at 2,500 rpm for approximately two minutes and then jump terminals TE1 and E1 of the test connector **(see illustration)**. Check the number of times the needle fluctuates in 10 seconds. It should fluctuate eight times or more. If it does not, warm the engine up again and repeat the test.

20 If the voltmeter still does not fluctuate eight times or more, remove the jumper wire from terminals TE1 and E1 of the test connector. Maintain engine speed at 2,500 rpm and measure the voltage between terminals VF1 and E1. If the voltage reading is more than 0 volts, then replace the oxygen sensor with a new part. If the voltage reading is 0 volts, access the self diagnostic codes (see Section 3) and check for any malfunctions.

21 If codes 21, 25 or 26 are obtained, then remove the PCV hose from the valve cover (see Section 8) and measure the voltage between VF1 and E1. If the voltage is 0 volts, replace the oxygen sensor. If the voltage reading is more than 0 volts, repair the over-rich running condition.

22 If codes other than 21, 25 or 26 are obtained, repair the particular sensor or circuit.

Replacement

Note: *Because it is installed in the exhaust manifold or pipe, which contracts when cool, the oxygen sensor may be very difficult to loosen when the engine is cold. Rather than risk damage to the sensor (assuming you are planning to reuse it in another manifold or pipe), start and run the engine for a minute or two, then shut it off. Be careful not to burn yourself during the following procedure.*

23 Disconnect the cable from the negative terminal of the battery.

Caution: If the stereo in your vehicle is equipped with an anti-theft system, make sure you have the correct activation code before disconnecting the battery.

24 Raise the vehicle and place it securely on jackstands.

25 Carefully disconnect the electrical connector from the sensor pigtail lead.

26 Remove the oxygen sensor from the exhaust system **(see illustration)**.

Caution: Excessive force may damage the threads.

Note: *Some oxygen sensors are threaded directly into the exhaust manifold while others are mounted in the exhaust manifold or pipe with two bolts.*

27 Anti-seize compound must be used on the threads of the sensor to facilitate future removal. The threads of new sensors will already be coated with this compound, but if an old sensor is removed and reinstalled, recoat the threads.

28 Install the sensor and tighten it securely.

29 Reconnect the electrical connector of the pigtail lead to the main engine wiring harness.

4.26 Slotted sockets are available for easing oxygen sensor removal

30 Lower the vehicle and reconnect the cable to the negative terminal of the battery.

Throttle Position Sensor (TPS)

General description

31 The Throttle Position Sensor (TPS) is located on the end of the throttle shaft on the throttle body (see Chapter 4). By monitoring the output voltage from the TPS, the ECM can alter fuel delivery based on throttle valve angle (driver demand). A broken or loose TPS can cause intermittent bursts of fuel from the injector and an unstable idle because the ECM thinks the throttle is moving. All the checks and replacement procedures are covered in Chapter 4.

MAP sensor

General Information

32 The MAP sensor monitors the intake manifold pressure changes resulting from changes in engine load and speed and converts the information into a voltage output. The ECM uses the MAP sensor to control fuel delivery and ignition timing. The ECM will receive information as a voltage signal. This signal can be detected using a voltmeter. Under ideal conditions, the voltage will vary from 4.0 volts with the engine off (no vacuum) to 0.5 volts with the engine idling (25 in-Hg vacuum).

Check

33 Turn the ignition On (do not start the engine). Disconnect the electrical connector and check the reference voltage from the MAP sensor on the yellow wire terminal. It should be approximately 5.0 volts **(see illustration)**.

34 Remove the vacuum hose from the MAP sensor and install a hand-held vacuum pump.

35 Reconnect the electrical connector to the MAP sensor. Backprobe the MAP sensor harness connector using straight pins on the light green/red wire (+) positive and brown

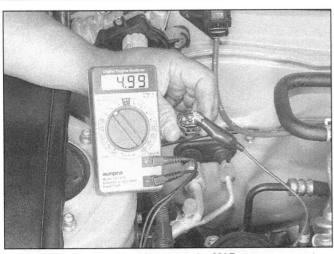

4.33 Check for reference voltage on the MAP sensor connector yellow wire terminal. It should be approximately 5.0 volts

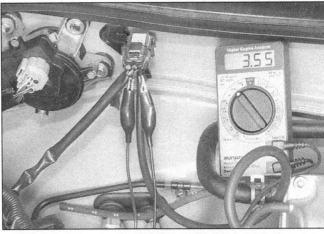

4.35 Install a vacuum pump to the MAP sensor and check for signal voltage on the light green/red (+) wire and brown wire (-) without vacuum applied. It should be approximately 3.0 to 4.0 volts

wire (-) negative **(see illustration)**. Without vacuum, the sensor voltage should be approximately 3.0 to 4.0 volts.

36 Use the hand-held vacuum pump and apply 25 in-Hg of vacuum to the MAP sensor and observe the voltage readings. The voltmeter should read approximately 0.5 to 1.5 volts **(see illustration)**.

37 If the test results are incorrect, replace the MAP sensor.

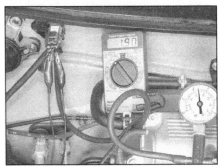

4.36 Now apply vacuum to the MAP sensor an observe that the voltage decreases to approximately 0.5 to 1.5 volts

Intake Air Temperature (IAT) sensor

General description

38 The intake air temperature sensor is located inside the air cleaner housing. This sensor is a resistor which changes value according to the temperature of the air entering the engine. Low temperatures produce a high resistance value (for example, at 68-degrees F the resistance is 2,000 to 3,000 ohms) while high temperatures produce low resistance values (at 176-degrees F the resistance is 200 to 400 ohms **(see illustration)**. The ECM supplies approximately 5-volts (reference voltage) to the air temperature sensor. The IAT sensor alters the voltage according to the temperature of the incoming air. The signal voltage sent back to the ECM will be high when the air temperature is cold and low when the air temperature is warm. Any problems with the air temperature sensor will usually set a code 24.

Check

39 To check the air temperature sensor, disconnect the two prong electrical connector **(see illustration)**. Turn the ignition key ON, but do not start the engine.

40 Measure the voltage (reference voltage) on the yellow/black wire terminal. The VOM should read approximately 5-volts **(see illustration)**.

41 If the reference voltage is not correct, have the ECM diagnosed by a dealer service department or other repair workshop.

42 Measure the resistance across the air temperature sensor terminals **(see illustration)**. The resistance should be HIGH when the air temperature is LOW. Next, start the engine and let it idle. Wait awhile and let the engine reach operating temperature.

4.38 The air intake temperature sensor resistance will DECREASE when the temperature of the air INCREASES

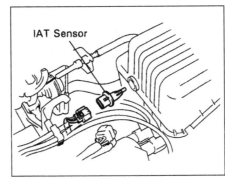

4.39 Location of the IAT sensor

4.40 Check the IAT sensor reference voltage on the yellow/black (+) wire

4.42 Checking the IAT sensor resistance

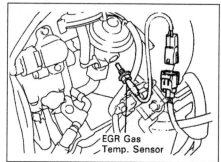

4.44 Disconnect the EGR gas temperature sensor connector and check the resistance of the sensor

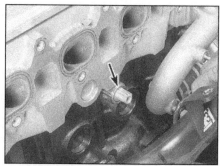

4.50 The knock sensor (arrowed) is located under the intake manifold

Turn the ignition OFF, disconnect the air temperature sensor and measure the resistance across the terminals. The resistance should be LOW when the air temperature is HIGH. If the sensor does not exhibit this change in resistance, replace it.

EGR temperature sensor

General Description

43 The EGR temperature sensor is mounted near the EGR valve. This sensor detects the temperature of the exhaust as it moves through the EGR valve. The information is sent to the ECM and in turn the EGR on/off time is regulated precisely and more efficiently. Any malfunction with the EGR temperature sensor will set a code 71.

Check

44 Disconnect the harness connector for the EGR temperature sensor **(see illustration)** and measure the resistance of the sensor at various temperatures. Refer to the Specifications listed in this Chapter for a list of the temperatures and the resistance values.

Replacement

45 Disconnect the harness connector for the EGR temperature sensor and using an open-end wrench, remove the sensor from the intake manifold.

46 Installation is the reverse of removal.

Vehicle speed sensor

General description

47 The Vehicle Speed Sensor (VSS) is located on the output section of the transmission (see Chapter 7B). The sensor is electronically controlled and sends a pulsing voltage signal to the ECM, which the ECM converts to miles per hour.

48 Any problems with the VSS and its circuit will set a code 42. Have the vehicle speed sensor, circuit and the ECM diagnosed by a dealership service department or other qualified repair workshop.

Knock sensor

General Description

49 Irregular octane levels in modern petrol can cause detonation in an engine. Detonation is sometimes referred to as "spark knock". The knock sensor sends a voltage signal to the ECM when no spark knock is occurring and the ECM provides normal advance. When the knock sensor detects abnormal vibration (spark knock), it turns off the circuit to the ECM, and distributor timing is retarded until the knock is eliminated. Any problems with the knock sensor or sensor circuit will set a code 52.

Check

50 The knock sensor is located on the firewall side of the engine block, under the

intake manifold **(see illustration)**. It will be necessary to remove the air intake plenum (see Chapter 4) and the intake manifold (see Chapter 2A) to gain access to the knock sensor.

51 Using an ohmmeter, check that there is no continuity between the terminal on the knock sensor and the body **(see illustration)**.

52 If continuity exists, replace the sensor.

Crankshaft Position Sensor

General description

53 The crankshaft position sensor is located in the timing belt cover near the crankshaft pulley on certain later models **(see illustration)**. The crankshaft position sensor relays a signal to the ECM to indicate the exact position (angle) of the crankshaft.

Check

54 Using an ohmmeter, measure the resistance of the crankshaft position sensor **(see illustration)**. It should be between 1,630 to 3,225 ohms depending on the temperature; the warmer the temperature of the sensor, the higher the resistance value. If the resistance is not within the specified range, replace the sensor with a new part.

55 To replace the sensor, remove the front pulley (see Chapter 2A), disconnect the electrical connector and remove the bolts from the crankshaft position sensor.

56 Installation is the reverse of removal.

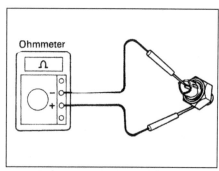

4.51 Check that NO continuity exists on the sensor terminal to the body of the sensor

4.53 Location of the crankshaft sensor near the timing belt cover

4.54 Check the resistance of the crankshaft sensor on the electrical connector

5 Evaporative Emission Control (EVAP) system

General description

1 This system is designed to trap and store fuel that evaporates from the fuel tank, throttle body and intake manifold that would normally enter the atmosphere in the form of hydrocarbon (HC) emissions.
2 The Evaporative Emission Control (EVAP) system consists of a charcoal-filled canister, the lines connecting the canister to the fuel tank, the Temperature Vacuum Valve (TVV) and a check valve **(see illustration)**.

3 Fuel vapors are transferred from the fuel tank and throttle body to a canister where they're stored when the engine isn't running. When the engine is running, the fuel vapors are purged from the canister by intake airflow and consumed in the normal combustion process.
4 The charcoal canister is equipped with a check valve that incorporates three check balls. Depending upon the running conditions and the pressure in the fuel tank, the check balls open and close the passageways to the TVV (consequently the throttle body) and fuel tank.

Check

5 Poor idle, stalling and poor driveability can be caused by an inoperative check valve, a damaged canister, split or cracked hoses or

hoses connected to the wrong fittings. Check the fuel filler cap for a damaged or deformed gasket (see Chapter 1).
6 Evidence of fuel loss or fuel odor can be caused by liquid fuel leaking from fuel lines, a cracked or damaged canister, an inoperative check valve, disconnected, misrouted, kinked, deteriorated or damaged vapor or control hoses.
7 Inspect each hose attached to the canister for kinks, leaks and cracks along its entyre length. Repair or replace as necessary.
8 Look for fuel leaking from the bottom of the canister. If fuel is leaking, replace the canister and check the hoses and hose routing.
9 Inspect the canister. If it's cracked or damaged, replace it.

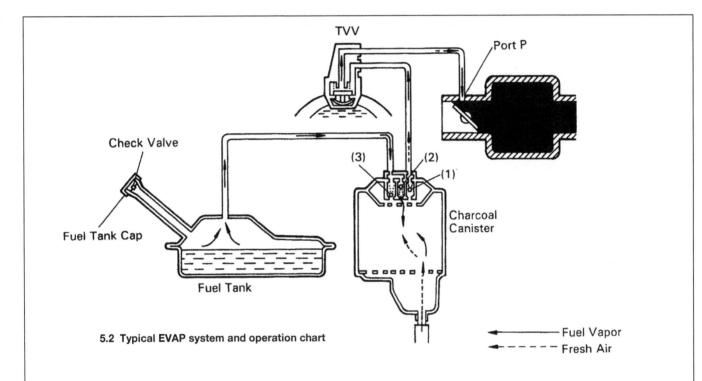

5.2 Typical **EVAP** system and operation chart

ECT	TVV	Throttle Position	Canister Check Valve			Check Valve in Cap	Evaporated Fuel (HC)
			(1)	(2)	(3)		
Below 35°C (95°F)	CLOSED	—	—	—	—	—	HC from tank is absorbed into the canister.
Above 54°C (129°F)	OPEN	Below port P	CLOSED	—	—	—	
		Above port P	OPEN	—	—	—	HC from canister is led into air intake chamber.
High pressure in tank	—	—	—	OPEN	CLOSED	CLOSED	HC from tank is absorbed into the canister.
High vacuum in tank	—	—	—	CLOSED	OPEN	OPEN	Air is led into the fuel tank.

5.10 Apply air pressure into the charcoal canister purge control valve A (inlet) and confirm that the valve allows the air to pass into the charcoal canister

5.11 Apply air pressure to the port A on the TVV (top port) and confirm that air does not pass through the valve when the temperature is below 95-degrees F

10 Check for a clogged filter or a stuck check valve. Using low pressure compressed air, blow into the canister tank pipe **(see illustration)**. Air should flow freely from the other pipes. If a problem is found, replace the canister.

11 Check the operation of the TVV. With the engine completely cold, use a hand-held pump and direct air into port A **(see illustration)**. Air should not pass through the TVV. Now warm the engine to operating temperature (above 129-degrees F) and observe that air passes through the TVV. Replace the valve if the test results are incorrect.

Charcoal canister replacement

12 Clearly label, then detach the vacuum hoses from the canister.
13 Remove the mounting clamp bolts, lower the canister with the bracket, disconnect the hoses from the check valve and remove it from the vehicle.
14 Installation is the reverse of removal.

6.1a Typical EGR system operation chart

To reduce NOx emissions, part of the exhaust gases are recirculated through the EGR valve to the intake manifold to lower the maximum combustion temperature.

ECT	RPM	VSV	Throttle Position	Pressure in the EGR Valve Pressure Chamber		EGR Vacuum Modulator	EGR Valve	Exhaust Gas
Below 47°C (117°F)	—	****	—	—		—	CLOSED	Not recirculated
Above 53°C (127°F)	Below 4,000 rpm	OFF	—	—		—	CLOSED	Not recirculated
		*** ON	Below port E	—		—	CLOSED	Not recirculated
			Between port E and port R	(1) LOW	* Pressure constantly alternating between low and high	OPENS passage to atmosphere	CLOSED	Not recirculated
				(2) HIGH		CLOSES passage to atmosphere	OPEN	Recirculated
			Above port R	(3) HIGH	**	CLOSES passage to atmosphere	OPEN	Recirculated (increase)
	Above 4,400 rpm	(4) OFF	—	—		—	CLOSED	Not recirculated

Remarks:
    * Pressure increase ——▶ Modulator closes ——▶ EGR valve opens ——▶ Pressure drops
                 EGR valve closes ◀—— Modulator opens ◀——

    ** When the throttle valve is positioned above port R, the EGR vacuum modulator will close the atmosphere passage and open the EGR valve to increase the exhaust gas, even if the exhaust pressure is insufficiently low.

    *** VSV switched ON when product of engine speed multiplied by vacuum sensor valve exceeds a specified valve.

    **** If terminals TE1 and E1 of data link connector 1 are connected, the VSV switches ON.

6 Exhaust Gas Recirculation (EGR) system

General description

1 To reduce oxides of nitrogen emissions, some of the exhaust gases are recirculated through the EGR valve to the intake manifold to lower combustion temperatures (see illustrations). The system is only fitted to certain models for use in territories where stringent exhaust emisson regulations are in force.

2 The EGR system consists of the EGR valve, the EGR modulator, vacuum switching valve (VSV), the Electronic Control Module (ECM) and the EGR gas temperature sensor.

Check

EGR valve

3 Start the engine and allow it to idle.
4 Detach the vacuum hose from the EGR valve and attach a hand-held vacuum pump in its place (see illustration).
5 Apply vacuum to the EGR valve. Vacuum should remain steady and the engine should run poorly.

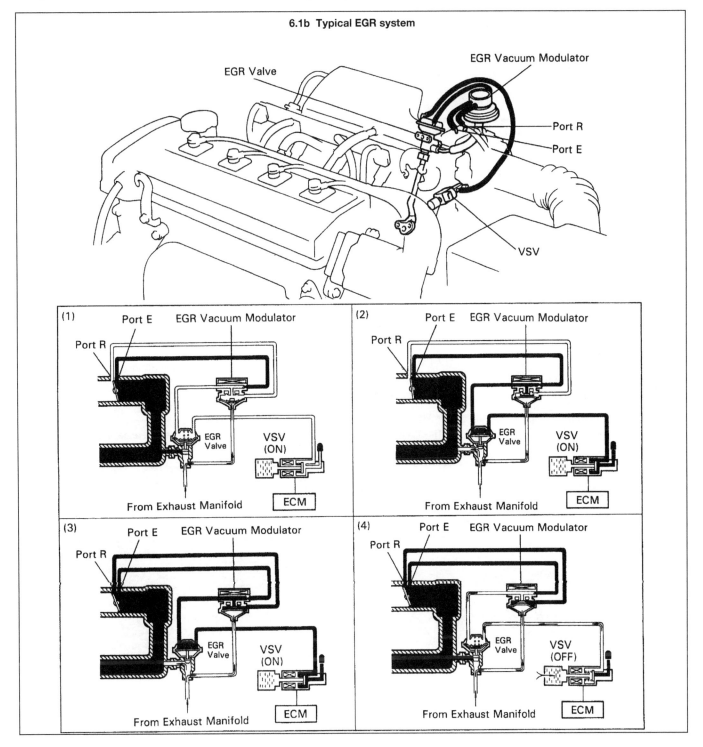

6.1b Typical EGR system

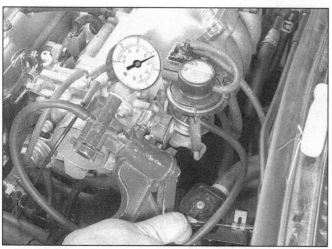

6.4 Apply vacuum to the EGR valve and confirm that the valve opens and allows exhaust gases to circulate. Once it is activated, the EGR valve should hold steady (no loss in vacuum)

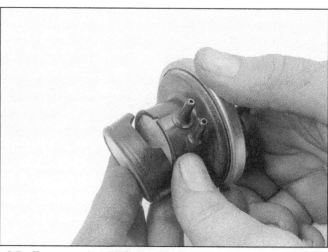

6.7a To remove the EGR vacuum modulator filters for cleaning, remove the cap . . .

a) If the vacuum doesn't remain steady and the engine doesn't run poorly, replace the EGR valve and recheck it.

b) If the vacuum remains steady but the engine doesn't run poorly, remove the EGR valve and check the valve and the intake manifold for blockage. Clean or replace parts as necessary and recheck.

EGR vacuum modulator filter

6 Remove the vacuum modulator.

7 Remove the cover and check the filters (see illustrations).

8 Clean or replace the filters, reinstall the cover and the modulator.

EGR system

9 Disconnect the hose from the EGR valve and install a three-way union and vacuum gauge between the EGR valve and the vacuum modulator (see illustration).

10 Start the engine and connect terminals TE1 and E1 on the test terminal (see illustration 3.3).

a) With the coolant temperature below 117-degrees F (cold), verify that the vacuum gauge indicates zero (no vacuum) at 2,500 rpm.

b) With the engine barely warm, verify that the vacuum gauge indicates low vacuum at 2,500 rpm.

c) With the engine fully warmed up, raise the rpm to 2,500 and confirm the vacuum gauge indicates low vacuum.

11 Check the operation of the VSV.

a) The VSV is located on the intake manifold.

b) Check the resistance of the VSV. It should be between 37 and 44 ohms (see illustration).

c) If the tests are incorrect, replace the VSV with a new part.

Component replacement

EGR valve

12 Disconnect the cable from the negative terminal on the battery.

6.7b . . . then pull out the two filters and blow them out with compressed air - be sure the coarse side of the outer filter faces the atmosphere (out) when reinstalling the filters

13 Remove the air cleaner housing (see Chapter 4).

14 Disconnect the accelerator cable from the throttle body (see Chapter 4).

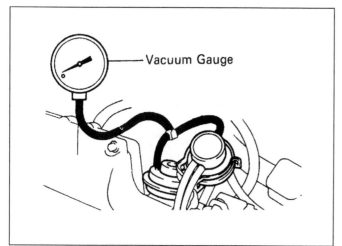

6.9 Install a vacuum gauge between the vacuum modulator and the EGR valve using a three way adapter

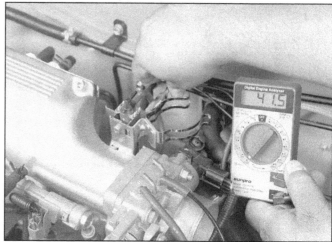

6.11 Check the resistance on the EGR VSV using an ohmmeter. It should be between 37 and 44 ohms

6.18 Remove the nuts that retain the EGR valve assembly to the engine

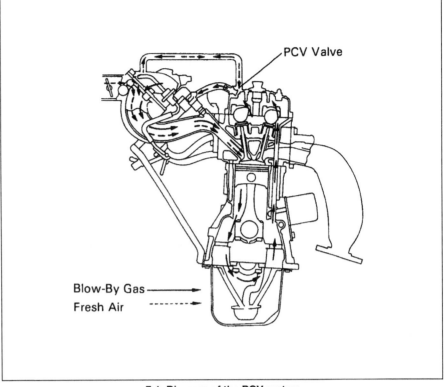

PCV Valve

Blow-By Gas

Fresh Air

7.1 Diagram of the PCV system

15 Remove the throttle body from the air intake plenum (see Chap-ter 4).
16 Remove the EGR vacuum modulator (see Steps 20 and 21).
17 Remove the EGR pipe.
18 Remove the EGR mounting bolts **(see illustration)** and separate the EGR valve from the engine compartment.
19 Installation is the reverse of removal.

EGR vacuum modulator

20 Label and disconnect the vacuum hoses and remove the EGR vacuum modulator from it's bracket.
21 Installation is the reverse of removal.

7 Positive Crankcase Ventilation (PCV) system

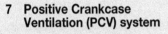

General description

1 The Positive Crankcase Ventilation (PCV) system reduces hydrocarbon emissions by scavenging crankcase vapors. It does this by circulating fresh air from the air cleaner through the crankcase, where it mixes with blow-by gases and is then rerouted through a PCV valve to the intake manifold **(see illustration)**.
2 The main components of the PCV system are the PCV valve, a fresh air intake and the vacuum hoses connecting these components to the engine.
3 To maintain idle quality, the PCV valve restricts the flow when the intake manifold vacuum is high. If abnormal operating conditions (such as piston ring problems) arise, the system is designed to allow excessive amounts of blow-by gases to flow back through the crankcase vent tube into the air cleaner to be consumed by normal combustion.

4 This system directs the blow-by into the throttle body which, over time, can cause an oily residue build up in the area near the throttle plate. Consequently, it's a good idea to periodically clean this residue from the throttle body. Refer to Chapter 4 for this cleaning procedure.

Check

5 To check the valve, first pull it out of the grommet in the valve cover and shake the valve. It should rattle, indicating that it's not clogged with deposits. If the valve does not rattle, replace it with a new one.
6 Start the engine and allow it to idle, then place your finger over the valve opening. If vacuum is felt, the PCV valve is working properly. If no vacuum is felt, the PCV valve may be bad or the hose may be plugged. Also, check for vacuum leaks at the valve, filler cap and all the hoses.

Replacement

7 Pull straight up on the valve to remove it. Check the rubber grommet for cracks and distortion. If it's damaged, replace it.
8 If the valve is clogged, the hose is also probably plugged. Remove the hose and clean it with solvent.
9 After cleaning the hose, inspect it for damage, wear and deterioration. Make sure it fits snugly on the fittings.
10 If necessary, install a new PCV valve.
11 Install the clean PCV hose. Make sure that the PCV valve and hose are secure.

8 Catalytic converter

General description

1 To reduce hydrocarbon, carbon monoxide and oxides of nitrogen emissions, all vehicles are equipped with a three-way catalyst system which oxidizes and reduces these chemicals, converting them into harmless nitrogen, carbon dioxide and water.
2 The catalytic converter is mounted in the exhaust system much like a muffler **(see illustration)**.

8.2 Be sure to spray penetrating lubricant onto the catalytic converter mounting bolts before attempting to unscrew them

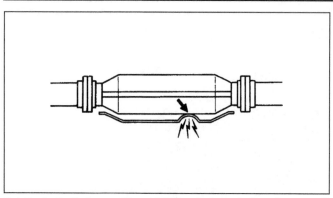

8.4 Periodically inspect the shield for dents and other damage - if a dent is deep enough to touch the surface of the converter, replace the shield

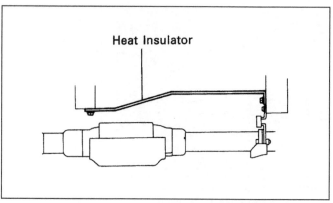

8.5 Periodically inspect the heat insulator to make sure there's adequate clearance between it and the converter

Check

3 Periodically inspect the catalytic converter-to-exhaust pipe mating flanges and bolts. Make sure that there are no loose bolts and no leaks between the flanges.

4 Look for dents in or damage to the catalytic converter protector **(see illustration)**. If any part of the protector is damaged or dented enough to touch the converter, repair or replace it.

5 Inspect the heat insulator for damage. Make sure that there is adequate clearance between the heat insulator and the catalytic converter **(see illustration)**.

Replacement

6 To replace the catalytic converter, refer to Chapter 4.

Chapter 7 Part A
Manual transmission

Contents

Degrees of difficulty

Easy, suitable for novice with little experience	**Fairly easy,** suitable for beginner with some experience	**Fairly difficult,** suitable for competent DIY mechanic	**Difficult,** suitable for experienced DIY mechanic	**Very difficult,** suitable for expert DIY or professional

Specifications

Torque wrench settings   Ft-lbs

Reversing light switch	30
Upper transmission-to-engine bolts **(see illustration 5.32)**	
Bolts A	47
Bolt B	34
Stiffener plate bolts	17
Lower transmission-to-engine bolts	17

1 General information

The vehicles covered by this manual are equipped with a 5-speed manual transmission or a 3- or 4-speed automatic transmission. Information on the manual transmission is included in this Part of Chapter 7. Service procedures for the automatic transmission are contained in Chapter 7, Part B.

The manual transmission is a compact, two-piece, lightweight aluminum alloy housing containing both the transmission and differential assemblies. A C150 transmission is used with the 1.3L engine; a C50 or C52 transmission is used with the 1.6L and 1.8L engines. All transmissions are virtually identical except for different first-gear ratios.

Because of the complexity, unavailability of replacement parts and special tools necessary, internal repair procedures for the manual transmission are beyond the scope of this manual. For readers who wish to tackle a transmission rebuild, exploded views and a brief *Manual transmission overhaul - general information* Section are provided. The bulk of information in this Chapter is devoted to removal and installation procedures.

2.1 To disconnect the shift cables from the transmission linkage, remove these two clips and washers (arrows)

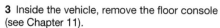
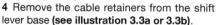

2.2 To detach the shift cable assembly from the cable bracket, remove these two retainers (arrows) with a pair of pliers

2.5 To disconnect the shift cables from the shift lever, remove these clips and washers (arrow)

2 Shift cables - removal and installation

Removal

1 In the engine compartment, remove the retaining clips and washers and disconnect the shift cables from the selecting bellcrank **(see illustration)**.

2 Remove the cable retainers from the cable bracket **(see illustration)**.

3 Inside the vehicle, remove the floor console (see Chapter 11).

4 Remove the cable retainers from the shift lever base **(see illustration 3.3a or 3.3b)**.

5 Remove the retaining clips and washers from the cable ends **(see illustration)** and disconnect the cables from the shift lever assembly.

6 Trace the cable assembly to the firewall and remove the weatherproofing grommet. Pull the cable assembly through the firewall.

Installation

7 Installation is the reverse of removal.

3 Shift lever - removal and installation

Removal

1 Remove the centre console (see Chapter 11).

2 Remove the shift cable retainers and disconnect both cables from the shift lever (see Section 2).

3 Remove the retaining bolts from the shift lever base **(see illustrations)** and detach the

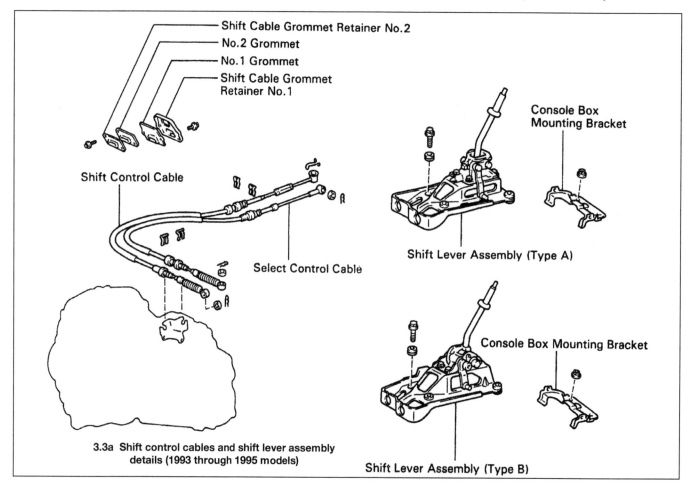

3.3a Shift control cables and shift lever assembly details (1993 through 1995 models)

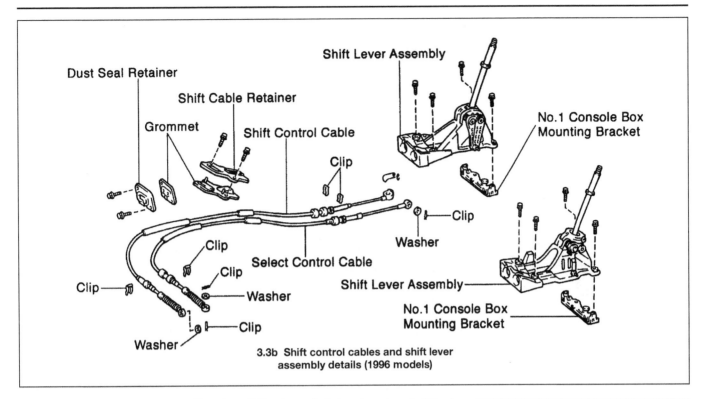

3.3b Shift control cables and shift lever
assembly details (1996 models)

shift lever from the vehicle. **Note:** *If you're replacing the shift lever assembly, it could be either of the two units shown in each illustration. Take the shift lever assembly with you when purchasing a replacement unit to ensure that you get the right unit for your vehicle.*

Installation

4 Installation is the reverse of removal.

4 Reversing light switch - check and replacement

Check

1 The reversing light switch is located on top of the transmission.
2 Turn the ignition key to the On position and move the shift lever to the Reverse position. The switch should close the reversing light circuit and turn on the reversing lights.
3 If it doesn't, check the reversing light fuse (see Chapter 12).
4 If the fuse is okay, verify that there's voltage available on the battery side of the switch (with the ignition turned to On).
5 If there's no voltage on the battery side of the switch, check the wire between the fuse and the switch; if there is voltage, put the shift lever in reverse and see if there's voltage on the ground side of the switch.
6 If there's no voltage on the ground side of the switch, replace the switch (see below); if there is voltage, note whether one or both reversing lights are out.

7 If only one bulb is out, replace it; if they're both out, the bulbs could be the problem, but it's more likely that the wire between the switch and the bulbs has an open somewhere.

Replacement

8 Disconnect the electrical connector from the reversing light switch **(see illustration)**.
9 Unscrew and remove the old switch.
10 To test the new switch before installation, simply check continuity across the switch terminals: with the plunger depressed, there should be continuity; with the plunger free, there should be no continuity.
11 Screw in the new switch and tighten it securely.
12 Connect the electrical connector.
13 Check the switch to ensure that the circuit is working properly.

4.8 Unplug the electrical connector from the back-up light switch (arrow)

5 Manual transmission - removal and installation

Removal

1 Disconnect the negative cable from the battery.
Caution: If the stereo in your vehicle is equipped with an anti-theft system, make sure you have the correct activation code before disconnecting the battery.
2 Remove the air cleaner assembly (see Chapter 4).
3 Remove the coolant reservoir (see Chapter 3).
4 Remove the clutch release cylinder and the clutch hydraulic line (see Chapter 8).
5 Unplug the electrical connectors from the reversing light switch (see Section 4) and the speed sensor (see Chapter 6).
6 Locate the ground cable on top of the transmission. Remove the cable retaining bolt and detach the ground cable from the transmission.
7 Disconnect the shift cables from the transmission (see Section 2).
8 Detach any wire harness clamps from the engine and/or transmission and set the harnesses aside.
9 Remove the upper starter mounting bolt (see Chapter 5).
10 Remove the two upper and the single front transmission-to-engine mounting bolts. Note the location of any ground connectors or brackets, so that they may be installed in their original location.

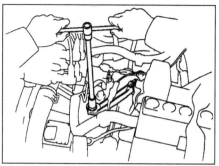

5.11a Remove the left engine mount stay

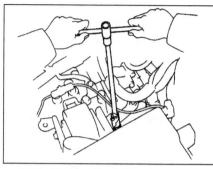

5.11b Remove the left engine mount retaining bolt

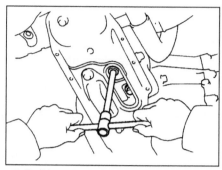

5.18 Disconnect the front engine mount

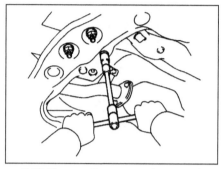

5.19 Remove the rear engine mount

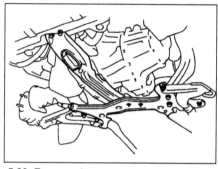

5.20 Remove the center support member

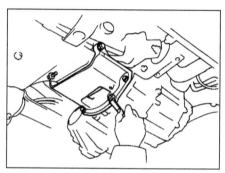

5.22 On 1.6L models, remove the stiffener plate

11 Remove the left engine mount stay and the left engine mount retaining bolt **(see illustrations)**.

12 Support the engine. This can be done from above by using an engine hoist, or by placing a jack (with a wood block as an insulator) under the engine oil pan. The engine must be supported at all times while the transmission is out of the vehicle.

13 Loosen the wheel nuts. Raise the vehicle and support it securely on jackstands. Remove the wheels.

14 Remove the splash shields (see Chapter 2).

15 Drain the transmission fluid (see Chapter 1).

16 Remove the driveshafts (see Chapter 8).

17 Remove the front exhaust pipe (see Chapter 4).

18 Disconnect the front engine mount **(see illustration)**.

19 Remove the rear engine mount **(see illustration)**.

20 Remove the centre support member **(see illustration)**.

21 Remove the starter motor (see Chapter 5).

22 On 1.6L models, remove the stiffener plate **(see illustration)**.

23 On 1.3L and 1.8L models, remove the bolts securing the rear engine plate or sump reinforcement section to the transmission **(see illustration)**.

24 Remove the left engine mount **(see illustration)**.

25 Support the transmission with a jack (preferably a special jack made for this purpose). If you're using a floor jack, be sure to place a wood block between the lifting pad and the transmission to protect the cast aluminum housing. Safety chains will help steady the transmission on the jack.

26 Remove the rest of the bolts securing the transmission to the engine.

27 Make a final check that all wires and hoses have been disconnected from the transmission.

28 Lower the left (driver's) end of the engine, then roll the transmission and jack toward the side of the vehicle. Once the input shaft is clear of the splines in the clutch hub, lower the transmission and remove it from under the vehicle. Try to keep the transmission as level as possible.

Caution: Do not depress the clutch pedal while the transmission is removed from the vehicle.

29 The clutch components can now be inspected (see Chapter 8). In most cases, new clutch components should be routinely installed whenever the transmission is removed.

Installation

30 If removed, install the clutch components (see Chapter 8).

31 With the transmission secured to the jack as on removal, raise it into position and then carefully slide it forward, engaging the input shaft with the splines in the clutch hub. Do not use excessive force to install the transmission - if the input shaft does not slide into place, readjust the angle of the transmission so it is level and/or turn the input shaft so the splines engage properly with the clutch.

32 Install the transmission-to-engine bolts **(see illustration)**. Tighten the bolts to the torque listed in this Chapter's Specifications.

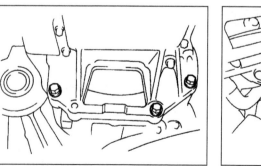

5.23 On 1.8L models, remove the engine rear end plate

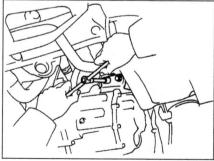

5.24 Remove the left engine mount

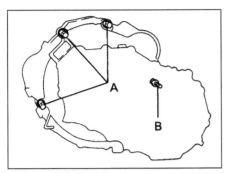

5.32 Tighten bolts A and B to the torque listed in this Chapter's Specifications

33 Install the transmission mount nuts and bolts. Tighten all nuts and bolts securely.

34 Install any suspension components which were detached or removed. Tighten all nuts and bolts to the torque listed in the Chapter 10 Specifications.

35 Remove the jacks supporting the transmission and the engine.

36 Install the various items removed previously. Refer to Chapter 4 for information regarding the exhaust pipe, Chapter 5 for the starter motor and Chapter 8 for the driveshafts.

37 Make sure that the wiring harness connectors for the reversing light switch and the speed sensor, and any other electrical devices, are plugged in. And make sure that all harness clamps are reattached to the engine and/or transmission.

38 If the transmission was drained, fill it with the specified lubricant to the proper level (see Chapter 1).

39 Lower the vehicle.

40 Connect the shift cables (see Section 3).

41 Connect the negative battery cable. Road test the vehicle to check for proper transmission operation and check for leakage.

6 Manual transmission overhaul - general information

1 Overhauling a manual transmission is a difficult job for the do-it-yourselfer. It involves the disassembly and reassembly of many small parts. Numerous clearances must be precisely measured and, if necessary, changed with select-fit spacers and snap-rings. As a result, if transmission problems arise, it can be removed and installed by a competent do-it-yourselfer, but overhaul should be left to a transmission repair workshop. Rebuilt transmissions may be available - check with your dealer parts department and auto parts stores. At any rate, the time and money involved in an overhaul is almost sure to exceed the cost of a rebuilt unit.

2 Nevertheless, it's not impossible for an inexperienced mechanic to rebuild a transmission if the special tools are available and the job is done in a deliberate step-by-step manner so nothing is overlooked.

3 The tools necessary for an overhaul include internal and external snap-ring pliers, a bearing puller, a slide hammer, a set of pin punches, a dial indicator and possibly a hydraulic press. In addition, a large, sturdy workbench and a vise or transmission stand will be required.

4 During disassembly of the transmission, make careful notes of how each piece comes off, where it fits in relation to other pieces and what holds it in place. Exploded views are included, over the next pages, **(see illustrations)** to show where the parts go - but actually noting how they are installed when you remove the parts will make it much easier to get the transmission back together.

5 Before taking the transmission apart for repair, it will help if you have some idea what area of the transmission is malfunctioning. Certain problems can be closely tied to specific areas in the transmission, which can make component examination and replacement easier. Refer to the *Fault finding* section for information regarding possible sources of trouble.

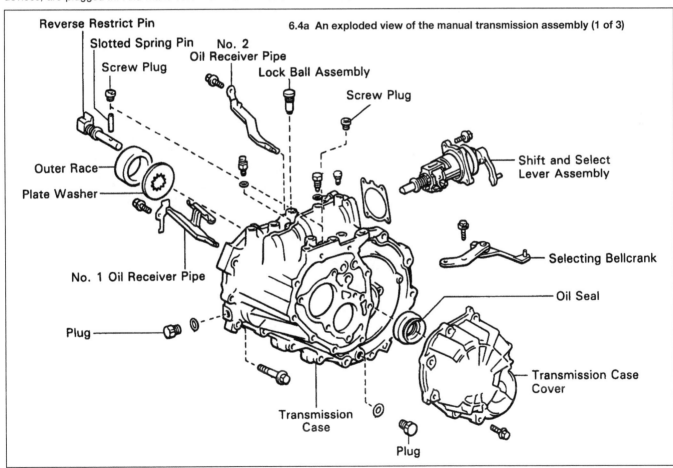

6.4a An exploded view of the manual transmission assembly (1 of 3)

Reverse Restrict Pin

Slotted Spring Pin

Screw Plug

No. 2 Oil Receiver Pipe

Lock Ball Assembly

Screw Plug

Shift and Select Lever Assembly

Outer Race

Plate Washer

No. 1 Oil Receiver Pipe

Selecting Bellcrank

Oil Seal

Plug

Transmission Case

Transmission Case Cover

Plug

6.4b An exploded view of the manual transmission assembly (2 of 3)

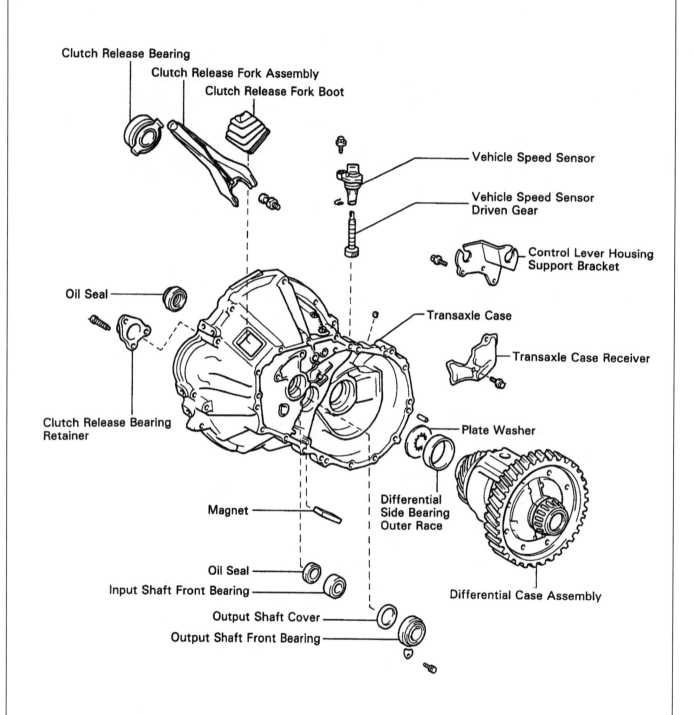

Clutch Release Bearing

Clutch Release Fork Assembly

Clutch Release Fork Boot

Vehicle Speed Sensor

Vehicle Speed Sensor Driven Gear

Control Lever Housing Support Bracket

Oil Seal

Transaxle Case

Transaxle Case Receiver

Clutch Release Bearing Retainer

Plate Washer

Magnet

Differential Side Bearing Outer Race

Oil Seal

Input Shaft Front Bearing

Output Shaft Cover

Output Shaft Front Bearing

Differential Case Assembly

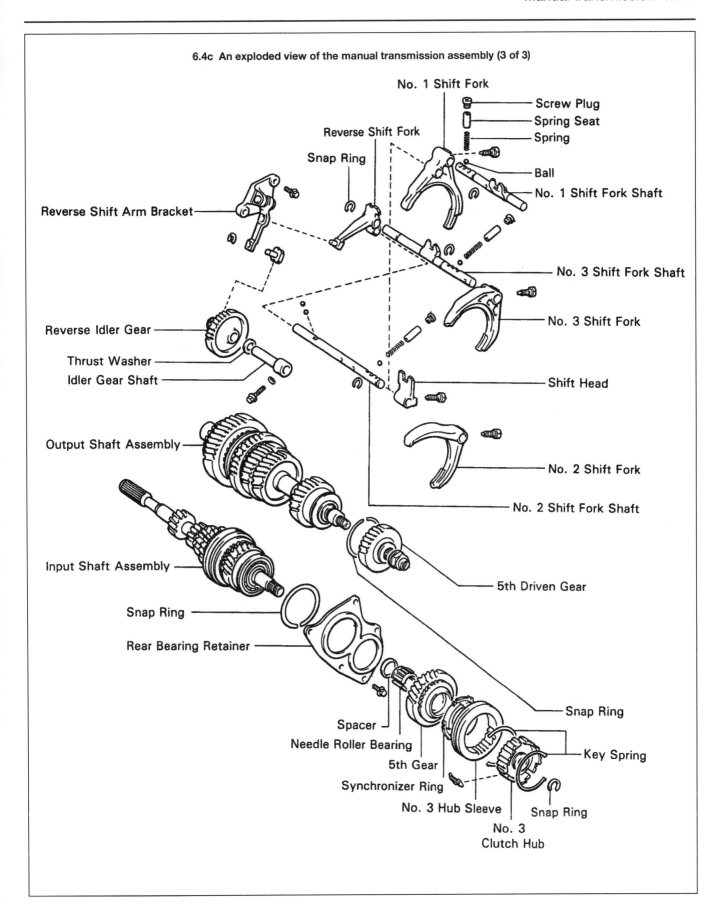

6.4c An exploded view of the manual transmission assembly (3 of 3)

Chapter 7 Part B
Automatic transmission

Contents

Degrees of difficulty

Easy, suitable for novice with little experience	Fairly easy, suitable for beginner with some experience	Fairly difficult, suitable for competent DIY mechanic 	Difficult, suitable for experienced DIY mechanic	Very difficult, suitable for expert DIY or professional

Specifications

Torque wrench settings	Ft-lbs
Neutral start switch	4
Torque converter-to-driveplate bolts	20
Transmission-to-engine bolts	47
Valve body bolts	7
Manual valve retaining bolts	7
Detent spring bolt(s)	7

1 General information

All vehicles covered in this manual are equipped with either a 5-speed manual transmission or a 3- or 4-speed automatic transmission. All information on the automatic transmission is included in this Part of Chapter 7. Information for the manual transmission can be found in Part A of this Chapter.

The A132L is a three-speed automatic transmission fitted to 4E-FE and 4A-FE engine models. Its shift points are controlled by the governor and the throttle valve. The A240L, fitted to 4A-FE and 7A-FE engine models is a four-speed automatic transmission with fourth gear being an overdrive gear. Both transmissions utilize a lock-up torque converter.

Because of the complexity of the automatic transmissions and the specialized equipment necessary to perform most service operations, this Chapter contains only those procedures related to general diagnosis, routine maintenance, adjustment and removal and installation.

If the transmission requires major repair work, it should be left to a dealer service department or an automotive or transmission repair workshop. You can, however, remove and install the transmission yourself and save the expense, even if the repair work is done by a transmission workshop.

2 Diagnosis - general

Note: Automatic transmission malfunctions may be caused by five general conditions: poor engine performance, improper adjustments, hydraulic malfunctions, mechanical malfunctions or malfunctions in the computer or its signal network. Diagnosis of these problems should always begin with a check of the easily repaired items: fluid level and condition (see Chapter 1), shift linkage adjustment and throttle linkage adjustment. Next, perform a road test to determine if the problem has been corrected or if more diagnosis is necessary. If the problem persists after the preliminary tests and corrections are completed, additional diagnosis should be done by a dealer service department or transmission repair workshop. Refer to the Fault finding section at the rear of this manual for information on symptoms of transmission problems.

Preliminary checks

1 Drive the vehicle to warm the transmission to normal operating temperature.
2 Check the fluid level as described in Chapter 1:
  a) If the fluid level is unusually low, add enough fluid to bring the level within the designated area of the dipstick, then check for external leaks (see below).
  b) If the fluid level is abnormally high, drain off the excess, then check the drained fluid for contamination by coolant. The presence of engine coolant in the automatic transmission fluid indicates that a failure has occurred in the internal radiator walls that separate the coolant from the transmission fluid (see Chapter 3).
  c) If the fluid is foaming, drain it and refill the transmission, then check for coolant in the fluid, or a high fluid level.

3 Check the engine idle speed. **Note:** *If the engine is malfunctioning, do not proceed with the preliminary checks until it has been repaired and runs normally.*

4 Check the throttle valve cable for freedom of movement. Adjust it if necessary (see Section 4). **Note:** *The throttle cable may function properly when the engine is shut off and cold, but it may malfunction once the engine is hot. Check it when cold and at normal engine operating temperature.*

5 Inspect the shift cable (see Section 5). Make sure that it's properly adjusted and that the cable operates smoothly.

Fluid leak diagnosis

6 Most fluid leaks are easy to locate visually. Repair usually consists of replacing a seal or gasket. If a leak is difficult to find, the following procedure may help.

7 Identify the fluid. Make sure it's transmission fluid and not engine oil or brake fluid (automatic transmission fluid is a deep red colour).

8 Try to pinpoint the source of the leak. Drive the vehicle several miles, then park it over a large sheet of cardboard. After a minute or two, you should be able to locate the leak by determining the source of the fluid dripping onto the cardboard.

9 Make a careful visual inspection of the suspected component and the area immediately around it. Pay particular attention to gasket mating surfaces. A mirror is often helpful for finding leaks in areas that are hard to see.

10 If the leak still cannot be found, clean the suspected area thoroughly with a degreaser or solvent, then dry it.

11 Drive the vehicle for several miles at normal operating temperature and varying speeds. After driving the vehicle, visually inspect the suspected component again.

12 Once the leak has been located, the cause must be determined before it can be properly repaired. If a gasket is replaced but the sealing flange is bent, the new gasket will not stop the leak. The bent flange must be straightened.

13 Before attempting to repair a leak, check to make sure that the following conditions are corrected or they may cause another leak. **Note:** *Some of the following conditions cannot be fixed without highly specialized tools and expertise. Such problems must be referred to a transmission workshop or a dealer service department.*

Gasket leaks

14 Check the pan periodically. Make sure the bolts are tight, no bolts are missing, the gasket is in good condition and the pan is flat (dents in the pan may indicate damage to the valve body inside).

15 If the pan gasket is leaking, the fluid level or the fluid pressure may be too high, the vent may be plugged, the pan bolts may be too tight, the pan sealing flange may be warped, the sealing surface of the transmission housing may be damaged, the gasket may be damaged or the transmission casting may be cracked or porous. If sealant instead of gasket material has been used to form a seal between the pan and the transmission housing, it may be the wrong sealant.

Seal leaks

16 If a transmission seal is leaking, the fluid level or pressure may be too high, the vent may be plugged, the seal bore may be damaged, the seal itself may be damaged or improperly installed, the surface of the shaft protruding through the seal may be damaged or a loose bearing may be causing excessive shaft movement.

17 Make sure the dipstick tube seal is in good condition and the tube is properly seated. Periodically check the area around the speedometer gear or sensor for leakage. If transmission fluid is evident, check the O-ring for damage.

Case leaks

18 If the case itself appears to be leaking, the casting is porous and will have to be repaired or replaced.

19 Make sure the oil cooler hose fittings are tight and in good condition.

Fluid comes out vent pipe or fill tube

20 If this condition occurs, the transmission is overfilled, there is coolant in the fluid, the case is porous, the dipstick is incorrect, the vent is plugged or the drain-back holes are plugged.

3 Oil seal replacement

1 Oil leaks frequently occur due to wear of the driveshaft oil seals and/or the speedometer drive gear oil seal and O-rings. Replacement of these seals is relatively easy, since the repairs can usually be performed without removing the transmission from the vehicle.

Driveshaft oil seals

2 The driveshaft oil seals are located on the sides of the transmission, where the inner ends of the driveshafts are splined into the differential side gears. If you suspect that a driveshaft oil seal is leaking, raise the vehicle and support it securely on jackstands. If the seal is leaking, you'll see lubricant on the side of the transmission, below the seal.

3 Remove the driveshaft (see Chapter 8).

4 Using a screwdriver or pry bar, carefully pry the oil seal out of the transmission bore **(see illustration)**.

5 If the oil seal cannot be removed with a screwdriver or pry bar, a special oil seal removal tool (available at auto parts stores) will be required.

6 Using a seal installer, a large section of pipe or a large deep socket as a drift, install the new oil seal. Drive it into the bore squarely and make sure it's completely seated **(see illustration)**. On A132L transmissions, a fully-seated seal should be flush with the surface of

3.4 Carefully pry out the driveshaft oil seal with a seal removal tool or a large screwdriver; make sure you don't damage the seal bore or the new seal may leak

3.6 Use a seal installer, a large socket or a piece of pipe to install the new seal

3.9 Unplug the speed sensor electrical connector (arrow), remove the bolt (arrow) and pull the speed sensor unit straight out of the transmission

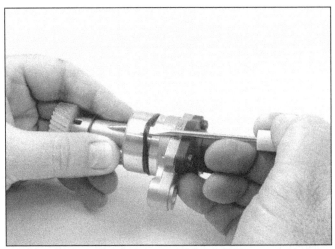

3.10 Remove the oil seal O-ring from the speed sensor with a small screwdriver; make sure you don't scratch the surface of the sensor or gouge the O-ring groove

the transmission housing; on A240L units, a fully-seated left seal should be recessed about 13/64-inch, a right seal about 1/8-inch.

7 Lubricate the lip of the new seal with multi-purpose grease, then install the driveshaft (see Chapter 8). Be careful not to damage the lip of the new seal.

Speed sensor O-ring

8 The speed sensor is located on the transmission housing. Look for lubricant around the sensor housing to determine if the O-ring is leaking.

9 Unplug the electrical connector and unbolt the vehicle speed sensor from the transmission (see illustration).

10 Using a scribe or a small screwdriver, remove the O-ring from the sensor (see illustration) and install a new O-ring. Lubricate the new O-ring with automatic transmission fluid to protect it during installation of the sensor.

11 Installation is the reverse of removal.

4 Throttle valve (TV) cable - check, adjustment and replacement

Check

1 Remove the duct between the air cleaner and the throttle body (see Chapter 4).

2 Have an assistant press the accelerator pedal all the way to the floor and hold it while you measure the distance between the end of the boot and the stopper on the cable.

3 If the measurement taken is as shown (see illustration), the cable is properly adjusted. If it's out-of-range, adjust it as follows.

Adjustment

4 Have your assistant continue to hold the pedal down while you loosen the adjusting nuts and adjust the cable housing so that the distance between the end of the boot and the stopper on the cable is within the range shown.

5 Tighten the adjusting nuts securely, recheck the clearance and make sure the throttle valve opens all the way when the throttle is depressed.

Replacement

6 Loosen the cable locknut and detach the cable from the bracket at the throttle body.

7 Disconnect the cable from the throttle linkage.

8 Detach the cable from the bracket on the transmission.

9 Follow the cable down to the front of the transmission, where it enters the transmission housing right behind the neutral start switch. Remove the cable hold-down bolt.

10 Remove the pan, drain the transmission fluid and remove the filter (see Chapter 1).

11 Remove the two oil tube bracket bolts and remove the oil tubes (see illustrations).

12 On A240L models, unplug the electrical connectors for the solenoids.

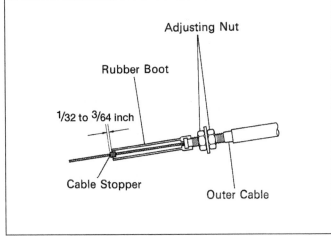

4.3 Throttle cable adjustment details

Adjusting Nut
Rubber Boot
1/32 to 3/64 inch
Cable Stopper
Outer Cable

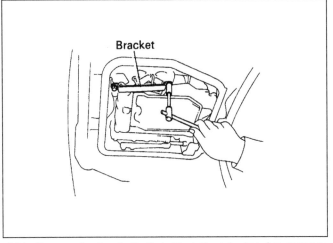

4.11a Remove the two bolts that attach the tube bracket, remove the bracket . . .

Bracket

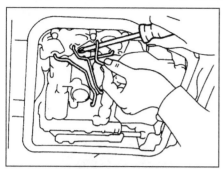

4.11b . . . and carefully pry out both ends of all four oil tubes - make sure you don't bend or kink the tubes (A132L transmission shown)

13 Remove the manual detent spring **(see illustration)**.
14 Remove the manual valve on A132L models then, on all models, remove the valve body **(see illustrations)**. On A132L models, the valve body is retained by 14 bolts, and on A240L models by 12 bolts. Note the different bolt lengths and their locations.
15 Disconnect the throttle valve cable from the cam on top of the valve body **(see illustration)**.
16 Installation is the reverse of removal. Be sure to tighten the valve body, manual valve and detent spring bolts to the torque listed in this Chapter's Specifications. Refer to Chapter 1 for the torque specifications for the pan bolts and the type and quantity of transmission fluid required to refill the transmission.

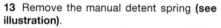

5   Shift cable - removal, installation and adjustment

Removal and installation

1 Disconnect the shift cable from the manual shift lever at the transmission and detach it

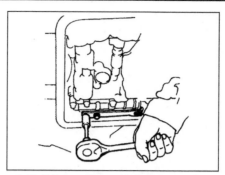

4.13 Remove the manual detent spring (A132L transmission shown)

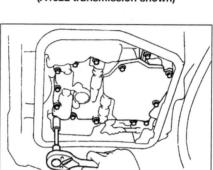

4.14b . . . remove the valve body retaining bolts and remove the valve body

from the bracket on the front of the transmission **(see illustrations)**.
2 Remove the centre console (see Chapter 11).
3 Remove the gear-position indicator panel retaining screws, lift up the gear-position indicator panel and disconnect the light bulb **(see illustrations)**. Tie the gear-position indicator panel to the shift lever handle so that you have room to work.
4 Remove the retaining clip and disconnect the shift cable from the shift lever **(see illustrations)**.

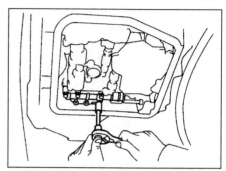

4.14a On A132L models, remove the manual valve . . .

4.15 Disengage the plug on the lower end of the throttle valve cable from the cam on top of the valve body

5 Remove the retaining clip from the front edge of the shift lever base **(see illustration)**.
6 Pull the cable through the grommet in the firewall.
7 Installation is the reverse of removal.
8 When you're done, adjust the shift cable.

Adjustment

9 Loosen the nut on the manual shift lever at the transmission **(see illustration 5.1A)**.
10 Push the lever toward the right side of the vehicle until it stops, then return it two notches to the Neutral position.

5.1a To disconnect the shift cable from the manual shift lever at the transmission, remove this nut

5.1b To detach the shift cable from the bracket on the front of the transmission, pry off this clip

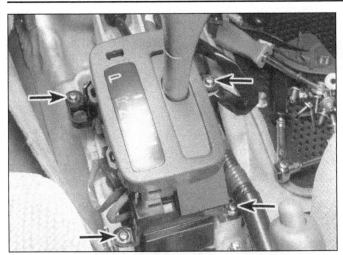

5.3a To detach the gear position indicator panel from the shift lever base, remove these four screws (arrows) . . .

5.3b . . . then detach the shift indicator panel light and raise the panel

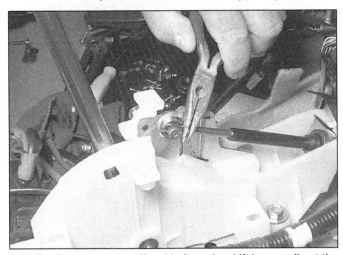

5.4a To disconnect the shift cable from the shift lever, pull out the retaining clip . . .

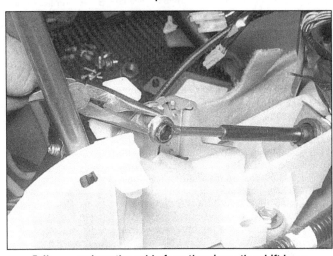

5.4b . . . and pry the cable from the pin on the shift lever

11 Move the shift lever inside the vehicle to the Neutral position.

12 While holding the lever with a slight pressure toward the Reverse position, tighten the nut securely.

13 Check the operation of the transmission in each shift lever position (try to start the engine in each gear - the starter should operate in the Park and Neutral positions only).

5.5 To detach the shift cable from the shift lever base, pry off this clip

6 Neutral start switch - check, adjustment and replacement

Adjustment

1 If the engine will start with the shift lever in any position other than Park or Neutral, adjust the neutral start switch.

2 Apply the park brake and block the rear wheels. Raise the front of the vehicle and place it securely on jackstands. Shift the transmission into Neutral.

3 Unplug the electrical connector from the switch and loosen the switch retaining bolts.

4 Touch the ohmmeter leads to the switch terminals inside the electrical connector and rotate the switch until there is continuity between the terminals, indicating that it's now in the Neutral position **(see illustration)**. Tighten the bolts securely.

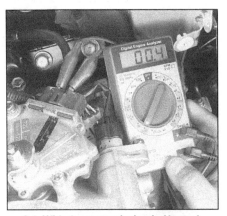

6.4 With the transmission in Neutral, check continuity with an ohmmeter as shown: loosen the switch retaining bolts, touch the leads of the ohmmeter to the switch terminals inside the electrical connector and rotate the switch until the meter indicates continuity and tighten the bolts

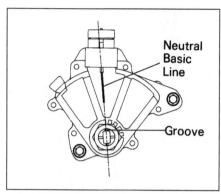

6.13 Rotate the switch until the neutral basic line aligns with the groove and tighten the bolts

Replacement

5 Disconnect the negative cable from the battery. **Caution:** *If the stereo in your vehicle is equipped with an anti-theft system, make sure you have the correct activation code before disconnecting the battery.*

6 Shift the transmission into Neutral.

7 Remove the nut and lift off the shift lever.

8 Unplug the electrical connector.

9 Using a screwdriver, prise back the tab on the lockwasher under the nut securing the switch to the valve shaft.

10 Unscrew the nut, and recover the lockwasher and shim(s).

11 Remove the retaining bolts and lift the switch off the shaft.

12 To install, line up the flats on the valve shaft with the flats in the switch and push the switch onto the shaft. Refit the shim(s), the lockwasher and securing nut. Tighten the securing nut, and bend over the lockwasher tab.

13 Rotate the switch until the neutral basic line aligns with the groove **(see illustration)**. Tighten the bolts securely and connect the electrical connector.

14 Install the shift lever, connect the negative battery cable and verify the engine will not start with the shift lever in any position other than Park or Neutral, if necessary follow the adjustment procedure above.

7 Transmission mount - check and replacement

Check

1 Insert a large screwdriver or prybar between the transmission mount and the body and try to pry it away from the body **(see illustration)**.

2 The transmission mount should not move excessively. If it does, replace the mount.

Replacement

3 To replace a mount, support the transmission with a jack, remove the nuts and bolts and remove the mount. It may be necessary to raise the transmission slightly to provide enough clearance to remove the mount.

4 Installation is the reverse of removal.

8 Automatic transmission - removal and installation

Removal

1 Detach the cable from the negative battery terminal. **Caution:** *If the stereo in your vehicle is equipped with an anti-theft system, make sure you have the correct activation code before disconnecting the battery.*

2 If you're planning to reuse the same transmission, simply remove the cable retaining clip from the bracket and disconnect the throttle valve cable from the linkage on the

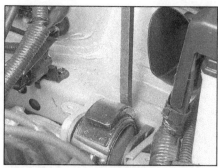

7.1 To check any of the three transmission mounts, insert a large screwdriver or prybar between the mount and the body as shown, and try to lever the mount from side to side or up and down - there should be a little movement, but it should be firm; if the mount moves too easily or looks cracked and torn, replace it (upper left transmission mount shown)

throttle body; if you're planning to replace the transmission, disconnect the throttle valve cable from the valve body (in either case, see Section 4).

3 Remove the air cleaner housing (see Chapter 4).

4 Remove the upper bolts from the left transmission mount **(see illustration)**. (There are two more bolts, but you won't be able to reach them until the vehicle is raised.)

5 Detach the ground cable **(see illustration)** from the transmission. Unplug the electrical connectors for the speed sensor (see Section 3), neutral start switch (see Section 6) and solenoid (A240L only), next to the neutral start switch on the front left corner of the transmission. Detach any wiring harness clamps from the transmission and set the wiring harnesses aside.

6 Remove the upper transmission-to-engine bolts **(see illustration)**. Remove the upper transmission-to-starter motor bolt (see Chapter 5).

8.4 Remove these bolts (arrows) from the upper side of the left transmission mount (there are two more bolts, but they're underneath, on the front side)

8.5 Remove this bolt (arrow) and detach the ground cable from the top of the transmission

8.6 Remove the two upper transmission-to-engine bolts (arrows); the bolt on the right (arrow) is the upper starter bolt

8.14a Remove the four front support brace bolts (arrows) . . .

7 Raise the vehicle and support it securely on jackstands.

8 Remove the engine under covers.

9 Disconnect the shift cable from the transmission (see Section 5).

10 Remove the exhaust pipe section between the exhaust manifold and the catalytic converter (see Chapter 4).

11 Drain the transmission fluid and on three-speed models, the differential fluid (see Chapter 1).

12 Remove the driveshafts (see Chapter 8). **Note:** *It's not absolutely necessary to completely remove the driveshafts; you can detach the inner CV joints and suspend them out of the way. However, you'll have more room to work if you remove the driveshafts. And this is a good time to inspect the CV joint boots for tears and deterioration and, if necessary, repack them with new CV joint grease (see Chapter 8).*

13 Support the engine using a hoist from above, or a jack and a wood block under the oil pan to spread the load.

14 Remove the bolts and nuts that attach the centre support brace and suspension member to the vehicle **(see illustrations)**.

15 Detach the starter motor leads, remove the lower starter-to-transmission bolt and remove the starter (see Chapter 5).

16 Detach the oil cooler line retaining clamps from the transmission, then disconnect the two line fittings from the transmission **(see illustration)**.

17 To detach the dipstick tube from the transmission, remove the single bracket bolt from the front of the bellhousing, then pull straight up on the tube.

18 Support the transmission with a jack - preferably a special jack made for this purpose. Safety chains will help steady the transmission on the jack.

19 Remove the remaining two bolts from the underside of the transmission mount **(see illustration)**. Remove the bolts from the front and rear mounts **(see illustration)** so that the engine can be tilted slightly to the left to allow easier removal and installation of the transmission.

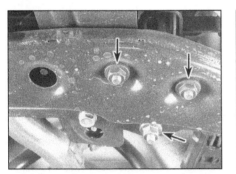

8.14b . . . the three rear support brace nuts (arrows) . . .

8.14c . . . and the five bolts (arrows) from each suspension member (left suspension member shown, right member identical)

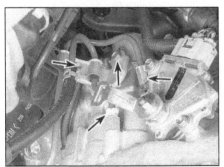

8.16 Unbolt the oil cooler line clamps (arrows) from the transmission, unscrew the line fittings (arrows) and disconnect the lines from the transmission

8.19a Remove these two bolts (arrows) from the underside of the left transmission mount

8.19b Remove the nut and through bolt (arrows) from the front and rear mounts (front mount shown, rear mount similar)

8.20 Mark the relationship of the torque converter to the driveplate to ensure proper dynamic balance when it's reattached, then remove all six torque converter bolts (bolt showing in access window) by rotating the crankshaft to bring each bolt to the bottom, where you can get at it

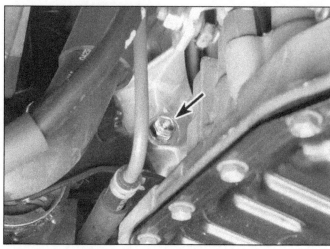

8.21 Remove this front lower transmission-to-engine bolt (arrow)

20 Remove the torque converter inspection cover. Mark the relationship of the torque converter to the driveplate so they can be installed in the same position **(see illustration)**. Remove the six torque converter mounting bolts. Turn the crankshaft for access to each one in turn.

21 Remove the lower engine-to-transmission bolts: the three lowest bolts are shown in **illustration 8.20**, and there's another bolt on the backside of the engine, right below the lower starter bolt. Remove the lower transmission-to-engine bolt, on the front side of the transmission **(see illustration)**.

22 Move the transmission to the side to disengage it from the engine block dowel pins and make sure the torque converter is detached from the driveplate. Secure the torque converter to the transmission so that it will not fall out during removal. Lower the transmission from the vehicle.

Installation

23 Make sure that the torque converter is securely engaged in the transmission prior to installation.

24 With the transmission secured to the jack,

raise it into position. Be sure to keep it level so the torque converter does not slide forward. Connect the cooler lines.

25 Move the transmission carefully into place until the dowel pins are engaged and the torque converter is engaged.

26 Rotate the torque converter to align the bolt holes with the holes in the driveplate. The match marks on the torque converter and driveplate, made during step 20, must align.

27 Install the lower transmission-to-engine bolts and tighten them to the torque listed in this Chapter's Specifications.

28 Install the torque converter-to-driveplate bolts. Tighten them to the torque listed in this Chapter's Specifications. Install the torque converter cover.

29 Install the support brace and suspension member. Tighten the bolts and nuts securely.

30 Remove the jacks supporting the transmission and the engine.

31 Install the starter motor (see Chapter 5). (It's easier to install the upper bolt after the vehicle has been lowered.)

32 Install the dipstick tube into the transmission and attach the dipstick bracket to the transmission.

33 Connect the oil cooler line fittings and the line retaining clamps to the transmission.

34 Install and/or connect the driveshafts to the transmission (see Chapter 8).

35 Install and adjust the neutral start switch (see Section 6).

36 Connect and adjust the shift cable (see Section 5) and the throttle valve cable (see Section 4).

37 Plug in the electrical connectors for the solenoid (A240L), neutral start switch and vehicle speed sensor. Make sure that the wiring harnesses are routed properly and clamped to the transmission housing.

38 Install the exhaust pipe between the exhaust manifold and the catalytic converter (see Chapter 4).

39 Remove the jackstands and lower the vehicle.

40 Install the upper transmission bolts and tighten them to the torque listed in this Chapter's Specifications. Install the upper starter motor bolt, if you haven't already done so.

41 Fill the transmission with the proper type and amount of fluid (see Chapter 1). Run the vehicle and check for fluid leaks.

Chapter 8
Clutch and driveshafts

Contents

Degrees of difficulty

| Easy, suitable for novice with little experience | | Fairly easy, suitable for beginner with some experience | | Fairly difficult, suitable for competent DIY mechanic | | Difficult, suitable for experienced DIY mechanic | | Very difficult, suitable for expert DIY or professional | |

Specifications

Clutch

Fluid type	See Chapter 1
Pedal freeplay	See Chapter 1
Driveshaft standard length	
Left driveshaft	21-17/64 inches
Right driveshaft	33-3/4 inches

Torque wrench settings

	Ft-lbs
Clutch master cylinder mounting nuts	9
Clutch pressure plate-to-flywheel bolts	14
Clutch release cylinder mounting bolts	9
Driveshaft/hub nut	159
Wheel nuts	See Chapter 1

1 General information

The information in this Chapter deals with components from the rear of the engine to the front wheels, except for the transmission, which is dealt with in Chapters 7A and 7B. For the purposes of this Chapter, these components are grouped into two categories: clutch and driveshafts. Separate Sections within this Chapter offer general descriptions and checking procedures for both groups.

Since nearly all the procedures covered in this Chapter involve working under the vehicle, make sure it's securely supported on sturdy jackstands or a hoist where the vehicle can be easily raised and lowered.

2 Clutch - description and check

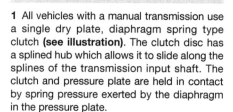

1 All vehicles with a manual transmission use a single dry plate, diaphragm spring type clutch **(see illustration)**. The clutch disc has a splined hub which allows it to slide along the splines of the transmission input shaft. The clutch and pressure plate are held in contact by spring pressure exerted by the diaphragm in the pressure plate.

2 The clutch release system is operated by hydraulic pressure. The hydraulic release system consists of the clutch pedal, a master cylinder and fluid reservoir, the hydraulic line, a slave cylinder which actuates the clutch release lever and the clutch release (or throw-out) bearing.

3 When pressure is applied to the clutch pedal to release the clutch, hydraulic pressure is exerted against the outer end of the clutch release lever. As the lever pivots, the shaft fingers push against the release bearing. The bearing pushes against the fingers of the diaphragm spring of the pressure plate assembly, which in turn releases the clutch plate.

4 Terminology can be a problem regarding the clutch components because common names have in some cases changed from that used by the manufacturer. For example, the driven plate is also called the clutch plate or disc, the pressure plate assembly is sometimes referred to as the clutch cover, the clutch release bearing is sometimes called a throw-out bearing, and the release cylinder is sometimes called the operating or slave cylinder.

5 Other than replacing components that have obvious damage, some preliminary checks should be performed to diagnose a clutch system failure.

a) The first check should be of the fluid level in the clutch master cylinder (see Chapter 1).

If the fluid level is low, add fluid as necessary and inspect the hydraulic clutch system for leaks. If the master cylinder reservoir has run dry, bleed the system (see Section 7) and retest the clutch operation.

b) To check "clutch spin down time," run the engine at normal idle speed with the transmission in Neutral (clutch pedal up - engaged). Disengage the clutch (pedal down), wait several seconds and shift the transmission into Reverse. No grinding noise should be heard. A grinding noise would most likely indicate a problem in the pressure plate or the clutch disc.

c) To check for complete clutch release, run the engine (with the parking brake applied to prevent movement) and hold the clutch pedal approximately 1/2-inch from the floor. Shift the transmission between 1st gear and Reverse several times. If the shift is not smooth, component failure is indicated. Check the release cylinder pushrod travel. With the clutch pedal depressed completely the release cylinder pushrod should extend substantially. If it doesn't, check the fluid level in the clutch master cylinder.

d) Visually inspect the clutch pedal bushing at the top of the clutch pedal to make sure there is no sticking or excessive wear.

e) Under the vehicle, check that the clutch release lever is solidly mounted on the ball stud.

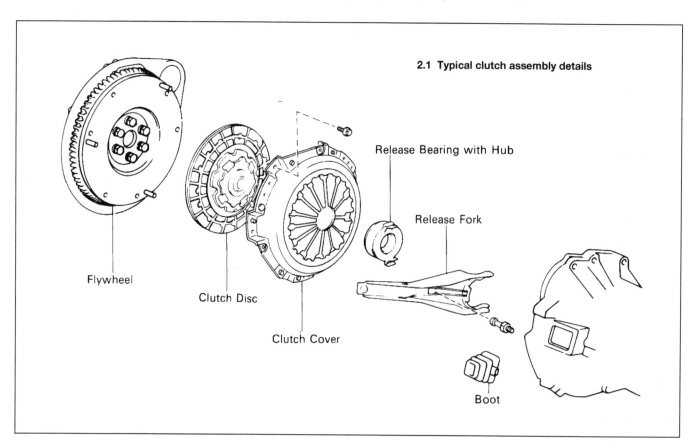

2.1 Typical clutch assembly details

Release Bearing with Hub

Release Fork

Flywheel

Clutch Disc

Clutch Cover

Boot

3 Clutch components -
removal, inspection and installation

⚠️ **Warning: Dust produced by clutch wear and deposited on clutch components may contain asbestos, which is hazardous to your health. DO NOT blow it out with compressed air and DO NOT inhale it. DO NOT use petrol or petroleum based solvents to remove the dust. Brake system cleaner should be used to flush the dust into a drain pan. After the clutch components are wiped clean with a rag, dispose of the contaminated rags and cleaner in a labeled, covered container.**

Removal

1 Access to the clutch components is normally by removing the transmission, leaving the engine in the vehicle. If the engine is being removed for major overhaul, then the opportunity should be taken to check the clutch for wear and replace worn components as necessary. However, the relatively low cost of the clutch components compared to the time and labor involved in gaining access to them warrants their replacement any time the engine or trans-mission is removed, unless they are new or in near-perfect condition. The following pro-cedures assume that the engine will stay in place.

2 Remove the release cylinder (see Section 6). Hang it out of the way with a piece of wire - it isn't necessary to disconnect the hose.

3 Remove the transmission from the vehicle (see Chapter 7A). Support the engine while the transmission is out. Preferably, an engine hoist should be used to support it from above.

HAYNES HINT *If a jack is used underneath the engine, make sure a piece of wood is used between the jack and oil pan to spread the load.*

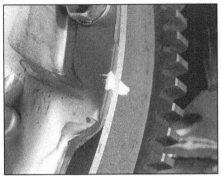

3.6 Mark the relationship of the pressure plate to the flywheel (in case you're going to reuse the same pressure plate)

Caution: The pick-up for the oil pump is very close to the bottom of the oil pan. If the pan is bent or distorted in any way, engine oil starvation could occur.

4 The release fork and release bearing can remain attached to the transmission for the time being.

5 To support the clutch disc during removal, install a clutch alignment tool through the clutch disc hub.

6 Carefully inspect the flywheel and pressure plate for indexing marks. The marks are usually an X, an O or a white letter. If they cannot be found, scribe marks yourself so the pressure plate and the flywheel will be in the same alignment during installation **(see illustration)**.

7 Slowly loosen the pressure plate-to-flywheel bolts. Work in a diagonal pattern and loosen each bolt a little at a time until all spring pressure is relieved. Then hold the pressure plate securely and completely remove the bolts, followed by the pressure plate and clutch disc.

Inspection

8 Ordinarily, when a problem occurs in the clutch, it can be attributed to wear of the clutch driven plate assembly (clutch disc).

3.10 Examine the clutch disc for evidence of excessive wear, such as smeared friction material, chewed-up rivets, worn hub splines and distorted damper cushions or springs

However, all components should be inspected at this time.

9 Inspect the flywheel for cracks, heat checking, score marks and other damage. If the imperfections are slight, a machine workshop can resurface it to make it flat and smooth. Refer to Chapter 2 for the flywheel removal procedure.

10 Inspect the lining on the clutch disc. There should be at least 1/16-inch of lining above the rivet heads. Check for loose rivets, distortion, cracks, broken springs and other obvious damage **(see illustration)**. As mentioned above, ordinarily the clutch disc is replaced as a matter of course, so if in doubt about the condition, replace it with a new one.

11 The release bearing should be replaced along with the clutch disc (see Section 4).

12 Check the machined surface and the diaphragm spring fingersof the pressure plate **(see illustrations)**. If the surface is grooved or otherwise damaged, replace the pressure plate assembly. Also check for obvious damage, distortion, cracking, etc. Light glazing can be removed with emery cloth or sandpaper. If a new pressure plate is indicated, new or factory rebuilt units are available.

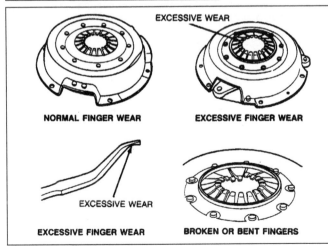

NORMAL FINGER WEAR

EXCESSIVE WEAR

EXCESSIVE FINGER WEAR

EXCESSIVE WEAR

EXCESSIVE FINGER WEAR

BROKEN OR BENT FINGERS

3.12a Replace the pressure plate if any of theseconditions are noted

3.12b Examine the pressure plate friction surface for score marks, cracks and evidence of overheating (blue spots)

3.14 Centre the clutch disc in the pressure plate with a clutch alignment tool

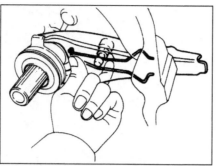

4.3 Reach behind the release lever and disengage the lever from the ball stud by pulling on the retention spring, then remove the lever and bearing

4.4 To check the operation of the bearing, hold it by the outer race and rotate the inner race while applying pressure - the bearing should turn smoothly - if it doesn't, replace it

Installation

13 Before installation, carefully wipe the flywheel and pressure plate machined surfaces clean. It's important that no oil or grease is on these surfaces or the lining of the clutch disc. Handle these parts only with clean hands.

14 Position the clutch disc and pressure plate with the clutch held in place with an alignment tool **(see illustration)**. Make sure it's installed properly (most replacement clutch plates will be marked "flywheel side" or something similar - if not marked, install the clutch disc with the damper springs or cushion toward the transmission).

15 Tighten the pressure plate-to-flywheel bolts only finger tight, working around the pressure plate.

16 Centre the clutch disc by ensuring the alignment tool is through the splined hub and into the recess in the crankshaft. Wiggle the tool up, down or side-to-side as needed to bottom the tool. Tighten the pressure plate-to-flywheel bolts a little at a time, working in a crisscross pattern to prevent distortion of the cover. After all of the bolts are snug, tighten them to the torque listed in this Chapter's Specifications. Remove the alignment tool.

17 Using high-temperature grease, lubricate the inner groove of the release bearing (see Section 4). Also place grease on the release lever contact areas and the transmission input shaft bearing retainer.

18 Install the clutch release bearing (see Section 4).

19 Install the transmission, release cylinder and all components removed previously, tightening all fasteners to the proper torque specifications.

4 Clutch release bearing and lever - removal, inspection and installation

⚠️ *Warning: Dust produced by clutch wear and deposited on clutch components may contain asbestos, which is hazardous to your health. DO NOT blow it out with compressed air and DO NOT inhale it. DO NOT use petrol or petroleum-based solvents to remove the dust. Brake system cleaner should be used to flush it into a drain pan. After the clutch components are wiped clean with a rag, dispose of the contaminated rags and cleaner in a labeled, covered container.*

Removal

1 Disconnect the negative cable from the battery.
Caution: If the stereo in your vehicle is equipped with an anti-theft system, make

sure you have the correct activation code before disconnecting the battery.

2 Remove the transmission (see Chapter 7).

3 Remove the clutch release lever from the ball stud, then remove the bearing from the lever **(see illustration)**.

Inspection

4 Hold the bearing by the outer race and rotate the inner race while applying pressure **(see illustration)**. If the bearing doesn't turn smoothly or if it's noisy, replace the bearing/hub assembly with a new one. Wipe the bearing with a clean rag and inspect it for damage, wear and cracks. Don't immerse the bearing in solvent - it's sealed for life and to do so would ruin it. Also check the release lever for cracks and bends.

Installation

5 Fill the inner groove of the release bearing with high-temperature grease. Also apply a light coat of the same grease to the transmission input shaft splines and the front bearing retainer **(see illustration)**.

6 Lubricate the release lever ball socket, lever ends and release cylinder pushrod socket with high-temperature grease **(see illustration)**.

7 Attach the release bearing to the release lever.

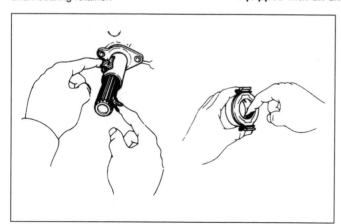

4.5 Apply a light coat of high-temperature grease to the transmission bearing retainer and also fill the release bearing groove

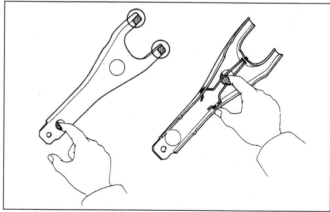

4.6 Apply high temperature grease to the release lever in the areas indicated

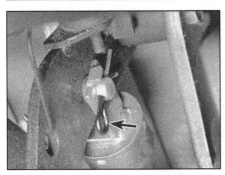

5.2 To release the clutch pushrod from the clutch pedal, remove this clip (arrow) and the clevis pin

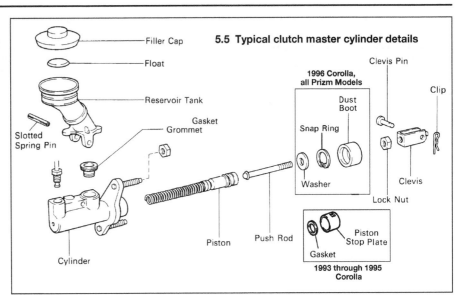

5.5 Typical clutch master cylinder details

Filler Cap

Float

Reservoir Tank

Gasket
Grommet

Slotted
Spring Pin

1996 Corolla, all Prizm Models

Clevis Pin

Dust Boot

Clip

Snap Ring

Washer

Clevis

Lock Nut

Cylinder

Piston

Push Rod

Gasket

Piston Stop Plate

1993 through 1995 Corolla

8 Slide the release bearing onto the transmission input shaft front bearing retainer while passing the end of the release lever through the opening in the clutch housing. Push the clutch release lever onto the ball stud until it's firmly seated.

9 Apply a light coat of high-temperature grease to the face of the release bearing where it contacts the pressure plate diaphragm fingers.

10 The remainder of installation is the reverse of the removalprocedure.

5   Clutch master cylinder - removal, overhaul and installation

Note: *Before beginning this procedure, contact local parts stores and dealer service departments concerning the purchase of a rebuild kit or a new master cylinder. Availability and cost of the necessary parts may dictate whether the cylinder is rebuilt or replaced with a new one. If you decide to rebuild the cylinder, inspect the bore as described in Step 11 before purchasing parts.*

Removal

1 Disconnect the negative cable from the battery.

Caution: If the stereo in your vehicle is equipped with an anti-theft system, make sure you have the correct activation code before disconnecting the battery.

2 Under the dashboard, disconnect the pushrod from the top of the clutch pedal. It's held in place with a clevis pin. To remove the clevis pin, remove the clip **(see illustration)**.

3 Disconnect the hydraulic line at the clutch master cylinder. If available, use a flare-nut wrench on the fitting, to protect the fitting from being rounded off. Have rags handy as some fluid will be lost as the line is removed.

Caution: Don't allow brake fluid to come into contact with paint, as it will damage it.

4 From under the dash, remove the nuts which attach the master cylinder to the firewall. Remove the master cylinder, again being careful not to spill any of the fluid.

Overhaul

5 Remove the reservoir cap and drain all fluid from the master cylinder. Drive out the spring pin **(see illustration)** with a hammer and punch, then carefully pry off the reservoir.

6 If you're working on a 1995 or earlier Corolla, use a small screwdriver and bend out the staked part of the piston stop plate until it's flush with the surface of the stop plate **(see illustration)**. Remove the stop plate, gasket and pushrod from the cylinder.

7 If you're working on a 1996 Corolla, remove the dust boot, depress the pushrod and remove the snap-ring with a pair of snap-ring pliers. Pull out the pushrod and washer.

8 Tap the master cylinder on a block of wood to eject the piston assembly from inside the bore **(see illustration)**. **Note:** *If the rebuild kit supplies a complete piston assembly, ignore the Steps which don't apply.*

9 Separate the spring from the piston.

10 Carefully remove the seal from the piston.

11 Inspect the bore of the master cylinder for deep scratches, score marks and ridges. The surface must be smooth to the touch. If the bore isn't perfectly smooth, the master cylinder must be replaced with a new or factory rebuilt unit.

12 If the cylinder will be rebuilt, use the new parts contained in the rebuild kit and follow any specific instructions which may have

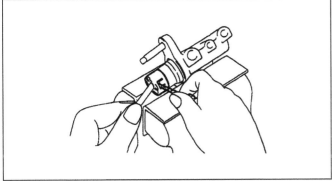

5.6 If you're working on a 1995 or earlier Corolla, use a small screwdriver to bend the staked part of the piston stop plate out until it's flush with the surface of the stop plate, then remove the stop plate, gasket and pushrod from the cylinder bore

5.8 Invert the cylinder and tap it against a block of wood to eject the piston

accompanied the rebuild kit. Wash all parts to be re-used with brake cleaner, denatured alcohol or clean brake fluid. DO NOT use petroleum-based solvents.

13 Attach the seal to the piston. The seal lips must face away from the pushrod end of the piston.

14 Assemble the spring on the other end of the piston.

15 Lubricate the bore of the cylinder and the seals with plenty of fresh brake fluid.

16 Carefully guide the piston assembly into the bore, being careful not to damage the seals. Make sure the spring end is installed first, with the pushrod end of the piston closest to the opening.

17 If you're working on a 1995 or earlier Corolla, position the pushrod and a new gasket in the bore, compress the spring and install a new stop plate. If you're working on a 1996 Corolla, install the pushrod and washer, depress the pushrod and install a new snap-ring, making sure it seats completely in its groove. Install a new dust boot.

18 Install the fluid reservoir with a new grommet. Drive in the spring pin with a small hammer and punch. Make sure the pin protrudes about 1/8-inch, or less, on each side of the reservoir bracket.

Installation

19 Position the master cylinder on the firewall, installing the mounting nuts finger-tight.

20 Connect the hydraulic line to the master cylinder, moving the cylinder slightly as necessary to thread the fitting properly into the bore. Don't cross-thread the fitting as it's installed.

21 Tighten the mounting nuts and the hydraulic line fitting securely.

22 Connect the pushrod to the clutch pedal.

23 Fill the clutch master cylinder reservoir with fresh brake fluid of the specified type (see Chapter 1) and then bleed the clutch system (see Section 7).

24 Check the clutch pedal height and freeplay (see Chapter 1).

---

6 Clutch release cylinder - removal, overhaul and installation

Note: *Before beginning this procedure, contact local parts stores and dealer service departments concerning the purchase of a rebuild kit or a new release cylinder. Availability and cost of the necessary parts may dictate whether the cylinder is rebuilt or replaced with a new one. If it's decided to rebuild the cylinder, inspect the bore as described in Step 8 before purchasing parts.*

Removal

1 Disconnect the negative cable from the battery.

Caution: If the stereo in your vehicle is equipped with an anti-theft system, make sure you have the correct activation code before disconnecting the battery.

2 Raise the vehicle and support it securely on jackstands.

3 Disconnect the hydraulic line at the release cylinder. If available, use a flare-nut wrench on the fitting, which will prevent the fitting from being rounded off **(see illustration)**. Have a small can and rags handy, as some fluid will be spilled as the line is removed.

4 Remove the release cylinder mounting bolts.

5 Remove the release cylinder.

6.3 Use a flare-nut wrench when disconnecting the hydraulic line fitting (left arrow) to prevent rounding off the corners of the tubing nut, then remove the two mounting bolts (right arrows)

Overhaul

6 Remove the pushrod and the boot **(see illustration)**.

7 Tap the cylinder on a block of wood to eject the piston and seal. Remove the spring from inside the cylinder.

8 Carefully inspect the bore of the cylinder. Check for deep scratches, score marks and ridges. The bore must be smooth to the touch. If any imperfections are found, the release cylinder must be replaced with a new one.

9 Using the new parts in the rebuild kit, assemble the components using plenty of fresh brake fluid for lubrication. Note the installed direction of the spring and the seal.

Installation

10 Install the release cylinder on the clutch housing. Make sure the pushrod is seated in the release fork pocket.

11 Connect the hydraulic line to the release cylinder. Tighten the connection.

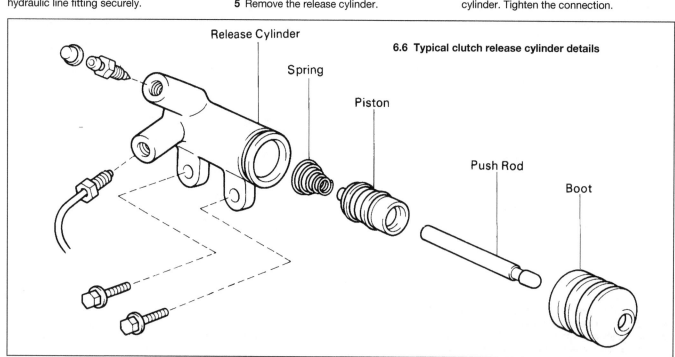

6.6 Typical clutch release cylinder details

Release Cylinder

Spring

Piston

Push Rod

Boot

12 Fill the clutch master cylinder with fresh brake fluid of the specified type (see Chapter 1).
13 Bleed the system (see Section 7).
14 Lower the vehicle and connect the negative battery cable.

7 Clutch hydraulic system - bleeding

1 The hydraulic system should be bled of all air whenever any part of the system has been removed or if the fluid level has been allowed to fall so low that air has been drawn into the master cylinder. The procedure is similar to bleeding a brake system.
2 Fill the master cylinder with fresh brake fluid of the specified type (see Chapter 1).
Caution: Do not re-use any of the fluid coming from the system during the bleeding operation or use fluid which has been inside an open container for an extended period of time.
3 Raise the vehicle and place it securely on jackstands to gain access to the release cylinder, which is located on the left side of the clutch housing.
4 Locate the bleeder valve on the clutch release cylinder (right above the fitting for the hydraulic fluid line). Remove the dust cap which fits over the bleeder valve and push a length of plastic hose over the valve. Place the other end of the hose into a clear container with about two inches of brake fluid in it. The hose end must be submerged in the fluid.
5 Have an assistant depress the clutch pedal and hold it. Open the bleeder valve on the release cylinder, allowing fluid to flow through the hose. Close the bleeder valve when fluid stops flowing from the hose. Once closed, have your assistant release the pedal.
6 Continue this process until all air is evacuated from the system, indicated by a full, solid stream of fluid being ejected from the bleeder valve each time and no air bubbles in the hose or container. Keep a close watch on the fluid level inside the clutch master cylinder reservoir; if the level drops too low, air will be sucked back into the system and the process will have to be started all over again.
7 Install the dust cap and lower the vehicle. Check carefully for proper operation before placing the vehicle in normal service.

8 Clutch start switch - check and replacement

Check

1 Check the clutch pedal height and freeplay and the pushrod freeplay (see Chapter 1).
2 Verify that the engine will not start when the clutch pedal is released. Verify that the engine will start when the clutch pedal is depressed all the way.

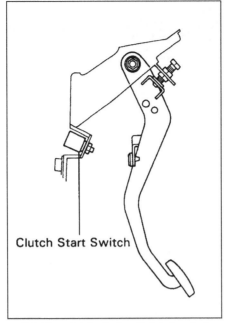

8.4 The clutch start switch is located under the dash on a bracket in front of the clutch pedal

3 If the clutch start switch doesn't perform as described, adjust and, if necessary, replace it.
4 Locate the switch **(see illustration)** and unplug the electrical connector.
5 Verify that there is continuity between the clutch start switch terminals when the switch is On (pedal depressed) **(see illustration)**.
6 Verify that no continuity exists between the switch terminals when the switch is Off (pedal released).
7 If the switch fails either of the tests, replace it.

Replacement

8 Remove the nut nearest the plunger end of the switch and unscrew the switch. Unplug the electrical connector.

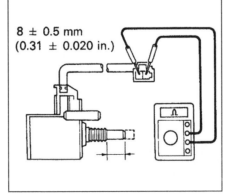

8.5 Using an ohmmeter, check the continuity of the clutch start switch - there should be continuity when the switch is On (pedal depressed) and no continuity when it's Off (pedal released)

9 Installation is the reverse of removal. The switch is self-adjusting, so there's no need for adjustment.
10 Verify again that the engine doesn't start when the clutch pedal is released, and does start when the pedal is depressed.

9 Driveshafts - general information and inspection

1 Power is transmitted from the transmission to the wheels through a pair of driveshafts. The inner end of each driveshaft is splined into the differential side gears. The outer ends of the driveshafts are splined to the axle hubs and locked in place by a large nut.
2 The inner ends of the driveshafts are equipped with sliding constant velocity joints, which are capable of both angular and axial motion. Each inner joint assembly consists of a tripod bearing and a joint housing (outer race) in which the joint is free to slide in and out as the driveshaft moves up and down with the wheel. The joints can be disassembled and cleaned in the event of a boot failure (see Section 11), but if any parts are damaged, the joints must be replaced as a unit.
3 The outer CV joints are the "Rzeppa" type, which consists of ball bearings running between an inner race and an outer cage, is capable of angular but not axial movement. The outer joints should be cleaned, inspected and repacked, but they cannot be disassembled. If an outer joint is damaged, it must be replaced along with the driveshaft (the outer joint and driveshaft are sold as a single component).
4 The boots should be inspected periodically for damage and leaking lubricant. Torn CV joint boots must be replaced immediately or the joints can be damaged. Boot replacement involves removal of the driveshaft (see Section 10). **Note:** *Some auto parts stores carry "split" type replacement boots, which can be installed without removing the driveshaft from the vehicle. This is a convenient alternative; however, the driveshaft should be removed and the CV joint disassembled and cleaned to ensure the joint is free from contaminants such as moisture and dirt which will accelerate CV joint wear.* The most common symptom of worn or damaged CV joints, besides lubricant leaks, is a clicking noise in turns, a clunk when accelerating after coasting and vibration at highway speeds. To check for wear in the CV joints and driveshaft shafts, grasp each driveshaft (one at a time) and rotate it in both directions while holding the CV joint housings, feeling for play indicating worn splines or sloppy CV joints. Also check the driveshaft shafts for cracks, dents and distortion.

10.4a Remove the cotter pin . . .

10.4b . . . and the nut lock

10.5 Use a large prybar to immobilize the hub while loosening the driveshaft hub nut

10 Driveshaft - removal and installation

Removal

1 Disconnect the cable from the negative terminal of the battery.
Caution: If the stereo in your vehicle is equipped with an anti-theft system, make sure you have the correct activation code before disconnecting the battery.
2 Set the parking brake.

10.6 Using a brass punch, strike the end of the driveshaft sharply with a hammer; when it breaks free, it will move noticeably

3 Loosen the front wheel nuts, raise the vehicle and support it securely on jackstands. Remove the wheel.
4 Remove the cotter pin and bearing nut lock from the driveshaft hub nut **(see illustrations)**.
5 Remove the driveshaft hub nut and washer. To prevent the hub from turning, wedge a prybar between two of the wheel studs and allow the prybar to rest against the ground or the floorpan of the vehicle **(see illustration)**.
6 To loosen the driveshaft from the hub splines, tap the end of the driveshaft with a soft-faced hammer or a hammer and a brass punch **(see illustration)**. **Note:** *Don't attempt to push the end of the driveshaft through the hub yet. Applying force to the end of the driveshaft, beyond just breaking it loose from the hub, can damage the driveshaft or transmission.* If the driveshaft is stuck in the hub splines and won't move, it may be necessary to remove the brake disc (see Chapter 9) and push it from the hub with a two-jaw puller after Step 8 is performed.
7 Remove the engine splash shields (see Chapter 1). Place a drain pan underneath the transmission to catch the lubricant that will spill out when the driveshafts are removed.
8 Remove the nuts and bolt securing the balljoint to the control arm, then pry the control arm down to separate the components (see Chapter 10)

9 Pull out on the steering knuckle and detach the driveshaft from the hub **(see illustration)**. Don't let the driveshaft hang by the inner CV joint after the outer end has been detached from the steering knuckle, as the inner joint could become damaged. Support the outer end of the driveshaft with a piece of wire, if necessary.
10 Carefully pry the inner CV joint out of the transmission **(see illustration)**.
11 Refer to Chapter 7 for the driveshaft oil seal replacementprocedure.

Installation

12 Installation is the reverse of the removal procedure, but with the following additional points:
a) *Push the driveshaft sharply in to seat the retaining ring on the inner CV joint in the groove in the differential side gear.*
b) *Tighten the driveshaft hub nut to the torque listed in this Chapter's Specifications, then install the nut lock and a new cotter pin.*
c) *Install the wheel and nuts, lower the vehicle and tighten the nuts to the torque listed in the Chapter 1 Specifications.*
d) *Check the transmission or differential lubricant and add, if necessary, to bring it to the proper level (see Chapter 1).*

10.9 Pull the steering knuckle out and slide the end of the driveshaft out of the hub

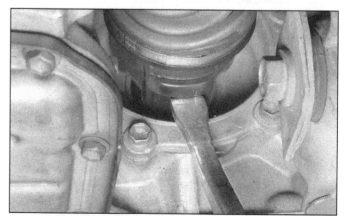

10.10 To separate the inner end of the driveshaft from the transmission, pry on the CV joint housing like this with a large screwdriver or prybar - you may need to give the prybar a sharp rap with a brass hammer

11.3 Lift the tabs on all the boot clamps with a screwdriver, then open the clamps

11.4 Remove the boot from the inner CV joint and slide the joint housingfrom the tripod

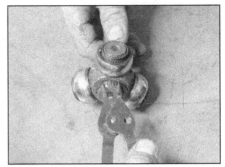

11.6 Remove the snap-ring with a pair of snap-ring pliers

11 Driveshaft boot replacement and CV joint inspection

Note: *If the CV joints must be overhauled (usually due to torn boots), explore all options before beginning the job. Complete rebuilt driveshafts are available on an exchange basis, which eliminates much time and work. Whichever route you choose to take, check on the cost and availability of parts before disassembling the vehicle.*

1 Remove the driveshaft (see Section 10).

Disassembly

2 Mount the driveshaft in a vise with wood lined jaws (to prevent damage to the driveshaft). Check the CV joint for excessive play in the radial direction, which indicates worn parts. Check for smooth operation throughout the full range of motion for each CV joint. If a boot is torn, disassemble the joint, clean the components and inspect for damage due to loss of lubrication and possible contamination by foreign matter.

3 Using a small screwdriver, pry the retaining tabs on the clamps up to loosen them and slide them off **(see illustration)**.

4 Using a screwdriver, carefully pry up on the edge of the outer boot and push it away from the CV joint. Old and worn boots can be cut off. Pull the inner CV joint boot back from the housing and slide the housing from the tripod **(see illustration)**. Mark the tripod and housing to ensure that they are reassembled properly.

5 Mark the tripod and driveshaft to ensure that they are reassembled properly.

6 Remove the tripod joint snap-ring with a pair of snap-ring pliers **(see illustration)**.

7 Use a hammer and a brass punch to drive the tripod joint from the driveshaft **(see illustration)**.

8 If you haven't already cut them off, remove both boots. If you're working on a right-hand driveshaft, you'll also have to cut off the clamp for the dynamic damper and slide the damper off, after first marking its position for reassembly.

Check

9 Thoroughly clean all components, including the outer CV joint assembly, with solvent until the old CV joint grease is completely removed. Inspect the bearing surfaces of the inner tripods and housings for cracks, pitting, scoring and other signs of wear. It's very difficult to inspect the bearing surfaces of the inner and outer races of the outer CV joint, but you can at least check the surfaces of the ball bearings themselves. If they're in good shape, the races probably are too; if they're not, neither are the races. If the inner CV joint is worn, you can buy a new inner CV joint and install it on the old driveshaft; if the outer CV joint is worn, you'll have to purchase a new outer CV joint *and* driveshaft (they're sold preassembled).

Reassembly

10 Wrap the splines on the end of the driveshaft with electrical tape to protect the boots from the sharp edges of the splines **(see illustration)**. Slide the clamps and boot(s) onto the driveshaft, then place the tripod on the shaft. **Note:** *If you're working on a right-hand driveshaft, be sure to install the dynamic damper and a new clamp before installing the inner boot.* Apply grease to the tripod assembly and inside the housing. Insert the tripod into the housing and pack the remainder of the grease around the tripod. **(see illustrations)**.

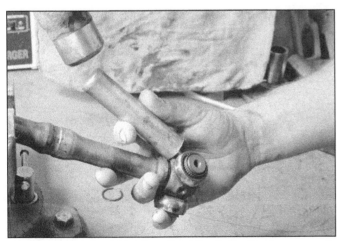

11.7 Drive the tripod joint from the driveshaft with a brass punch and hammer; be careful not to damage the bearing surfaces or the splines on the shaft

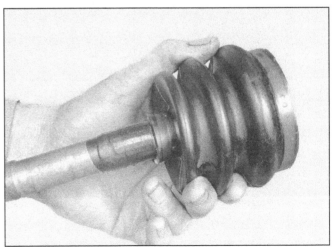

11.10a Wrap the splined area of the axleshaft with tape to prevent damageto the boots when removing or installing them

11.10b Install the tripod with the recessed portion of the splines facing the axleshaft

11.10c Place grease at the bottom of the CV joint housing

11.10d Install the boot and clamps onto the axleshaft, then insert the tripod into the housing, followed by the rest of the grease

11 Slide the boot into place, making sure both ends seat in their grooves. Adjust the length of the driveshaft to the dimension listed in this Chapter's Specifications **(see illustration)**.

12 Equalize the pressure in the boot, then tighten and secure the boot clamps **(see illustrations)**.

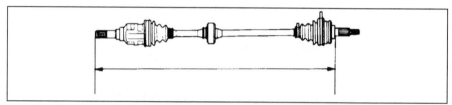

11.11 The driveshaft standard length should be set to the dimension listed in this Chapter's Specifications before the boot clamps are tightened

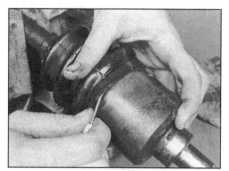

11.12a Equalize the pressure inside the boot by inserting a small, dull screwdriver between the boot and the outer race

11.12b To install the new clamps, bend the tang down . . .

11.12c . . . then tap the tabs over tohold it in place

Chapter 9
Braking system

Contents

Degrees of difficulty

Easy, suitable for novice with little experience	**Fairly easy,** suitable for beginner with some experience	**Fairly difficult,** suitable for competent DIY mechanic 🔧	**Difficult,** suitable for experienced DIY mechanic 🔧	**Very difficult,** suitable for expert DIY or professional 🔧

Specifications

General

Brake fluid type	See Chapter 1
Brake pedal height	
Right-hand drive models	5.85 to 6.24 inches
Left-hand drive models	5.46 to 5.85 inches
Brake pedal freeplay	0.04 to 0.24 inches
Brake pedal reserve distance	At least 2.76 inches
Brake light switch-to-pedal clearance	0.02 to 0.09 inches
Servo unit pushrod-to-master cylinder piston clearance	0.0 inch

Front disc brakes

Minimum brake pad thickness	See Chapter 1
Disc thickness	
Standard	0.709 inches or 0.866 inches
Minimum*	
For 0.709 inch disc	0.669 inches
For 0.866 inch disc	0.837 inches
Disc runout limit	0.002 inch

Rear drum brakes

Minimum brake shoe lining thickness	See Chapter 1
Drum inside diameter*	
Standard	7.874 inches
Maximum*	7.913 inches

Rear disc brakes

Minimum brake pad thickness	See Chapter 1
Disc thickness	
Standard	0.354 inches
Minimum*	0.315 inches
Disc runout limit	0.006 inch

*Note: If different specifications are cast into the disc or drum, they supersede information printed here.

Parking brake

Parking brake lever travel	4 to 7 clicks

Torque wrench settings

	Ft-lbs
Brake hose-to-caliper banjo bolts	22
Front caliper-to-torque plate	25
Front caliper torque plate-to-steering knuckle	65
Rear caliper-to-torque plate	14
Rear caliper torque plate-to-axle carrier	33
Master cylinder-to-brake servo unit nuts	9
Servo unit mounting nuts	9
Wheel cylinder mounting bolts	7
Wheel nuts	See Chapter 1

1 General information

The vehicles covered by this manual are equipped with hydraulically operated front and rear brake systems. The front brakes are disc type and the rear brakes are drum or disc type according to model. Both the front and rear brakes are self adjusting. The disc brakes automatically compensate for pad wear, while the drum brakes incorporate an adjustment mechanism which is activated as the parking brake is applied.

Hydraulic system

The hydraulic system consists of two separate circuits. The master cylinder has separate reservoirs for the two circuits, and, in the event of a leak or failure in one hydraulic circuit, the other circuit will remain operative. A dual proportioning valve on the bulkhead provides brake balance between the front and rear brakes. On models with ABS, a load sensing proportioning valve limits hydraulic pressure to the rear brakes according to vehicle loading.

Servo unit

The servo unit, utilizing engine manifold vacuum and atmospheric pressure to provide assistance to the hydraulically operated brakes, is mounted on the bulkhead in the engine compartment.

Parking brake

The parking brake operates the rear brakes only, through cable actuation. It's activated by a lever mounted in the centre console.

Service

After completing any operation involving disassembly of any part of the brake system, always test drive the vehicle to check for proper braking performance before resuming normal driving. When testing the brakes, perform the tests on a clean, dry, flat surface. Conditions other than these can lead to inaccurate test results.

Test the brakes at various speeds with both light and heavy pedal pressure. The vehicle should stop evenly without pulling to one side or the other. Avoid locking the brakes, because this slides the tyres and diminishes braking efficiency and control of the vehicle.

Tyres, vehicle load and wheel alignment are factors which also affect braking performance.

2 Anti-lock Brake System (ABS) - general information

1 The anti-lock brake system (ABS) **(see illustration)** is designed to maintain vehicle steerability, directional stability and optimum deceleration under severe braking conditions and on most road surfaces. It does so by monitoring the rotational speed of each wheel and controlling the brake line pressure to each wheel during braking. This prevents the wheel from locking up.

Components

Actuator assembly

2 The actuator assembly consists of an electric hydraulic pump and four solenoid valves. The electric pump provides hydraulic pressure to charge the reservoirs in the actuator, which supplies pressure to the braking system. The pump and reservoirs are housed in the actuator assembly. The solenoid valves modulate brake line pressure during ABS operation. The body contains four valves - one for each wheel.

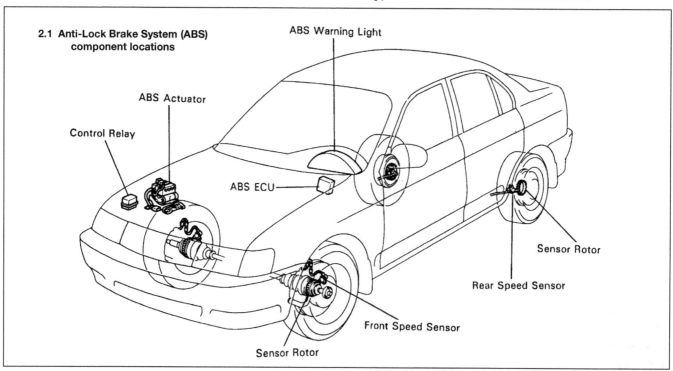

2.1 Anti-Lock Brake System (ABS) component locations

3.5 Before removing the caliper, be sure to depress the piston into the bottom of its bore in the caliper with a large C-clamp to make room for the new pads

3.6a Always wash the brakes with brake cleaner before disassembling anything

Speed sensors

3 The wheel speed sensors, which are located at each wheel, generate small electrical pulsations when the toothed sensor rotors are turning, sending a variable voltage signal to the ABS electronic control unit (ECU) indicating wheel rotational speed.

4 The front speed sensors are mounted on the front steering knuckles in close relationship to the toothed sensor rotors, which are integral with the outer constant velocity (CV) joints.

5 The rear wheel sensors are bolted to the brake backing plates or axle carriers. The sensor rotors are integral with the rear hub assemblies.

ABS computer

6 The ABS electronic control unit (ECU), which is mounted under the dashboard, is the "brain" of the ABS system. The function of the ECU is to accept and process information received from the wheel speed sensors to control the hydraulic line pressure, avoiding wheel lock up. The ECU also constantly monitors the system, even under normal driving conditions, to find faults within the system.

7 If a problem develops within the system, an "ABS" light will glow on the dashboard. A diagnostic code will also be stored in the ECU, which, when retrieved by a service technician, will indicate the problem area or component.

Diagnosis and repair

8 If a dashboard warning light comes on and stays on while the vehicle is in operation, the ABS system requires attention. Although a special electronic ABS diagnostic tester is necessary to properly diagnose the system, the home mechanic can perform a few preliminary checks before taking the vehicle to a dealer service department or other repair workshop which is equipped with a tester.

a) Check the brake fluid level in the reservoir.
b) Check that all electrical connectors are securely connected.
c) Check the fuses.

9 If the above preliminary checks do not rectify the problem, the vehicle should be diagnosed and repaired by a dealer service department or other repair workshop.

3 Front disc brake pads - replacement

⚠️ *Warning: Disc brake pads must be replaced on both front wheels at the same time - never replace the pads on only one wheel. Also, the dust created by the brake system may contain asbestos, which is harmful to your health. Never blow it out with compressed air and don't inhale any of it. An approved filtering mask should be worn when working on the brakes. Do not, under any circumstances, use petroleum-based solvents to clean brake parts. Use brake system cleaner only!*

1 Remove the cap from the brake fluid reservoir.

2 Loosen the wheel nuts, raise the front of the vehicle and support it securely on jackstands. Block the wheels at the opposite end.

3 Remove the wheel. **Note:** *All four front brake pads must be replaced at the same time, but to avoid mixing up parts, work on only one brake assembly at a time.*

4 Inspect the brake disc carefully as outlined in Section 7. If machining is necessary, follow the information in that Section to remove the disc, at which time the pads can be removed as well.

5 Push the piston back into its bore to provide room for the new brake pads. A C-clamp can be used to accomplish this **(see illustration)**. As the piston is depressed to the

bottom of the caliper bore, the fluid in the master cylinder will rise. Make sure that it doesn't overflow. If necessary, siphon off some of the fluid.

6 Follow the accompanying photos **(illustrations 3.6a through 3.6u)**, for the actual pad replacement procedure. Be sure to stay in order and read the caption under each illustration. Note that two brake caliper types are used on these cars, the type PE54 and type PD51. The photographic sequence depicts the PE54 caliper but both types are virtually identical apart from minor differences in the sliding pin arrangement **(see illustrations 4.4a and 4.4b)**.

7 When reinstalling the caliper, be sure to tighten the mounting bolts to the torque listed in this Chapter's Specifications. After the job has been completed, firmly depress the brake pedal a few times to bring the pads into contact with the disc. Check the level of the brake fluid, adding some if necessary. Check the operation of the brakes carefully before placing the vehicle into normal service.

3.6b Remove the bolts indicated by the upper and lower arrows. On PE54 calipers, counterhold the sliding pins with a wrench while removing the bolts. The brake hose union (middle arrow) shouldn't be unscrewed unless the caliper is being removed for overhaul)

3.6c Remove the caliper . . .

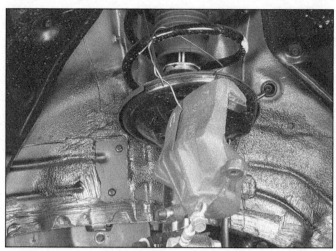

3.6d . . . and hang it from the strut coil spring with a piece of coat hanger or wire; do not allow the caliper to hang by the brake hose

3.6e Remove the upper anti-squeal spring . . .

3.6f . . . and the lower anti-squeal spring but note that on some later calipers these springs aren't fitted

3.6g Remove the outer shim . . .

3.6h . . . and, where fitted, the inner shim from the outer brake pad

3.6i Remove the outer brake pad

3.6j Remove the outer shim . . .

3.6k . . . and, where fitted, the inner shim from the inner brake pad

3.6l Remove the inner brake pad

3.6m Remove the four pad support plates; inspect the plates for damage and replace as necessary (good plates should "snap" into place in the torque plate; if they're weak or distorted, replace them)

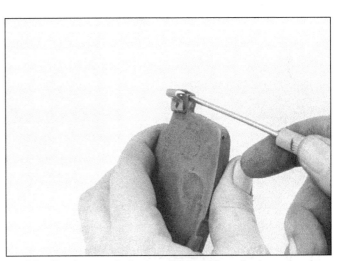

3.6n Pry the wear indicator off the old inner brake pad and transfer it to the new inner pad (if the wear indicator is worn or bent, replace it)

3.6o Install the pad support plates, the new inner brake pads and the shims; make sure the ears on the pad are properly engaged with the pad support plates as shown

3.6p Install the pad support plates, the outer pad and the shims

3.6q Install the upper and lower anti-squeal springs; make sure both springs are properly engaged with the pads as shown

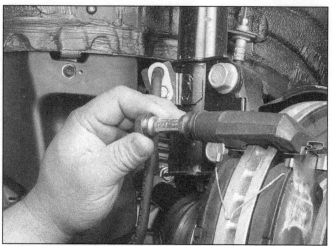

3.6r On the PE54 caliper, pull out the upper and lower sliding pins and clean them off (if either rubber boot is damaged, remove it by prying the flange of the metal bushing that retains the boot) . . .

3.6s . . . apply a coat of high-temperature grease to the PE54 caliper sliding pins before installing them

3.6t Install the caliper and tighten the caliper bolts to the torque listed in this Chapter's Specifications

3.6u If you have difficulty installing the caliper over the new pads, use a C-clamp to bottom the piston in its bore, then try again - it should now slip over the pads

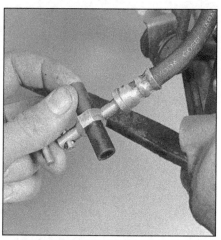

4.2 Using a piece of rubber hose of the appropriate size, plug the brake line; this will prevent brake fluid from leaking out and dirt and moisture from contaminating the fluid in the hose

4 Front disc brake caliper - removal, overhaul and installation

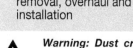 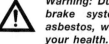 **Warning: Dust created by the brake system may contain asbestos, which is harmful to your health. Never blow it out with compressed air and don't inhale any of it. An approved filtering mask should be worn when working on the brakes. Do not, under any circumstances, use petroleum-based solvents to clean brake parts. Use brake system cleaner.**

Note: If an overhaul is indicated (usually because of fluid leakage), explore all options before beginning the job. New and factory rebuilt calipers are available on an exchange basis, which makes this job quite easy. If it's decided to rebuild the calipers, make sure a rebuild kit is available before proceeding. Always rebuild the calipers in pairs - never rebuild just one of them.

Removal

1 Loosen the front wheel nuts, raise the front of the vehicle and place it securely on jackstands. Remove the wheel.
2 Remove the bolt and disconnect the brake hose from the caliper (see illustration 3.6b). Plug the brake hose to keep contaminants out of the brake system and to prevent losing any more brake fluid than is necessary (see illustration).
3 Refer to Section 3 for the caliper removal procedure (it's part of the brake pad replacement procedure).

Overhaul

4 To overhaul the caliper, remove the boot set ring and the boot (see illustrations). Before you remove the piston, place a wood block or some rags between the piston and caliper to prevent damage as it is removed.
5 To remove the piston from the caliper, apply compressed air to the brake fluid hose connection on the caliper body (see illustration). Use only enough pressure to ease the piston out of its bore.

 Warning: Be careful not to place your fingers between the piston and the caliper, as the piston may come out with some force.

6 Inspect the mating surfaces of the piston and caliper bore wall. If there is any scoring, rust, pitting or bright areas, replace the complete caliper unit with a new one.

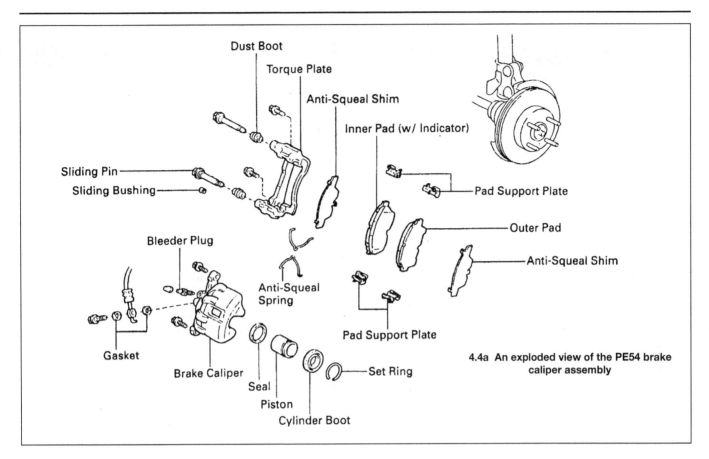

4.4a An exploded view of the PE54 brake caliper assembly

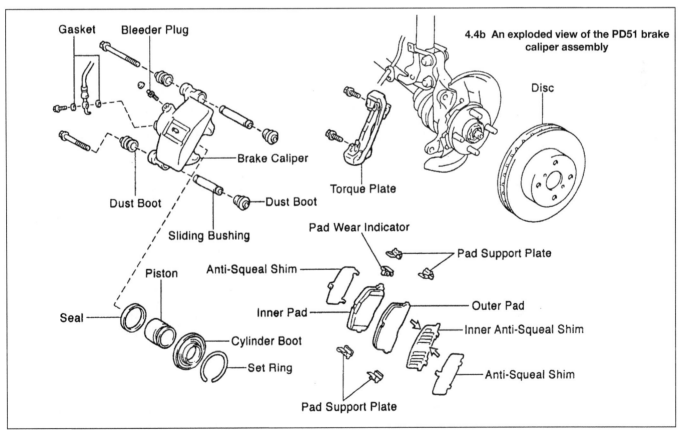

4.4b An exploded view of the PD51 brake caliper assembly

4.4c Using a screwdriver, remove the cylinder boot set ring

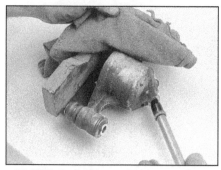

4.5 With the caliper padded to catch the piston, use compressed air to force the piston out of its bore - make sure your hands or fingers are not between the piston and caliper

4.7 To remove the seal from the caliper bore, use a plastic or wooden tool, such as a pencil

7 If these components are in good condition, remove the piston seal from the caliper bore using a wooden or plastic tool **(see illustration)**. Metal tools may damage the cylinder bore.

8 On PD51 calipers, push the sliding bushings out of the caliper ears **(see illustration)** and remove the dust boots from both ends.

9 Wash all the components with brake system cleaner.

10 To reassemble the caliper, you should already have the correct rebuild kit for your vehicle.

11 Submerge the new piston seal and the piston in brake fluid and install them into the caliper bore. Do not force the piston into the bore, but make sure it is squarely in place, then apply firm (but not excessive) pressure to install it.

12 Install the new piston dust boot and set ring.

13 Lubricate the sliding bushings with silicone-based grease (supplied in the kit) and push them into the caliper ears. Install the dust boots.

Installation

14 Install the caliper by reversing the removal procedure. Remember to replace the copper sealing washers (gaskets) at the brake hose-to-caliper connection (new washers normally come with the rebuild kit).

15 Bleed the brake circuit according to the procedure in Section 12. Make sure there are

no leaks from the hose connections. Test the brakes carefully before returning the vehicle to normal service.

5 Rear disc brake pads - replacement

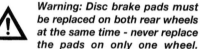

⚠️ *Warning: Disc brake pads must be replaced on both rear wheels at the same time - never replace the pads on only one wheel. Also, the dust created by the brake system may contain asbestos, which is harmful to your health. Never blow it out with compressed air and don't inhale any of it. An approved filtering mask should be worn when working on the brakes. Do not, under any circumstances, use petroleum-based solvents to clean brake parts. Use brake system cleaner only!*

1 Remove the cap from the brake fluid reservoir.

2 Loosen the rear wheel nuts, raise the rear of the vehicle and support it securely on jack-stands. Block the wheels at the opposite end.

3 Remove the wheel and release the parking brake. **Note:** *All four rear brake pads must be replaced at the same time, but to avoid mixing up parts, work on only one brake assembly at a time.*

4 Remove the upper and lower sliding bolts and ease the caliper off the pads and torque plate **(see illustration 6.5)**.

5 Hang the caliper from the strut coil spring with a piece of coat hanger or wire; do not allow the caliper to hang by the brake hose and parking brake cable.

6 Remove the outer anti squeal shim and the outer brake pad, followed by the inner shim and inner brake pad.

7 Remove the two pad support plates; inspect the plates for damage and replace as necessary (good plates should "snap" into place in the torque plate; if they're weak or distorted, replace them).

8 Inspect the brake disc carefully as outlined in Section 7. If machining is necessary, follow the information in that Section to remove the disc, at which time the pads can be removed as well.

9 Install the pad support plates, the new brake pads and the shims. Make sure the ears on the pads are properly engaged with the pad support plates and install the inner pad with the wear indicator at the top.

10 Before the caliper can be installed over the new (thicker) brake pads, the self-adjusting mechanism must be retracted. To do this, turn the caliper piston clockwise, using a pair of circlip pliers engaged with the two stopper groves in the piston face. Keep turning the piston until it turns freely, then align the stopper groves with the protrusion on the caliper housing **(see illustration)**.

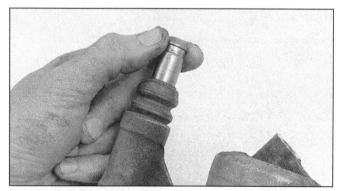

4.8 On PD51 calipers, push out each sliding bushing through the boot, pull it free, then remove the dust boots

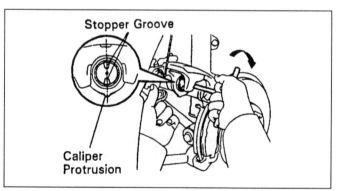

5.10 Retract the caliper piston by turning it clockwise until it turns freely, then align the stopper grooves and caliper protrusion

11 Slide the caliper back over the pads while at the same time engaging the protrusion on the back of the inner pad with the stopper groove in the caliper piston.

12 Install the upper and lower sliding bolts and tighten the bolts to the torque listed in this Chapter's Specifications.

13 Install the wheel, then lower the vehicle to the ground. Tighten the nuts to the torque listed in the Chapter 1 Specifications.

14 After the job has been completed, firmly depress the brake pedal a few times to automatically adjust the rear brakes and bring the pads into contact with the disc. Check the level of the brake fluid, adding some if necessary. Check the operation of the brakes carefully before placing the vehicle into normal service.

6 Rear disc brake caliper - removal, overhaul and installation

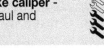

⚠️ *Warning: Dust created by the brake system may contain asbestos, which is harmful to your health. Never blow it out with compressed air and don't inhale any of it. An approved filtering mask should be worn when working on the brakes. Do not, under any circumstances, use petroleum-based solvents to clean brake parts. Use brake system cleaner.*

Note: *If an overhaul is indicated (usually because of fluid leakage), explore all options before beginning the job. New and factory rebuilt calipers are available on an exchange basis, which makes this job quite easy. If it's decided to rebuild the calipers, make sure a rebuild kit is available before proceeding. Always rebuild the calipers in pairs - never rebuild just one of them.*

Removal

1 Loosen the rear wheel nuts, raise the rear of the vehicle and place it securely on jackstands. Remove the wheel.

2 Remove the bolt and disconnect the brake hose from the caliper. Plug the brake hose to keep contaminants out of the brake system and to prevent losing any more brake fluid than is necessary **(see illustration 4.2)**.

3 Disconnect the parking brake cable at the caliper end by removing the pin clip then pulling out the hole pin while pushing the parking brake crank. Remove the outer cable retaining clip and remove the cable.

4 Refer to Section 5 for the caliper removal procedure (it's part of the brake pad replacement procedure).

Overhaul

5 To overhaul the caliper, push the sliding bushings out of the caliper ears and remove the dust boots and main pin boots from both ends **(see illustration)**.

6 Using a screwdriver, remove the cylinder boot set ring and the cylinder boot.

7 Using circlip pliers engaged with the two stopper groves in the piston face, turn the piston anti-clockwise and remove it from the caliper.

8 Inspect the mating surfaces of the piston and caliper bore wall. If there is any scoring, rust, pitting or bright areas, replace the complete caliper unit with a new one.

9 If these components are in good condition, remove the piston seal from the caliper bore using a wooden or plastic tool. Metal tools may damage the cylinder bore.

10 Overhaul of the parking brake and adjusting bolt components is not recommended as special tools are needed and many of these parts cannot be purchased individually. Check the operation of the adjusting mechanism by moving the parking brake crank by hand and checking that the adjusting bolt moves smoothly. If there is any problem with these components, replace the complete caliper unit with a new one.

11 Wash all the components with brake system cleaner.

12 To reassemble the caliper, you should already have the correct rebuild kit for your vehicle.

13 Submerge the new piston seal in brake fluid and install it into the caliper bore.

14 Submerge the new piston in brake fluid and engage it with the adjusting bolt in the caliper bore. Using circlip pliers engaged with the two piston stopper groves, turn the piston clockwise until it turns freely, then align the stopper groves with the protrusion on the caliper housing.

15 Install the new piston dust boot and set ring.

16 Lubricate the sliding bushings with silicone-based grease (supplied in the kit) and push them into the caliper ears. Install the dust boots and main pin boots.

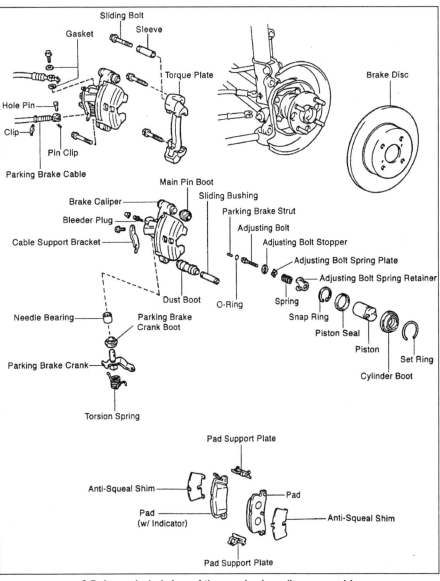

6.5 An exploded view of the rear brake caliper assembly

7.2 To remove the front caliper torque plate, remove these two bolts (arrowed); the pad support plates might fall off while the torque plate is removed, so it's a good idea to note how they're installed before removing the torque plate

7.3 The brake pads on this vehicle were obviously neglected, as they wore down to the backing plate and cut deep grooves into the disc - wear this severe means the disc must be replaced

Installation

17 Install the caliper by reversing the removal procedure. Remember to replace the copper sealing washers (gaskets) at the brake hose-to-caliper connection (new washers normally come with the rebuild kit).

18 Bleed the brake circuit according to the procedure in Section 12. Make sure there are no leaks from the hose connections. Test the brakes carefully before returning the vehicle to normal service.

---

7 Brake disc - inspection, removal and installation

Inspection

1 Loosen the wheel nuts, raise the vehicle and support it securely on jackstands.

Remove the wheel and install two nuts to hold the disc in place.

2 Remove the brake caliper as outlined in Section 4 (front disc) or Section 6 (rear disc). It isn't necessary to disconnect the brake hose. After removing the caliper bolts, suspend the caliper out of the way with a piece of wire **(see illustration 3.6d)**. Remove the two torque plate-to-steering knuckle or axle carrier bolts **(see illustration)** and detach the torque plate.

3 Visually inspect the disc surface for score marks and other damage. Light scratches and shallow grooves are normal after use and may not always be detrimental to brake operation, but deep scoring - over 0.039-inch (1.0 mm) - requires disc removal and refinishing by an automotive machine workshop **(see illustration)**. Be sure to check both sides of the disc. If pulsating has been noticed during application of the brakes, suspect disc runout.

4 To check disc runout, place a dial indicator at a point about 1/2-inch from the outer edge

of the disc **(see illustration)**. Set the indicator to zero and turn the disc. The indicator reading should not exceed the specified allowable runout limit. If it does, the disc should be refinished by an automotive machine workshop. **Note:** *The discs should be resurfaced regardless of the dial indicator reading, as this will impart a smooth finish and ensure a perfectly flat surface, eliminating any brake pedal pulsation or other undesirable symptoms related to questionable discs. At the very least, if you elect not to have the discs resurfaced, remove the glaze from the surface with emery cloth or sandpaper, using a swirling motion* **(see illustration)**.

5 It's absolutely critical that the disc not be machined to a thickness under the specified minimum thickness. The minimum wear (or discard) thickness is cast into the inside of the disc **(see illustration)**. The disc thickness can be checked with a micrometer **(see illustration)**.

7.4a To check disc runout, mount a dial indicator as shown and rotate the disc

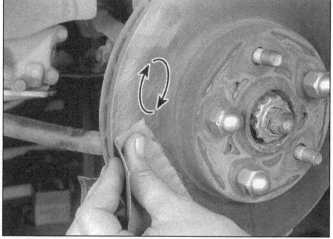

7.4b Using a swirling motion, remove the glaze from the disc surface with sandpaper or emery cloth

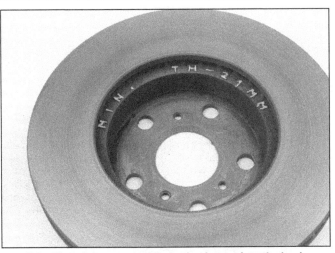

7.5a The minimum wear dimension is cast into the back side of the disc

7.5b Use a micrometer to measure disc thickness

Removal

6 Remove the nuts which were installed to hold the disc in place and remove the disc from the hub.

Installation

7 Place the disc in position over the threaded studs.

8 Install the torque plate and caliper assembly over the disc and position it on the steering knuckle or axle carrier. Tighten the torque plate and caliper bolts to the torques listed in this Chapter's Specifications.

9 Install the wheel, then lower the vehicle to the ground. Tighten the nuts to the torque listed in the Chapter 1 Specifications. Depress the brake pedal a few times to bring the brake pads into contact with the disc. Bleeding won't be necessary unless the brake hose was disconnected from the caliper. Check the operation of the brakes carefully before driving the vehicle.

8 Rear drum brake shoes - replacement

⚠ **Warning:** *Drum brake shoes must be replaced on both wheels at the same time - never replace the shoes on only one wheel. Also, the dust created by the brake system may contain asbestos, which is harmful to your health. Never blow it out with compressed air and don't inhale any of it. An approved filtering mask should be worn when working on the brakes. Do not, under any circumstances, use petroleum-based solvents to clean brake parts. Use brake system cleaner only!*
Caution: *Whenever the brake shoes are replaced, the return and hold-down springs should also be replaced. Due to the continuous heating/cooling cycle the*
springs are subjected to, they lose tension over a period of time and may allow the shoes to drag on the drum and wear at a much faster rate than normal.

1 Loosen the wheel nuts, raise the rear of the vehicle and support it securely on jackstands. Block the front wheels to keep the vehicle from rolling.

2 Release the parking brake.

3 Remove the wheel. **Note:** *All four rear brake shoes must be replaced at the same time, but to avoid mixing up parts, work on only one brake assembly at a time.*

4 Follow the accompanying illustrations for the brake shoe replacement procedure **(see illustrations 8.4a through 8.4ff)**. Be sure to stay in order and read the caption under each illustration. **Note:** *If the brake drum cannot be easily pulled off the axle and shoe assembly, make sure the parking brake is completely released. If the drum still cannot be pulled off, the brake shoes will have to be retracted.*

8.4a Mark the relationship of the drum to the hub, so the drum will retain its dynamic balance after reassembly

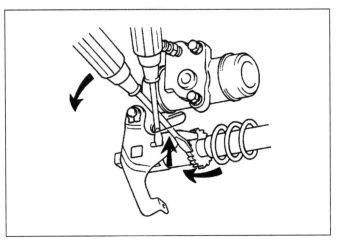

8.4b If the brake drum is hanging up on the shoes because of excessive wear, insert two screwdrivers through the hole in the backing plate, push the adjuster lever away from the star wheel and turn the star wheel to retract the brake shoes

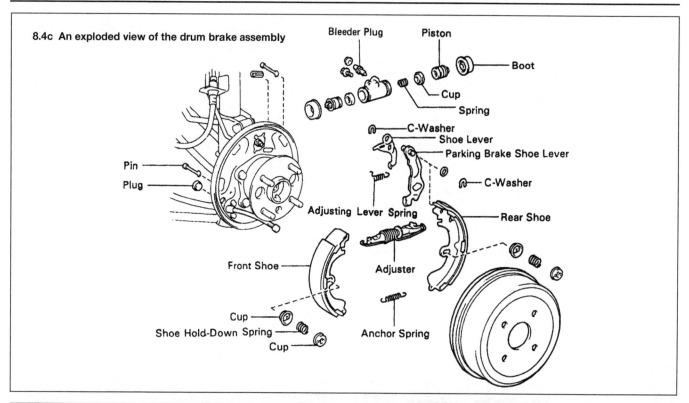

8.4c An exploded view of the drum brake assembly

Bleeder Plug
Piston
Boot
Cup
Spring
C-Washer
Shoe Lever
Parking Brake Shoe Lever
C-Washer
Adjusting Lever Spring
Rear Shoe
Pin
Plug
Front Shoe
Adjuster
Cup
Shoe Hold-Down Spring
Cup
Anchor Spring

8.4d Before removing anything, place a drain pan under the brake assembly, clean the brake assembly with brake cleaner and allow it to dry; DO NOT USE COMPRESSED AIR TO BLOW OFF BRAKE DUST! (hub removed for clarity)

8.4e Unhook the return spring from its hole in the front shoe . . .

8.4f . . . then pull the other end out of the hole in the rear shoe and remove the adjuster and spring

8.4g Using a hold-down spring tool, remove the hold-down spring by pushing in and rotating it 1/4-turn . . .

8.4h . . . remove the outer cup, the spring and the inner cup . . .

8.4i . . . and pull the pin through the backing plate

8.4j Remove the front shoe and unhook the anchor spring from the rear shoe

8.4k Remove the rear shoe hold-down spring, cups and pin

8.4l Flip the rear shoe over, force the spring back from the parking brake lever as shown . . .

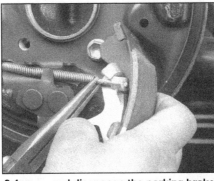

8.4m . . . and disengage the parking brake cable from the parking brake lever

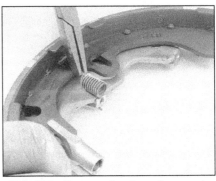

8.4n Take the rear shoe to a clean work bench and unhook the adjusting lever spring from the shoe

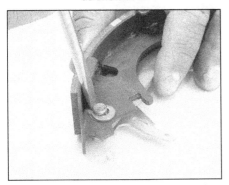

8.4o Pry off the C-washer (don't lose the shim underneath) . . .

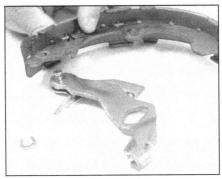

8.4p . . . and remove the parking brake lever and the adjusting lever from the old rear shoe

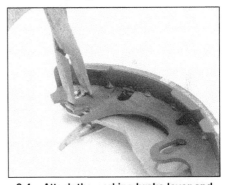

8.4q Attach the parking brake lever and adjusting lever to the new rear shoe and secure them with a new C-washer (don't forget the shim)

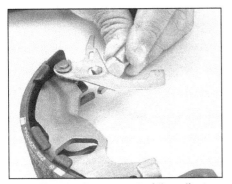

8.4r Engage the rear part of the adjuster with the shoe lever as shown . . .

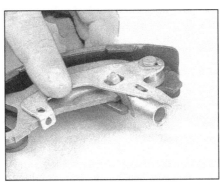

8.4s . . . rotate the shoe lever back against the rear shoe . . .

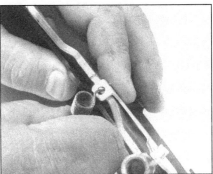

8.4t . . . hook the short end of the adjusting lever spring into the shoe lever . . .

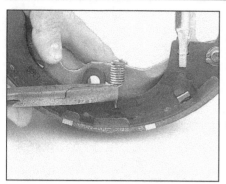

8.4u . . . and hook the long end of the spring into the hole in the rear shoe

8.4v Apply high-temperature grease to the friction points of the backing plate

8.4w Insert the pin for the rear shoe hold-down spring through the hole in the backing plate

This is done by first removing the plug from the backing plate. With the plug removed, push the lever off the adjuster star wheel with a narrow screwdriver while turning the adjuster wheel with another screwdriver, moving the shoes away from the drum (see illustration 8.4b). The drum should now come off.
5 Before reinstalling the drum, it should be checked for cracks, score marks, deep scratches and hard spots, which will appear as small discoloured areas. If the hard spots cannot be removed with fine emery cloth or if any of the other conditions listed above exist, the drum must be taken to an automotive

machine workshop to have it resurfaced. **Note:** Professionals recommend resurfacing the drums each time a brake job is done. Resurfacing will eliminate the possibility of out-of-round drums. If the drums are worn so much that they can't be resurfaced without exceeding the maximum allowable diameter (stamped into the drum), then new ones will be required **(see illustration)**. At the very least, if you elect not to have the drums resurfaced, remove the glaze from the surface with emery cloth using a swirling motion.
6 Install the brake drum on the axle flange.
7 Mount the wheel and install the nuts. Using

a screwdriver inserted through the adjusting hole in the backing plate **(see illustration 8.4b)**, turn the adjuster star wheel until the brake shoes drag on the drum as the drum is rotated, then back off the star wheel until the shoes don't drag. Lower the vehicle and tighten the nuts to the torque listed in the Chapter 1 Specifications.
8 Make a number of forward and reverse stops and operate the parking brake to adjust the brakes until satisfactory pedal action is obtained.
9 Check the operation of the brakes carefully before driving the vehicle.

8.4x Attach the parking brake cable to the parking brake lever

8.4y Bring the rear shoe into position, insert the hold-down pin through the shoe, install the inner cup on the pin . . .

8.4z . . . install the hold-down spring and outer cup . . .

8.4aa . . . compress the spring with a brake spring tool, give the outer cup a 1/4-turn twist and lock it down

8.4bb Place the adjuster assembly in position and insert it into the rear part of the adjuster that you installed on the rear shoe on the bench

8.4cc Attach the anchor spring to the rear shoe . . .

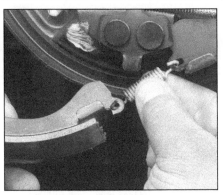

8.4dd . . . attach it to the front shoe . . .

8.4ee . . . place the front shoe in position and hook both ends of the return spring into their respective holes in the front and rear shoes

8.4ff Install the front shoe hold-down pin, spring and inner and outer cups and lock the hold-down assembly into place with a brake spring tool

9 Wheel cylinder - removal, overhaul and installation

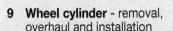

Note: *If an overhaul is indicated (usually because of fluid leaks or sticky operation), explore all options before beginning the job. New wheel cylinders are available, which makes this job quite easy. If it's decided to rebuild the wheel cylinder, make sure a rebuild kit is available before proceeding. Never overhaul only one wheel cylinder - always rebuild both of them at the same time.*

Removal

1 Raise the rear of the vehicle and support it securely on jackstands. Block the front wheels to keep the vehicle from rolling.
2 Remove the rear brake shoe assembly (see Section 8).
3 Remove all dirt and foreign material from around the wheel cylinder.
4 Disconnect the brake line **(see illustration)** with a flare-nut wrench, if available. Don't pull the brake line away from the wheel cylinder.
5 Remove the wheel cylinder mounting bolts.
6 Detach the wheel cylinder from the brake backing plate and place it on a clean workbench. Immediately plug the brake line to prevent fluid loss and contamination.

Overhaul

7 Remove the bleeder screw, cups, pistons, boots and spring assembly from the wheel cylinder body **(see illustration 8.4c)**.
8 Clean the wheel cylinder with brake fluid, denatured alcohol or brake system cleaner.

 Warning: Do not, under any circumstances, use petroleum-based solvents to clean brake parts!

9 Use filtered, unlubricated compressed air to dry the wheel cylinder and blow out the passages.
10 Check the bore for corrosion and score marks - the cylinder must be replaced with a new one if the bore is corroded or scored.
11 Lubricate the new cups with brake fluid.
12 Assemble the brake cylinder components. Make sure the cup lips face in.

Installation

13 Place the wheel cylinder in position and install the bolts finger tight. Connect the brake line to the cylinder, being careful not to cross-thread the fitting. Tighten the wheel cylinder bolts to the torque listed in this Chapter's Specifications.
14 Tighten the brake line securely and install the brake shoe assembly (see Section 8).
15 Bleed the brakes (see Section 12).
16 Check the operation of the brakes carefully before driving the vehicle.

8.5 The maximum drum diameter is cast into the drum

10 Master cylinder - removal, overhaul and installation

Note: *Before deciding to overhaul the master cylinder, check on the availability and cost of a new or factory rebuilt unit and also the availability of a rebuild kit. If you decide to rebuild the cylinder, inspect the bore as described in Step 12 before purchasing parts.*

Removal

1 Remove the air cleaner assembly (see Chapter 4).
2 Unplug the electrical connector for the fluid level warning switch **(see illustration)**.

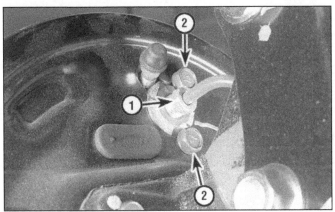

9.4 Disconnect the brake line fitting (1), then remove the two wheel cylinder bolts (2)

10.2 Unplug the electrical connector for the fluid level warning switch (arrow points to the left master cylinder mounting nut)

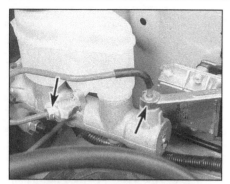

10.4 Loosen the brake line fittings (arrowed) with a flare-nut wrench

3 Remove as much brake fluid as possible from the reservoir.

HAYNES HiNT *An ideal way to remove fluid from the master cylinder reservoir is to use a clean syringe or an old poultry baster.*

4 Place rags under the fittings and prepare caps or plastic bags to cover the ends of the lines once they're disconnected.
Caution: Brake fluid will damage paint. Cover all body parts and be careful not to spill fluid during this procedure. Loosen the fittings at the ends of the brake lines where they enter the master cylinder (see illustration). To prevent rounding off the flats, use a flare-nut wrench, which wraps around the fitting hex.
5 Pull the brake lines away from the master cylinder and plug the ends to prevent contamination.
6 Remove the three nuts attaching the master cylinder to the servo unit **(see illustration)**. Pull the master cylinder off the studs to remove it. Again, be careful not to spill the fluid as this is done. Remove and discard the old gasket between the master cylinder and the servo unit.

Overhaul

7 Before attempting the overhaul of the master cylinder, obtain the proper rebuild kit, which will contain the necessary replacement parts and also any instructions which may be specific to your model.
8 Remove the reservoir retaining screw, pull off the reservoir and remove the grommets **(see illustrations)**.
9 Place the cylinder in a vise and use a punch or Phillips screwdriver to depress the pistons until they bottom against the other end of the master cylinder. Hold the pistons in this position and remove the stopper bolt from the master cylinder **(see illustration)**.
10 Carefully remove the snap-ring at the end of the master cylinder **(see illustration)**.
11 The internal components can now be removed from the bore **(see illustrations)**. Make a note of the proper order of the components so they can be returned to their original locations. **Note:** *The two springs are different, so pay particular attention to their installed order.*
12 Carefully inspect the bore of the master cylinder. Any deep score marks or other damage will mean a new master cylinder is required. DO NOT attempt to hone the bore.
13 Replace all parts included in the rebuild kit, following any instructions in the kit. Clean all re-used parts with brake system cleaner.

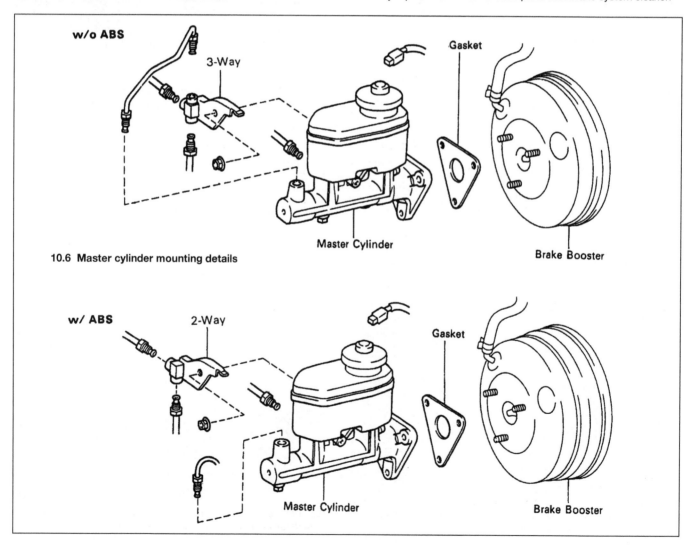

10.6 Master cylinder mounting details

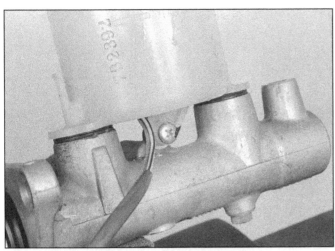

10.8a The brake fluid reservoir is retained by a screw

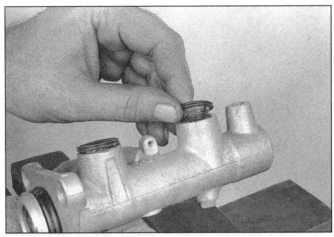

10.8b After the reservoir has been removed, pull the grommets from the master cylinder body; if they're hard, cracked or damaged, or have been leaking, replace them

 Warning: Do not use any petroleum-based solvents. During reassembly, lubricate all parts liberally with clean brake fluid.

14 Push the assembled components into the bore, bottoming them against the end of the master cylinder, then install the stopper bolt.

15 Install the new snap-ring, making sure it's seated properly in the groove.

16 Install the reservoir grommets, reservoir and screw.

10.9 Using a Phillips screwdriver, depress the pistons, then remove the stopper bolt; be sure to replace the sealing washer for the stopper bolt

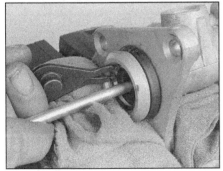

10.10 Depress the pistons again and remove the snap-ring with a pair of snap-ring pliers

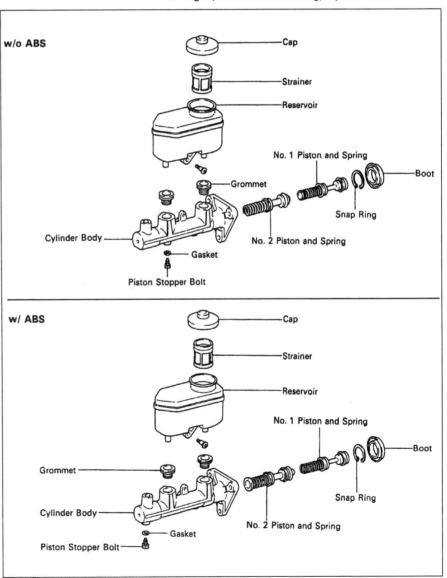

10.11a An exploded view of the master cylinder assembly

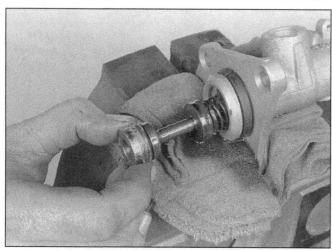

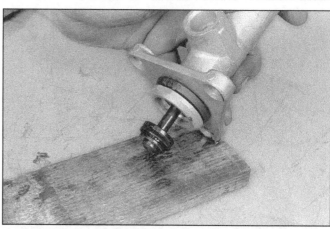

10.11b After the snap-ring has been removed, the primary (No. 1) piston assembly can be removed

10.11c Remove the cylinder from the vise and tap it against a block of wood until the secondary (No. 2) piston is exposed. Pull the piston assembly STRAIGHT OUT - if it becomes even slightly cocked, the bore may be damaged

17 Before installing the master cylinder, it should be bench bled. Since you'll have to apply pressure to the master cylinder piston and, at the same time, control flow from the brake line outlets, the master cylinder should be mounted in a vise, with the jaws of the vise clamping on the mounting flange.

18 Insert threaded plugs into the brake line outlet holes and snug them down so no air will leak past them, but not so tight that they can't be easily loosened.

19 Fill the reservoir with brake fluid of the recommended type (see Chapter 1).

20 Remove one plug and push the piston assembly into the bore to expel the air from the master cylinder. A large Phillips screwdriver can be used to push on the piston assembly.

21 To prevent air from being drawn back into the master cylinder, the plug must be replaced and snugged down before releasing the pressure on the piston.

22 Repeat the procedure until only brake fluid is expelled from the brake line outlet hole. When only brake fluid is expelled, repeat the procedure at the other outlet hole and plug. Be sure to keep the master cylinder

reservoir filled with brake fluid to prevent the introduction of air into the system.

23 Since high pressure isn't involved in the bench bleeding procedure, an alternative to the removal and replacement of the plugs with each stroke of the piston assembly is available. Before pushing in on the piston assembly, remove the plug as described in Step 20. Before releasing the piston, however, instead of replacing the plug, simply put your finger tightly over the hole to keep air from being drawn back into the master cylinder. Wait several seconds for brake fluid to be drawn from the reservoir into the bore, then depress the piston again, removing your finger as brake fluid is expelled. Be sure to put your finger back over the hole each time before releasing the piston, and when the bleeding procedure is complete for that outlet, replace the plug and tighten it before going on to the other port.

Installation

24 Install the master cylinder over the studs on the servo unit and tighten the nuts only finger-tight at this time. Don't forget to use a new gasket.

25 Thread the brake line fittings into the master cylinder. Since the master cylinder is still a bit loose, it can be moved slightly so the fittings thread in easily. Don't strip the threads as the fittings are tightened.

26 Tighten the mounting nuts to the torque listed in this Chapter's Specifications. Tighten the brake line fittings securely.

27 Fill the master cylinder reservoir with fluid, then bleed the master cylinder and the brake system (see Section 12). To bleed the master cylinder on the vehicle, have an assistant depress the brake pedal and hold it down. Loosen the fitting to allow air and fluid to escape **(see illustration)**. Tighten the fitting, then allow your assistant to return the pedal to its rest position. Repeat this procedure on both fittings until the fluid is free of air bubbles. Check the operation of the brake system carefully before driving the vehicle.

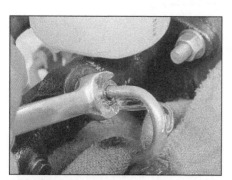

10.27 Have an assistant depress the brake pedal and hold it down, then loosen the fitting nut, allowing the air and fluid to escape; repeat this procedure on both fittings until the fluid is clear of air bubbles

11 Brake hoses and lines - inspection and replacement

Inspection

1 About every six months, with the vehicle raised and supported securely on jackstands, the rubber hoses which connect the steel brake lines with the front and rear brake assemblies should be inspected for cracks, chafing of the outer cover, leaks, blisters and other damage. These are important and vulnerable parts of the brake system and inspection should be complete. A light and mirror will be helpful for a thorough check. If a hose exhibits any of the above conditions, replace it with a new one.

Replacement

Front brake hose

2 Loosen the wheel nuts, raise the vehicle and support it securely on jackstands. Remove the wheel.

3 At the frame bracket, unscrew the brake line fitting from the hose **(see illustration)**.

11.3 Unscrew the brake line threaded fitting with a flare-nut wrench to protect the fitting corners from being rounded off

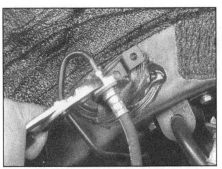

11.4 Pull off the U-clip with a pair of pliers

Use a flare-nut wrench to prevent rounding off the corners. If the bracket begins to bend, hold the hose fitting with an open-end wrench.

4 Remove the U-clip from the female fitting at the bracket with a pair of pliers **(see illustration)**, then pass the hose through the bracket.

5 At the caliper end of the hose, remove the banjo fitting bolt, then separate the hose from the caliper. Note that there are two copper sealing washers on either side of the fitting - they should be replaced with new ones during installation.

6 Remove the U-clip from the strut bracket, then feed the hose through the bracket.

7 To install the hose, pass the caliper fitting end through the strut bracket, then connect the fitting to the caliper with the banjo bolt and copper washers. Make sure the locating on the fitting is engaged with the hole in the caliper, then tighten the bolt to the torque listed in this Chapter's Specifications.

8 Push the metal support into the strut bracket and install the U-clip. Make sure the hose isn't twisted between the caliper and the strut bracket.

9 Route the hose into the frame bracket, again making sure it isn't twisted, then connect the brake line fitting, starting the threads by hand. Install the U-clip, then tighten the fitting securely.

10 Bleed the caliper (see Section 12).

11 Install the wheel and nuts, lower the vehicle and tighten the nuts to the torque listed in the Chapter 1 Specifications.

Rear brake hose

12 The rear brake hose serves as the flexible connection between two rigid metal lines, one on the body and the other on the axle. Both ends of the hose are attached to these metal lines with threaded fittings and U-clips. Refer to Steps 2, 3 and 4 above. Be sure to bleed the wheel cylinder or rear caliper when you're done (see Section 12).

Metal brake lines

13 When replacing brake lines, be sure to use the correct parts. Don't use copper tubing for any brake system components. Purchase steel brake lines from a dealer or auto parts store.

14 Prefabricated brake line, with the tube ends already flared and fittings installed, is available at auto parts stores and dealer parts departments. These lines are also bent to the proper shapes.

15 When installing the new line, make sure it's securely supported in the brackets and has plenty of clearance between moving or hot components.

16 After installation, check the master cylinder fluid level and add fluid as necessary. Bleed the brake system (see Section 12) and test the brakes carefully before driving the vehicle in traffic.

12 Brake hydraulic system - bleeding

 Warning: Wear eye protection when bleeding the brake system. If the fluid comes in contact with your eyes, immediately rinse them with water and seek medical attention.
Note: *Bleeding the hydraulic system is necessary to remove any air that manages to find its way into the system when it's been opened during removal and installation of a hose, line, caliper or master cylinder.*

1 You'll probably have to bleed the system at all four brakes if air has entered it due to low fluid level, or if the brake lines have been disconnected at the master cylinder.

2 If a brake line was disconnected only at a wheel, then only that caliper or wheel cylinder must be bled.

3 If a brake line is disconnected at a fitting located between the master cylinder and any of the brakes, that part of the system served by the disconnected line must be bled.

4 Remove any residual vacuum from the brake servo unit by applying the brake several times with the engine off.

5 Remove the master cylinder reservoir cover and fill the reservoir with brake fluid. Reinstall the cover. **Note:** *Check the fluid level often during the bleeding operation and add fluid as necessary to prevent the fluid level from falling low enough to allow air bubbles into the master cylinder.*

6 Have an assistant on hand, as well as a supply of new brake fluid, a clear plastic container partially filled with clean brake fluid, a length of 3/16-inch plastic, rubber or vinyl tubing to fit over the bleeder valve and a wrench to open and close the bleeder valve.

7 Beginning at the rear wheel furthest away from the master cylinder, loosen the bleeder valve slightly, then tighten it to a point where it's snug but can still be loosened quickly and easily.

8 Place one end of the tubing over the bleeder valve and submerge the other end in brake fluid in the container **(see illustration)**.

9 Have the assistant pump the brakes slowly a few times to get pressure in the system, then hold the pedal down firmly.

10 While the pedal is held down, open the bleeder valve just enough to allow a flow of fluid to leave the valve. Watch for air bubbles to exit the submerged end of the tube. When the fluid flow slows after a couple of seconds, close the valve and have your assistant release the pedal.

11 Repeat Steps 9 and 10 until no more air is seen leaving the tube, then tighten the bleeder valve and proceed to the diagonally opposite front wheel, then the other rear wheel and, finally, the remaining front wheel, in that order, and perform the same procedure. Be sure to check the fluid in the master cylinder reservoir frequently.

12 Never use old brake fluid. It contains moisture which will deteriorate the brake system components.

13 Refill the master cylinder with fluid at the end of the operation.

14 Check the operation of the brakes. The pedal should feel solid when depressed, with no sponginess. If necessary, repeat the entyre process.

 Warning: Do not operate the vehicle if you're in doubt about the effectiveness of the brake system.

13 Servo unit - check, removal and installation

Operating check

1 Depress the brake pedal several times with the engine off and make sure there's no change in the pedal reserve distance.

2 Depress the pedal and start the engine. If the pedal goes down slightly, operation is normal.

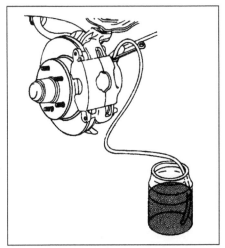

12.8 When bleeding the brakes, a hose is connected to the bleed screw at the caliper or wheel cylinder and then submerged in brake fluid - air will be seen as bubbles in the tube and container (all air must be expelled before moving to the next wheel)

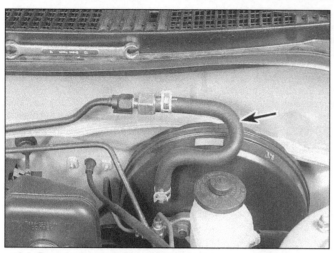

13.6 Detach this hose (arrowed) from the servo unit; make sure you don't puncture or tear the hose during removal

13.10a To disconnect the servo unit pushrod from the brake pedal, remove the retaining clip and clevis pin (centre arrow); to detach the servo from the firewall, remove the four mounting nuts (arrows, upper right nut not visible in this photo)

Airtightness check

3 Start the engine and turn it off after one or two minutes. Depress the brake pedal slowly several times. If the pedal depresses less each time, the servo unit is airtight.

4 Depress the brake pedal while the engine is running, then stop the engine with the pedal depressed. If there's no change in the pedal reserve travel after holding the pedal for 30 seconds, the servo unit is airtight.

Removal

5 Servo units shouldn't be disassembled. They require special tools not normally found in most automotive repair stations or workshops. Because of its critical relationship to brake performance, the servo unit should be replaced with a new or rebuilt one.

6 Disconnect the hose leading from the engine to the servo unit (see illustration). Be careful not to damage the hose when removing it from the servo unit fitting.

7 Remove the brake master cylinder (see Section 10).

8 Remove the steering column lower finish panel (see Chapter 11).

9 Remove the pedal return spring.

10 Locate the pushrod clevis connecting the servo unit to the brake pedal (see illustrations). Remove the clevis pin retaining clip with pliers and pull out the pin.

11 Remove the four nuts and washers holding the brake servo unit to the bulkhead (see illustration 13.10a); you may need a light to see them.

12 Slide the servo unit straight out from the bulkhead until the studs clear the holes.

Installation

13 Installation is basically the reverse of removal. Tighten the servo unit mounting nuts to the torque listed in this Chapter's Specifications. Be sure to use a new clevis retaining clip if the old clip is loose.

14 If the servo unit is being replaced, the clearance between the master cylinder piston and the pushrod in the vacuum servo unit must be measured and, if necessary, adjusted. Using a depth micrometer or vernier calipers, measure the distance from the seat (recessed area) in the master cylinder to the master cylinder mounting flange. Next, measure the distance from the end of the vacuum servo unit pushrod to the mounting face of the servo unit (including gasket) where the master cylinder mounting flange seats. The measurements should be the same (see illustration). If not, turn the adjusting screw on the end of the servo unit pushrod until the clearance is within the specified limit (see illustration).

15 After the final installation of the master cylinder and brake hoses and lines, the brake pedal height and freeplay must be adjusted and the system must be bled. See the appropriate Sections of this Chapter for the procedures.

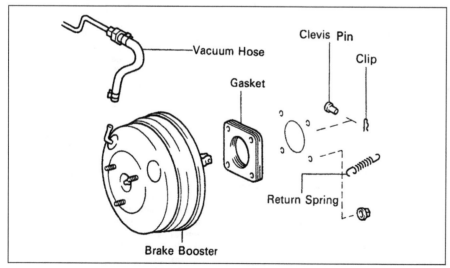

13.10b Servo unit installation details

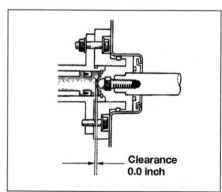

13.14a There should be no clearance between the servo pushrod and the master cylinder pushrod, but no interference either; if there is interference between the two, the brakes may drag; if there is clearance, there will be excessive brake pedal travel

13.14b To adjust the length of the servo pushrod, hold the serrated portion of the rod with a pair of pliers and turn the adjusting screw in or out, as necessary, to achieve the desired setting

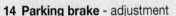

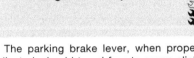

14 Parking brake - adjustment

1 The parking brake lever, when properly adjusted, should travel four to seven clicks, when a moderate pulling force is applied. If it travels less than the specified minimum number of clicks, there's a chance the parking brake might not be releasing completely and the brake shoes or brake pads might be dragging on the drum or disc. If the lever can be pulled up more than the specified maximum number of clicks, the parking brake may not hold adequately on an incline, allowing the car to roll.
2 To gain access to the parking brake cable adjuster, remove the centre console (see Chapter 11).
3 Loosen the locknut (the upper nut) while holding the adjusting nut (lower nut) with a wrench **(see illustration)**. Turn the adjusting nut until the desired travel is attained. Tighten the locknut.
4 Install the centre console.

14.3 Loosen the locknut, then turn the adjusting nut until the desired handle travel is obtained

15 Parking brake cables - replacement

Equalizer-to-parking brake cable

1 Loosen the rear wheel nuts, raise the rear of the vehicle and support it securely on jackstands. Block the front wheels. Remove the wheel.
2 Make sure the parking brake is completely released then, on drum brake models, remove the brake drum.
3 On drum brake models, remove the brake shoes and disconnect the cable from the parking brake lever (see Section 8). Remove the two cable retaining bolts from the backing plate **(see illustration)** and pull the cable through the backing plate.
4 On disc brake models, disconnect the cable at the caliper end by removing the pin clip then pulling out the hole pin while pushing the parking brake crank. Remove the outer cable retaining clip and remove the cable.
5 Unbolt the cable clamp near the forward end of the strut rod **(see illustration)**.

15.3 On drum brake models, unscrew the bolts (arrowed) from the backing plate and pass the cable through

15.5 Remove this nut (arrowed) and detach this cable bracket from the frame near the forward end of the strut rod

6 Unbolt the cable clamp from the floor pan, just to the left of the centre tunnel **(see illustration)**.
7 Remove the exhaust pipe and catalytic converter heat shields (see Chapter 4).
8 Unclamp the cable from the rear retaining bracket, pull the nylon bushing out of the front bracket and disconnect the cable from the equalizer **(see illustration)**.
9 Installation is the reverse of removal. Apply a light coat of grease to the portion of the cable end that engages with the equalizer.

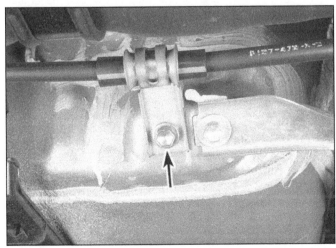

15.6 Remove this bolt (arrowed) and detach this cable bracket from the floor pan

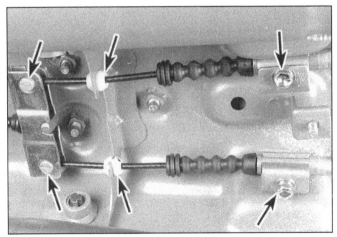

15.8 Remove the clamp retaining bolt (right arrows), pry the nylon bushing out of the bracket (centre arrows) and disengage the forward end of the cable from the equalizer (left arrows)

10 Adjust the parking brake when you're done (see Section 14).

Equalizer-to-brake lever cable

11 Remove the centre console (see Chapter 11).

12 With the lever in the down (off) position, remove the locknut and the adjusting nut (see Section 14) and detach the cable from the lever.

13 Raise the rear of the vehicle and place it securely on jackstands.

14 Remove the exhaust pipe and catalytic converter heat shields (see Chapter 4).

15 Turn the cable end 90-degrees and disconnect it from the equalizer **(see illustration 15.8)**.

16 Pry out the rubber grommet from the floorpan and pull the cable through the hole in the pan.

17 Installation is the reverse of removal. Apply a light coat of grease to the portion of the cable end that engages with the equalizer. And coat the sealing edge of the rubber grommet with silicone to ensure that it remains watertight.

18 Adjust the parking brake lever when you're done (see Section 14).

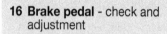

16 Brake pedal - check and adjustment

Pedal height

1 Measure the pedal height from the upper face of the pedal rubber to the asphalt sheet on the firewall **(see illustration)** and compare your measurement to the pedal height listed in this Chapter's Specifications. If the pedal height is incorrect, adjust it as follows:

2 Remove the steering column lower finish panel and air duct.

3 Unplug the electrical connector from the brake light switch.

4 Loosen the brake light switch locknut and remove the brake light switch.

5 Loosen the pushrod locknut.

6 Adjust the pedal height by turning the pedal pushrod.

7 Tighten the pushrod locknut.

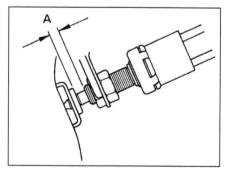

16.10 Clearance "A" is the distance between the brake light switch and the pedal arm

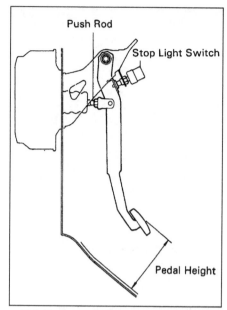

16.1 Brake pedal height is the distance between the pedal and the firewall asphalt sheet when the pedal is released

8 Install the brake light switch and turn it until it lightly contacts the pedal stopper.

9 Back off the brake light switch one turn.

10 Measure the distance (clearance "A") between the brake light switch and the pedal **(see illustration)** and compare your measurement to the clearance listed in this Chapter's Specifications. If the clearance is not as specified, repeat the previous two steps and try again.

11 Tighten the brake light switch locknut.

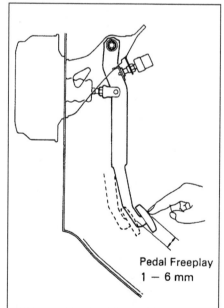

16.16 Brake pedal freeplay is the distance between the pedal when it's released and the point at which some resistance is first felt when the pedal is depressed

12 Plug in the brake light switch electrical connector.

13 Verify that brake lights come on when the brake pedal is depressed, and go off when the brake pedal is released.

14 Check the pedal freeplay (see below).

Pedal freeplay

15 Stop the engine, if it's running, and depress the brake pedal several times until there's no more vacuum left in the servo unit.

16 Push the brake pedal by hand until you feel some resistance, then measure the distance between the pedal fully released position and this point at which you can feel resistance **(see illustration)**. Compare your measurement with the pedal freeplay listed in this Chapter's Specifications. If the pedal freeplay is incorrect, adjust it as follows:

17 Check the brake light switch clearance. If the brake light switch clearance is okay, troubleshoot the brake system.

Pedal reserve

18 Start the engine, depress the brake pedal a few times, then press down hard and hold it.

19 Pedal reserve travel is measured from the floor to the top of the pedal while it's being depressed. Compare your measurement to the pedal reserve listed in this Chapter's Specifications.

20 If the pedal reserve is less than specified, check the adjustment of the rear brakes and/or the servo unit pushrod-to-master cylinder piston clearance. If the brake pedal feels spongy, bleed the brake system (see Section 12).

17 Brake light switch - check and replacement

Check

1 The brake light switch is located on a bracket at the top of the brake pedal **(see illustration 16.1)**. The switch activates the brake lights at the rear of the vehicle when the pedal is depressed.

2 To check the brake light switch, simply note whether the brake lights come on when the pedal is depressed and go off when the pedal is released. If they don't, adjust the switch as described in Section 16 (adjusting the switch is part of brake pedal adjustment).

3 If the lights still don't come on, either the switch is not getting voltage, the switch itself is defective, or the circuit between the switch and the lights is defective. There is always the remote possibility that all of the brake light bulbs are burned out, but this is not very likely.

4 Use a voltmeter or test light to verify that there's voltage present at one side of the switch connector. If no voltage is present, troubleshoot the circuit from the switch to the fuse box. If there is voltage present, check for voltage on the other terminal when the brake pedal is depressed. If no voltage is present, replace the switch. If there is voltage present, troubleshoot the circuit from the switch to the brake lights (see the *Wiring diagrams* at the end of Chapter 12).

Replacement

5 Disconnect the negative battery cable from the battery.
6 Unplug the electrical connector for the brake light switch.
7 Loosen the locknut **(see illustration 16.10)** and unscrew the switch from the pedal bracket.
8 Installation is the reverse of removal.
9 Adjust the brake pedal and brake light switch (see Section 16).

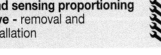

18 Load sensing proportioning valve - removal and installation

Note: *Due to the specialised equipment required to check and accurately adjust the brake fluid pressure after refitting (or reconnecting) the valve, you are advised to leave this job to a Toyota dealer or suitably equipped specialist. The following procedure is given for circumstances where the task must be undertaken, but it is vitally important that the brake fluid pressure is checked and adjusted as necessary by a dealer (or other suitably equipped specialist) upon completion.*

⚠️ **Warning: If the fluid pressure is not checked and accurately adjusted, braking system performance may be severely impaired.**

Removal

1 Position the car over an inspection pit or raise it on a hoist. Alternatively car ramps may be used at the front and rear but the car must be level and with its weight on the wheels.
2 To minimise fluid loss, remove the master cylinder reservoir filler cap and place a piece of polythene over the filler neck. Secure the polythene with an elastic band ensuring that an airtight seal is obtained.
3 Loosen the fittings at the ends of the brake lines where they enter the proportioning valve. To prevent rounding off the flats, use a flare-nut wrench, which wraps around the fitting hex.
4 Pull the brake lines away from the valve and plug the ends to prevent contamination.
5 Remove the locknut and adjusting nut and remove the spring retaining bracket from the suspension member.
6 Remove the three bolts and remove the valve and mounting bracket assembly.

Installation

7 Install the valve and tighten the three bolts.
8 Install the spring retaining bracket and temporarily tighten the locknut below the adjusting nut. Turn the adjusting nut and locknut to set the spring length to the initial set-up dimension of approximately 4-1/8 inches **(see illustration)**. Tighten the locknut while counterholding the adjusting nut.
9 Reconnect the brake lines then bleed the brake system (see Section 12).
10 Lower the vehicle to the ground and have the brake fluid pressure checked and if necessary adjusted by a Toyota dealer.

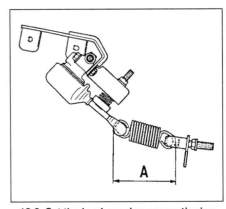

18.8 Set the load sensing proportioning valve spring length "A" to an initial set-up dimension of 4-1/8 inches when installing

Chapter 10
Suspension and steering systems

Contents

Degrees of difficulty

| Easy, suitable for novice with little experience | | Fairly easy, suitable for beginner with some experience | | Fairly difficult, suitable for competent DIY mechanic | | Difficult, suitable for experienced DIY mechanic | | Very difficult, suitable for expert DIY or professional | |

Specifications

Torque wrench settings

Ft-lbs

Front suspension

Balljoints
Balljoint-to-control arm bolt/nuts	105
Balljoint-to-steering knuckle nut	87

Control arm
Front pivot bolt	161
Rear pivot stud nut (1993 through 1995)	101
Rear pivot bolt (1996)	129

Front stabilizer bar
Bracket
Rear bolt	37
Front bolt	108
Nut	14
Link nuts	33

Front struts
Strut-to-steering knuckle bolts/nuts	203
Strut upper mounting nuts	29
Suspension support-to-piston rod nut	34

Rear suspension

No. 1 (front) suspension arm nuts/bolts
1995 and earlier	87
1996	92

No. 2 (rear) suspension arm nuts/bolts
1995 and earlier	87
1996	92
Rear hub and bearing assembly-to-rear axle carrier	59

Rear stabilizer bar
Link nuts	33
Bushing retainer bolts	14

Rear struts
Strut-to-axle carrier nuts/bolts	105
Strut upper mounting nuts	29
Suspension support-to-piston rod nut	36
Strut rod nuts/bolts	67

Torque wrench settings (continued)

Steering   Ft-lbs

Airbag module Torx screws	4
Steering gear bracket bolts/nuts	43
Steering wheel nut	25
Tie-rod ends	
Tie-rod end-to-steering knuckle nut	36
Tie-rod end locknut	41
U-joint-to-pinion shaft pinch bolt	26
Power steering pressure line banjo bolts	40

1 General information

The front suspension **(see illustration)** is a MacPherson strut design. The upper end of each strut/coil spring assembly is attached to the vehicle's body strut support. The lower end of the strut assembly is connected to the upper end of the steering knuckle. The steering knuckle is attached to a balljoint mounted on the outer end of the suspension control arm. A stabilizer bar reduces body roll.

The rear suspension **(see illustration)** also utilizes strut/coil spring assemblies. The upper end of each strut is attached to the vehicle body. The lower end of each strut is attached to an axle carrier. The carrier is located by a pair of suspension arms on each side, and a longitudinally mounted strut rod between the body and each carrier.

The rack-and-pinion steering gear is located behind the engine/transmission assembly on the firewall and actuates the tie-rods, which are attached to the steering knuckles. The inner ends of the tie-rods are protected by rubber boots which should be inspected periodically for secure attachment, tears and leaking lubricant.

The power assist system consists of a belt-driven pump and associated lines and hoses. The fluid level in the power steering pump reservoir should be checked periodically (see Chapter 1).

The steering wheel operates the steering shaft, which actuates the steering gear through universal joints. Looseness in the steering can be caused by wear in the steering shaft universal joints, the steering gear, the tie-rod ends and loose retaining bolts.

1.1 Front suspension components

1 Front stabilizer bar	3 Control arm	6 Right driveshaft assembly	9 Support brace
2 Stabilizer bar bushing clamp	4 Balljoint	7 Left driveshaft assembly	10 Suspension crossmember
	5 Strut/coil spring assembly	8 Rack-and-pinion steering gear	

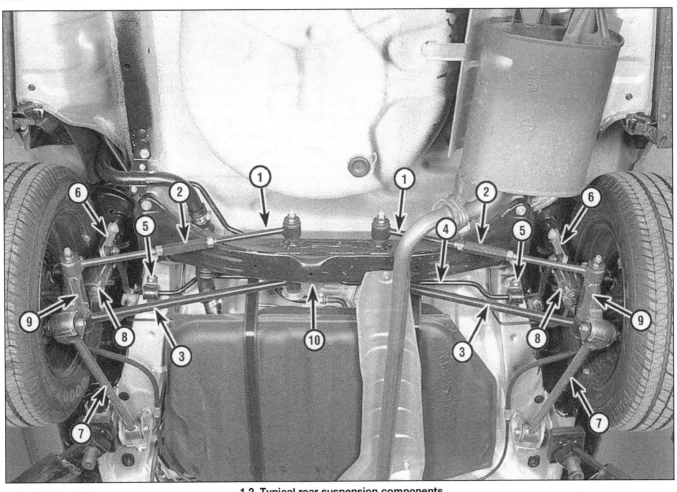

1.2 Typical rear suspension components

1	No. 2 lower suspension arm	3	No. 1 lower suspension arm	6	Stabilizer link	9	Rear axle carrier
2	No. 2 arm toe adjuster	4	Rear stabilizer bar	7	Strut rod	10	Rear suspension crossmember
		5	Stabilizer bushing clamp	8	Strut/coil spring assembly		

Precautions

Frequently, when working on the suspension or steering system components, you may come across fasteners which seem impossible to loosen. These fasteners on the underside of the vehicle are continually subjected to water, road grime, mud, etc., and can become rusted or "frozen," making them extremely difficult to remove. In order to unscrew these stubborn fasteners without damaging them (or other components), be sure to use lots of penetrating oil and allow it to soak in for a while. Using a wire brush to clean exposed threads will also ease removal of the nut or bolt and prevent damage to the threads. Sometimes a sharp blow with a hammer and punch will break the bond between a nut and bolt threads, but care must be taken to prevent the punch from slipping off the fastener and ruining the threads. Heating the stuck fastener and surrounding area with a torch sometimes helps too, but isn't recommended because of the obvious dangers associated with fire. Long

breaker bars and extension, or "cheater," pipes will increase leverage, but never use an extension pipe on a ratchet - the ratcheting mechanism could be damaged. Sometimes tightening the nut or bolt first will help to break it loose. Fasteners that require drastic measures to remove should always be replaced with new ones.

Since most of the procedures dealt with in this Chapter involve jacking up the vehicle and working underneath it, a good pair of jackstands will be needed. A hydraulic floor jack is the preferred type of jack to lift the vehicle, and it can also be used to support certain components during various operations.

 Warning: Never, under any circumstances, rely on a jack to support the vehicle while working on it. Whenever any of the suspension or steering fasteners are loosened or removed they must be inspected and, if necessary, replaced with

new ones of the same part number or of original equipment quality and design. Torque specifications must be followed for proper reassembly and component retention. Never attempt to heat or straighten any suspension or steering components. Instead, replace any bent or damaged part with a new one.

2 Strut assembly (front) - removal, inspection and installation

Removal

1 Loosen the wheel nuts, raise the vehicle and support it securely on jackstands. Remove the wheel.

2 Unbolt the brake hose bracket from the strut. If the vehicle is equipped with ABS, detach the speed sensor wiring harness from the strut by removing the clamp bracket bolt.

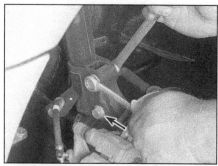

2.3 To detach the strut assembly from the steering knuckle, remove the two nuts, then knock out the bolts with a hammer and punch

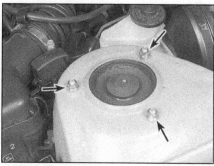

2.5 To detach the upper end of the strut assembly from the body, remove the upper mounting nuts (arrows)

3 Remove the strut-to-knuckle nuts **(see illustration)** and knock the bolts out with a hammer and punch.

4 Separate the strut from the steering knuckle. Be careful not to overextend the inner CV joint. Also, don't let the steering knuckle fall outward and strain the brake hose.

5 Support the strut and spring assembly with one hand and remove the three strut-to-body nuts **(see illustration)**. Remove the assembly out from the wingwell.

Inspection

6 Check the strut body for leaking fluid, dents, cracks and other obvious damage which would warrant repair or replacement.

7 Check the coil spring for chips or cracks in the spring coating (this will cause premature spring failure due to corrosion). Inspect the spring seat for cuts, hardness and general deterioration.

8 If any undesirable conditions exist, proceed to the strut disassembly procedure (see Section 3).

Installation

9 Guide the strut assembly up into the wingwell and insert the upper mounting studs through the holes in the body. Once the studs protrude, install the nuts so the strut won't fall back through. This is most easily accomplished with the help of an assistant, as the strut is quite heavy and awkward.

10 Slide the steering knuckle into the strut flange and insert the two bolts. Install the nuts and tighten them to the torque listed in this Chapter's Specifications.

11 Connect the brake hose bracket to the strut and tighten the bolt securely. If the vehicle is equipped with ABS, install the speed sensor wiring harness bracket.

12 Install the wheel and nuts, then lower the vehicle and tighten the nuts to the torque listed in the Chapter 1 Specifications.

13 Tighten the upper mounting nuts to the torque listed in this Chapter's Specifications.

14 Drive the vehicle to an alignment workshop to have the front end alignment checked, and if necessary, adjusted.

3 Strut/spring assembly - replacement

1 If the struts or coil springs exhibit the telltale signs of wear (leaking fluid, loss of damping capability, chipped, sagging or cracked coil springs) explore all options before beginning any work. The strut/shock absorber assemblies are not serviceable and must be replaced if a problem develops. However, strut assemblies complete with springs may be available on an exchange basis, which eliminates much time and work. Whichever route you choose to take, check on the cost and availability of parts before disassembling your vehicle.

⚠️ *Warning: Disassembling a strut is potentially dangerous and utmost attention must be directed to the job, or serious injury may result. Use only a high-quality spring compressor and carefully follow the manufacturer's instructions furnished with the tool. After removing the coil spring from the strut assembly, set it aside in a safe, isolated area.*

Disassembly

2 Remove the strut assembly following the procedure described in the previous Section.

3.3 Install the spring compressor according to the tool manufacturer's instructions and compress the spring until all pressure is relieved from the upper spring seat

Mount the strut assembly in a vise. Line the vise jaws with wood or rags to prevent damage to the unit and don't tighten the vise excessively.

3 Following the tool manufacturer's instructions, install the spring compressor (which can be obtained at most auto parts stores or equipment yards on a daily rental basis) on the spring and compress it sufficiently to relieve all pressure from the upper spring seat **(see illustration)**. This can be verified by wiggling the spring.

4 Loosen the damper shaft nut with a socket wrench **(see illustration)**.

5 Remove the nut and suspension support **(see illustration)**. Inspect the bearing in the suspension support for smooth operation. If it doesn't turn smoothly, replace the suspension support. Check the rubber portion of the suspension support for cracking and general deterioration. If there is any separation of the rubber, replace it.

6 Lift the spring seat and upper insulator from the damper shaft **(see illustration)**. Check the rubber spring seat for cracking and hardness, replacing it if necessary.

7 Carefully lift the compressed spring from the assembly **(see illustration)** and set it in a safe place.

⚠️ *Warning: Never place your head near the end of the spring!*

8 Slide the rubber bumper off the damper shaft.

9 Check the lower insulator (if equipped) for wear, cracking and hardness and replace it if necessary.

Reassembly

10 If the lower insulator is being replaced, set it into position with the dropped portion seated in the lowest part of the seat. Extend the damper rod to its full length and install the rubber bumper **(see illustration)**.

11 Carefully place the coil spring onto the lower insulator, with the end of the spring resting in the lowest part of the insulator **(see illustration)**.

12 Install the upper insulator and spring seat, making sure that the flats in the hole in the seat match up with the flats on the damper shaft **(see illustration)**.

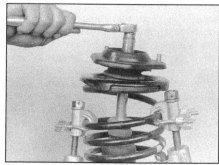

3.4 Remove the damper shaft nut

3.5 Lift the suspension support off the damper shaft

3.6 Remove the spring seat from the damper shaft

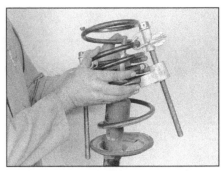

3.7 Remove the compressed spring assembly - keep the ends of the spring pointed away from your body

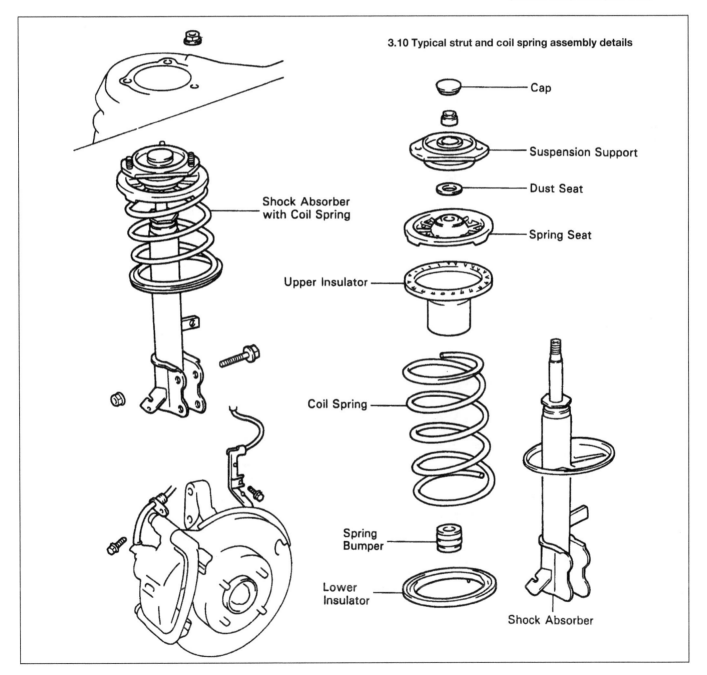

3.10 Typical strut and coil spring assembly details

Cap

Suspension Support

Dust Seat

Spring Seat

Shock Absorber with Coil Spring

Upper Insulator

Coil Spring

Spring Bumper

Lower Insulator

Shock Absorber

3.11 When installing the spring, make sure the end fits into the recessed portion of the lower seat (arrow)

3.12 The flats on the damper shaft (arrow) must match up with the flats in the spring seat

4.2 To detach the front stabilizer bar from the control arms, remove these two nuts (arrows) from each link

13 Install the dust seal and suspension support to the damper shaft.

14 Install the nut and tighten it to the torque listed in this Chapter's Specifications.

15 Install the strut assembly following the procedure outlined previously (see Section 2).

4 Stabilizer bar and bushings (front) - removal and installation

Removal

1 Loosen the front wheel nuts. Raise the front of the vehicle and support it securely on jackstands. Apply the parking brake and block the rear wheels to keep the vehicle from rolling off the stands. Remove the front wheels.

2 Remove the stabilizer bar link **(see illustration)**. If the ballstud turns with the nut, use an Allen wrench to hold the stud.

3 Unbolt the stabilizer bar bushing clamps **(see illustration)**.

4 Unbolt the front exhaust pipe from the flange in front of the catalytic converter (see Chapter 4) and pull it down far enough to remove the stabilizer bar.

5 While the stabilizer bar is off the vehicle, slide off the retainer bushings and inspect them. If they're cracked, worn or deteriorated, replace them. It's also a good idea to inspect the stabilizer bar link. To check it, flip the balljoint stud side to side five or six times as shown **(see illustration)**, then install the nut. Using an inch-pound torque wrench, turn the nut continuously one turn every two to four seconds and note the torque reading on the fifth turn. It should be about 0.4 to 8.7 in-lbs. If it isn't, replace the link assembly.

6 Clean the bushing area of the stabilizer bar with a stiff wire brush to remove any rust or dirt.

Installation

7 Lubricate the inside and outside of the new bushing with vegetable oil (used in cooking) to simplify reassembly.

Caution: Don't use petroleum or mineral-based lubricants or brake fluid - they will lead to deterioration of the bushings.

8 Installation is the reverse of removal **(see illustration)**.

5 Control arm - removal, inspection and installation

Removal

1 Loosen the wheel nuts on the side to be dismantled, raise the front of the vehicle, support it securely on jackstands and remove the wheel.

2 Remove the bolt and two nuts holding the control arm to the steering knuckle. Use a prybar to disconnect the control arm from the steering knuckle **(see illustrations)**.

3 Remove the control arm front pivot bolt **(see illustration)**.

4 Remove the rear pivot bolt **(see illustration)**. **Note:** *It's not necessary to*

4.3 To detach the front stabilizer bar from the vehicle, remove this nut (left arrow) and these two bolts (arrows) from the bushing clamps (left clamp shown, right identical)

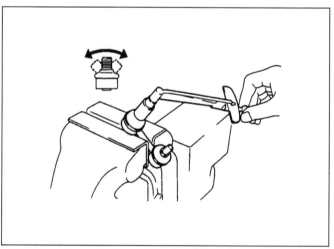

4.5 Check the balljoint in the stabilizer bar link as described in the text

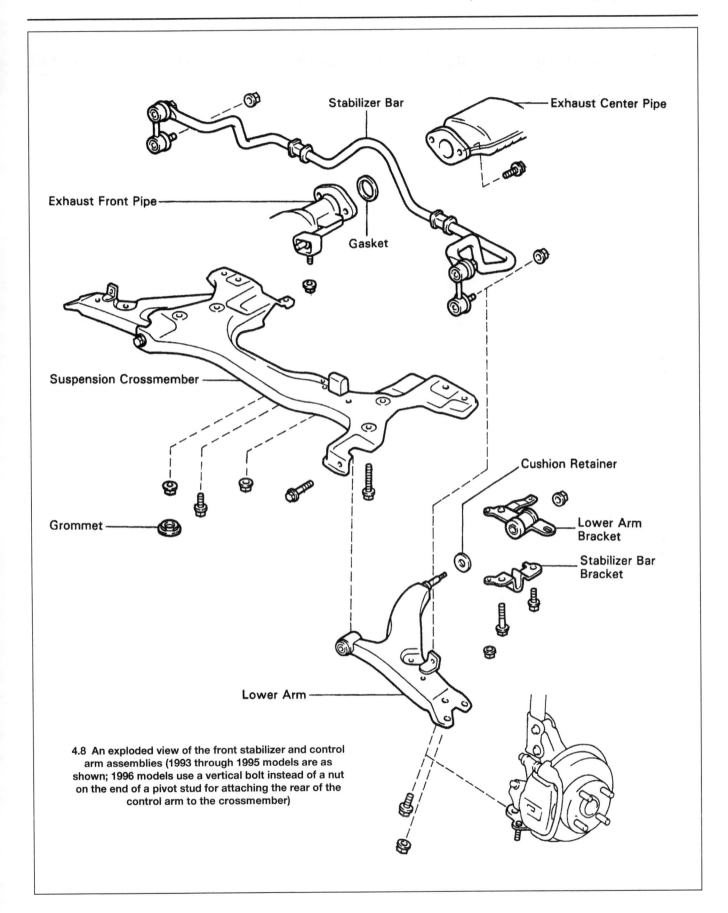

4.8 An exploded view of the front stabilizer and control arm assemblies (1993 through 1995 models are as shown; 1996 models use a vertical bolt instead of a nut on the end of a pivot stud for attaching the rear of the control arm to the crossmember)

5.2a To detach the control arm from the steering knuckle balljoint, remove this bolt and these two nuts (arrows) . . .

5.2b . . . and pry the control arm and balljoint apart with a large prybar or screwdriver

5.3 To detach the front of the control arm from the frame, remove this pivot bolt (arrow)

remove the nut and two bolts that retain the control arm bracket unless you're replacing the bushing.

5 Remove the control arm.

Inspection

6 Check the control arm for distortion and the bushings for wear, replacing parts as necessary. Do not attempt to straighten a bent control arm.

Installation

7 Installation is the reverse of removal **(see illustration 4.8)**. Tighten all of the fasteners to the torque values listed in this Chapter's Specifications. **Note:** *Before tightening the pivot bolts, raise the outer end of the control arm with a floor jack to simulate normal ride height.*

8 Install the wheel and nuts, lower the vehicle and tighten the nuts to the torque listed in the Chapter 1 Specifications.

9 It's a good idea to have the front wheel alignment checked, and if necessary, adjusted after this job has been performed.

6 Balljoints - replacement

1 Loosen the wheel nuts, raise the vehicle and support it securely on jackstands. Remove the wheel.

2 Remove the cotter pin (if equipped) from the balljoint stud and loosen the nut (but don't remove it yet).

3 Separate the balljoint from the steering knuckle with a balljoint separator **(see illustration)**. Lubricate the rubber boot with grease and work carefully, so as not to tear the boot. Remove the balljoint stud nut. The clearance between the balljoint stud and the CV joint is very tight. To remove the stud nut, you'll have to alternately back off the nut a turn or two, pull down the stud, turn the nut another turn or two, etc. until the nut is off.

4 Remove the bolt and nuts securing the balljoint to the control arm. Separate the balljoint from the control arm with a prybar **(see illustration 5.2b)**.

5 To install the balljoint, insert the balljoint stud through the hole in the steering knuckle and install the nut, but don't tighten it yet. Don't push the balljoint stud all the way up into and through the hole; instead, thread the nut onto the stud as soon as the stud protrudes through the hole, then turn the nut to draw the stud up through the hole.

6 Attach the balljoint to the control arm and install the bolt and nuts, tightening them to the torque listed in this Chapter's Specifications.

7 Tighten the balljoint stud nut to the torque listed in this Chapter's Specifications and install a new cotter pin. If the cotter pin hole doesn't line up with the slots on the nut, tighten the nut additionally until it does line up - don't loosen the nut to insert the cotter pin.

8 Install the wheel and nuts. Lower the vehicle and tighten the nuts to the torque listed in the Chapter 1 Specifications.

5.4 To detach the rear end of the control arm from the frame on a 1996 model, remove this bolt (arrow); to detach the rear end of the arm on earlier models, remove the nut that attaches the pivot stud to the lower arm bracket and bushing (see illustration 4.8)

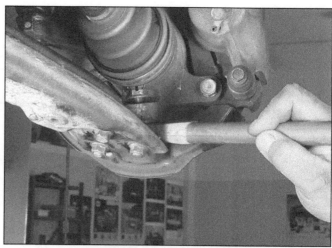

6.3 Separate the balljoint from the steering knuckle with a wedge-type forked balljoint separator

7 Steering knuckle and hub - removal and installation

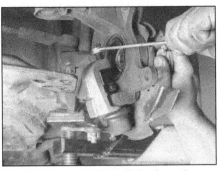

7.11 Remove the balljoint from the steering knuckle

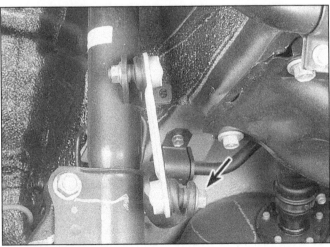

9.2 To detach the rear stabilizer bar links from the stabilizer bar, remove this nut (arrow) and pivot the link out of the way

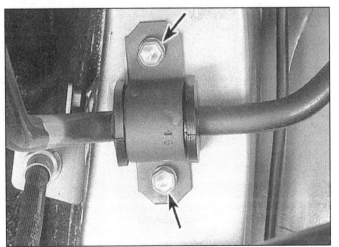

9.3 To detach the rear stabilizer bar from the vehicle body, remove the bolts (arrows) from the bushing clamps

⚠ **Warning:** *Dust created by the brake system may contain asbestos, which is harmful to your health. Never blow it out with compressed air and don't inhale any of it. Do not, under any circumstances, use petroleum-based solvents to clean brake parts. Use brake cleaner or denatured alcohol only.*

Removal

1 Loosen the wheel nuts, raise the vehicle and support it securely on jackstands. Remove the wheel.
2 Remove the cotter pin and the bearing nut lock from the driveshaft hub nut.
3 Remove the driveshaft hub nut and washer. To prevent the hub from turning, wedge a prybar between two of the wheel studs and allow the prybar to rest against the ground or the floorpan of the vehicle.
4 To loosen the driveshaft from the hub splines, tap the end of the driveshaft with a soft-faced hammer or a hammer and a brass punch. **Note:** *Don't attempt to push the end of the driveshaft through the hub yet. Applying force to the end of the driveshaft, beyond just breaking it loose from the hub, can damage the driveshaft or transmission*
5 Remove the brake caliper and the brake disc (see Chapter 9), and disconnect the brake hose from the strut.
6 If the vehicle is equipped with ABS, disconnect and remove the wheel speed sensor.
7 Loosen, but don't remove the strut-to-steering knuckle nuts and bolts (see Section 2).
8 Separate the tie-rod end from the steering knuckle arm (see Section 17).
9 Remove the balljoint-to-lower arm bolt and nuts **(see illustrations 5.2a and 5.2b).**

10 Push the driveshaft from the hub and support the end of the driveshaft with a piece of wire.
11 Using a balljoint separator tool **(see illustration)** or a small puller, remove the balljoint from the steering knuckle.
12 The strut-to-knuckle bolts can now be removed.
13 Carefully separate the steering knuckle from the strut.

Installation

14 Guide the knuckle and hub assembly into position, inserting the driveshaft into the hub.
15 Push the knuckle into the strut flange and install the bolts and nuts, but don't tighten them yet.
16 If you removed the balljoint from the old knuckle, and are planning to use it with the new knuckle, connect the balljoint to the knuckle and tighten the balljoint stud nut to the torque listed in this Chapter's Specifications.
17 Attach the balljoint to the control arm (see Section 5), but don't tighten the bolt and nuts yet.
18 Attach the tie-rod to the steering knuckle arm (see Section 17). Tighten the strut bolt nuts, the balljoint-to-control arm bolt and nuts and the tie-rod nut to the torque listed in this Chapter's Specifications.

19 Place the brake disc on the hub and install the caliper as outlined in Chapter 9.
20 Install the driveshaft/hub nut and tighten it to the torque listed in the Chapter 8 Specifications.
21 Install the wheel and nuts.
22 Lower the vehicle and tighten the nuts to the torque listed in the Chapter 1 Specifications.
23 Drive the vehicle to an alignment workshop to have the front alignment checked and, if necessary, adjusted

8 Hub and bearing assembly (front) - removal and installation

Due to the special tools and expertise required to press the hub and bearing from the steering knuckle, this job should be left to a professional mechanic. However, the steering knuckle and hub may be removed and the assembly taken to a dealer service department or other repair workshop. See Section 7 for the steering knuckle and hub removal procedure.

9 Stabilizer bar and bushings (rear) - removal and installation

Removal

Note: *On certain models it may be necessary to lower the fuel tank to provide sufficient clearance to remove the stabilizer bar (see Chapter 4).*
1 Loosen the rear wheel nuts. Raise the rear of the vehicle and place it securely on jackstands. Remove the rear wheels.
2 Remove the stabilizer bar-to-link nut **(see illustration)**. If the ballstud turns with the nut, use a hex wrench to hold the stud.
3 Unbolt the stabilizer bar bushing clamps from the body **(see illustration)**.

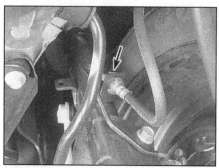

10.3 Remove the clip (arrow) and pass the hose fitting through the slot in the bracket

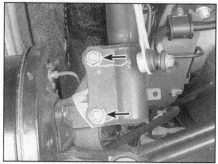

10.6 To detach the rear strut from the axle carrier, remove these two nuts (arrows) and drive out the bolts with a hammer and punch

10.7 To detach the upper end of the rear strut from the vehicle, remove these three nuts (arrows)

4 The stabilizer bar can now be removed from the vehicle. Pull the retainers off the stabilizer bar (if they haven't fallen off already) using a rocking motion.
5 Check the bushings for wear, hardness, distortion, cracking and other signs of deterioration, replacing them if necessary. Also check the link bushings for these signs.
6 Using a wire brush, clean the areas of the bar where the bushings ride. Installation is the reverse of the removal procedure. If necessary, use a light coat of vegetable oil to ease bushing and U-bracket installation (don't use petroleum-based products or brake fluid, as these will damage the rubber).
7 To inspect the links, refer to Step 5 in Section 4.

Installation
8 Installation is the reverse of removal.

10 Strut assembly (rear) - removal, inspection and installation

Removal
1 On models with a one-piece rear seat, remove the rear seat back; on models with separate rear seat backs, remove the rear side seat backs; on Estate models, remove the rear strut cover (the plastic trim piece/cup holder on top of the side trim panel, attached by a single screw) (see Chapter 11).
2 Loosen the rear wheel nuts, raise the rear of the vehicle and support it securely on jackstands. Remove the wheel.
3 Remove the clip and detach the brake hose from the bracket on the strut **(see illustration)**. If the vehicle is equipped with ABS, detach the ABS sensor wire from the strut.
4 Disconnect the stabilizer bar link from the strut **(see illustration 9.2)**.
5 Support the axle carrier with a floor jack.
6 Loosen the strut-to-axle carrier bolt nuts **(see illustration)**.
7 Remove the three upper strut-to-body mounting nuts **(see illustration)**.
8 Lower the axle carrier with the jack and remove the two strut-to-axle carrier bolts.
9 Remove the strut assembly.

Inspection
10 Follow the inspection procedures described in Section 3. If you determine that the strut assembly must be disassembled for replacement of the strut or the coil spring, refer to Section 3.
11 When reassembling the strut, make sure the suspension support is aligned as shown **(see illustration)**.

Installation
12 Maneuver the assembly up into the wingwell and insert the mounting studs through the holes in the body. Install the nuts, but don't tighten yet.
13 Push the axle carrier into the strut lower bracket and install the bolts and nuts, tightening them to the torque listed in this Chapter's Specifications.
14 Connect the stabilizer bar link to the strut bracket.
15 Attach the brake hose to the strut bracket and install the clip. If the vehicle is equipped with ABS, attach the ABS wire to the strut.
16 Install the wheel and nuts, lower the vehicle and tighten the nuts to the torque listed in the Chapter 1 Specifications.
17 Tighten the three strut upper mounting nuts to the torque listed in this Chapter's Specifications.
18 Repeat Steps 2 through 17 for the other strut.
19 Install the seat, rear side seat backs or rear strut covers (see Chapter 11).

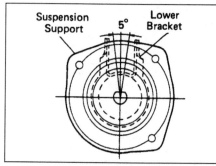

10.11 Install the suspension support with the flat side facing forward and the strut-to-axle carrier bracket within 5-degrees of the middle of the distance between the two outer holes

11 Strut rod - removal and installation

Removal
1 Loosen the wheel nuts, raise the vehicle and support it securely on jackstands. Remove the wheel.
2 Remove the strut rod-to-axle carrier bolt **(see illustration)**.
3 Remove the strut rod-to-body bracket bolt **(see illustration)** and detach the rod from the vehicle.

11.2 To disconnect the strut rod from the axle carrier, remove this nut and bolt (arrows)

11.3 To disconnect the strut rod from the body, remove this nut and bolt (arrows)

12.4 To detach the suspension arms from the axle carrier, remove this nut and bolt (if you're only removing the No. 2 arm, it isn't necessary to pull the bolt out)

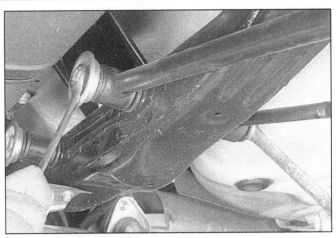

12.5 To detach the No. 2 (rear) suspension arms from the suspension crossmember, remove the nut and washer; to remove the No. 1 (front) arms, remove the centre exhaust pipe and lower the suspension crossmember so the bolt can be pulled out

Installation

4 Installation is the reverse of the removal procedure, but don't tighten the bolts until the suspension is raised by a jack to simulate normal ride height. Be sure to tighten the bolts to the torque listed in this Chapter's Specifications. Tighten the wheel nuts to the torque listed in the Chapter 1 Specifications.

12 Suspension arms - removal and installation

Removal

1 Loosen the rear wheel nuts, raise the rear of the vehicle and support it securely on jackstands.
2 Block the front wheels and remove the rear wheel.

No. 2 (rear) suspension arms

3 Where a load-sensing proportioning valve is fitted, unscrew the locknut securing the valve lower spring anchor to the right-hand No.2 suspension arm. Take care not to alter the position of the adjusting nut fitted just above. It is advisable to mark the adjusting nut and the spring anchor threads with quick drying paint so that the relative positions can be maintained.
4 Remove the nut and washer from the outer end of the suspension arm at the axle carrier **(see illustration)**.
5 Remove the nut and washer from the inner end of the suspension arm at the suspension crossmember **(see illustration)**.
6 Remove the No. 2 suspension arm.
Caution: Do NOT loosen the locknuts and turn the adjusting tube; moving this tube will affect the rear wheel toe adjustment.

No. 1 (front) suspension arms

7 Loosen the nut and bolt securing the inner end of the arms **(see illustration 12.5)**. Also loosen the nut and bolt attaching the outer ends of the arms to the axle carrier **(see illustration 12.4)**. Remove the exhaust system centre pipe and the exhaust pipe insulator (see Chapter 4). Where a load-sensing proportioning valve is fitted, disconnect the lower spring anchor (see Step 3).

8 Support the suspension crossmember with a floor jack. Remove the four bolts retaining the crossmember **(see illustration)**. Lower the crossmember far enough to allow the long through bolt at the inner end of the suspension arm to be pulled forward, out of the crossmember.

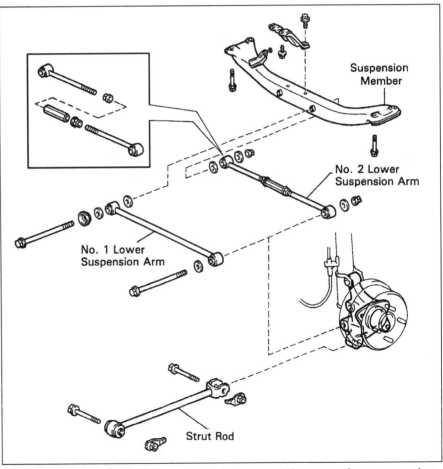

12.8 An exploded view of the rear suspension arms and the suspension crossmember

Suspension Member

No. 2 Lower Suspension Arm

No. 1 Lower Suspension Arm

Strut Rod

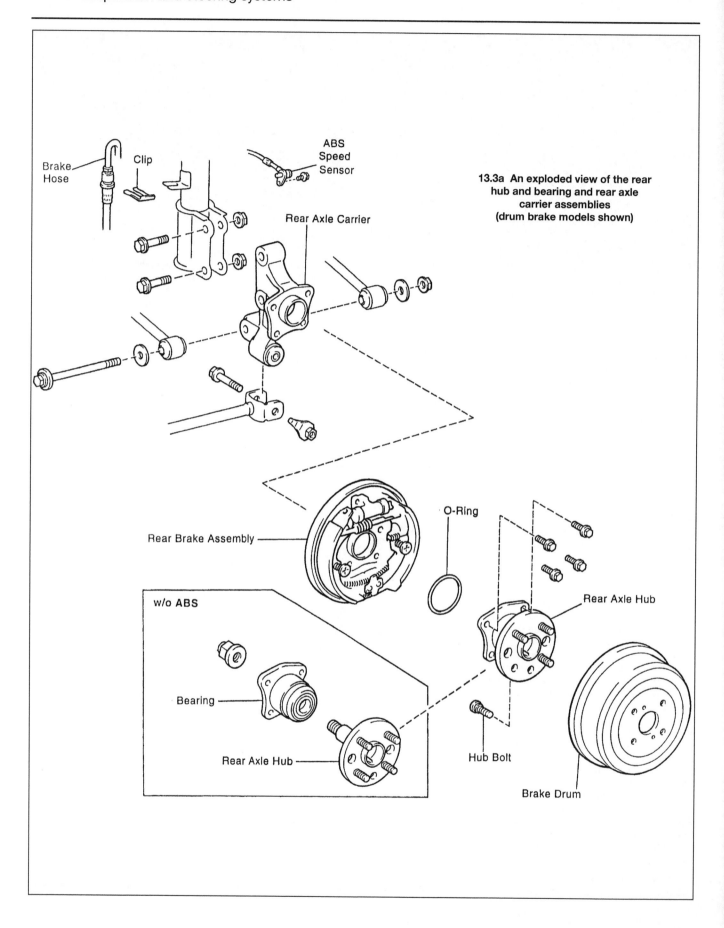

Brake Hose

Clip

ABS Speed Sensor

Rear Axle Carrier

13.3a An exploded view of the rear hub and bearing and rear axle carrier assemblies (drum brake models shown)

Rear Brake Assembly

O-Ring

Rear Axle Hub

w/o ABS

Bearing

Rear Axle Hub

Hub Bolt

Brake Drum

9 Remove the front suspension arm-to-rear axle carrier nut and bolt.
10 Remove the front suspension arm-to-suspension crossmember nut and bolt.
11 Remove the No. 1 suspension arm.

Installation

12 Installation is the reverse of removal. Be sure to tighten all suspension fasteners to the torque listed in this Chapter's Specifications. If you replaced a No. 2 suspension arm, have the rear wheel toe adjusted by an alignment workshop as soon as you're done.
13 Install the wheel and nuts, then lower the vehicle to the ground. Tighten the wheel nuts to the torque listed in the Chapter 1 Specifications.
14 Have the rear wheel alignment checked by a dealer service department or an alignment workshop.

13 Hub and bearing assembly (rear) - removal and installation

Warning: Dust created by the brake system may contain asbestos, which is harmful to your health. Never blow it out with compressed air and don't inhale any of it. Do not use petroleum-based solvents. Use brake system cleaner only.
Note: *Due to the special tools required to replace the bearing, the hub and bearing assembly should not be disassembled by the home mechanic. The assembly can be removed, however, and taken to a dealer service department or other repair workshop to have the bearing replaced.*

Removal

1 Loosen the wheel nuts, raise the vehicle and support it securely on jackstands. Remove the wheel.

2 Pull the brake drum from the hub (drum brake models) or remove the rear disc and caliper (disc brake models) (see Chapter 9).
3 Remove the four hub-to-axle carrier bolts, accessible by turning the hub flange so that the large circular cutout exposes each bolt **(see illustrations)**.
4 Remove the hub and bearing assembly from its seat, maneuvering it out through the brake assembly.
5 Remove the old O-ring from the hub seat.
6 On models without anti-lock brakes the rear axle hub can be removed from the bearing to allow replacement of the bearing. Due to the special tools required to do this, you'll have to take the hub and bearing assembly to an automotive machine workshop and have the old bearing pulled off the hub and a new bearing pressed on (you can re-use the hub itself, as long as it's in good condition). Make sure the hub retaining nut is tightened to the torque listed in this Chapter's Specifications. On models equipped with anti-lock brakes, the hub and bearing must be replaced as an assembly.

Installation

7 Apply a light coat of oil to the new O-ring and install it on the outer circumference of the raised hub in the backing plate **(see illustration)**.
8 Position the hub and bearing assembly on the axle carrier and align the holes in the backing plate. Install the bolts. A magnet is useful in guiding the bolts through the hub flange and into position. After all four bolts have been installed, tighten them to the torque listed in this Chapter's Specifications.
9 Install the brake drum, or disc and caliper, and the wheel. Lower the vehicle and tighten the nuts to the torque listed in the Chapter 1 Specifications.

14 Rear axle carrier - removal and installation

Warning: Dust created by the brake system may contain asbestos, which is harmful to your health. Never blow it out with compressed air and don't inhale any of it. Do not, under any circumstances, use petroleum-based solvents to clean brake parts. Use brake system cleaner only.

Removal

1 Loosen the wheel nuts, raise the vehicle and support it on jackstands. Block the front wheels and remove the rear wheel.
2 Remove the rear brake drum (drum brake models) or remove the rear disc and caliper (disc brake models) Detach the brake line from the bracket on the strut **(see illustration 10.3)**.
3 Remove the rear hub and bearing assembly (see Section 13).
4 Detach the backing plate and rear brake assembly (drum brake models) from the axle carrier. It isn't necessary to disassemble the brake shoe assembly or disconnect the parking brake cable from the backing plate. Suspend the backing plate and brake assembly from the coil spring with a piece of wire. Be careful not to kink the brake line.
5 On models with ABS, remove the wheel speed sensor from the axle carrier **(see illustration 13.3a)**.
6 Loosen, but don't remove the strut-to-axle carrier bolts **(see illustration 10.6)**.
7 Remove the suspension arm-to-axle carrier bolt, nut and washers and remove the rear strut rod-to-axle carrier bolt **(see illustrations 11.2 and 12.3)**.
8 Remove the loosened strut-to-axle carrier bolts while supporting the carrier so it doesn't fall and detach the axle carrier from the strut bracket.

13.3b To remove the four bolts which attach the hub and bearing assembly to the rear axle carrier, rotate the hub flange and align one of the holes in the flange with each of the bolts

13.7 Apply a light coat of oil to a new O-ring and install it on the raised hub of the backing plate; don't push the O-ring down against the face of the backing plate - when the hub/bearing assembly is installed, the O-ring will seat in its groove around the inside of the hub nut bore as the hub/bearing assembly is tightened

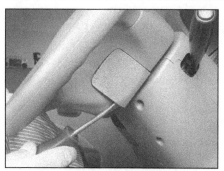

16.2a To access the airbag module retaining screws, remove the cover on each side of the steering wheel

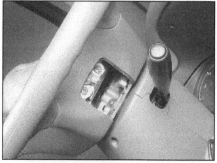

16.2b There is one T30 Torx retaining screw (shown) on the right side of the steering wheel and, on some models, there are two T30s on the left side

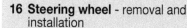

16.2c Back out the Torx screws until the airbag module is free, but don't try to remove them from the screw case

Installation

9 Inspect the carrier bushing for cracks, deformation and signs of wear. If it is worn out, take the carrier to a dealer service department or other repair workshop to have the old one pressed out and a new one pressed in.

10 Push the axle carrier into the strut bracket, aligning the two bolt holes. Insert the two strut-to-carrier bolts and tighten them to the torque listed in this Chapter's Specifications.

11 Install the suspension arm-to-axle carrier bolt (from the front), washers and nut. Tighten the nut by hand.

12 Connect the strut rod to the axle carrier and tighten the nut and bolt finger tight.

13 Place a jack under the carrier and raise it to simulate normal ride height.

14 Tighten the suspension arm bolt/nut and the strut rod bolt/nut to the torque values listed in this Chapter's Specifications. Remove the floor jack from under the rear axle carrier.

15 On models with ABS, reattach the wheel speed sensor to the axle carrier.

16 Attach the brake backing plate to the axle carrier, install the hub and tighten the four bolts to the torque listed in this Chapter's Specifications.

17 Connect the brake line to the strut bracket and install the clip. Make sure the hose isn't twisted.

18 Install the rear brake drum or disc and caliper (see Chapter 9).

19 Install the wheel and nuts.

20 Lower the vehicle and tighten the nuts to the torque listed in the Chapter 1 Specifications.

15 Steering system - general information

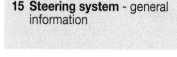

All models are equipped with rack-and-pinion steering. The steering gear is bolted to the engine cradle and operates the steering knuckles via tie-rods. The inner ends of the tie-rods are protected by rubber boots which should be inspected periodically for secure attachment, tears and leaking lubricant.

On models with power steering, the power assist system consists of a belt-driven pump and associated lines and hoses. The fluid level in the power steering pump reservoir should be checked periodically (see Chapter 1).

The steering wheel operates the steering shaft, which actuates the steering gear through universal joints. Looseness in the steering can be caused by wear in the steering shaft universal joints, the steering gear, the tie-rod ends and loose retaining bolts.

16 Steering wheel - removal and installation

⚠ **Warning: These models are equipped with airbags. The airbag is armed and can deploy (inflate) whenever the battery is connected. To prevent accidental deployment (and possible injury), turn the ignition key to LOCK and disconnect the negative battery cable whenever working near airbag components. After the battery is disconnected, wait at least two minutes before beginning work (the system has a back-up capacitor that must fully discharge). For more information see Chapter 12.**

Removal

1 Turn the ignition key to Off, then disconnect the cable from the negative terminal of the battery. If the vehicle is equipped with an airbag system, wait at least two minutes before proceeding.

Caution: If the stereo in your vehicle is equipped with an anti-theft system, make sure you have the correct activation code before disconnecting the battery.

2 Turn the steering wheel so the wheels are pointing straight ahead, then pry off the small covers (where fitted) on either side of the steering wheel and loosen the T30 Torx screws that attach the airbag module to the steering wheel (see illustrations). Loosen each screw until the groove in the circumference of the screw catches on the screw case (see illustration). Note that, on some models, there are two screws on the left and one screw on the right.

3 Pull the airbag module off the steering wheel (see illustration) and disconnect the module electrical connector (see illustration).

⚠ **Warning: Set the airbag module down with the trim side facing up.**

4 Unplug the electrical connector for the cruise control (if equipped).

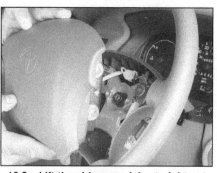

16.3a Lift the airbag module straight out from the steering wheel ...

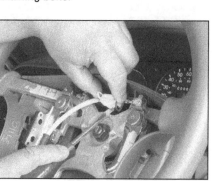

16.3b ... flip up the locking tab on the electrical connector for the module and unplug the connector

16.5 After removing the steering wheel nut, mark the relationship of the steering wheel to the shaft before removing the wheel

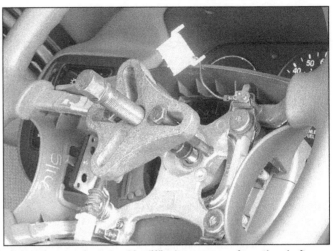

16.6 If the steering wheel is difficult to remove from the shaft, use a steering wheel puller to remove it

5 Remove the steering wheel retaining nut, then mark the relationship of the steering shaft to the hub (if marks don't already exist or don't line up) to simplify installation and ensure steering wheel alignment **(see illustration)**.
6 Use a puller to disconnect the steering wheel from the shaft **(see illustration)**.

Installation

7 Make sure that the front wheels are facing straight ahead. Turn the spiral cable anti-clockwise by hand until it becomes harder to turn the cable. Rotate the cable clockwise about three turns and align the two red pointers **(see illustration)**.
8 To install the wheel, align the mark on the steering wheel hub with the mark on the shaft and slip the wheel onto the shaft. Install the nut and tighten it to the torque listed in this Chapter's Specifications.
9 Plug in the cruise control connector.
10 Plug in the electrical connector for the airbag module and flip down the locking tab.
11 Make sure the airbag module electrical connector is positioned correctly and that the wires don't interfere with anything **(see illustration)**, then install the airbag module and tighten the Torx retaining screws to the torque listed in this Chapter's Specifications.
12 Connect the negative battery cable.

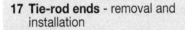

16.7 Verify that the front wheels are pointing straight ahead and turn the spiral cable anti-clockwise by hand until it becomes hard to turn the cable, then rotate the spiral cable clockwise three turns and align the red marks (the spiral cable will rotate about three turns to the left or right of centre)

17 Tie-rod ends - removal and installation

Removal

1 Loosen the wheel nuts. Raise the front of the vehicle, support it securely on jackstands,

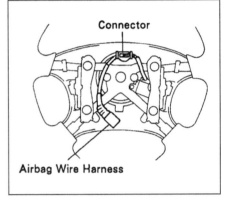

16.11 Before installing the airbag module, make sure that no wiring interferes with, or is pinched between, other parts; if you route the airbag harness as shown, it should be fine

block the rear wheels and set the parking brake. Remove the front wheel.
2 Remove the cotter pin **(see illustration)** and loosen the nut on the tie-rod end stud.
3 Hold the tie rod with a pair of locking pliers or wrench and loosen the lock nut enough to mark the position of the tie-rod end in relation to the threads **(see illustrations)**.

17.2 Remove the cotter pin from the castle nut and loosen - but don't remove - the nut

17.3a Loosen the locknut . . .

17.3b . . . then mark the position of the tie-rod end in relation to the threads

17.4 Disconnect the tie-rod from the steering knuckle arm with a puller

18.3a The outer ends of the steering gear boots are secured by band-type clamps; they're easily released with a pair of pliers

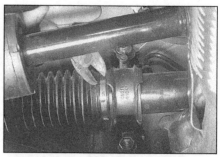

18.3b The inner ends of the steering gear boots are retained by boot clamps which must be cut off and discarded

4 Disconnect the tie rod from the steering knuckle arm with a puller **(see illustration)**. Remove the nut and detach the tie-rod.
5 Unscrew the tie-rod end from the tie-rod.

Installation

6 Thread the tie-rod end on to the marked position and insert the tie-rod stud into the steering knuckle arm. Tighten the lock nut securely.
7 Install the castle nut on the stud and tighten it to the torque listed in this Chapter's Specifications. Install a new cotter pin. If the hole for the cotter pin doesn't line up with one of the slots in the nut, turn the nut an additional amount until it does.
8 Install the wheel and nuts. Lower the vehicle and tighten the nuts to the torque listed in the Chapter 1 Specifications.
9 Have the alignment checked by a dealer service department or an alignment workshop.

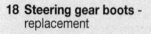

18 Steering gear boots - replacement

1 Loosen the nuts, raise the vehicle and support it securely on jackstands. Remove the wheel.
2 Remove the tie-rod end and lock nut (see Section 17).
3 Remove the outer steering gear boot clamp with a pair of pliers **(see illustration)**. Cut off the inner boot clamp with a pair of diagonal cutters **(see illustration)**. Slide off the boot.

4 Before installing the new boot, wrap the threads and serrations on the end of the steering rod with a layer of tape so the small end of the new boot isn't damaged.
5 Slide the new boot into position on the steering gear until it seats in the groove in the steering rod and install new clamps.
6 Remove the tape and install the tie-rod end (see Section 17).
7 Install the wheel and nuts. Lower the vehicle and tighten the nuts to the torque listed in the Chapter 1 Specifications.

19 Steering gear - removal and installation

⚠ *Warning: These models are equipped with airbags. Make sure the steering shaft is not turned while the steering gear is removed or you could damage the airbag system. To prevent the shaft from turning, turn the ignition key to the lock position before beginning work or run the seat belt through the steering wheel and clip the seat belt into place.*

Removal

1 Loosen the front wheel nuts, raise the front of the vehicle and support it securely on jackstands. Apply the parking brake and remove the wheels. Remove the engine splash shields.

2 If equipped with power steering, place a drain pan under the steering gear. Detach the power steering pressure and return lines **(see illustration)** and cap the ends to prevent excessive fluid loss and contamination.
3 Remove the universal joint cover **(see illustration)**. Mark the relationship of the lower universal joint to the steering gear input shaft and remove the lower intermediate shaft pinch bolt **(see illustration)**.
4 Separate the tie-rod ends from the steering knuckle arms (see Section 17).
5 Support the steering gear and remove the steering gear bracket-to-firewall mounting bolts **(see illustration)**. Separate the intermediate shaft from the steering gear input shaft and remove the steering gear assembly.

⚠ *Warning: Do NOT turn the steering wheel while the steering gear is removed. If the steering*

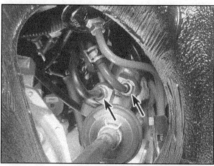

19.2 Disconnect the power steering line fittings (arrows)

19.3a Remove the universal joint cover bolts (arrows) and remove the cover (only three cover bolts are visible in this photo - there are actually five)

19.3b Mark the relationship of the universal joint to the steering gear input shaft and loosen the U-joint pinch bolt (arrow)

19.5 Remove the lower bolt (arrow) and the upper nut (arrow) from the right steering gear bracket, then remove the nut and bolt from the left bracket (not visible here)

20.7 Loosen the fluid return hose clamp (left arrow) and detach the return hose from the power steering pump; remove the pressure line banjo bolt (right arrow) and disconnect the pressure line from the pump

20.10 Working from underneath, detach these two vacuum lines (arrows) from the power steering pump

20.11a Besides the pivot bolt, you'll need to remove the adjuster bolt (left arrow) to remove the pump; if you want to remove the pump bracket, remove the two bolts (arrows) at the right as well

wheel is inadvertently turned, remove the steering wheel and centre the spiral cable (see Section 16).
6 Check the steering gear mounting grommets for excessive wear or deterioration, replacing them if necessary.

Installation

7 Raise the steering gear into position and connect the U-joint, aligning the marks.
8 Install the mounting brackets and bolts and tighten them to the torque listed in this Chapter's Specifications.
9 Connect the tie-rod ends to the steering knuckle arms (see Section 17).
10 Install the U-joint pinch bolt and tighten it to the torque listed in this Chapter's Specifications.
11 If equipped with power steering, connect the power steering pressure and return hoses to the steering gear and fill the power steering pump reservoir with the recommended fluid (see Chapter 1).
12 Lower the vehicle and bleed the steering system (see Section 21).

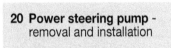

20 Power steering pump -
removal and installation

Removal

1 Disconnect the cable from the negative battery terminal.
Caution: If the stereo in your vehicle is equipped with an anti-theft system, make sure you have the correct activation code before disconnecting the battery.
2 Using a large syringe, suck as much fluid out of the power steering fluid reservoir as possible. Place a drain pan under the vehicle to catch any fluid that spills out when the hoses are disconnected.

4E-FE engines

3 Loosen the clamp and disconnect the fluid return hose from the pump.
4 Unscrew the pressure line to pmp union nut, and detach the line from the pump.

5 Detach the two vacuum lines from the pump air control vale.
6 Loosen the pivot bolt (above) and adjster bolt (below) and remove the drivebelt (see Chapter 1). Remove the pivot and adjuster bolts, then remove the pump from the vehicle.

4A-FE and 7A-FE engines

7 Loosen the clamp and disconnect the fluid return hose from the pump **(see illustration)**.
8 Remove the pressure line-to-pump banjo bolt **(see illustration 20.7)**, then detach the line from the pump. Remove and discard the

copper sealing washers. They must be replaced when installing the pump.
9 Raise the front of the vehicle and place it securely on jackstands.
10 Working from underneath the vehicle, detach the two vacuum lines from the pump **(see illustration)**.
11 Loosen the pivot bolt (underneath) and adjuster bolt (above) and remove the drivebelt (see Chapter 1). Remove the pivot, adjuster and mounting bolts **(see illustrations)**, then remove the pump from the vehicle.

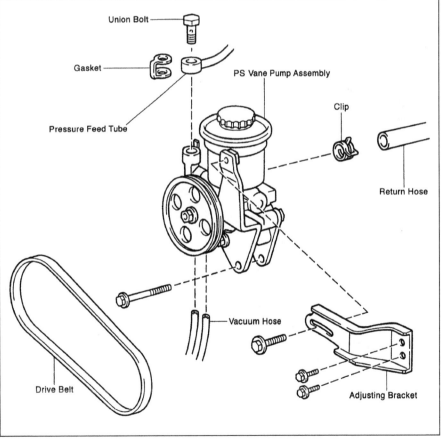

20.11b An exploded view of the power steering pump and mounting bracket assembly as fitted to 4A-FE and 7A-FE engines

Installation

12 Installation is the reverse of removal. Be sure to tighten the pressure line banjo bolt to the torque listed in this Chapter's Specifications. Adjust the drivebelt tension following the procedure described in Chapter 1.

13 Top up the fluid level in the reservoir (see Chapter 1) and bleed the system (Section 21).

21 Power steering system - bleeding

1 Following any operation in which the power steering fluid lines have been disconnected, the power steering system must be bled to remove all air and obtain proper steering performance.

2 With the front wheels in the straight ahead position, check the power steering fluid level and, if low, add fluid of the specified type (see Chapter 1) until it reaches the Cold mark on the dipstick.

3 Start the engine and allow it to run at fast idle. Recheck the fluid level and add more if necessary to reach the Cold mark on the dipstick.

4 Bleed the system by turning the wheels from side to side, without hitting the stops. This will work the air out of the system. Keep the reservoir full of fluid as this is done.

5 When the air is worked out of the system, return the wheels to the straight ahead position and leave the vehicle running for several more minutes before shutting it off.

6 Road test the vehicle to be sure the steering system is functioning normally and noise free.

7 Recheck the fluid level to be sure it is up to the Hot mark on the dipstick while the engine is at normal operating temperature. Add fluid if necessary (see Chapter 1).

22 Wheels and tyres - general information

1 All vehicles covered by this manual are equipped with metric-sized fiberglass or steel belted radial tyres **(see illustration)**. Use of other size or type of tyres may affect the ride and handling of the vehicle. Don't mix different types of tyres, such as radials and bias belted, on the same vehicle as handling may be seriously affected. It's recommended that tyres be replaced in pairs on the same axle, but if only one tyre is being replaced, be sure it's the same size, structure and tread design as the other.

2 Because tyre pressure has a substantial effect on handling and wear, the pressure on all tyres should be checked at least once a month or before any extended trips (see Chapter 1).

3 Wheels must be replaced if they are bent, dented, leak air, have elongated bolt holes, are heavily rusted, out of vertical symmetry or if the nuts won't stay tight. Wheel repairs that use welding or peening are not recommended.

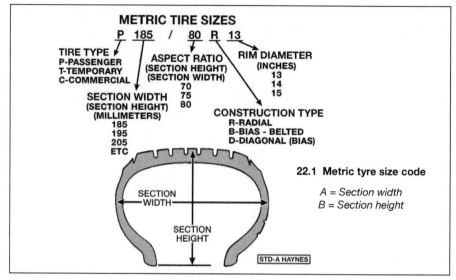

22.1 Metric tyre size code

A = Section width
B = Section height

4 Tyre and wheel balance is important in the overall handling, braking and performance of the vehicle. Unbalanced wheels can adversely affect handling and ride characteristics as well as tyre life. Whenever a tyre is installed on a wheel, the tyre and wheel should be balanced by a workshop with the proper equipment.

23 Wheel alignment - general information

A wheel alignment refers to the adjustments made to the wheels so they are in proper angular relationship to the suspension and the ground. Wheels that are out of proper alignment not only affect vehicle control, but also increase tyre wear. The front end angles normally measured are camber, caster and toe-in **(see illustration)**. Camber and toe-in are adjustable on 1996 models. Toe-in is the only adjustable angle on 1995 and earlier models. The only adjustment possible on the rear is toe-in. The other angles should be measured to check for bent or worn suspension parts.

Getting the proper wheel alignment is a very exacting process, one in which complicated and expensive machines are necessary to perform the job properly. Because of this, you should have a technician with the proper equipment perform these tasks. We will, however, use this space to give you a basic idea of what is involved with a wheel alignment so you can better understand the process and deal intelligently with the workshop that does the work.

Toe-in is the turning in of the wheels. The purpose of a toe specification is to ensure parallel rolling of the wheels. In a vehicle with zero toe-in, the distance between the front edges of the wheels will be the same as the distance between the rear edges of the wheels. The actual amount of toe-in is normally only a fraction of an inch. On the front end, toe-in is controlled by the tie-rod end

position on the tie-rod. On the rear end, it's controlled by altering the length of the rear (No.2) suspension arm. Incorrect toe-in will cause the tyres to wear improperly by making them scrub against the road surface.

Camber is the tilting of the wheels from vertical when viewed from one end of the vehicle. When the wheels tilt out at the top, the camber is said to be positive (+). When the wheels tilt in at the top the camber is negative (-). The amount of tilt is measured in degrees from vertical and this measurement is called the camber angle. This angle affects the amount of tyre tread which contacts the road and compensates for changes in the suspension geometry when the vehicle is cornering or traveling over an undulating surface. It is adjusted using special camber adjusting bolts.

Caster is the tilting of the front steering axis from the vertical. A tilt toward the rear is positive caster and a tilt toward the front is negative caster.

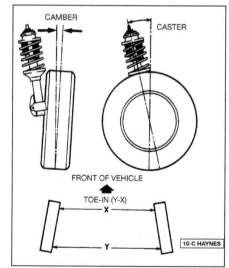

23.1 Camber, caster and toe-in angles

Chapter 11
Bodywork and fittings

Contents

Degrees of difficulty

| Easy, suitable for novice with little experience | Fairly easy, suitable for beginner with some experience | Fairly difficult, suitable for competent DIY mechanic | Difficult, suitable for experienced DIY mechanic | Very difficult, suitable for expert DIY or professional |

1 General information

The models covered by this manual feature a "unibody" construction, using a floor pan with front and rear frame side rails which support the body components, front and rear suspension systems and other mechanical components. Certain components are particularly vulnerable to accident damage and can be unbolted and repaired or replaced. Among these parts are the body moldings, bumpers, bonnet and boot lids and all glass.

Only general body maintenance practices and body panel repair procedures within the scope of the do-it-yourselfer are included in this Chapter.

2 Body - maintenance

1 The condition of your vehicle's body is very important, because the resale value depends a great deal on it. It's much more difficult to repair a neglected or damaged body than it is to repair mechanical components. The hidden areas of the body, such as the wheel wells, the frame and the engine compartment, are equally important, although they don't require as frequent attention as the rest of the body.
2 Once a year, or every 12 000 miles, it's a good idea to have the underside of the body steam cleaned. All traces of dirt and oil will be removed and the area can then be inspected carefully for rust, damaged brake lines, frayed electrical wires, damaged cables and other problems. The front suspension components should be greased after completion of this job.
3 At the same time, clean the engine and the engine compartment with a steam cleaner or water soluble degreaser.
4 The wheel wells should be given close attention, since undercoating can peel away and stones and dirt thrown up by the tyres can cause the paint to chip and flake, allowing rust to set in. If rust is found, clean down to the bare metal and apply an anti-rust paint.
5 The body should be washed about once a week. Wet the vehicle thoroughly to soften the dirt, then wash it down with a soft sponge and plenty of clean soapy water. If the surplus dirt is not washed off very carefully, it can wear down the paint.
6 Spots of tar or asphalt thrown up from the road should be removed with a cloth soaked in solvent.
7 Once every six months, wax the body and chrome trim. If a chrome cleaner is used to remove rust from any of the vehicle's plated parts, remember that the cleaner also removes part of the chrome, so use it sparingly.

3 Vinyl trim - maintenance

Don't clean vinyl trim with detergents, caustic soap or petroleum-based cleaners. Plain soap and water works just fine, with a soft brush to clean dirt that may be ingrained. Wash the vinyl as frequently as the rest of the vehicle.

After cleaning, application of a high quality rubber and vinyl protectant will help prevent oxidation and cracks. The protectant can also be applied to weatherstripping, vacuum lines and rubber hoses, which often fail as a result of chemical degradation, and to the tyres.

4 Upholstery and carpets - maintenance

1 Every three months remove the carpets or mats and clean the interior of the vehicle (more frequently if necessary). Vacuum the upholstery and carpets to remove loose dirt and dust.

2 Leather upholstery requires special care. Stains should be removed with warm water and a very mild soap solution. Use a clean, damp cloth to remove the soap, then wipe again with a dry cloth. Never use alcohol, petrol, nail polish remover or thinner to clean leather upholstery.

3 After cleaning, regularly treat leather upholstery with a leather wax. Never use car wax on leather upholstery.

4 In areas where the interior of the vehicle is subject to bright sunlight, cover leather seats with a sheet if the vehicle is to be left out for any length of time.

5 Body repair - minor damage

Repair of minor scratches

1 If the scratch is superficial and does not penetrate to the metal of the body, repair is very simple. Lightly rub the scratched area with a fine rubbing compound to remove loose paint and built-up wax. Rinse the area with clean water.

2 Apply touch-up paint to the scratch, using a small brush. Continue to apply thin layers of paint until the surface of the paint in the scratch is level with the surrounding paint. Allow the new paint at least two weeks to harden, then blend it into the surrounding paint by rubbing with a very fine rubbing compound. Finally, apply a coat of wax to the scratch area.

3 If the scratch has penetrated the paint and exposed the metal of the body, causing the metal to rust, a different repair technique is required. Remove all loose rust from the bottom of the scratch with a pocket knife, then apply rust inhibiting paint to prevent the formation of rust in the future. Using a rubber or nylon applicator, coat the scratched area with glaze-type filler. Before the glaze filler in the scratch hardens, wrap a piece of smooth cotton cloth around the tip of a finger. Dip the cloth in thinner and then quickly wipe it along the surface of the scratch. This will ensure that the surface of the filler is slightly hollow. The scratch can now be painted over as described earlier in this section.

HAYNES HiNT *If required, the filler can be mixed with thinner to provide a very thin paste, which is ideal for filling narrow scratches.*

Repair of dents

4 When repairing dents, the first job is to pull the dent out until the affected area is as close as possible to its original shape. There is no point in trying to restore the original shape completely as the metal in the damaged area will have stretched on impact and cannot be restored to its original contours. It is better to bring the level of the dent up to a point which is about 1/8-inch below the level of the surrounding metal. In cases where the dent is very shallow, it is not worth trying to pull it out at all.

5 If the back side of the dent is accessible, it can be hammered out gently from behind using a soft-face hammer.

HAYNES HiNT *Hold a block of wood firmly against the opposite side of the metal to absorb the hammer blows and prevent the metal from being stretched.*

6 If the dent is in a section of the body which has double layers, or some other factor makes it inaccessible from behind, a different technique is required. Drill several small holes through the metal inside the damaged area, particularly in the deeper sections. Screw long, self-tapping screws into the holes just enough for them to get a good grip in the metal. Now the dent can be pulled out by pulling on the protruding heads of the screws with locking pliers.

7 The next stage of repair is the removal of paint from the damaged area and from an inch or so of the surrounding metal. This is done with a wire brush or sanding disk in a drill motor, although it can be done just as effectively by hand with sandpaper. To complete the preparation for filling, score the surface of the bare metal with a screwdriver or the tang of a file, or drill small holes in the affected area. This will provide a good grip for the filler material. To complete the repair, see the subsection on filling and painting later in this Section.

Repair of rust holes or gashes

8 Remove all paint from the affected area and from an inch or so of the surrounding metal using a sanding disk or wire brush mounted in a drill motor. If these are not available, a few sheets of sandpaper will do the job just as effectively.

9 With the paint removed, you will be able to determine the severity of the corrosion and decide whether to replace the whole panel, if possible, or repair the affected area. New body panels are not as expensive as most people think and it is often quicker to install a new panel than to repair large areas of rust.

10 Remove all trim pieces from the affected area except those which will act as a guide to the original shape of the damaged body, such as headlight shells, etc. Using metal snips or a

hacksaw blade, remove all loose metal and any other metal that is badly affected by rust. Hammer the edges of the hole in to create a slight depression for the filler material.

11 Wire brush the affected area to remove the powdery rust from the surface of the metal. If the back of the rusted area is accessible, treat it with rust inhibiting paint.

12 Before filling is done, block the hole in some way. This can be done with sheet metal riveted or screwed into place, or by stuffing the hole with wire mesh.

13 Once the hole is blocked off, the affected area can be filled and painted. See the following subsection on filling and painting.

Filling and painting

14 Many types of body fillers are available, but generally speaking, body repair kits which contain filler paste and a tube of resin hardener are best for this type of repair work. A wide, flexible plastic or nylon applicator will be necessary for imparting a smooth and contoured finish to the surface of the filler material. Mix up a small amount of filler on a clean piece of wood or cardboard (use the hardener sparingly). Follow the manufacturer's instructions on the package, otherwise the filler will set incorrectly.

15 Using the applicator, apply the filler paste to the prepared area. Draw the applicator across the surface of the filler to achieve the desired contour and to level the filler surface. As soon as a contour that approximates the original one is achieved, stop working the paste. If you continue, the paste will begin to stick to the applicator. Continue to add thin layers of paste at 20-minute intervals until the level of the filler is just above the surrounding metal.

16 Once the filler has hardened, the excess can be removed with a body file. From then on, progressively finer grades of sandpaper should be used, starting with a 180-grit paper and finishing with 600-grit wet-or-dry paper. Always wrap the sandpaper around a flat rubber or wooden block, otherwise the surface of the filler will not be completely flat. During the sanding of the filler surface, the wet-or-dry paper should be periodically rinsed in water. This will ensure that a very smooth finish is produced in the final stage.

17 At this point, the repair area should be surrounded by a ring of bare metal, which in turn should be encircled by the finely feathered edge of good paint. Rinse the repair area with clean water until all of the dust produced by the sanding operation is gone.

18 Spray the entire area with a light coat of primer. This will reveal any imperfections in the surface of the filler. Repair the imperfections with fresh filler paste or glaze filler and once more smooth the surface with sandpaper. Repeat this spray-and-repair procedure until you are satisfied that the surface of the filler and the feathered edge of the paint are perfect. Rinse the area with clean water and allow it to dry completely.

19 The repair area is now ready for painting. Spray painting must be carried out in a warm, dry, windless and dust free atmosphere. These conditions can be created if you have access to a large indoor work area, but if you are forced to work in the open, you will have to pick the day very carefully. If you are working indoors, dousing the floor in the work area with water will help settle the dust which would otherwise be in the air. If the repair area is confined to one body panel, mask off the surrounding panels. This will help minimize the effects of a slight mismatch in paint colour. Trim pieces such as chrome strips, door handles, etc., will also need to be masked off or removed. Use masking tape and several thickness of newspaper for the masking operations.

20 Before spraying, shake the paint can thoroughly, then spray a test area until the spray painting technique is mastered. Cover the repair area with a thick coat of primer. The thickness should be built up using several thin layers of primer rather than one thick one. Using 600-grit wet-or-dry sandpaper, rub down the surface of the primer until it is very smooth. While doing this, the work area should be thoroughly rinsed with water and the wet-or-dry sandpaper periodically rinsed as well. Allow the primer to dry before spraying additional coats.

21 Spray on the top coat, again building up the thickness by using several thin layers of paint. Begin spraying in the centre of the repair area and then, using a circular motion, work out until the whole repair area and about two inches of the surrounding original paint is covered. Remove all masking material 10 to 15 minutes after spraying on the final coat of paint. Allow the new paint at least two weeks to harden, then use a very fine rubbing compound to blend the edges of the new paint into the existing paint. Finally, apply a coat of wax.

6 Body repair - major damage

1 Major damage must be repaired by an auto body workshop specifically equipped to perform unibody repairs. These workshops have the specialized equipment required to do the job properly.

2 If the damage is extensive, the body must be checked for proper alignment or the vehicle's handling characteristics may be adversely affected and other components may wear at an accelerated rate.

3 Due to the fact that all of the major body components (bonnet, wings, etc.) are separate and replaceable units, any seriously damaged components should be replaced rather than repaired. Sometimes the components can be found in a wrecking yard that specializes in used vehicle components, often at considerable savings over the cost of new parts.

7 Hinges and locks - maintenance

Once every 3000 miles, or every three months, the hinges and latch assemblies on the doors, bonnet and boot should be given a few drops of light oil or lock lubricant. The door latch strikers should also be lubricated with a thin coat of grease to reduce wear and ensure free movement. Lubricate the door and boot locks with spray-on graphite lubricant.

8 Windscreen and fixed glass - replacement

Replacement of the windscreen and fixed glass requires the use of special fast-setting adhesive/caulk materials and some specialized tools. It is recommended that these operations be left to a dealer or a workshop specializing in glass work.

9 Bonnet - removal, installation and adjustment

Note: *The bonnet is heavy and somewhat awkward to remove and install - at least two people should perform this procedure.*

Removal and installation

1 Make marks around the bolt heads to ensure proper alignment during installation **(see illustration)**.

2 Use blankets or pads to cover the cowl area of the body and wings. This will protect the body and paint as the bonnet is lifted off.

3 Disconnect any cables or wires that will interfere with removal.

4 Have an assistant support the bonnet. Remove the hinge-to-bonnet bolts.

5 Lift off the bonnet.

6 Installation is the reverse of removal.

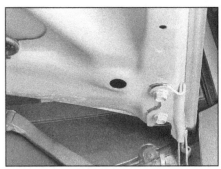

9.1 Before removing the bonnet, make marks around the hinge plate

Adjustment

7 Fore-and-aft and side-to-side adjustment of the bonnet is done by moving the hinge plate slot after loosening the bolts.

8 Scribe a line around the entyre hinge plate so you can judge the amount of movement **(see illustration 9.1)**

9 Loosen the bolts or nuts and move the bonnet into correct alignment. Move it only a little at a time. Tighten the hinge bolts and carefully lower the bonnet to check the position.

10 If necessary after installation, the entire bonnet latch assembly can be adjusted up-and-down as well as from side-to-side on the radiator support so the bonnet closes securely, flush with the wings. To make the adjustment, scribe a line around the bonnet latch mounting bolts to provide a reference point, then loosen them and reposition the latch assembly, as necessary **(see illustration)**. Following adjustment, retighten the mounting bolts.

11 Finally, adjust the bonnet bumpers on the radiator support so the bonnet, when closed, is flush with the wings **(see illustration)**.

12 The bonnet latch assembly, as well as the hinges, should be periodically lubricated with white, lithium-base grease to prevent binding and wear.

9.10 Loosen the bonnet latch bolts, move the latch and retighten bolts, then close the bonnet to check the fit - repeat the procedure until the bonnet is flush with the fenders

9.11 Adjust the bonnet height by screwing the bonnet bumpers in-or-out

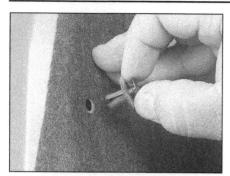

10.2 Unscrew the plastic retainer, then pull it out

10.3 Scribe a mark around the bolt heads to help with lid realignment on installation

10.8 Loosen the bolts, then adjust the latch and striker position

10 Boot lid - removal, installation and adjustment

Removal

1 Open the boot lid and cover the edges of the boot compartment with pads or cloths to protect the painted surfaces when the lid is removed.
2 Remove the boot lid trim cover **(see illustration)**.
3 Make alignment marks around the hinge mounting bolts **(see illustration)**.
4 While an assistant supports the lid, remove the lid-to-hinge bolts on both sides and lift it off.

Installation and adjustment

5 Installation is the reverse of removal. **Note:** *When reinstalling the boot lid, align the lid-to-hinge bolts with the marks made during removal.*
6 After installation, close the lid and make sure it's in proper alignment with the surrounding panels.
7 Forward-and-backward and side-to-side adjustments are made by loosening the hinge-to-lid bolts and gently moving the lid into correct alignment.
8 To adjust the lid so it is flush with the body when closed, loosen the mounting bolts and move the lock and striker **(see illustration)**.

11 Tailgate (Estate models) - removal, installation and adjustment

Note: *The rear tailgate is heavy and somewhat awkward to remove and install - at least two people should perform this procedure.*

Removal

1 Open the tailgate and cover the edges of the compartment with pads or cloths to protect the painted surfaces when the lid is removed.
2 Disconnect any cables or wire harness connectors attached to the tailgate that would interfere with removal.
3 Use a marking pen to make alignment marks around the hinge mounting flanges **(see illustration)**.
4 Have an assistant support the tailgate and detach the support struts (see Section 12).
5 While an assistant supports the tailgate, remove the lid-to-hinge bolts on both sides and lift it off.

Installation and adjustment

6 Installation is the reverse of removal. **Note:** *When reinstalling the tailgate, align the hinges with the marks made during removal.*
7 After installation, close the tailgate and make sure it's in proper alignment with the surrounding panels.
8 Adjustments to the tailgate position are made by loosening the hinge to tailgate bolts or nuts and gently moving the tailgate into correct alignment.

9 The tailgate latch position can be adjusted by loosening the adjusting bolts and moving the latch. The latch striker can be adjusted by loosening the mounting screws and gently tapping it into position with a plastic hammer **(see illustration)**.

12 Tailgate support strut - replacement

⚠ *Warning: The support strut is filled with pressurized gas - do not disassemble this component. If it is faulty replace it with a new one.*

Note: *The rear tailgate is heavy and somewhat awkward to hold securely while replacing the struts - at least two people should perform this procedure.*
1 Open the tailgate and support it in the open position. Remove the bolts at the ends and detach the strut from the tailgate **(see illustration)**.
2 Installation is the reverse of the removal procedure.

13 Door trim panel - removal and installation

Removal

1 Disconnect the negative cable from the battery. **Caution:** *If the stereo in your vehicle is equipped with an anti-theft system, make*

11.3 Draw a line around the hinge plate on the tailgate before removing the bolts

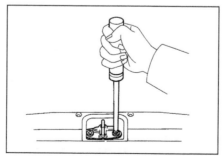

11.9 Adjust the lock striker by loosening the mounting screws slightly and tapping the striker with a soft-faced hammer

12.1 After supporting the tailgate, remove the bolts at each end and detach the support strut

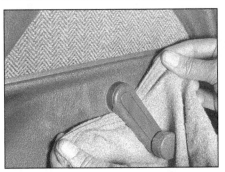

13.2a Work a cloth up behind the regulator handle and move it back-and-forth . . .

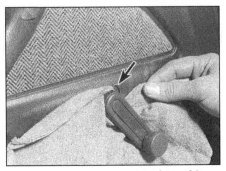

13.2b . . . until the retainer (arrow) is pushed up so you can remove it

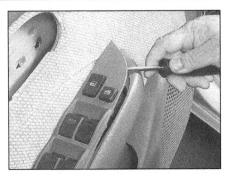

13.2c Pry up on the power window switch and remove it

sure you have the correct activation code before disconnecting the battery.

2 On manual window regulator equipped models, remove the window crank by working a cloth back-and-forth behind the handle to dislodge the retainer **(see illustrations)**. A special tool is available for this purpose but it's not essential. With the retainer removed, pull off the handle. On power window models, pry out the switch assembly, unplug the electrical connector and remove it **(see illustration)**.

3 Remove the outside mirror trim cover (see Section 18).

4 Remove the inside door handle (see Section 15). Remove the door trim panel retaining screws and door pull/armrest assemblies **(see illustrations)**.

5 Insert a wide putty knife, a thin screwdriver or a special trim panel removal tool between

the trim panel and door to disengage the retaining clips. Work around the outer edge until the panel is free.

6 Once all of the clips are disengaged, detach the trim panel, unplug any electrical connectors and remove the trim panel from the vehicle by gently pulling it up and out **(see illustration)**.

7 For access to the inner door remove the plastic watershield. Peel back the plastic cover, taking care not to tear it **(see illustration)**. Remove the plastic grommets, if necessary.

Installation

8 To install the trim panel, first press the watershield back into place. If necessary, add more sealant to hold it in place.

9 Prior to installation of the door panel, be sure to reinstall any clips in the panel which

may have come out during the removal procedure and stayed in the door.

10 Plug in any electrical connectors and place the panel in position. Press it into place until the clips are seated and install any retaining screws and armrest/door pulls. Install the manual regulator window crank or power switch assembly.

14 Door - removal, installation and adjustment

Removal and installation

1 Remove the door trim panel (see Section 13). Disconnect any electrical connectors and push them through the door opening so they won't interfere with removal.

2 Position a jack or jackstands under the door or have an assistant on hand to support the door when the hinge bolts are removed **(see illustration)**. **Note:** *If a jack or stand is used, place a rag between it and the door to protect the door's paint.*

3 Remove the door stop strut bolt **(see illustration)**.

4 Scribe around the door bolts **(see illustration)**.

5 Remove the hinge-to-door bolts and carefully detach the door. Installation is the reverse of removal.

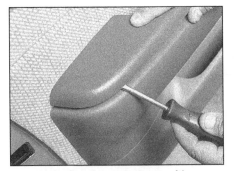

13.4a Pry the arm rest up with a screwdriver

13.4b Remove the armrest screws

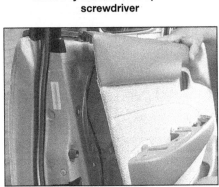

13.6 Use a trim panel removal tool to detach the trim panel retaining clips, then pull the door trim up and out to remove it

13.7 If the plastic watershield is peeled off carefully it can be reused

14.2 Use two jackstands padded with rags to support the door during the removal and installation procedures

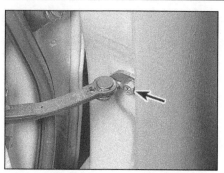

14.3 Remove the bolt (arrow) and detach the stop strut

Adjustment

6 Following installation, make sure the door is aligned properly. Adjust it if necessary as follows:

a) *Up-and-down and forward-and-backward adjustments are made by loosening the hinge-to-body bolts and moving the door, as necessary. A special offset tool may be required to reach some of the bolts (see illustration).*

b) *In-and-out and up-and-down adjustments are made by loosening the door side hinge bolts and moving the door, as*

necessary. A special offset tool may be required to reach some of the bolts (see illustration).

c) The door lock striker can also be adjusted both up-and-down and sideways to provide a positive engagement with the locking mechanism. This is done by loosening the screws and moving the striker, as necessary (see illustration).

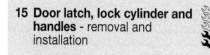

15 Door latch, lock cylinder and handles - removal and installation

1 Remove the door trim panel and the plastic watershield (Section 13).

Door latch

Removal

2 Reach behind the inside the door panel and disconnect the control links from the latch.
3 Remove the latch retaining screws from the end of the door (see illustration).
4 Detach the door latch and (if equipped) the door lock solenoid.

Installation

5 Installation is the reverse of removal.

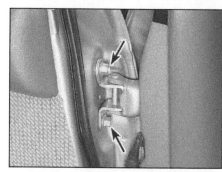

14.4 Before loosening or removing them, mark the door bolt locations (arrows)

Lock cylinder and outside handle

Removal

6 Disconnect the control link from the lock cylinder and outside handle.
7 Remove the outside handle retention bolts and pull the handle and lock cylinder from the door (see illustration).
8 Use a screwdriver to pry the retaining clip off and remove the lock cylinder from the door.

Installation

9 Installation is the reverse of removal.

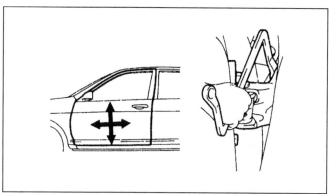

14.6a When adjusting the door up-and-down or forward-and-backward a special wrench such as this one will make the job easier

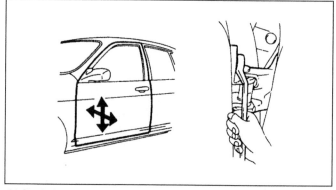

14.6b Adjust the door up-and-down or in-and-out after loosening the hinge to door bolts

14.6c Adjust the door lock striker by loosening the mounting screws (arrows) and gently tapping the striker in the desired direction

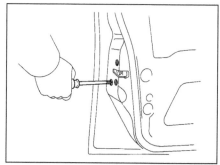

15.3 Remove the latch screws from the end of the door

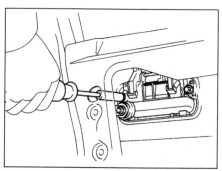

15.7 The outside handle retention bolts can be reached through access holes in the door frame

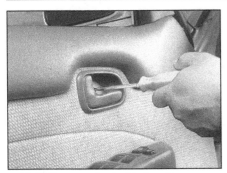

15.10 Remove the inside handle screw

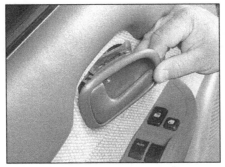

15.11a Rotate the handle out for access to the link

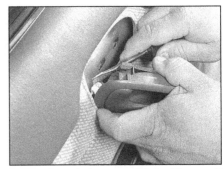

15.11b Detach the control link with a small screwdriver

Inside handle

Removal

10 Remove the retaining screw **(see illustration)**.
11 Pull the handle free, disconnect the link from the inside handle control and remove the handle from the door **(see illustrations)**.

Installation

12 Installation is the reverse of removal.

16 Door window glass - removal and installation

Removal

1 Remove the door trim panel and the plastic watershield (Section 13).
2 Lower the window glass.
3 Carefully pry the inner weatherstrip out of the door window opening.
4 Place a rag inside the door panel to help prevent scratching the glass and remove the two glass mounting bolts.
5 Remove the glass by pulling it up.

Installation

6 Installation is the reverse of the removal procedure.

17 Bumpers - removal and installation

Caution: If the stereo in your vehicle is equipped with an anti-theft system, make sure you have the correct activation code before disconnecting the battery.

Removal

1 Apply the parking brake, raise the vehicle and support it securely on jackstands.
2 Disconnect the cable from the negative battery terminal and disconnect any wiring that would interfere with bumper removal.
3 Remove the bumper cover if equipped, taking care to avoid damaging the cover and the bumper.

4 Working under the vehicle remove the bumper retention bolts **(see illustrations)**.
5 Pull the bumper assembly from the vehicle.

Installation

6 Installation is the reverse of the removal procedure.

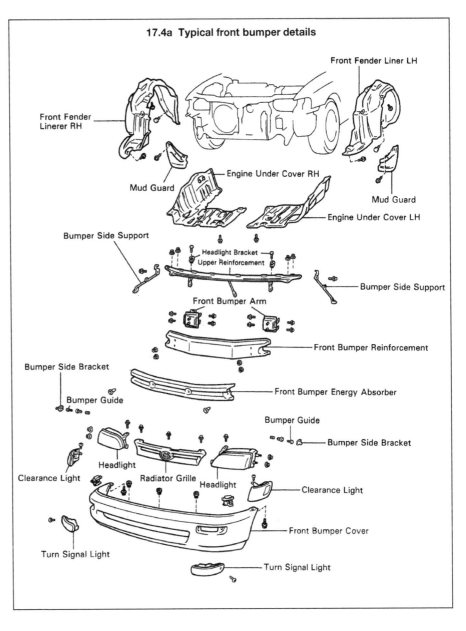

17.4a Typical front bumper details

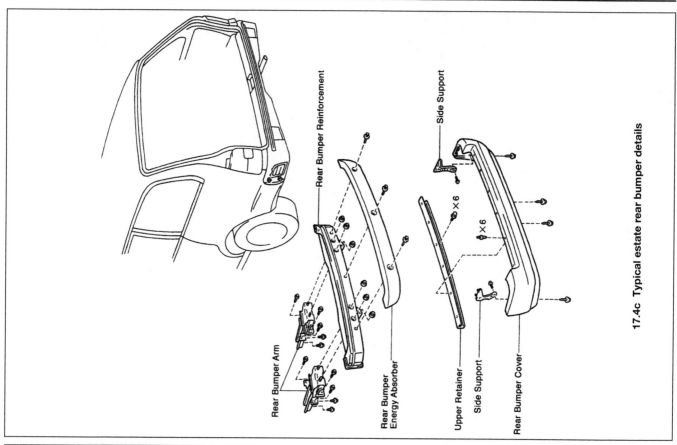

17.4c Typical estate rear bumper details

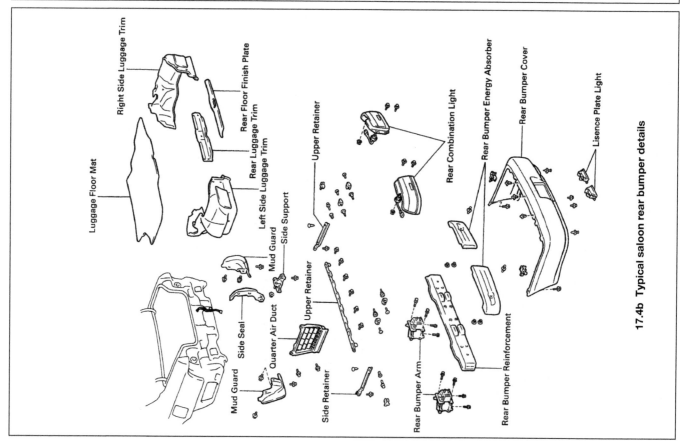

17.4b Typical saloon rear bumper details

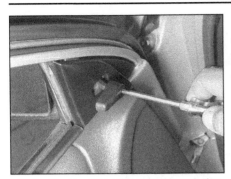

18.1a Remove the screw and detach the control handle

18.1b Detach the cover and lift it out (power mirror shown)

18.2a Remove the three bolts securing the outside mirror to the door

18 Outside mirror - removal and installation

Removal

1 On manually operated mirrors, remove the control handle **(see illustration)**. Detach the mirror cover by using a small screwdriver to pry the retainers free from the door **(see illustration)**.
2 Remove the three retaining nuts and detach the mirror **(see illustration)**. On power mirrors, unplug the electrical connector **(see illustration)**.

Installation

3 Installation is the reverse of removal.

19 Seats - removal and installation

Front seats

Removal

1 Remove the retaining bolts, unplug any electrical connectors and lift the seats from the vehicle **(see illustration)**.

Installation

2 Installation is the reverse of removal.

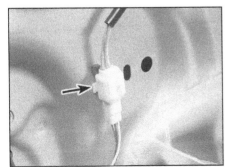

18.2b Unplug the power mirror electrical connector (arrow)

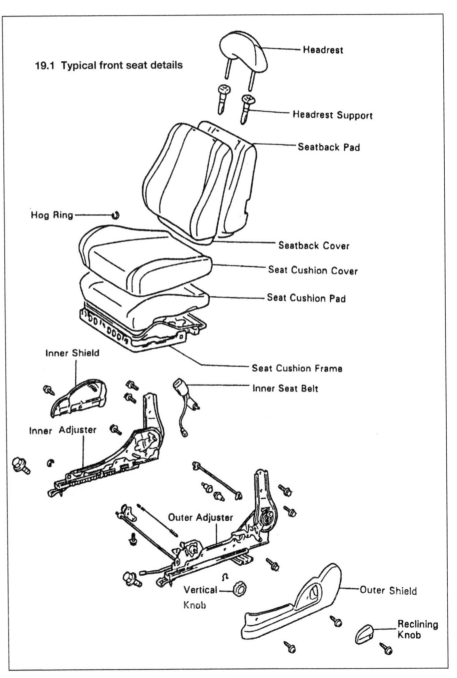

19.1 Typical front seat details

- Headrest
- Headrest Support
- Seatback Pad
- Hog Ring
- Seatback Cover
- Seat Cushion Cover
- Seat Cushion Pad
- Seat Cushion Frame
- Inner Seat Belt
- Inner Shield
- Inner Adjuster
- Outer Adjuster
- Vertical Knob
- Outer Shield
- Reclining Knob

Rear seats

Removal

3 On saloon models, lift the front of the cushion up, then pull it out toward the front of the vehicle. Remove the seat back retaining bolts, then lift up on the back to release the seat back from the body.**(see illustration)**.

4 On estate models, remove the retaining bolts at the base of the seat cushion, pull the back of the cushion up and remove it from the vehicle. Remove the seat back pivot retaining bolts and remove the seat back from the vehicle.

Installation

5 Installation is the reverse of removal.

---

20 Instrument cluster bezel - removal and installation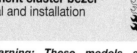

⚠ *Warning: These models are equipped with airbags. The airbag is armed and can deploy (inflate) anytime the battery is connected. To prevent accidental deployment (and possible injury), turn the ignition key to LOCK and disconnect the negative battery cable whenever working near airbag components. After the battery is disconnected, wait at least two minutes before beginning work (the system has a back-up capacitor that must fully discharge). For more information see Chapter 12.*

20.2a Remove the two screws at the top of the bezel

20.2b Use a screwdriver to detach the clips at each end of the bezel

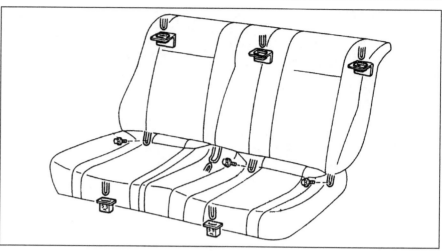

19.3 Typical rear seat details

Caution: If the stereo in your vehicle is equipped with an anti-theft system, make sure you have the correct activation code before disconnecting the battery.

Removal

1 Disconnect the cable from the negative battery terminal.

2 Remove the two screws along the top of the bezel, then detach the two clips at the lower edges by prying with a screwdriver **(see illustrations)**.

3 Grasp the bezel securely and remove it **(see illustration)**.

Installation

4 Installation is the reverse of the removal procedure.

---

21 Glovebox - removal and installation

⚠ *Warning: These models are equipped with airbags. The airbag is armed and can deploy (inflate) anytime the battery is connected. To prevent accidental deployment (and possible injury), turn the ignition key to LOCK and disconnect the negative battery cable whenever working*

20.3 Detach the bezel and lift it off

near airbag components. After the battery is disconnected, wait at least two minutes before beginning work (the system has a back-up capacitor that must fully discharge). For more information see Chapter 12.
Caution: If the stereo in your vehicle is equipped with an anti-theft system, make sure you have the correct activation code before disconnecting the battery.

Removal

1 Disconnect the cable from the negative battery terminal. Remove the screws, pull the glove box out of the instrument panel and lower it for access to the airbag connector **(see illustration)**. Detach the connector from the clips and remove the glovebox assembly **(see illustration)**.

Installation

2 Installation is the reverse of removal.

---

22 Centre trim panel - removal and installation

⚠ *Warning: These models are equipped with airbags. The airbag is armed and can deploy (inflate) anytime the battery is*

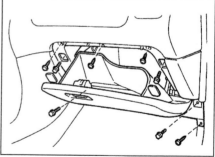

21.1a Glovebox installation details

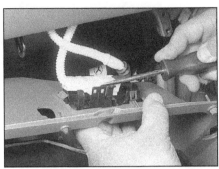

21.1b Lower the glove box and detach the airbag connector from the clips (**DO NOT** unplug the airbag connector unless you plan to remove the airbag module)

22.3a Detach the trim panel, pull it out and turn it over for access to the electrical connectors

22.3b Unplug the connectors

connected. *To prevent accidental deployment (and possible injury), turn the ignition key to LOCK and disconnect the negative battery cable whenever working near airbag components. After the battery is disconnected, wait at least two minutes before beginning work (the system has a back-up capacitor that must fully discharge). For more information see Chapter 12.*
Caution: If the stereo in your vehicle is equipped with an anti-theft system, make sure you have the correct activation code before disconnecting the battery.

Removal

1 Disconnect the cable from the negative battery terminal.

Upper trim panel

2 Pull off the heater/air conditioning control knobs.
3 Detach the retaining clips at each corner using a small screwdriver, then remove the panel and unplug the electrical connectors (**see illustrations**).

Lower trim panel

4 Remove the two screws along the upper edge, then pull the panel out and unplug the electrical connectors (**see illustration**).

Installation

5 Installation is the reverse of the removal procedure.

22.4 Remove the screws and pull the lower trim panel out

23 Steering column cover - removal and installation

⚠ *Warning: These models are equipped with airbags. The airbag is armed and can deploy (inflate) anytime the battery is connected. To prevent accidental deployment (and possible injury), turn the ignition key to LOCK and disconnect the negative battery cable whenever working near airbag components. After the battery is disconnected, wait at least two minutes before beginning work (the system has a back-up capacitor that must fully discharge). For more information see Chapter 12.*
Caution: If the stereo in your vehicle is equipped with an anti-theft system, make sure you have the correct activation code before disconnecting the battery.

Removal

1 Remove the steering column cover screws.
2 Separate the cover halves and detach them from the steeringcolumn.
3 Disconnect any electrical connections and the covers.

Installation

4 Installation is the reverse of the removal procedure.

24 Steering column lower finish panel - removal and installation

⚠ *Warning: These models are equipped with airbags. The airbag is armed and can deploy (inflate) anytime the battery is connected. To prevent accidental deployment (and possible injury), turn the ignition key to LOCK and disconnect the negative battery cable whenever working near airbag components. After the battery is disconnected, wait at least two minutes*

before beginning work (the system has a back-up capacitor that must fully discharge). For more information see Chapter 12.
Caution: If the stereo in your vehicle is equipped with an anti-theft system, make sure you have the correct activation code before disconnecting the battery.

Removal

1 Remove the two screws and detach the bonnet release handle.
2 Remove the retaining bolts, disconnect any electrical connections and pull the panel off (**see illustration**).

Installation

3 Installation is the reverse of the removal procedure.

25 Console - removal and installation

⚠ *Warning: These models are equipped with airbags. The airbag is armed and can deploy (inflate) anytime the battery is connected. To prevent accidental deployment (and possible injury), turn the ignition key to LOCK and disconnect the negative battery cable whenever working near airbag components. After the battery is*

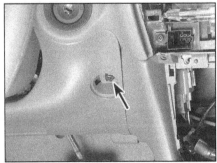

24.2 Remove the screws (some of which are under covers like this one), then detach the finish panel

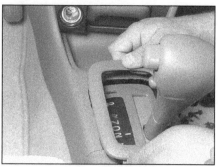

25.2 On automatic transmission models, detach the shifter bezel with a screwdriver, then lift it off

25.4a Remove the carpet piece inside the console for access, then remove the retaining screws

25.4b Pull the rear console back to detach the clips

disconnected, wait at least two minutes before beginning work (the system has a back-up capacitor that must fully discharge). For more information see Chapter 12.
Caution: If the stereo in your vehicle is equipped with an anti-theft system, make sure you have the correct activation code before disconnecting the battery.

Removal

1 Disconnect the cable from the negative battery terminal.
2 On manual shift models, unscrew the shift knob. On automatic models detach the shift bezel **(see illustration)**.

Rear console

3 Remove the centre trim panels (Section 22).
4 Remove retaining screws, lift the console up, detach the clips then remove the console **(see illustrations)**.

Front console

5 Remove the screws retaining the front console to the instrument panel, then lift detach the console **(see illustration)**.

Installation

6 Installation is the reverse of the removal procedure.

26 Instrument panel/facia - removal and installation

⚠ *Warning: These models are equipped with airbags. The airbag is armed and can deploy (inflate) anytime the battery is connected. To prevent accidental deployment (and possible injury), turn the ignition key to LOCK and disconnect the negative battery cable whenever working near airbag components. After the battery is disconnected, wait at least two minutes before beginning work (the system has a back-up capacitor that must fully discharge). For more information see Chapter 12.*
Caution: If the stereo in your vehicle is equipped with an anti-theft system, make sure you have the correct activation code before disconnecting the battery.

Removal

1 Disconnect the cable from the negative battery terminal.
2 Remove drivers airbag module and the steering wheel (see Chapter 10).
3 Remove the glove box assembly (see section 21), disconnect the passenger airbag

module electrical connector and remove the airbag module **(see illustration)**. The electrical connectors used in the airbag system are a twin-lock design; use the proper method for disconnecting these connectors or damage to the connector may occur (see Chapter 12).

⚠ *Warning: Store the airbag modules in a safe place with the airbag face (the trim side) pointing up.*

4 Remove the instrument cluster bezel (see Section 20) and remove the instrument cluster (see Chapter 12).
5 Remove the centre trim panel (see Section 22), remove the radio (see chapter 12) and the heater and air conditioning control panel (see Chapter 3).
6 Remove the steering column covers (see Section 23) and the lower finish panel (see Section 24).
7 Remove the front and rear console panels (see Section 25).
8 Remove the front door scuff plates and the front-pillar garnish moldings from both sides **(see illustration)**.
9 Remove the key lock cylinder (see Chapter 12). Remove the bolts retaining the steering column to the instrument panel and reinforcement brace and lower the steering column **(see illustration)**.

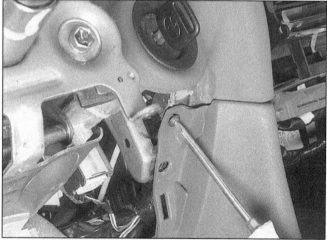

25.5 Remove the screws on each side and detach the front console from the instrument panel

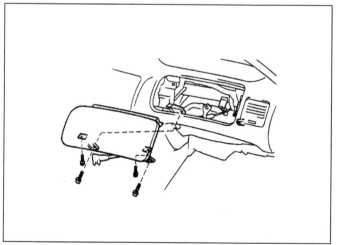

26.3 Passenger airbag module installation details

**26.8 Instrument panel and related components -
exploded view**

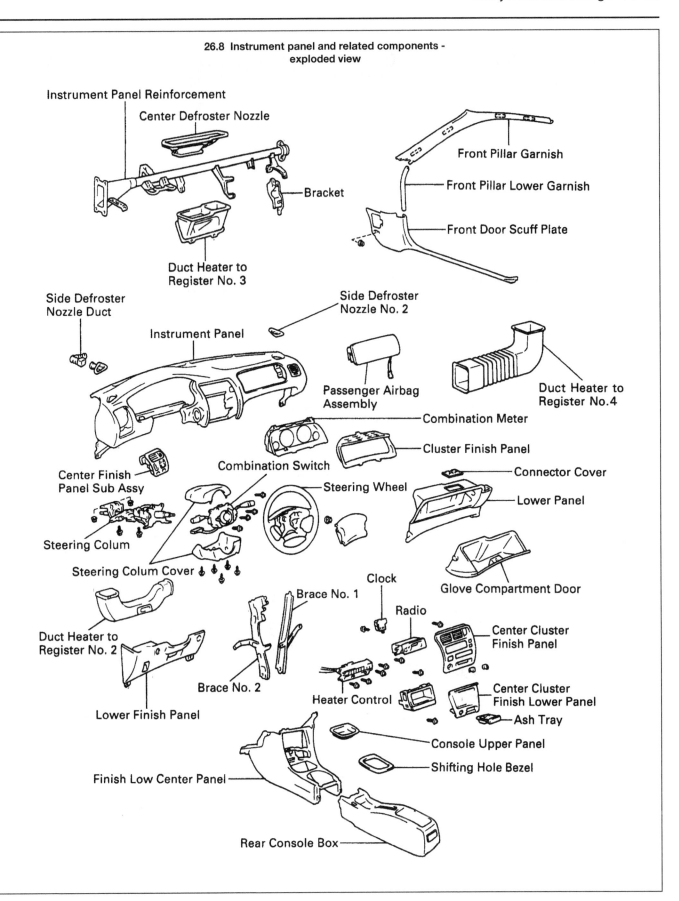

Instrument Panel Reinforcement

Center Defroster Nozzle

Bracket

Front Pillar Garnish

Front Pillar Lower Garnish

Front Door Scuff Plate

Duct Heater to
Register No. 3

Side Defroster
Nozzle Duct

Side Defroster
Nozzle No. 2

Instrument Panel

Passenger Airbag
Assembly

Duct Heater to
Register No.4

Combination Meter

Cluster Finish Panel

Connector Cover

Center Finish
Panel Sub Assy

Combination Switch

Steering Wheel

Lower Panel

Steering Colum

Steering Colum Cover

Clock

Glove Compartment Door

Radio

Duct Heater to
Register No. 2

Brace No. 1

Center Cluster
Finish Panel

Brace No. 2

Heater Control

Center Cluster
Finish Lower Panel

Lower Finish Panel

Ash Tray

Console Upper Panel

Shifting Hole Bezel

Finish Low Center Panel

Rear Console Box

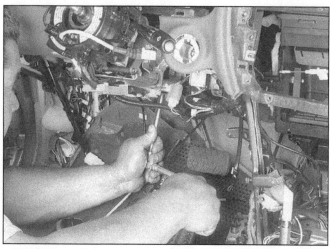

26.9 Remove the steering column retaining bolts and lower the column

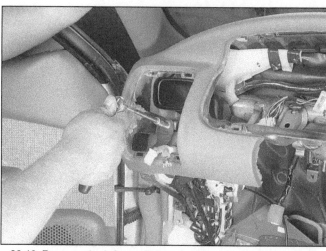

26.10 Remove the left ventilation duct for access to one of the instrument panel retaining bolts

10 Carefully pry out the left ventilation duct, disconnect the electrical connectors and remove the instrument panel retaining bolt behind the duct **(see illustration)**.

11 The main instrument panel wiring harness will remain with the panel when you remove it. Disconnect any remaining connectors. Detach the fuse box from the body and remove it with the panel and harness. Disconnect the electrical connectors from the heater case and remove the ground wire terminals from the centre brace.

12 Remove the remaining instrument panel retaining bolts, grasp the instrument panel firmly and pull it sharply to the rear to release the five clips along the base of the windscreen **(see illustration)**. Remove the instrument panel from the vehicle.

Installation

13 Carefully remove the wiring harness and the ventilation and defroster ducts and transfer them to the new instrument panel.

14 Guide the instrument panel into position, press the tabs into the five retaining clips and install the retaining bolts.

15 The remainder of installation is the reverse of removal.

27 Radiator grille - removal and installation

Removal

1 Remove three screws along the top of the grille **(see illustration)**.

2 Pull the top of the grille out for access and disengage the two retaining clips with a screwdriver **(see illustration)**.

3 Once the retaining clips are disengaged, pull the grille out and remove it.

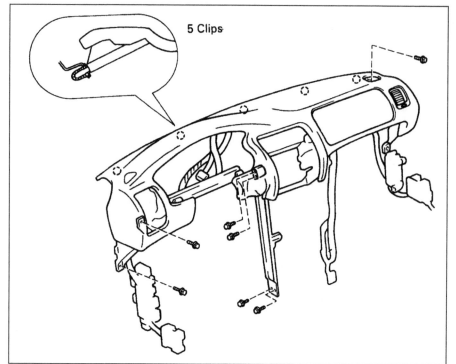

26.12 Instrument panel installation details

5 Clips

27.1 Remove the three Phillips-head screws along the top of the grille

27.2 Reach behind the grill and detach the clips by squeezing the side together as you pull the grille out

Installation

4 Installation is the reverse of removal.

28 Cowl louver - removal and installation

Removal

1 Mark the position of the windscreen wiper blades on the windscreen with a wax marking pen.
2 Remove the wiper arms.
3 Remove the cowl louver retaining screws, disconnect the windscreen washer hoses and detach the cowl from the vehicle **(see illustration)**.

Installation

4 Installation is the reverse of removal. Make sure to align the wiper blades with the marks made during removal.

29 Seat belts - check

 Warning: Later models are equipped with pyrotechnic seat belt pretensioners. Do not attempt to remove a seat belt retractor unit on models so equipped, as personal injury could result if the correct procedures are not followed exactly. Leave any work involving seat belt removal and refitting to your Toyota dealer.
1 Check the seat belts, buckles, latch plates and guide loops for any obvious damage or signs of wear.
2 Make sure the seat belt reminder light comes on when the key is turned on.
3 The seat belts are designed to lock up during a sudden stop or impact, yet allow free movement during normal driving. The retractors should hold the belt against your chest while driving and rewind the belt when the buckle is unlatched.
4 If any of the above checks reveal problems with the seat-belt system, have any parts replaced, as necessary, by a Toyota dealer **(see illustrations)**.

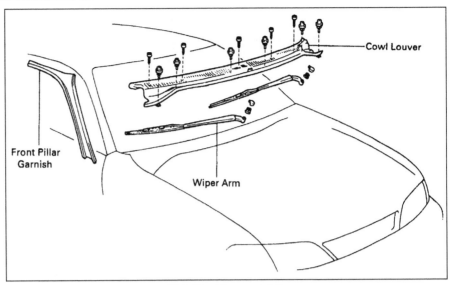

28.3 Cowl louver details

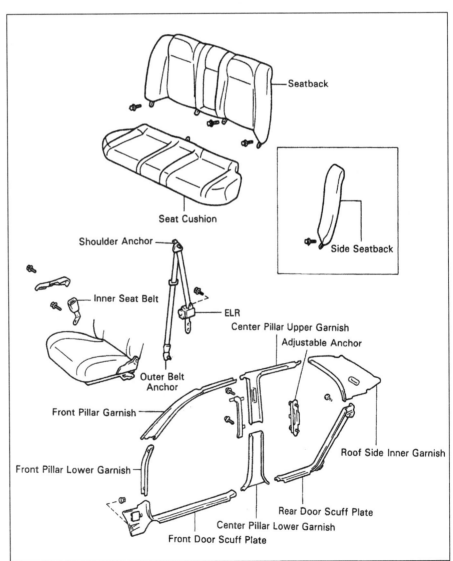

29.4a Typical saloon seat belt details

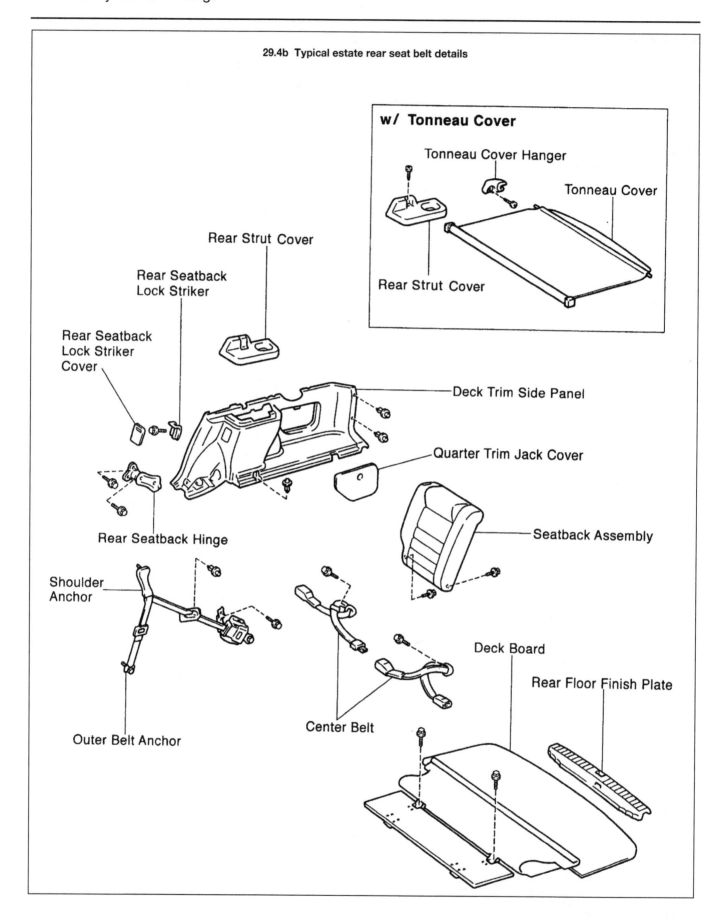

29.4b Typical estate rear seat belt details

w/ Tonneau Cover

Tonneau Cover Hanger

Tonneau Cover

Rear Strut Cover

Rear Strut Cover

Rear Seatback Lock Striker

Rear Seatback Lock Striker Cover

Deck Trim Side Panel

Quarter Trim Jack Cover

Rear Seatback Hinge

Seatback Assembly

Shoulder Anchor

Deck Board

Rear Floor Finish Plate

Outer Belt Anchor

Center Belt

Chapter 12
Body electrical system

Contents

Degrees of difficulty

Easy, suitable for novice with little experience	Fairly easy, suitable for beginner with some experience	Fairly difficult, suitable for competent DIY mechanic	Difficult, suitable for experienced DIY mechanic	Very difficult, suitable for expert DIY or professional

1 General information

The electrical system is a 12-volt, negative earth type. Power for the lights and all electrical accessories is supplied by a lead/acid-type battery which is charged by the alternator.

This Chapter covers repair and service procedures for the various electrical components not associated with the engine. Information on the battery, alternator, distributor and starter motor can be found in Chapter 5.

It should be noted that when portions of the electrical system are serviced, the cable should be disconnected from the negative battery terminal to prevent electrical shorts and/or fires.

Caution: If the stereo in your vehicle is equipped with an anti-theft system, make sure you have the correct activation code before disconnecting the battery.

2 Electrical fault finding - general information

A typical electrical circuit consists of an electrical component, any switches, relays, motors, fuses, fusible links or circuit breakers related to that component and the wiring and electrical connectors that link the component to both the battery and the chassis. To help you pinpoint an electrical circuit problem, wiring diagrams are included at the end of this Chapter.

Before tackling any troublesome electrical circuit, first study the appropriate wiring diagrams to get a complete understanding of what makes up that individual circuit. Trouble spots, for instance, can often be narrowed down by noting if other components related to the circuit are operating properly. If several components or circuits fail at one time, chances are the problem is in a fuse or earth connection, because several circuits are often routed through the same fuse and earth connections.

Electrical problems usually stem from simple causes, such as loose or corroded connections, a blown fuse, a melted fusible link or a bad relay. Visually inspect the condition of all fuses, wires and connections in a problem circuit first.

If testing instruments are going to be utilized, use the diagrams to plan ahead of time where you will make the necessary connections in order to accurately pinpoint the trouble spot.

The basic tools needed for electrical fault finding include a circuit tester or voltmeter (a 12-volt bulb with a set of test leads can also be used), a continuity tester, which includes a bulb, battery and set of test leads, and a jumper wire, preferably with a circuit breaker incorporated, which can be used to bypass electrical components. Before attempting to locate a problem with test instruments, use the wiring diagram(s) to decide where to make the connections.

Voltage checks

Voltage checks should be performed if a circuit is not functioning properly. Connect one lead of a circuit tester to either the negative battery terminal or a known good earth. Connect the other lead to a electrical connector in the circuit being tested, preferably nearest to the battery or fuse. If the bulb of the tester lights, voltage is present, which means that the part of the circuit between the electrical connector and the battery is problem free. Continue checking the rest of the circuit in the same fashion. When you reach a point at which no voltage is present, the problem lies between that point and the last test point with voltage. Most of the time the problem can be traced to a loose connection. Note: Keep in mind that some circuits receive voltage only when the ignition key is in the Accessory or Run position.

Finding a short-circuit

One method of finding shorts in a circuit is to remove the fuse and connect a test light or voltmeter in its place to the fuse terminals. There should be no voltage present in the circuit. Move the wiring harness from side to side while watching the test light. If the bulb goes on, there is a short to earth somewhere in that area, probably where the insulation has rubbed through. The same test can be performed on each component in the circuit, even a switch.

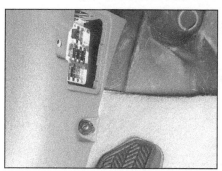

3.1a The main fuse block is located in the driver's side kick panel, under a cover

3.1b A fuse and relay block is located in the engine compartment

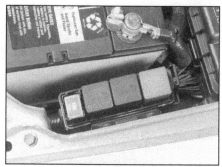

3.1c On air-conditioned models, fuse and relay block is located next to the battery

Earth check

Perform a earth test to check whether a component is properly earthed. Disconnect the battery and connect one lead of a self-powered test light, known as a continuity tester, to a known good earth. Connect the other lead to the wire or earth connection being tested. If the bulb goes on, the earth is good. If the bulb does not go on, the earth is not good.

Continuity check

A continuity check is done to determine if there are any breaks in a circuit - if it is passing electricity properly. With the circuit off (no power in the circuit), a self-powered continuity tester can be used to check the circuit. Connect the test leads to both ends of the circuit (or to the "power" end and a good earth), and if the test light comes on the circuit is passing current properly. If the light doesn't come on, there is a break somewhere in the circuit. The same procedure can be used to test a switch, by connecting the continuity tester to the power in and power out sides of the switch. With the switch turned On, the test light should come on.

Finding an open circuit

When diagnosing for possible open circuits, it is often difficult to locate them by sight because oxidation or terminal misalignment are hidden by the electrical connectors. Merely wiggling an electrical connector on a sensor or in the wiring harness may correct the open circuit condition. Remember this when an open circuit is indicated when diagnosing a circuit. Intermittent problems may also be caused by oxidized or loose connections.

Electrical fault finding is simple if you keep in mind that all electrical circuits are basically electricity running from the battery, through the wires, switches, relays, fuses and fusible links to each electrical component (light bulb, motor, etc.) and to earth, from which it is passed back to the battery. Any electrical problem is an interruption in the flow of electricity to and from the battery.

3 Fuses - general information

The electrical circuits of the vehicle are protected by a combination of fuses, circuit breakers and fusible links. The fuse blocks are located under the instrument panel on the left and right (some models) sides of the dashboard, and in the engine compartment next to the battery (see illustrations).

Each of the fuses is designed to protect a specific circuit, and the various circuits are identified on the fuse panel itself.

Three types of miniaturized fuses are employed in the fuse block. These compact fuses, with blade terminal design, allow fingertip removal and replacement. If an electrical component fails, always check the fuse first. A blown fuse is easily identified through the clear plastic body. Visually inspect the element for evidence of damage (see illustration). If a continuity check is called for on the type A fuse, the blade terminal tips are exposed in the fuse body.

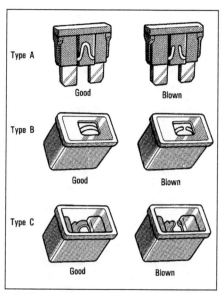

3.3 Three types of fuses are used on these models - all can be visually checked

Be sure to replace blown fuses with the correct type. Fuses of different ratings are physically interchangeable, but only fuses of the proper rating should be used. Replacing a fuse with one of a higher or lower value than specified is not recommended. Each electrical circuit needs a specific amount of protection. The amperage value of each fuse is molded into the fuse body.

If the replacement fuse immediately fails, don't replace it again until the cause of the problem is isolated and corrected. In most cases, this will be a short circuit in the wiring caused by a broken or deteriorated wire.

4 Fusible links - general information

Some circuits are protected by fusible links. The links are used in circuits which are not ordinarily fused, such as the ignition circuit.

The fusible links on these models are similar to fuses in that they can be visually checked to determine if they are melted.

To replace a fusible link, first disconnect the negative cable from the battery. Unplug the burned-out link and replace it with a new one (available from your dealer or auto parts store). Always determine the cause for the overload which melted the fusible link before installing a new one.

Caution: If the stereo in your vehicle is equipped with an anti-theft system, make sure you have the correct activation code before disconnecting the battery.

5 Circuit breakers - general information

Because on some models the circuit breaker resets itself automatically, an electrical overload in a circuit breaker protected system will cause the circuit to fail momentarily, then come back on. If the circuit does not come back on, check it immediately. Note, however, that some circuit breakers must be reset manually. Once the condition is corrected, the circuit breaker will resume its normal function.

To reset a manual circuit breaker, first disconnect the cable from the negative battery terminal. Remove the circuit breaker, insert a pin into the reset hole and push in until you hear a click **(see illustration)**. Once the circuit breaker is reset, it's a good idea to use an ohmmeter to make sure there is continuity across the terminals before reinstalling it **(see illustration)**.
Caution: If the stereo in your vehicle is equipped with an anti-theft system, make sure you have the correct activation code before disconnecting the battery.

6 Relays - general information

Several electrical accessories in the vehicle use relays to transmit the electrical signal to the component. If the relay is defective, that component will not operate properly.

The various relays are mounted in several locations throughout the vehicle.

If a faulty relay is suspected, it can be removed and tested by a dealer or other qualified workshop. Defective relays must be replaced as a unit.

7 Turn signal/hazard flashers - check and replacement

Warning: These models are equipped with airbags. The airbag is armed and can deploy (inflate) anytime the battery is connected. To prevent accidental deployment (and possible injury), turn the ignition key to LOCK and disconnect the negative battery cable whenever working near airbag components. After the battery is disconnected, wait at least two minutes before beginning work (the system has a reversing capacitor that must fully discharge). For more information see Section 27.
Caution: If the stereo in your vehicle is equipped with an anti-theft system, make sure you have the correct activation code before disconnecting the battery.

Check

1 The turn signal/hazard flasher, a small canister shaped unit located in the main fuse block, flashes the turn signals **(see illustration 3.1a)**.
2 When the flasher unit is functioning properly, an audible click can be heard during its operation. If the turn signals fail on one side or the other and the flasher unit does not make its characteristic clicking sound, a faulty turn signal bulb is indicated.
3 If both turn signals fail to blink, the problem may be due to a blown fuse, a faulty flasher unit, a broken switch or a loose or open connection. If a quick check of the fuse box indicates that the turn signal fuse has blown,

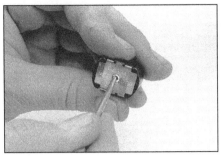

5.2a Insert a pin or paper clip into the circuit breaker reset hole and push it in to reset it

check the wiring for a short before installing a new fuse.

Replacement

4 To replace the flasher, simply pull it out of the fuse block.
5 Make sure that the replacement unit is identical to the original. Compare the old one to the new one before installing it.
6 Installation is the reverse of removal.

8 Combination switch - removal and installation

Warning: These models are equipped with airbags. The airbag is armed and can deploy (inflate) anytime the battery is connected. To prevent accidental deployment (and possible injury), turn the ignition key to LOCK and disconnect the negative battery cable whenever working near airbag components. After the battery is disconnected, wait at least two minutes before beginning work (the system has a reversing capacitor that must fully discharge). For more information see Section 27.
Caution: If the stereo in your vehicle is equipped with an anti-theft system, make sure you have the correct activation code before disconnecting the battery.

Removal

1 Disconnect the negative cable at the battery.

8.4 Remove the four combination switch mounting screws (arrows)

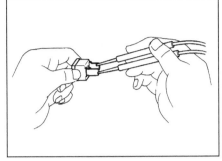

5.2b After resetting, check the circuit breaker for continuity

2 Disable the drivers airbag (see Section 27) and remove the steering wheel (see Chapter 10).
3 Remove the steering column cover and the lower finish panel (see Chapter 11).
4 Remove the combination switch retaining screws **(see illustration)**.
5 Trace the wiring harness down the steering column to the connector. Release the wiring retainer clamps, if equipped, slide the switch off the column and unplug the connector **(see illustration)**.

Installation

6 Installation is the reverse of removal. Refer to Chapter 10 and centre the spiral cable before installing the steering wheel.

9 Steering column switches - check and replacement

Warning: These models are equipped with airbags. The airbag is armed and can deploy (inflate) anytime the battery is connected. To prevent accidental deployment (and possible injury), turn the ignition key to LOCK and disconnect the negative battery cable whenever working near airbag components. After the battery is disconnected, wait at least two minutes before beginning work (the system has a reversing capacitor that must fully discharge). For more information see Section 27.

8.5 Slip the combination switch off the steering column and unplug the connector (arrow)

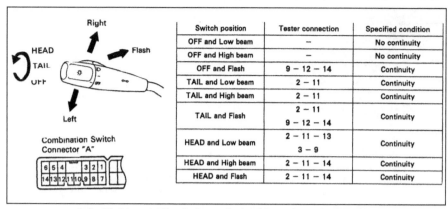

Switch position	Tester connection	Specified condition
OFF and Low beam	—	No continuity
OFF and High beam	—	No continuity
OFF and Flash	9 – 12 – 14	Continuity
TAIL and Low beam	2 – 11	Continuity
TAIL and High beam	2 – 11	Continuity
TAIL and Flash	2 – 11 9 – 12 – 14	Continuity
HEAD and Low beam	2 – 11 – 13 3 – 9	Continuity
HEAD and High beam	2 – 11 – 14	Continuity
HEAD and Flash	2 – 11 – 14	Continuity

9.4a Light control switch terminal guide and continuity table

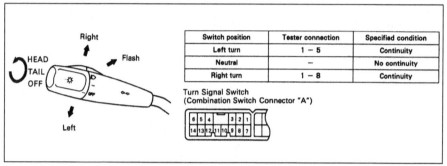

Switch position	Tester connection	Specified condition
Left turn	1 – 5	Continuity
Neutral	—	No continuity
Right turn	1 – 8	Continuity

9.4b Turn signal switch terminal guide continuity table

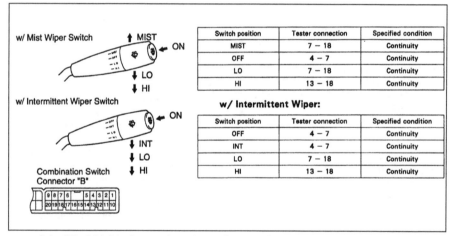

Switch position	Tester connection	Specified condition
MIST	7 – 18	Continuity
OFF	4 – 7	Continuity
LO	7 – 18	Continuity
HI	13 – 18	Continuity

w/ Intermittent Wiper:

Switch position	Tester connection	Specified condition
OFF	4 – 7	Continuity
INT	4 – 7	Continuity
LO	7 – 18	Continuity
HI	13 – 18	Continuity

9.4c Windshield wiper and washer switch terminal guide and continuity table

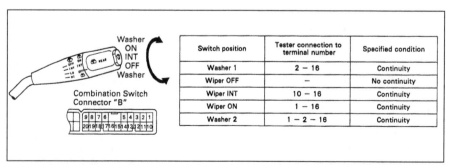

Switch position	Tester connection to terminal number	Specified condition
Washer 1	2 – 16	Continuity
Wiper OFF	—	No continuity
Wiper INT	10 – 16	Continuity
Wiper ON	1 – 16	Continuity
Washer 2	1 – 2 – 16	Continuity

9.4d Rear window wiper and washer switch terminal guide and continuity table

Caution: If the stereo in your vehicle is equipped with an anti-theft system, make sure you have the correct activation code before disconnecting the battery.

1 Disconnect the negative cable at the battery.

2 Remove the steering column cover and lower finish panel (see Chapter 11).

3 Trace the wiring harness from the component to be checked to the harness connector.

Check

4 Unplug the electrical connector and using an ohmmeter, check for continuity between the indicated terminals with the various switches in each of the indicated positions **(see illustrations)**.

5 If the continuity is not as specified, replace the defective switch.

Replacement

6 Remove the combination switch (see Section 8). Remove the four screws retaining the airbag spiral cable and remove the spiral cable from the combination switch.

7 Remove the retaining screws from the switch being replaced and remove the defective switch from the switch body **(see illustration)**.

8 Separate the wiring harness of the switch being replaced from the main wiring harness and remove the terminals from the connector.

9 Release the tabs from the terminal cover at the rear of the connector. From the front of the connector, insert a small screwdriver or pick, pry down on the locking and remove the terminal from the rear **(see illustration)**.

10 Insert the terminals from the new switch into the connector, pushing in until they are securely locked in place.

11 The remainder or installation is the reverse of removal. Refer to Chapter 10 and centre the spiral cable before installing the steering wheel.

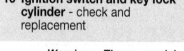

10 Ignition switch and key lock cylinder - check and replacement

 Warning: These models are equipped with airbags. The airbag is armed and can deploy (inflate) anytime the battery is connected. To prevent accidental deployment (and possible injury), turn the ignition key to LOCK and disconnect the negative battery cable whenever working near airbag components. After the battery is disconnected, wait at least two minutes before beginning work (the system has a reversing capacitor that must fully discharge). For more information see Section 27.

Caution: If the stereo in your vehicle is equipped with an anti-theft system, make sure you have the correct activation code before disconnecting the battery.

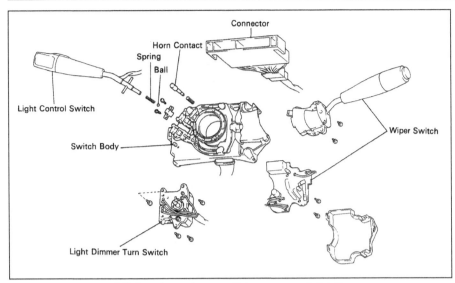

9.7 Steering column switch component details

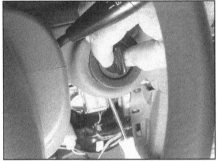

9.9 To remove a terminal from the connector, pry down on the locking lug and pull the terminal out from the rear

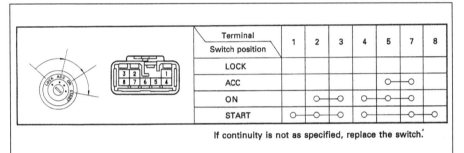

Terminal / Switch position	1	2	3	4	5	7	8
LOCK							
ACC					○—○		
ON		○—○		○—○	○—○		
START	○—○—○			○		○—○—○	

If continuity is not as specified, replace the switch.

10.5 Ignition switch terminal guide and continuity table

10.9 With the key in the ACC position. push in on the release button and pull the lock cylinder straight out

Ignition switch

1 Disconnect the negative cable at the battery.
2 Remove the steering wheel (see Chapter 10).
3 Remove the steering column cover and lower finish panel (see Chapter 11).

Check

4 Trace the wire from the switch to the connector and unplug the connector.
5 Use an ohmmeter to check for continuity at the indicated terminals with the switch in each indicated position (see illustration).
6 Replace the switch if continuity is not as specified.

Replacement

7 Remove the screw(s) retaining the switch to the rear of the lock cylinder housing and remove the switch.
8 Installation is the reverse of removal. Refer to Chapter 10 and centre the spiral cable before installing the steering wheel.

Key lock cylinder

9 With the key in the Accessory position, insert a small screwdriver or punch in the hole in the casting and press the release button while pulling the lock cylinder straight out. Remove it from the steering column (see illustration).

10 Installation is the reverse of removal. Refer to Chapter 10 and centre the spiral cable before installing the steering wheel.

11 Rear window demister switch - check and replacement

Warning: These models are equipped with airbags. The airbag is armed and can deploy (inflate) anytime the battery is connected. To prevent accidental deployment (and possible injury), turn the ignition key to LOCK and disconnect the negative battery cable whenever working near airbag components. After the battery is disconnected, wait at least two minutes before beginning work (the system has a reversing capacitor that must fully discharge). For more information see Section 27.
Caution: If the stereo in your vehicle is equipped with an anti-theft system, make sure you have the correct activation code before disconnecting the battery.

1 Detach the cable from the negative battery terminal.
2 Remove the centre trim panel and turn it over for access to the demister switch.
3 Use an ohmmeter to check for continuity at the indicated terminals with the switch in the indicated position (see illustration).
4 Replace the switch if the continuity is not as specified.

Condition	Tester connection to terminal number	Specified condition
Switch OFF	—	No continuity
Switch ON	4 – 6	Continuity
Illumination circuit	1 – 3	Continuity

11.3 Demister switch terminal guide and continuity table

12 Rear window demister - check and repair

1 The rear window demister consists of a number of horizontal elements baked onto the glass surface.
2 Small breaks in the element can be repaired without removing the rear window.

Check

3 Turn the ignition switch and demister system switches to On.
4 When measuring voltage during the next two tests, wrap a piece of aluminum foil around the tip of the voltmeter negative probe and press the foil against the wire with your finger (see illustration).
5 Check the voltage at the centre of each heat wire (see illustration). If the voltage is 5-volts, the wire is okay (there is no break). If the voltage is 10-volts, the wire is broken between the centre of the element and the positive end. If the voltage is 0-volts the wire is broken between the centre of the element and earth.
6 Connect the negative lead to a good body earth. The reading should stay the same.
7 To find the break, place the voltmeter positive lead against the demister positive terminal. Place the voltmeter negative lead with the foil strip against the heat wire at the positive terminal end and slide it toward the negative terminal end. The point at which the voltmeter deflects from zero to several volts is the point at which the heat element is broken (see illustration). Note: If the heat element is not broken, the voltmeter will indicate no voltage at the positive end of the heat element but gradually increase to about 12-volts.

Repair

8 Repair the break in the element using a repair kit specifically recommended for this purpose, available from auto parts stores.
9 Prior to repairing a break, turn off the system and allow it to cool off for a few minutes.
10 Lightly buff the element area with fine steel wool, then clean it thoroughly with rubbing alcohol.
11 Use masking tape to mask off the area being repaired.
12 Carry out the repair, following the instructions provided with the repair kit.

13 Radio and speakers - removal and installation

⚠️ Warning: These models are equipped with airbags. The airbag is armed and can deploy (inflate) anytime the battery is connected. To prevent accidental deployment (and possible injury), turn the ignition key to LOCK and disconnect the negative battery cable whenever working near airbag components. After the battery is disconnected, wait at least two minutes before beginning work (the system has a reversing capacitor that must fully discharge). For more information see Section 27.
Caution: If the stereo in your vehicle is equipped with an anti-theft system, make sure you have the correct activation code before disconnecting the battery.

Radio

Removal

1 Disconnect the negative cable at the battery.
2 Remove the centre trim panel (see Chapter 11).
3 Remove the mounting screws or bolts and pull the housing out of the dash (see illustrations).
4 Remove the screws or nuts, pull the radio out, then unplug the electrical connector and the aerial lead and lift the radio out.

Installation

5 Installation is the reverse of removal.

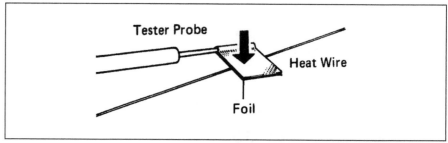

12.4 When measuring the voltage at the rear window demister grid, wrap a piece of aluminum foil around the negative probe of the voltmeter and press the foil against the wire with your finger

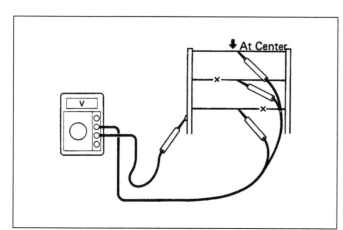

12.5 To determine if a wire has broken, place the voltmeter positive lead against the demister positive terminal and check the voltage with the negative lead at the centre of each wire - if the voltage is 5-volts, the wire is unbroken; if the voltage is 10-volts, the wire is broken between the centre of the wire and the positive end; if the voltage is 0-volts, the wire is broken between the centre of the wire and ground

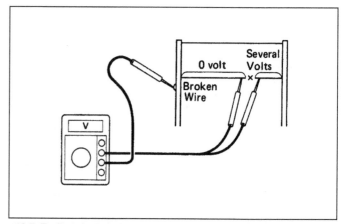

12.7 To find the break, place the voltmeter positive lead against the demister positive terminal, place the voltmeter negative lead with the foil strip against the heat wire at the positive terminal end and slide it toward the negative terminal end - the point at which the voltmeter deflects from zero to several volts is the point at which the wire is broken

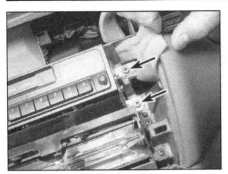

13.3a Remove the mounting screws . . .

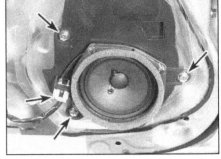

13.3b . . . pull the radio/bracket unit out, unplug the power connector and disconnect the antenna cable

13.7 Typical front door mounted speaker screws (arrows)

Speakers

Removal

6 Remove the front door trim panel (see Chapter 11).
7 Remove the speaker retaining screws/nuts. Unplug the electrical connector and remove the speaker (see illustration).

Installation

8 Installation is the reverse of removal.

---

14 Aerial - removal and installation

Removal

1 Remove the two Phillips-head screws.

15.3a Use a small screwdriver to pry up on the air intake retainer

15.3b Lift the air intake duct out

2 Detach the aerial, pull out the cable and unplug it.

Installation

3 Installation is the reverse of removal.

---

15 Headlight bulb - replacement

⚠️ *Warning: These models are equipped with halogen gas-filled bulbs which are under pressure and may shatter if the surface is scratched or the bulb is dropped. Wear eye protection and handle the bulbs carefully, grasping only the base whenever possible. Do not touch the surface of the bulb with your fingers because the oil from your skin could cause it to overheat and fail prematurely.*

HAYNES HiNT *If you do touch the bulb surface, clean it with methylated spirit.*

Caution: If the stereo in your vehicle is equipped with an anti-theft system, make sure you have the correct activation code before disconnecting the battery.
1 Open the bonnet.

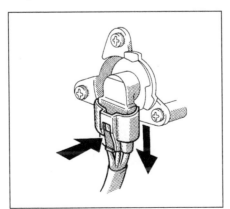

15.4 Depress the lever and unplug connector

2 Disconnect the cable from the negative battery terminal.
3 Where necesary, remove the air intake duct for access to the back of the housing (see illustrations).
4 Press the lock release and unplug the electrical connector from the bulb assembly (see illustration).
5 Rotate bulb assembly anti-clockwise and withdraw it from the headlight housing. Without touching the glass with your bare fingers, insert the new assembly into the headlight housing, install and rotate it clockwise to lock it in place (see illustration).
6 Plug in the electrical connector and reconnect the battery. Test the headlight operation, then close the bonnet.

---

16 Headlights - adjustment

Note: *It is important that the headlights are aimed correctly. If adjusted incorrectly they could blind the driver of an oncoming vehicle and cause a serious accident or seriously reduce your ability to see the road. The headlights should be checked for proper aim every 12 months and any time a new headlight is installed or front end body work is performed. It should be emphasized that the following procedure is only an interim step which will provide temporary adjustment until the headlights can be adjusted by a properly equipped workshop.*

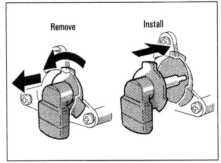

15.5 Rotate the bulb holder anti-clockwise and withdraw it from the housing (when viewed from behind)

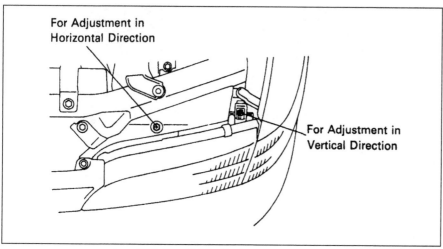

16.1 Headlight adjustment screws

1 These models have two adjustment screws, one to the side controlling left-and-right movement and one below the light for up-and-down movement that are accessible from behind the headlight housing **(see illustration)**.

2 There are several methods of adjusting the headlights. The simplest method requires a blank wall, masking tape and a level floor.

3 Position masking tape vertically on the wall in reference to the vehicle centreline and the centrelines of both headlights.

4 Position a horizontal tape line in reference to the centreline of all the headlights. **Note:** *It*

may be easier to position the tape on the wall with the vehicle parked only a few inches away.

5 Adjustment should be made with the vehicle parked 25 feet from the wall, sitting level, the fuel tank half-full and no unusually heavy load in the vehicle.

6 Starting with the low beam adjustment, position the high intensity zone so it is two inches below the horizontal line and two inches to the right of the headlight vertical line. Twist the adjustment screws until the desired level has been achieved.

7 With the high beams on, the high intensity zone should be vertically centreed with the exact centre just below the horizontal line. **Note:** *It may not be possible to position the headlight aim exactly for both high and low beams. If a compromise must be made, keep in mind that the low beams are the most used and have the greatest effect on driver safety.*

8 Have the headlights adjusted by a dealer service department at the earliest opportunity.

17 Composite headlight housing - removal and installation

Removal

1 Disconnect the cable from the negative battery terminal.

Caution: If the stereo in your vehicle is equipped with an anti-theft system, make sure you have the correct activation code before disconnecting the battery.

2 Remove the radiator grille (Chapter 11).

3 Remove the parking light housing (Section 18).

4 Remove the retaining bolts and nuts, detach the housing by pulling it straight out, then withdraw it from the vehicle **(see illustrations)**.

5 Remove the headlight bulb (Section 15).

Installation

6 Installation is the reverse of removal.

18 Bulb replacement

Front parking and side marker

1 Remove the retaining screw and detach the housing by sliding it forward **(see illustration)**.

2 Unplug the electrical connector and rotate the bulb holders anti-clockwise to replace the bulbs **(see illustration)**.

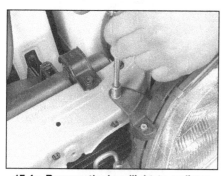

17.4a Remove the headlight-to-radiator crossmember bolt

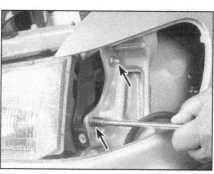

17.4b After removing the parking light assembly, the two side retaining nuts (arrows) are accessible

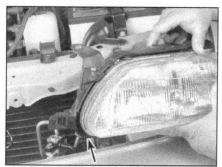

17.4c Pull the headlight straight out to detach the retainer at the lower corner (arrow)

18.1 Remove the retaining screw (arrow) and push the lens housing forward (in the direction arrowed) to detach it

18.2 Unplug the connector and rotate the bulb holders to remove them from the housing

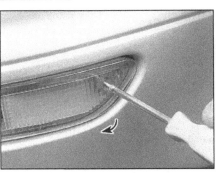

18.3 Remove the turn signal light screw and rotate the housing out of the fender

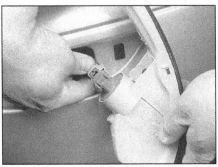

18.4a Unplug the electrical connector

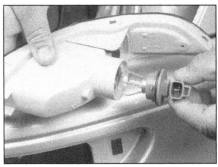

18.4b Rotate the bulb holder anti-clockwise and pull it out

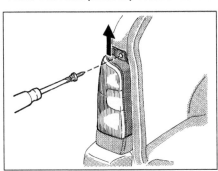

18.5a Boot trim panel clip retainer details

Turn signal

3 Remove the retaining screw and detach the housing by rotating it forward out of the bumper **(see illustration)**.
4 Unplug the electrical connector and rotate the bulb holder anti-clockwise to remove it **(see illustrations)**.

Rear side marker, turn signal, brake, tail and reversing lights

Saloon

5 Remove the two screws retaining the housing, open the boot lid and detach the trim cover for access, then remove the nut and pull the housing out **(see illustrations)**.
6 Rotate the bulb holders anti-clockwise and replace the bulbs **(see illustration)**.

Estate

7 Remove the retaining screw and lift the housing up to remove **(see illustration)**.
8 Rotate the bulb holders anti-clockwise and replace the bulbs **(see illustration)**.

License plate light

Saloon

9 Depress the tab and rotate the light housing down for access to the bulb holder **(see illustration)**.
10 Rotate the holder anti-clockwise to remove it, the pull the bulb straight out **(see illustration)**.

Estate

11 Remove the screws and lower the housing **(see illustration)**.

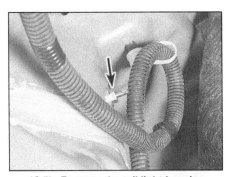

18.5b Remove the tail light housing retaining nut (arrow)

18.6 Rotate the bulb holder anti-clockwise to remove it

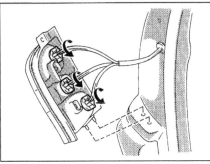

18.7 Remove the Estate tail light screws and lift the housing straight up

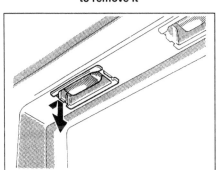

18.8 Estate tail light bulb details

18.9 Press the tab in and lower the Saloon license plate light housing

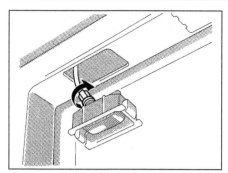

18.10 Saloon license plate bulb details

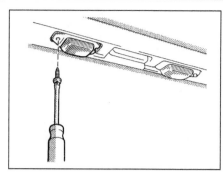

18.11 Estate number plate housing screws

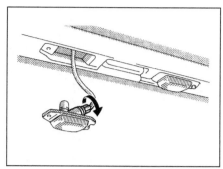

18.12 Estate number plate bulb details

12 Remove the bulb holder by turning it anti-clockwise, then pull the bulb out of the holder (see illustration).

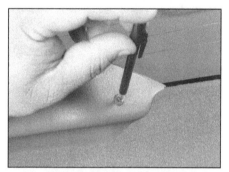

18.13a Use a ball-point pen to push in on the centre of the retainers

High mounted brake light

Saloon

13 Use a ball-point pen to push in the centres of retainers the pry the retainers out with a small screwdriver and remove the light cover (see illustrations).

14 Remove the housing bolts, lift the housing up for access, then rotate the holder anti-clockwise to remove it and pull the bulb straight out (see illustrations).

Estate

15 Pry the light cover off, remove the bulb holder by turn it anti-clockwise, then pull the bulb out of the holder (see illustration).

Interior lights

16 Use a small screwdriver to pry off the lens.

17 Detach the bulb from the terminal. It may be necessary to pry the bulb out, if this is the case, pry only at the end of the bulb (otherwise the glass may shatter (see illustration).

Instrument cluster illumination

18 To gain access to the instrument cluster illumination lights, the instrument cluster will have to be removed (see Section 21). The bulbs can then be removed and replaced from the rear of the cluster (see illustration).

19 Daytime Running Lights (DRL) - general information

The Daytime Running Lights (DRL) system, used on some models, turns the headlights on whenever the engine is started. The only

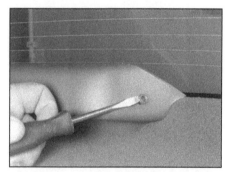

18.13b Use a screwdriver to pry out the retainers

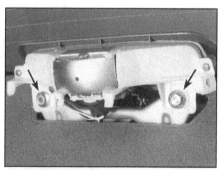

18.14a Remove the nuts and lift the housing up for access to the bulb holder

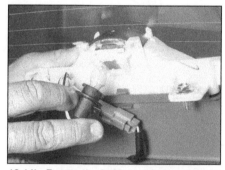

18.14b Rotate the holder anti-clockwise to remove it - the bulb pulls straight out

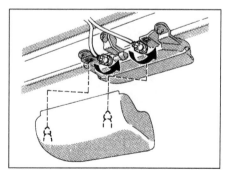

18.15 Estate high-mounted brake light details

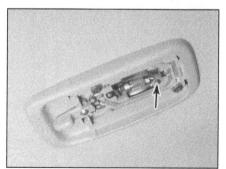

18.17 Pry carefully at the bulb clip (arrow) and detach the bulb

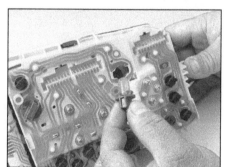

18.18 Rotate the instrument cluster bulb anti-clockwise and lift it out

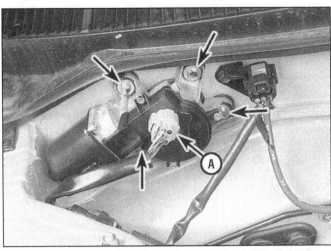

20.5 Unplug the wiper motor connector (A), remove the bolts (arrows) and detach the motor

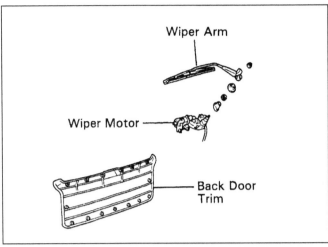

20.7 Rear wiper arm details

exception is when the engine is on when the parking brake is engaged. Once the parking brake is released, the lights will remain on as long as the ignition switch is on, even if the parking brake is later applied.

The DRL system supplies reduced power to the headlights so they won't be too bright for daytime use while prolonging headlight life.

20 Wiper motor - check and replacement

⚠️ Warning: These models are equipped with airbags. The airbag is armed and can deploy (inflate) anytime the battery is connected. To prevent accidental deployment (and possible injury), turn the ignition key to LOCK and disconnect the negative battery cable whenever working near airbag components. After the battery is disconnected, wait at least two minutes before beginning work (the system has a reversing capacitor that must fully discharge). For more information see Section 27.

21.3 Remove the instrument cluster screws

Caution: If the stereo in your vehicle is equipped with an anti-theft system, make sure you have the correct activation code before disconnecting the battery.

1 The windscreen wiper motor is located on the right (passenger) side of the underbonnet compartment and the rear wiper motor is mounted in the tailgate.

Check

Windscreen washer/wiper switch

2 Refer to Section 9 for the wiper and washer switch check procedure.

Wiper motor

3 If a motor doesn't work or doesn't park properly and the switch checks out okay, the relay or the motor must be replaced.

Replacement

Windscreen wiper motor

4 Disconnect the cable from the negative battery terminal.
5 Unplug the electrical connector, remove the motor bracket retaining bolts, then lower the wiper motor and bracket assembly and remove it from the vehicle (see illustration).

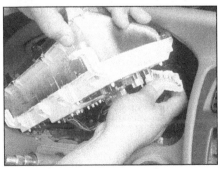

21.4 Unplug the electrical connectors and remove the cluster

6 Installation is the reverse of removal.

Rear wiper motor

7 Remove the wiper arm, then remove the shaft spindle nuts and washers (see illustration).
8 Unplug the electrical connector, detach the wiper linkage, remove the retaining bolts and lower the motor through the tailgate access hole as an assembly.
9 Installation is the reverse of removal.

21 Instrument cluster - removal and installation

⚠️ Warning: These models are equipped with airbags. The airbag is armed and can deploy (inflate) anytime the battery is connected. To prevent accidental deployment (and possible injury), turn the ignition key to LOCK and disconnect the negative battery cable whenever working near airbag components. After the battery is disconnected, wait at least two minutes before beginning work (the system has a reversing capacitor that must fully discharge). For more information see Section 27.
Caution: If the stereo in your vehicle is equipped with an anti-theft system, make sure you have the correct activation code before disconnecting the battery.
1 Disconnect the cable from the negative battery terminal.
2 Remove the instrument cluster bezel (see Chapter 11).
3 Remove the retaining screws and pull the cluster forward (see illustration).
4 Unplug the electrical connectors and remove the cluster (see illustration).
5 Installation is the reverse of the removal procedure.

22.4 Disconnect the electrical connector and remove the bolts (arrows) and detach the horn

22 Horn - check and replacement

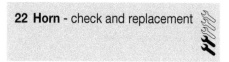

Check

1 Disconnect the electrical connector from the horn.
2 Test the horn by connecting battery voltage to the two terminals with a pair of jumper wires.
3 If the horn doesn't sound, replace it. If it does sound, the problem lies in the switch, relay or the wiring between components.

Replacement

4 Disconnect the electrical connector and remove the bracket bolt (see illustration).
5 Installation is the reverse of removal.

23 Cruise control system - description and check

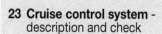

1 The cruise control system (where fitted) maintains vehicle speed with an ECU (computer) located in the passenger compartment and actuator located near the battery in the engine compartment. The actuator is connected to the throttle linkage by a cable or rod. Besides the actuator, the system consists of the brake switch, clutch switch, control switches, a relay and associated wiring (see illustration). Some features of the system requires special testers and diagnostic procedures which are beyond the scope of the home mechanic. Listed below are some general procedures that may be used to locate common problems.
2 Locate and check the fuse (see Section 3).
3 Have an assistant operate the brake lights while you check their operation (voltage from the brake light and (if equipped) clutch switch deactivates the cruise control).
4 If the brake lights don't come on or don't shut off, correct the problem and retest the cruise control. Check the clutch switch (Chapter 8).
5 Visually inspect the vacuum hose (if

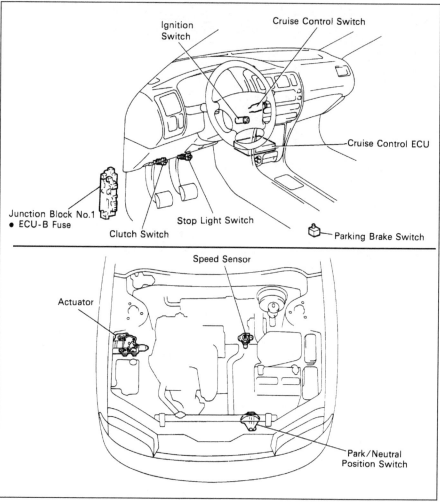

23.1 Typical cruise control system component layout

equipped) connected to the servo and check the control linkage between the cruise control servo and the throttle linkage and replace as necessary.
6 Cruise control systems use a variety of speed sensing devices. On these models the speed sensor pickup is located in the transmission. Remove the bolt and detach the sensor, rotate the sensor and check it with a digital voltmeter while it's rotating (see Chapter 6). If the resistance doesn't vary as the cable rotates, the sensor is defective.
7 Test drive the vehicle to determine if the cruise control is now working. If it isn't, take it to a dealer service department or an automotive electrical specialist for further diagnosis and repair.

24 Central locking system - description and check

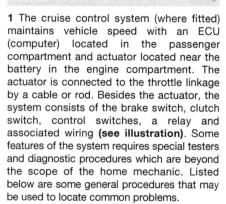

1 The central locking system operates the door lock actuators mounted in each door. The system consists of the switches,

actuators and associated wiring (see illustration). Diagnosis can usually be limited to simple checks of the wiring connections and actuators for minor faults which can be easily repaired.
2 Central locking systems are operated by bi-directional solenoids located in the doors. The lock switches have two operating positions: Lock and Unlock. These switches activate a relay which in turn connects voltage to the door lock solenoids. Depending on which way the relay is activated, it reverses polarity, allowing the two sides of the circuit to be used alternately as the feed (positive) and earth side.
3 Always check the circuit protection first. Some vehicles use a combination of circuit breakers and fuses.
4 Operate the door lock switches in both directions (Lock and Unlock) with the engine off. Listen for the faint click of the relay operating.
5 If there's no click, check for voltage at the switches. If no voltage is present, check the wiring between the fuse panel and the switches for shorts and opens.

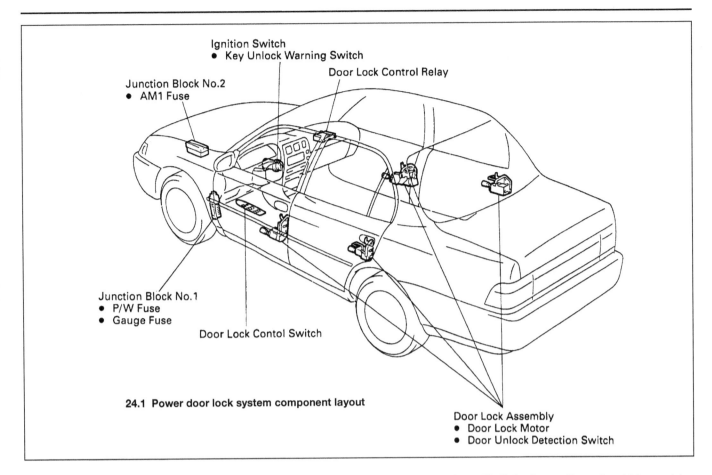

24.1 Power door lock system component layout

Ignition Switch
● Key Unlock Warning Switch

Door Lock Control Relay

Junction Block No.2
● AM1 Fuse

Junction Block No.1
● P/W Fuse
● Gauge Fuse

Door Lock Contol Switch

Door Lock Assembly
● Door Lock Motor
● Door Unlock Detection Switch

6 If voltage is present but no click is heard, test the switch for continuity. Replace the switch if there's no continuity in both switch positions **(see illustrations)**.

7 If the switch has continuity but the relay doesn't click, check the wiring between the switch and relay for continuity. Repair the wiring if there's no continuity.

8 If the relay is receiving voltage from the switch but is not sending voltage to the solenoids, check for a bad earth at the relay case. If the relay case is earthing properly, replace the relay.

9 If all but one lock solenoids operate, remove the trim panel from the affected door (see Chapter 11). and check for voltage at the solenoid while the lock switch is operated. One of the wires should have voltage in the Lock position; the other should have voltage in the unlock position.

10 If the inoperative solenoid is receiving voltage, replace the solenoid.

11 If the inoperative solenoid isn't receiving voltage, check for an open or short in the wire between the lock solenoid and the relay. **Note:** *It's common for wires to break in the portion of the harness between the body and door (opening and closing the door fatigues and eventually breaks the wires).*

25 Electric windows - description and check

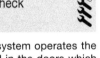

1 The electric window system operates the electric motors mounted in the doors which lower and raise the windows. The system consists of the control switches, the motors (regulators), glass mechanisms and associated wiring **(see illustration)**.

2 Electric windows are wired so they can be lowered and raised from the master control switch by the driver or by remote switches located at the individual windows. Each window has a separate motor which is reversible. The position of the control switch determines the polarity and therefore the direction of operation. Some systems are equipped with relays that control current flow to the motors.

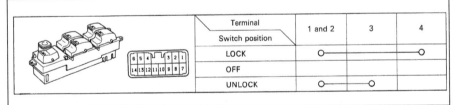

Terminal Switch position	1 and 2	3	4
LOCK	o———————————o		
OFF			
UNLOCK	o————————o		

24.6a Power door lock master switch terminal guide and continuity table

Terminal Switch position	2	3	4
LOCK		o————————o	
OFF			
UNLOCK	o————————————o		

24.6b Power door lock switch terminal guide and continuity table

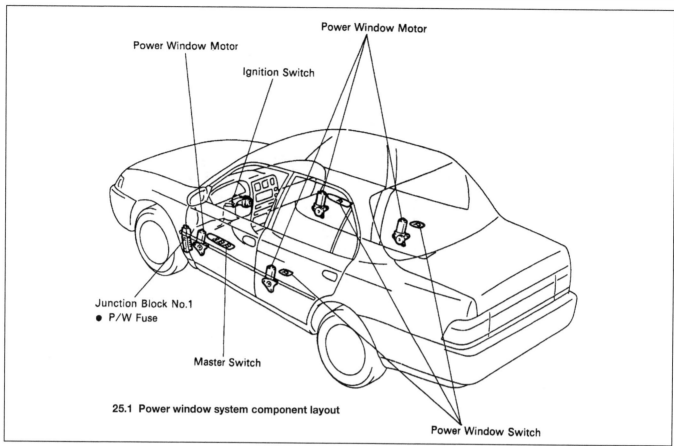

25.1 Power window system component layout

3 Some vehicles are equipped with a separate circuit breaker for each motor in addition to the fuse or circuit breaker protecting the whole circuit. This prevents one stuck window from disabling the whole system.

4 The electric windows will only operate when the ignition switch is ON. In addition, when activated the window lockout switch at the master control switch disables the switches at the passenger's window also. Always check these items before diagnosing a window problem.

5 These procedures are general in nature, so if you can't find the problem using them, take the vehicle to a dealer service department.

6 If the electric windows don't work at all, check the fuse or circuit breaker.

7 If only the rear windows are inoperative, or if the windows only operate from the master control switch, check the rear window lockout switch for continuity in the unlocked position (see illustration). Replace it if it doesn't have continuity.

8 Check the wiring between the switches and fuse panel for continuity. Repair the wiring, if necessary.

9 If only one window is inoperative from the master control switch, try the other control switch at the window. **Note:** *This doesn't apply to the drivers door window.*

10 If the same window works from one switch, but not the other, check the switch for continuity (see illustration).

11 If the switch tests OK, check for a short or open in the wiring between the affected switch and the window motor.

12 If one window is inoperative from both switches, remove the trim panel from the affected door and check for voltage at the motor while the switch is operated.

13 If voltage is reaching the motor, disconnect the glass from the regulator (see Chapter 11). Move the window up and down by hand while checking for binding and damage. Also check for binding and damage to the regulator. If the regulator is not damaged and the window moves up and down smoothly, replace the motor. If there's binding or damage, lubricate, repair or replace parts, as necessary.

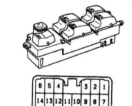

Switch position	Tester connection to terminal number	Specified condition
UP	6 − 7 − 8	Continuity
	1 − 2 − 13	
OFF	1 − 2 − 6 − 13	Continuity
DOWN	1 − 2 − 6	Continuity
	7 − 8 − 13	

25.7 Power window master switch terminal guide and continuity table

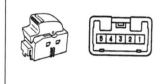

Switch position	Tester connection to terminal number	Specified condition
UP	1 − 5	Continuity
	3 − 4	
OFF	1 − 2	Continuity
	3 − 4	
DOWN	1 − 2	Continuity
	4 − 5	

25.10 Door window switch terminal guide and continuity table

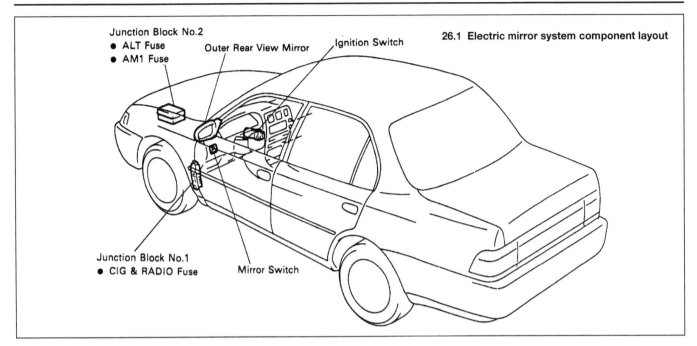

Junction Block No.2
● ALT Fuse
● AM1 Fuse

Outer Rear View Mirror

Ignition Switch

26.1 Electric mirror system component layout

Junction Block No.1
● CIG & RADIO Fuse

Mirror Switch

14 If voltage isn't reaching the motor, check the wiring in the circuit for continuity between the switches and motors. You'll need to consult the wiring diagram for the vehicle. Some window circuits are equipped with relays. If equipped, check that the relays are earthed properly and receiving voltage from the switches. Also check that each relay sends voltage to the motor when the switch is turned on. If it doesn't, replace the relay.

15 Test the windows after you are done to confirm proper repairs.

26 Electric rear view mirrors - description and check

1 The electric rear view mirrors use two motors to move the glass; one for up and down adjustments and one for left-right adjustments (see illustration).

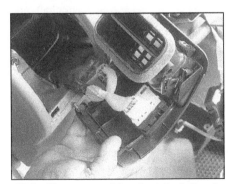

26.6a Use a screwdriver to detach the air register/mirror switch from the instrument panel; press in on the clips and push the mirror switch out

2 The control switch has a selector portion which sends voltage to the left or right side mirror. With the ignition key in the ACC position, roll down the windows and operate the mirror control switch through all functions (left-right and up-down) for both the left and right side mirrors.

3 Listen carefully for the sound of the electric motors running in the mirrors.

4 If the motors can be heard but the mirror glass doesn't move, there's probably a problem with the drive mechanism inside the mirror. Remove and disassemble the mirror to locate the problem.

5 If the mirrors don't operate and no sound comes from the mirrors, check the CIG/Radio fuse in the fuse block located under the left side of the dash (see Section 3).

6 If the fuse is OK, remove the air register/switch panel from the instrument panel for access the back of the mirror control switch without disconnecting the wires attached to it (see illustration). Turn the ignition ON and check for voltage at the switch. There should be voltage at one terminal. If there's no voltage at the switch, check for an open or short in the wiring between the fuse panel and the switch (see illustration).

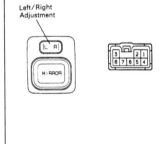

Left/Right
Adjustment

Switch position	Tester connection to terminal number	Specified condition
OFF	–	No continuity
UP	3 – 7 4 – 8	Continuity
DOWN	3 – 4 7 – 8	Continuity
LEFT	1 – 8 3 – 7	Continuity
RIGHT	1 – 3 7 – 8	Continuity

RIGHT SIDE

Switch position	Tester connection to terminal number	Specified condition
OFF	–	No continuity
UP	3 – 7 6 – 8	Continuity
DOWN	3 – 6 7 – 8	Continuity
LEFT	3 – 7 5 – 8	Continuity
RIGHT	3 – 5 7 – 8	Continuity

26.6b Power mirror switch terminal guide and continuity table

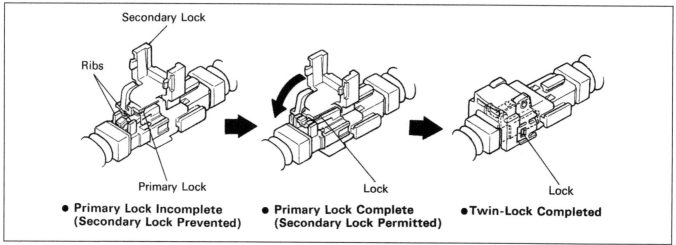

27.8 Each connector used in the airbag system uses a two stage locking system for security purposes - use care when disconnecting the airbag module connectors

7 If there's voltage at the switch, disconnect it. Check the switch for continuity in all its operating positions. If the switch does not have continuity, replace it.

8 Re-connect the switch. Locate the wire going from the switch to earth. Leaving the switch connected, connect a jumper wire between this wire and earth. If the mirror works normally with this wire in place, repair the faulty earth connection.

9 If the mirror still doesn't work, remove the mirror and check the wires at the mirror for voltage. Check with ignition ON and the mirror selector switch on the appropriate side. Operate the mirror switch in all its positions. There should be voltage at one of the switch-to-mirror wires in each switch position (except the neutral "off" position).

10 If there's no voltage in each switch position, check the wiring between the mirror and control switch for opens and shorts.

11 If there's voltage, remove the mirror and test it off the vehicle with jumper wires. Replace the mirror if it fails this test.

27 Airbag - general information

1 A Supplemental Restraint System (SRS), more commonly known as "airbags", is available in various versions as standard or optional equipment depending on model and territory. This system is designed to protect the driver and front seat passenger from serious injury in the event of a head-on or frontal collision. It consists of airbag modules in the centre of the steering wheel and the right side of the instrument panel, two crash sensors mounted at the front of the vehicle (1995 and earlier models) and a centre airbag sensor assembly located inside the passenger compartment.

2 On certain models, pyrotechnic seat belt pretensioners are built into the retractor units to tighten the seat belts in the event of a head-on or frontal collision.

Airbag modules

3 The airbag modules contain a housing incorporating the cushion (airbag) and inflator unit. The inflator assembly is mounted on the back of the housing over a hole through which gas is expelled, inflating the bag almost instantaneously when an electrical signal is sent from the system. The specially wound wire that carries this signal to the driver's module is called a spiral cable. The spiral cable is a flat, ribbon-like electrically conductive tape which is wound many times so that it can transmit an electrical signal regardless of steering wheel position.

Sensors

4 On 1995 and earlier models, the system has three sensors: two crash sensors at the front of the vehicle behind the bumper and above the wheel arches and a safing sensor in the centre airbag sensor assembly located in the centre console. On 1996 models, all sensors are located in the centre airbag sensor assembly.

5 The front crash sensors are basically pressure sensitive switches that complete an electrical circuit during an impact of sufficient G force. The electrical signal from the crash sensors is sent to the safing sensor in the centre airbag sensor assembly, which then completes the circuit and inflates the airbag.

Centre airbag sensor assembly

6 The centre airbag sensor contains the safing sensor and an on-board microprocessor which monitors the operation of the system. It checks this system every time the vehicle is started, causing the "AIRBAG" warning light to go on, then off, if the system is operating properly. If there is a fault in the system, the light will go on and stay on and the centre airbag sensor assembly will store fault codes indicating the nature of the fault. If the AIRBAG light goes on and stays on, the vehicle should be taken to your dealer immediately for service.

Seat belt pretensioners

7 In addition to the airbag units, the Supplemental Restraint System may also incorporate pyrotechnical seat belt pretensioners operated by gas cartridges in the belt retractor assemblies. The pyrotechnical units are also triggered by the centre airbag assembly, in conjunction with the airbag, to tighten the seat belts and provide additional collision protection.

Servicing components near the SRS system

8 Nevertheless, there are times when you need to remove the steering wheel, radio or service other components on or near the instrument panel. At these times, you'll be working around components and wiring harnesses for the SRS system. SRS system wiring is easy to identify; they're all covered by a bright yellow conduit. Do not unplug the connectors for the SRS system wiring, except to disable the system (see illustration). And do not use electrical test equipment on the SRS system wiring. ALWAYS DISABLE THE SRS SYSTEM BEFORE WORKING NEAR THE SRS SYSTEM COMPONENTS OR RELATED WIRING.

Disabling the SRS system

9 Turn the steering wheel to the straight ahead position, place the ignition switch in Lock and remove the key. Disconnect the cable from the negative battery terminal. Wait two minutes for the reversing capacitor to discharge.

10 Unplug the yellow connectors at the base of the steering column and under the right side of the instrument panel as described in the following steps.

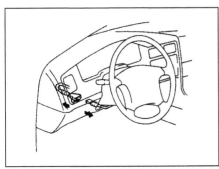

27.11 Remove the steering column lower finish panel for access to the driver's airbag module connector

Driver's side airbag

11 Remove the steering column lower finish panel below the instrument panel (see Chapter 11) and unplug the yellow steering column harness connector **(see illustration)**.

Passenger's side airbag

12 Open the glove box and remove the access cover (see Chapter 11).
13 Unplug the yellow electrical connector from the passenger inflator module **(see illustration)**.

Enabling the SRS system

14 After you've disabled the airbag and performed the necessary service, plug in the steering column (driver's side) and passenger side airbag connectors. Reinstall the lower finish panel and the glove box access cover.
15 Connect the cable to the negative battery terminal.

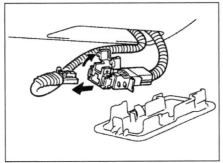

27.13 Remove the access cover inside the glove box for access to the passenger's airbag module connector

16 Turn the ignition key to On and verify that the "AIRBAG" warning light comes on for approximately six seconds, then goes off.

28 Wiring diagrams - general information

Since it isn't possible to include all wiring diagrams for every year covered by this manual, the following diagrams are those that are typical and most commonly needed.

Prior to diagnosing any circuits, check the fuse and circuit breakers (if equipped) to make sure they are in good condition. Make sure the battery is properly charged and has clean, tight cable connections (see Chapter 1).

When checking the wiring system, make sure that all electrical connectors are clean, with no broken or loose pins. When unplugging an electrical connector, do not pull on the wires, only on the connector housings themselves.

The following abbreviations are used on the wiring diagrams.

ABS	Anti-Lock Braking System
A/C	Air Conditioner
ACV	Air Control valve
A/T	Automatic Transmission
COMB.	Combination
ECU	Electronic Control Unit
EFI	Electronic Fuel Injection
Ex.	Except
FL	Fusible Link
H/B	Hatchback
IIA	Integrated Ignition Assembly
ISC	Idle Speed Control
J/B	Junction Block
L/B	Liftback
LH	Left-Hand
LHD	Left-Hand Drive
M/T	Manual Transmission
O/D	Overdrive
PTC	Positive Temperature Coefficient
RH	Right-Hand
RHD	Right-Hand Drive
S/D	Saloon (Sedan)
SW	Switch
TEMP.	Temperature
VSV	Vacuum Switching Valve
W/G	Estate (Wagon)
w/	With
w/o	Without

Wire colors are indicated by an alphabetical code.

B	=	Black	L	=	Blue	R	= Red
BR	=	Brown	LG	=	Light Green	V	= Violet
G	=	Green	O	=	Orange	W	= White
GR	=	Gray	P	=	Pink	Y	= Yellow

The first letter indicates the basic wire color and the second letter indicates the color of the stripe.

Example: L — Y

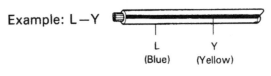

L
(Blue)

Y
(Yellow)

28.4 Wiring diagram colour code chart

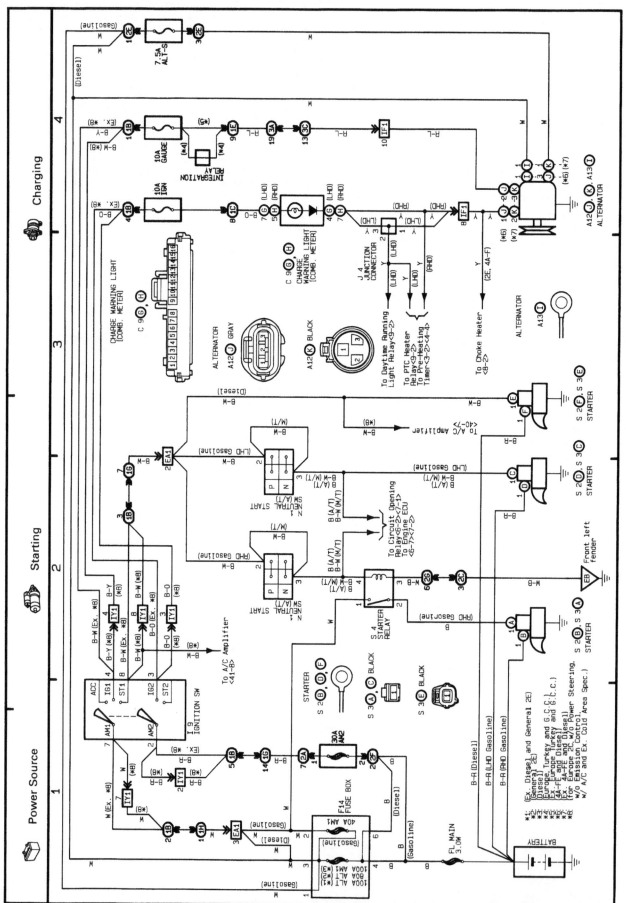

Wiring diagram for charge and start

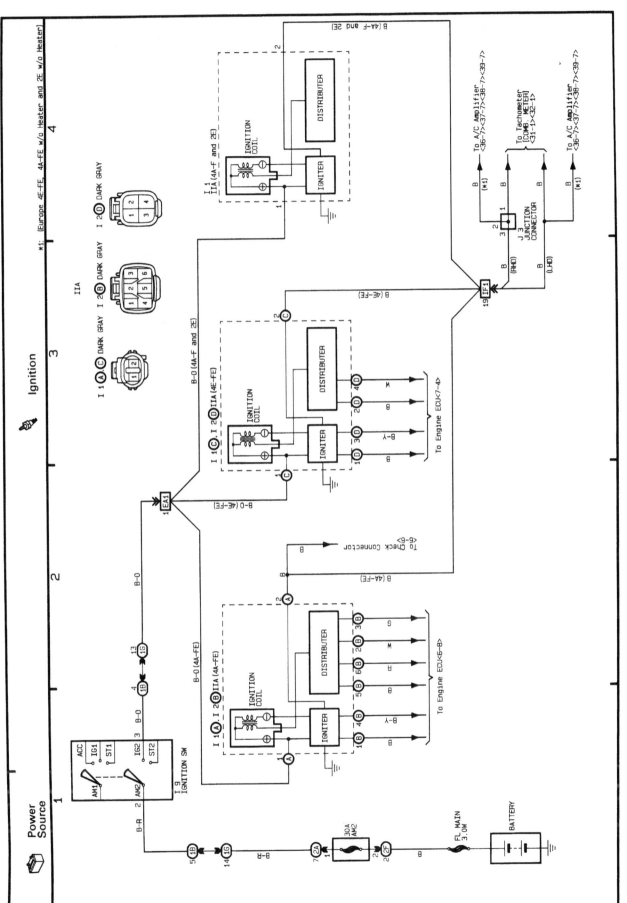

Wiring diagram for ignition

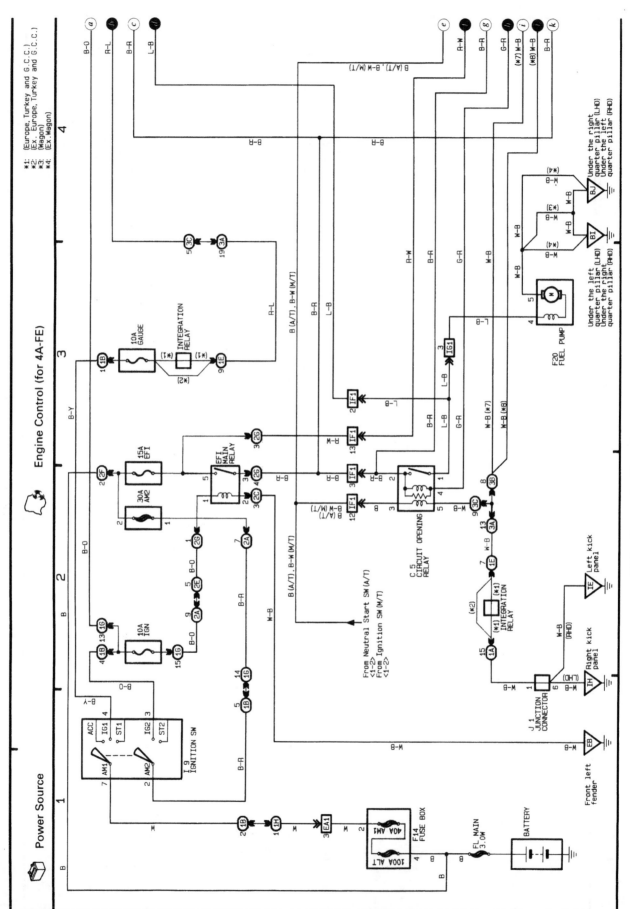

Wiring diagram for 4A engine management

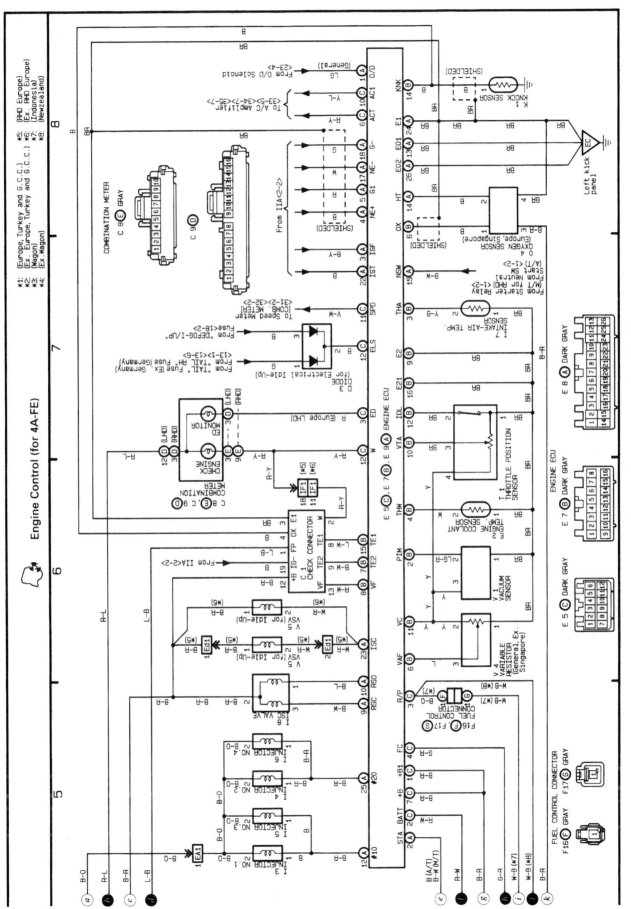

Wiring diagram for 4A engine management (continued)

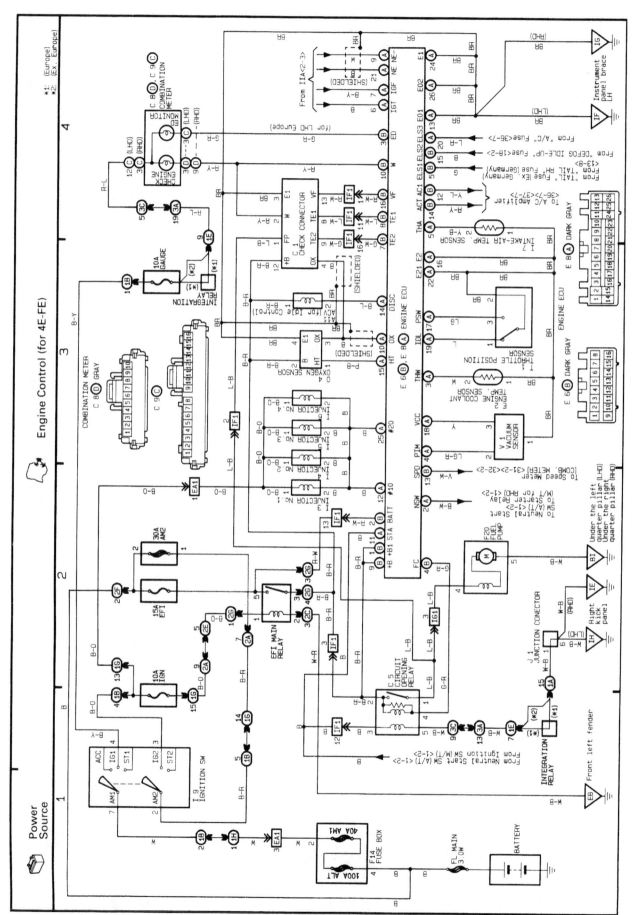

Wiring diagram for 4E engine management

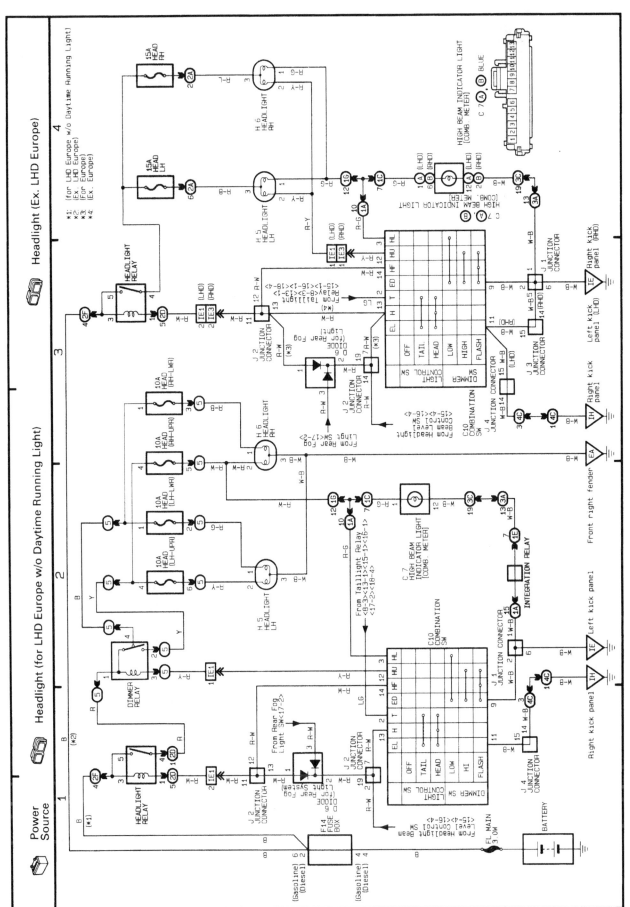

Wiring diagram for headlights

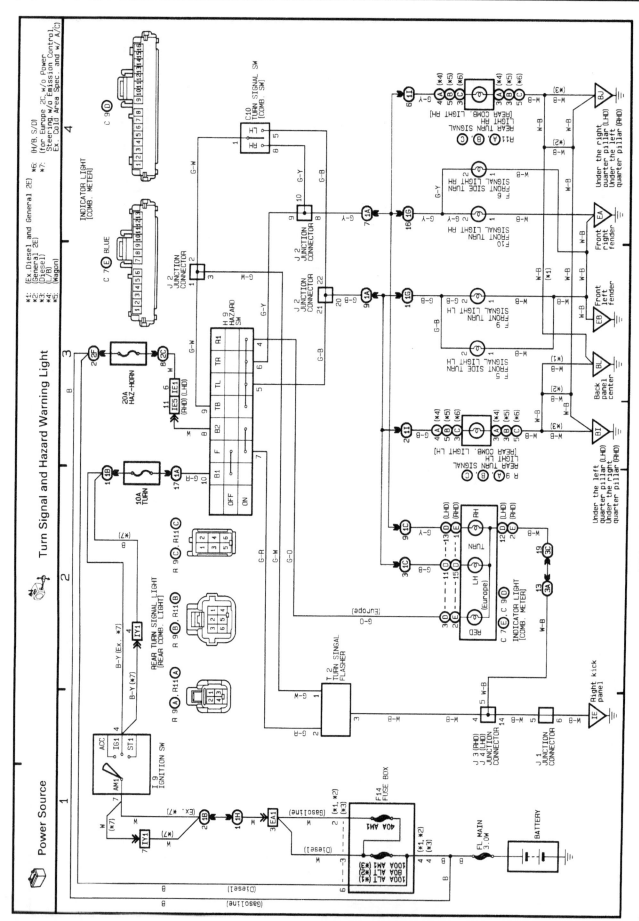

Wiring diagram for direction indicators

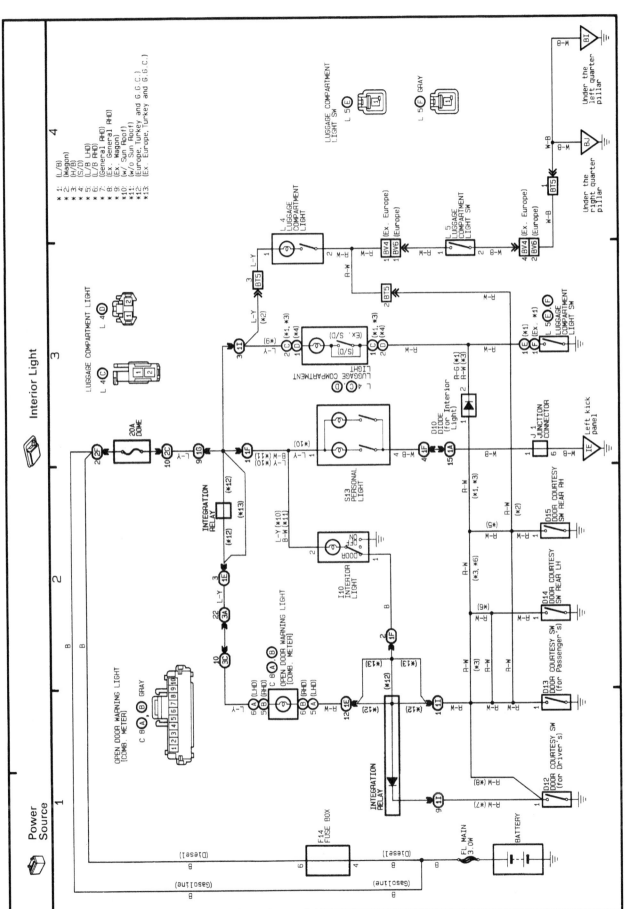

Wiring diagram for interior lights

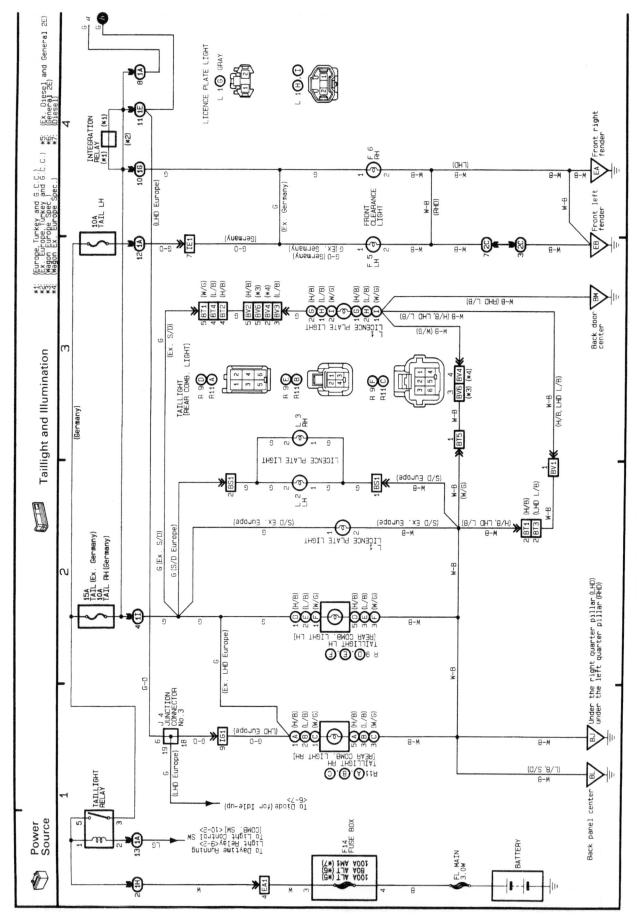

Taillight and Illumination

Wiring diagram for rear lights and instrument lighting

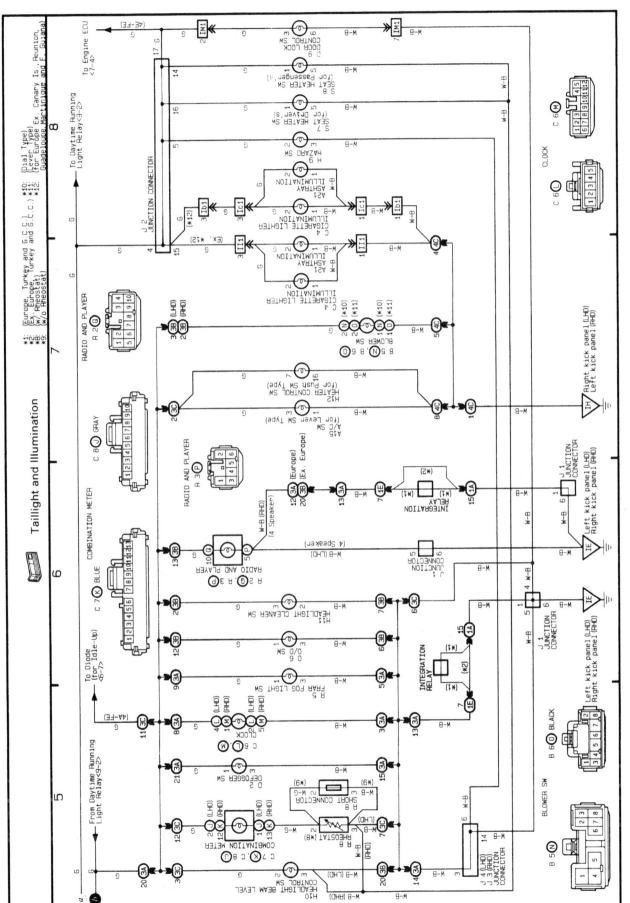

Taillight and Illumination

Wiring diagram for rear lights and instrument lighting (continued)

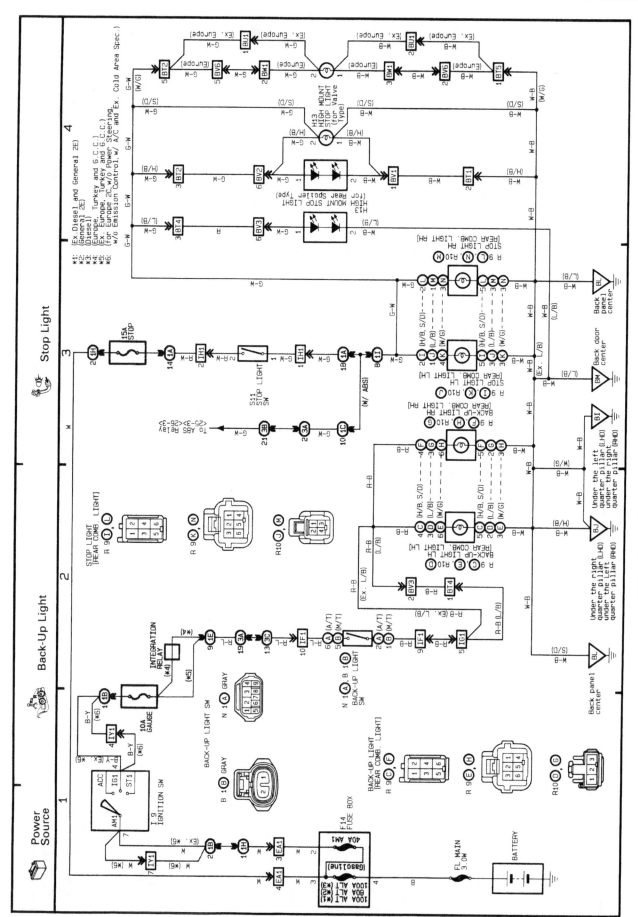

Wiring diagram for stop lights and reversing lights

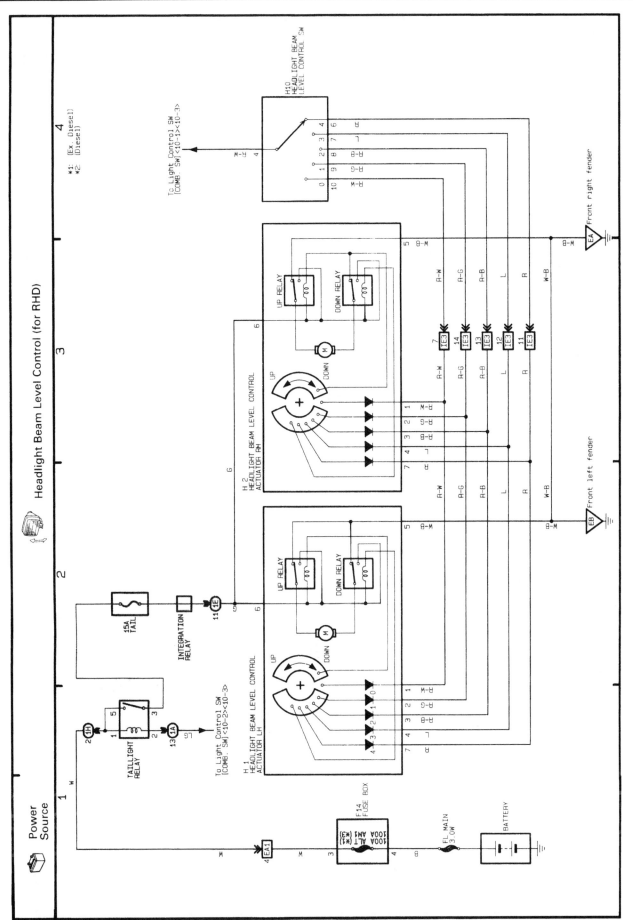

Wiring diagram for headlight beam control

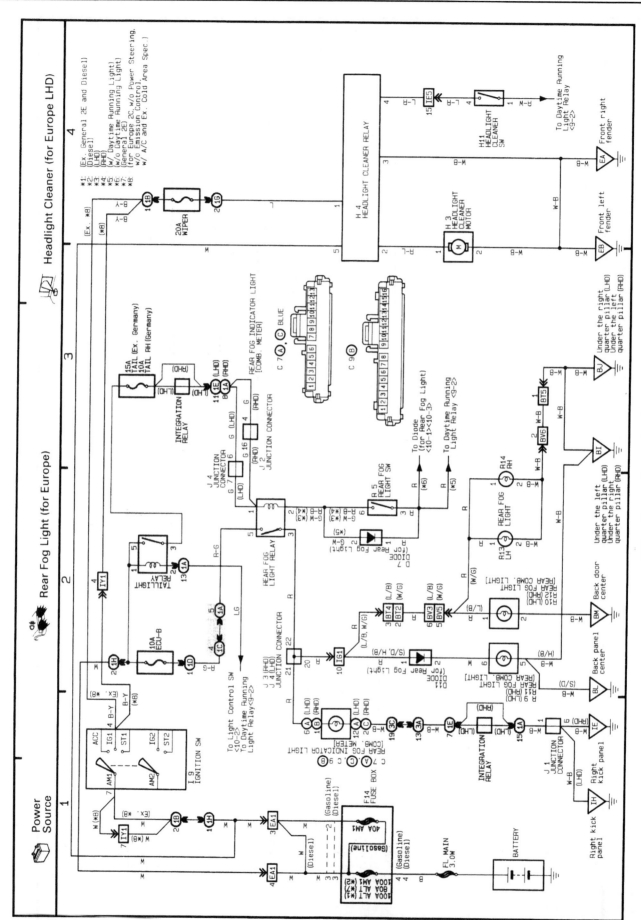

Wiring diagram for rear fog lights

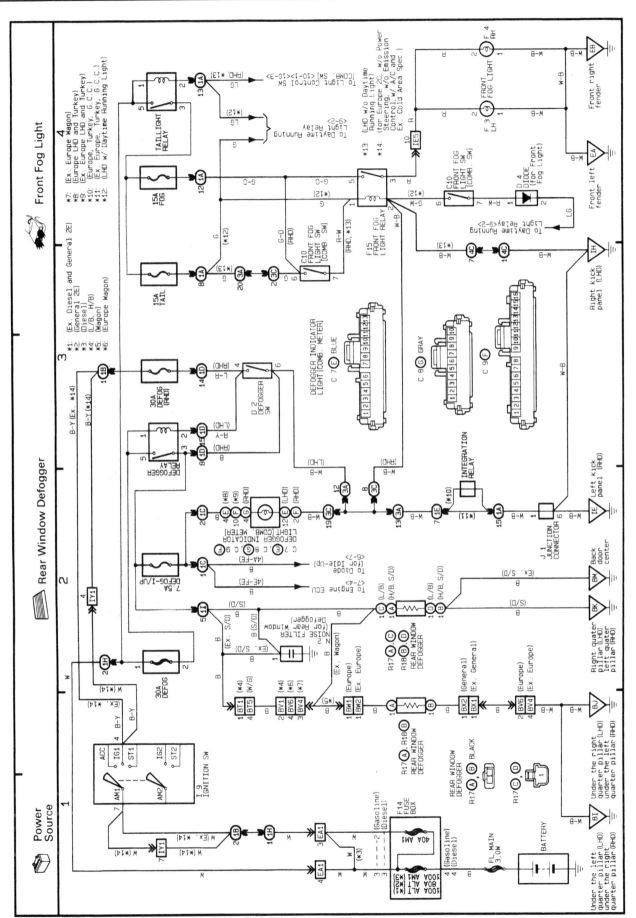

Wiring diagram for front fog lights and heated rear window

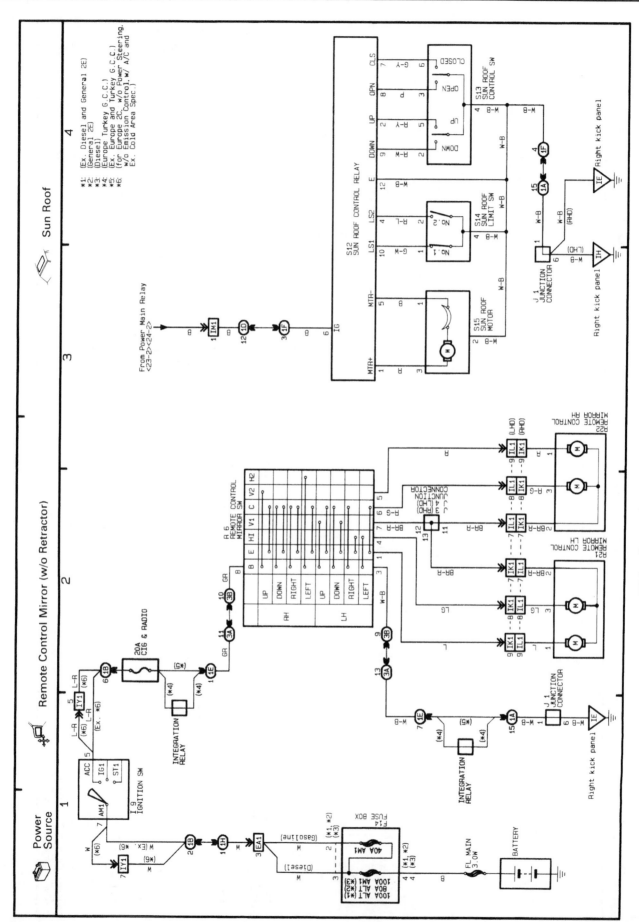

Wiring diagram for electric mirrors and sunroof

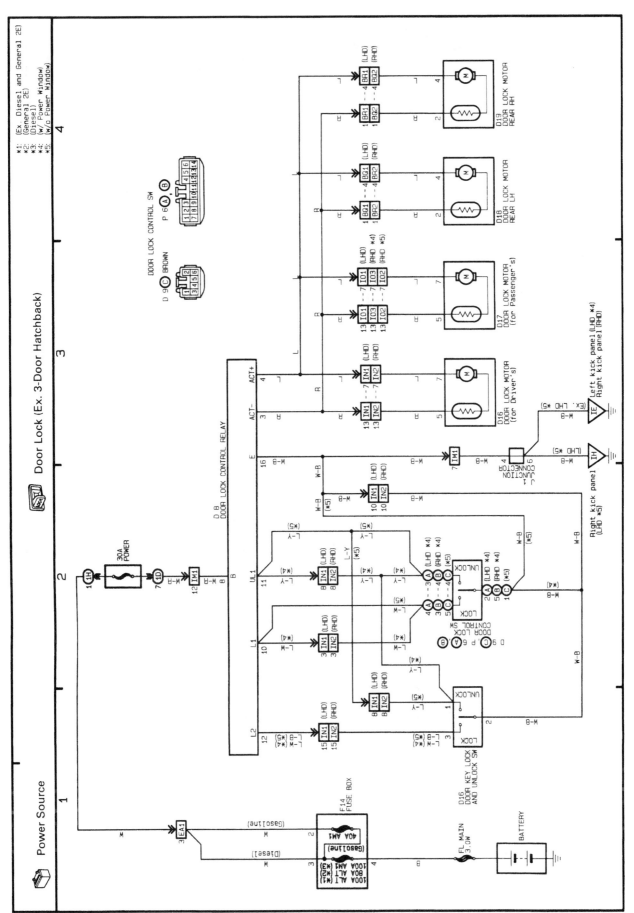

Wiring diagram for central locking

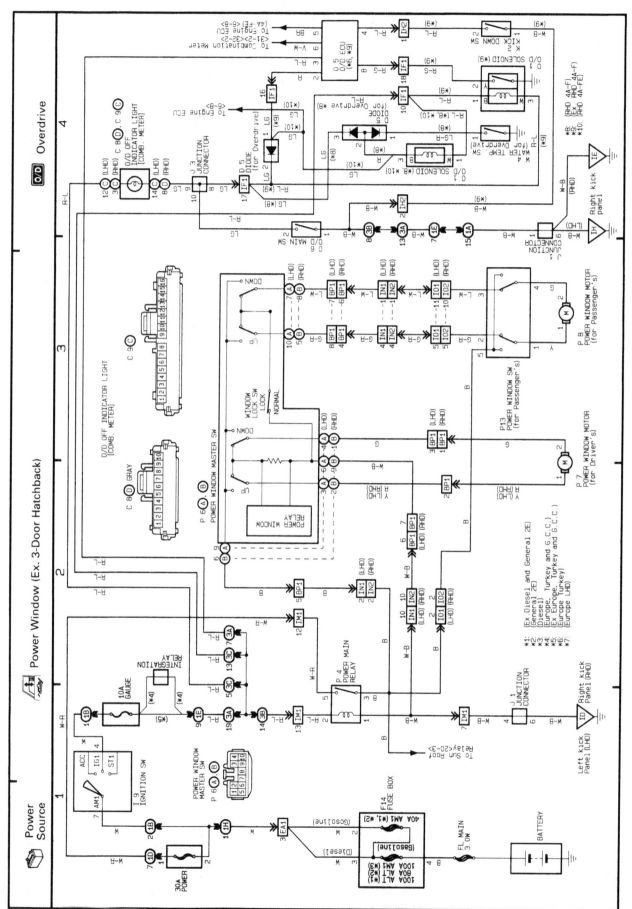

Wiring diagram for electric windows

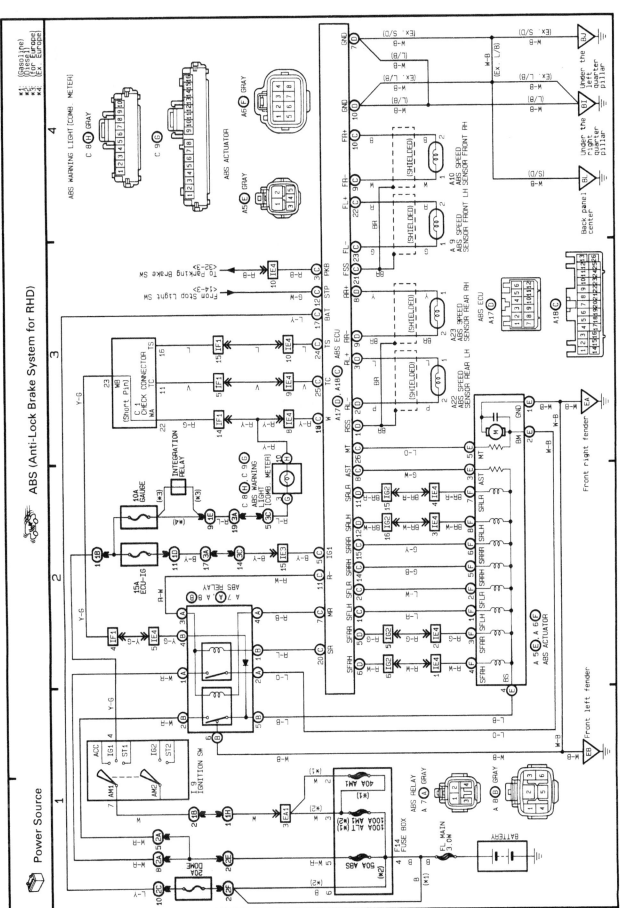

Wiring diagram for ABS

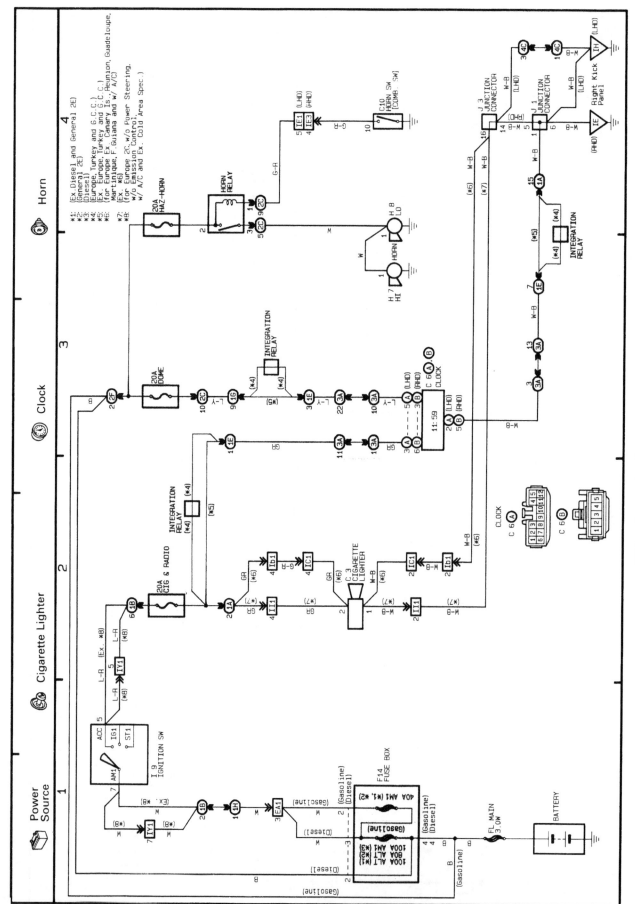

Wiring diagram for cigarette lighter, clock and horn

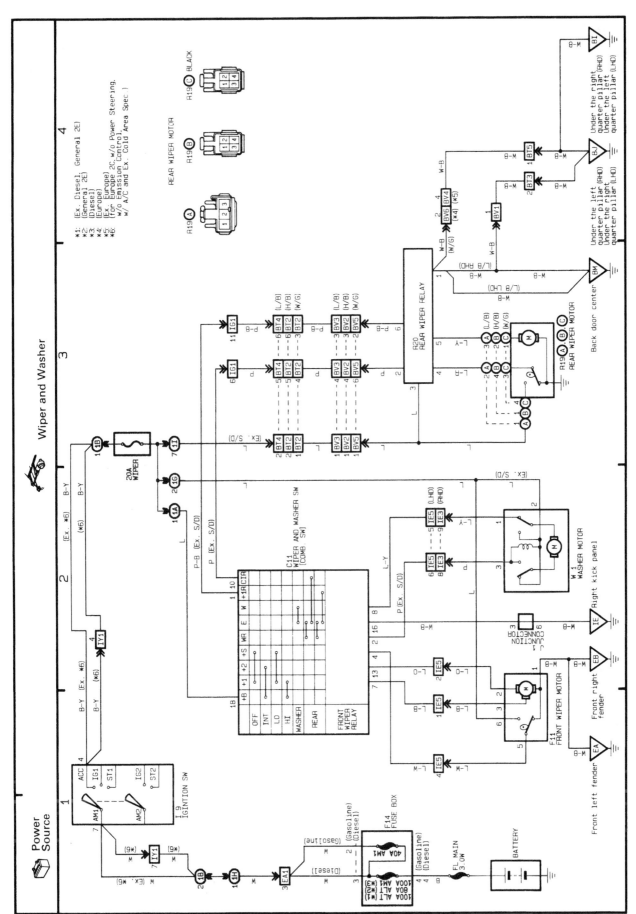

Wiring diagram for wipers and washers

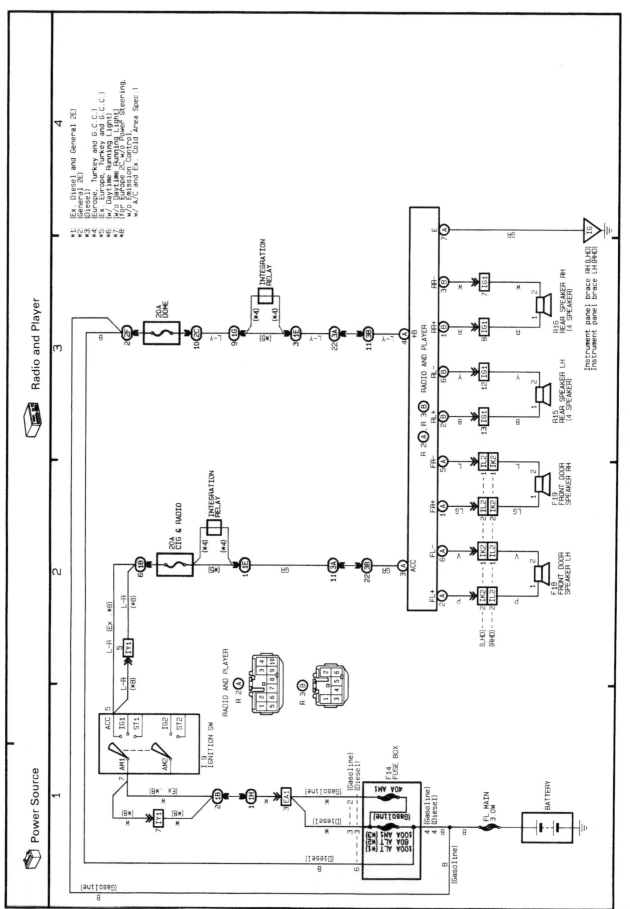

Wiring diagram for radio

Wiring diagram for instruments

Combination Meter (for RHD)

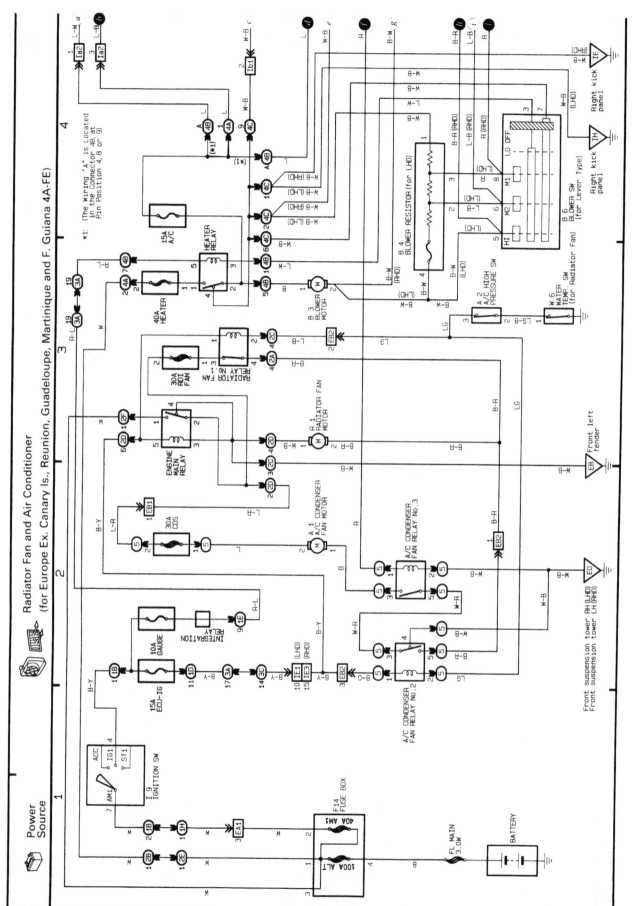

Radiator Fan and Air Conditioner
(for Europe Ex. Canary Is., Reunion, Guadeloupe, Martinique and F. Guiana 4A-FE)

Power Source

Wiring diagram for radiator fan and air conditioning

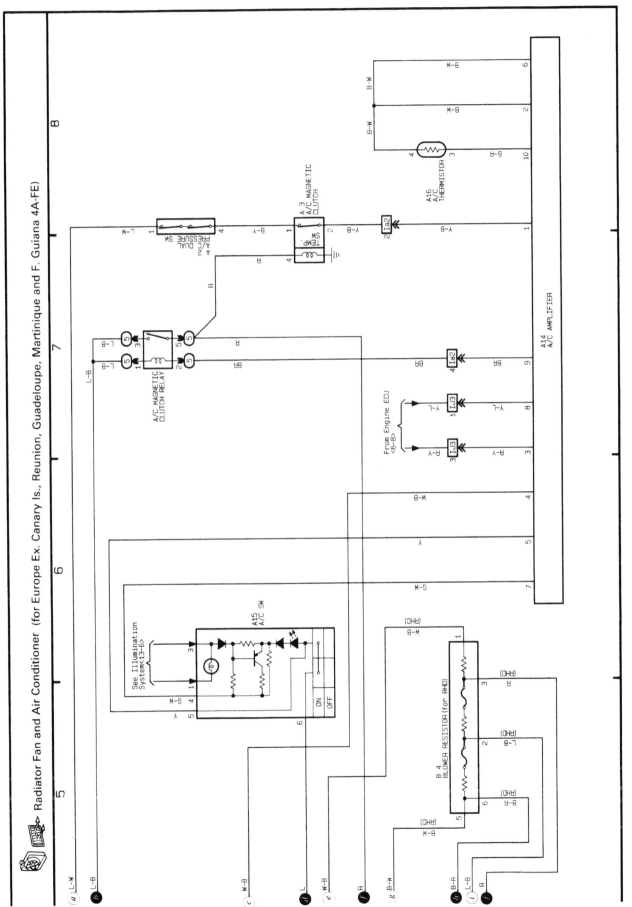

Wiring diagram for radiator fan and air conditioning (continued)

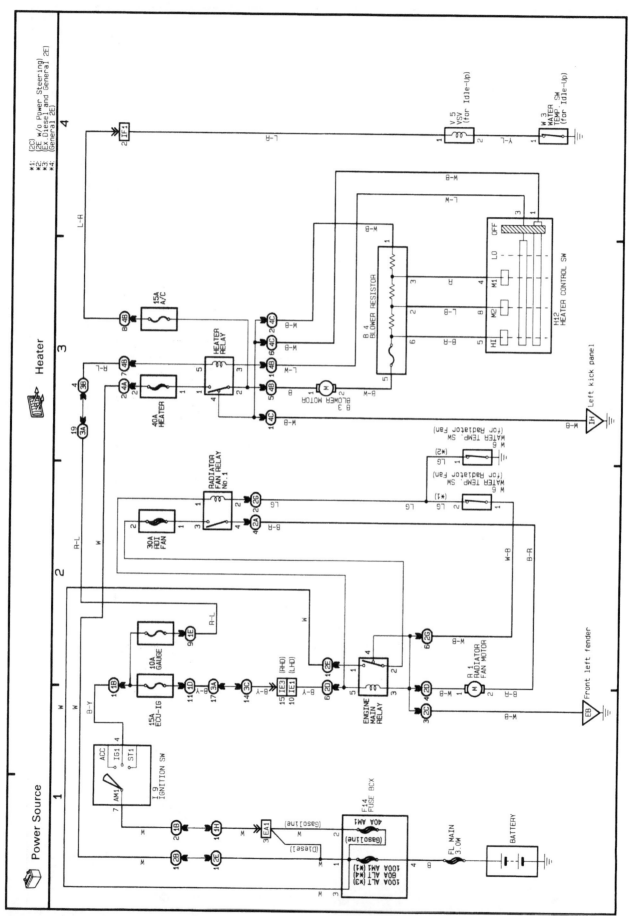

Wiring diagram for heater

Reference REF•1

Dimensions and Weights

Note: *All figures are approximate, and may vary according to model. Refer to manufacturer's data for exact figures.*

Dimensions
Overall length
  Saloon models . . . . 168.1 inches
  Liftback models . . . . 169.1 inches
  Hatchback models . . . . 161.2 inches
  Estate models . . . . 167.7 inches
Width . . . . 66.3 inches
Overall height
  Saloon models . . . . 54.3 inches
  Liftback models . . . . 54.1 inches
  Hatchback models . . . . 54.3 inches
  Estate models . . . . 56.1 inches
Wheelbase . . . . 97.0 inches
Front track . . . . 57.5 inches
Rear track . . . . 57.1 inches

Weights
Gross vehicle weight . . . . 3439 to 3803 lbs according to model
Maximum towing weight . . . . Refer to your Toyota dealer for weights and legal requirements concerning anticipated gradients and altitudes.

Conversion factors

Length (distance)

Inches (in)	x 25.4	= Millimetres (mm)	x 0.0394 =	Inches (in)
Feet (ft)	x 0.305	= Metres (m)	x 3.281 =	Feet (ft)
Miles	x 1.609	= Kilometres (km)	x 0.621 =	Miles

Volume (capacity)

Cubic inches (cu in; in³)	x 16.387	= Cubic centimetres (cc; cm³)	x 0.061 =	Cubic inches (cu in; in³)
Imperial pints (Imp pt)	x 0.568	= Litres (l)	x 1.76 =	Imperial pints (Imp pt)
Imperial quarts (Imp qt)	x 1.137	= Litres (l)	x 0.88 =	Imperial quarts (Imp qt)
Imperial quarts (Imp qt)	x 1.201	= US quarts (US qt)	x 0.833 =	Imperial quarts (Imp qt)
US quarts (US qt)	x 0.946	= Litres (l)	x 1.057 =	US quarts (US qt)
Imperial gallons (Imp gal)	x 4.546	= Litres (l)	x 0.22 =	Imperial gallons (Imp gal)
Imperial gallons (Imp gal)	x 1.201	= US gallons (US gal)	x 0.833 =	Imperial gallons (Imp gal)
US gallons (US gal)	x 3.785	= Litres (l)	x 0.264 =	US gallons (US gal)

Mass (weight)

Ounces (oz)	x 28.35	= Grams (g)	x 0.035 =	Ounces (oz)
Pounds (lb)	x 0.454	= Kilograms (kg)	x 2.205 =	Pounds (lb)

Force

Ounces-force (ozf; oz)	x 0.278	= Newtons (N)	x 3.6 =	Ounces-force (ozf; oz)
Pounds-force (lbf; lb)	x 4.448	= Newtons (N)	x 0.225 =	Pounds-force (lbf; lb)
Newtons (N)	x 0.1	= Kilograms-force (kgf; kg)	x 9.81 =	Newtons (N)

Pressure

Pounds-force per square inch (psi; lbf/in²; lb/in²)	x 0.070	= Kilograms-force per square centimetre (kgf/cm²; kg/cm²)	x 14.223 =	Pounds-force per square inch (psi; lbf/in²; lb/in²)
Pounds-force per square inch (psi; lbf/in²; lb/in²)	x 0.068	= Atmospheres (atm)	x 14.696 =	Pounds-force per square inch (psi; lbf/in²; lb/in²)
Pounds-force per square inch (psi; lbf/in²; lb/in²)	x 0.069	= Bars	x 14.5 =	Pounds-force per square inch (psi; lbf/in²; lb/in²)
Pounds-force per square inch (psi; lbf/in²; lb/in²)	x 6.895	= Kilopascals (kPa)	x 0.145 =	Pounds-force per square inch (psi; lbf/in²; lb/in²)
Kilopascals (kPa)	x 0.01	= Kilograms-force per square centimetre (kgf/cm²; kg/cm²)	x 98.1 =	Kilopascals (kPa)
Millibar (mbar)	x 100	= Pascals (Pa)	x 0.01 =	Millibar (mbar)
Millibar (mbar)	x 0.0145	= Pounds-force per square inch (psi; lbf/in²; lb/in²)	x 68.947 =	Millibar (mbar)
Millibar (mbar)	x 0.75	= Millimetres of mercury (mmHg)	x 1.333 =	Millibar (mbar)
Millibar (mbar)	x 0.401	= Inches of water (inH₂O)	x 2.491 =	Millibar (mbar)
Millimetres of mercury (mmHg)	x 0.535	= Inches of water (inH₂O)	x 1.868 =	Millimetres of mercury (mmHg)
Inches of water (inH₂O)	x 0.036	= Pounds-force per square inch (psi; lbf/in²; lb/in²)	x 27.68 =	Inches of water (inH₂O)

Torque (moment of force)

Pounds-force inches (lbf in; lb in)	x 1.152	= Kilograms-force centimetre (kgf cm; kg cm)	x 0.868 =	Pounds-force inches (lbf in; lb in)
Pounds-force inches (lbf in; lb in)	x 0.113	= Newton metres (Nm)	x 8.85 =	Pounds-force inches (lbf in; lb in)
Pounds-force inches (lbf in; lb in)	x 0.083	= Pounds-force feet (lbf ft; lb ft)	x 12 =	Pounds-force inches (lbf in; lb in)
Pounds-force feet (lbf ft; lb ft)	x 0.138	= Kilograms-force metres (kgf m; kg m)	x 7.233 =	Pounds-force feet (lbf ft; lb ft)
Pounds-force feet (lbf ft; lb ft)	x 1.356	= Newton metres (Nm)	x 0.738 =	Pounds-force feet (lbf ft; lb ft)
Newton metres (Nm)	x 0.102	= Kilograms-force metres (kgf m; kg m)	x 9.804 =	Newton metres (Nm)

Power

Horsepower (hp)	x 745.7	= Watts (W)	x 0.0013 =	Horsepower (hp)

Velocity (speed)

Miles per hour (miles/hr; mph)	x 1.609	= Kilometres per hour (km/hr; kph)	x 0.621 =	Miles per hour (miles/hr; mph)

Fuel consumption*

Miles per gallon (mpg)	x 0.354	= Kilometres per litre (km/l)	x 2.825 =	Miles per gallon (mpg)

Temperature

Degrees Fahrenheit = (°C x 1.8) + 32   Degrees Celsius (Degrees Centigrade; °C) = (°F - 32) x 0.56

* It is common practice to convert from miles per gallon (mpg) to litres/100 kilometres (l/100km), where mpg x l/100 km = 282

Spare parts are available from many sources, including maker's appointed garages, accessory shops, and motor factors. To be sure of obtaining the correct parts, it will sometimes be necessary to quote the vehicle identification number. If possible, it can also be useful to take the old parts along for positive identification. Items such as starter motors and alternators may be available under a service exchange scheme - any parts returned should be clean.

Our advice regarding spare parts is as follows.

Officially appointed garages

This is the best source of parts which are peculiar to your car, and which are not otherwise generally available (eg, badges, interior trim, certain body panels, etc). It is also the only place at which you should buy parts if the vehicle is still under warranty.

Accessory shops

These are very good places to buy materials and components needed for the maintenance of your car (oil, air and fuel filters, light bulbs, drivebelts, greases, brake pads, tough-up paint, etc). Components of this nature sold by a reputable shop are of the same standard as those used by the car manufacturer.

Besides components, these shops also sell tools and general accessories, usually have convenient opening hours, charge lower prices, and can often be found close to home. Some accessory shops have parts counters where components needed for almost any repair job can be purchased or ordered.

Motor factors

Good factors will stock all the more important components which wear out comparatively quickly, and can sometimes supply individual components needed for the overhaul of a larger assembly (eg, brake seals and hydraulic parts, bearing shells, pistons, valves). They may also handle work such as cylinder block reboring, crankshaft regrinding, etc.

Tyre and exhaust specialists

These outlets may be independent, or members of a local or national chain. They frequently offer competitive prices when compared with a main dealer or local garage, but it will pay to obtain several quotes before making a decision. When researching prices, also ask what "extras" may be added - for instance fitting a new valve and balancing the wheel are both commonly charged on top of the price of a new tyre.

Other sources

Beware of parts or materials obtained from market stalls, car boot sales or similar outlets. Such items are not invariably sub-standard, but there is little chance of compensation if they do prove unsatisfactory. In the case of safety-critical components such as brake pads, there is the risk not only of financial loss, but also of an accident causing injury or death.

Second-hand components or assemblies obtained from a car breaker can be a good buy in some circumstances, but his sort of purchase is best made by the experienced DIY mechanic.

Vehicle Identification

Modifications are a continuing and unpublicised process in vehicle manufacture, quite apart from major model changes. Spare parts manuals and lists are compiled upon a numerical basis, the individual vehicle identification numbers being essential to correct identification of the component concerned.

When ordering spare parts, always give as much information as possible. Quote the vehicle model, year of manufacture, VIN and engine numbers as appropriate.

The *Vehicle Identification Number (VIN)* is located in the centre of the bulkhead in the engine compartment **(see illustration)**. On certain models, the number is also stamped on a tag fixed to the facia, which can be read through the windscreen.

The *Manufacturer's plate* is located toward the left-hand side of the bulkhead in the engine compartment and gives the vehicle build code specifications as well as carrying a duplication of the vehicle identification number

The *engine number* is located on the forward facing side of the cylinder block for all engine types **(see illustration)**.

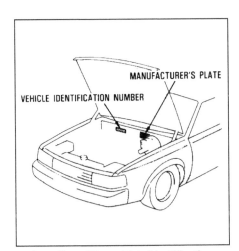

Location of the vehicle identification number and manufacturer's identification plate

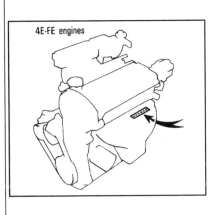
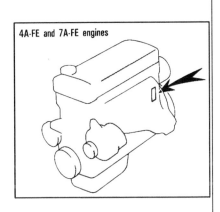

Engine number locations

The jack supplied with the vehicle tool kit should only be used for changing the roadwheels - see *"Wheel changing"* at the front of this manual. When jacking up the vehicle to carry out repair or maintenance tasks, a pillar or trolley type jack of suitable lifting capacity must be used, supplemented with axle stands positioned only beneath the appropriate points under the vehicle **(see illustration)**.

Never work under, around or near a raised vehicle unless it is adequately supported in at least two places with axle stands.

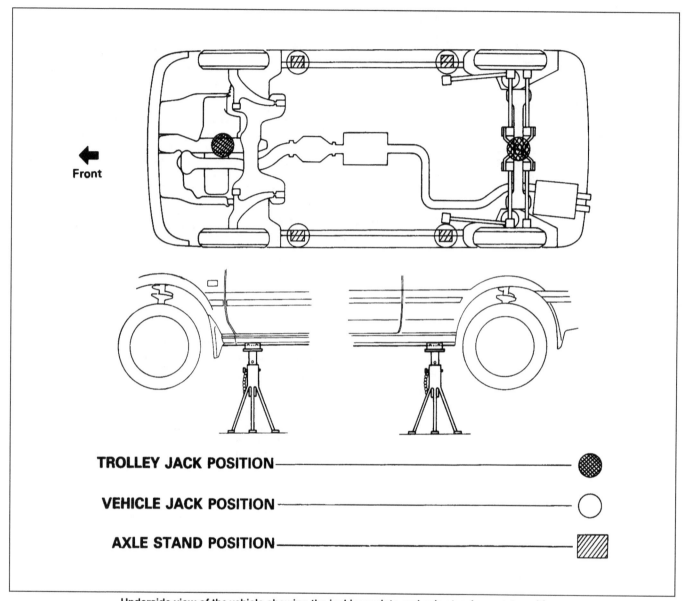

TROLLEY JACK POSITION ⬤

VEHICLE JACK POSITION ◯

AXLE STAND POSITION ▨

Underside view of the vehicle showing the jacking points and axle stand support positions

Radio/cassette unit anti-theft system - precaution

The radio/cassette unit fitted as standard or optional equipment may be equipped with a built-in security code, to deter thieves. If the power source to the unit is cut, the anti-theft system will activate. Even if the power source is immediately reconnected, the radio/cassette unit will not function until the correct security code has been entered. Therefore, if you do not know the correct security code for the radio/cassette unit **do not** disconnect either of the battery terminals, or remove the radio/cassette unit from the vehicle.

To enter the correct security code, follow the instructions provided with the radio/cassette player or vehicle handbook.

If an incorrect code is entered, the unit will become locked, and cannot be operated.

If this happens, or if the security code is lost or forgotten, seek the advice of your Toyota dealer.

Whenever servicing, repair or overhaul work is carried out on the car or its components, observe the following procedures and instructions. This will assist in carrying out the operation efficiently and to a professional standard of workmanship.

Joint mating faces and gaskets

When separating components at their mating faces, never insert screwdrivers or similar implements into the joint between the faces in order to prise them apart. This can cause severe damage which results in oil leaks, coolant leaks, etc upon reassembly. Separation is usually achieved by tapping along the joint with a soft-faced hammer in order to break the seal. However, note that this method may not be suitable where dowels are used for component location.

Where a gasket is used between the mating faces of two components, a new one must be fitted on reassembly; fit it dry unless otherwise stated in the repair procedure. Make sure that the mating faces are clean and dry, with all traces of old gasket removed. When cleaning a joint face, use a tool which is unlikely to score or damage the face, and remove any burrs or nicks with an oilstone or fine file.

Make sure that tapped holes are cleaned with a pipe cleaner, and keep them free of jointing compound, if this is being used, unless specifically instructed otherwise.

Ensure that all orifices, channels or pipes are clear, and blow through them, preferably using compressed air.

Oil seals

Oil seals can be removed by levering them out with a wide flat-bladed screwdriver or similar implement. Alternatively, a number of self-tapping screws may be screwed into the seal, and these used as a purchase for pliers or some similar device in order to pull the seal free.

Whenever an oil seal is removed from its working location, either individually or as part of an assembly, it should be renewed.

The very fine sealing lip of the seal is easily damaged, and will not seal if the surface it contacts is not completely clean and free from scratches, nicks or grooves. If the original sealing surface of the component cannot be restored, and the manufacturer has not made provision for slight relocation of the seal relative to the sealing surface, the component should be renewed.

Protect the lips of the seal from any surface which may damage them in the course of fitting. Use tape or a conical sleeve where possible. Lubricate the seal lips with oil before fitting and, on dual-lipped seals, fill the space between the lips with grease.

Unless otherwise stated, oil seals must be fitted with their sealing lips toward the lubricant to be sealed.

Use a tubular drift or block of wood of the appropriate size to install the seal and, if the seal housing is shouldered, drive the seal down to the shoulder. If the seal housing is unshouldered, the seal should be fitted with its face flush with the housing top face (unless otherwise instructed).

Screw threads and fastenings

Seized nuts, bolts and screws are quite a common occurrence where corrosion has set in, and the use of penetrating oil or releasing fluid will often overcome this problem if the offending item is soaked for a while before attempting to release it. The use of an impact driver may also provide a means of releasing such stubborn fastening devices, when used in conjunction with the appropriate screwdriver bit or socket. If none of these methods works, it may be necessary to resort to the careful application of heat, or the use of a hacksaw or nut splitter device.

Studs are usually removed by locking two nuts together on the threaded part, and then using a spanner on the lower nut to unscrew the stud. Studs or bolts which have broken off below the surface of the component in which they are mounted can sometimes be removed using a stud extractor. Always ensure that a blind tapped hole is completely free from oil, grease, water or other fluid before installing the bolt or stud. Failure to do this could cause the housing to crack due to the hydraulic action of the bolt or stud as it is screwed in.

When tightening a castellated nut to accept a split pin, tighten the nut to the specified torque, where applicable, and then tighten further to the next split pin hole. Never slacken the nut to align the split pin hole, unless stated in the repair procedure.

When checking or retightening a nut or bolt to a specified torque setting, slacken the nut or bolt by a quarter of a turn, and then retighten to the specified setting. However, this should not be attempted where angular tightening has been used.

For some screw fastenings, notably cylinder head bolts or nuts, torque wrench settings are no longer specified for the latter stages of tightening, "angle-tightening" being called up instead. Typically, a fairly low torque wrench setting will be applied to the bolts/nuts in the correct sequence, followed by one or more stages of tightening through specified angles.

Locknuts, locktabs and washers

Any fastening which will rotate against a component or housing during tightening should always have a washer between it and the relevant component or housing.

Spring or split washers should always be renewed when they are used to lock a critical component such as a big-end bearing retaining bolt or nut. Locktabs which are folded over to retain a nut or bolt should always be renewed.

Self-locking nuts can be re-used in non-critical areas, providing resistance can be felt when the locking portion passes over the bolt or stud thread. However, it should be noted that self-locking stiffnuts tend to lose their effectiveness after long periods of use, and should then be renewed as a matter of course.

Split pins must always be replaced with new ones of the correct size for the hole.

When thread-locking compound is found on the threads of a fastener which is to be re-used, it should be cleaned off with a wire brush and solvent, and fresh compound applied on reassembly.

Special tools

Some repair procedures in this manual entail the use of special tools such as a press, two or three-legged pullers, spring compressors, etc. Wherever possible, suitable readily-available alternatives to the manufacturer's special tools are described, and are shown in use. In some instances, where no alternative is possible, it has been necessary to resort to the use of a manufacturer's tool, and this has been done for reasons of safety as well as the efficient completion of the repair operation. Unless you are highly-skilled and have a thorough understanding of the procedures described, never attempt to bypass the use of any special tool when the procedure described specifies its use. Not only is there a very great risk of personal injury, but expensive damage could be caused to the components involved.

Environmental considerations

When disposing of used engine oil, brake fluid, antifreeze, etc, give due consideration to any detrimental environmental effects. Do not, for instance, pour any of the above liquids down drains into the general sewage system, or onto the ground to soak away. Many local council refuse tips provide a facility for waste oil disposal, as do some garages. If none of these facilities are available, consult your local Environmental Health Department, or the National Rivers Authority, for further advice.

With the universal tightening-up of legislation regarding the emission of environmentally-harmful substances from motor vehicles, most vehicles have tamperproof devices fitted to the main adjustment points of the fuel system. These devices are primarily designed to prevent unqualified persons from adjusting the fuel/air mixture, with the chance of a consequent increase in toxic emissions. If such devices are found during servicing or overhaul, they should, wherever possible, be renewed or refitted in accordance with the manufacturer's requirements or current legislation.

OIL CARE
FOLLOW THE CODE

OIL BANK LINE
0800 66 33 66
www.oilbankline.org.uk

Note: It is antisocial and illegal to dump oil down the drain. To find the location of your local oil recycling bank, call this number free.

Introduction

A selection of good tools is a fundamental requirement for anyone contemplating the maintenance and repair of a motor vehicle. For the owner who does not possess any, their purchase will prove a considerable expense, offsetting some of the savings made by doing-it-yourself. However, provided that the tools purchased meet the relevant national safety standards and are of good quality, they will last for many years and prove an extremely worthwhile investment.

To help the average owner to decide which tools are needed to carry out the various tasks detailed in this manual, we have compiled three lists of tools under the following headings: *Maintenance and minor repair, Repair and overhaul,* and *Special*. Newcomers to practical mechanics should start off with the *Maintenance and minor repair* tool kit, and confine themselves to the simpler jobs around the vehicle. Then, as confidence and experience grow, more difficult tasks can be undertaken, with extra tools being purchased as, and when, they are needed. In this way, a *Maintenance and minor repair* tool kit can be built up into a *Repair and overhaul* tool kit over a considerable period of time, without any major cash outlays. The experienced do-it-yourselfer will have a tool kit good enough for most repair and overhaul procedures, and will add tools from the *Special* category when it is felt that the expense is justified by the amount of use to which these tools will be put.

Maintenance and minor repair tool kit

The tools given in this list should be considered as a minimum requirement if routine maintenance, servicing and minor repair operations are to be undertaken. We recommend the purchase of combination spanners (ring one end, open-ended the other); although more expensive than open-ended ones, they do give the advantages of both types of spanner.

☐ *Combination spanners:*
Metric - 8 to 19 mm inclusive
☐ *Adjustable spanner - 35 mm jaw (approx.)*
☐ *Spark plug spanner (with rubber insert) - petrol models*
☐ *Spark plug gap adjustment tool - petrol models*
☐ *Set of feeler gauges*
☐ *Brake bleed nipple spanner*
☐ *Screwdrivers:*
Flat blade - 100 mm long x 6 mm dia
Cross blade - 100 mm long x 6 mm dia
Torx - various sizes (not all vehicles)
☐ *Combination pliers*
☐ *Hacksaw (junior)*
☐ *Tyre pump*
☐ *Tyre pressure gauge*
☐ *Oil can*
☐ *Oil filter removal tool*
☐ *Fine emery cloth*
☐ *Wire brush (small)*
☐ *Funnel (medium size)*
☐ *Sump drain plug key (not all vehicles)*

Repair and overhaul tool kit

These tools are virtually essential for anyone undertaking any major repairs to a motor vehicle, and are additional to those given in the *Maintenance and minor repair* list. Included in this list is a comprehensive set of sockets. Although these are expensive, they will be found invaluable as they are so versatile - particularly if various drives are included in the set. We recommend the half-inch square-drive type, as this can be used with most proprietary torque wrenches.

The tools in this list will sometimes need to be supplemented by tools from the *Special* list:

☐ *Sockets (or box spanners) to cover range in previous list (including Torx sockets)*
☐ *Reversible ratchet drive (for use with sockets)*
☐ *Extension piece, 250 mm (for use with sockets)*
☐ *Universal joint (for use with sockets)*
☐ *Flexible handle or sliding T "breaker bar" (for use with sockets)*
☐ *Torque wrench (for use with sockets)*
☐ *Self-locking grips*
☐ *Ball pein hammer*
☐ *Soft-faced mallet (plastic or rubber)*
☐ *Screwdrivers:*
Flat blade - long & sturdy, short (chubby), and narrow (electrician's) types
Cross blade – long & sturdy, and short (chubby) types
☐ *Pliers:*
Long-nosed
Side cutters (electrician's)
Circlip (internal and external)
☐ *Cold chisel - 25 mm*
☐ *Scriber*
☐ *Scraper*
☐ *Centre-punch*
☐ *Pin punch*
☐ *Hacksaw*
☐ *Brake hose clamp*
☐ *Brake/clutch bleeding kit*
☐ *Selection of twist drills*
☐ *Steel rule/straight-edge*
☐ *Allen keys (inc. splined/Torx type)*
☐ *Selection of files*
☐ *Wire brush*
☐ *Axle stands*
☐ *Jack (strong trolley or hydraulic type)*
☐ *Light with extension lead*
☐ *Universal electrical multi-meter*

Sockets and reversible ratchet drive

Brake bleeding kit

Torx key, socket and bit

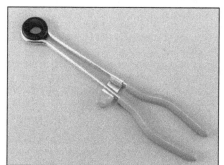

Hose clamp

Angular-tightening gauge

Special tools

The tools in this list are those which are not used regularly, are expensive to buy, or which need to be used in accordance with their manufacturers' instructions. Unless relatively difficult mechanical jobs are undertaken frequently, it will not be economic to buy many of these tools. Where this is the case, you could consider clubbing together with friends (or joining a motorists' club) to make a joint purchase, or borrowing the tools against a deposit from a local garage or tool hire specialist. It is worth noting that many of the larger DIY superstores now carry a large range of special tools for hire at modest rates.

The following list contains only those tools and instruments freely available to the public, and not those special tools produced by the vehicle manufacturer specifically for its dealer network. You will find occasional references to these manufacturers' special tools in the text of this manual. Generally, an alternative method of doing the job without the vehicle manufacturers' special tool is given. However, sometimes there is no alternative to using them. Where this is the case and the relevant tool cannot be bought or borrowed, you will have to entrust the work to a dealer.

☐ Angular-tightening gauge
☐ Valve spring compressor
☐ Valve grinding tool
☐ Piston ring compressor
☐ Piston ring removal/installation tool
☐ Cylinder bore hone
☐ Balljoint separator
☐ Coil spring compressors (where applicable)
☐ Two/three-legged hub and bearing puller
☐ Impact screwdriver
☐ Micrometer and/or vernier calipers
☐ Dial gauge
☐ Stroboscopic timing light
☐ Dwell angle meter/tachometer
☐ Fault code reader
☐ Cylinder compression gauge
☐ Hand-operated vacuum pump and gauge
☐ Clutch plate alignment set
☐ Brake shoe steady spring cup removal tool
☐ Bush and bearing removal/installation set
☐ Stud extractors
☐ Tap and die set
☐ Lifting tackle
☐ Trolley jack

Buying tools

Reputable motor accessory shops and superstores often offer excellent quality tools at discount prices, so it pays to shop around.

Remember, you don't have to buy the most expensive items on the shelf, but it is always advisable to steer clear of the very cheap tools. Beware of 'bargains' offered on market stalls or at car boot sales. There are plenty of good tools around at reasonable prices, but always aim to purchase items which meet the relevant national safety standards. If in doubt, ask the proprietor or manager of the shop for advice before making a purchase.

Care and maintenance of tools

Having purchased a reasonable tool kit, it is necessary to keep the tools in a clean and serviceable condition. After use, always wipe off any dirt, grease and metal particles using a clean, dry cloth, before putting the tools away. Never leave them lying around after they have been used. A simple tool rack on the garage or workshop wall for items such as screwdrivers and pliers is a good idea. Store all normal spanners and sockets in a metal box. Any measuring instruments, gauges, meters, etc, must be carefully stored where they cannot be damaged or become rusty.

Take a little care when tools are used. Hammer heads inevitably become marked, and screwdrivers lose the keen edge on their blades from time to time. A little timely attention with emery cloth or a file will soon restore items like this to a good finish.

Working facilities

Not to be forgotten when discussing tools is the workshop itself. If anything more than routine maintenance is to be carried out, a suitable working area becomes essential.

It is appreciated that many an owner-mechanic is forced by circumstances to remove an engine or similar item without the benefit of a garage or workshop. Having done this, any repairs should always be done under the cover of a roof.

Wherever possible, any dismantling should be done on a clean, flat workbench or table at a suitable working height.

Any workbench needs a vice; one with a jaw opening of 100 mm is suitable for most jobs. As mentioned previously, some clean dry storage space is also required for tools, as well as for any lubricants, cleaning fluids, touch-up paints etc, which become necessary.

Another item which may be required, and which has a much more general usage, is an electric drill with a chuck capacity of at least 8 mm. This, together with a good range of twist drills, is virtually essential for fitting accessories.

Last, but not least, always keep a supply of old newspapers and clean, lint-free rags available, and try to keep any working area as clean as possible.

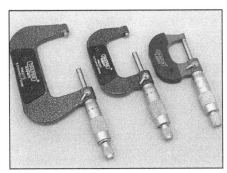

Micrometers

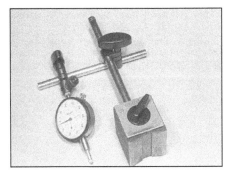

Dial test indicator ("dial gauge")

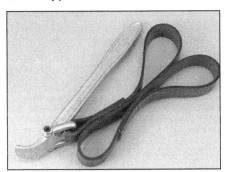

Strap wrench

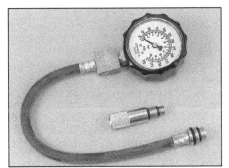

Compression tester

Fault code reader

This is a guide to getting your vehicle through the MOT test. Obviously it will not be possible to examine the vehicle to the same standard as the professional MOT tester. However, working through the following checks will enable you to identify any problem areas before submitting the vehicle for the test.

Where a testable component is in borderline condition, the tester has discretion in deciding whether to pass or fail it. The basis of such discretion is whether the tester would be happy for a close relative or friend to use the vehicle with the component in that condition. If the vehicle presented is clean and evidently well cared for, the tester may be more inclined to pass a borderline component than if the vehicle is scruffy and apparently neglected.

It has only been possible to summarise the test requirements here, based on the regulations in force at the time of printing. Test standards are becoming increasingly stringent, although there are some exemptions for older vehicles.

An assistant will be needed to help carry out some of these checks.

The checks have been sub-divided into four categories, as follows:

1 Checks carried out **FROM THE DRIVER'S SEAT**

2 Checks carried out **WITH THE VEHICLE ON THE GROUND**

3 Checks carried out **WITH THE VEHICLE RAISED AND THE WHEELS FREE TO TURN**

4 Checks carried out on **YOUR VEHICLE'S EXHAUST EMISSION SYSTEM**

---

1 Checks carried out **FROM THE DRIVER'S SEAT**

Handbrake

☐ Test the operation of the handbrake. Excessive travel (too many clicks) indicates incorrect brake or cable adjustment.

☐ Check that the handbrake cannot be released by tapping the lever sideways. Check the security of the lever mountings.

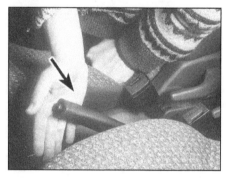

Footbrake

☐ Depress the brake pedal and check that it does not creep down to the floor, indicating a master cylinder fault. Release the pedal, wait a few seconds, then depress it again. If the pedal travels nearly to the floor before firm resistance is felt, brake adjustment or repair is necessary. If the pedal feels spongy, there is air in the hydraulic system which must be removed by bleeding.

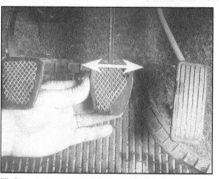

☐ Check that the brake pedal is secure and in good condition. Check also for signs of fluid leaks on the pedal, floor or carpets, which would indicate failed seals in the brake master cylinder.

☐ Check the servo unit (when applicable) by operating the brake pedal several times, then keeping the pedal depressed and starting the engine. As the engine starts, the pedal will move down slightly. If not, the vacuum hose or the servo itself may be faulty.

Steering wheel and column

☐ Examine the steering wheel for fractures or looseness of the hub, spokes or rim.

☐ Move the steering wheel from side to side and then up and down. Check that the steering wheel is not loose on the column, indicating wear or a loose retaining nut. Continue moving the steering wheel as before, but also turn it slightly from left to right.

☐ Check that the steering wheel is not loose on the column, and that there is no abnormal

movement of the steering wheel, indicating wear in the column support bearings or couplings.

Windscreen, mirrors and sunvisor

☐ The windscreen must be free of cracks or other significant damage within the driver's field of view. (Small stone chips are acceptable.) Rear view mirrors must be secure, intact, and capable of being adjusted.

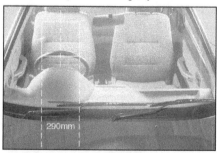

☐ The driver's sunvisor must be capable of being stored in the "up" position.

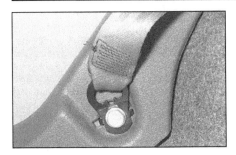

Seat belts and seats

Note: *The following checks are applicable to all seat belts, front and rear.*

☐ Examine the webbing of all the belts (including rear belts if fitted) for cuts, serious fraying or deterioration. Fasten and unfasten each belt to check the buckles. If applicable, check the retracting mechanism. Check the security of all seat belt mountings accessible from inside the vehicle.

☐ Seat belts with pre-tensioners, once activated, have a "flag" or similar showing on the seat belt stalk. This, in itself, is not a reason for test failure.

☐ The front seats themselves must be securely attached and the backrests must lock in the upright position.

Doors

☐ Both front doors must be able to be opened and closed from outside and inside, and must latch securely when closed.

2 Checks carried out WITH THE VEHICLE ON THE GROUND

Vehicle identification

☐ Number plates must be in good condition, secure and legible, with letters and numbers correctly spaced – spacing at (A) should be at least twice that at (B).

☐ The VIN plate and/or homologation plate must be legible.

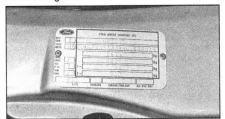

Electrical equipment

☐ Switch on the ignition and check the operation of the horn.

☐ Check the windscreen washers and wipers, examining the wiper blades; renew damaged or perished blades. Also check the operation of the stop-lights.

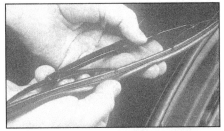

☐ Check the operation of the sidelights and number plate lights. The lenses and reflectors must be secure, clean and undamaged.

☐ Check the operation and alignment of the headlights. The headlight reflectors must not be tarnished and the lenses must be undamaged.

☐ Switch on the ignition and check the operation of the direction indicators (including the instrument panel tell-tale) and the hazard warning lights. Operation of the sidelights and stop-lights must not affect the indicators - if it does, the cause is usually a bad earth at the rear light cluster.

☐ Check the operation of the rear foglight(s), including the warning light on the instrument panel or in the switch.

☐ The ABS warning light must illuminate in accordance with the manufacturers' design. For most vehicles, the ABS warning light should illuminate when the ignition is switched on, and (if the system is operating properly) extinguish after a few seconds. Refer to the owner's handbook.

Footbrake

☐ Examine the master cylinder, brake pipes and servo unit for leaks, loose mountings, corrosion or other damage.

☐ The fluid reservoir must be secure and the fluid level must be between the upper (**A**) and lower (**B**) markings.

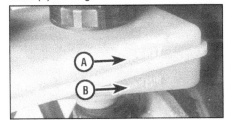

☐ Inspect both front brake flexible hoses for cracks or deterioration of the rubber. Turn the steering from lock to lock, and ensure that the hoses do not contact the wheel, tyre, or any part of the steering or suspension mechanism. With the brake pedal firmly depressed, check the hoses for bulges or leaks under pressure.

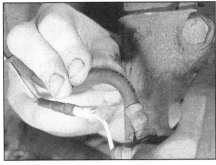

Steering and suspension

☐ Have your assistant turn the steering wheel from side to side slightly, up to the point where the steering gear just begins to transmit this movement to the roadwheels. Check for excessive free play between the steering wheel and the steering gear, indicating wear or insecurity of the steering column joints, the column-to-steering gear coupling, or the steering gear itself.

☐ Have your assistant turn the steering wheel more vigorously in each direction, so that the roadwheels just begin to turn. As this is done, examine all the steering joints, linkages, fittings and attachments. Renew any component that shows signs of wear or damage. On vehicles with power steering, check the security and condition of the steering pump, drivebelt and hoses.

☐ Check that the vehicle is standing level, and at approximately the correct ride height.

Shock absorbers

☐ Depress each corner of the vehicle in turn, then release it. The vehicle should rise and then settle in its normal position. If the vehicle continues to rise and fall, the shock absorber is defective. A shock absorber which has seized will also cause the vehicle to fail.

Exhaust system

☐ Start the engine. With your assistant holding a rag over the tailpipe, check the entire system for leaks. Repair or renew leaking sections.

3 Checks carried out **WITH THE VEHICLE RAISED AND THE WHEELS FREE TO TURN**

Jack up the front and rear of the vehicle, and securely support it on axle stands. Position the stands clear of the suspension assemblies. Ensure that the wheels are clear of the ground and that the steering can be turned from lock to lock.

Steering mechanism

☐ Have your assistant turn the steering from lock to lock. Check that the steering turns smoothly, and that no part of the steering mechanism, including a wheel or tyre, fouls any brake hose or pipe or any part of the body structure.
☐ Examine the steering rack rubber gaiters for damage or insecurity of the retaining clips. If power steering is fitted, check for signs of damage or leakage of the fluid hoses, pipes or connections. Also check for excessive stiffness or binding of the steering, a missing split pin or locking device, or severe corrosion of the body structure within 30 cm of any steering component attachment point.

Front and rear suspension and wheel bearings

☐ Starting at the front right-hand side, grasp the roadwheel at the 3 o'clock and 9 o'clock positions and rock gently but firmly. Check for free play or insecurity at the wheel bearings, suspension balljoints, or suspension mountings, pivots and attachments.
☐ Now grasp the wheel at the 12 o'clock and 6 o'clock positions and repeat the previous inspection. Spin the wheel, and check for roughness or tightness of the front wheel bearing.

☐ If excess free play is suspected at a component pivot point, this can be confirmed by using a large screwdriver or similar tool and levering between the mounting and the component attachment. This will confirm whether the wear is in the pivot bush, its retaining bolt, or in the mounting itself (the bolt holes can often become elongated).

☐ Carry out all the above checks at the other front wheel, and then at both rear wheels.

Springs and shock absorbers

☐ Examine the suspension struts (when applicable) for serious fluid leakage, corrosion, or damage to the casing. Also check the security of the mounting points.
☐ If coil springs are fitted, check that the spring ends locate in their seats, and that the spring is not corroded, cracked or broken.
☐ If leaf springs are fitted, check that all leaves are intact, that the axle is securely attached to each spring, and that there is no deterioration of the spring eye mountings, bushes, and shackles.

☐ The same general checks apply to vehicles fitted with other suspension types, such as torsion bars, hydraulic displacer units, etc. Ensure that all mountings and attachments are secure, that there are no signs of excessive wear, corrosion or damage, and (on hydraulic types) that there are no fluid leaks or damaged pipes.
☐ Inspect the shock absorbers for signs of serious fluid leakage. Check for wear of the mounting bushes or attachments, or damage to the body of the unit.

Driveshafts (fwd vehicles only)

☐ Rotate each front wheel in turn and inspect the constant velocity joint gaiters for splits or damage. Also check that each driveshaft is straight and undamaged.

Braking system

☐ If possible without dismantling, check brake pad wear and disc condition. Ensure that the friction lining material has not worn excessively, (A) and that the discs are not fractured, pitted, scored or badly worn (B).

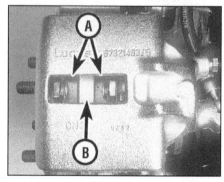

☐ Examine all the rigid brake pipes underneath the vehicle, and the flexible hose(s) at the rear. Look for corrosion, chafing or insecurity of the pipes, and for signs of bulging under pressure, chafing, splits or deterioration of the flexible hoses.
☐ Look for signs of fluid leaks at the brake calipers or on the brake backplates. Repair or renew leaking components.
☐ Slowly spin each wheel, while your assistant depresses and releases the footbrake. Ensure that each brake is operating and does not bind when the pedal is released.

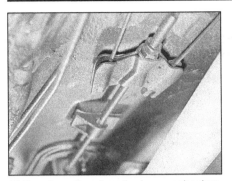

☐ Examine the handbrake mechanism, checking for frayed or broken cables, excessive corrosion, or wear or insecurity of the linkage. Check that the mechanism works on each relevant wheel, and releases fully, without binding.

☐ It is not possible to test brake efficiency without special equipment, but a road test can be carried out later to check that the vehicle pulls up in a straight line.

Fuel and exhaust systems

☐ Inspect the fuel tank (including the filler cap), fuel pipes, hoses and unions. All components must be secure and free from leaks.

☐ Examine the exhaust system over its entire length, checking for any damaged, broken or missing mountings, security of the retaining clamps and rust or corrosion.

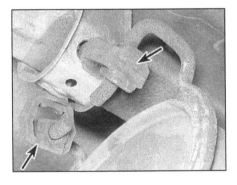

Wheels and tyres

☐ Examine the sidewalls and tread area of each tyre in turn. Check for cuts, tears, lumps, bulges, separation of the tread, and exposure of the ply or cord due to wear or damage. Check that the tyre bead is correctly seated on the wheel rim, that the valve is sound and properly seated, and that the wheel is not distorted or damaged.

☐ Check that the tyres are of the correct size for the vehicle, that they are of the same size and type on each axle, and that the pressures are correct.

☐ Check the tyre tread depth. The legal minimum at the time of writing is 1.6 mm over at least three-quarters of the tread width. Abnormal tread wear may indicate incorrect front wheel alignment.

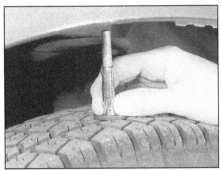

Body corrosion

☐ Check the condition of the entire vehicle structure for signs of corrosion in load-bearing areas. (These include chassis box sections, side sills, cross-members, pillars, and all suspension, steering, braking system and seat belt mountings and anchorages.) Any corrosion which has seriously reduced the thickness of a load-bearing area is likely to cause the vehicle to fail. In this case professional repairs are likely to be needed.

☐ Damage or corrosion which causes sharp or otherwise dangerous edges to be exposed will also cause the vehicle to fail.

4 Checks carried out on YOUR VEHICLE'S EXHAUST EMISSION SYSTEM

Petrol models

☐ Have the engine at normal operating temperature, and make sure that it is in good tune (ignition system in good order, air filter element clean, etc).

☐ Before any measurements are carried out, raise the engine speed to around 2500 rpm, and hold it at this speed for 20 seconds. Allow the engine speed to return to idle, and watch for smoke emissions from the exhaust tailpipe. If the idle speed is obviously much too high, or if dense blue or clearly-visible black smoke comes from the tailpipe for more than 5 seconds, the vehicle will fail. As a rule of thumb, blue smoke signifies oil being burnt (engine wear) while black smoke signifies unburnt fuel (dirty air cleaner element, or other carburettor or fuel system fault).

☐ An exhaust gas analyser capable of measuring carbon monoxide (CO) and hydrocarbons (HC) is now needed. If such an instrument cannot be hired or borrowed, a local garage may agree to perform the check for a small fee.

CO emissions (mixture)

☐ At the time of writing, for vehicles first used between 1st August 1975 and 31st July 1986 (P to C registration), the CO level must not exceed 4.5% by volume. For vehicles first used between 1st August 1986 and 31st July 1992 (D to J registration), the CO level must not exceed 3.5% by volume. Vehicles first

used after 1st August 1992 (K registration) must conform to the manufacturer's specification. The MOT tester has access to a DOT database or emissions handbook, which lists the CO and HC limits for each make and model of vehicle. The CO level is measured with the engine at idle speed, and at "fast idle". The following limits are given as a general guide:

At idle speed -
CO level no more than 0.5%
At "fast idle" (2500 to 3000 rpm) -
CO level no more than 0.3%
(Minimum oil temperature 60°C)

☐ If the CO level cannot be reduced far enough to pass the test (and the fuel and ignition systems are otherwise in good condition) then the carburettor is badly worn, or there is some problem in the fuel injection system or catalytic converter (as applicable).

HC emissions

☐ With the CO within limits, HC emissions for vehicles first used between 1st August 1975 and 31st July 1992 (P to J registration) must not exceed 1200 ppm. Vehicles first used after 1st August 1992 (K registration) must conform to the manufacturer's specification. The MOT tester has access to a DOT database or emissions handbook, which lists the CO and HC limits for each make and model of vehicle. The HC level is measured with the engine at "fast idle". The following is given as a general guide:

At "fast idle" (2500 to 3000 rpm) -
HC level no more than 200 ppm
(Minimum oil temperature 60°C)

☐ Excessive HC emissions are caused by incomplete combustion, the causes of which can include oil being burnt, mechanical wear and ignition/fuel system malfunction.

Diesel models

☐ The only emission test applicable to Diesel engines is the measuring of exhaust smoke density. The test involves accelerating the engine several times to its maximum unloaded speed.

Note: *It is of the utmost importance that the engine timing belt is in good condition before the test is carried out.*

☐ The limits for Diesel engine exhaust smoke, introduced in September 1995 are:
Vehicles first used before 1st August 1979:
Exempt from metered smoke testing, but must not emit "dense blue or clearly visible black smoke for a period of more than 5 seconds at idle" or "dense blue or clearly visible black smoke during acceleration which would obscure the view of other road users".
Non-turbocharged vehicles first used after 1st August 1979: 2.5m-1
Turbocharged vehicles first used after 1st August 1979: 3.0m-1

☐ Excessive smoke can be caused by a dirty air cleaner element. Otherwise, professional advice may be needed to find the cause.

Engine

- ☐ Engine backfires
- ☐ Engine difficult to start when cold
- ☐ Engine difficult to start when hot
- ☐ Engine fails to rotate when attempting to start
- ☐ Engine hesitates on acceleration
- ☐ Engine idles erratically
- ☐ Engine lacks power
- ☐ Engine misfires at idle speed
- ☐ Engine misfires throughout the driving speed range
- ☐ Engine noises
- ☐ Engine rotates, but will not start
- ☐ Engine runs-on after switching off
- ☐ Engine stalls
- ☐ Engine starts, but stops immediately
- ☐ Oil pressure warning light illuminated with engine running
- ☐ Starter motor noisy or excessively-rough in engagement

Cooling system

- ☐ Corrosion
- ☐ External coolant leakage
- ☐ Internal coolant leakage
- ☐ Overcooling
- ☐ Overheating

Fuel and exhaust systems

- ☐ Excessive fuel consumption
- ☐ Excessive noise or fumes from exhaust system
- ☐ Fuel leakage and/or fuel odour

Clutch

- ☐ Clutch fails to disengage (unable to select gears)
- ☐ Clutch slips (engine speed increases, with no increase in vehicle speed)
- ☐ Judder as clutch is engaged
- ☐ Noise when depressing or releasing clutch pedal
- ☐ Pedal travels to floor - no pressure or very little resistance

Manual transmission

- ☐ Jumps out of gear
- ☐ Lubricant leaks
- ☐ Noisy in neutral with engine running
- ☐ Noisy in one particular gear
- ☐ Vibration

Automatic transmission

- ☐ Engine will not start in any gear, or starts in gears other than Park or Neutral
- ☐ Fluid leakage
- ☐ General gear selection problems
- ☐ Transmission fluid brown, or has burned smell
- ☐ Transmission slips, shifts roughly, is noisy, or has no drive in forward or reverse gears
- ☐ Transmission will not downshift (kickdown) with accelerator fully depressed

Driveshafts

- ☐ Clicking or knocking noise on turns (at slow speed on full-lock)
- ☐ Vibration when accelerating or decelerating

Braking system

- ☐ Brake pedal feels spongy when depressed
- ☐ Brakes binding
- ☐ Excessive brake pedal effort required to stop vehicle
- ☐ Excessive brake pedal travel
- ☐ Judder felt through brake pedal or steering wheel when braking
- ☐ Noise (grinding or high-pitched squeal) when brakes applied
- ☐ Rear wheels locking under normal braking
- ☐ Vehicle pulls to one side under braking

Suspension and steering systems

- ☐ Excessive pitching and/or rolling around corners, or during braking
- ☐ Excessive play in steering
- ☐ Excessively-stiff steering
- ☐ Lack of power assistance
- ☐ Tyre wear excessive
- ☐ Vehicle pulls to one side
- ☐ Wandering or general instability
- ☐ Wheel wobble and vibration

Electrical system

- ☐ Battery will not hold a charge for more than a few days
- ☐ Ignition warning light fails to come on
- ☐ Ignition warning light remains illuminated with engine running
- ☐ Lights inoperative

Introduction

The vehicle owner who does his or her own maintenance according to the recommended service schedules should not have to use this section of the manual very often. Modern component reliability is such that, provided those items subject to wear or deterioration are inspected or renewed at the specified intervals, sudden failure is comparatively rare. Faults do not usually just happen as a result of sudden failure, but develop over a period of time. Major mechanical failures in particular are usually preceded by characteristic symptoms over hundreds or even thousands of miles. Those components which do occasionally fail without warning are often small and easily carried in the vehicle.

With any fault-finding, the first step is to decide where to begin investigations. Sometimes this is obvious, but on other occasions, a little detective work will be necessary. The owner who makes half a dozen haphazard adjustments or replacements may be successful in curing a fault (or its symptoms), but will be none the wiser if the fault recurs, and ultimately may have spent more time and money than was necessary. A calm and logical approach will be found to be more satisfactory in the long run. Always take into account any warning signs or abnormalities that may have been noticed in the period preceding the fault - power loss, high or low gauge readings, unusual smells, etc - and remember that failure of components such as fuses or spark plugs may only be pointers to some underlying fault.

The pages which follow provide an easy reference guide to the more common problems which may occur during the operation of the vehicle. These problems and their possible causes are grouped under headings denoting various components or systems, such as Engine, Cooling system, etc. The Chapter and/or Section which deals with the problem is also shown in brackets. Whatever the fault, certain basic principles apply. These are as follows:

Verify the fault. This is simply a matter of being sure that you know what the symptoms are before starting work. This is particularly important if you are investigating a fault for someone else, who may not have described it very accurately.

Don't overlook the obvious. For example, if the vehicle won't start, is there petrol in the tank? (Don't take anyone else's word on this particular point, and don't trust the fuel gauge either!) If an electrical fault is indicated, look for loose or broken wires before digging out the test gear.

Cure the disease, not the symptom. Substituting a flat battery with a fully-charged one will get you off the hard shoulder, but if the underlying cause is not attended to, the new battery will go the same way. Similarly, changing oil-fouled spark plugs for a new set will get you moving again, but remember that the reason for the fouling (if it wasn't simply an incorrect grade of plug) will have to be established and corrected.

Don't take anything for granted. Particularly, don't forget that a "new" component may itself be defective (especially if it's been rattling around in the boot for months), and don't leave components out of a fault diagnosis sequence just because they are new or recently fitted. When you do finally diagnose a difficult fault, you'll probably realise that all the evidence was there from the start.

Engine

Engine fails to rotate when attempting to start

☐ Battery terminal connections loose or corroded (Chapter 1).
☐ Battery discharged or faulty (Chapter 1).
☐ Broken, loose or disconnected wiring in the starting circuit (Chapter 5 and 12).
☐ Defective starter solenoid or switch (Chapter 5).
☐ Defective starter motor (Chapter 5).
☐ Flywheel ring gear or starter pinion teeth loose or broken (Chapters 2A, 2B, or 5).
☐ Automatic transmission not in Park/Neutral position (Chapter 7B).

Engine rotates, but will not start

☐ Fuel tank empty.
☐ Battery discharged (engine rotates slowly) (Chapter 1).
☐ Battery terminal connections loose or corroded (Chapter 1).
☐ Ignition components damp or damaged (Chapters 1 and 5).
☐ Broken, loose or disconnected wiring in the ignition circuit (Chapters 1 and 5).
☐ Worn, faulty or incorrectly-gapped spark plugs (Chapter 1).
☐ Major mechanical failure (eg camshaft drive) (Chapters 2A or 2B).

Engine difficult to start when cold

☐ Battery discharged (Chapter 1).
☐ Battery terminal connections loose or corroded (Chapter 1).
☐ Worn, faulty or incorrectly-gapped spark plugs (Chapter 1).
☐ Other ignition system fault (Chapters 1 and 5).
☐ Engine management system fault (Chapters 1, 4, 5 or 6).
☐ Low cylinder compressions (Chapters 2A or 2B).

Engine difficult to start when hot

☐ Air filter element dirty or clogged (Chapter 1).
☐ Engine management system fault (Chapters 1, 4, 5 or 6).
☐ Low cylinder compressions (Chapters 2A or 2B).

Starter motor noisy or excessively-rough in engagement

☐ Flywheel ring gear or starter pinion teeth loose or broken (Chapters 2A, 2B or 5).
☐ Starter motor mounting bolts loose or missing (Chapter 5).
☐ Starter motor internal components worn or damaged (Chapter 5).

Engine starts but stops immediately

☐ Loose or faulty electrical connections in the ignition circuit (Chapters 1 and 5).
☐ Engine management system fault (Chapters 1, 4, 5 or 6).
☐ Vacuum leak at the intake manifold (Chapters 1, 2A, 2B, 4, or 6).

Engine idles erratically

☐ Engine management system fault (Chapters 1, 4, 5 or 6).
☐ Air filter element clogged (Chapter 1).
☐ Vacuum leak at the inlet manifold or associated hoses (Chapters 1, 2A, 2B, 4, or 6).
☐ Worn, faulty or incorrectly-gapped spark plugs (Chapter 1).
☐ Incorrect valve clearances (Chapter 1).
☐ Uneven or low cylinder compressions (Chapters 2A or 2B).
☐ Camshaft lobes worn (Chapters 2A or 2B).
☐ Timing belt incorrectly-tensioned (Chapters 2A).

Engine misfires at idle speed

☐ Worn, faulty or incorrectly-gapped spark plugs (Chapter 1).
☐ Faulty spark plug HT leads (Chapter 1).
☐ Engine management system fault (Chapters 1, 4, 5 or 6).
☐ Vacuum leak at the inlet manifold or associated hoses (Chapters 1, 2A, 2B, 4, or 6).
☐ Incorrect valve clearances (Chapter 2A).
☐ Uneven or low cylinder compressions (Chapters 2A or 2B).
☐ Disconnected, leaking or perished crankcase ventilation hoses (Chapters 1 and 6).

Engine misfires throughout the driving speed range

☐ Fuel filter choked (Chapter 1).
☐ Fuel pump faulty or delivery pressure low (Chapter 4).
☐ Fuel tank vent blocked or fuel pipes restricted (Chapter 4).
☐ Vacuum leak at the inlet manifold or associated hoses (Chapters 1, 2A, 2B, 4, or 6).
☐ Worn, faulty or incorrectly-gapped spark plugs (Chapter 1).
☐ Faulty spark plug HT leads (Chapter 1).
☐ Faulty ignition coil (Chapter 5).
☐ Engine management system fault (Chapters 1, 4, 5 or 6).
☐ Uneven or low cylinder compressions (Chapters 2A or 2B).

Engine hesitates on acceleration

☐ Worn, faulty or incorrectly-gapped spark plugs (Chapter 1).
☐ Engine management system fault (Chapters 1, 4, 5 or 6).
☐ Vacuum leak at the inlet manifold or associated hoses (Chapters 1, 2A, 2B, 4, or 6).

Engine (continued)

Engine stalls

- ☐ Engine management system fault (Chapters 1, 4, 5 or 6).
- ☐ Vacuum leak at the inlet manifold or associated hoses (Chapters 1, 2A, 2B, 4, or 6).
- ☐ Fuel filter choked (Chapter 1).
- ☐ Fuel pump faulty or delivery pressure low (Chapter 4).
- ☐ Fuel tank vent blocked or fuel pipes restricted (Chapter 4).

Engine lacks power

- ☐ Engine management system fault (Chapters 1, 4, 5 or 6).
- ☐ Timing belt incorrectly fitted or incorrectly tensioned (Chapter 2A).
- ☐ Fuel filter choked (Chapter 1).
- ☐ Fuel pump faulty or delivery pressure low (Chapter 4).
- ☐ Uneven or low cylinder compressions (Chapters 2A or 2B).
- ☐ Worn, faulty or incorrectly-gapped spark plugs (Chapter 1).
- ☐ Vacuum leak at the inlet manifold or associated hoses (Chapters 1, 2A, 2B, 4, or 6).
- ☐ Brakes binding (Chapters 1 and 9).
- ☐ Clutch slipping (Chapter 8).
- ☐ Automatic transmission fluid level incorrect (Chapter 1).

Engine backfires

- ☐ Engine management system fault (Chapters 1, 4, 5 or 6).
- ☐ Timing belt incorrectly fitted or incorrectly tensioned (Chapter 2A).
- ☐ Vacuum leak at the inlet manifold or associated hoses (Chapters 1, 2A, 2B, 4, or 6).

Oil pressure warning light illuminated with engine running

- ☐ Low oil level or incorrect oil grade (Chapter 1).
- ☐ Faulty oil pressure warning light switch (Chapter 2A).
- ☐ Worn engine bearings and/or oil pump (Chapters 2A or 2B).
- ☐ High engine operating temperature (Chapter 3).
- ☐ Oil pressure relief valve defective (Chapters 2A).
- ☐ Oil pick-up strainer clogged (Chapters 2A).

Engine runs-on after switching off

- ☐ Idle speed excessively high (Chapter 4).
- ☐ Engine management system fault (Chapters 1, 4, 5 or 6).
- ☐ Excessive carbon build-up in engine (Chapters 2A or 2B).
- ☐ High engine operating temperature (Chapter 3).

Engine noises

Pre-ignition (pinking) or knocking during acceleration or under load

- ☐ Incorrect grade of fuel.
- ☐ Vacuum leak at the inlet manifold or associated hoses (Chapters 1, 2A, 2B, 4, or 6).
- ☐ Excessive carbon build-up in engine (Chapters 2A or 2B).

Whistling or wheezing noises

- ☐ Leaking inlet manifold gasket (Chapter 2A).
- ☐ Leaking exhaust manifold gasket or downpipe-to-manifold joint (Chapter 4).
- ☐ Leaking vacuum hose (Chapters 1, 2A, 2B, 4, or 6).
- ☐ Blowing cylinder head gasket (Chapters 2A or 2B).

Tapping or rattling noises

- ☐ Incorrect valve clearance adjustment (Chapter 2A).
- ☐ Worn valve gear or camshaft (Chapters 2A or 2B).
- ☐ Worn timing belt or tensioner (Chapter 2A).
- ☐ Ancillary component fault (water pump, alternator, etc) (Chapters 3 and 5).

Knocking or thumping noises

- ☐ Worn big-end bearings (regular heavy knocking, perhaps less under load) Chapter 2B).
- ☐ Worn main bearings (rumbling and knocking, perhaps worsening under load) Chapter 2B).
- ☐ Piston slap (most noticeable when cold) (Chapter 2B).
- ☐ Ancillary component fault (water pump, alternator, etc) (Chapters 3 and 5).

Cooling system

Overheating

- ☐ Insufficient coolant in system (Chapter 1).
- ☐ Thermostat faulty (Chapter 3).
- ☐ Radiator core blocked or grille restricted (Chapter 3).
- ☐ Radiator electric cooling fan(s) or coolant temperature sensor faulty Chapter 3).
- ☐ Engine management system fault (Chapters 1, 4, 5 or 6).
- ☐ Pressure cap faulty (Chapter 3).
- ☐ Auxiliary drivebelt worn or slipping (Chapter 1).
- ☐ Inaccurate coolant temperature gauge sender (Chapter 3).
- ☐ Airlock in cooling system (Chapter 1).

Overcooling

- ☐ Thermostat faulty (Chapter 3).
- ☐ Inaccurate coolant temperature gauge sender (Chapter 3).

External coolant leakage

- ☐ Deteriorated or damaged hoses or hose clips (Chapter 1).
- ☐ Radiator core or heater matrix leaking (Chapter 3).
- ☐ Pressure cap faulty (Chapter 3).
- ☐ Water pump seal leaking (Chapter 3).
- ☐ Boiling due to overheating (Chapter 3).
- ☐ Core plug leaking (Chapter 2D).

Internal coolant leakage

- ☐ Leaking cylinder head gasket (Chapters 2A or 2B).
- ☐ Cracked cylinder head or cylinder bore (Chapter 2B).

Corrosion

- ☐ Infrequent draining and flushing (Chapter 1).
- ☐ Incorrect antifreeze mixture, or inappropriate antifreeze type (Chapters 1 and 3).

Fuel and exhaust systems

Excessive fuel consumption
☐ Unsympathetic driving style, or adverse conditions.
☐ Air filter element dirty or clogged (Chapter 1).
☐ Engine management system fault (Chapters 1, 4, 5 or 6).
☐ Tyres under-inflated (Chapter 1).

Fuel leakage and/or fuel odour
☐ Damaged or corroded fuel tank, pipes or connections (Chapters 1 and 4).
☐ Charcoal canister and/or connecting pipes leaking (Chapters 1 and 6).

Excessive noise or fumes from exhaust system
☐ Leaking exhaust system or manifold joints (Chapters 1 or 4).
☐ Leaking, corroded or damaged silencers or pipe (Chapters 1 or 4).
☐ Broken mountings, causing body or suspension contact (Chapters 1 or 4).

Clutch

Pedal travels to floor - no pressure or very little resistance
☐ Air in clutch hydraulic system (Chapter 8).
☐ Incorrect clutch adjustments (Chapter 8).
☐ Broken clutch release bearing or fork (Chapter 8).
☐ Broken diaphragm spring in clutch pressure plate (Chapter 8).

Clutch fails to disengage (unable to select gears)
☐ Air in clutch hydraulic system (Chapter 8).
☐ Incorrect clutch adjustments (Chapter 8).
☐ Broken clutch release bearing or fork (Chapter 8).
☐ Clutch disc sticking on transmission input shaft splines (Chapter 8).
☐ Clutch disc sticking to flywheel or pressure plate (Chapter 8).
☐ Faulty pressure plate assembly (Chapter 8).

Clutch slips (engine speed increases, with no increase in vehicle speed)
☐ Incorrect clutch adjustments (Chapter 8).
☐ Clutch disc linings excessively worn (Chapter 8).
☐ Clutch disc linings contaminated with oil or grease (Chapter 8).
☐ Faulty pressure plate or weak diaphragm spring (Chapter 8).

Judder as clutch is engaged
☐ Clutch disc linings contaminated with oil or grease (Chapter 8).
☐ Clutch disc linings excessively worn (Chapter 8).
☐ Faulty or distorted pressure plate or diaphragm spring (Chapter 8).
☐ Worn or loose engine/transmission mountings (Chapters 2A or 7A).
☐ Clutch disc hub or transmission input shaft splines worn (Chapter 8).

Noise when depressing or releasing clutch pedal
☐ Worn clutch release bearing (Chapter 8).
☐ Worn or dry clutch pedal bushes (Chapter 8).
☐ Faulty pressure plate assembly (Chapter 8).
☐ Pressure plate diaphragm spring broken (Chapter 8).
☐ Broken clutch disc cushioning springs (Chapter 8).

Manual transmission

Noisy in neutral with engine running
☐ Input shaft bearings worn (noise apparent with clutch pedal released, but not when depressed) (Chapter 7A).*
☐ Clutch release bearing worn (noise apparent with clutch pedal depressed, possibly less when released) (Chapter 8).

Noisy in one particular gear
☐ Worn, damaged or chipped gear teeth (Chapter 7A).*

Difficulty engaging gears
☐ Clutch fault (Chapter 8).
☐ Worn or damaged gear linkage (Chapter 7A).
☐ Worn synchroniser assemblies (Chapter 7A).*

Jumps out of gear
☐ Worn or damaged gear linkage (Chapter 7A).
☐ Worn synchroniser assemblies (Chapter 7A).*
☐ Worn selector forks (Chapter 7A).*

Vibration
☐ Lack of oil (Chapter 1).
☐ Worn bearings (Chapter 7A).*

Lubricant leaks
☐ Leaking oil seal (Chapter 7A).
☐ Leaking housing joint (Chapter 7A).*

Although the corrective action necessary to remedy the symptoms described is beyond the scope of the home mechanic, the above information should be helpful in isolating the cause of the condition, so that the owner can communicate clearly with a professional mechanic.

Automatic transmission

Note: *Due to the complexity of the automatic transmission, it is difficult for the home mechanic to properly diagnose and service this unit. For problems other than the following, the vehicle should be taken to a dealer service department or automatic transmission specialist.*

Fluid leakage

☐ Automatic transmission fluid is usually deep red in colour. Fluid leaks should not be confused with engine oil, which can easily be blown onto the transmission by airflow.

☐ To determine the source of a leak, first remove all built-up dirt and grime from the transmission housing and surrounding areas, using a degreasing agent, or by steam-cleaning. Drive the vehicle at low speed, so airflow will not blow the leak far from its source. Raise and support the vehicle, and determine where the leak is coming from. The following are common areas of leakage:

a) Transmission fluid sump (Chapters 1 and 7B).
b) Dipstick tube (Chapters 1 and 7B).
c) Transmission-to-fluid cooler pipes/unions (Chapter 7B).
d) Speedometer drive pinion O-ring.
e) Driveshaft oil seals (Chapter 7B).

Transmission fluid brown, or has burned smell

☐ Transmission fluid level low, or fluid in need of renewal (Chapter 1).

General gear selection problems

☐ Chapter 7B deals with checking and adjusting the selector cable on automatic transmissions. The following are common problems which may be caused by a poorly-adjusted cable:
a) Engine starting in gears other than Park or Neutral.
b) Indicator on gear selector lever pointing to a gear other than the one actually being used.
c) Vehicle moves when in Park or Neutral.
d) Poor gear shift quality or erratic gear changes.
Refer to Chapter 7B for the selector cable adjustment procedure.

Transmission will not downshift (kickdown) with accelerator pedal fully depressed

☐ Low transmission fluid level (Chapter 1).
☐ Incorrect throttle valve cable adjustment (Chapter 7B).

Engine will not start in any gear, or starts in gears other than Park or Neutral

☐ Neutral start switch faulty or incorrectly adjusted (Chapter 7B).
☐ Incorrect throttle valve adjustment (Chapter 7B).

Transmission slips, is noisy, or has no drive in forward or reverse gears

☐ There are many probable causes for the above problems, but the home mechanic should be concerned with only one possibility - fluid level. Before taking the vehicle to a dealer or transmission specialist, check the fluid level and condition of the fluid as described in Chapter 1. Correct the fluid level as necessary, or change the fluid if needed. If the problem persists, professional help will be necessary.

Driveshafts

Clicking or knocking noise on turns (at slow speed on full-lock)

☐ Lack of constant velocity joint lubricant (Chapter 8).
☐ Worn outer constant velocity joint (Chapter 8).

Vibration when accelerating or decelerating

☐ Worn inner constant velocity joint (Chapter 8).
☐ Bent or distorted driveshaft (Chapter 8).

Braking system

Note: *Before assuming that a brake problem exists, make sure that the tyres are in good condition and correctly inflated, that the front wheel alignment is correct, and that the vehicle is not loaded with weight in an unequal manner. Apart from checking the condition of all pipe and hose connections, any faults occurring on the Anti-lock Braking System (ABS) should be referred to a Ford dealer for diagnosis.*

Vehicle pulls to one side under braking

☐ Worn, defective, damaged or contaminated front or rear brake pads/shoes on one side (Chapters 1 or 9).
☐ Seized or partially-seized front or rear brake caliper/wheel cylinder piston (Chapter 9).
☐ A mixture of brake pad/shoe lining materials fitted between sides (Chapters 1 or 9).
☐ Brake caliper mounting bolts loose (Chapter 9).
☐ Rear brake backplate mounting bolts loose (Chapter 9).
☐ Worn or damaged steering or suspension components (Chapter 10).

Noise (grinding or high-pitched squeal) when brakes applied

☐ Brake pad or shoe friction lining material worn down to metal backing (Chapters 1 or 9).
☐ Excessive corrosion of brake disc or drum (may be apparent after the vehicle has been standing for some time) (Chapters 1 or 9).

Excessive brake pedal travel

☐ Inoperative rear brake self-adjust mechanism (Chapter 9).
☐ Incorrect brake pedal adjustment (Chapter 9).
☐ Faulty master cylinder (Chapter 9).
☐ Air in hydraulic system (Chapter 9).

Brake pedal feels spongy when depressed

☐ Air in hydraulic system (Chapter 9).
☐ Deteriorated flexible rubber brake hoses (Chapter 9).
☐ Master cylinder mounting nuts loose (Chapter 9).
☐ Faulty master cylinder (Chapter 9).

Braking system (continued)

Excessive brake pedal effort required to stop vehicle

- [ ] Faulty vacuum servo unit (Chapter 9).
- [ ] Disconnected, damaged or insecure brake servo vacuum hose (Chapter 9).
- [ ] Primary or secondary hydraulic circuit failure (Chapter 9).
- [ ] Seized brake caliper or wheel cylinder piston(s) (Chapter 9).
- [ ] Brake pads or brake shoes incorrectly fitted (Chapter 9).
- [ ] Incorrect grade of brake pads or brake shoes fitted (Chapters 1 or 9).
- [ ] Brake pads or brake shoe linings contaminated (Chapters 1 or 9).

Brakes binding

- [ ] Seized brake caliper or wheel cylinder piston(s) (Chapter 9).
- [ ] Incorrect brake pedal adjustment (Chapter 9).
- [ ] Faulty handbrake mechanism (Chapter 9).
- [ ] Faulty master cylinder (Chapter 9).

Judder felt through brake pedal or steering wheel when braking

- [ ] Excessive run-out or distortion of front discs or rear drums (Chapter 9).
- [ ] Brake pad or brake shoe linings worn (Chapters 1 or 9).
- [ ] Brake caliper or rear brake backplate mounting bolts loose (Chapter 9).
- [ ] Wear in suspension or steering components or mountings (Chapter 10).

Rear wheels locking under normal braking

- [ ] Rear brake shoe linings contaminated (Chapter 1).
- [ ] Faulty brake pressure regulator or load sensing proportioning valve (Chapter 9).

Suspension and steering systems

Note: *Before diagnosing suspension or steering faults, be sure that the trouble is not due to incorrect tyre pressures, mixtures of tyre types, or binding brakes.*

Vehicle pulls to one side

- [ ] Faulty or damaged tyre (Chapter 1).
- [ ] Excessive wear in suspension or steering components (Chapter 10).
- [ ] Incorrect front wheel alignment (Chapter 10).
- [ ] Accident damage to steering or suspension components (Chapter 10).

Wheel wobble and vibration

- [ ] Front roadwheels out of balance (vibration felt mainly through the steering wheel) (Chapter 1).
- [ ] Rear roadwheels out of balance (vibration felt throughout the vehicle) Chapter 1).
- [ ] Roadwheels damaged or distorted (Chapter 1).
- [ ] Faulty or damaged tyre (Chapter 1).
- [ ] Worn steering or suspension joints, bushes or components (Chapter 10).
- [ ] Roadwheel nuts loose (Chapter 1).
- [ ] Wear in driveshaft joint, or loose driveshaft nut (vibration worst when under load) (Chapter 8).

Excessive pitching and/or rolling around corners, or during braking

- [ ] Defective shock absorbers (Chapter 10).
- [ ] Broken or weak coil spring and/or suspension component (Chapter 10).
- [ ] Worn or damaged anti-roll bar or mountings (Chapter 10).

Wandering or general instability

- [ ] Incorrect front wheel alignment (Chapter 10).
- [ ] Worn steering or suspension joints, bushes or components (Chapter 10).
- [ ] Tyres out of balance (Chapter 1).
- [ ] Faulty or damaged tyre (Chapter 1).
- [ ] Roadwheel nuts loose (Chapter 1).
- [ ] Defective shock absorbers (Chapter 10).

Excessively-stiff steering

- [ ] Lack of steering gear lubricant (Chapter 10).
- [ ] Seized track-rod end balljoint or suspension balljoint (Chapter 10).
- [ ] Broken or slipping power steering pump drivebelt (Chapter 1).
- [ ] Incorrect front wheel alignment (Chapter 10).
- [ ] Steering rack or column bent or damaged (Chapter 10).

Excessive play in steering

- [ ] Worn steering column universal joint(s) or flexible coupling (Chapter 10).
- [ ] Worn steering tie-rod balljoints (Chapter 10).
- [ ] Worn rack-and-pinion steering gear (Chapter 10).
- [ ] Worn steering or suspension joints, bushes or components (Chapter 10).

Lack of power assistance

- [ ] Broken or slipping drivebelt (Chapter 1).
- [ ] Incorrect power steering fluid level (Chapter 1).
- [ ] Restriction in power steering fluid hoses (Chapter 10).
- [ ] Faulty power steering pump (Chapter 10).
- [ ] Faulty rack-and-pinion steering gear (Chapter 10).

Tyre wear excessive

Tyres worn on inside or outside edges

- [ ] Tyres under-inflated (wear on both edges) (Chapter 1).
- [ ] Incorrect camber or castor angles (wear on one edge only) (Chapter 10).
- [ ] Worn steering or suspension joints, bushes or components (Chapter 10).
- [ ] Excessively-hard cornering.
- [ ] Accident damage.

Tyre treads exhibit feathered edges

- [ ] Incorrect toe setting (Chapter 10).

Tyres worn in centre of tread

- [ ] Tyres over-inflated (Chapter 1).

Tyres worn on inside and outside edges

- [ ] Tyres under-inflated (Chapter 1).

Tyres worn unevenly

- [ ] Tyres out of balance (Chapter 1).
- [ ] Excessive wheel or tyre run-out (Chapter 1).
- [ ] Worn shock absorbers (Chapter 10).
- [ ] Faulty tyre (Chapter 1).

Electrical system

Note: *For problems associated with the starting system, refer to the faults listed under "Engine" earlier in this Section.*

Battery will not hold a charge for more than a few days

☐ Battery defective internally (Chapter 5).
☐ Battery terminal connections loose or corroded (Chapter 1).
☐ Auxiliary drivebelt worn or incorrectly-adjusted (Chapter 1).
☐ Alternator not charging at correct output (Chapter 5).
☐ Alternator or voltage regulator faulty (Chapter 5).
☐ Short-circuit causing continual battery drain (Chapters 5 and 12).

Ignition (no-charge) warning light remains illuminated with engine running

☐ Auxiliary drivebelt broken, worn, or incorrectly-adjusted (Chapter 1).
☐ Alternator brushes worn, sticking, or dirty (Chapter 5).
☐ Alternator brush springs weak or broken (Chapter 5).
☐ Internal fault in alternator or voltage regulator (Chapter 5).
☐ Broken, disconnected, or loose wiring in charging circuit (Chapter 5).

Ignition (no-charge) warning light fails to come on

☐ Warning light bulb blown (Chapter 12).
☐ Broken, disconnected, or loose wiring in warning light circuit (Chapters 5 and 12).
☐ Alternator faulty (Chapter 5).

Lights inoperative

☐ Bulb blown (Chapter 12).
☐ Corrosion of bulb or bulbholder contacts (Chapter 12).
☐ Blown fuse (Chapter 12).
☐ Faulty relay (Chapter 12).
☐ Broken, loose, or disconnected wiring (Chapter 12).
☐ Faulty switch (Chapter 12).

A

ABS (Anti-lock brake system) A system, usually electronically controlled, that senses incipient wheel lockup during braking and relieves hydraulic pressure at wheels that are about to skid.

Air bag An inflatable bag hidden in the steering wheel (driver's side) or the dash or glovebox (passenger side). In a head-on collision, the bags inflate, preventing the driver and front passenger from being thrown forward into the steering wheel or windscreen.

Air cleaner A metal or plastic housing, containing a filter element, which removes dust and dirt from the air being drawn into the engine.

Air filter element The actual filter in an air cleaner system, usually manufactured from pleated paper and requiring renewal at regular intervals.

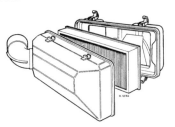

Air filter

Allen key A hexagonal wrench which fits into a recessed hexagonal hole.

Alligator clip A long-nosed spring-loaded metal clip with meshing teeth. Used to make temporary electrical connections.

Alternator A component in the electrical system which converts mechanical energy from a drivebelt into electrical energy to charge the battery and to operate the starting system, ignition system and electrical accessories.

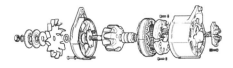

Alternator (exploded view)

Ampere (amp) A unit of measurement for the flow of electric current. One amp is the amount of current produced by one volt acting through a resistance of one ohm.

Anaerobic sealer A substance used to prevent bolts and screws from loosening. Anaerobic means that it does not require oxygen for activation. The Loctite brand is widely used.

Antifreeze A substance (usually ethylene glycol) mixed with water, and added to a vehicle's cooling system, to prevent freezing of the coolant in winter. Antifreeze also contains chemicals to inhibit corrosion and the formation of rust and other deposits that would tend to clog the radiator and coolant passages and reduce cooling efficiency.

Anti-seize compound A coating that reduces the risk of seizing on fasteners that are subjected to high temperatures, such as exhaust manifold bolts and nuts.

Anti-seize compound

Asbestos A natural fibrous mineral with great heat resistance, commonly used in the composition of brake friction materials. Asbestos is a health hazard and the dust created by brake systems should never be inhaled or ingested.

Axle A shaft on which a wheel revolves, or which revolves with a wheel. Also, a solid beam that connects the two wheels at one end of the vehicle. An axle which also transmits power to the wheels is known as a live axle.

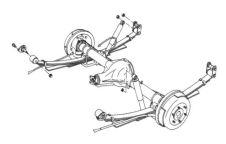

Axle assembly

Axleshaft A single rotating shaft, on either side of the differential, which delivers power from the final drive assembly to the drive wheels. Also called a driveshaft or a halfshaft.

B

Ball bearing An anti-friction bearing consisting of a hardened inner and outer race with hardened steel balls between two races.

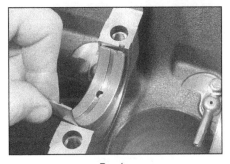

Bearing

Bearing The curved surface on a shaft or in a bore, or the part assembled into either, that permits relative motion between them with minimum wear and friction.

Big-end bearing The bearing in the end of the connecting rod that's attached to the crankshaft.

Bleed nipple A valve on a brake wheel cylinder, caliper or other hydraulic component that is opened to purge the hydraulic system of air. Also called a bleed screw.

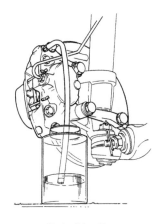

Brake bleeding

Brake bleeding Procedure for removing air from lines of a hydraulic brake system.

Brake disc The component of a disc brake that rotates with the wheels.

Brake drum The component of a drum brake that rotates with the wheels.

Brake linings The friction material which contacts the brake disc or drum to retard the vehicle's speed. The linings are bonded or riveted to the brake pads or shoes.

Brake pads The replaceable friction pads that pinch the brake disc when the brakes are applied. Brake pads consist of a friction material bonded or riveted to a rigid backing plate.

Brake shoe The crescent-shaped carrier to which the brake linings are mounted and which forces the lining against the rotating drum during braking.

Braking systems For more information on braking systems, consult the *Haynes Automotive Brake Manual*.

Breaker bar A long socket wrench handle providing greater leverage.

Bulkhead The insulated partition between the engine and the passenger compartment.

C

Caliper The non-rotating part of a disc-brake assembly that straddles the disc and carries the brake pads. The caliper also contains the hydraulic components that cause the pads to pinch the disc when the brakes are applied. A caliper is also a measuring tool that can be set to measure inside or outside dimensions of an object.

Camshaft A rotating shaft on which a series of cam lobes operate the valve mechanisms. The camshaft may be driven by gears, by sprockets and chain or by sprockets and a belt.

Canister A container in an evaporative emission control system; contains activated charcoal granules to trap vapours from the fuel system.

Canister

Carburettor A device which mixes fuel with air in the proper proportions to provide a desired power output from a spark ignition internal combustion engine.

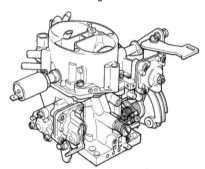

Carburettor

Castellated Resembling the parapets along the top of a castle wall. For example, a castellated balljoint stud nut.

Castellated nut

Castor In wheel alignment, the backward or forward tilt of the steering axis. Castor is positive when the steering axis is inclined rearward at the top.

Catalytic converter A silencer-like device in the exhaust system which converts certain pollutants in the exhaust gases into less harmful substances.

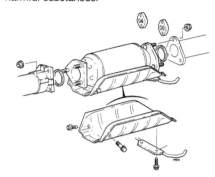

Catalytic converter

Circlip A ring-shaped clip used to prevent endwise movement of cylindrical parts and shafts. An internal circlip is installed in a groove in a housing; an external circlip fits into a groove on the outside of a cylindrical piece such as a shaft.

Clearance The amount of space between two parts. For example, between a piston and a cylinder, between a bearing and a journal, etc.

Coil spring A spiral of elastic steel found in various sizes throughout a vehicle, for example as a springing medium in the suspension and in the valve train.

Compression Reduction in volume, and increase in pressure and temperature, of a gas, caused by squeezing it into a smaller space.

Compression ratio The relationship between cylinder volume when the piston is at top dead centre and cylinder volume when the piston is at bottom dead centre.

Constant velocity (CV) joint A type of universal joint that cancels out vibrations caused by driving power being transmitted through an angle.

Core plug A disc or cup-shaped metal device inserted in a hole in a casting through which core was removed when the casting was formed. Also known as a freeze plug or expansion plug.

Crankcase The lower part of the engine block in which the crankshaft rotates.

Crankshaft The main rotating member, or shaft, running the length of the crankcase, with offset "throws" to which the connecting rods are attached.

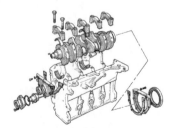

Crankshaft assembly

Crocodile clip See Alligator clip

D

Diagnostic code Code numbers obtained by accessing the diagnostic mode of an engine management computer. This code can be used to determine the area in the system where a malfunction may be located.

Disc brake A brake design incorporating a rotating disc onto which brake pads are squeezed. The resulting friction converts the energy of a moving vehicle into heat.

Double-overhead cam (DOHC) An engine that uses two overhead camshafts, usually one for the intake valves and one for the exhaust valves.

Drivebelt(s) The belt(s) used to drive accessories such as the alternator, water pump, power steering pump, air conditioning compressor, etc. off the crankshaft pulley.

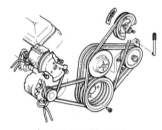

Accessory drivebelts

Driveshaft Any shaft used to transmit motion. Commonly used when referring to the axleshafts on a front wheel drive vehicle.

Driveshaft

Drum brake A type of brake using a drum-shaped metal cylinder attached to the inner surface of the wheel. When the brake pedal is pressed, curved brake shoes with friction linings press against the inside of the drum to slow or stop the vehicle.

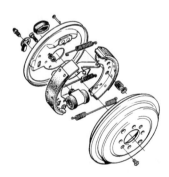

Drum brake assembly

E

EGR valve A valve used to introduce exhaust gases into the intake air stream.

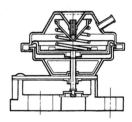

EGR valve

Electronic control unit (ECU) A computer which controls (for instance) ignition and fuel injection systems, or an anti-lock braking system. For more information refer to the *Haynes Automotive Electrical and Electronic Systems Manual*.

Electronic Fuel Injection (EFI) A computer controlled fuel system that distributes fuel through an injector located in each intake port of the engine.

Emergency brake A braking system, independent of the main hydraulic system, that can be used to slow or stop the vehicle if the primary brakes fail, or to hold the vehicle stationary even though the brake pedal isn't depressed. It usually consists of a hand lever that actuates either front or rear brakes mechanically through a series of cables and linkages. Also known as a handbrake or parking brake.

Endfloat The amount of lengthwise movement between two parts. As applied to a crankshaft, the distance that the crankshaft can move forward and back in the cylinder block.

Engine management system (EMS) A computer controlled system which manages the fuel injection and the ignition systems in an integrated fashion.

Exhaust manifold A part with several passages through which exhaust gases leave the engine combustion chambers and enter the exhaust pipe.

Exhaust manifold

F

Fan clutch A viscous (fluid) drive coupling device which permits variable engine fan speeds in relation to engine speeds.

Feeler blade A thin strip or blade of hardened steel, ground to an exact thickness, used to check or measure clearances between parts.

Feeler blade

Firing order The order in which the engine cylinders fire, or deliver their power strokes, beginning with the number one cylinder.

Flywheel A heavy spinning wheel in which energy is absorbed and stored by means of momentum. On cars, the flywheel is attached to the crankshaft to smooth out firing impulses.

Free play The amount of travel before any action takes place. The "looseness" in a linkage, or an assembly of parts, between the initial application of force and actual movement. For example, the distance the brake pedal moves before the pistons in the master cylinder are actuated.

Fuse An electrical device which protects a circuit against accidental overload. The typical fuse contains a soft piece of metal which is calibrated to melt at a predetermined current flow (expressed as amps) and break the circuit.

Fusible link A circuit protection device consisting of a conductor surrounded by heat-resistant insulation. The conductor is smaller than the wire it protects, so it acts as the weakest link in the circuit. Unlike a blown fuse, a failed fusible link must frequently be cut from the wire for replacement.

G

Gap The distance the spark must travel in jumping from the centre electrode to the side

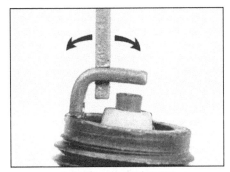

Adjusting spark plug gap

electrode in a spark plug. Also refers to the spacing between the points in a contact breaker assembly in a conventional points-type ignition, or to the distance between the reluctor or rotor and the pickup coil in an electronic ignition.

Gasket Any thin, soft material - usually cork, cardboard, asbestos or soft metal - installed between two metal surfaces to ensure a good seal. For instance, the cylinder head gasket seals the joint between the block and the cylinder head.

Gasket

Gauge An instrument panel display used to monitor engine conditions. A gauge with a movable pointer on a dial or a fixed scale is an analogue gauge. A gauge with a numerical readout is called a digital gauge.

H

Halfshaft A rotating shaft that transmits power from the final drive unit to a drive wheel, usually when referring to a live rear axle.

Harmonic balancer A device designed to reduce torsion or twisting vibration in the crankshaft. May be incorporated in the crankshaft pulley. Also known as a vibration damper.

Hone An abrasive tool for correcting small irregularities or differences in diameter in an engine cylinder, brake cylinder, etc.

Hydraulic tappet A tappet that utilises hydraulic pressure from the engine's lubrication system to maintain zero clearance (constant contact with both camshaft and valve stem). Automatically adjusts to variation in valve stem length. Hydraulic tappets also reduce valve noise.

I

Ignition timing The moment at which the spark plug fires, usually expressed in the number of crankshaft degrees before the piston reaches the top of its stroke.

Inlet manifold A tube or housing with passages through which flows the air-fuel mixture (carburettor vehicles and vehicles with throttle body injection) or air only (port fuel-injected vehicles) to the port openings in the cylinder head.

J

Jump start Starting the engine of a vehicle with a discharged or weak battery by attaching jump leads from the weak battery to a charged or helper battery.

L

Load Sensing Proportioning Valve (LSPV) A brake hydraulic system control valve that works like a proportioning valve, but also takes into consideration the amount of weight carried by the rear axle.

Locknut A nut used to lock an adjustment nut, or other threaded component, in place. For example, a locknut is employed to keep the adjusting nut on the rocker arm in position.

Lockwasher A form of washer designed to prevent an attaching nut from working loose.

M

MacPherson strut A type of front suspension system devised by Earle MacPherson at Ford of England. In its original form, a simple lateral link with the anti-roll bar creates the lower control arm. A long strut - an integral coil spring and shock absorber - is mounted between the body and the steering knuckle. Many modern so-called MacPherson strut systems use a conventional lower A-arm and don't rely on the anti-roll bar for location.

Multimeter An electrical test instrument with the capability to measure voltage, current and resistance.

N

NOx Oxides of Nitrogen. A common toxic pollutant emitted by petrol and diesel engines at higher temperatures.

O

Ohm The unit of electrical resistance. One volt applied to a resistance of one ohm will produce a current of one amp.

Ohmmeter An instrument for measuring electrical resistance.

O-ring A type of sealing ring made of a special rubber-like material; in use, the O-ring is compressed into a groove to provide the sealing action.

O-ring

Overhead cam (ohc) engine An engine with the camshaft(s) located on top of the cylinder head(s).

Overhead valve (ohv) engine An engine with the valves located in the cylinder head, but with the camshaft located in the engine block.

Oxygen sensor A device installed in the engine exhaust manifold, which senses the oxygen content in the exhaust and converts this information into an electric current. Also called a Lambda sensor.

P

Phillips screw A type of screw head having a cross instead of a slot for a corresponding type of screwdriver.

Plastigage A thin strip of plastic thread, available in different sizes, used for measuring clearances. For example, a strip of Plastigage is laid across a bearing journal. The parts are assembled and dismantled; the width of the crushed strip indicates the clearance between journal and bearing.

Plastigage

Propeller shaft The long hollow tube with universal joints at both ends that carries power from the transmission to the differential on front-engined rear wheel drive vehicles.

Proportioning valve A hydraulic control valve which limits the amount of pressure to the rear brakes during panic stops to prevent wheel lock-up.

R

Rack-and-pinion steering A steering system with a pinion gear on the end of the steering shaft that mates with a rack (think of a geared wheel opened up and laid flat). When the steering wheel is turned, the pinion turns, moving the rack to the left or right. This movement is transmitted through the track rods to the steering arms at the wheels.

Radiator A liquid-to-air heat transfer device designed to reduce the temperature of the coolant in an internal combustion engine cooling system.

Refrigerant Any substance used as a heat transfer agent in an air-conditioning system. R-12 has been the principle refrigerant for many years; recently, however, manufacturers have begun using R-134a, a non-CFC substance that is considered less harmful to

the ozone in the upper atmosphere.

Rocker arm A lever arm that rocks on a shaft or pivots on a stud. In an overhead valve engine, the rocker arm converts the upward movement of the pushrod into a downward movement to open a valve.

Rotor In a distributor, the rotating device inside the cap that connects the centre electrode and the outer terminals as it turns, distributing the high voltage from the coil secondary winding to the proper spark plug. Also, that part of an alternator which rotates inside the stator. Also, the rotating assembly of a turbocharger, including the compressor wheel, shaft and turbine wheel.

Runout The amount of wobble (in-and-out movement) of a gear or wheel as it's rotated. The amount a shaft rotates "out-of-true." The out-of-round condition of a rotating part.

S

Sealant A liquid or paste used to prevent leakage at a joint. Sometimes used in conjunction with a gasket.

Sealed beam lamp An older headlight design which integrates the reflector, lens and filaments into a hermetically-sealed one-piece unit. When a filament burns out or the lens cracks, the entire unit is simply replaced.

Serpentine drivebelt A single, long, wide accessory drivebelt that's used on some newer vehicles to drive all the accessories, instead of a series of smaller, shorter belts. Serpentine drivebelts are usually tensioned by an automatic tensioner.

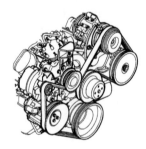

Serpentine drivebelt

Shim Thin spacer, commonly used to adjust the clearance or relative positions between two parts. For example, shims inserted into or under bucket tappets control valve clearances. Clearance is adjusted by changing the thickness of the shim.

Slide hammer A special puller that screws into or hooks onto a component such as a shaft or bearing; a heavy sliding handle on the shaft bottoms against the end of the shaft to knock the component free.

Sprocket A tooth or projection on the periphery of a wheel, shaped to engage with a chain or drivebelt. Commonly used to refer to the sprocket wheel itself.

Starter inhibitor switch On vehicles with an

automatic transmission, a switch that prevents starting if the vehicle is not in Neutral or Park.

Strut See MacPherson strut.

T

Tappet A cylindrical component which transmits motion from the cam to the valve stem, either directly or via a pushrod and rocker arm. Also called a cam follower.

Thermostat A heat-controlled valve that regulates the flow of coolant between the cylinder block and the radiator, so maintaining optimum engine operating temperature. A thermostat is also used in some air cleaners in which the temperature is regulated.

Thrust bearing The bearing in the clutch assembly that is moved in to the release levers by clutch pedal action to disengage the clutch. Also referred to as a release bearing.

Timing belt A toothed belt which drives the camshaft. Serious engine damage may result if it breaks in service.

Timing chain A chain which drives the camshaft.

Toe-in The amount the front wheels are closer together at the front than at the rear. On rear wheel drive vehicles, a slight amount of toe-in is usually specified to keep the front wheels running parallel on the road by offsetting other forces that tend to spread the wheels apart.

Toe-out The amount the front wheels are closer together at the rear than at the front. On front wheel drive vehicles, a slight amount of toe-out is usually specified.

Tools For full information on choosing and using tools, refer to the *Haynes Automotive Tools Manual*.

Tracer A stripe of a second colour applied to a wire insulator to distinguish that wire from another one with the same colour insulator.

Tune-up A process of accurate and careful adjustments and parts replacement to obtain the best possible engine performance.

Turbocharger A centrifugal device, driven by exhaust gases, that pressurises the intake air. Normally used to increase the power output from a given engine displacement, but can also be used primarily to reduce exhaust emissions (as on VW's "Umwelt" Diesel engine).

U

Universal joint or U-joint A double-pivoted connection for transmitting power from a driving to a driven shaft through an angle. A U-joint consists of two Y-shaped yokes and a cross-shaped member called the spider.

V

Valve A device through which the flow of liquid, gas, vacuum, or loose material in bulk may be started, stopped, or regulated by a movable part that opens, shuts, or partially obstructs one or more ports or passageways. A valve is also the movable part of such a device.

Valve clearance The clearance between the valve tip (the end of the valve stem) and the rocker arm or tappet. The valve clearance is measured when the valve is closed.

Vernier caliper A precision measuring instrument that measures inside and outside dimensions. Not quite as accurate as a micrometer, but more convenient.

Viscosity The thickness of a liquid or its resistance to flow.

Volt A unit for expressing electrical "pressure" in a circuit. One volt that will produce a current of one ampere through a resistance of one ohm.

W

Welding Various processes used to join metal items by heating the areas to be joined to a molten state and fusing them together. For more information refer to the *Haynes Automotive Welding Manual*.

Wiring diagram A drawing portraying the components and wires in a vehicle's electrical system, using standardised symbols. For more information refer to the *Haynes Automotive Electrical and Electronic Systems Manual*.

Note: *References throughout this index relate to 'Chapter number'•'page number'*

Preserving Our Motoring Heritage

< The Model J Duesenberg Derham Tourster. Only eight of these magnificent cars were ever built – this is the only example to be found outside the United States of America

Almost every car you've ever loved, loathed or desired is gathered under one roof at the Haynes Motor Museum. Over 300 immaculately presented cars and motorbikes represent every aspect of our motoring heritage, from elegant reminders of bygone days, such as the superb Model J Duesenberg to curiosities like the bug-eyed BMW Isetta. There are also many old friends and flames. Perhaps you remember the 1959 Ford Popular that you did your courting in? The magnificent 'Red Collection' is a spectacle of classic sports cars including AC, Alfa Romeo, Austin Healey, Ferrari, Lamborghini, Maserati, MG, Riley, Porsche and Triumph.

A Perfect Day Out

Each and every vehicle at the Haynes Motor Museum has played its part in the history and culture of Motoring. Today, they make a wonderful spectacle and a great day out for all the family. Bring the kids, bring Mum and Dad, but above all bring your camera to capture those golden memories for ever. You will also find an impressive array of motoring memorabilia, a comfortable 70 seat video cinema and one of the most extensive transport book shops in Britain. The Pit Stop Cafe serves everything from a cup of tea to wholesome, home-made meals or, if you prefer, you can enjoy the large picnic area nestled in the beautiful rural surroundings of Somerset.

> John Haynes O.B.E., Founder and Chairman of the museum at the wheel of a Haynes Light 12.

< Graham Hill's Lola Cosworth Formula 1 car next to a 1934 Riley Sports.

The Museum is situated on the A359 Yeovil to Frome road at Sparkford, just off the A303 in Somerset. It is about 40 miles south of Bristol, and 25 minutes drive from the M5 intersection at Taunton.
Open 9.30am - 5.30pm (10.00am - 4.00pm Winter) 7 days a week, *except Christmas Day, Boxing Day and New Years Day*
Special rates available for schools, coach parties and outings Charitable Trust No. 292048